PROFESSIONAL FOOD PREPARATION

PROFESSIONAL FOOD PREPARATION

MARGARET E. TERRELL

University of Washington, Seattle

JOHN WILEY & SONS, INC.

NEW YORK • LONDON • SYDNEY • TORONTO

Library of Congress Catalogue Card Number: 72-129865

ISBN 0-471-85201-5

Printed in the United States of America

10 9 8 7 6 5 4 3 2 1

Preface

The techniques and equipment of large-quantity food preparation differ considerably from cooking in the home. With the professional food-preparation student in mind, this book is designed to serve as a text for those beginning their study of large-quantity cooking; it should also be useful as a reference for those who direct or supervise food-production employees. A review of the principles, simply stated, has been included with a discussion of large-quantity methods and a description of the operation and care of the equipment commonly used in large kitchens.

Variation exists in the amount of study of food-preparation principles students have had before enrolling in classes in large-quantity cooking. Four-year professional programs normally require courses in basic sciences and in principles of food preparation to be taken first. Such instruction in two-year occupational programs is of necessity greatly limited. A review of the reasons for the recommended methods is believed to have value in promoting understanding and acceptance of the suggested procedures.

Guidance in the care and operation of equipment helps to promote better production of food and to ensure greater safety for individuals who use the equipment, resulting in a substantial saving in equipment expense. Equipment requirements differ in large kitchens in terms of the volume and type of food prepared. Since there is much similarity in equipment designed to perform specific functions, only representative items have been chosen from among the numerous makes and models for description in this book. Knowledge of the operation and care of these should provide a basis for understanding others. A discussion of equipment typical of that used in the specific work areas of a kitchen is included at the beginning of each section. Although this information may be taught in an equipment class, it can be understood more effectively if combined with the uses for which the equipment was designed.

A major focus in large-quantity or professional food preparation is directed toward pleasing the public rather than satisfying a family. It is essential that students develop not only a sensitive awareness of the basic elements of excellence in foods and a knowledge of the procedures for producing them but also the ability to relate them to public food acceptance, food safety, and economic considerations in production and sale. It is to be expected that students at this period of their experience will have uncertain judgment of food quality and will have given little thought to tastes other than their own. Words are inadequate in developing clear concepts of food quality. First-hand experience is needed in which students will have the opportunity to sample, analyze, and compare foods and note preferences. This training will enable them to establish goals for the production of food that has high acceptance value.

MARGARET E. TERRELL

Seattle, Washington
September 1970

Contents

SECTION I.   INTRODUCTION TO LARGE QUANTITY
PREPARATION OF FOOD

    1. Organization of Food Production   3
    2. Utensils and Small Equipment   23
    3. Aspects With General Application in Food
       Production   55

BIBLIOGRAPHY   89

SECTION II.   PROCESSING EQUIPMENT AND
PREPARATION METHODS FOR FRUITS,
VEGETABLES, SAUCES AND SOUPS

    4. Vegetable Processing Equipment   93
    5. Steam Cooking Equipment   115
    6. Preparation of Fruits and Vegetables   133
    7. Sauce Preparation   159
    8. Soup Production   182

BIBLIOGRAPHY   192

SECTION III.   THE PANTRY

    9. Pantry Equipment—Refrigeration
       Equipment, Work Tables, Slicing Machine,
       and Beverage Equipment   197
    10. Salads and Salad Dressings   222
    11. Sandwich Making   247

SECTION IV.   COOKING SECTION

12. Meat Preparation and Cooking Equipment   283
13. Dairy Products and Eggs   308
14. Poultry   337
15. Fish and Shellfish   352
16. Selection and Preparation of Beef   372
17. Selection and Preparation of Veal   403
18. Selection and Preparation of Lamb   416
19. Pork and Variety Meats   434

BIBLIOGRAPHY   457

SECTION V.   THE BAKE SHOP

20. Bakery Equipment—Mixer, Bun Cutter,
    Dough Roller and Sheeter, Proof Box   463
21. Bread Making   485
22. Cakes and Cookies   504
23. Pastry, Fillings and Puddings   526

BIBLIOGRAPHY   546

APPENDIX.   EQUIVALENT MEASURES OF FOODS   549
            FOOD QUANTITIES FOR 100 PORTIONS   559
            DEFINITION OF TERMS IN FOOD PREPARATION   574
            LIST OF TABLES   585

INDEX   587

PROFESSIONAL FOOD PREPARATION

SECTION I

Introduction to Large-Quantity Preparation of Food

CHAPTER 1   Organization of Food Production
CHAPTER 2   Utensils and Small Equipment
CHAPTER 3   Aspects with General Application
            in Food Production
            Bibliography for Section I

1.

Organization of Food Production

The preparation of food in large quantity affords employment for one out of every six persons employed in the retail trades. Public food service is one of America's most important industries, not only because of immense dollar volume, but also because it affects the welfare and pleasure of so many people. Food is a necessity for life and well-being and directly influences the health and contentment of those who consume it. The pleasure that good food provides causes people to use it as an expression of friendship and hospitality. It has certain therapeutic values for those who are ill. Business men, recognizing good meals as effective tools of influence, budget sizable amounts for "expense-account dining." Persons concerned with children's welfare and their education for a healthy and happy life give special thought to choice of food and the development of good food habits.

The characteristics of large kitchens vary in relation to specific aspects emphasized in the food preparation and service. Many are organized for the purpose of providing complete meal service to large groups in residence halls, retirement homes, hospitals, and commercial restaurants. Special foods and highly individualized service are characteristic of hospitals and certain restaurants. Other establishments serve lunch to students and workers. Short-order and specialty-food places cater to specific demands for certain foods and a particular type of preparation. Away-from-home meals may be as simple as a drive-in snack or as elaborate as a dinner in a fine hotel.

The equipment required and the organization of work are affected not only by the volume and the character of the food served, but also by the extent of the preparation done. Many large kitchens prepare all or most of the items served. Others depend partially or entirely on commercially prepared foods. Facilities suitable for one may be inefficient for the other. Quick means of heating, such as a microwave cooker, may be desirable for heat-and-serve foods but unsatisfactory where complete preparation is done. Mixers and cutters that aid in large quantity manipulation of materials are not

3

needed for food that has been prepared. The food quality obtainable and the cost involved in each system call for continual analysis by those responsible for choosing a suitable plan of operation.

Many operators recognize important values to be gained through having the major preparation of food done in their own kitchens. Shortage of personnel qualified to prepare consistently acceptable food in large quantity is a factor that has helped to promote the use of commercially prepared foods. Although there are many policies and conditions that may affect the success of a food establishment, a matter of major significance is the quality of the food served. The subject matter in this book is limited to those aspects that directly affect quality in large quantity production of food. Included are discussions of materials to be used, equipment operation and care, and recommended techniques for the preparation of food.

ORGANIZATION OF A LARGE KITCHEN

The organization of a large kitchen is influenced by the type and volume of food produced. In a smaller unit, such as a home, one person may be able to perform all of the activities required for the preparation of a simple meal. When the volume is large and the help of several people is required, the activities are divided into sections or departments in which specific types of preparation are done. Raw foods that require preprocessing may move from the receiving area to the section of the kitchen in which preliminary preparation, such as meat cutting or vegetable cleaning and paring, is done. Other items may go directly to the cooking section, salad and sandwich pantry, and the bake shop. In a large kitchen each department has separate work centers with space allotted according to the number of persons required for the specific tasks performed there. A large cooking section, for example, may have one area for meat roasting and entree preparation, one for short-order cooking, such as broiling, griddling, and deep frying, another for sauce and soup preparation, and one for cooking vegetables. A bake shop may have separate work centers for bread, cake, pastry, cookies, and puddings.

Observation of employees in a large kitchen should help students of food preparation to understand the different divisions of work. It is also helpful in visualizing the processing that occurs on each menu item, and the departments that share in the preparation of a meal. It is well to consider the supplies used, the state in which they are received, and the storage requirements both before and after preparation.

Job titles for food-production employees signify the kind of work done and the extent of an individual's responsibility. A person who is sufficiently well informed about needs and work methods to plan and direct work serves as a manager. Different titles are used for the top manager; these depend on the qualifications required and the specific responsibilities in the position. Food production may be managed by a food director, dietitian, food manager, chef, head cook, or cook-manager. A food director is expected to have competence in any matter which normally affects the successful functioning of the food operation, and is frequently responsible for the administration of more than one place. A university education in food management or business administration plus practical experience are usually required.

Dietitians are employed in food establishments in which special attention is paid to the nutritional welfare of the group served and food quality is stressed. In order to qualify as a dietitian, a person must have taken a carefully planned university program in the science of human nutrition and food preparation and have had experience through internship or practice under professional supervision in large-quantity food production and service. Dietitians are frequently employed as food directors.

Both areas of responsibility and qualifications vary for other managers of food production. A food manager usually plans for the food requirements in a specific establishment. This may involve more than one type of preparation and service. In a hotel it may include food served in the main dining room, the coffee shop, room service, and the banquet rooms. An ability to satisfy patrons with food produced and served within specified financial limitations is important. University education is an asset and experience is essential for success. A chef or head cook is responsible for planning and directing activities in one kitchen, which may or may not prepare food for more than one type of service. Special training is highly desirable and experience is essential. A cook-manager functions in kitchens in which the food to be prepared is simple or the number to be served is small. There are many openings for these employees in school food service, small clubs, and nursing homes. Special training and experience are needed for success.

Cooks, bakers, and butchers are recognized as department heads. They perform activities that call for superior skill in their respective areas and they are responsible for supervising the work of persons in their sections. Second to them in level of skill and responsibility are the sauce chef or cook, vegetable cook, short-order or grill cook, pantry supervisor, sandwich maker, salad maker, and pastry cook. Their work calls for skill in special types of preparation.

Large kitchens require many helpers. These positions are excellent for people who are learning the trade and need to develop special skills. There are many specially suited to this work and who enjoy doing it enough to continue in their positions. These jobs include assistant cooks, kitchen helpers, baker's helpers, and vegetable-preparation workers.

ORGANIZATION OF WORK

Preparation for Production

There are seven steps that should be followed carefully by those getting ready to prepare food. Habits developed through routinely observing these steps will help toward avoiding many unfortunate errors.

1. Know and observe rules for safety and sanitation.
2. Understand specific requirements or assignments.
3. Check recipe calculations to be sure that they are correct.
4. Collect supplies that will be required immediately.
5. Assemble needed equipment, and be sure that it is available and in condition for use.
6. Plan for the progress of work.
7. Allot time for the work to be done.

Guard Safety and Sanitation

FOOD SAFETY AND SANITATION. The food-handling practices of every food worker are important to the welfare of those who consume the food he has handled. Carelessness can lead to serious illness from food poisoning. The poisoning may be caused by injurious bacteria in food as a result of unsanitary practices or to poisonous materials in foods. Cleaning agents, pesticides, and similar poisonous materials are sometimes mistaken for food supplies. These should always be clearly marked and stored in areas away from foods.

Persons who work with food should have clean bodies, a clean uniform, and, most important, clean hands. The uniform is a "badge of office" for persons working with foods. Cleanliness of the uniform and general appearance of the person should be a matter of pride and fostered in students as well as with food employees. Every food production area, including a classroom, should have facilities for hand washing. It should become a well-established habit to wash the hands before handling food or equipment used for food and after handling any dirty object. Every person handling food has the responsibility for protecting food from contamination. A hairnet or cap should be worn by food workers to prevent dandruff or hair from falling into the food. Those around food should be made aware that a saliva spray is emitted when people talk, sneeze, or cough. All persons should avoid doing this near food. Clean equipment and freedom from pests or pets in food areas are also important for safe sanitation.

Safety protection includes storing food under conditions that protect it from contamination and retard the growth of bacteria. Protection from roaches, flies, rodents, and other common pests calls for alertness on the part of all food employees. The existence of pests should be called to the attention of the manager for special exterminator service. Promptness of action is important.

Holding time and temperature are important factors in food safety. One bacterium may not cause illness, but under favorable conditions one can multiply into several trillion within a few hours. In order to retard the growth of bacteria, hot foods should be held at temperatures above 140°F and cold foods at temperatures below 45°F. When hot foods are to be refrigerated, they should not be completely air-cooled at room temperature, but should be placed in shallow containers and refrigerated immediately. For quick, even cooling, the containers should be arranged in the refrigerator so that air can circulate around them. Special precaution should be taken with poultry and egg products, custard mixtures, potato salad, meats, dairy foods, dressings, cream puddings, sauces and other foods most favorable to bacterial growth. Left-over foods should be used as soon as possible; foods that spoil readily should not be held over 24 hours without freezing.

The development of the following habits by persons working in the kitchen area ensures proper safety and sanitation.

1. Workers must handle all utensils carefully. Plates should be picked up by spreading the fingers on the underside and placing the thumb on the edge; glasses should always be carried by the bottom; handles should be used when touching cups or silverware.

2. Persons should avoid touching food whenever possible by using tongs, spoon, or fork when handling it; the tasting spoon must be clean and should never be returned to the food after it is used.

3. Surfaces should be clean and well organized. People working in the kitchen area should be sure that no one leans, sits, or places commercial packages (which have an unknown sanitation history) on the surfaces on which food is prepared. They must be certain also that all equipment is properly cleaned before it is used, and that spillage is wiped up promptly before it can cause an accident.

4. No one with a communicable disease, a cold, sores, or an infected wound should work with food.

SAFETY FROM INJURY. Persons in large kitchens work with power tools, sharp instruments, and high temperatures; any of these can cause serious injury. Surprise factors, such as slick spots on floors, blind corners, or collision with other hurrying workers, are common conditions that tend to promote accidents. Prevention calls for strict observance of safety precautions. Alertness

TABLE 1.1 FOOD POISONING CAUSES AND PREVENTION

Type of Poison	Food Most Likely to be Involved	Contaminating Factors	Suggested Methods for Prevention
Clostridium Botulinum (often fatal)	Protein foods, such as canned green beans and fish, under anaerobic conditions. Toxin is deadly poison.	Improper cleaning and processing.	Thorough cleaning and proper processing. Discard questionable foods. Toxin is destroyed by boiling for 20 min. More than 6 hrs. of boiling is needed to kill the spores.
Brucellosis (undulant fever)	Milk or dairy products.	Use of raw milk that is not certified.	Pasteurization of milk and other dairy products.
Parasitic Dysentery	Contaminated food, milk, and water.	Contaminated food and water supply. Employees who have not washed after going to toilet.	Proper cleanliness habits of food employees, plus sanitary food and water supply.
Salmonella	Poultry, eggs, egg products, dairy foods, shellfish, and meats. It is wide spread in nature.	Use of raw shellfish and poultry products. Lack of sanitation. Bacteria grow at temperatures between 44° and 115°F.	Safe food and proper sanitation in food handling. These foods must not be eaten raw.
Staphyloccus	Dressings, salads, mixtures of both meats and vegetables.	Persons with cuts, sores, or boils and are careless in handling food.	Heat food to 190°F to kill bacteria. Refrigerate food and prevent handling that might contaminate it.

TABLE 1.1 (*Continued*)

Type of Poison	Food Most Likely to be Involved	Contaminating Factors	Suggested Methods for Prevention
Streptococcus	Milk, milk products, and ham.	People who are carriers and those who are careless in sanitation.	Pasteurize foods, segregate infected people from working with food.
Trichinosis	Pork and pork products.	Infected products and lack of adequate cooking.	Cook above 150°F. When holding, freeze below −16.6°F.
Tuberculosis	Raw milk.	Use of raw milk, use of common cups and towels. Lack of proper sanitation.	Use pasteurized milk. Do not allow infected people to work with food. Proper sanitation.
Typhoid	Polluted water, foods, milk, and shellfish.	Use of contaminated products. Lack of care in food handling.	Proper cooking and sanitation. Good refrigeration and good food habits.
Chemical	Any food or beverage.	Carelessness in use and storage. Unlabelled or mislabelled chemicals.	Keep all poisonous chemicals well marked and stored away from food areas.

TABLE 1.2 CONTROL OF DISEASE-CARRYING PESTS

Pests	Habits	Control Measures
Ants	Ants live, store food, and raise young in hills. They feed on sweets and meats, and crawl over filth as well as food.	Keep the place clean to eliminate food supply. Find the hill in which they live and use a chemical exterminator.
Flies	The eggs are laid in filth, rotting food, and human waste. They lay 100 to 125 eggs, which hatch in 1 to 2 days. They carry filth on bodies, legs, and wings.	Screen them out. Shut off food supply by tightly covering garbage and protecting food supplies. Kill flies by spray or trap.
Lice	Lice use pets and humans as hosts. Their eggs hatch in 2 to 3 wk. They carry typhus and relapsing fever.	Keep pets out of food areas and be certain food workers are clean. Destroy lice with chemical controls.
Mosquitoes	They breed in stagnant water and drains and multiply rapidly, with a 10-day life cycle. They carry disease on their bodies and transmit it by biting.	Screen doors and windows. Eliminate water that can serve as a breeding place. Use chemical controls.

TABLE 1.2 (*Continued*)

Pests	Habits	Control Measures
Roaches	These insects like dark, damp, warm places. They lay 25 to 30 eggs, and live 5 yr. Roaches have an offensive odor and carry disease on bodies and feet; they often enter on delivery packages.	Eliminate food and moisture through clean housekeeping (no crumbs, or dripping drains and faucets). Watch alertly and use insecticides to eliminate them.
Rodents	These mammals produce 5 litters of 6 to 9 per yr and live 2 to 3 yr. They like food, warmth, and moisture and live in trash, lumber piles, rockeries, sewers, and walls. Good swimmers, they can gnaw through wood and jump 2 to 3 ft. Rodents carry fleas that can transmit typhus and bubonic plague.	Eliminate food and nesting places. Close garbage cans tightly; use metal, vermin-proof storage containers for food. Elimination requires pesticides or an exterminator service.

TABLE 1.3 TEMPERATURES RELATED TO FOOD SAFETY

Temperature	Description
212°F	Boiling point of water at sea level.
	Water vaporizes enough at temperatures higher than 180°F to interfere with rinsing action in dishwashers.
180°F	Proper rinse spray temperature for dishwashing.
170°F	Use temperatures above this for sanitizing tableware and utensils. Most bacteria are killed at 165°F.
145–165°F	Holding temperature for hot food during service.
140°F	Kills or retards growth of harmful bacteria. Washing temperature for dish machines. Some bacterial growth may occur.
120°F	Pre-rinse temperature in dishwashing.
60–120°F	Hazardous temperatures favorable to the growth of bacteria.
40–60°F	Some growth of food poisoning bacteria.
45°F	Maximum storage temperature for perishable foods.
44–45°F	Short period storage for most perishable foods. Retards growth of bacteria. Use for fresh fruits and vegetables (except bananas).
38–45°F	Dairy products.
33–38°F	Meat and poultry.
32–40°F	Slow growth of bacteria that causes spoilage.
23–30°F	Fish and shellfish.
−10 to −30°F	Frozen food storage.

is constantly needed in kitchens where many people are busily doing a variety of jobs, situations are constantly changing, and distractions are numerous.

The most frequent injuries result from cuts, burns, and falls. The usefulness of a knife depends on the keenness of its cutting edge. A dull knife, however, may cut because the force needed to use it may cause the knife to slip. Knives should be stored where the cutting edges are protected and a worker does not strike the edge when reaching for a knife. Knives should never be placed where they are covered by food or equipment and cannot be seen; for example, under water in a sink. When using a knife, a person should hold it firmly in a proper cutting position and cut away from himself.

Burns often result from picking up hot pans without adequate protection. Any carelessness when reaching into ovens or over open flames or when using steam equipment is hazardous. Manufacturers install safety devices on most equipment, but they cannot control the human factor. Each individual must be concerned with his own and his fellow workers' safety; he must keep alert to hazards and work to prevent accidents. Both salt, for extinguishing stove-top or oven fires, and a lid, for smothering a deep-fat fire, should be available. Workers must be careful to avoid spattering water into hot fat and permitting handles of cooking pots to project where they may be hit. Persons in cooking sections should know how that specific institution handles each type of fire, and the location and use of its fire extinguisher.

Safe footing is essential to prevent falls. Common causes of falls include slick flooring materials like concrete; worn spots, broken floor boards, or other uneven areas; and unexpected items on the floor, such as a curling mat, equipment that is out of place, or scraps of food. Defective equipment (for example, weak supports, bent shelves on storage racks, and sticking casters on carts) can also cause accidents. It is the responsibility of ownership

(a)   (b)   (c)

Figure 1.1 National testing laboratories permit the use of their symbols on equipment that meets their design and construction standards. (a) American Gas Association, (b) Underwriters Laboratories, and (c) National Sanitation Foundation.

to provide safe flooring materials and equipment, but it is up to the workers to prevent accidents by using reasonable care when handling equipment and to follow the recommended work procedures.

Respect for electrical power is also important for safety. Households may use 120 volts for lighting and equipment; institutions use 240 volts and it is very important that power equipment be properly grounded. Most heavy-duty equipment is three phase and has a three-pronged plug-in with two wires that each carry 120 volts and a neutral or ground wire. These should be completely encased with insulating material. Copper, an excellent electrical conductor, is commonly used for carrying the current, but water, other metals, and the human body can also conduct electricity if the circuit is complete.

Conditions for safety require that insulation on electrical lines or cords be complete. Connections with cut, worn, or broken insulation should be repaired immediately. Electrical connections should never be handled by someone who has wet hands or is standing in water. Switches should be located so that they can be reached without touching metal equipment. "Stop" switches on a machine should be placed where they can be easily reached in an emergency.

Power equipment has been designed to be of service. The electrical horsepower helps make work quicker and easier; it enables workers to handle larger volumes at lower production costs. Used carelessly, however, the horsepower can cause serious physical injury, ruin materials, and result in expensive repairs. For safety and efficiency, equipment should be operated by those who understand and follow the directions for its use.

The heavy equipment and large volume of materials handled in big kitchens may result in strained muscles and back injury if lifting is done unwisely. No one should attempt lifting loads beyond his strength. In lifting, the chin should be kept up, the arms and back straight. When a worker is lifting from a low level he should stand close to the load with his feet apart and flat on the ground and the body weight well balanced. Then he should grasp the load firmly from two sides with the fingers extending underneath, and gradually lift or put down the load. When lifting in this way, it is important to bend the knees rather than the back; this permits the legs to exert the required force and take the strain off the back. All persons should remember to ask for help rather than risk strain or accident.

Be Sure of the Job Requirements

Time may be saved and expensive errors avoided by making sure that directions are correctly understood before work begins. This is true of both class assignments and job instructions. Before the preparation of food begins the following questions must be answered.

1. What items are to be prepared?
2. How much of each item is needed for a specified number of portions of a stated size?
3. Which recipe or method of preparation is to be used?
4. At what time is the food to be served?
5. Are there any special requirements of form or condition of service?
6. Where is it to be delivered for service or holding?

Check Calculations for Accuracy

Recipes frequently need to be adjusted for the number of portions required. Errors are likely to occur when recipes are reduced, enlarged, or retyped. A mistake in only one item may spoil the product. Check whether there have been omissions of any items that are normally required, such as leavening or seasoning. When checking calculations it is necessary to be familiar with commonly used abbreviations and the fractional units of weight and volume.

TABLE 1.4 COMMONLY USED ABBREVIATIONS WITH WEIGHT AND VOLUME EQUIVALENTS

Abbreviation	Equal Volume	Equal Weight
Bu—bushel	4 pk	Approx. 50 lb (potatoes, apples)
pk—peck	8 qt	Approx. 12½ lb fruit
gal—gallon	4 qt	8 lb liquid
qt—quart	2 pt	2 lb liquid
pt—pint	2 c	1 lb liquid
c—cup	16 tbsp	8 oz liquid
tbsp—tablespoon	3 tsp	½ oz liquid
tsp—teaspoon	1 tsp	5 g or .175 oz liquid
oz—ounce	2 tbsp liquid	1 oz
lb—pound	1 pt liquid	16 oz
g—gram	pinch	.035 oz
kg—kilogram	2½ c (scant)	1 lb, 3½ oz
l—litre	4½ c	2.21 lb

Standardized recipes are among the most valuable possessions of a well-run food establishment. Proportions in recipes should not be changed without the approval of the management. A recipe is standardized by carefully adjusting ingredients and their proportions to produce products of acceptable quality and in amounts sufficient for the desired number of portions of specified size. Helpful information that should be stated in standardized recipes include:

1. The name of the recipe, the number and size of portions.
2. The ingredients, with statement of amount in weight and/or volume and description, such as melted fat, cooked or uncooked rice.
3. The order and method of combining ingredients.
4. The equipment used in processing.
5. The appearance or condition at various stages when it is needed to guide preparation.
6. The processing time.
7. The temperature used in processing.
8. Any special directions needed to guard quality, control portion size, or add appeal.

When changes are made in recipes, the changes should be *written down* and rechecked because one error may lower quality or cause a total loss of the product. The following recipe illustrates this.

BEEF NOODLE CASSEROLE   100 portions (6 oz)

Ingredients	Weight	Volume
Noodles, raw	3 lb	1 gal
Onions, finely chopped	5 lb	3¾ qt
Green peppers, chopped	2 lb	2 qt
Parsley, finely chopped	3 oz	2¼ c
Shortening	12 oz	1½ c
Raw beef, cubed	6 lb	3¾ qt
Tomato soup	9 lb	1½ No. 10 cans or 2⅛ gal
Corn, whole kernel, drained	5 lb	2½ qt
Mushrooms, canned, sliced	3 lb	4½ qt
Cheddar cheese, diced	2 lb	2 qt
Worcestershire sauce	1 tbsp	1 tbsp
Salt	4 oz	½ c

PROCEDURE:

1. Cook noodles in 2 gallons of boiling water to which ¼ cup of salt has been added. Rinse and drain.
2. Saute onions, green pepper and parsley in shortening. Add beef and cook until brown.
3. Mix all ingredients together.
4. Scale 10 pounds of mixture into each of 4 greased serving pans (12 × 20 × 2¼ in.), each to yield 25 portions of approximately 6 ounces each.
5. Bake in 350°F oven for 30 minutes or until nicely browned.

When this recipe is reduced for 25 portions there is a change of pounds to ounces, of quarts to cups, and tablespoons to teaspoons. This is where errors frequently occur. The abbreviations for tablespoons and teaspoons may cause difficulty also. Calculations should be checked carefully before one proceeds with the preparation.

BEEF NOODLE CASSEROLE   25 portions (6 oz)

Ingredients	Weight	Volume
Noodles, raw	12 oz	1 qt
Onions, finely chopped	1¼ lb	3¼ c
Green peppers, chopped	8 oz	2 c
Parsley, finely chopped	¾ oz	½ c, plus 1 tbsp
Shortening	3 oz	6 tbsp
Raw beef, cubed	1½ lb	3¾ c
Tomato soup	2¼ lb	4½ c
Corn, whole kernel, drained	1¼ lb	2½ c
Mushrooms, canned, sliced	12 oz	4½ c
Cheddar cheese, diced	8 oz	2 c
Worcestershire sauce	¾ tsp	¾ tsp
Salt	1 oz	2 tbsp

Collect Supplies

Satisfactory results often depend on the use of specific materials. One should know that the needed items are available before preparation begins; fewer errors are likely to occur when work can proceed without interruption to get supplies. Time and effort can often be saved by using a tray or cart to collect several items at one time.

ASSEMBLE EQUIPMENT. The condition of the equipment also should be ascertained before preparation starts. Certain pieces of large equipment, such as ovens and mixers, may be shared by more than one department of a kitchen, and more than one person may be planning to use them at the same time. The required use of equipment changes from day to day. A variation in demand because of menu selections or special catering often imposes a need for extra space or special equipment. A shortage of equipment may prohibit certain types of preparation. Since searching for items disrupts the work-flow and increases the likelihood of error and time loss, the processing steps that indicate the required equipment should be examined before food preparation is begun. Chapter 2 contains a list of small items that should be available in the various production departments.

Plan for the Progress of Work

The assignment is reviewed in terms of the number of different items and the best order of preparation. The materials and equipment are arranged in the work center so that the activities can go forward in the quickest, easiest manner. One of the rules for simplifying work is to place frequently used materials within normal reach and occasionally used items at maximum reach (see Figure 1.2).

Since recipes indicate the steps to be followed in preparing food, materials and equipment can be arranged in the best order of procedure so that both hands can be used in a smooth, rythmic flow of work. Figure 1.3 shows an arrangement of materials that permits a person to stand erect and use both hands while breading food.

The following are suggestions to keep in mind when analyzing activities for ways to minimize motion. (a) Place items where they will be used by the hand that picks them up. (b) Place items where other things will not have to be moved to get to the one required. (c) Systematize storage to eliminate searching for needed articles. (d) Store items in or near the work center where they will be used most frequently. (e) Keep the work center compact in arrangement to eliminate the need for maximum reach and extra steps. A cart or other mobile item helps in arranging a compact work center beside such stationary equipment as mixers, tables, or cooking equipment (see Figure 1.4).

Allot the Time Required for Preparation

Timing is an important factor in preparation and service of high quality foods. The majority of foods are best at the point when preparation is completed. In order to insure best quality for those who dine either early or late in a meal period preparation must be started at successive time periods so as to provide a continually fresh supply. This is known as rotation preparation.

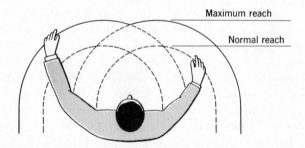

Figure 1.2 Worker demonstrating convenient and maximum reach.

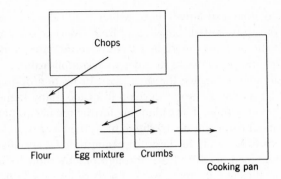

Figure 1.3   The flow of work in breading chops.

It is necessary to operate within established time schedules when serving the public. Diners are impatient for service at the scheduled periods and are hard to pacify if they are kept waiting beyond the appointed time. When cooks are nervous about food being ready on time, they tend to prepare food so far in advance of service that the bloom of goodness is lost before the food is served. Such food has the quality of a leftover the first time it appears. Careful planning of time for preparation can prevent this.

Knowledge of the amount of time required to do jobs is needed in order to allot the right amount for each stage of processing. Cooks and bakers may have several products in various stages of completion at the same time. It is necessary to organize the activities so that adequate attention can be given to each item and so that all will be completed at the time desired. A baker, for example, may prepare a pudding that requires chilling, pies that need to

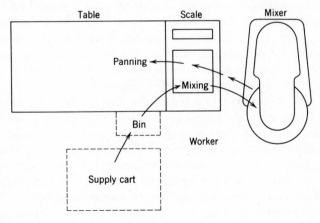

Figure 1.4   The arrangement of a work center for mixing and panning food.

cool enough to hold attractive shape when cut, cakes to be baked and frosted, and rolls to be raised, baked, and fresh from the oven at the time of service. All of the activities must be carefully coordinated and time allowances made for the specific tasks in order to accomplish this.

Many factors may influence the time plan. Protection of quality calls for planning so that a crisis does not develop from too many items demanding attention at the same time. Time planning for the use of equipment needs to avoid conflict in schedules for use by different workers and overloads. Suitable allowance needs to be made for best processing time for specific items. Each person preparing food needs to learn through practice how to judge his personal speed or efficiency in doing work. Foods differ in length of time they can be held after preparation before quality is lowered appreciably. Information on such points furnishes a basis for allotting time for each activity in the preparation of food.

SUGGESTED LABORATORY EXPERIENCE

1. Spend time (equivalent to a laboratory period) observing workers in a large kitchen. Identify the employees by work title and list jobs each was performing.

   Note: Students will be in food production areas where personnel are required to wear clean uniforms for proper sanitation. It is to be expected that students will be attired in fresh uniforms also.

2. Spend time (equivalent to a laboratory period) timing activities performed by a specific employee. List activities, state amount of time for each, and total amount of work or volume of material produced per hour.

3. On the basis of observation, estimate the amount of time required to prepare a specific recipe for a given number of portions. Calculate the cost per portion for preparation labor at .03, .06, and .08 cents per minute. Subtract the labor cost per portion from the sale price. How much per portion is left to cover food and other expenses?

4. Spend time (equivalent to a laboratory period) observing a production worker preparing a specific recipe. List pieces of equipment used and the food items required. Note arrangement for work. List number of times work was interrupted to get supplies or a piece of equipment giving amount of time spent. Note conditions or practices that protected sanitation.

5. Prepare an instruction sheet for employees that briefly states major points to be observed by them in protecting the sanitation of food.

6. Enlarge a family-size recipe to one sufficient for 100 portions, giving all information recommended for a standardized recipe.

7. Reduce a 50-portion recipe to one for 12 portions.

REVIEW QUESTIONS AND ANSWERS

1. What is meant by safe food?

Food prepared under sanitary conditions that does not contain harmful bacteria or poisonous materials.

2. List essential conditions for food safety.

Clean food and food equipment, proper temperature, freedom from contamination, and safe holding limits.

3. What are the chief causes of food poisoning?

Harmful bacteria and materials in food that are injurious to health.

4. What foods are most likely to contain botulinum?

Improperly cleaned and poorly processed protein foods such as green beans.

5. What should be done with food that is thought to be infected?

It should be discarded. One *never* tastes food to determine spoilage.

6. Name the kinds of infection that may result from the use of raw milk.

Brucellosis (undulant fever), typhoid, streptococcus, tuberculosis, and possibly dysentery and salmonella.

7. What is the best way to insure against these?

The strict use of pasteurized milk, obtained from a reliable source and handled in a sanitary manner.

8. What are the safe temperatures for temporary holding of food?

Temperatures above 140 and below 45° retard the growth of bacteria.

9. What are the most hazardous temperatures?

Those between 60 and 120°F are favorable to the growth of bacteria.

10. How do insects affect the sanitation of food?

They carry dirt on bodies from crawling on filth, and deposit it by lighting or crawling on food.

11. What are the most common pests to infest food areas?

Roaches, flies, mosquitoes, and rodents.

12. What means may be used to keep food areas free of pests?

Clean housekeeping, vigilant attention, preventive screens, and prompt extermination if they enter.

13. What are the three most important points for food workers to observe in guarding food safety?

Clean hands, clean uniforms, and clean practices in food handling.

14. Before beginning work, what information should a food-preparation worker have?

Items to be prepared, quantity required, recipes to be used, methods of procedure, time and place food will be needed, and any special characteristics relating to form or condition desired.

15. When is it of special importance to check accuracy of a recipe?

When recipe has not been standardized, after adjusting quantities for more or fewer portions, and after copying or retyping.

16. What are the commonest errors made when enlarging or reducing a recipe?

Abbreviations, fractional measurements of larger units, and mathematical calculations.

17. Why should materials and equipment be assembled before starting preparation?

To make sure that all items will be available so work can progress without interruption and with less chance of error.

18. On what principles should plans for work be based?

Proper manipulation and sequence for best quality and expenditure of minimum effort and time.

19. How can work be done most quickly and easily?

By having needed items located within easy reach where one item will not have to be moved to reach another and work can progress with the fewest steps.

20. On what basis should one allow time for doing jobs?

Time required by worker to perform tasks, coordination of tasks and equipment use, and rotation of production to meet quality, quantity, and time requirements.

21. What is meant by rotation of preparation?

Beginning final stage of preparation at successive times in order to have a fresh supply within a limited period.

2.

Utensils and Small Equipment

Proper tools help improve the quality of work and make it easier to accomplish. Small equipment needed by most of the preparation departments include food containers, cutting tools, means of measurement, and utensils for manipulation, such as forks, spatulas, and stirring spoons. An item's usefulness is influenced strongly by the material and its gauge, and the article's size and form in relation to specific uses. Important selection points also include its sanitary properties, durability, ease of maintenance, and good appearance.

Each material used in kitchen equipment has certain advantages and disadvantages that affect its usefulness. The following list shows some common materials with their strong and weak points; suggestions for their use and recommendations for their care are also included.

ALUMINUM. *Where used*: Pots, pans, mixing bowls, colanders, measuring spoons, cups, pitchers, and equipment legs, feet, and facing.

Advantages: Light weight; rapid, even, heat distribution; bright appearance; relatively low cost; cleanable and sanitary.

Disadvantages: Soft metal, easily scratched or dented; oxidizes readily in presence of air and moisture and is attacked by alkalis.

Recommended care: Clean with mild soap and use very fine steel wool if required to remove soil. Avoid strong alkaline detergents and coarse abrasives. Avoid hitting or rough treatment.

CHINA AND
GLASSWARE. *Where used*: Baking dishes, mixing bowls, and measures.

23

Advantages: Heat-proof glass is desired by some cooks for liquid measures. Its slow heat conduction is good in egg cookery. Good appearance, easy to clean, relatively low cost.

Disadvantages: Heavy, fragile, and easily broken. The hazard of broken fragments makes it unsuitable for institution use.

Recommended care: Avoid use of abrasives that will etch the surface. Wash with regular dishwashing detergents, soaking to soften soil for complete removal if necessary.

COPPER.   *Where used*: Water pans for hot tables, cladding on cooking pots, and equipment trim.

Advantages: Excellent heat conductor; bright, warm appearance when polished.

Disadvantages: Soft, easily dented; toxic metal which forms a poisonous oxide, (vertigris); requires frequent polishing for good appearance.

Recommended care: Avoid contact with foods. Avoid scratching or denting soft metal. Wash with regular pot detergents, rinse well, dry, and polish with copper polish.

IRON, CAST.   *Where used*: Cooking surfaces, such as grills and frying pans, and tops and framework of ranges.

Advantages: Provides steady, uniform distribution of heat; it is sturdy and will support the weight of heavy utensils and food; it is nontoxic.

Disadvantages: Will rust, and rust discolors food; it has a dark, dull color and is heavy.

Recommended care: Wash with regular pot detergents, rinse thoroughly and dry completely. Cover with salt-free oil if allowed to stand for extended periods.

IRON,
ENAMELLED. *Where used*: Food containers and equipment facing, such as refrigerators and cabinets.

Advantages: Bright, colorful appearance and resistance to food acids.

Disadvantages: Tendency to chip on impact, heat craze and crack.

Recommended care: Wash with mild detergents, rinse thoroughly and allow to dry.

IRON,
RETINNED.   *Where used*: Pots, pans, spoons, whips, ladles and mixing bowls (including those for the power mixer). May be called tin-coated steel or hotel steel.

Advantages: Low cost, sturdy, nontoxic, bright in appearance, fairly durable except for retinning and conducts heat well.

Disadvantages: With heavy use it requires the expense of retinning because iron rusts where tin has worn off; it is also heavy.

Recommended care: Wash with regular pot detergents, rinse thoroughly and air dry. Avoid abrasion that will remove the tin coating.

IRON, ZINC COATED (CALLED GALVANIZED IRON OR GALVANEAL).
Where used: Tables, sinks, and wall facings.

Advantages: Low cost and fairly sturdy.

Disadvantages: Zinc is toxic, wears off readily and leaves iron exposed to air and moisture so that it rusts readily.

Recommended care: Wash with soap and water. Protect from acids that attack zinc. Rub with salt-free oil to protect iron from rusting.

SHEET
STEEL.   *Where used*: Bread pans, roasting pans, and light weight skillets.

Advantages: Inexpensive, sturdy and a good heat conductor.

Disadvantages: Dark color; it rusts easily and is heavy.

Recommended care: Wash with regular pot detergents, rinse well at a high temperature to promote complete drying. Oil with salt-free oil if allowed to stand for a long time.

STAINLESS
STEEL.   *Where used*: Tables, sinks, carts, pots and pans, colanders, bowls, and the various utensils used for manipulating foods during preparation.

Advantages: Bright appearance, easy to maintain, durable, nontoxic, rust free, sturdy.

Disadvantages: Heavy, spotty conductor of heat, high cost.

Recommended care: Wash with detergents, rinse well and air dry. When using abrasives, protect good appearance by rubbing in direction of the grain. Avoid use of abrasives on polished surfaces.

PLASTICS AND HARD
RUBBER.   *Where used*: Cutting boards, equipment bumpers, bowls, spatulas, trays, garbage cans and utensil handles.

Advantages: Color may be used, warm work surfaces. It is less dulling to knives than metal, less absorptive and may be cleaned more thoroughly than wood and is a good insulator.

Disadvantages: Surface becomes marred with use or abrasion, rubber is softened by oils, plastic may crack.

Recommended care: Wash in hot soapy water, rinse with very hot water and air dry. Avoid excess heat, such as range top or direct flame.

WOOD.   *Where used*: Table tops, butcher blocks, cutting boards and utensil handles.

Advantages: Relatively low cost. It is a good surface for cutting and chopping and is a good insulator.

Disadvantages: Will absorb food juices and become unsanitary and is impossible to sterilize.

Recommended care: Never allow to soak; wash quickly in hot soapy water, rinse well and wipe dry with clean cloth or air dry. Stand on side or end to fully dry on both sides. Meat blocks should be scraped and cleaned with steel block brush. Wipe up liquids immediately and prevent soaking into the block.

Assembly of needed utensils is simplified and many steps are saved if the items are stored in or adjacent to the specific work area in which they are used. Economy is served when several workers can share the use of equipment. Even with some duplication of items, the total number needed in central storage would be less than the number required if each section had its own. Because time and effort saving depends on the location of the storage area it should be reasonably close to the work area in which the items are used. A centrally located pot-washing section helps to conserve steps, both in delivering soiled equipment and in picking up clean items. For convenience in checking commonly needed small equipment, the pieces that should be available for each department are listed below.

RECEIVING AND STORAGE AREA

Box opener, to lift tops and pull out nails
Box cutter for pasteboard cartons
Crowbar for large heavy crates
Pliers
Hammer
Screwdriver

Scales, capacity appropriate for amounts normally received
Scoops, grocery type, aluminum
Spindle or clip board for orders and delivery slips
Storage containers, such as bins or cans
Stepladder

VEGETABLE PREPARATION SECTION

Bowls, assorted large sizes
Bowl rack, mobile for large bowls
Colander, stainless or hotel steel
Cutter and grater (hand or machine attachment)
Cutting board, 15 x 20 x 1 to 1¾ in., rubber, plastic, or maple
Knives, French, 10 to 12 in. blade paring, Hotel parer
utility, 6 in. blade, s/s

Hand parer, swivel-action blade
Potato-ball cutter
Storage carts or racks with removable pans (see Figure 2.1)
Pots, stock, aluminum, 15 qt, shallow
Overhead spray attachment above sink with trigger faucet control
Vegetable brushes
Steam cooker pans, both solid and perforated

SALAD AND SANDWICH PREPARATION

Bowls, s/s, assorted sizes
Can opener, heavy duty table model
Colander, large, s/s or aluminum
Cutters, melon ball and corregated
Cutting board, 15 x 20 x 1 to 1¾ in., rubber, plastic, or maple
Egg slicer
Knives, French, 10 in. blade paring
salad or utility, s/s, 6 to 7 in.

Measures, aluminum or s/s, cup, pt, qt, gal; glass cup, pt and qt
Molds, aluminum, individual
Pans, dish, aluminum or s/s, 14 qt
steam table or pudding, s/s
sandwich filling containers, s/s
Scales, utility for formulas and portions
Scoops, ice cream Nos. 12, 16, 20, 30, 40

SALAD AND SANDWICH PREPARATION (*Continued*)

Spoons, measuring, s/s or aluminum
   solid stirring, s/s
   perforated stirring, s/s
   tasting, teaspoons
Spatulas, wide blade, s/s, 6 and 10 in.
   sandwich spreaders
   rubber or plastic
Strainer, reinforced bowl, 8 in.
Tongs, s/s, 6 and 8 in.
Trays, plastic, 14 x 18 in.
Supply cart or rack for supplies
Bottle opener
Forks, serving, 2 tine, 10 to 12 in.
   table

MEAT PREPARATION

Brush, steel, block
Cleaver, 7 to 8 in. blade
Knives, boning, light
   French, 10 to 12 in. blade
   slicing, 12 in. blade
   steak or butcher, 10 to 12 in.
Pans, s/s, 12 x 20 x 1 in.
   s/s, 12 x 20 x 2¼ in.

Saw, butchers, 24 in.
Scales, portion
Sharpening stones, carborundum, 8 x 2 x 1 in.
Steel, butchers, 12 to 14 in.
Trays or baking sheets for portion-ready meats

COOKING SECTION

Boiler, double, aluminum, 4 or 8 qt
Bowls, mixing, s/s, 1½ qt, 3 qt, 5 qt, 8 qt, 13 qt
Can opener, heavy duty table model
Cannister set
Casseroles, individual, 5, 6, or 8 oz
Colander, large aluminum or s/s
Cutter, biscuit, 2 or 2½ in.
Cutting board, 15 x 20 x 1 to 1¾ in.
   rubber, plastic, or maple
Dredges for salt, pepper, flour
Forks, two tines, 12 and 20 in.
Counter pans, s/s, whole or fraction of 12 x 20 in.
Knives, French, 10 to 12 in. blade
   boning, 5 to 6 in.
   paring, hotel parer
   slicing, 12 in.
   utility, s/s, 6 in.
Ladles, s/s, 2, 4, 8, 16 oz
Measures, aluminum, cup, qt, 2 qt, gal.
Paddles for stock kettles, aluminum or heat-resistant plastic or s/s, 24, 36, or 48 in.
Griddle scraper
Cake turner, 11 in. handle
Pitchers, s/s or aluminum, gal cap
Rolling table or cart, 3 deck, s/s
China cap strainer, s/s or retinned steel
Funnel, aluminum, ½ pt
Egg slicer
Flour sifter, tinned steel, 8 c

COOKING SECTION (*Continued*)

Pans, baking sheets, 18 x 26 x 1½
in. tinned steel or aluminum
dish, aluminum, 14 or 20 qt
fry, steel, 4 and 7 in. for individual egg cooking
frying, cast iron or aluminum
10 to 12 x 2 in.
roasting, aluminum or steel with
lugs, 16 x 20 x 5 in. ap-
proximately
sauce, aluminum, hotel steel or
s/s 1½, 2½, 4½, 12 qt
Pots, stock, aluminum, s/s or hotel
steel 12, 16, or 20 qt
Scales for formulas and portioning
Scoops, s/s, Nos. 12, 16, and 20
Skimmer, s/s or aluminum, 5 in.
Spatulas, 6, 8, 10, 12 in. blades

offset, approx. 3 x 6¼ in.
rubber
Spoons, measuring, s/s or aluminum
perforated serving, s/s
solid serving, s/s
long-handled basting, solid
long-handled basting, slotted
tasting, tea or dessert size
Scoops, flour, aluminum, for bins,
I lb
Steamer baskets, tall, narrow, or
wide; solid or perforated
Steak tenderer (maul)
Thermometer, meat and deep fat
Whips, tinned steel wire, sanitary
handle, 8, 12, 16, 24, 36 in.

BAKERY SECTION

Beaters, egg, rotary
Bowls, mixing, s/s, 1½, 3, 5, and
8 qt mixing retinned steel, 12
and 25 qt with mobile stand
Cutters, biscuit, 2 or 2½ in. cooky,
assorted
Knives, French, 10 in. blade
paring
utility, 6 in. s/s blade
Measures, aluminum or s/s with
pouring lip, cup, pt, qt, gal,
heat-proof glass 8, 16, 32 oz
Muffin pans, aluminum or hotel
steel, 2 and 2½ in. diameter
Pans, baking sheets, aluminum
or hotel steel, 18 x 26 x 1½ in.
pie, aluminum or hotel steel
pudding, s/s or aluminum
cake, round, 9¼ x 1½ in.

square, 8 x 8 x 2 in.
loaf, aluminum or steel, 10 x 4
x 4 in.
tube, aluminum, 9¼ x 4 in.
Parer, swivel-action blade
Pastry bags
Pastry tips, set
Peel, if needed for deep oven
Rolling pin, revolving handles,
15 x 3½ in.
Scales, formula and portioning
Brushes, pastry
Corer, apple
Cups, custard, 4 or 5 oz cap.
Cutting board, 12 x 15 x 1 to 1¾
in. rubber, plastic, or maple
Divider, dough (chopping knife)
Scoops, grocer, aluminum, 1 lb
Scoops, ice cream, s/s with plastic

BAKERY SECTION (*Continued*)

handle Nos. 20, 30, 40, and 60

Scraper, dough

Sieve, flour, aluminum, 14 in. diameter

Spatulas, s/s, straight, 6, 8, and 12 in.

offset cake turner

offset pie server

rubber scraper, large

Spoons, measuring, s/s or aluminum

serving, solid, s/s

serving, slotted, s/s

tasting, tea or dessert size

long-handled stirring, s/s

Spice cannisters

Truck or mobile table, s/s, 2 or 3 decks

Strainers, reinforced bowl, 8 in. and 3 in.

china cap for pureeing fruit

Icing grate, ½ in. mesh, 11 x 18 in.

Whips, tinned-steel wire, 8, 12, 16, and 24 in.

SELECTION AND CARE OF SMALL EQUIPMENT

The usefulness of many small pieces of equipment is influenced by their size, design, material, and sturdiness. These features should be well adapted to the purpose for which an item is selected. A kitchen fork, for example, needs to have a handle long enough to turn hot, spattering food without burning the hand. Two tines are better than four, because they make fewer punctures in the food and require less effort to pierce it. Repeated use and such heavy loads as roasts require a sturdy construction and material.

Cannisters

These are to be used for spices and other seasonings. Small compartments built into a cook's or baker's table at high shelf height are convenient and neat appearing. When these have not been provided, it is well to have a cannister set appropriately sized for amounts of seasonings used within a fairly limited time. The preservation of flavor calls for good closure and neatness is served by having a uniform set rather than a heterogeneous assortment of sacks and boxes. Since the cannisters are handled frequently, often with sticky fingers, they should be wiped with a damp cloth daily, and thoroughly cleaned and air dried before being filled.

Carts

Many steps may be saved in kitchen work through the use of carts to move foods into storage, from storage to production areas, and from production to service areas. Carts add flexibility in the arrangement of work centers through furnishing an easy-to-reach space for supplies or completed products. They should be selected carefully for size, which should be large enough for the volume of material required, but small enough to move easily through busy kitchen aisles. A cart should be sturdy enough to support the maximum load to be carried and have wheels or casters of a type that will not clog or stick. The cart should be well bumpered to prevent it from damaging walls and other equipment if it rolls without proper control. Its material and construction should permit thorough scrubbing and steam cleaning.

Casseroles and Custard Cups

These are service items as well as production equipment. It is well when selecting them, therefore, to consider portion control and display possibilities for food. Will the food look attractive when served in the particular container, and will the casserole or cup harmonize with the other tableware? Will heat-resistant opaque china or transparent glass be the most attractive?

China-Cap Strainer, Collanders, and Wire Strainers

Each of these, designed for straining liquids from foods, have particular uses. Wire strainers are small and light weight, range in size from 2 or 3 inches to

Figure 2.1 Carts designed for modular pans.

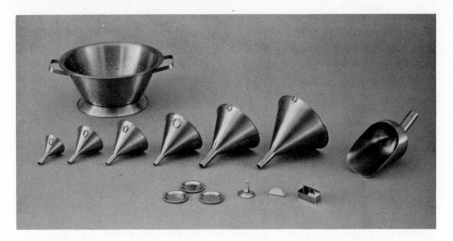

Figure 2.2   Colander, funnels, and scoop. (Courtesy of the Vollrath Company.)

8 or 9 inches in diameter, and are used for straining small amounts. Those measuring 5 inches or more in diameter should have two crisscross wires below the bowl as reinforcement. The mesh may be fine or coarse as required. The material is usually tin-coated wire. Colanders for heavier materials are available in sizes from 15 to 18 inches in diameter. They are made of tin-coated steel, stainless steel, and aluminum, and are fashioned with a foot or base to hold the bowl above the liquid as it drains off. They should be equipped with sturdy handles at the top of both sides. A smaller colander, sauce-pan shape, is available in 1 to 4 quart sizes. It is equipped with a hook on one side and a handle on the other so that it can be rested on top of another pan. This is called a soup strainer or French hotel colander. The purpose of the cone-shaped China cap is chiefly for straining sauces and pureeing foods. If it is to be used as a fruit or vegetable press, it needs a maul fashioned to fit the contours of the cone-shaped China cap. China caps are made of stainless steel, hotel steel, and aluminum. The pressure applied in its use makes sturdy material and construction necessary.

Containers for Food

In spite of the wide range in size and characteristics of containers there are certain specifications that are desirable in both storage containers and serving pans. Any container should have a size and shape appropriate for its use. It should be sanitary, durable, and designed for both convenience and appearance. Thought should be given to how the filled container is to be moved, and how well the food is protected. The container should help to protect quality and prevent contamination.

Figure 2.3   China-cap strainer. (Courtesy of William Hodges & Co., Inc.)

Figure 2.4   Suitable capacity, vermin proof, and Mobile are desirable qualities for storage containers. (Courtesy of Bloomfield Industries, Inc.)

Mobility is an important aspect in convenience. Foods in storage are in a temporary stopping place and need to be moved to be used. Movement should be made easy by putting wheels under heavy objects and limiting bulk and weight. Rehandling is reduced when processed foods are placed in pans that fit into a rack that can be moved into storage, rolled from there to the cooking equipment, and from there to the serving table. Serving pans (approximately 12 × 20 inches), baking sheets (18 × 26 inches), and cafeteria trays (14 × 18 inches) have become sufficiently standardized to be used by manufacturers as modules for measurements in large equipment. Carts, ovens, steam cookers, refrigerators, and serving tables may be selected to accommodate these measurements.

The serving pan that measures approximately 12 × 20 inches is designed to fit a serving table opening that measures $11\frac{7}{8} \times 19\frac{7}{8}$ (200). Pans are made to fit the entire opening or may be in four fractions of this measurement, which, with the use of a cross bar, permit them to be fitted into this space. Depths of the pans may be approximately $2\frac{1}{4}$, 4, and 6 inches. Tight fitting covers are obtainable to fit each size. Utilization of these pans in the various stages of processing and storage of food helps to reduce rehandling. The small sizes are satisfactory for gravy, sauces, and sandwich fillings; the larger ones are useful in vegetable preparation and roasting. All sizes are useful and attractive for display of food on a serving table.

When selecting cooking pots consider the metal and its gauge along with the size and shape. It is well to remember that iron, steel, and aluminum are better conductors of heat than stainless steel. How much cooking and what kind of food is to be cooked in the pot? Some cooks choose stainless steel because of its bright appearance, durability, and ease of cleaning, and ignore its spotty heating and the tendency of food to stick to it. Those who wish steady, even distribution of heat select iron or steel, or aluminum for fast

Figure 2.5 Sizes obtainable in serving pans include full, half (long), two-thirds/one-third, half/one-fourth, and one-sixth/one-ninth. (Courtesy of the Vollrath Company.)

heating. A round shape is best for stirring; a flat bottom that fits tightly over the heat source is the quickest to warm and the most economical of fuel. Since sauce pans are used for a variety of purposes it is well to have them in assorted sizes. They should have sturdy handles securely fastened to the pan.

Pans for frying need to be conditioned to prevent sticking. The lightweight, hotel-style, fry pan used for egg cookery is an example. The pans should be scrubbed with scouring powder and steel wool, then rinsed thoroughly and dried. Next, they should be heated until just too hot to

Figure 2.6 Sauce pans and round serving containers. (Courtesy of the Vollrath Company.)

Figure 2.7   Stock pots and dolly for moving large pots. (Courtesy of the Vollrath Company.)

touch with the bare hand, rubbed with cooking oil, and set aside for a day. Before it is used the pan should be sprinkled with a teaspoonful or more of salt and rubbed vigorously for a minute with a paper towel. The salt is then wiped out with a fresh paper towel and the pan is ready. In cleaning, pans should be wiped with a paper towel, *not* washed. If they are washed, it is well to rub them again with salt; this prevents sticking.

Cutting Boards

Laminated maple cutting boards are widely used in large kitchens, but from the standpoint of sanitation are much less desirable than those made of materials that will not absorb juices. The pieces of maple sometimes separate sufficiently to provide a lodging place for soil. Wood boards that have been impregnated with chemicals and compressed under great pressure until they are impervious to absorption are sanitary because they can be cleaned by scalding. Hard rubber and plastic are fashioned into boards about 1 inch thick; these provide sanitary cutting surfaces that are thoroughly cleanable. Selection of size should be done with thought for the quantity of material to be chopped and the way in which the board is to be used. Small, easy-to-handle boards (10 × 12 × 1 in.) are frequently preferred by workers for cutting small amounts of food. In the cooking and pantry sections where considerable slicing and chopping are done, it is often desirable to have more than one size.

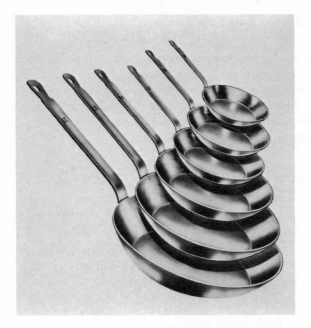

Figure 2.8   French style fry pans. (Courtesy of Bloomfield Industries, Inc.)

Figure 2.9   Cutting boards should be cleanable and impervious to absorption.

Knives and Sharpening Tools

Knives are among the most important tools in food preparation. A keen edge and the proper shape have so much value for efficient work that many food workers are encouraged to own their knives and to be responsible for keeping them in good condition. The knives used most frequently are the French knife, salad or utility knife, and the paring knife. Suggested specifications for this equipment are the following:

FRENCH KNIFE. 10 to 12-inch blade of sturdy weight and reinforced heel, well balanced, of carbon steel that takes and holds a keen edge, with a firmly riveted, sanitary handle.

SALAD OR UTILITY KNIFE. $6\frac{1}{2}$ to 8-inch stainless-steel blade, slender shape, good balance, with firmly riveted, sanitary handle.

PARING KNIFE. 3-inch blade, carbon steel that takes and holds a keen edge and a sanitary handle large enough in diameter to hold for extended periods without causing the hand to cramp.

There are knives in numerous sizes and shapes to fit special purposes, such as a grapefruit knife, bread knife, and steak slicer. Need will determine the advisability of purchase. The knives that are needed by a meat cutter in addition to those listed above include:

BUTCHER KNIFE. 10 to 12-inch blade of sturdy weight, well balanced, and of carbon steel that takes and holds a keen edge, with a firmly riveted, sanitary handle.

BONING KNIFE. 6-inch slender but sturdy blade of carbon steel that takes and holds a keen edge, with a sanitary, firmly riveted handle.

MEAT SLICER. 12-inch flexible blade in straight line, slender shape, of carbon steel that takes and holds a keen edge, with a firmly riveted, sanitary handle.

CLEAVER OR BONE CLIPPER. Carbon steel, size and shape suitable for trimming chops, dressing poultry or other intended use.

A carborundum stone for sharpening knives and a 12 to 14-inch steel should be readily available for use by food workers. A sharpening stone measuring $8 \times 2 \times 1$ inches is a satisfactory size for use. Electric sharpeners may be desirable for use by those who are less skillful in sharpening or who are using inexpensive, difficult-to-sharpen blades like stainless steel. Those who have respect for their knives will be cautious about sharpening them on an electric sharpener, because although it is a quick, easy way of putting an edge on knives it may cause irregularities in the straight edge that lessen the usefulness of the knife. Uneven pressure on the knife during sharpening

Figure 2.10 Knives and steel used in large-quantity food preparation. Courtesy, Russell Harrington Cutlery, Inc.

or irregular length of grinding time at any point can cause this. A novice can quickly damage a knife on a power-driven sharpener.

In the sharpening of dull knives, the coarse side of the carborundum stone is used first and the final finishing is done with the fine side. A straight line should be maintained on the cutting edge from the heel to the tip; this requires uniform sharpening motion and pressure as the edge moves against the stone. Curves worn in the center of the cutting edge spoils its usefulness for cutting or chopping against a flat surface.

The condition of the stone is important to effectiveness in sharpening. Care should be taken to wear the stone evenly, for if the knife is always moved in the same way and in the same place it will wear grooves in the carborundum. Dry stones should be dampened with water or mineral oil, *not* cooking oil, before use. (Cooking oil causes the stone to become gummy.) The stone should be wiped after each use, and washed with soap and water if it becomes soiled.

In sharpening, the carborundum is placed on a damp cloth on the table. (This helps prevent the stone from slipping.) Then the angle of the stone is arranged to permit a free, easy arc in the arm movement when sharpening. When the motion is to the right, the stone forms an angle of approximately 60° with the front line of the table (see Figure 2.11); when the motion is to the left, the stone should be shifted to make the angle approximately 45°. The sharpening motion may be either pushing the knife forward from tip to

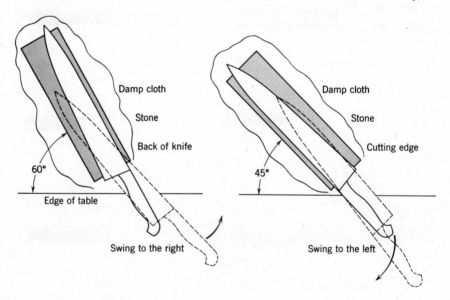

Figure 2.11   Motion for sharpening knife on a carborundum stone.

heel or drawing it back from heel to tip, as long as whichever motion used is followed consistently. *It should never be moved back and forth.* When the knife is drawn back, moving from heel to tip with the cutting edge turned toward the left, the arm is moved in an arc back and away from the body. When the cutting edge is turned toward the right, the angle of the stone should be adjusted, and the knife swung in an arc to the left.

The angle of the knife against the stone is important. The knife and the stone should form an angle of approximately 20 degrees (see Figure 2.12). If the angle is less the stone brushes the bevel on the sides of the knife and does not sharpen the edge. If the angle is greater, the edge is removed or turned to the side. When the knife is in use, a fine edge may develop burrs or areas where the edge is slightly bent. If this happens it may be trued by stroking it at a 20° angle against a magnetized steel. The blade should be cleaned after the knife has been sharpened.

A keen edge adds to the usefulness of knives but presents a hazard if they are not handled wisely. Knives should never be laid on work surfaces where they may be covered by food or equipment, but always placed where their presence can be observed. A worker picking up an item should not be in danger of striking the keen edge and being cut. One should be careful not to drop knives; this damages the knives and may also cause a foot injury. Knives should be stored, with the sharp edges protected from being damaged or dangerous, in a location within easy reach of the work center.

A French knife is gripped in the manner that permits the easiest action, the best control of motion, and the use of the necessary force. Three motions commonly used are (a) the rocking of the heel up and down from the tip, (b) raising the entire blade and chopping down, and (c) a slicing motion in which the knife is moved forward and back. In the first type of motion, the fingers of the left hand may be placed on the tip of the knife to steady and hold it in position, while the right hand grasps the handle and moves up and down with an easy motion of the wrist and arm. Where more perfect control and force are required, in dicing or cutting julienne strips, for example, a closed grip on the handle is needed. The knife is gripped with the first finger on the right side of the knife blade and the thumb on the left, with the other fingers wrapped around the handle near the heel of the blade (see Figure 2.13).

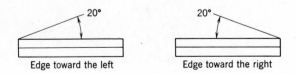

20°	20°
Edge toward the left	Edge toward the right

Figure 2.12   Angle of the knife on the stone when sharpening.

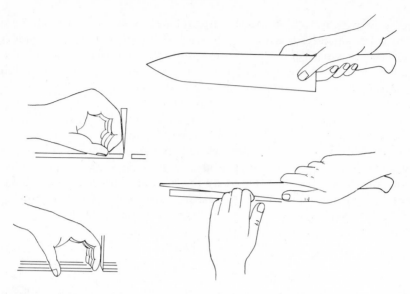

Figure 2.13   Position of the hands in holding both knife and materials for control and use of force in cutting.

It is necessary to be alert when using a French knife to make cuts of food that are uniform in size and shape, and to avoid cutting oneself. This means controlling the action of the knife and the finger tips holding the food. The following are some hints in the correct use of this tool. (a) Keep moving the tips back as the cutting proceeds. (b) Keep the second joints of the fingers

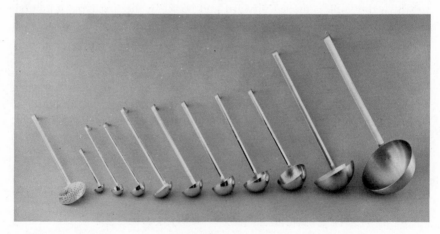

Figure 2.14   A skimmer and ladles ranging in capacity from $\frac{1}{2}$ ounce to 72 ounces. (Courtesy of the Vollrath Company.)

at right angles with the cutting surface. (c) Allow the side of the knife blade to ride against the projecting finger or fingers. Avoid being cut by (a) keeping finger tips curled back, (b) holding the knife blade at right angles with the cutting surface and flat against the projecting fingers, and (c) avoiding raising the knife higher than the fingers.

Ladles and Scoops

Many ladles and scoops are sufficiently standardized to serve as convenient measures for ingredients or portions. They are of special value in portioning tasks as filling muffin pans, dropping cookies, scooping desserts, and ladling soup and sauces. The size numbers of scoops refer to the number of scoops (level) in a quart.

TABLE 2.1 SCOOP AND LADLE SIZES

Number	Volume	Approximate Weight Liquid	
Scoops			
No. 6	⅔ c	5 oz	
No. 8	½ c	4 oz	
No. 10	⅜ c	3¼ oz	
No. 12	⅓ c	2⅔ oz	
No. 16	¼ c	2 oz	
No. 20	3⅕ tbsp	1½ oz	
No. 24	2⅔ tbsp	1⅓ oz	
No. 30	2⅕ tbsp	1 oz	
No. 40	1⅗ tbsp	0.8 oz	
No. 60	1 tbsp	0.5 oz	
		Bowl Dia. (in.)	Handle Length (in.)
Ladles			
1 oz	2 tbsp	1¾	10
2 oz	¼ c	2⅜	9⅜
4 oz	½ c	3⅜	12⅝
6 oz	¾ c	3½	12⅜
8 oz	1 c	4	12⅝
12 oz	1½ c	4⅜	12⅛
24 oz	3 c	6	18⅛
32 oz	1 qt	8⅛	17

Measuring Equipment

Accurate means of measure are needed for receiving and issuing supplies, measuring ingredients for formulas, and portioning foods for service. Weight is the quickest, easiest, and most accurate means of measure in most instances. Good scales are indispensable in large kitchens. Scales are needed that (a) accurately weigh the largest amount and indicate the smallest gradation regularly used, (b) retain accuracy, (c) indicate weights in easily legible form, (d) have a platform large enough for containers commonly used for ingredients, and (e) subtract the weight of the tare (weight of the container) from the weight of the ingredients.

The cooking section and the bakery use scales daily, not only for measuring the ingredients for recipes, but also for scaling (weighing) food into containers for cooking and serving. Uniform weights of food placed in standardized pans aids in portioning because a given number of portions of specified size per pan may be obtained. Heavy duty scales are needed for this. The light weight, spring-balance scales that are widely used are not sufficiently accurate or sturdy, but their compact size and low cost promote their use in many kitchens. They are better than no scales at all, but their accuracy varies $\frac{1}{8}$ to $\frac{1}{5}$ ounce or more and they need to be checked frequently.

Scales are tools to promote precision and their value is in relation to their accuracy. The steel spring in the small spring-balance scales becomes fatigued through continued use and its degree of accuracy becomes undependable. The service life of both it and the larger, more expensive models can be prolonged through proper care. Scales should be placed where they set level and where they receive a minimum amount of jarring. Portable ones should always be handled by the base. Objects should be removed from the platform when the scale is not in use. Since gummy build-up of soil interferes with accuracy scales should be kept clean by wiping with a damp cloth or washing with soap and water. It is desirable for heavy duty scales to have sealed-in mechanisms that protect them from soil, and exterior finishes that are streamlined and easy to keep clean.

Accurate volume measures are needed also. These may be made of glass, aluminum, stainless steel, or tinned steel. Metal measures for dry ingredients, if graduated to the top edge, may be levelled by removing excess material with a straight edged knife or spatula. Glass measures with capacity extending above the last graduation, are preferable for liquids. In measuring, the container should be set on a flat surface and filled until the bottom of the meniscus (curved surface) is even with the desired measure or graduation. Personal preference may determine whether spoon measures should be separate or have the tablespoon, teaspoon, and fractions of the teaspoon fastened together.

Figure 2.15   A heavy duty scale with easy to read dial, convenient tare adjustment and platform large enough for institution pans. (Courtesy of the Toledo Scale Company.)

Figure 2.16   Convenience and accuracy require measures that range in capacity from one-fourth teaspoon to one gallon.

Some foods, spices, for example, may be more conveniently measured by volume than by weight because of their character or the small amount needed. (See the table for Equivalent Measures of Foods in the Appendix.) In measuring, soda, baking powder, cream of tartar, cornstarch, spices, and other ingredients that tend to settle firmly, first should be stirred, then placed in the measure to overflowing and leveled to exact measure with a straight edged instrument. All measures need to be level to be accurate. Flour should be sifted once before it is measured and then handled lightly. It should not be pressed or shaken down. Brown sugar, on the other hand, should be packed into the measure firmly enough to hold its shape when turned out unless the recipe indicates that it is to be lightly packed. Granulated sugar should be handled lightly and should not be shaken down. If it is lumpy powdered sugar should be sifted or pressed through a sieve, then measured lightly into the measure with a spoon or a scoop, and leveled with a straight edged knife or spatula. Syrups, molasses, melted fat, oil, and other viscous material that

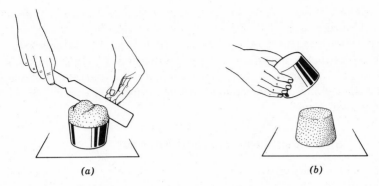

Figure 2.17   Points in measuring dry ingredients. (*a*) Fill to overflowing and level with a straight edge. (*b*) Pack brown sugar until it holds the shape of the measure.

tends to adhere to the measure should be scraped out of the container with a rubber spatula in order to get the full measure. Tablespoons and teaspoons are used to measure amounts less than $\frac{1}{4}$ cup.

In America, volume is measured by cups, pints, quarts, and gallons, and weight by ounces and pounds. The metric system is used in most European countries; often, it is used here in the calculation and preparation of special diets. The volume is measured in litres and the weight in grams. Americans must have a knowledge of equivalent measures if they wish to use recipes from other countries and to understand these weights when they are used in hospitals.

TABLE 2.2 EQUIVALENT MEASURES

Metric Measures	Pound Weights	Volume
1 g	.035	⅕ tsp liquid
	(.035 × g = oz)	
15 g	½ oz	1 tbsp liquid
28.35 g	1 oz	2 tbsp liquid
	(28.35 × oz = g)	
100 g	3½ oz	Scant ½ c
114 g	4 oz	½ c liquid
226.78 g	8 oz	1 c liquid
1 kg—1000 g	2.21 lb	4½ c liquid (1.06 qt)
1 l		(l × .95 = qt)
453.59	1 lb	1 pt liquid
500 g—1 demilitre	1.1 lb	1 pt liquid generous

British weight and volume for pints, quarts, and gallons differ from those in the United States. The British pint contains 20 fluid ounces and the United States pint has 16 ounces. Their quarts weigh 40 fluid ounces which is equivalent to $4\frac{3}{4}$ cups liquid in the United States. They call five fluid ounces a gill. Familiarity with fractional amounts of a larger measure is useful when reducing or increasing recipes, or when translating amounts to the one that is easiest to use.

Spatulas, Skimmers, and Spoons

These are important manipulative tools. Spatulas may vary in length from the sandwich spreader with a $3\frac{1}{2}$-inch blade to one that has a 12-inch blade. Width may range from $\frac{3}{4}$ inch to $6\frac{1}{4}$ inches. Some need to be flexible (those used for loosening food from a baking pan) and others should have rigidity (those used for frosting cakes or turning hamburgers). When lifting tender material from a deep pan or when working over a hot surface, such as a grill, it is important that the spatula be offset instead of straight. It is desirable to have the spatulas for salads and sandwiches made of stainless steel. Those for the majority of kitchen uses may be of carbon steel. Rubber spatulas are needed for removing pasty or viscous material from containers and for combining light mixtures with a folding motion.

Offset spatula   Pie server

Straight spatula   Cook's fork

Ball cutter

Figure 2.18   Spatulas, cook's fork, and ball cutter. (Courtesy of Russell Harrington Cutlery, Inc.)

Skimmers are used for removing congealed fat from the top of stock and for straining solids out of liquids. They may be either the scroll or the perforated type. The flat, perforated disc approximately 5 inches in diameter and fastened to a hooked handle is the type most often preferred. They may be made of stainless steel or retinned steel (see Figure 2.14).

Every kitchen needs small spoons for tasting, medium-sized spoons for stirring and service, and long-handled spoons for basting and manipulating foods during preparation. Many steps can be saved and good practice promoted by having tasting spoons in a convenient location in every production department. They also are needed for manipulating small mixtures. Spoons need to be appropriate in size for the size of the container and the volume of material that is being handled. A variation in size is desirable. Both solid-bowl and perforated or slotted spoons are needed. Stainless steel is the preferred material but retinned-steel spoons are satisfactory and lower in cost. Either material needs to be of sufficiently heavy gauge for sturdiness.

Thermometers and Timers

Thermometers and timers are indicators of significant factors in food preparation. Reliable thermostats on ovens and deep-fat fryers are valuable aids, but there are times (as in roasting meat) when a thermometer is needed to show when a desired temperature has been reached. Oven and deep-fat thermometers are useful in determining the actual temperature of slow heating equipment and the reliability of the temperature registered by the equipment. A thermometer should be chosen for (a) accuracy in registering temperature, (b) appropriateness for specific use, (c) sturdiness to wishstand repeated use,

Figure 2.19   Perforated spoons, slotted spoons, three-cornered stirring spoons, and solid spoons have particular uses. (Courtesy of the Vollrath Company.)

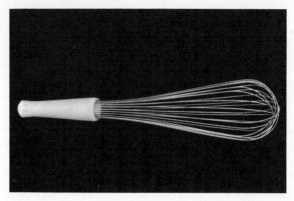

Figure 2.20   Flexible piano wire whip with plastic handle. (Courtesy of William Hodges & Co., Inc.)

and (d) clearly indicated temperatures that are easy to read. Dropping or subjecting thermometers of glass to rapid, extreme changes in temperature is likely to damage them. All thermometers should be handled carefully and cleaned thoroughly after each use.

Timers installed on equipment are always in place and very convenient to use. When an oven, steamer, or other large piece of equipment lacks a timer it is a good idea to supply a portable one. This can be labor saving through reducing inspection time. The accuracy of the timer should be checked periodically against a time piece of known accuracy.

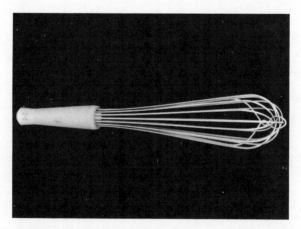

Figure 2.21   French hotel whip of sturdy wire reinforced, set in plastic handle. (Courtesy of William Hodges & Co., Inc.)

Whips and Beaters

Whips are constructed of stainless or retinned steel wire set into a handle of wood or metal. For sanitary reasons, it is important to select those that are set or sealed into the handle in a manner that makes them completely cleanable and eliminates lodging places for soil. The size of the whip and the flexibility of the wire should be appropriate for the intended use. Those that are used for stirring or beating a large volume or a thick mass need strength and rigidity. Those to be used for thin foods, such as cream or eggs, should be light and flexible. Rotary beaters are needed for foods that require rapid agitation and are in amounts too small to use the power mixer.

SUGGESTED LABORATORY EXPERIENCE

1. Visit a large kitchen or an equipment supply house where a variety of utensils may be seen. Identify the utensils and discuss their intended purposes. Evaluate material and construction for use and durability, and sanitation.

2. Visit specific departments in a large kitchen and inventory kind and number of items of small equipment available for each department. Note whether used by one or more workers and where stored.

3. Sharpen a French knife with a carborundum stone until it is sharp enough to slice a ripe tomato into smooth slices $\frac{1}{4}$ inch thick.

4. Demonstrate proper technique for holding a French knife when
   (a) chopping parsley,   (c) dicing potatoes or making julienne strips,
   (b) making celery rings,   (d) shredding cabbage.

5. Prepare an instruction sheet for employees briefly stating points for safety when handling and storing knives.

6. Condition an iron or steel fry pan to prevent sticking.

7. Weigh and compare the following:
   (a) 1 cup of flour dipped from the bin or sack and leveled with a spatula and 1 cup of sifted flour placed gently in the cup by spoonsful and leveled. After weighing, strike cup of sifted flour on the table, and note the change in level of flour in the cup.
   (b) 1 cup of brown sugar poured loosely into the cup without packing and 1 cup of brown sugar firmly packed so that it holds its shape when turned out of the cup.
   (c) Weigh 1 quart container. Fill it with water to an exact quart measure and weigh it on a spring-balance scale. Subtract the weight of the container. Repeat with a large scale. Compare the weights. Are adjustments needed?

8. Convert the following:
   (a) 57 grams into ounces,
   (b) 5 ounces into grams,
   (c) 20 tablespoons into cups,
   (d) 12 pints into gallons,
   (e) $1\frac{1}{2}$ quarts into liquid pounds,
   (f) $2\frac{1}{2}$ ounces liquid into tablespoons,
   (g) $\frac{1}{6}$ pint into fractions of a cup,
   (h) 40 ounces into pounds.

REVIEW QUESTIONS AND ANSWERS

1. What are the nontoxic metals most commonly used for kitchen utensils?

Stainless steel, aluminum, and retinned or hotel steel.

2. What are the chief advantages of each?

Stainless steel—durable, easy to maintain, does not rust or react with foods.
Aluminum—rapid, uniform heat conduction, bright appearance, relatively low cost.
Retinned steel—fairly durable, sturdy, relatively low cost, good heat conductor.

3. What points should be considered when storing small equipment?

Convenience for use, protection from soil, and where it would be easy to find.

4. What features affect usefulness of small equipment?

Appropriateness of size, design, material, and sturdiness.

5. What qualities are important in carts?

Size and sturdiness appropriate to carry weight and volume normally required, size and wheels that promote ease of movement, well bumpered to prevent damage.

6. How does modularity of food pans reduce labor?

Modularity reduces rehandling of food in order for pans to fit equipment.

7. What qualities are desirable in a cutting board?

A sanitary surface that causes the least dulling of knives, a size that is appropriate and easy to handle, and possible to clean easily and thoroughly.

8. What are the chief uses for a French knife?

Chopping, shredding, dicing, and mincing foods.

9. Is it a suitable knife for slicing meat?

No. A slender bladed slicing knife is more flexible and will do a better job.

10. Why is stainless steel used for salad and utility knives?

For its stainless quality. Carbon steel tends to develop a dark oxide that may rub off on food being cut.

11. Why is it important to maintain an even pressure on a blade as it is being sharpened?

To avoid developing irregularities in the straight edge of the knife.

12. At what degree of angle should a blade be held in relation to the stone when sharpening?

20°.

13. Why is this angle important?

If the angle is greater the edge is removed, and if it is too little the blade rests on the bevel or side and the edge is not sharpened.

14. What treatment should be given to the stone before using it for sharpening?

It should be moistened with mineral oil or water.

15. Why is the stone placed on a damp cloth during sharpening?

To prevent slipping.

16. How can one avoid wearing grooves in the carborundum stone?

By using the entire surface of the stone when sharpening and not making the strokes in only one area.

17. What is the purpose of the magnetized steel?

To true up the edge and remove burrs or turned spots that form on the edge during use.

18. List common cutting accidents to be avoided.

Knife slipping when using force, dropping knife on feet, striking sharp edge when knife is hidden under objects or improperly stored.

19. How can cutting accidents be avoided?

Keep knives where they can be seen, be alert when using them, hold them firmly when using, cut in direction away from person, store properly when not in use.

20. What volume and liquid weight is contained in scoops Nos. 8, 16, 30, and 60?

No. 8—$\frac{1}{2}$ cup or 4 ounces liquid; No. 16—$\frac{1}{4}$ cup or 2 ounces liquid; No. 30—$2\frac{1}{5}$ tablespoon or 1 ounce liquid; and No. 60—1 tablespoon or $\frac{1}{2}$ ounce liquid.

21. Why is it important for scoops and ladles to be standardized?

So that they are useful in preparing and portioning foods.

22. What is the most accurate means of measuring ingredients?

Weight.

23. List important points in selection of scales.

Accuracy in weighing, amounts normally required, durable retention of accuracy, easy to read weights, platform of proper size, and subtraction of tare.

24. List points to observe in care of scales.

Set level, avoid jarring, keep clean, remove objects from platform when not in use, and lift by the base when moving.

25. What is a skimmer and how is it used?

It is a utensil with a perforated disc or scroll fastened to a handle and used to remove congealed fat from stock or to strain solids from liquids.

26. Why should production departments have tasting spoons?

To promote sanitary sampling of foods for judging quality, to reduce time and steps in searching for a spoon, and to encourage tasting to insure quality.

27. Why should baking powder and cornstarch be stirred before measuring by volume?

These foods tend to settle and a more consistently accurate measure can be obtained if they are stirred before measuring.

28. What is the chief value of a timer?

By giving warning of specified times it reduces labor time and effort spent in inspection.

29. List desired properties of a thermometer.

Accurate temperatures appropriate for intended use, sturdiness to withstand frequent use, and temperatures shown in a manner that can be read easily.

30. List the important selection points for whips.

Appropriate size and sturdiness, flexible or rigid according to need for intended use, and sanitary construction.

3.

Aspects with General Application in Food Production

Successful operation of a large quantity food establishment calls for the consistent production of good food. In order to do this, those responsible for producing the food need to have reliable judgment of food quality and be able to choose suitable materials and control methods in its production. Extensive studies have been made in both research laboratories and practical kitchen work to determine what materials, conditions, and techniques are required for satisfactory results. Trial and error methods are too expensive for both individuals who hope to build a reputation for their ability in food production and food establishments that hope to attract a profitable clientele. Obtaining dependable results calls for following reliable procedures.

JUDGMENT OF QUALITY

Appreciation of excellence in quality in each food product serves as both a guide and a stimulus in its production. Excellence is measured by the degree of acceptability of a food of specific quality by the majority of people. This means that those who cater to the public must be sensitive, not only to specific characteristics of foods, but also to the popular reaction to foods. Exact definitions of excellence may appear elusive at times because of differences in taste; for example, one group may describe an excellent biscuit as one that has high volume, light color, tender, bready texture, and a rich, wheaty flavor and another may prefer thin, rich, flaky, well-browned, crusty biscuits.

The principles and procedures recommended in this text are based on qualities that have been judged as generally acceptable by laboratory panels composed of persons familiar with public preferences. The qualities described can be useful as guides for those who are learning to evaluate qualities. Before

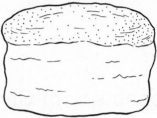

Figure 3.1 Does your public prefer a rich, crisp, shallow biscuit or one that is tall and light but less rich?

preparing a product, a person should have in mind both the qualities of the product he wishes to produce and the conditions that are required to produce them. It is at this point that a person can be effective in controlling materials or procedures. The difference in the biscuits, for example, may result from the variation in kneading and length of baking time and temperature. Products should be regularly analyzed after production to evaluate the acceptability of their various characteristics. How enjoyable is the quality? What are the most appealing features? What elements are objectionable? How may the product be improved?

Acceptance of a quality that is too low is hazardous to success. Conscientious workers have been known to lose their jobs because they accepted inferior quality as satisfactory when they did not know or appreciate better quality. Caterers have been known to fail in spite of diligent effort, because of their lack of understanding of public preferences and inability to give people food of the quality they desired. The development of quality judgment is a highly significant part of large quantity food preparation.

Words are inadequate in developing appreciation of the fine gradations of excellence. Clear concepts of quality are best developed through firsthand experience. In order to develop quality judgment, an individual needs to have an opportunity to sample, analyze, and compare foods of superior quality. A beginner may faithfully follow a recipe but be unable to evaluate the results accurately if he is unfamiliar with acceptable standards. Experience with products of commonly accepted quality gives him a basis for comparing the quality of the product he has prepared.

It is well to develop a habit of noting preferences shown by people in their selection of food because "actions speak louder than words" in showing food preferences. People sometimes complain about food when they are unhappy about something else. Some may say they like a food, but avoid eating it. It is important to note where patronage is heavy, which foods sell in the largest volume, and, especially, what foods are selected repeatedly. The qualities of specific foods with particular appeal or enjoyment value can then be analyzed.

The elements of excellence that add delight to the enjoyment of food are often fragile. Such qualities have sufficient strength, however, to cause people to walk an extra distance and pay a higher price for meals. Included are such things as sharpness of temperature, the bloom of freshness, delectable flavor, and beauty of appearance. A one-time happening is insufficient for success. Patrons require assurance that they will not be disappointed. Even one failure raises doubts. Quality must be consistent to be reassuring. This means that those who prepare food need to be skillful in following the procedures essential in producing good food consistently. Development of skill requires practice in using right techniques until the techniques have become second nature, or the most natural way to perform the activity.

UTILIZATION OF MATERIALS

Substitutions

The lack of one ingredient can sometimes delay or prevent the production of a product. In many instances, another food may be substituted in a recipe without greatly changing the quality of the product. In order to do this, it is necessary to understand product qualities and to know which foods may be substituted for others. Table 3.1 lists the measurements of common foods that are required in their substitution for specific measurements of other foods.

Leavening Agents

The leavening agents used in batters and doughs to make them light and porous are classified as physical, chemical, and biological leavens. The physical leavens commonly used are steam and air. Popover and cream-puff batters are examples of leavening by steam. When these batters are baked at high temperatures, steam is formed from moisture in the batter and causes the batter to swell during baking. Air may be incorporated into batters by beating and in doughs by folding and kneading. Air may be incorporated into egg whites and folded into batters. During baking, the high temperature causes the air to expand; this makes the product light and porous.

Chemical leavening is brought about by the gas (carbon dioxide) formed through the action of an alkaline ingredient, usually soda (sodium bicarbonate), with an acid, such as those found in baking powders or in sour milk or molasses. The acid ingredient in baking powder may be (a) a tartrate, which liberates its gas quickly in the presence of moisture at room temperature, has very little residue flavor, and is satisfactory for use by those who work quickly and bake products immediately; (b) the acid phosphate,

TABLE 3.1 INGREDIENT SUBSTITUTIONS

Recipe Item	Amount	Substitute Ingredients
Baking powder	1 tsp	¼ tsp soda + ⅝ tsp cream of tartar.
Butter	1 c	⅞ to 1 c hydrogenated fat + ½ tsp salt, ⅞ c oil + ½ tsp salt, 1 c margarine, or ⅞ c clarified chicken fat + ½ tsp salt.
Chocolate	1 oz sq	3 tbsp cocoa + 1 tbsp fat.
Cocoa	3 tbsp	Reduce fat in recipe 1 tbsp, add 1 oz chocolate.
Cornstarch (thickening)	1 tbsp	2 tbsp flour (approximately).
Cream (18 to 20%)	1 c	⅞ c milk + 3 tbsp fat.
Cream (32 to 40%)	1 c	¾ c milk + ⅓ c fat.
Egg, whole	1 lge	3 tbsp slightly beaten egg, 2 egg yolks, or 2 tbsp whole egg solids + 2½ tbsp water.
Egg yolk	1	1⅓ tbsp frozen egg yolk or 2 tbsp dried egg yolk + 2 tsp water (lukewarm).
Egg white	1	2 tsp dried white + 2 tbsp water (lukewarm), or 2 tbsp frozen egg white.
Flour, all-purpose	1 c	1 c + 2 tbsp cake flour, 1 c less 2 tbsp cornmeal, 1 c graham flour, 1 c rye flour, 1½ c bread flour, or 1 c rolled oats.

which liberates gas more slowly but at mixing temperatures; and (c) sodium aluminum sulfate, which, when combined with calcium acid phosphate, becomes a double-acting powder that liberates part of the gas at room temperature but continues to react, thus releasing most of the gas at baking temperature. Since it has a bitter residue flavor great care must be taken to

TABLE 3.1 (*Continued*)

Recipe Item	Amount	Substitute Ingredients
Flour, cake	1 c	1 c less 2 tbsp all-purpose flour.
Flour (thickening)	1 tbsp	½ to ¾ tbsp cornstarch, potato starch, or arrowroot; 2 tbsp granular cereal; 1 whole egg, 2 yolks, or 2 whites; or 1 tbsp granular tapioca.
Honey	1 c	1¼ c sugar and ¼ c liquid.
Milk, fresh, whole	1 c	½ c evaporated milk + ½ c water, ¼ c nonfat milk solids + water to make ⅞ c + 1 tbsp butter, or 1 c sour milk or buttermilk + ½ tsp soda (decrease baking powder 2 tsp).
Milk, sour or buttermilk	1 c	1 tbsp lemon juice or vinegar + fresh milk to make 1 c.
Sugar, granulated	1 c	1⅓ c brown sugar, lightly packed; 1½ c powdered sugar; 1¼ to 1½ c corn syrup less ¼ to ½ c liquid; 1 c honey less ¼ to ⅓ c liquid; or 1⅓ c molasses less ⅓ c liquid.
Tapioca, granular	1 tbsp	2 tbsp pearl tapioca, 1 tbsp flour (for thickening), or 2 tbsp granular cereal.
Tomatoes, canned	1 c	1⅓ c diced fresh tomatoes, simmered 10 minutes (reduced to 1 c).
Yeast, active dry	1 pkg (¼ oz)	1 cake compressed yeast.

use only the amount required for leavening. Nevertheless, it is the best type to use if the batters must be held for a period before baking. Differences in baking powder make it important to follow the manufacturer's directions carefully.

The leavening power of $\frac{1}{2}$ teaspoon of soda with either 1 cup of sour milk or $\frac{1}{2}$ cup of molasses is equal to that of 2 teaspoons of baking powder. Baking powder may be added if additional leavening is required by the recipe.

Because the leavening gas begins to escape as soon as soda and acid are mixed with liquid, it is best to sift the soda and baking powder with the flour before incorporating it into the other ingredients, rather than adding it directly to the liquid.

The biological leavens are bacteria and yeast. Bacteria has very limited use in leavening. The bacteria in cornmeal causes a fermentation with escaping gas that is utilized for leavening salt-rising bread. Yeast is widely used and may be procured in either the compressed or dry-active state. The yeast plants multiply in the presence of moisture and sugar, and liberate carbon dioxide gas which leavens the dough. Temperatures above 110°F kill the yeast plants, and temperatures lower than 65°F retard their growth.

Thickening and Jelling Agents

Various ingredients are used to develop a thicker consistency in liquids. Table 3.2, pp. 62-63, lists those most commonly used.

Seasoning of Food

A knowledge of flavoring materials and harmony of flavors should serve as a guide for developing the most appealing flavor quality. The purpose of seasoning is to increase the palatability of food. The seasoner needs to be aware of the most appealing natural flavors in foods and must know when and how to enhance them. There are instances when it is well to support delicate flavors and other times when strong or objectionable flavors need to be masked or subdued. In no part of food preparation is greater sensitivity required.

Interest and delectable taste can often be developed through a skillful use of herbs and spices. It is necessary to develop a sensitive discernment for each of the flavoring materials and a fairly precise knowledge of the amounts to use. A person who is unfamiliar with herbs and spices can acquaint himself with them by steeping a small amount in hot water, savoring the aroma, and sipping the brew for flavor. This exercise helps in distinguishing one flavor from another. It is necessary to taste a flavor added to a recipe to know what effect it will have on the palatability of specific foods or food combinations. Addition of seasonings to a recipe should be made cautiously; only a small amount of one should be used until its influence on flavor can be determined. The development of appealing flavor blends can be regarded as one of the fine, creative adventures in cooking. (See Table 3.3 for seasonings.)

Foods depend on volatile oils or esters for flavor. These escape from some foods more rapidly than from others. When one readily detects aroma from a food, he can know that flavor-giving substances are being lost. Much of the aromatic quality of spices and herbs is lost upon standing unless they are kept in tightly closed containers. Since fresh products have the most flavor they should be purchased in quantities that can be used within one season.

Toppings, Garnishes, and Accompaniments

Toppings, garnishes, and accompaniments are used to add extra appeal to fine foods. They should be used with restraint and only when needed to add interest by furnishing contrasting color, form, texture, and flavor to the dish with which they are used. Browned crumbs can make a simple, creamed casserole appear rich and golden. A sprig of green watercress can add freshness to a salad or an entree, and cherry red may catch admiring attention. Garnishes should always be appropriate to the food with which they are served, and should harmonize in flavor. They should be edible and should add enjoyment to the food quality.

The term *topping* is used here to denote food finishes that are sprinkled on, or poured over, the food. *Garnishes* are decorative or ornamental touches like a sprig of parsley on a plate. An *accompaniment* may serve as a garnish, but its chief function is to enhance the eating pleasure of the food it accompanies with contrasting texture and flavor; for example, a spiced fruit or relish served with a bland meat. Since it is often difficult to classify these foods into three distinct groups it may be just as well to think of them collectively as additions that enhance food appeal.(Table 3.4).

The person who wants to make a good impression takes a last glimpse of himself in the mirror before appearing in public. Well-prepared food deserves similar concern for appearance before it is presented to diners. At this time it should be noted whether the best things have been done to make it attractive and delectable.

CONTROL OF CONDITIONS

From the time items are delivered to a kitchen until they are prepared for service many conditions may influence the ultimate quality of food. Humidity, temperature, and length of holding time in storage have a pronounced effect. Because of variations in storage requirements for different products, storage needs (with the exception of those for frozen foods) are included with the directions for the preparation of specific products.

TABLE 3.2 THICKENING AND JELLING AGENTS

Agent	Use	Amount for 1 gal		Precautions	Characteristics
		Weight	Volume		
Agar	Salad and desserts	1.11 oz	3⅓ tbsp	Soak in 1½ c cold liquid before adding to hot liquid.	Rigid, transparent, gel.
Egg, whole	Desserts and sauces	20 oz	2½ c	Cook at slow heat. Overcooking causes curdling and weeping.	Firm gel when baked. Thickened, but soft when stirred.
yolk	Desserts and sauces	18 oz	2 c		
Flour, cake	Thin soups, medium sauces	4 oz 8 to 10 oz	1 c 2 to 2½ c	Mix with cold liquid or fat before adding to hot liquid.	Opaque paste.
bread	Thin soups, medium sauces	5 oz 10 to 12 oz	1¼ c 2¼ to 3 c	Acid causes thinning ; sugar reduces thickening power.	
Waxy maize starch	Frozen sauces and gravies	2½ to 3 oz	⅜ to ½ c	Blend with cold liquid or fat, then add to hot liquid. Thickens at 158 to 176°F.	Transparent paste, freezes well.
Waxy rice flour	Frozen sauces and gravies	4 to 5 oz	2 to 2½ c	Mix with cold liquid or fat, then add to hot liquid. Thickens at 158 to 176°F.	Forms opaque paste.

TABLE 3.2 (Continued)

Agent	Use	Amount for 1 gal		Precautions	Characteristics
		Weight	Volume		
Gelatin, granulated, unflavored	Salad and desserts	2 oz	½ c	Soak in 2 c cold water, then dissolve in hot liquid. Add sugar after gelatin is dissolved. Enzyme in raw pineapple prevents jelling.	Firm, quivery, transparent.
Gum tragacanth	Salad dressings and sauce	½ to 1 oz thin 1½ to 2¼ oz thick	1½ to 3 tbsp	Thickening power and amount required varies. Dissolve in hot or cold water. Thinned by acid, salt, and heat.	Thick and mucilaginous but not rigid.
Irish moss	Puddings and sauces	1 to 1¼ oz (thick paste) 4½ to 7 oz (stiff mold)	3 to 4 tbsp 1 to 1½ c	Soak in cold water, then heat to 140°F. Melts at 81 to 106°F.	Thick, mucilaginous gel. Acid plus heat causes thinning.
Cornstarch and rice	Sauces and puddings	2½ oz	½ c	Mix with cold liquid before adding to hot liquid. Thinned by acid. Add acid after thickened.	Transparent when fully cooked.
Potato starch and arrowroot	Fruit sauces and puddings	2½ oz	½ c	Thickens at 158 to 175°F. Thinned by higher heat and stirring.	Very transparent paste.
Tapioca, quick cooking	Soup or pie filling	1 to 3½ oz	⅓ to ½ c	Stir while cooking. Becomes sticky if stirred after cooling.	Transparent paste, good for pie filling.
	Puddings	9 oz	1½ c		

63

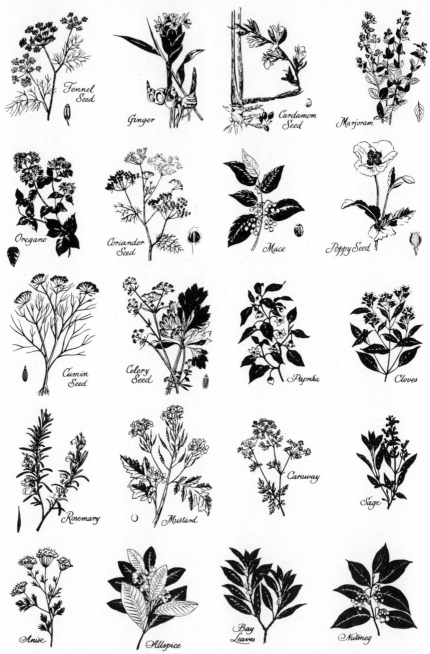

Figure 3.2 Spices and herbs used in cooking. (Courtesy of the American Spice Trade Association.)

TABLE 3.3 SUGGESTED USES OF HERBS, SPICES, AND OTHER SEASONING MATERIALS

Seasoning	Eggs and Cheese	Meats and Poultry	Fish and Shellfish	Vegetables and Fruits	Breads and Desserts
Herbs					
Basil	Omelets, cheese spread.	Beef, lamb and veal roasts, hamburgers, sausage, spaghetti and meatball, lamb chops, and stews.	Shrimp, tuna, crabmeat, and salmon.	Tomato dishes, carrots, peas, onions, beans, and eggplant.	
Bay leaf		Boiled meat, soup, stews, chicken, and turkey.	Baked or poached fish.	Tomato, rice, carrots, and green beans.	
Dill	Cottage cheese, cream cheese, and mayonnaise.	Lamb chops.	Fish.	Cabbage, cauliflower, and green beans.	
Marjorum	Souffles.	Beef, lamb and veal roasts, meat loaf, stuffings, and bouillon.	Baked or creamed fish.	Carrots, onions, Brussels sprouts, peas, potatoes, and zuchini.	
Mint	Cream cheese.	Lamb and veal.	Baked and broiled fish.	Carrots, peas, spinach, and green beans.	
Oregano	Cheese spreads, omelets.	Pork, veal, lamb, meat loaf, hamburgers, chicken, pheasant, and stuffings.	Shrimp and fish stuffings.	Potatoes, onions, peas, mushrooms, green beans, and tomatoes.	

TABLE 3.3 (*Continued*)

Seasoning	Eggs and Cheese	Meats and Poultry	Fish and Shellfish	Vegetables and Fruits	Breads and Desserts
Parsley	Egg dishes, cheese spreads.	Beef, lamb, pork, and veal stews, soups, casseroles; poultry dishes.	All fish and shellfish.	In or over any vegetable dish, rice.	
Rosemary	Omelets.	Beef, lamb, veal, and pork dishes; chicken fricassee, turkey, and duck.	Baked or poached fish and broiled salmon.	Cauliflower, spinach, peas, cucumber, mushrooms, and fruit cups.	
Sage	Cheddar, cream and cottage cheese.	Pork, lamb and poultry stuffings.	Chowder and fish stuffings.	Eggplant, lima beans, onions, peas, and tomatoes.	
Savory	All egg dishes.	All meats and poultry.	Fish, butters, and stuffings.	Beans, peas, cabbage, rice, carrots, tomatoes, and sauerkraut.	
Thyme	Eggs, cottage and cream cheese.	Beef, pork, and lamb stews; liver pate, chicken and turkey.	Crabmeat, lobster, scallops, and shrimp.	Beets, onions, green beans, tomatoes, and mushrooms.	
Tarragon		Chicken, duck, turkey, goose, and liver pate.	Baked salmon, crabmeat, lobster, shrimp, and poached fish.	Asparagus, beans, beets, tomatoes, and spinach.	

TABLE 3.3 (*Continued*)

Seasoning	Eggs and Cheese	Meats and Poultry	Fish and Shellfish	Vegetables and Fruits	Breads and Desserts
Spices and Seeds					
Allspice		Potroast, spiced beef, sausage, lamb, pork, veal.	Poached fish.	Apples, peaches, cabbage, and tomatoes.	Cakes, cookies, fruit pies, plum pudding, and mincemeat.
Anise seed			Poached fish.	Carrots.	Cookies.
Caraway	Cheese spreads.	Soups, goulash, pot roast, stews, liver, and pork.	Poached fish.	Apples, beets, and cabbage.	Rye bread, cookies, cakes, pastry, and biscuits.
Celery seed	Cheese spreads.	Beef, pork, veal, and poultry.		Potato and cabbage; salads and dressings.	
Chili powder	Cheeses.	Pot roast, all Mexican dishes, and stews.		Potato and corn chips; rice.	
Cinnamon		Ham glaze, pork roast, and pot roast.		Squash, sweet potatoes, apples, and peaches.	Breads, cakes, rolls, cookies, and doughnuts.
Cloves		Ham, pork, beef, stew, and sausage.	Poached fish.	Beans, apples, tomatoes, and cranberries.	Bread, cookies, fruitcake, and gingerbread.

TABLE 3.3 (*Continued*)

Seasoning	Eggs and Cheese	Meats and Poultry	Fish and Shellfish	Vegetables and Fruits	Breads and Desserts
Curry powder	Creamed eggs, deviled eggs, and cheese spreads.	Beef, pork, lamb, veal, and chicken.	Poached and baked fish.	Tomatoes, carrots, rice, bananas, and apples.	Biscuits and breads.
Ginger		Steak, pot roast, Chinese dishes, and poultry.		Apples, pears, figs, tomato soup, and sweet potatoes.	Gingerbread, cake, cookies, and pies.
Mace	Eggnog and custard.	Steak, meatballs, pot roast, lamb, sausage, and veal.		Carrots and cauliflower.	Yellow or white cake, cookies, and breads.
Mustard	Cheese spreads and deviled eggs.	Soups, ham, pork, beef, and chicken.	Broiled or poached seafood.	Most vegetables and sauces.	Biscuits and yeast buns.
Nutmeg	Eggnogs, custards, and cream cheese.	Meat balls, sausage, and beef.	Poached and fried fish.	Carrots, spinach, and sweet potatoes.	Bread, cake, and cookies.
Paprika	Poached eggs.	Veal and chicken.	Baked, fried, poached fish.	Asparagus and spinach.	Bread and crackers.
Pepper (black or white)	Eggs.	All poultry, game, and meat stuffings.	All fish.	All vegetables.	Dough with meat fillings.

69

TABLE 3.3 (*Continued*)

Seasoning	Eggs and Cheese	Meats and Poultry	Fish Shellfish	Vegetables and Fruits	Breads and Desserts
Cayenne		Spicy stews.	Baked fish.	Corn and onions.	
Poppy and sesame seeds	Cheese mixtures and egg dishes.	Cream soups, meat and poultry stuffing, creamed dishes, veal, and poultry.	Baked and poached fish.		Bread and rolls; sweet-roll fillings and cakes.
Saffron		Veal and poultry.	Soups and creamed fish.		

Fruits, Sauces, and Wines

Apple	Fresh with cheese.	Lamb and chicken curries ; stews and pork glaze.		Red and white cabbage.	Cakes, tortes, and pies.
Barbecue sauce		Beef and poultry dishes.		Potatoes.	
Chili sauce	Cheese spreads.	Beef, lamb, pork, and veal.	Baked fish, shellfish, and fish cocktail.	Baked beans, onions, and potatoes.	

TABLE 3.3 (*Continued*)

Seasoning	Eggs and Cheese	Meats and Poultry	Fish and Shellfish	Vegetables and Fruits	Breads and Desserts
Claret wine	Cheese appetizers.	Soups, stews, hamburgers, beef and lamb.		Beets and spinach.	
Horse radish	Egg and cheese appetizers.	Beef, pork, ham, and poultry.			
Lemon (rind or juice)		Ham, veal, and poultry.	Juice with all dishes.	Juice with artichokes, asparagus, beans, beets, broccoli, spinach, honeydew, and casaba.	Cookies, cakes, pies, puddings, and breads.
Orange (rind or juice)		Duck, pork, veal; stuffings for meat and poultry		Beets, onion, cauliflower, carrots, and fruit cups.	Breads, cakes, cookies, pies, and puddings.
Hot pepper sauce	Cheese mixtures.	Beef, lamb, pork, veal, and poultry.	Baked fish.	Asparagus, broccoli, cauliflower, potatoes, and tomatoes.	
Sherry	Egg dishes and cheese spreads.	Veal and poultry.	Poached and creamed fish; Newbergs and Thermidors.		Puddings and pie fillings.

TABLE 3.3 (*Continued*)

Seasoning	Eggs and Cheese	Meats and Poultry	Fish and Shellfish	Vegetables and Fruits	Breads and Desserts
Soy		Pork and poultry dishes. Soups, stews, and casseroles.		Rice, green beans, peas, and most other vegetables.	
Stock (beef or chicken)		Pork and poultry dishes. Soups, stews, and casseroles.		Rice, green beans, peas, and most other vegetables.	
Tomato sauce	Egg dishes and cheese mixtures.	Beef, pork, veal, and poultry.	Baked fish; fish canapes and cocktails.	Baked beans, artichokes, eggplant, and green beans.	
Vermouth	Cheese mixtures.	Beef and lamb steaks and chops; meat canapes.			
Worcester-shire sauce	Egg or cheese mixtures.	Pork and veal.	Broiled or fried fish.	Peas.	

TABLE 3.4 TOPPING, GARNISH, AND ACCOMPANIMENT SUGGESTIONS

Food	Toppings	Garnishes	Accompaniments
Soup (broth)		Thin lemon slice (chicken bouillon, beef consomme, clear tomato, or clam nectar).	Cheese sticks, any crisp wafers, Melba toast, corn chips, or potato chips.
Soup (cream)	Crushed cereal flakes, slivered almonds, chopped cashews, snipped chives (minced, fresh), herbs, grated cheese, crushed corn or potato chips, or sour cream and nutmeg.	Sprig of watercress, whipped cream, popcorn, croutons, strips of salami, or sliced chicken or ham, olives, paprika, sieved egg yolk, or thin slices of frankfurters.	Same as above.
Egg dishes	Grated cheese, minced ham, crumbled crisp bacon, chopped sauted mushrooms, chopped olives, parsley, or green pepper.	Sprig of watercress or parsley, bacon slice, radish rose, tomato wedge, olives, or paprika.	Broiled tomato slice, marmelade, toast points, or hot biscuits.
Casseroles	Buttered bread crumbs, browned crumbs and cheese or chopped nuts, crushed cereal, corn or potato chips, chow-mein noodles, crushed crackers, fried onion ring, chopped green onion, or toasted sesame seed.	Green pepper strips or rings, sliced olives, paprika, tomato wedges, cherry tomatoes, bacon strips, pickle fan, orange slices, or carrot curls.	Spiced fruit (peach, apple, prune, apricot, or Mandarin oranges), carrot sticks in ripe olive, broiled tomato, hot biscuit, or toast.

73

TABLE 3.4 (*Continued*)

Food	Toppings	Garnishes	Accompaniments
Fish	Caper sauce, lemon butter, grated cheese, slivered almonds, shrimp sauce, buttered crumbs, crushed chips, or minced green pepper.	Cucumber slices, twisted lemon slice, lemon slice with half of it dipped in paprika or parsley, tomato wedges, or hard-cooked egg slice, wedge, or quarter.	Lemon wedge, tartar sauce, cucumber slices, baked tomato, Mandarin orange segments, grapefruit segments sprinkled with chopped parsley, or stuffed eggs.
Beef steak (including hamburger)	Fried onion rings, snipped chives, crumbled blue cheese, sliced mushrooms, dip in garlic oil before broiling, vermouth, or sauterne.	Mushroom caps, anchovie fillets, fried onion rings, pickle fan, parsley sprigs, or radish roses.	Meat sauces, pickle relish, potato chips, green onions, or French-fried potatoes.
Roast beef	Au jus, brown gravy, or minced parsley.	Watercress sprigs, curly chicory, spiced crabapple, or kumquats (fresh or preserved).	Horseradish, mustard sauce, spiced fruit, catsup, or chili sauce.
Lamb (chops, roasts, and stews)	Chopped ripe olives seasoned with oregano, minced parsley, or crumbled blue cheese.	Mint jelly, pineapple chunk rolled in minced mint leaves, watercress sprig, olives, or radish rose.	Minted pear, stuffed celery, tomato slices, or orange or lemon shells filled with pineapple.

TABLE 3.4 (*Continued*)

Food	Toppings	Garnishes	Accompaniments
Pork, goose, and duck	Fruit glaze.	Broiled tomato slice, water-melon pickles, cucumber pickles, green or stuffed olives, celery, radishes, cranberry jelly, grapes, orange slice, or currant jelly.	Apple and red cabbage, apple-sauce, pineapple, spiced prune filled with plum butter, chutney, Philadelphia relish, cinnamon-apple rings, or Mandarin oranges.
Chicken and turkey	Chopped or slivered almonds, buttered bread crumbs, chopped green onion or chive, chopped hard-cooked egg, or crushed cereal.	Watercress sprig, preserved kumquat, salted almonds or cashews, pimiento, avocado balls or slices, carrot curls, or Mandarin orange segments.	Cranberry sauce, spiced apri-cots, peaches, crabapples, or prunes, sauted banana, broiled tomato, stuffed celery, or chutney.
Vegetables	Browned bread crumbs, brushed corn or potato chips, minced parsley, chopped peanuts, al-monds, or cashews, chopped egg, crumbled crisp bacon, grated cheese, or sauted chopped mushrooms.	Mushroom caps, pimiento, chopped green pepper, green pepper ring, parsley, chopped chives, sliced olives, quartered or sliced hard-cooked egg, thin lemon slice or wedge, or toasted nuts.	Drawn butter, mayonnaise, hollandaise, chili sauce, catsup, or French dressing.

TABLE 3.4 (*Continued*)

Food	Toppings	Garnishes	Accompaniments
Desserts	Chopped nuts, meringue, chopped candied fruit, cake or cookie crumbs, whipped cream, plain or toasted coconut, creme de menthe or cacao, crumbled macaroons, crushed peanut brittle, crushed peppermint candy, grated chocolate, crushed sweet cereals, marshmallow cream and shaved chocolate, orange marmelade, diced bananas and nutmeg, sauces (caramel, cherry, custard, chocolate, rum, butterscotch, strawberry, raspberry, maple, and mixed fruit), or frostings.	Candied fruit, banana slices, maraschino cherry, fresh blueberries, strawberries, or raspberries, cubes of bright gelatin, grape cluster, whipped cream, red jelly, peach slices, hard sauce, chocolate shot, sprinkles, cinnamon candies, marshmallows, gum drops, toasted nuts or coconut, orange sections, or citron angelica.	Cake, cookies, lady fingers, spiced applesauce (with gingerbread), graham crackers, ice cream, waffles, fruit (fresh or stewed), or cream puddings.

Cooking Temperatures

The quality of many foods is directly influenced by the temperature at which they are cooked. Recipes should be followed closely with regard to temperature. The equipment should be checked for accuracy of control and speed of temperature recovery in order to be sure that the proper temperatures are provided. The speed of temperature recovery when a cold load of food is placed in an oven or in deep fat determines in large degree whether the proper temperature is provided during a major portion of the cooking period. A reliable thermostat may regulate temperature but it cannot insure speed of recovery; this must be provided by effective heating elements.

When it is necessary to cope with equipment-on-hand, slow recovery can be partially offset by preheating to a higher temperature than the one required; this makes up for loss of heat during loading and the lowering of temperature caused by the cold food. The thermostat may then be changed to the temperature required during cooking. If the oven thermometer or control is not reliable, a portable thermometer may be procured and placed on the deck where the food is to be baked. The temperature of an oven may also be checked by the speed with which flour or unglazed white paper will brown. Times and temperatures are as follows:

1. A slow oven (250 to 325°) produces a light brown in 5 minutes.
2. A moderate oven (325 to 375°) makes it golden brown in 5 minutes.
3. A hot oven (375 to 425°) produces a deep, dark brown in 5 minutes.
4. A very hot oven (425 to 500°) makes it a deep, dark brown in 3 minutes.

If a deep-fat fryer is not equipped with a reliable temperature control, a deep-fry thermometer should be used to determine the exact temperature of the fat. A bread-browning test may be used when both the thermometer and the automatic control are lacking. The times and temperatures for browning inch cubes of day-old bread are the following:

1. At 370°F they brown in 60 seconds.
2. At 375°F they brown in 40 seconds.
3. At 390°F they brown in 20 seconds.

Frozen Foods

Frozen foods hold an important place in large-quantity food service. Large quantities are processed in individual kitchens; they are also available commercially prepared. Advance preparation and freezing provides a means of coping with unusually large amounts with limited labor and equipment. A large percentage of the items classified as "convenience foods" are pre-

TABLE 3.5 COOKING TEMPERATURES

Fahrenheit (degrees)	Centigrade (degrees)	Term for Temperature	Food Prepared	Approximate Cooking Time
140	60	Very low	Internal temp., rare beef	3 to 48 hr
160	71		Internal temp., med. beef	3 to 48 hr
170	77		Internal temp., well-done beef	3 to 48 hr
200	93	Low	Below boiling; eggs	3 to 15 min
212	100		Boiling water at sea level	
240	115	Very slow	Steam vegetables	
250	121	Very slow	Meringue shells	1 hr
250	121		Large turkeys, 18 to 24 lb	6½ to 7½ hr
275	135		Crisp crackers, freshen cereals	3 to 5 min
300	149	Slow	Roast beef, veal, lamb, ham to internal temp. 170°F	
325	163		Small poultry, chicken, pheasant	1½ to 2 hr
325			Standing rib	1 to 2 hr
350	177	Moderate	Cakes, cookies, breads, pies, and casseroles	varies with size

TABLE 3.5 (*Continued*)

Fahrenheit (degrees)	Centigrade (degrees)	Term for Temperature	Food Prepared	Approximate Cooking Time
370	188		French fries, precook drain, and fry at 390°F	5 to 7 min, until brown
370	188		Doughnuts and fritters	2 to 5 min
			oysters and clams fried	2 min
			fish fillets fried	4 min
390	200		Croquettes of cooked food, fried	2 min
			eggplant, onion rings	4 to 6 min
400	205	Hot	Bake potatoes, onions, squash, cookies, coffee cake, muffins	40 to 60 min
425	218		Cookies, breads, rolls	
450	232		Biscuits, pastry	10 to 20 min
475	246	Very hot		
500 to 525	260 to 274		Baked Alaska	
550 to 575	288 to 301	Extremely hot	Broil meats, poultry	

(In order to convert a Fahrenheit temperature to Centigrade, subtract 32, multiply by 5, and divide by 9. To change Centigrade temperature to Fahrenheit, multiply by 9, divide by 5, and add 32.)

processed foods preserved by freezing. The large quantity of frozen food used emphasizes the importance of controlling the conditions in freezing and storage that are essential for preservation of good quality.

Insurance of good quality in frozen foods requires (a) understanding the characteristics of the specific food item, (b) packaging to shut out the air and protect the product, (c) freezing and storage at a low temperature, and (d) maintenance of uniform temperature. Some foods, such as custards and some creamed dishes, do not freeze well. Some, such as turkey, fatty or shell fish, and uncooked batters and yeast doughs, are good when first frozen, but do not hold well for extended periods. Others, such as starch-thickened puddings and sauces, require some modification for best results. Waxy cereal flours and starches, rather than wheat flour or cornstarch, are recommended for thickening.

The lowering of temperature slows the chemical reactions that cause deterioration in foods. The quality rating of a specific food is approximately the same, for example, when held 6 months at 10°F, 12 months at 0°F, and 3 years at −20°F. Equipment that provides, and uniformly maintains, a low temperature is needed for processing and storing frozen foods. Widely fluctuating temperatures permit softening and refreezing of the product which results in the formation of large crystals that lower the quality. Flavor changes and some dehydration occurs. Quality loss speeds up approximately five times for every 5 to 10° rise in temperature from 0 to 30°F. Good, natural flavor tends to be lost and off-flavors are absorbed at the higher temperatures.

Frozen foods purchased from commercial firms should be carefully checked when they are received to determine whether their storage history has affected their quality. Only quantities which the kitchen can store properly and use within a suitably limited period should be purchased at one time. Commercial storage companies and venders are usually better equipped than kitchens for holding foods at a low, uniform temperature. Unless food is to be used immediately, it should be stored immediately after delivery and not allowed to set in a warm kitchen.

Food service establishments located near markets should use their low-temperature storage for immediate turnover only, and should hold frozen products a minimum length of time. The more quickly food is used after freezing the better the quality is likely to be. Freezing does not improve the quality of many products, it merely gives it better storage life. Foods vary in the length of time they may be held without serious deterioration in quality (Table 3.6).

Packages for frozen items should be selected for convenience as well as for protection of the food. Packaging may be done in kitchen containers, semi-rigid foil, regular aluminum foil, plastic film, or cardboard. The use of

TABLE 3.6 APPROXIMATE STORAGE LIMITS FOR FOODS HELD AT 0°F

Items	Length of Storage
Apricots, peaches, raspberries and strawberries, fruit pies	12 months
Broccoli, cauliflower, cut corn, carrots, limas, peas, spinach, squash	12 months
Asparagus, green beans, Brussel sprouts, corn-on-the-cob, mushrooms	8 months
Beef steaks, lamb chops	12 months
Stew beef, veal chops and cutlets	10 months
Pork chops, poultry, lean fish (haddock and cod), shrimp	6 months
Sausage, smoked pork, variety meats	4 months
Bacon, fatty fish (salmon, swordfish, and tuna), oysters, clams	3 months
Lobsters, crabs	2 months
Soups, casseroles, French fries, cakes, cookies, yeast bread	4 months
Quick breads, sandwiches, rolls	2 months
Pumpkin and chiffon pies	1 month

kitchen containers should be limited to those items that are to be used within a short period of time, so that needed utensils are not tied up in storage. Casserole items to be reheated and served on a steam table may be frozen in a serving pan, then removed, wrapped for storage, and returned to the serving pan at the time of use, or frozen in semi-rigid foil pans that fit the serving table. Disposable foil pans reduce handling and dishwashing. Foods freeze more rapidly and thaw more quickly if stored in small amounts or shallow packages.

Most fruits and vegetables require blanching to stop enzyme action before freezing. (See Table 6.3 for time required for blanching fruits and vegetables.)

When cooking foods to be frozen, it is well to make allowance for the cooking that occurs when the food is reheated by cooking them less than would be required for immediate service. Pastes, such as spaghetti, may be cooked until barely tender. Potatoes should be avoided in stews that are to be frozen because they tend to become mushy. When frozen, custards in pies and timbals tend to separate and meringues toughen. Cream puffs freeze well if they are packed carefully to avoid crushing, but they should not be filled until ready for use. Meringue shells may be stored filled or unfilled;

Figure 3.3   Flexible foil shuts out air during frozen-food storage, and containers sized to fit the serving table reduce handling. (Courtesy of Kaiser Aluminum.)

if filled with whipped cream or ice cream, they should be frozen before wrapping.

Changes for Altitude

Certain adjustments may need to be made for altitude cooking. The atmospheric pressure is decreased as the elevation increases. Boiling temperatures and steam pressures are affected. The boiling point of water is 1°F lower for every 500-foot increase in elevation, 1°C lower for every 960-foot rise.

When using steam equipment it is necessary to add ½ pound of pressure for each additional 1000 feet in altitude to obtain the same temperature as at sea level.

Cake recipes need some adjustment when baked at different altitudes. The temperatures should be increased from 2 to 3 degrees for each 1000 feet above sea level. The baking time is shorter. The quality may be improved through making certain changes in ingredient proportions. Those given in Table 3.10 are approximate and need adjustments for specific localities.

Candy makers also need to note temperature adjustments for best results at different altitudes.

TABLE 3.7 FROZEN FOOD PREPARATION

Food	Preparation for Freezing	Thawing Time	Preparation for Use
Baked Goods			
Cakes, angel	Bake, cool, place in box to prevent crushing, overwrap.	2 or 3 hr	Frost, if desired, just before serving.
layer and cupcakes	Bake, cool, place on cardboard or sheet pan, and overwrap.	1 hr	Frost just before serving.
Breads, quick	Bake, cool, place in rigid container, and overwrap.	1 to 3 hr or in 350°F oven for 15 to 30 min	May be reheated.
yeast	Bake, cool, wrap or rich-roll dough may be shaped, not baked.	1 to 3 hr	Let unbaked rise and then bake.
Pies and shells	Place in pans (not paper), freeze, then wrap.	1 to 1½ hr chiffon 30 to 35 min for baked fruit 40 to 45 min for unbaked fruit	Bake at 375°F. Bake at 425°F.
Cookies, baked	Place in rigid container and overwrap.	15 to 60 min	Crisp in 325°F oven for 5 min.
unbaked	Wrap rolls in foil or pliofilm, and soft dough in refrigerator container.	Only until dough can be handled	If shaped, may be baked without thawing.
Casseroles (stews, meat mixtures, etc.)	Freeze in the baking container.	10 to 12 hr in the refrigerator if in shallow container	Reheat in oven.

TABLE 3.7 (*Continued*)

Food	Preparation for Freezing	Thawing Time	Preparation for Use
Fish	Wrap whole raw fish.	Overnight in the refrigerator	Thaw partially, then cook.
	Wrap steaks, fillets, and pieces to be taken apart before thawing.		May be cooked without thawing by increasing cooking time and lowering temperature.
Fruits	Blanch, drain, add sugar or syrup if desired, use ¼ tsp ascorbic acid and ¼ c water to 1 qt if it is needed to prevent discoloration.	3 to 5 hr per lb in refrigerator	Allow for sugar used in fruit when preparing recipe.
Meats, roasts	Wrap raw meat in size desired for cooking.	5 to 8 hr per lb in refrigerator	Allow additional time if roasting is started before meat is thawed.
chops and steaks	Wrap for ease in handling.	5 to 8 hr per lb	May be broiled when partially thawed. Thaw completely when breaded.
Poultry	Wrap whole or in pieces.	2 hr per lb in refrigerator	Cook as soon as thawed.
Vegetables	Blanch (4 min), drain thoroughly, and package.		Cook without thawing in steam cooker or in boiling water. Separate gently with fork after steaming 3 min.

TABLE 3.8 BOILING POINT OF WATER AT DIFFERENT ALTITUDES

Altitude (ft)	Boiling Point of Water (°F)	(°C)
Sea level	212.0	100.0
2000	208.4	98.4
5000	203.0	95.0
7500	198.4	92.4

TABLE 3.9 TEMPERATURES OF STEAM PRESSURES AT DIFFERENT ALTITUDES

Temperature (°F)	(°C)	Steam Pressures (psi) at Different Altitudes (sea level)	(4000 ft)	(6000 ft)	(7500 ft)
228	109	5	7	8	9
240	115	10	12	13	14
250	121	15	17	18	19
259	126	20	22	23	24

TABLE 3.10 INGREDIENT ADJUSTMENT FOR DIFFERENT ALTITUDES

Ingredient	Altitude (2000 to 3000 ft)	(5000 ft)	(7500 ft)	(10,000 ft)
Baking powder for each tsp, decrease	⅛ tsp	⅛ to ¼ tsp	¼ to ½ tsp	½ to ⅞ tsp
Sugar for each cup, decrease	0 to 1 tbsp	0 to 2 tbsp	1 to 2 tbsp	2 to 4 tbsp
Shortening for each cup, decrease			1 to 2 tbsp	2 to 4 tbsp
Liquid for each cup, add	1 to 2 tbsp	2 to 3 tbsp	3 to 4 tbsp	4 tbsp
Flour for each cup, add			1 to 2 tbsp	2 tbsp

TABLE 3.11 COOKING TEMPERATURES FOR CANDY AT DIFFERENT ALTITUDES

Product	Test	(sea level)	Cooking Temperatures (2000 ft)	(5000 ft)	(7500 ft)
Syrup	Spins 2-inch thread when dropped from spoon.	110 to 112°C 230 to 234°F	113 to 115°C 235 to 239°F	114 to 117°C 238 to 245°F	117 to 120°C 237 to 243°F
Fondant, fudge panocha	Forms soft ball in very cold water and softens on removal from water.	112 to 115°C 234 to 240°F	114 to 117°C 237 to 243°F	117 to 120°C 248 to 253°F	120 to 123°C 248 to 253°F
Caramels	Forms firm ball in very cold water, and does not soften on removal from water.	118 to 120°C 244 to 248°F	120 to 124°C 248 to 255°F	123 to 127°C 253 to 261°F	126 to 130°C 259 to 266°F
Divinity, marshmallows, popcorn balls	Forms hard ball in very cold water, yet plastic	121 to 130°C 250 to 266°F	123 to 132°C 253 to 270°F	126 to 135°C 259 to 275°F	129 to 128°C 264 to 280°F
Butterscotch taffies	Forms threads in very cold water that are hard but not brittle.	132 to 143°C 270 to 290°F	134 to 145°C 273 to 293°F	137 to 148°C 279 to 298°F	140 to 151°C 284 to 304°F
Brittle, glace	Forms hard, brittle threads when dropped in very cold water.	149 to 154°C 300 to 310°F	151 to 156°C 302 to 313°F	154 to 159°C 309 to 318°F	157 to 162°C 315 to 324°F

SUGGESTED LABORATORY EXPERIENCE

1. Evaluate the quality of the following products procured from at least three different sources:
   (a) white loaf bread,
   (b) frozen peas (cook for 5 minutes before sampling), and
   (c) commercially prepared chocolate pudding.
2. Observe menu items, size of portions, and price in a cafeteria, and find out from the manager how many portions of each item were sold. Estimate what qualities affected the sale of each item.
3. Use each of the following to thicken 1 cup of liquid and compare the consistency, appearance, and flavor (heat $\frac{3}{4}$ cup of the liquid, stir $\frac{1}{4}$ cup gradually into the thickening agent, and then stir into hot liquid):
   (a) 2 tablespoons pastry flour,
   (b) 1 tablespoon instant tapioca,
   (c) 1 tablespoon cornstarch, and
   (d) 1 tablespoon waxy maize or rice starch.
4. Test oven temperatures by browning flour at different settings and noting time required for a specific color.
5. Change the following temperatures to Fahrenheit: 60°C, 107°C, 37°C, and 260°C.
6. Identify flavorings (herbs and spices) that have been steeped in hot water. Suggest foods in which they may be used.
7. Assemble materials for use as garnishes. Prepare sample garnishes. Arrange plate meals with and without garnishes and evaluate their appearance.

REVIEW QUESTIONS AND ANSWERS

1. How do people show their food preferences?

In their choice of foods and by the dining rooms they patronize.

2. How can an individual improve his judgment of food quality?

By sampling, analyzing, and comparing foods that have a high acceptance rating and by broadening his experience with food.

3. What are the different types of leavening?

Physical, chemical, and biological.

4. Give an example of each.

Physical—steam and air; chemical—acid and alkaline reaction, as in baking powder; and biological—yeast or bacteria.

5. Name three commonly used thickening agents.

Starch, eggs, and gelatin.

6. State the range of temperatures for slow, moderate, hot, and very hot ovens.

Slow—250° to 325°F; moderate—325° to 375°F; hot—375° to 425°F; very hot —425° to 500°F.

7. What foods should be cooked at low temperatures?

Protein foods such as meat, eggs, and milk.

8. What foods should be cooked at high temperatures?

Baked potatoes, squash, cookies, and pastry.

9. At what temperature should frozen foods be held?

For best results −20°F or lower is required.

10. How can Fahrenheit temperatures be converted to Centigrade?

By subtracting 32, multiplying by 5, and dividing by 9.

11. What is a food topping?

Food items that are sprinkled on, or poured over, other foods.

12. Distinguish between a garnish and an accompaniment.

A garnish is an ornamental addition; an accompaniment is a food item served with another food, such as applesauce with pork.

13. Can spices and herbs be kept indefinitely without deterioration?

Quality becomes lower because of flavor loss.

14. Do all foods keep equally well when frozen?

No. All foods should be used as soon as possible after freezing for best quality; many have definite time limits for palatability.

15. Does the fluctuation of temperature affect quality of frozen foods?

Yes. Flavor, dehydration, and texture may be affected.

16. ½ tsp of soda plus 1 cup of sour milk or molasses is equal to the leavening power of how much baking powder?

2 teaspoons.

17. At what temperatures are yeast destroyed.

At 110°F or above.

18. What is the effect on yeast plants of temperature of 65°F or below?

Their growth is retarded and some may be destroyed at very low temperatures.

19. Why is a baking powder containing sodium aluminum sulfate and calcium acid phosphate called double acting?

Because it liberates only part of its gas at room temperature and releases most of the gas at baking temperature.

20. Why is it important to use only the amount of this kind of baking powder that is required for leavening?

Because it has a bitter residue that may affect the flavor of the product.

21. What type of baking powder has very little residue flavor?

A tartrate baking powder.

22. Why is it desirable to use another type of baking powder?

This type releases its gas quickly and its strength may be lost before the product is baked.

23. How can best flavor of herbs and spices be insured?

Use them while they are fresh; store them in tightly closed containers.

24. How may the flavor quality of herbs and spices be sampled?

By steeping them in boiling water.

25. How may an oven temperature be checked without the use of a thermometer?

By checking the time required to brown flour to a given shade.

26. How may the temperature of hot fat be determined?

By checking the browning time of bread cubes.

27. How does altitude affect boiling temperature?

The boiling temperature is 1°F lower for every 500-foot rise in altitude.

28. What adjustment should be made for altitude in cake-baking temperatures?

Increase the baking temperature 2 or 3 degrees for every 1000 feet in altitude and decrease baking time.

29. What adjustment is needed in cooking with steam for change in altitude?

$\frac{1}{2}$ pound more pressure is needed for each additional 1000 feet of altitude to produce temperatures comparable to those at sea level.

30. Are other adjustments recommended in food prepared at high altitudes?

Certain ingredient changes are needed in bakery items made at high altitudes.

BIBLIOGRAPHY

American Dietetic Association, "Standardizing Recipes for Institutional Use." Published by The American Dietetic Assoc., 620 N. Michigan Ave., Chicago, 60611.

American Home Economics Association, "Handbook of Food Preparation," by the American Home Economics Assoc., 1600 Twentieth St. N.W., Washington, D.C., 1964 Edition.

Department of Foods and Nutrition, Kansas State University, "Practical Cookery," New York: Wiley, 1966.

Folsom, LeRoi A., "How to Master the Tools Of Your Trade," Guilford, Conn.: Dimensions Press, 1965.

General Mills, "Betty Crocker Cook Book," New York: McGraw Hill, 1961.

Griswold, Ruth M., "The Experimental Study of Foods," Boston: Houghton Mifflin, 1962.

Haskell, W. H., "A Training Course in Sanitation for Food Service Workers," *Institutions Magazine*, 1801 Prairie Avenue, Chicago.

Kotschevar, Lendal H., and Terrell, Margaret E., "Food Service Planning: Layout and Equipment," New York: Wiley, 1961.

Kotchevar, Lendal H., "Quantity Food Production," Berkeley, California: McCutchan, 1964.

Longree, Karla, "Quantity Food Sanitation," New York: Wiley-Interscience, 1967.

Lukowski, R. F. and Esbach, C. E., "Employee Training in Food Service Establishments," Food Management Program Leaflet 7, GPC 3/63 AMA, Cooperative Extension Service, College of Agriculture, University of Massachusetts, Amherst, 1963.

Marsh, Dorothy B., "The New Good Housekeeping Cookbook," New York: Harcourt, Brace & World, 1963.

McWilliams, Margaret, "Food Fundamentals," New York: Wiley, 1966.

The Pillsbury Company, "The Pillsbury Family Cook Book," Minneapolis: Pillsbury, 1963.

Terrell, Margaret E., "Large Quantity Recipes," Philadelphia: Lippincott, 1951.

Tresslar, Donald K., W. B. Van Arsdel, M. J. Copley, et al., "The Freezing Preservation of Foods," (4 vol.), Westport, Conn.: AVI, 1968.

U.S. Department of Health, Education and Welfare, Public Health Service, "Food Service Sanitation Manual," Washington, D.C.: PHS Publication No. 934, 1962.

West, Bessie B., LeVelle Wood, and Virginia Harger, "Food Service in Institutions," New York: Wiley, 1966.

White, Philip L., "Let's Talk About Food," American Medical Association, Chicago, 1967.

SECTION II

Processing Equipment and Preparation Methods for Vegetables, Sauces, and Soups

CHAPTER 4   Vegetable-Processing Equipment

CHAPTER 5   Steam-Cooking Equipment

CHAPTER 6   Preparation of Fruits and Vegetables

CHAPTER 7   Sauces

CHAPTER 8   Soup Preparation

Bibliography for Section II

4.

Vegetable Processing Equipment

Vegetables are available in large markets in various stages of preparation for use. The potatoes, for example, may be cleaned, graded, and sacked without further treatment. These require paring and shaping for use in kitchens. Other supplies may have been pared, but not cut. Some may have been formed in the size and shape desired for cooking, such as sliced, shredded, diced, or French fries. It also is possible to purchase potatoes that are fully cooked and require only heating before service. Market supplies of the various vegetables are limited to those items and methods of processing used in profitably large volume. Because of the perishable nature of fresh vegetables, only those markets that will support a profitable business offer a suitably wide and competitive selection.

The availability of the commercially processed products at a time when managers have been plagued by labor problems has caused many managers to question the feasibility of investing in equipment, space, and labor to process vegetables in kitchens. There are many questions that must be answered and evaluated in arriving at the best solution. The first questions pertain to market supplies. How available are the specific supplies required? How satisfactory is the quality and how dependable is the quantity and quality of the supply? Some large kitchens are located where suitably fresh supplies of processed products are not readily available.

Many points in addition to the cost of the item are involved in economic considerations. Availability of needed equipment, the volume of material required, and the possibility of fully utilizing the time of workers who must be present for other activities need to be considered. Flexibility in operation and assurance of the freshest and most desirable quality are important considerations when choosing the plan of operation. The influence of cost on the choice of a plan emphasizes the importance of making accurately calculated comparisons of direct costs.

The following example demonstrates the type of calculations that should be made. Answers to certain questions are needed in order to make the calculations. What is the total time required for processing a given amount of vegetable to a specified stage of preparation? Research has shown that 100 pounds of potatoes or carrots may be pared in a mechanical peeler in approximately 35 to 40 minutes. The average waste on either potatoes or carrots is from 25 to 28 pounds, or approximately 28 percent. What is the current price for 100 pounds of No. 1 potatoes? What is the current labor rate per hour for personnel who prepare vegetables? In order to determine the price per pound of pared potatoes, take the total cost of the 100 pounds, add the cost of labor for 40 minutes, and divide the sum by the total weight of the pared potatoes (100 pounds minus the weight of the waste). If the cost of potatoes is $5.00 per 100 pounds and the price of labor is $2.40 per hour or $1.60 for 40 minutes, the total cost would be $6.60. This, divided by 72 pounds (100 pounds minus 28 pounds of waste), would be about 9.17 cents per pound. What is the current price per pound of commercially pared potatoes? If the price is 12 cents per pound, the difference between the two costs would be 2.83 cents. How many potatoes are used daily by the kitchen? If only a few are used the difference may be negligible. If 100 pounds are used daily the saving would be $2.83 per day or about $85 per month and $1,020 per year. Over the 10-year depreciation period for equipment, this may be enough to cover the cost of space and equipment for preparation.

When planning a mode of operation, it is valuable to carefully evaluate the advantages to be gained through following each of the available methods. The temptation is strong, often, to follow another's practice or the one that appears to be the modern method or the "thing done." The availability of satisfactory supplies, the comparative costs and quality, the volume required, and the specific needs of each operation all should be considered in planning procedure.

Vegetable processing equipment includes that used for paring, slicing, dicing, shredding, chopping, and cutting into shoestrings, julienne strips, or cuts for French frying. Most of these modern machines are power driven. Labor costs prohibit hand methods except for occasional, small quantities of specific items that may be required.

PARING EQUIPMENT

Operation

Mechanical peelers vary in capacity from 10 to 70 pounds, and all operate in a similar manner. The general design is an upright cylinder with a rotating disc in the bottom. The irregular surface of the disc throws the vegetables against the side of the cylinder. The side of the cylinder and the disc, or the disc only, are covered with abrasive carborundum that removes the skin from the surface of the vegetables. A flow of water from the top of the cylinder flushes out the peelings. The depth of the paring is governed by the length of time the vegetables remain in the peeler while it is operating. The time most suitable for a specific peeler should be noted. The peelers with carborundum on both sides and bottom are slightly faster than those with carborundum on the bottom plate only. Research has shown that the most satisfactory length of time for the paring machine operation is about three minutes in most instances. Approximately 10 minutes are required for the handwork to complete removal of spots, or the paring of 15 pounds of potatoes, after 3 minutes in the mechanical peeler.

DIRECTIONS FOR OPERATING A VEGETABLE PEELER

1. Close and fasten the door at the front.
2. Turn on the water, so that the potatoes will move freely and the peelings will be flushed away.
3. Start the motor by turning the switch to ON. Note that this is done before the potatoes or other vegetables are put into the peeler.
4. Pour in the vegetables, filling the cylinder not to exceed ⅔ full.
5. Allow the vegetables to remain while the machine operates for 3 minutes or until a satisfactory paring has been done.
6. Turn off the water. (So that it will not flow into the container placed to receive the vegetables.)

Figure 4.1 Peeler located for vegetables to empty into the sink.

7. Open the door and allow the vegetables to empty from the peeler while the machine continues to operate. It is well to hold the door so that the vegetables will not be thrown beyond the container.

8. Shut off the motor.

Fruits and some vegetables are hand pared using a swivel-action parer and/or paring knife. Mechanical apple parers are available but few large kitchens have them. Because of the amount used and the irregularity of need, it is generally considered better economy to purchase apples for pie, pudding, and sauce in one of the preprocessed forms, such as canned or frozen, and to hand pare any small amount needed.

Cleaning of Equipment

Good sanitation requires that mechanical peelers be thoroughly cleaned each day after they have been used. Cleaning can be done most easily immediately after use before the soil has had time to dry on the surfaces.

STEPS IN CLEANING A VEGETABLE PEELER

1. Flush the inside of the machine to remove all parings and soil. (The overhead hose with a strong spray is especially desirable for this.)

2. Remove the disc and rinse the base thoroughly.

3. Replace the disc, being careful not to drop or chip it.

4. Empty and clean the trap which catches the parings, unless the machine is installed so that the parings go into a disposal unit. (Where a disposal is used, run sufficient water through the unit to flush away any parings that may lodge in the disposal.)

5. Clean the outside of the machine with warm water and mild soap. Wipe the door and chute.

Hand parers and knives should be washed in soapy water, rinsed well, dried, and stored. Knives should be kept sharpened for most effective use. (See knife sharpening in Chapter 2.)

FOOD CUTTERS

Slicing, dicing, shredding, and the making of julienne strips can be done quickly with a sharp French knife by a person who has developed this skill. (See Chapter 2 for the description of the use of a French knife.) This is an important skill for those who prepare food in large quantity. There are many instances when this method of preparation can be used more efficiently than a machine method because of the small quantity required for a special need. Practice is required for developing and maintaining skill.

Power-driven machines provide the means for rapidly processing large quantities of food. Food cutters have long been popular for chopping vegetables for soup, salads, and entrees. The fineness of the food particles is determined by the length of operating time. There are three types of cutters in common use, any of which may be preferred by particular operators. They are identified here as (a) Food Cutter and attachments, (b) Vertical Cutter/Mixer, and (c) Vegetable Cutter and Slicer.

Food Cutter and Attachments

The cutting is done by a pair of knives that revolve rapidly in a rotating bowl. A plow in the lid helps to turn the food and carry it under the knives. Attachments for cutting in different forms may be applied on the motor hub.

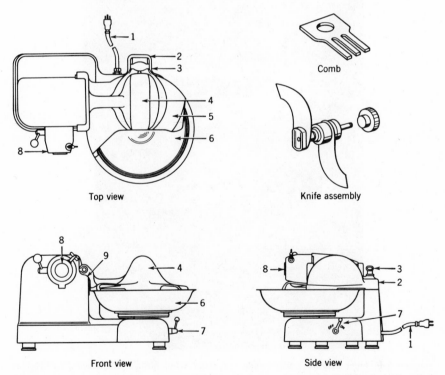

Figure 4.2 Food cutter: (1) electric cord, (2) location of comb, (3) cover-lock knob, (4) location of knives, (5) bowl cover, (6) bowl, (7) switch, (8) attachment hub, and (9) cover hinge.

ASSEMBLY AND OPERATION OF THE FOOD CUTTER

1. Place bowl in position and rotate counter-clockwise to stop.

2. Place knives on the knife shaft. Note that the leader knife is beveled on one side only. This knife is to be on the shaft first, nearest the motor.

3. Screw the hand knob into position to hold the knives securely in place.

4. Place the comb on the dowel, so that the knives move through the teeth of the comb as they turn.

5. Place the bowl cover in a raised position, with the slots against the hinge-rod, so that the slots slide into position on the flat surface of the hinge-rod. (Make sure that the cover slot is completely down against the rod before hinging the cover.)

6. Be sure that the switch is in an *off* position.

7. Place the food to be cut in the bowl, filling the bowl from one-third to

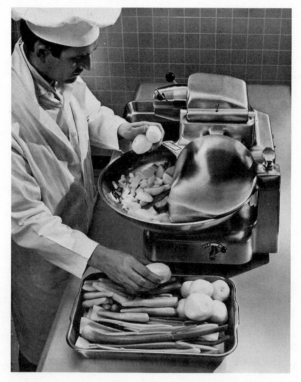

Figure 4.3 Food may be added while the cutter is operating. (Courtesy of the Hobart Manufacturing Company.)

half full depending on the nature of the material. More food may be added when the machine is in motion. (Use care not to overload the machine and to add food in such a way that the cuts are fairly uniform in size.)

8. Close the cover, pressing the knob down firmly over the comb position. Turn the knob so that it is parallel with the knife shaft.

9. Turn the switch to *on* position. *Keep hands from under cover or in bowl.*

10. To stop the machine, turn switch to *off* position and permit knives to stop turning before lifting the cover. *Do not lift cover until knives have stopped.*

11. To open cover, turn lock knob to a right angle with the machine and lift.

12. Unscrew hand knob on the knife shaft, slide off knife assembly, and place it to one side for cleaning. Remove food from the bowl.

CLEANING AND CARE OF THE FOOD CUTTER

1. When the switch is in an *off* position and the knives stopped, open the cover fully so that the flat area of the hinge-rod or pin is in alignment with slot of the cover. Lift off the cover.

2. If knives have not been removed as indicated in Point 12 above, remove the knife assembly as a unit. (The two knives and their collar and bushings.)

3. Lift off the comb from its dowel.

4. Turn bowl clockwise to its stop and lift off.

5. Wash the parts in hot soapy water, rinse thoroughly in clear water, drain well, and permit to air dry.

6. Wipe the machine with a damp cloth or, if necessary, wash with soapy water and rinse.

7. Periodic lubrication of the bowl drive gear is needed. A yearly check may be done by the manufacturer's service technician or done by the operator in these three steps:

   a. Turn off power supply and remove bowl.
   b. Remove bowl drive-cover disc and bowl drive-retaining screws. Lift off bowl drive disc.
   c. Remove pipe plug. Using a small rod (approximately $\frac{1}{8}$ in.) as a dip-stick, check the amount of lubricant. When using the dip-stick, make sure to clear the worm wheel. (It is approximately $2\frac{7}{16}$ inches from the face to the bottom of the cavity.) The measurement from the top surface down for a minimum of lubrication should be $2\frac{1}{8}$ inches and for a maximum the measurement should be $1\frac{3}{4}$ inches. (Use "Texaco Multigear EP-140" Texaco, Inc. or equivalent for replenishment.)

The food cutter and mixer are often equipped with hubs to operate attachments. It is important when selecting attachments to make sure that the make and hub size of the attachments correspond with the machine for them to fit and be usable. Attachments are available for dicing, slicing, grating, shredding, and for cutting julienne pieces and French fries. When using the attachments on the food cutter, it is good practice to remove the knife unit. Food cutters have a special clutch that allows the operator to throw the attachment drive in or out of gear. When an attachment is in use on the mixer, the speed may be adjusted with the mixer clutch; this needs to be done so that there is sufficient power to drive the extra unit.

There are three basic parts or attachment units. These are the Back Case which fits into the hub first, and catches and directs the cut material into the receiving container; the Front, which may be a hopper and level feed, a tubular feed with stomp, or a dicer attachment; and the plate

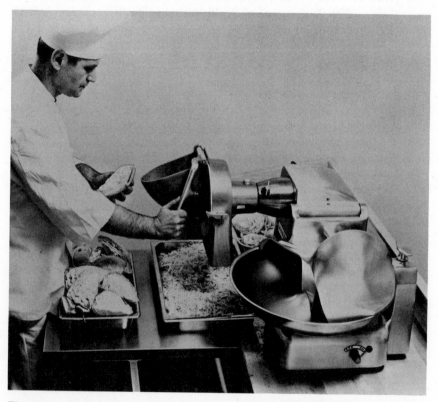

Figure 4.4 Food cutter with an attachment in position on the attachment hub. (Courtesy of the Hobart Manufacturing Company.)

of knife and shaft units. The Front is supported on the Back Case by dowels or pins that fit through holes in bosses or supports on the Back Case to form a hinge; it is closed by a case latch on the right side. It is important to store plate or knife and shaft units in a manner that preserves the keenness of their cutting edges. (See parts illustrated in Figure 4.6.)

METHOD OF ASSEMBLING AND USING ATTACHMENT PLATES

1. Stop the machine (mixer and food cutter).
2. Attach back case to the socket of the machine with the thumb screw.
3. Drop hinge pins of the front into holes in bosses of back case.
4. Select plate and shaft assembly (such as slicer or grater plate) to be used. Lift plunger (*b*, Fig. 4.6) and insert plate and shaft assembly into drive position. Release plunger.
5. Close the front and fasten latch.
6. Set slice adjustment to proper thickness (if slicer plate is used).
7. Start machine. Set at speed to produce best results.
8. Raise feed-plate lever.
9. Place commodity to be prepared in hopper and gently press down on the feed-plate lever. Too much pressure crushes the food and causes irregularity in the slices.

Figure 4.5   Dicer attachment in operation. (Courtesy of the Hobart Manufacturing Company.)

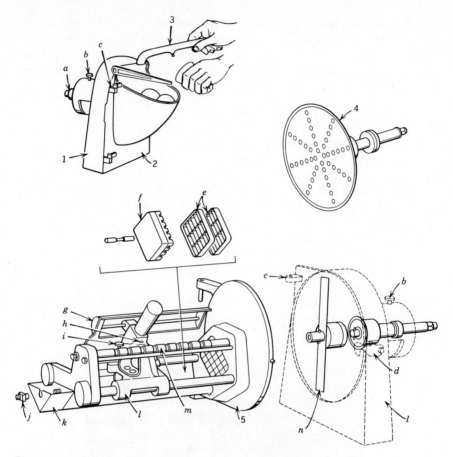

Figure 4.6 Attachments for vegetable processing. 1. Back case: (*a*) shaft that fits into hub, (*b*) plunger, (*c*) hinge. 2. Hopper front. 3. Lever feed. 4. Grater plate. 5. Dicer front: (*d*) case latch, (*e*) cutting frames, (*f*) grid, (*g*) safety guard, (*h*) power feed stud, (*i*) clamp screw (grid plate), (*j*) lock knob, (*k*) hopper, (*l*) pusher, (*m*) lead-screw, and (*n*) two-blade knife.

METHOD OF ASSEMBLING AND OPERATING THE HOBART DICER

1. Attach the back case. Lift the plunger and insert the main drive shaft unit.

2. Mount the dicer front on the hinge supports on the back case.

3. Insert rotating knife and turn slightly to the right. The knife locks in place on the back of the dicer front.

4. Close and lock the dicer. It may be necessary to turn the lead screw by hand until the drive engages the knife shaft.

5. Select knife frames and grid plate of the size desired.

6. Keep grid plate and frames together as one unit and, using right hand, insert grid-plate studs into the pusher from the under side of dicer assembly.

7. Use left hand to tighten hex-head grid-plate screw. *Note:* When changing the pusher plate it is not necessary to completely remove this clamp screw. *Always* be sure that the clamp screw is hand tight before operating the machine.

8. Push complete pusher assembly forward, guiding knife frames with left hand. *Note:* When the pusher plate is in forward position, it acts as a location guide for the hopper.

9. Slide the hopper forward into position onto two guide pins. Raise the rear of the hopper into position and tighten the lock knob. The hopper holds the frames in place as well as acting as a chute for the product being cut.

10. When operating the dicer *make sure the correct knife cutting frame and pusher plate* are assembled according to instructions. Without turning on machine, manually engage pusher and cutting frames to be sure dicer is operating properly. Place the product (no longer than $3\frac{1}{2}$ inches for the $\frac{1}{4}$ inch size (only) to be diced in the hopper, small end forward. Engage the pusher by applying a firm downward pressure on the handle. This makes contact with the lead screw. The product then slides forward into the cutting frames; the pusher disengages at the end of the lead screw. Always allow the pusher to travel the full length of travel before attempting to disengage the handle. Return pusher and place additional material in the hopper and continue.

Attachment equipment needs to be thoroughly cleaned after use. The more quickly it is cleaned before food juices and particles have dried, the easier the cleaning is. Parts should then be stored together where they are easy to find when needed.

CARE AND CLEANING OF FOOD PROCESSING ATTACHMENTS

1. Periodic lubrication of the attachment drive-gear case is needed. This may be done yearly by the manufacturer's service technician or by the operator in the following steps.

    a. Turn off the power supply.
    b. Remove thumb screw and withdraw hub cover.
    c. Remove six hex-head screws and withdraw the attachment hub (with worm wheel).
    d. The lubricant should be at the gasket line, where the lower gear case cover attaches to the gear case. *Note:* No lubricant is used in this cavity on machines without the attachment drive. Use "Gearep #65"

(Standard Oil Co., Ohio) or medium weight transmission oil with a Saybolt viscosity of 60 to 90 at 210°F if additional lubricant is needed.

2. To clean case, front and plate assembly:

    a. Stop the power unit.

    b. Release latch and open slicer front.

    c. Lift plunger and withdraw the rotating unit.

    d. Shredder and grater plates are easily removed from the plate hub by rotating plate counter-clockwise to release the eyeslots from the shouldered studs.

    e. All parts (case, front and rotating unit) may be immersed in warm soapy water for cleaning. Rinse in clear water and dry immediately. It is important that juices be cleaned from slicer before they are dry. When using the adjustable slicer unit, make sure it is cleaned frequently to assure easy thickness adjustment. Use a drop of tasteless oil on the adjustment threads after cleaning.

3. To clean and care for the dicer attachment:

    a. The dicer may be wiped with a damp cloth, or when more thorough cleaning is necessary, it may be immersed in warm, soapy water, rinsed, and dried.

    b. At periodic intervals, apply mineral oil to the slide rods and bearings for proper operation of the pusher. It is important to keep the slide rods clean and free of food deposits.

    c. *Do not allow* food to harden on the cutting frames and pusher. Clean immediately after use while food is easily removed.

    d. Knife may be sharpened with carborundum stone when it becomes dull.

    e. Knife should clear the front support by $\frac{1}{32}$ inches. To arrive at this clearance, adjust screw in knife hub as required.

    f. When the power feed stud becomes worn it may be replaced. To do this remove the acorn retaining nut and push the old stud from the engaging arm. A slot insures proper alignment of the new stud at installation.

Vertical Cutter/Mixer

The operation of the vertical cutter/mixer is similar to that of a home size electric blender. It operates with a great deal more power than a home blender and with such speed as to make it necessary for a user to be alert in controlling the time of operation. It chops lettuce for salad in $1\frac{1}{2}$ seconds; this is approximately the time required to turn the machine on and off. It may be used for chopping vegetables, meats, cheese, and bread crumbs and for mixing certain bakery products. Meat may be chopped most satisfactorily when it is slightly frozen (but not colder than 22°F).

Water is poured into the bowl when chopping vegetables. This permits the vegetables to move freely during the chopping process and lessens bruising. Some water is absorbed by the vegetables, increasing their weight. It is desirable when placing this piece of equipment to locate a water faucet near it to serve both as the source needed when chopping and a convenience when cleaning. A hose extending from the sink may be used. A floor drain near the machine is also a great convenience.

Several sizes are available. The smallest has a 15-quart capacity. This is a portable unit that may be placed on a mobile stand or clamped on a sturdy work table or ledge. The bowl of this model is removable for emptying or cleaning. The larger models, 25-, 40-, 60-, and 80-quart capacities, have tilting bowls that are counterbalanced for ease in handling. The mixing baffle, which cleans the sides of the bowl and moves products into the cutter blades, is operated by hand on 15- and 25-quart models but may be manually or electrically operated on the larger models.

The knives move with speed and force. It is important that the edges of the blades be kept true and sharp. The edges should be trued daily with a regular butcher's steel to remove any burrs (where the edge is slightly turned sideways). An oilstone (one furnished by manufacturer) should be used to hone the edges every two weeks (or after heavy use). Be cautious about using the machine to cut meats or other foods that are frozen very hard (below 22°F and whole grain breads) because they will have a dulling effect on the blades.

The knives are assembled on the shaft with rings that provide proper pitch or positioning (see Figure 4.7). The three slant rings are numbered and are to be used in order of the numbering with No. 1 at the top, No. 2 in between the blades, and No. 3 at the bottom, with the sharpened side of the blade turned toward the bottom. A spacer ring may be used above or below this knife assembly to raise or lower the location of the knives on the shaft. The knives should be set low with the spacer ring above the knives when the bowl is to be operated more than half full. A knurled nut, with left hand thread, holds the knife shaft and the various attachments on the drive shaft. One should be able to turn it with the fingers, but if it sticks the special wrench for turning and pin for holding that are provided with the machine may be used. However, these tools should not be used to tighten the nut when assembling the machine; only the fingers should be employed.

The mixing baffle may be assembled in position by placing the shaft through the round hole in the center of the cover, then slipping the handle on it, and fastening it in position with a knurled nut. When the baffle is in

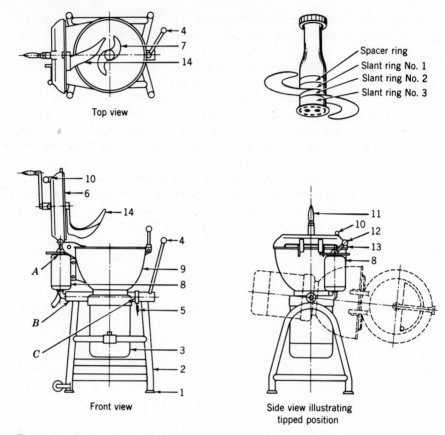

Top view

Spacer ring
Slant ring No. 1
Slant ring No. 2
Slant ring No. 3

Front view

Side view illustrating
tipped position

Figure 4.7 Views showing the parts of the cutter/mixer: (1) rubber foot, (2) tubular steel chassis, (3) motor housing, (4) bowl-position lever, (5) lock pin, (6) bowl cover, (7) knives, (8) switch box, (9) bowl, (10) cover knob, (11) handle crank, (12) switch handle, (13) cover hinge, (14) mixing baffle, (*A*) grease nipple for drum switch, (*B*) and (*C*) points for fitting grease.

use during the machine operation, it is to be turned slowly in a clockwise direction. An occasional jerk in the opposite direction shakes loose foods that cling to it.

The machine cannot be turned on when the lid is open, but the knives may still revolve with force after the machine has been turned off. Safety requires that the lid *not* be opened until the knives have come to a full stop. The machine has two speeds and the switch handle should be moved firmly and without hesitation when changing from one speed to the other. The lid has an inspection opening for viewing material during operation or for adding seasonings. The speed of the operation requires strict attention in order to stop the machine when the proper degree of cutting or mixing has been

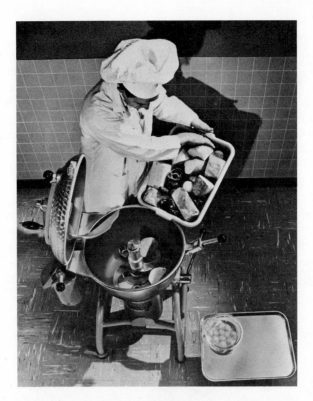

Figure 4.8 Vertical cutter/mixer open to receive ingredients for preparation of meat loaf. (Courtesy of the Hobart Manufacturing Company.)

done. At the end of the operation, most of the food may be dipped out by hand. If the knives are turned on briefly at high speed they shake loose the food that adheres to them. Then the knife shaft should be removed and the remainder of the food should be taken from the bowl.

The cutter/mixer may be cleaned between uses in these steps: (a) Pour warm water and detergent into the bowl. (b) Close and operate for 10 seconds. (c) Empty and add clean, hot water to rinse. (d) Operate 5 seconds. (e) Empty and wipe dry. At the end of each day of use the mixing baffle and sight cover should be taken off for a complete cleaning. (a) Open the cover and loosen the knurled nut of the hand crank (see Figure 4.7). (b) Slip off the hand crank and pull the mixing baffle (no. 14) out of the cover. (c) Loosen the cover knob and slide the sight cover hold bar aside and lift the sight cover off the bowl cover hub. (d) Before reassembly, lubricate the bowl cover hub with a small amount of neutral petroleum (vaseline). All of the parts and bowl should be washed with warm water and mild soap, rinsed with clean water, permitted to dry, and reassembled. The exterior parts of the machine should be regularly wiped with a damp cloth and polished dry.

Grease should be applied with the grease gun to the fittings B and C (see Figure 4.7) about every two weeks. Two pushes of grease from the grease gun are sufficient. The grease nipple for the drum switch (shown as A in Figure 4.7) should be lubricated only twice a year. The motor is packed in semi-permanent lubricant, and requires attention about every 5 to 7 years. A competent industrial electrician should be asked to do this and to check the bearings.

Vegetable Cutter and Slicer

The vegetable cutter and slicer has slots or entries for cutting vegetables into different forms. When the switch located at the rear of the base is snapped on, a red reflector light goes on to indicate that the unit is ready for operation. The cutting mechanism is enclosed, for safety, and stops automatically when the lid is lifted. Plungers are used to feed the entries. Figures 4.9, 4.10, and

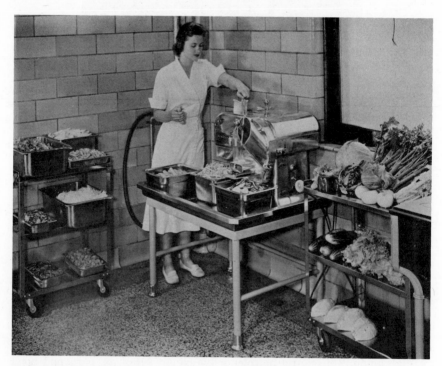

Figure 4.9   Demonstration of vegetable cutter and slicer. (Courtesy of Qualheim, Inc.)

4.11 indicate methods to be followed in the operation, care, and maintenance of this machine.

SUGGESTED USES FOR VEGETABLE CUTTER AND SLICER

1. Set thickness of slicer to $\frac{1}{16}$ inch entry #1 (Bias Slicing). For quantity feeding, push one piece on top of other, using plunger on last piece.

2. *American Fries.* Set thickness to $\frac{3}{16}$ inch and feed through entry #1.

3. *Potato chips.* Set thickness to $\frac{1}{64}$ inch and feed through entry #1.

4. *Cucumber slices.* Set thickness to $\frac{1}{16}$ inch and feed through entry #1.

5. *Radish slices.* Set thickness to $\frac{1}{32}$ inch and feed through entry #1.

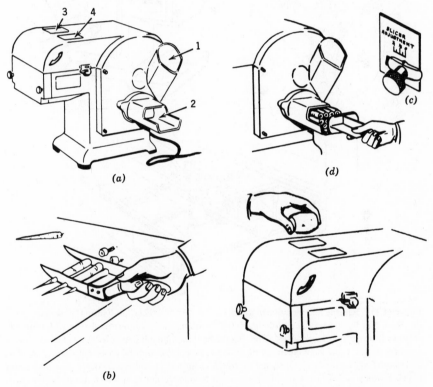

Figure 4.10   Points in the operation of a vegetable cutter and slicer: (*a*) The vegetable cutter and slicer has four basic entries for specific cutting operations: (1) bias slicing, (2) horizontal slicing, (3) $\frac{7}{16} \times \frac{7}{16}$ inch-strip cutting and rough chopping, and (4) $\frac{3}{16} \times \frac{3}{16}$-inch strip cutting and fine chopping. (*b*) Vegetables are trimmed with a trimmer to fit entries. (*c*) An adjustment device on the right side of the machine controls the thickness of slices from 0 to $\frac{1}{4}$ inches. (*d*) A plunger is used to feed vegetables into the machine. (Courtesy of Qualheim, Inc.)

6. *Chopped lettuce and cabbage.* Quarter and feed into entry #3. Use plunger. If finer chopping is desired, feed into entry #4 instead of #3.

7. *Julienne cuts of beets, apples, pears, pineapple.* Put through entry #4.

8. *Chopped onion or egg.* Put through entry #4, using plunger for each onion or full hopper of hard cooked eggs.

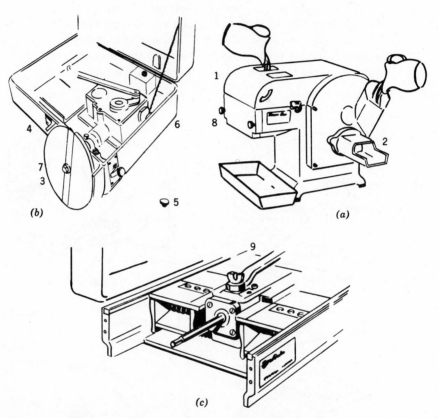

Figure 4.11   Rinsing and cleaning of a vegetable cutter and slicer. (*a*) Rinsing: place pan under the entry that has been used. While machine is running, pour 2-quart pitcher of water into the entry to flush cutting mechanism. This should be done immediately after use before the juices have dried. For a thorough cleaning, the unit can be opened and the parts removed for washing and rinsing at the sink. (*b*) Open for thorough cleaning: (1) raise top cover, (2) remove four knurled knobs and front plate, (3) use wrench to remove hexagon half nut and lock washer, (4) remove 12-inch knife, (5) remove adjusting arm guard by unscrewing knurled knob, (6) unscrew knurled knob (when reassembling, be sure that the knob is rescrewed back into the hole in the slicer disk, the flat side of knife is in front, and the lock washer and hexagon nut No. 3 are replaced firmly), (7) pull off slicer disk, (8) remove knurled knobs and end plate, and (9) unscrew wing nut and slide out cutting head (this must be replaced tightly on reassembly of unit).

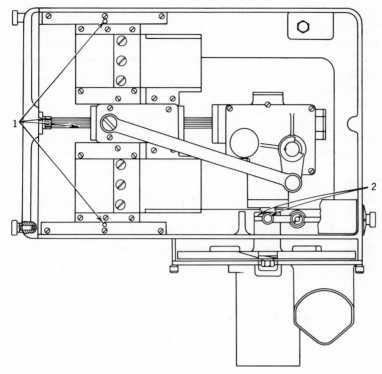

Figure 4.12 Vegetable cutter and slicer lubrication. Lubricate daily: raise top cover and oil points indicated by arrows (1) cutting-head guide oil holes, end-bearing oil hole, and spline shaft; (2) slicer-adjusting ring and slicer shaft.

9. *Sliced onions.* Stop unit, set slicer adjustment to thickness desired. Place two onions into entry #1, place plunger on top of last onion, snap on switch and complete operation.

10. *Sliced carrots.* Load hopper #2 for horizontal slicing. Set at desired thickness ($\frac{1}{8}$ inch suggested), start unit and feed through with plunger. (See Figure 4.10.)

SUGGESTED LABORATORY EXPERIENCE

1. Pare potatoes in a vegetable peeler as follows (weigh potatoes before and after peeling):
   (a) permit machine to operate 2 minutes,
   (b) allow peeling for 3 minutes,
   (c) peel for 5 minutes.

Calculate the difference in waste per pound, and the value of the loss per 100 pounds.

2. Keep a record of the time required to remove spots or paring. Compare the difference in labor time required to finish potatoes pared in the machine:
   (a) for 2 minutes,
   (b) for 3 minutes,
   (c) for 5 minutes.
   Calculate the difference in labor cost to do 100 pounds if the worker was paid 3 cents per minute.
3. Assemble, use, disassemble, and clean the food cutter.
4. Slice carrots for cooking using (a) French knife and (b) food slicer. Compare appearance and evaluate difference in labor time. (Include cleaning time.)
5. Shred cabbage for slaw using (a) French knife and (b) machine attachment. Note time required (including cleaning time) per pound of shredded cabbage and the appearance of the slaw from each method.

REVIEW QUESTIONS AND ANSWERS

1. In what forms may potatoes be purchased?

(a) Graded and sacked, without paring; (b) pared, but not cut; (c) pared and cut ready for cooking; and (d) cooked, to be reheated.

2. What is the best form for large food units to purchase?

The one that provides the best quality, convenience, economy, and dependable supply.

3. What factors are to be considered when evaluating economy?

Pro rata cost of facilities for a 10-year period (depreciation period), cost of labor required for equal state of preparation, and market price for the items.

4. Describe the paring operation in a mechanical peeler.

A rotating disc, covered with carborundum and irregular in shape, throws the potatoes against the sides in a motion that turns them and as they fall against the carborundum on the sides or disc, the skin is removed.

5. What is the average time required for the machine operation in paring?

About 3 minutes.

6. List 8 steps in order for operating a vegetable peeler.

Close and fasten door; turn on water; start motor; pour in vegetables; pare for

7. Approximately how much time is required to finish paring 10 pounds of potatoes?

3 minutes; turn off water; open door for potatoes to spill out; when peeler is empty, shut off motor.

About 15 minutes.

8. When assembling the knives on a food cutter, which knife should be placed on the shaft first, the one that is bevelled on one side or on both sides?

The one that is bevelled on one side.

9. How are the knives held in place?

By a hand knob.

10. What is the purpose of the comb and where should it be placed?

Place on the dowel at the back of the machine, behind the bowl. The knives pass through it, and it removes adhering food and prevents food from being thrown back of the bowl.

11. List three important precautions to observe when working with a food cutter.

(a) Make sure that the switch is in an *off* position while assembling the cutter. (b) Keep hands from under the cover or in the bowl when it is operating. (c) Do not lift the lid until the knives have stopped revolving.

12. What condition is required for the attachments to be usable on a power machine, such as a cutter or mixer?

The hub sizes must correspond.

13. What are the three attachment parts?

(a) Back case, (b) plate or knife and shaft, and (c) front.

14. What forms may be provided by use of different attachment plates?

Grating, slices, dices, shreds, julienne pieces, and French fries.

15. When is the best time to clean a food cutter?

Immediately after use before the juices and food particles have dried.

16. How should it be cleaned?

Take it apart and wash it in warm, soapy water, rinse thoroughly with clean, hot water.

17. Why is water added when cutting vegetables in a cutter/mixer?

They move freely in the water; this allows them to be chopped more uniformly and prevents bruising.

18. Why should a butcher's steel be used on the knives?

To slightly sharpen and straighten or true the edges of the blades.

19. How and when are the knives to be sharpened?

Hone with the oilstone that is supplied by the manufacturer. Sharpen every two weeks or after continued, heavy use.

20. What is the purpose of the mixing baffle? How is it operated?

The mixing baffle moves food away from the sides of the bowl and into the cutter blades. It is operated by hand in models smaller than 40 quarts and by motor in the large models.

21. What is the purpose of the spacer ring in the knife assembly?

It is for positioning the knives. The knives are set low with the spacer ring above the assembly when chopping is done with the bowl more than half full.

22. What are the other three rings called and why are they used?

Slant rings are used to provide the proper pitch to the blades.

23. Should the ground or sharpened side of the blade be turned toward the top or the bottom of the bowl?

Turn the sharpened side of the blade toward the bottom.

24. How is the knife shaft fastened in the bowl?

It is held by a knurled nut that is to be tightened with the fingers.

25. Which direction should the mixing baffle be turned?

Clockwise.

26. How many speeds does the cutter/ mixer have?

Two.

27. Must the machine be stopped to change speeds?

No.

28. How often should the machine be greased?

Use grease gun to grease fittings every two weeks and the drum switch twice a year. The motor should be checked by a competent industrial electrician every five to seven years.

29. What are the basic cutting operations of the Vegetable Cutter and Slicer?

The machine has four entries for the four basic cutting operations: (a) bias slicing, (b) horizontal slicing, (c) strip cutting and rough chopping, and (d) strip cutting and fine chopping.

30. How is the thickness of slices controlled?

By a slicer adjustment on the right side of the machine.

31. How should the machine be cleaned?

It may be flushed between uses by pouring water through every entry while the machine is running, before food juices have dried. It may be opened and parts removed for washing at the sink.

32. How often should it be lubricated?

Daily. Oil the cutting head, end bearing, spline shaft, slicer-adjusting ring, and slicer shaft.

5.

Steam Cooking Equipment

The largest percentage of cooked vegetables are prepared by boiling or steaming. Steam cooking is preferred over boiling for large quantity cooking of fruits and vegetables, not only because it is a fast and convenient method, but also because it retains more of the ascorbic acid (vitamin C). The comparative cost of operating steam equipment is low.

The source of steam for operating the equipment may be from (a) a steam generating plant or boiler, or (b) it may be generated in the equipment by means of electricity or gas. The steam pressure in the equipment influences the temperature and the cooking time required (see Tables 3.9 and 3.5). If the equipment is to be connected to a line carrying high pressure steam, a reducing valve is required to reduce the pressure for the equipment that should have 5 pounds. A pressure of 5 pounds is best for free-venting steam cookers and for self-generating steamers that control their temperature by means of a thermostat.

When steam is highly saturated, water tends to collect in the chamber during cooking. When the door is opened the water pours out on the floor. This places the operator in danger of being burned as well as making the floor wet and slippery. This excess water in the cooking chamber can be avoided by installing a trap close to the reducing valve before the steam line reaches it. This drains off most of the condensation in the line and also protects the reducing valve because an excessive amount of water may damage its diaphragm.

STEAM COOKERS

Many fruits and vegetables can be cooked in a steam cooker without added water. They may be cooked in perforated pans, if the cooking juices are not to be retained, or in solid pans if the juices are to be saved for soups and sauces. The capacity of steam cookers varies from a small, single-compartment cooker that accommodates only three $12 \times 20 \times 2\frac{1}{2}$ inch serving pans, to the set of three wide-compartment cookers with intermediate shelves that have a capacity of 12 to 16 serving pans. The wide steamers accommodate 12×20 inch pans, placed side by side on a shelf. The large cookers may be in combinations of one, two, or three compartments. Shelves that slide out when the door is opened and timers on the door to signal the cooking time add to convenience, but are optional and must be requested when purchasing the equipment.

Frozen foods may be cooked in the steamers from the frozen state, but results are more satisfactory if the food is thawed before cooking. This is especially true of a large, frozen mass of food in which the exterior may become overcooked before heat has penetrated the interior. It is important to establish schedules for cooking time as it is affected in a specific establishment by (a) the altitude, (b) the amount of steam pressure, and (c) the time required by the items to be cooked. Cooking is quickest when the compartment is preheated before cooking the food.

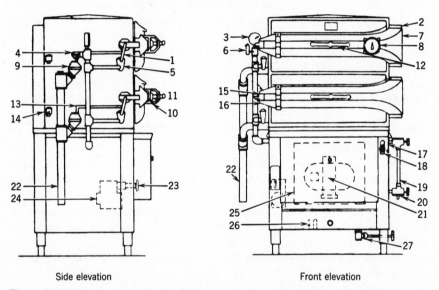

Side elevation   Front elevation

Figure 5.1   A large steam cooker in which steam is generated by gas heat: (1) valve lever with handle, (2) door-arm hinge, (3) steam-pressure gauge, (4) safety gauge, (5) compartment-steam valve, (6) steam-manifold air vent, (7) door arm, (8) timer, (9) compartment-discharge valve, (10) door retainer, (11) door-arm wheel screw, (12) door-arm handle bar, (13) valve lever (short), (14) compartment vent, (15) door-arm latch, (16) door-arm latch pin, (17) water valve, (18) water connection, (19) water-gauge glass, (20) water-gauge set, (21) handhole plate, (22) drain valve, (23) gas valve, (24) gas connection, (25) boiler, (26) pilot generator leads, (burner), (27) boiler-drain valve. (Courtesy of the Cleveland Range Company.)

The Large-Compartment Steam Cooker

OPERATION

1. Check the source of the steam supply. If the equipment is self-generating type or has a kitchen boiler, the first step is to turn on water to the boiler. Some have a float valve that automatically controls the level of the water, on others the water should be allowed to run until the gauge shows the boiler to be approximately ¾ full. Next, light or turn on the heat for the boiler. The Pressure Gauge (3) indicates when the pressure is sufficient for cooking.

2. Pre-heat the cooking equipment until the gauge shows approximately 4 psi (pressure per square inch). The handle that locks the door closure operates the steam valve. This is a safety device that prevents opening the door before the steam has been turned off.

3. To open the compartment door, push the steam valve handle (1) back. Next revolve the door wheel or bar (12) counter-clockwise until loose, then release latch (15) and swing the door open. To close the door and seal it, shut the door, rehook catch, and turn wheel or bar clockwise to seal it. To turn on steam, pull valve handle (1) forward. *Note*: Tightening door sealer excessively wears out gaskets quickly. Use only enough force to stop leakage of steam. *Caution*: Do not tighten doors when they are open or unlatched.

4. At the end of the normal cooking day, turn the gas valve or electric switch to *off* position. On direct connected steam models, the external steam supply should be closed.

CARE AND CLEANING OF LARGE COMPARTMENT STEAM COOKERS

1. Flush out boiler at least weekly and more often in areas where there is likely to be a high degree of mineral deposits. Shut off the heat before draining and flushing.

2. Close the water-supply valve (17).

3. Open the drain valve (27) and let the pressure force the water, steam, and impurities out of the boiler.

4. *Allow the boiler to cool* for 15 minutes before opening the water supply valve to refill the boiler. *Cold water must never be allowed to enter a hot, empty boiler.*

5. The steamer compartment should be cool when it is cleaned. Remove the shelves and shelf supports for scrubbing at the sink. Wash thoroughly with warm water and mild detergent, rinse thoroughly with hot water and allow to air dry.

6. Wash compartments inside and outside with warm water and a mild detergent, rinse well. Dry and polish outside surfaces with a soft cloth.

7. Replace shelf supports and shelves, being sure that they are firmly in place.

8. Permit doors of compartments to be open a few inches when the steamer is not in use. This allows the interior to dry and prolongs the life of the gaskets.

9. Occasionally add a small amount of lubricant to the end of the door wheel screw and the first inch of thread so that the wheel or sealer turns easily.

Small, Single Compartment Steam Cookers

Installation of the small electric-powered steam cookers calls for water, drain, and power connections. The steam is generated within the cooking chamber. When the power switch (6) is in the *on* position, the signal light (5) glows to indicate the start of the heating cycle. When the temperature of the cooking chamber reaches approximately 360°F, the signal light ceases to glow. With the chamber at 320°F, a spray of water is admitted when the 60-minute timer (2) is turned to some setting. The water hits the hot chamber and is immediately flashed into steam. Steam can be generated in the cooking chamber whether the door is opened or closed.

During the first 20 minutes of the steaming operation, the drain (9) and exhaust valves (12) remain open. With the door closed, the steam forces air and liquids out of the cooking chamber through these outlets. The valves close at the end of 20 seconds, and steam pressure builds up to 15 psi. This pressure is maintained automatically throughout the cooking cycle by the control circuit which admits a spray of water into the chamber as it is needed to generate more steam. Water is admitted into the cooking chamber only at chamber pressures between 12 and 13 psi.

An exhaust-pressure switch opens and closes the exhaust valve during the operating cycle to maintain chamber pressure at approximately 15 psi. At the end of the operating cycle, the timer shuts off and the drain and exhaust valves open [(9) and (12)] to permit condensates and steam to escape. After the pressure in the chamber has been relieved, the door can be opened.

An automatic power-control thermostat holds the temperature of the cooking chamber at approximately 360°F. Should the circuits malfunction and the chamber overheat, a safety thermostat opens at a temperature between 450 and 470°F. Whenever the safety thermostat operates, all the circuits become de-energized until the cooking chamber cools down. Pressing the reset button (4) closes the safety thermostat and restores all circuits to the normal operating condition. Should the exhaust valve fail to open, the safety (10) operates to relieve chamber pressure. The safety valve is equipped with a lever for periodic manual operation.

OPERATION OF THE ELECTRIC-POWERED STEAM COOKER

1. Check source of water supply for steam. Is the water supplied by a directly connected water line or must it be poured into the chamber man-

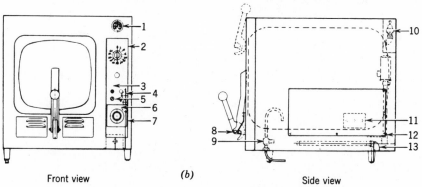

Front view   **(b)**   Side view

Figure 5.2   (*a*) Small electric-powered steam cooker. (*b*) Diagrams showing the parts of the cooker pictured in (*a*): (1) pressure gauge, (2) timer, (3) fuse mounting, (4) safety thermostat reset button, (5) signal light, (6) power switch, (7) browning-unit timer, (8) door handle and latch, (9) drain outlet, (10) safety valve, (11) terminal block, (12) exhaust outlet, and (13) water outlet. (Courtesy of the General Electric Company.)

ually? (If it is poured directly into the chamber, first check to be sure that the drain plug is securely in place, then pour 6 quarts of water into the chamber.)

2. Be sure that pan supports are securely in position.

3. Turn switch (6) to *on* position and preheat chamber for approximately 9 minutes.

4. Insert from one to three 12 × 20 × $2\frac{1}{2}$ inch pans of food into the rack or slides.

5. Close the door and engage the latch, and lock the door handle (8) in the upright position.

6. Set the timer for the required cooking time. (If less than 6 minutes, turn timer to the right past and then back to the time required.)

7. At the end of the required time the steam automatically exhausts. When pressure reaches zero the door can be opened.

8. Remove food, season, and prepare for service.

9. During standby periods, allow power switch to remain *on* and the chamber door to be ajar. Be sure that water is at 6-quart level for steamers that require water to be poured into the chamber, and that the water supply is changed after cooking strong flavored foods, flushing the chamber before refilling.

USE OF THE BROWNING UNIT

Follow directions 3, 4, and 5 above. The browning unit has a separate timer (7). Set the timer for the required time. Do not use the browning unit more than 30 minutes per cooking cycle to avoid overheating the cooking chamber, and *never use the browning unit with the door in a fully raised position.* To do so will damage the door and the gasket.

CARE AND CLEANING OF SMALL ELECTRIC-POWERED STEAM COOKERS

1. Turn power *off* and let chamber cool.

2. Remove drain syphon (9), by pulling upward with a slight twisting motion, and remove drain pan.

3. Wash inner surfaces with a fiber bristle brush and warm water with a noncaustic compound. Do not use steel wool or metallic abrasives for these might cause trouble with the solenoid valve.

4. Wash and brush the spray nozzle at the bottom center of the cooking chamber. Do not allow food particles to fall into the drain.

5. Place a stopper in the drain, and add 2 quarts of hot solution of water and noncaustic cleaning compound. Allow solution to remain for a short time.

6. Remove all nonsoluble particles and then remove the stopper and drain the cleaning solution out of the chamber.

7. Rinse with clean hot water.

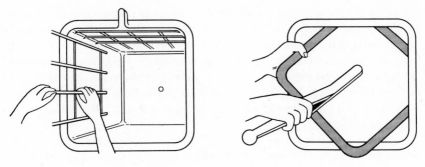

Figure 5.3 Removal of pan racks and door.

8. Wash drain syphon and pan thoroughly, making sure that the inner wall of the syphon is clean. Rinse in clean, hot water and replace in cooking chamber.

9. Fill drain pan with 2 quarts of hot water, close chamber door, and operate steamer through a 5-minute cycle to flush the drain line.

10. Safety valve. It is recommended that at least once a week the safety valve (10) be operated manually while the steamer is pressurized. Use a long-handled kitchen tool to actuate the valve lever and to protect the hands from the steam blow-off.

11. The pan supports may be removed by lifting the front, sliding them back, and lifting them away from the wall. The door may be removed by releasing its spring attachment or sliding it off the retaining bar, and lifting it out for more thorough cleaning. This is necessary when meat and starchy foods are cooked in the steamer frequently.

STEAM KETTLES

Steam kettles are designed on a principle similar to that of a double boiler. Steam to heat the kettle circulates between an inner kettle and a jacket or outer kettle. The temperature depends on the steam pressure used and is regulated in some kettles by turning the steam off or on. A steam pressure of 5 pounds is commonly used.

Steam kettles are available in a wide range of sizes (from 2 to over 100 gallons in capacity) so selection for size is important. Size should be chosen first, by the type of food prepared in it and second, by the amounts cooked. It is better to have two small kettles than one so large that the food cannot be properly manipulated during preparation. Large volume due to weight results in excess crushing of tender foods.

Kettles that range in size from 2 to 20 gallons are satisfactory for rotation cooking of vegetables. When cooking vegetables, the kettle is approximately three-fourths full of water and vegetables. When drained after cooking, the vegetable volume would be equal to approximately one-half to two-thirds of the kettle capacity, depending on the character of the vegetables. The yield in $\frac{1}{2}$-cup portions from a 2-gallon kettle would be from 30 to 40 portions at the end of each period required for cooking, and about 300 portions from a 20-gallon kettle.

A strainer basket to fit the kettle is a valuable aid when cooking vegetables. The vegetables can be lifted from the water in one quick motion; this results in less handling and crushing. Since many of the milder flavored vegetables can be cooked in the hot liquid from the previous batch the time of heating

Figure 5.4 Small tilt kettles mounted over a sink and large wall-hung steam kettles promote ease of use and cleaning.

water to cooking temperature can be saved. Faster draining by means of the basket saves the worker time and speeds production for faster service.

The kettles for preparing entrees or thickened mixtures may be larger. Where manipulation of the food during cooking is required, the height, diameter, and depth of the kettle should be restricted in terms of convenient reach. The size of a 40-gallon kettle and the volume of material it may contain should be considered a maximum for women workers. Tender foods in a mass of this weight must be stirred or manipulated carefully if they are not to be mashed beyond recognition. Larger kettles are useful for cooking stock or other highly fluid mixtures for which handling and protection of texture does not present a problem.

Kettles may be stationary or tilting, mounted on a pedestal or legs, or wall-hung. Stationary kettles are equipped with a draw-off faucet. A water supply faucet (hot and cold) should be installed adjacent to the kettle for a water supply for cooking and for cleaning the kettle. Kettle accessories that are offered, include (a) a strainer basket, (b) a solid or perforated disc for the bottom of the stationary kettle over the drain, (c) swivel-drain strainer, and (d) a support for holding a container at the kettle.

The drains for steam kettles need to be adequate and located to reduce the hazard of wet floors. It is sometimes difficult to control the liquid from overflowing the drain. Figure 5.4 shows the small kettles mounted above a sink which catches any spill occurring when the kettles are tilted forward. The shallow sink (8 inches deep) also provides a place for containers while they are being filled. A swivel drain with strainer is satisfactory for stationary kettles. It permits the drain basket to be either under the faucet or pushed to one side so a pan can set there. (See Figure 5.7.)

The pipe which carries the steam to the kettle from a remote boiler is in the support or pedestal. This promotes a good appearance with a minimum of pipes and easy floor cleaning. There is only one valve to open to admit steam into the jacket. A safety valve controls the pressure by opening the exhaust pipe when it reaches the equipment's safety limit.

OPERATION OF A STATIONARY STEAM KETTLE

1. Close valve in the draw-off faucet (6). (See Figure 5.6.)

2. Place disc (3) inside on the bottom of the kettle covering the opening of the draw-off faucet.

3. Fill kettle (not exceeding approximately ¾ full) with food to be cooked or with water in which it is to be cooked.

Note: Thickening agents such as flour, cornstarch and eggs, do not cook into the draw-off valve if the valve is filled with water prior to cooking the thickened mixtures.

Figure 5.5 Large kettles may have a motor-powered stirring device for thickened mixtures and a jacket designed for both heating and cooling. (Courtesy of the Groen Manufacturing Company.)

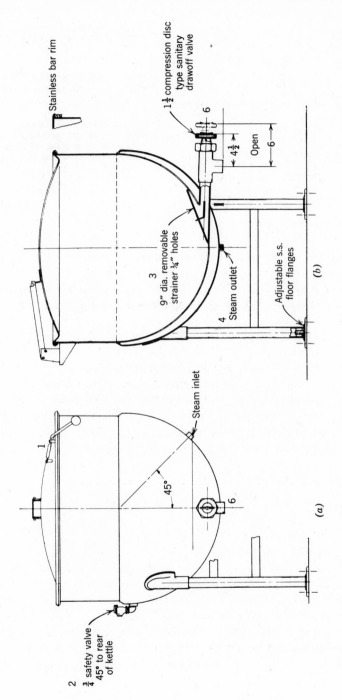

Stainless bar rim

$1\frac{1}{2}$ compression disc
type sanitary
drawoff valve

6

$4\frac{1}{2}$

Open

6

3
9" dia. removable
strainer ¼" holes

Steam outlet

4

Adjustable s.s.
floor flanges

(b)

1

Steam inlet

45°

6

2
¾ safety valve
45° to rear
of kettle

(a)

Figure 5.6 Stationary kettle mounted on legs, showing exterior and jacket cross-sections: (a) front and (b) side views. (Courtesy of Groen Manufacturing Company.)

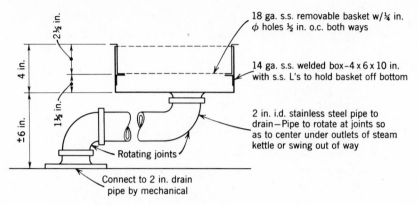

18 ga. s.s. removable basket w/¼ in.
φ holes ½ in. o.c. both ways

14 ga. s.s. welded box–4 x 6 x 10 in.
with s.s. L's to hold basket off bottom

2 in. i.d. stainless steel pipe to
drain—Pipe to rotate at joints so
as to center under outlets of steam
kettle or swing out of way

Rotating joints

Connect to 2 in. drain
pipe by mechanical

Figure 5.7   A drain basket with removable strainer.

4. Close the lid (1) for quick heating of the kettle contents. The lid may either remain closed or be raised during cooking.

5. Turn on steam control valve (5) by turning it counter-clockwise. For the highest temperature open valve completely. Partially close valve for simmering temperature.

6. When cooking is completed, close the steam control valve, and remove food to prevent overcooking. Schedule cooking so that it is coordinated with the speed of service and ready just at the time it is needed.

7. When removing food from the kettle: (a) the stock or liquid may be drawn off through the draw-off valve before the solids are removed; (b) the food may be strained from the broth; or (c) if particles are small enough to pass through the draw-off opening, the valve may be fully opened to allow the food to pour into a container placed under the faucet.

OPERATION OF A STEAM TRUNNION OR TILT-KETTLE

1. Adjust kettle so that it is in a level upright position.

2. Fill kettle (not to exceed ¾ full) with food or water in which food is to be cooked.

3. Turn on steam control valve.

4. When food is cooked it may be strained from broth or kettle tilted to permit food to flow from the pouring lip. To tilt large kettle, turn wheel (1) counter-clockwise gradually to pouring position. Note: Be sure swinging water faucet is out of the way before tilting kettle.

Small kettles are available with electronic heat control that are excellent for sauce making and batch cooking of foods. Accurately controlled heat with a range of 150 to 430°F is supplied to the kettle. The kettle may be tilted from an upright to a full pouring position by means of a lever. It then remains in a pouring position until the operator moves it back. It is made of satin-polished aluminum with a chrome-plated steel outer shell.

OPERATION OF ELECTRONIC-CONTROLLED KETTLE

1. *Vegetable or Boiling-type Cooking*

Preheat by setting "Full Range" Control at 400° and setting Selector Switch at "Full Range" Position. The Trunnion Kettle automatically maintains the 400°F temperature when empty.

  a. Add required amount of water and bring to a boil.
  b. Insert the food load into the Food Container. When cooking vege-tables use the Trunnion Kettle Basket (optional equipment at extra cost). Add salt when water begins to boil.

Figure 5.8   (*a*) Small steam trunnion kettles. (Courtesy of Market Forge.)

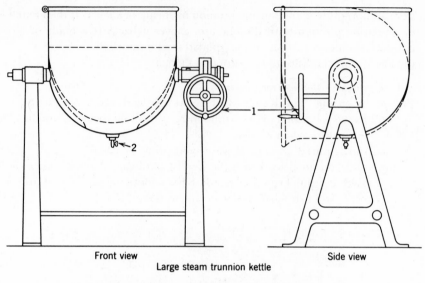

Front view   Side view
Large steam trunnion kettle

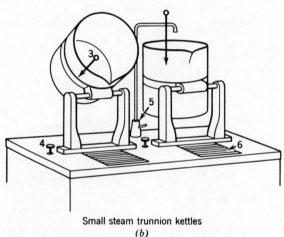

Small steam trunnion kettles
(b)

Figure 5.8 (*continued*)
(*b*) Tilting-type steam kettles. (1) Tilting control wheel, (2) bleeder valve, (3) trunnion handle, (4) steam-control valve, (5) water-fill faucet, and (6) kettle-drain plate.

c. Set Selector Switch at the "Boiling Range" position.
d. Set the "Boiling Range" Control Dial for the rate of boiling desired to finish cooking the food.
e. Remove the food by (a) lifting out the strainer basket, or (b) tilting the kettle forward and emptying contents into a serving container.

Figure 5.9 (*a*) Electronic-control trunnion kettle. (*b*) Diagram of (*a*) showing tilting control lever, (2) three-position selector switch, (3) *full-range* control dial, (4) *boiling-range* control dial, (5) signal light, (6) leveling adjustment, (7) counter-balance mechanism. (Courtesy, General Electric Company.)

2. *Sauteing or Braising*
Preheat by setting "Full Range" Control Dial at 300 to 325°F and setting Selector Switch at "Full Range" Position.

    a. Add required amount of cooking fat.

    b. Insert food load when the fat has melted.

    c. If faster browning is desired, increase the "Full Range" Control Dial setting to a higher temperature. Use Trunnion Kettle Cover (optional equipment at extra cost) when braising or stewing.

d. When food is cooked, remove it by tilting Food Container forward and emptying contents into a suitable serving container.

e. Turn off the switch.

CLEANING OF STEAM AND ELECTRONIC-CONTROL KETTLES

1. Kettles are easiest to clean immediately after the food has been removed. If the work schedules do not permit this, fill the kettle with water above the food line and permit it to soak until it can be scrubbed.

2. When ready to clean the kettle, turn on the steam or electricity and heat the water. Add a mild, noncaustic cleaning compound.

3. Scrub thoroughly with a brush to remove all of the food soil.

4. Use a bottle brush to scrub the draw-off valve of the stationary kettles.

5. Drain or pour out all of the soapy water, rinse with clean water and drain.

6. Wash the exterior with the soapy water, giving attention to the framework and any pipes connected to the kettle. Wipe off with a damp cloth and dry with a soft, dry cloth.

SUGGESTED LABORATORY EXPERIENCE

1. Demonstrate operation of the equipment, emphasizing safety features.
2. Heat an equal amount of water to boiling and note the time required by each of the following methods:
   (a) in a covered sauce or soup pot on the range, and
   (b) in a steam kettle with the steam valve completely open.
3. Cook potatoes and note time required for equal tenderness and the condition or appearance of the product, cooked by the following methods:
   (a) in water in pot on the range,
   (b) in steam kettle in water, and
   (c) in steam cooker in a perforated basket without water. (Be sure that the cooker has been properly preheated before use.)
4. During the steaming process note the pressure registered by the gauge.
5. When cool, take steamer apart for thorough cleaning, clean and reassemble.

REVIEW QUESTIONS AND ANSWERS

1. List the chief values of cooking by steam.

Fast, convenient, low-cost means of cooking. More vitamin C is retained than in cooking vegetables in water.

2. What is meant by psi?

Pressure per square inch.

3. How much pressure is used in large cooking equipment?

From 5 to 15 pounds.

4. What is a chief cause of water collecting in the steam cooker?

Highly saturated steam.

5. How can this be avoided?

Draining off the water by having a trap installed on the steam line before it reaches the reducing valve.

6. What is meant by self-generating?

The steam for cooking is generated in the item of equipment, by gas or electric heat.

7. Is it necessary to preheat the steam cooker before using it?

It is desirable to preheat the cooker until the gauge registers 4 pounds of pressure.

8. How may the door be opened when it is time to cook a product?

Turn off the steam, revolve the door wheel or bar counter-clockwise until loose, release the latch, and swing the door open.

9. What is the gasket?

The rubber around the edge of the door, which when the door is closed forms a seal that prevents steam escaping.

10. How tight should a door wheel be tightened when closing a steamer?

Just tight enough to prevent steam from escaping. Tighten with the hands and do not use a tool to tighten.

11. What happens when the door is tightened excessively?

The gaskets wear out quickly; this permits steam to escape into the kitchen.

12. Should the door of the steam cooker be closed or remain open when it is not in use?

Permit the doors to be open a few inches when they are not in use, to allow it to dry?

13. What should be used for cleaning the compartments and parts?

Warm water and a mild detergent, and then a clean, hot water rinse.

14. What is the source of steam in the small, electric, steam cookers?

Water may be poured into the compartment or dripped in automatically from a water line. It is converted to steam by the heat of the electrically heated chamber.

15. How is pressure developed?

Valves close automatically as the chamber heats until pressure builds up to 15 psi.

16. What releases the pressure?

When the timer shuts off, the drain and exhaust valves open and allow steam to escape.

17. What holds the door closed after the handle has been released?

The pressure of the steam in the chamber.

18. At what temperature does the safety thermostat react?

Between 450 and 470°F.

19. Can the cooker be used immediately after this has happened?

All circuits are de-energized and the cooker must cool down. The reset button may then be pressed to close the safety thermostat and restore the circuits to operating condition.

20. Should the door be open or closed when using the browning unit?

It should *never* be fully raised, nor completely closed, but almost closed. Leave open just enough for moisture to escape while browning.

21. May steel wool be used for cleaning the inside of the chamber?

No.. Do not use steel wool or metallic abrasives as these may affect the solenoid valves.

22. How can a safety valve be tested?

By activating it manually, with a long-handled tool to protect the hands, while there is pressure in the chamber.

23. On what should the selection of size of a steam kettle be based?

Type of food to be prepared and the volume required at one time.

24. What are the chief draw-backs of having very large kettles?

Weight of food is too hard to handle and tender foods are crushed and not well prepared.

25. What are the two main types of steam kettles?

Tilting and stationary.

26. In what ways may kettles be mounted?

On legs or pedestals, or wall mounted.

27. List conveniences to consider when installing or purchasing kettles.

A convenient water supply for cooking or cleaning, a swivel drain with strainer, a strainer basket for the kettle, a disc to cover the drain in the kettle, and a support for holding pans.

28. How may one prevent thickening agents from clogging the drain from the kettle?

By filling the drain with liquid before thickening has been added to the contents.

29. What is a trunnion kettle?

This is another term for a tilting kettle.

30. What is an electronic kettle?

An electrically heated kettle that has thermostatically controlled temperatures.

6.

Preparation of
Fruits and Vegetables

Brightly colored, flavorful fruits and vegetables give variety and zest to meals. They are liked by most people and constitute one-fourth of the food eaten in the United States. They supply nutrients important to good health. In terms of the amount consumed "they provide over nine-tenths of the nation's ascorbic acid, about two-thirds of the vitamin A, a quarter of the iron, about a fifth of the carbohydrates, and 7% of the protein. They supply enough of the B vitamins to make them important sources in the aggregate."[1]

The term "garden fresh" is often used to denote best quality. There is a bloom of goodness in flavor and texture at the time these products are harvested but their color, texture, flavor, and nutrients deteriorate upon standing. The loss of goodness is more rapid in some items than in others. A few hours after picking, the loss of sugar and toughening of texture can be detected readily in corn, peas, and berries. Thiamine, riboflavin, niacin, ascorbic acid, and minerals are water soluble and may be lost through excessive cutting and soaking in water. Vitamin A and ascorbic acid (vitamin C) are sensitive to oxidation and light. Addition of an alkali such as soda to cooking water increases the loss of thiamine and ascorbic acid. Some of the glutamic acid that enhances the flavor is lost during storage.

Qualities of natural goodness, which are essential for excellence, are fragile and require careful protection. Care must begin with harvesting and carry through storage, preparation, and service. In spite of the simplicity of the care required, no food is more often left on plates because of poor quality or inferior preparation. No item in the meal exhibits the alertness and skill of those responsible for food production and service more quickly. Factors that affect quality include storage time, temperature, humidity, and light, and

[1] R. A. Seelig, "Nutrition: Fruit and Vegetable Facts and Pointers," United Fresh Fruit and Vegetable Association, Wyatt Building, Washington, D.C.

methods of processing and cooking. The best quality calls for the shortest possible time between garden patch and plate. It demands immediate refrigeration, prevention from drying, protection from light, and proper processing procedures.

√ STORAGE

Refrigeration slows deterioration. It should begin as soon as fruits and vegetables are harvested and continue through marketing and holding time in kitchens. Proper covering of products and control of humidity in storage areas helps to prevent drying. Frequent changes in refrigerator temperature (typical in kitchens because of the repeated opening and closing of refrigerator doors) causes fairly rapid dehydration. Excessive drying can be reduced by storing the food in covered containers or plastic bags and maintaining a constant temperature. Fruits and vegetables lose less of their volatile flavor substances at low temperatures. Wholesale warehouses store many fruits and vegetables at as low a temperature above freezing as possible and with controlled humidity.

A great deal of the surface of leafy vegetables is exposed to drying. It is important to clean and refrigerate them as soon as they are delivered to the kitchen. They should be washed thoroughly in a large amount of water to remove sand and soil. If the vegetables have not drained fully before storage, it is well to use a rack or drainsert in the bottom of the vegetable container to keep them from standing in the water that drains off. (See Figure 6.1.)

V PREPROCESSING

The term preprocessing refers to the initial cleaning and paring of fruits and vegetables in preparation for cooking or salad making. This may be done in the institution kitchen or the food may be purchased from a commercial firm in a preprocessed condition. Paring or cutting of fresh produce speeds deterioration and the food should not be held after paring but used as soon as possible. When preprocessed products are purchased to reduce kitchen labor, it is important to remember that these are fragile products that need to be used immediately for best quality.

When calculation is made of the cost of prepared material for a recipe, the percentage loss for preparation should be included; for example, if the loss is 50%, the cost of the prepared material would be two times the price per pound as purchased. Accuracy in calculation calls for consideration of the percentage waste on the amount required to make up the loss per pound.

TABLE 6.1 MAINTAINING THE FRESH QUALITY IN PRODUCE IN WHOLESALE WAREHOUSES

Fresh Fruits

Fresh Vegetables

Store at 32°F and 80% Relative Humidity

Apples	Figs		Artichokes	Cauliflower	Horseradish	Radishes
Apricots	Grapes		Asparagus	Celeriac	Kohlrabi	Rhubarb
Blackberries	Nectarines	Pomegranates	Beans, Lima	Celery	Leeks, Green	Rutabagas
Cherries	Oranges	Prunes	Beets	Corn, Sweet	Lettuce	Spinach
Coconuts	Peaches	Quinces	Broccoli	Endive	Mushrooms	Salsify
Cranberries	Pears	Raspberries	Brussel	Escarole	Onions,	Squash
Dates	Persimmons	Strawberries	Sprouts	Garlic, dry	Green	(yellow
Dewberries	Plums	Tangerines	Cabbage	Greens	Parsnips	summer)
			Carrots	(General)	Peas, Green	Turnips

Store at 50°F and 80 to 85% Relative Humidity

Avocados	Limes	Olives	Beans, Green	Okra	Potatoes	Sweet
Grapefruit	Mangoes	Papayas	Cucumbers	Onions, dry	Pumpkins	Potatoes
Lemons	Melons	Pineapples	Eggplants	Peppers,	Squash	Tomatoes
				sweet	(hard shell)	(ripe)

Commodities Requiring Special Conditions

Bananas for ripening: 58 to 68°F,
  90 to 95% relative humidity.
Bananas, ripe (for holding): 55 to 60°F,
  75 to 90% relative humidity.

Green tomatoes, for ripening: 55 to 70°F.
  85 to 90% relative humidity.
Pears, for ripening: 60 to 65°F,
  85 to 95% relative humidity.

Courtesy, United States Department of Agriculture.

135

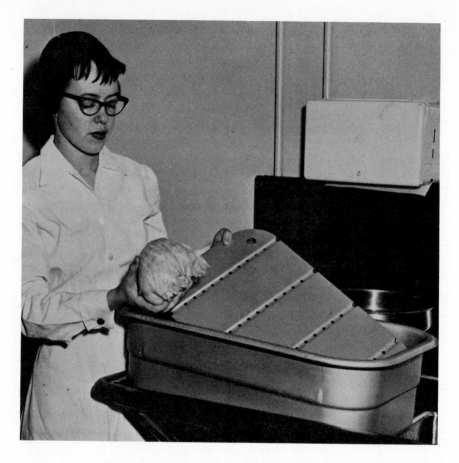

Figure 6.1   Vegetable storage container with drainsert.

This is determined by proportion; for example, if the percentage loss is 25%, the cost of the prepared weight would be one and one-third times the price per pound as purchased, not one and one-fourth, and 20% would be one and one-fourth times the A.P. price, not one and one-fifth. The average percentage should be observed in the specific kitchen for accuracy in calculating actual costs. There is likely to be variation in the percentage loss as affected by the condition of the products procured and the specific care and methods of preparation.

TABLE 6.2 FRUIT AND VEGETABLE PREPROCESSING WITH TYPICAL PER CENT LOSS

Product	Initial Processing	Preparation Loss
Fruit		
Apples and pears	Store under refrigeration in original package until time for use. Wash. Pare as required and place in solution to retard browning.	10% not pared 24 to 28% pared
Apricots	Refrigerate in original container until time for use. Wash. Leave whole or cut in half and remove pit.	6%
Avocado	Hold where cool in original container. Select mellow fruit. Cut in half lengthwise, remove pit, and peel. Place in citrus juice or other solution to retard discoloration.	25%
Banana	Place in common storage at cool or room temperature. Peel as needed and place in fruit juice or other solution to retard discoloration.	28 to 30%
Blackberries, boysenberries, raspberries, and similar berries	Sort carefully and remove any foreign matter or spoiled fruit. Wash under a spray. Drain well in sieve.	3 to 5%
Blueberries, cranberries, and currants	Sort carefully and remove stems, blossoms and foreign matter or spoiled fruit. Wash with hands in container of clean water.	3 to 8%
Canteloupe, casaba melon, and honeydew	Wash well. Cut into portions of desired size or weight.	45 to 50% pared

137

TABLE 6.2 (*Continued*)

Product	Initial Processing	Preparation Loss
Cherries	Refrigerate in original container until needed. Wash. Remove stems and foreign matter and spoiled fruit. Swivel action parer is useful in removing pits.	12 to 15%
Grapefruit and oranges	Refrigerate in original container until needed. Peel with sharp salad knife cutting through outer edge of segments. Use slender-bladed paring knife inserted at the center of fruit to strip out segments. (Figure 6.2.)	40 to 55% pared without membrane
Grapes	Refrigerate in original container until needed. Wash thoroughly, stem and cut in half and remove seeds or use swivel action parer to fish out seeds and leave large grapes whole.	11% seeded
Kumquats	Wash. Slice across, unpeeled for salad garnish.	5%
Peaches	Refrigerate in original container until needed. Scald until skin will strip off easily. Peel, cut as desired, and place immediately in syrup or other solution to retard discoloration.	20 to 24%
Pineapple	Place where cool. Large fruit is easiest to handle if cut into pieces for paring. Wash with brush. Cut off both top and bottom and discard. Fruit may be sliced across into rings or split from top to bottom through the center and cut into wedges or fingers of equal size, cutting from top to bottom. The slices or fingers may then be pared, taking care to remove the eyes.	40 to 50%
Plums	Wash. Serve whole, or cut in half and remove pits.	5 to 6%

TABLE 6.2 (*Continued*)

Product	Initial Processing	Preparation Loss
Rhubarb	Carefully remove all of the leaf as this part is injurious to health. Remove hard part at the base of the stem. Wash. Slice across stems into pieces of desired width.	10 to 15%
Strawberries	Refrigerate in original container until needed. Wash with a spray and drain immediately. Stem.	10 to 14%
Watermelon	Refrigerate until time for service. Wash melons and cut into pieces of desired size or weight.	50 to 55%
Vegetables		
Artichokes (French or globe)	Wash thoroughly, using a brush as needed. Cut off about 1 inch of top and tips of leaves. Remove tough bottom leaves and stems. Dip cut surface in lemon juice or other solution to prevent discoloration.	15 to 20%
Jersalem	Pare thin. May be whole, quartered, or sliced.	
Asparagus	Wash thoroughly, removing scales that contain sand and soil. Cut tips 4½ to 5 inches long. Reserve remainder of stalks for soup or cuts. Arrange tips in serving pans for steaming.	30 to 40% 50% cooked
Beans (fresh, green or wax)	Wash. Remove ends and spots. Leave whole, cut into even lengths or shred as desired.	10 to 15%
Green limas	Shell, wash, and drain well.	60%

139

TABLE 6.2 (*Continued*)

Product	Initial Processing	Preparation Loss
Beets	Cut off tops and roots to approximately ½-inch length. Wash with a brush. Cook with skin on, then peel. Serve whole or cut.	18%= tops 25% pared
Broccoli	Remove coarse, yellowed leaves and tough portion of stalk. Wash thoroughly, drain. Cut into 4½ to 5 inch lengths and split large stalks to make uniform for uniform cooking and attractive service. Arrange in serving pans for steaming. Tender portions of the remainder or the entire stems may be cut into 1-inch pieces for service as cuts.	30 to 40%
Brussel sprouts	Remove coarse yellow leaves and trim stalks. Wash. Soak for a few minutes in salt water, drain.	15 to 20%
Cabbage	Remove coarse, discolored leaves and trim stalks. Wash. Cut into wedges or shred as desired for use.	15 to 20%
Carrots	Remove tops. Peel by hand or in mechanical peeler. Cut as desired for use.	20 to 25%
Cauliflower	Remove leaves, stalks and any discoloration. Wash carefully. Leave whole or break into flowerlets. Place in serving pans for steaming.	40 to 50% 55% cooked
Celery	Trim off root end, leaves and spots. Clean thoroughly, using brush as needed. Reserve tough outer stems for cooking or mincing.	20 to 30%
Corn (sweet)	Keep refrigerated. Use as soon as possible. Remove husks and silks just before cooking.	45% cut from cob
Cucumber	Wash. Pare only if the skin is tough. Slice or dice as used.	10 to 25% depending on paring

TABLE 6.2 (*Continued*)

Product	Initial Processing	Preparation Loss
Eggplant	Wash. Pare only if the skin is tough. Cut shortly before use. Dip in lemon juice to prevent discoloration.	10 to 25%
Lettuce	Trim off discolored leaves, core. Wash, drain, and refrigerate.	25 to 35%
Mushrooms	Wash, using a soft brush if needed. Do not pare.	0 to 5%
Okra	Wash. Cut off stems. Leave whole or slice as desired.	15 to 20%
Onions	Pare off thin outer skin. Wash. Cut as needed.	8 to 15%
Parsley	Trim off excess stem, discard discolored leaves, wash in large amount of water. Shake off water, drain well, and refrigerate in covered container.	15 to 25%
Parsnips	Pare, rinse. Cut or leave whole as desired.	25 to 30%
Peas (green or black-eyed)	Shell and wash.	50 to 60%
Peppers (green)	Wash. Remove stem, seeds and inside membrane.	18 to 25%
Potatoes (white)	Peel or leave skin on and scrub thoroughly. Dip pared potatoes in anti-oxidant solution, drain, and store in polyethylene bags in batch quantities.	25 to 28%
Potatoes (sweet)	Scrub, steam in skins, and pare. If they are to be mashed, paring may be done before cooking.	20 to 25%
Squash (summer pattypan, yellow chayote and zucchini)	Wash, remove stem and blossom ends. Pare only if skin is tough. Remove coarse seeds and cut or leave whole as desired.	5 to 15%

141

TABLE 6.2 (*continued*)

Product	Initial Processing	Preparation Loss
Squash (winter acorn, banana, and Hubbard)	Wash. Cut in half, remove seeds and fiber. Cut into serving pieces. Pare if desired.	10 to 20% 30 to 35% cooked
Radishes	Remove tops and roots. Wash. Refrigerate.	35 to 40% with tops
Rutabagas	Pare. Rinse and cut into pieces as desired.	15 to 20%
Spinach and other greens	Wash thoroughly in large amount of water to remove dirt and sand. Remove foreign matter, yellow leaves, roots and tough fiber. Drain well and refrigerate until time for cooking.	25 to 30%
Tomatoes	Wash and drain if to be used with skin on. For peeling, scald with boiling water until skin can be removed easily. Plunge quickly into cold water. Skin and trim away hard stem core. Cut as desired for service.	5 to 10%
Turnips	Remove tops. Tops may be washed well and used as greens. Pare turnips. Rinse and cut as desired for service.	20 to 24%
Watercress	Wash. Remove discolored pieces. Drain well. Refrigerate.	8 to 10%

Mincing, shredding, and other cutting of fruits and vegetables should be done as close to the time of cooking or service as possible. Cutting exposes more surface to oxidation of vitamins and to leaching out of vitamins, minerals, and flavoring substances in the water in which they are prepared. The skin of fruits and vegetables protect from oxidation and loss of valuable nutrients.

Figure 6.2   Use a sharp knife when paring and sectioning fruit, and pare as near time for use as possible to protect vitamin content. (Courtesy of the U.S. Fish and Wildlife Service.)

Tannins present in varying amounts in fruits and vegetables cause browning of cut surfaces that are exposed to the air. Various means are used to prevent this. Oxygen is required for the enzymatic action that causes browning. Oxygen may be kept from the product by immersing it in water, as with potatoes after paring. The surface may be covered with a sugar syrup, as in the preparation of fruit. Oxygen may be shut out through vacuum packing. Browning may be reduced or delayed through the use of inhibitors or antioxidants, such as a salt solution or ascorbic acid. Pineapple juice and citrus juice reduce browning of cut surfaces of apples, pears, peaches, and other fruits with high tannin contents. Fruits for drying are usually bleached with sulphur dioxide. The enzymes that cause browning are killed by heating, as in scalding and steaming.

Salad Greens

Salad greens are grown close to the ground and it is natural for sand and soil to sift between the leaves. Some of the coarse, soiled outer leaves are removed in the field and others are left to protect the more tender leaves during shipment. Salad materials should be inspected for quality and given proper care as soon as they are delivered to the kitchen. Allowing them to wither in a warm kitchen increases the amount lost through trimming; thus early refrigeration is important. Lukewarm water cleans the greens better than cold water. When using lukewarm water, clean them quickly and refrigerate them immediately. The salad greens tend to become limp in the warm water, but they regain crispness as soon as they are chilled. If greens are to be used as soon as cleaned, the washing may be done in cold water to avoid temporary loss of crispness.

When cleaning head lettuce, remove the tough, discolored outer leaves. Cut out the core with a circular motion that removes it in a cone shape. Permit a strong flow of water to pour into the head from the faucet or move the head up and down in the water in such a way as to force water between the leaves. This cleans away the grit and soil and helps to loosen the leaves so that they separate more easily. The heads should be placed with the cut area down so that all the water drains out of the head. Lettuce stores best if the leaves are not separated until shortly before it is used.

Promote crispness by keeping salad greens covered while in storage; this helps prevent dehydration. Metal containers that have a drainsert to hold the vegetables out of the water that drains off of them are satisfactory. The cover may be one that fits the pan, or a sheet of plastic that can be tucked closely around the greens. A wet towel may be used as a cover. Plastic bags are very good for storing well-drained salad greens. Plastic bags that are used repeatedly should be washed after use in a mild soap and chlorine solution (1 teaspoon of chlorox or purex to 1 gallon of water) and thoroughly rinsed with clean water. This helps to keep them fresh and prevents decomposed particles from causing spoilage of the salad greens. Keep salad greens refrigerated.

Fruits

Many fruits are served in their natural form and require cleaning only. Berries and other small fruits are cleaned better by a spray than immersion in a large amount of water. An overhead hose equipped with a trigger-operated spray nozzle is good for washing fruits and leafy vegetables. Less of the nutrients in strawberries are lost if they are hulled after washing. Fruits that are high in tannins should be placed in a solution of salt, sugar, or ascorbic acid or in pineapple or citrus juice as soon as they are pared.

COOKING METHODS

When cooking fruits and vegetables, special attention should be directed to preserving their appealing color, texture, flavor, and valuable nutrients. The length of cooking time and the acidity or alkalinity of the liquid in which they are cooked have a great deal of influence. Each of the fruits and vegetables has specific characteristics that are to be considered when choosing a method of preparation. Both fruits and vegetables naturally contain organic acids which combine with the water in cooking to form weak acid solutions, except in communities where the water is strongly alkaline. The solutions are less acid when the products are cooked uncovered so that the volatile acids can escape.

The green color in fruits and vegetables is due to a green pigment, chlorophyll, which changes color in an acid medium. Prolonged cooking in even a very mild acid solution causes the fresh green color to change to an unattractive olive green; thus, one should be especially careful not to overcook. The addition of a small amount of soda or another alkali to the water does intensify the green color, but it also causes undesirable results. The alkali softens the texture, making it mushy or slippery, and destroys much of the thiamine and ascorbic acid vitamins. In order to prevent the vitamin loss in areas where the water is naturally alkaline, it may be advisable to add a small amount of cream of tartar, lemon juice, or vinegar to the water in which the vegetables are boiled. An important rule to remember is to cook green vegetables uncovered and for the shortest time required for obtaining palatable tenderness.

The yellow color pigments are known as carotinoids. These are found in such yellow vegetables as carrots and sweet potatoes. They are nutritionally important as precursors of vitamin A. The yellow pigments are stable and little affected by either acid or alkaline solutions. A short cooking time in a small amount of water, however, helps to preserve good flavor and valuable nutrients.

The third group of pigments are the flavonoids that include flavones and anthocyanins. The colors in this group are best when cooking is done in an acid medium. The flavones and flavonols are colorless when prepared in an acid solution, but turn yellow in an alkaline medium or with prolonged cooking. These are found in light-colored vegetables like potatoes, white cabbage, and yellow-skinned onions. Anthocyanins, found in red cabbage and blueberries, become red-blue in acid and an unattractive blue-green in alkaline solutions. There is sufficient acid in fruits and vegetables to protect the color, except where the water for cooking is alkaline. As a safeguard for color, an acid fruit (such as tart apple) may be added when cooking red cabbage or other foods containing anthocyanin pigments. Special care is needed when making blueberry muffins to have a slight excess of acid in the batter and to avoid an excess of soda which would make the berries blue-green.

Boiling and Steaming

Boiling and steaming are popular methods of cooking the majority of vegetables. Baking, deep-frying, and broiling add menu variety. When cooking vegetables by boiling, it is best to use a minimum of water, cook them until crisp-tender and in a rotation of batches that will be served within a 15 to 20 minute serving period. The successive batches should be adjusted in quantity according to the number served within that period of time. The water should be boiling when the vegetables are added and should be brought quickly to boiling temperature again. Short, quick cooking is best for retention of natural flavor and the water-soluble vitamins.

Steam cookers are favored for speed and convenience of preparation in large quantity. Retention of ascorbic acid (vitamin C) has been found to be greater when vegetables are cooked in a steamer without water than when they are boiled.[1] Many of the tender, easily broken vegetables such as asparagus, broccoli, and cauliflower can be arranged in serving pans and cooked without water. This arrangement in the pans during preprocessing eliminates additional handling until the vegetables are to be served. Each $12 \times 20 \times 2\frac{1}{2}$ inch serving pan holds from 20 to 30 portions, depending on

[1] J. Gordon and I. Noble, "Effect of Cooking Method on Vegetables," *Journal of The American Dietetic Association*, **35**, 578–581 (1959).

the item and the size of the portions. The amount of pressure used in cooking affects the time required for cooking (see Table 6.1). The range of pressure is from free venting to 15 pounds. The free venting operate without pressure and the time required for cooking is similar to that required for boiling vegetables. Small establishments that do not have a steam cooker find the utensil-size potato steamer useful. It has a pan for water that is heated on top of the range. Steam is formed and escapes into and cooks the food placed in a container on top of the water pan.

The effect of sugar and the osmosis influence results when stewing fruit. Solutions have a tendency to seek a common level of concentration. The solvent or weaker solution diffuses into the heavier one if the membranes separating them are permeable. When fruits are stewed in water, for example, osmotic pressure causes water to be taken up by the cell sap (which is more concentrated) and this causes the cells to rupture during cooking. A heavy syrup, being more concentrated than the cell sap, acts in reverse. It draws juice from the cells, thus causing them to shrivel. Sugar produces firmness in the cellulose or structural fiber and preserves and darkens the color. It removes sharpness or harshness in flavor. Heavy syrup tends to mask delicate flavors like that of pears.

The different varieties of fruit vary in their responses to sugar and to cooking. An understanding of the differences helps in choosing a variety and a method of preparation that will yield the quality desired; for example, those who prefer an applesauce that cooks into a smooth puree choose Trans-

Figure 6.3   Steamed new potatoes with peas, water chestnuts and button mushrooms. (Courtesy of Pacific Kitchen.)

parent or Gravenstein varieties and cook them with little or no sugar, while those who wish apple segments to hold their shape select Jonathan, Winesap, and Pippins and cook them in a syrup that has at least one part sugar to two parts water. The cooking should be done gently, without stirring. The cooking of strawberries illustrates the influence of sugar on color and texture. The dark color and firm texture of the berries in jam are very different from the pale, limp fruit cooked without sugar. The texture of pineapple canned in juice is more tender than that canned in a heavy syrup, and the natural flavor is more pronounced.

Dried fruit and dried vegetables require soaking to shorten cooking time. They take up water and increase in size most rapidly if the water is hot when it is poured over them. The soaking may be done in the steam kettle or other container in which they are to be cooked. It requires 3 to 5 hours soaking time, depending on the item and the temperature and alkalinity of the water. If soda is added to speed the tenderizing of legumes (1 teaspoon to 1 gallon of water), it should be added to the soaking water and this solution should be discarded and fresh water added before cooking.

Because the characteristics of potatoes differ according to varieties, they should be selected for the specific purposes for which they are used. Cobblers and red Triumphs are waxy and do not lose their smooth, close texture when cooked. These are the most suitable for hash-browns, stews, and salads in which it is desirable for pieces to hold their shape. A mealy potato, such as a Russet, is more satisfactory for baking and whipping. Specific gravity can be used to determine mealiness. Starchy or mealy potatoes sink in a room-temperature solution of 20 ounces of salt to one gallon of water (1.08 sp. gr.) and waxy potatoes float on a room temperature solution of $14\frac{1}{2}$ ounces of salt to one gallon of water (1.07 sp. gr.).

Storing or maturing of potatoes at the right temperature affects cooking quality. Low temperatures (40°F and lower) during storage increases the sugar content that is used up in respiration at higher temperatures. Potatoes that have a high sugar content brown too readily and have a poor flavor because of caramelization. Potatoes that are to be used for frying or hash-browning should be held 2 or 3 weeks at 50° to 60°F.

Baking

When baking potatoes or winter squash the oven temperature should be high enough to drive off excess moisture (400 to 450°F). Precooking by steam and finishing in the oven shortens cooking time. This method produces satisfactory results with apples, carrots, onions, parsnips, sweet potatoes, and squash. Ovens can be used for steaming by putting the food in tightly covered pans in the oven. Baked white potatoes are best if they are not steamed, either by precooking in the steamer or by wrapping in foil. Many find the crisp surface of a well-scrubbed potato more attractive and less tedious to handle when it is not foil wrapped. Baking time can be reduced through the use of aluminum pins put through the center of the potatoes while they are baking.

Deep Frying

For deep frying, select fat that has a high smoke point and mild, sweet flavor. Vegetable fats that do not contain an emulsifier have a smoke point of

Figure 6.4 Two fry kettles, each 20 feet long with a capacity of 3000 pounds per hour, cook the French fries for the U.S. Naval Academy at Annapolis.

approximately 440°F when they are heated for the first time. The smoke point of a fat is lowered each time it is heated; that of vegetable fats is about 365°F after use. The smoke point of the vegetable fats containing an emulsifier are about 360°F on first use. The frying temperature required for the majority of foods is 375°F. The absorption of fat by foods is lowest when the fats used have a high smoke point.

Proper care helps to prolong the frying life of fat. There is decomposition of the fat at smoking temperature that produces a disagreeable flavor in food. Exposure of the surface of the oil during frying affects the smoke point. It is best, therefore, to use a deep frying container rather than a shallow one. Particles of food or sediment in the fat lowers the smoking point. The fat should be filtered through cheesecloth or a fine strainer after use and the fry kettle carefully cleaned. The frying life can be prolonged further by replacing 20% of the total weight of the fat with fresh fat before the fat is used again.

Minimum absorption of fat is desirable. The longer the frying period, the greater the fat absorption. Frying time can be shortened by precooking foods that require longer cooking periods than needed for heating and browning. Asparagus, carrots, cauliflower, and fruits, except bananas, may be steamed until almost done, then dipped in batter and deep fried. Potatoes should be dried well and fried without coating. They may be processed in one operation or two. Which method is most advantageous depends on the speed of output required. Approximately seven minutes continuous cooking in 375°F fat is required for the one step method. In the two step method, the potatoes are precooked by boiling, steaming, or deep frying until tender but not browned. In the second step they are browned in 375°F fat for two minutes. The precooking or blanching may be done well in advance of the final cooking, and the potatoes may be refrigerated or frozen until needed. Browning time is shortened by having the potatoes free of moisture and warmed in the oven or warming closet before frying.

Sauteing

Certain fruits and vegetables are delicious sauted (grilled or pan-fried in a small amount of fat). This is a favorite method of preparation for breakfast potatoes. The hashed potatoes may be made from boiled or steamed potatoes or from pre-blanched, shredded potatoes. If cooked slowly without stirring, they become well browned and crisp on the under surface. They present an attractive appearance if carefully turned out on the plate with the brown surface uppermost. Tomato slices are often grilled and served as a meat accompaniment. Fried apples are enjoyed as a breakfast fruit or to accompany entrees. Fruits and vegetables that need extra cooking for tenderness may be braised by adding a small amount of water and tightly covering the container in which they are cooked.

Broiling

Broiling is a quick method of cooking used for tender foods. The browning developed from the high heat adds flavor and an appealing appearance. There are several fruits and vegetables, such as grapefruit and tomatoes, that are tender enough to cook in this manner. Their juiciness tends to interfere with ready browning, and calls for seasoning with material that will promote the development of attractive color. Oil, cheese, bread crumbs, or sauces may be used on vegetables, and butter, oil, and sugar mixtures on fruit. Piping-hot broiled grapefruit, for example, is delightful as a beginner at breakfast or dinner.

TABLE 6.3 MINUTES REQUIRED FOR COOKING VEGETABLES

Vegetables	Steam Kettle or Range Top	Steam Cooker psi 5 lbs	Steam Cooker psi 15 lbs	Oven 400°F	Fry Kettle 375°F	Blanching for Freezing
Artichokes, globe	35 to 45	20 to 30	10 to 15			
Jerusalem	25 to 35	15 to 25	10 to 12			
Asparagus, tips	5 to 10	5 to 8	½ to 1½		4 to 6	3
cuts or stalks	10 to 20	8 to 10	1 to 2			4
frozen	5 to 10	10 to 12	1 to 2			
Beans, green or wax	10 to 20	10 to 12	1 to 3			3
frozen	10 to 20	10 to 12	1 to 3			3
Beans, dry limas	25 to 30	25 to 35	15 to 25			
Beets, small new	30 to 45	35 to 45	5 to 10			25 to 30
large old	45 to 90	45 to 90	10 to 20			45 to 50
Broccoli, cut, fresh	10 to 15	7 to 10	2 to 4			3
frozen	10 to 15	4 to 6	1 to 2			
Brussel Sprouts	10 to 20	8 to 12	1 to 3			3
frozen	5 to 10	8 to 10	1 to 3			
Cabbage, shredded	5 to 8	5 to 8	½ to 1½			1½
wedges	10 to 15	8 to 10	2 to 3			
red, wedges	10 to 15	8 to 10	2 to 3			1½

Variation in time allows for differences in size and maturity of vegetables. Use minimum time whenever possible. Test for doneness by piercing with a sharp fork. (See the Appendix for the portion sizes and quantities required for 100 portions.)

TABLE 6.3 (*Continued*)

Vegetables	Steam Kettle or Range Top	Steam Cooker 5 lbs	Steam Cooker psi 15 lbs	Oven 400°F	Fry Kettle 375°F	Blanching for Freezing
Canned vegetables	10 to 15	5 to 8	3 to 4			
Carrots, young, whole	15 to 25	15 to 25	3 to 5			5
sliced	10 to 20	8 to 10	1½ to 3			
mature, sliced	15 to 25	15 to 20	3 to 5			
Cauliflower, whole	15 to 20	10 to 15	10			
flowerets	8 to 12	8 to 10	1½ to 3			
frozen	8 to 10	6 to 8	1½ to 3			
Celery, sliced	10 to 20	10 to 12	2 to 3			3
Corn on cob	5 to 15	5 to 10	½ to 1½			7 to 9
Corn, frozen	3 to 5	2 to 3	2 to 3			
Eggplant, pieces	10 to 20	10 to 15			5 to 10	
Kohlrabi, sliced	20 to 25	15 to 20				
Kale	5 to 10	6 to 8				
Mixed vegetables, frozen	10 to 20	8 to 15	2 to 4			
Okra, sliced	10 to 15	10 to 15	2 to 4			3
Onions, small whole	15 to 25	12 to 15	3 to 5	40 to 45		
medium	20 to 40	15 to 20	5 to 8			
rings					4 to 6	

TABLE 6.3 (*Continued*)

Vegetables	Steam Kettle or Range Top	Steam Cooker 5 lbs	Steam Cooker psi 15 lbs	Oven 400°F	Fry Kettle 375°F	Blanching for Freezing
Parsnips, whole	20 to 40	20 to 25	8 to 10	30 to 45		2
quartered	10 to 20	15 to 20	4 to 8			
Peas, green	8 to 20	5 to 10	1 to 2			1½
frozen	4 to 7	3 to 4	1			
Potatoes, white, whole	25 to 40	20 to 25	8 to 12	45 to 60		
French cut		10 to 12	3 to 5		3 to 5	
Julienne					2 to 4	
Sweet potatoes, whole	25 to 35	30 to 40	5 to 8	30 to 45		
Rutabagas, cubed	20 to 30	15 to 25	4 to 7			
Spinach, fresh	3 to 10	8 to 10				2
frozen	2 to 4	3 to 5	½ to 1			
Squash, summer	10 to 20	8 to 12	1½ to 3	30 to 45		
zucchini	6 to 8	5 to 8	1 to 2	40 to 60		
acorn	20 to 30	15 to 20	6 to 12	40 to 60		
Hubbard	15 to 20	15 to 20	6 to 12			3 to 5
Swiss Chard	7 to 10					
Tomatoes, whole	7 to 15		½ to 1	15 to 30		
Turnips, whole	20 to 30	20 to 30	8 to 10			
sliced or diced	15 to 20	15 to 20	1½ to 2			

SUGGESTED LABORATORY EXPERIENCE

1. Weigh apples before and after paring and practice paring apples with a swivel-action parer. Cut apples into uniform dices or julienne strips using a French knife. Calculate percentage paring loss, and cost per prepared pound.

2. Place pieces of apple in each of the following solutions or manner indicated below and set aside for an hour. Note which solutions are most effective in retarding discoloration and which are best in terms of the intended use of the apples.
   (a) Pineapple juice.
   (b) Ascorbic acid solution.
   (c) Salt solution (use 1 tsp to 1 qt water).
   (d) Syrup made with 2 cups of water and 1 cup of sugar.
   (e) Plain water, with no addition.
   (f) Allow a small amount to stand without treatment.

3. Wash lettuce, separate the head and place part of it in the refrigerator without covering, and part in a plastic bag. Leave it over night and note the condition of crispness of each the next day.

4. Separate a head of romaine or other lettuce and wash half of it in water that feels warm to the hand and the other half in very cold water. Place each, when drained, into separate plastic bags. Refrigerate over night or for several hours. Compare crispness and general condition.

5. Compare time and effort required and percent waste in peeling tomatoes or peaches that have and have not been scalded with boiling water before peeling.

6. Note cooking time indicated in Table 6.1 for vegetables. Select five vegetables and cook them for the shortest length of time stated. Test for doneness. If a longer time is required, note the exact time. Set up rotation plans for preparing these vegetables for serving five persons per minute and 20 persons per minute.

7. Bake potatoes as follows until tender, note time required for each and compare palatability:
   (a) a Cobbler or Triumph and a Russet variety in 350°F oven, no covering;
   (b) a Cobbler or Triumph and a Russet variety in 400°F oven, no covering;
   (c) a Russet variety wrapped in foil in 400°F oven;
   (d) a Russet variety with surface oiled before baking;
   (e) a Russet variety, not covered pierced with aluminum pin through center.

8. Deep fry vegetables as follows and note time required for palatable doneness:

(a) potatoes steamed until tender, held warm in oven until fried;

(b) potatoes steamed until tender, refrigerated, fried without warming;

(c) potatoes deep fried from raw state after drying carefully with towel;

(d) asparagus or green beans dipped in batter and fried without pre-cooking;

(e) asparagus or green beans steamed until tender, dipped and fried.

REVIEW QUESTIONS AND ANSWERS

1. Vegetables are an important source of what vitamins?

Ascorbic acid (vitamin C) and vitamin A.

2. What effect does cutting and soaking of vegetables in water have on vitamins?

Thiamine, riboflavin, niacin, and ascorbic acid are water soluble and are lost.

3. What other factors or conditions may destroy the vitamin content?

Vitamin A and ascorbic acid are sensitive to light and oxidation, and thiamine and ascorbic acid are destroyed by alkali such as soda.

4. What conditions are desirable for storage or holding of vegetables?

Short storage period, refrigerated temperature, proper humidity, protection from dehydration and light.

5. What fruits should be held at a temperature above 50°F?

Bananas, pineapple, avocado, papayas, and grapefruit.

6. What is the result of holding potatoes under 40°F until time of use?

The sugar content remains high as it is not used up through respiration, and the potato is less satisfactory for frying.

7. What is the effect of tannins on fruits and vegetables that are cut?

Enzymatic action results in browning of cut surfaces.

8. How can the browning be retarded or stopped?

Shut out oxygen, use an anti-oxidant or inhibitor or heat the product to kill the enzyme.

9. How may the crisp quality of salad greens be protected?

Clean promptly, keep under refrigeration, and protect from drying.

10. What are two of the factors important to control when cooking vegetables to preserve good color, flavor, and texture?

Length of cooking time for palatable tenderness and the acidity or alkalinity of the liquid in which they are cooked.

11. Are more vitamins preserved by boiling or steaming?

By steaming.

12. Name the chief color pigments in fruits and vegetables.

Green—chlorophyll; yellow or orange—carotinoids; and the flavonoids that include those that are colorless and the red-blue color pigments.

13. Is an acid or alkaline medium better for an attractive green color?

A slightly alkaline or very dilute acid medium.

14. Is cooking water likely to be acid or alkaline?

It depends upon the water in the specific area of the country. The natural acid in the fruit or vegetable will cause the solution to be mildly acid unless the water in the region is alkaline.

15. Why is it better for the water to be slightly acid rather than alkaline in spite of the effect on the green color?

In order that the thiamine and ascorbic acid are not destroyed.

16. How may the acid content be assured in an area where the water is alkaline?

By adding a small amount of lemon juice, cream of tartar, or vinegar to the cooking water.

17. What affects carotinoids?

They are stable and little affected by either acid or alkaline solutions.

18. What effect does an alkaline solution have on anthocyamins?

It changes them from red-blue to blue-green. It is well to take extra precaution that the medium is acid.

19. What is meant by rotation cooking?

Cooking in successive batches so as to insure a fresh supply for service.

20. What factors are to be considered when planning rotation cooking?

The length of time required for cooking and the quantity to be used in a given period of time.

21. How does osmosis affect the cooking of fruit?

When cooked in a syrup of heavier concentration than the cell sap, liquid is drawn by osmosis from the cell, and when the concentration is lower the cells take up the liquid and tend to rupture.

22. What is the influence of sugar in the cooking of fruit?

It tends to preserve and darken color and makes texture firmer.

23. What type of potato is best for baking or mashing?

Mealy varieties that are low in protein, such as the Russet varieties.

24. What is the desirable frying temperature for the majority of foods?

375°F.

25. What is the influence of use on fat?

It lowers the smoke point.

26. List other conditions that affect the smoke point.

Kind of fat used, amount of surface exposed during frying, sediment or particles of food in the fat.

27. What conditions influence the amount of fat absorbed by food?

Temperature at which frying is done, and length of frying time.

28. How may frying time be shortened?

By precooking or blanching.

29. How may blanching be done?

By boiling, steaming, or frying.

30. Is it essential to thaw frozen food before cooking in a steam cooker?

Only if the mass is so large that the exterior would be overcooked before heat penetrated to the inside.

7.

Sauces

Sauces are dressings used to complement foods that need some additional quality to make the foods more palatable or interesting. Enjoyable qualities may be imparted by adding moisture to foods that are too dry or more richness to those that lack pleasing substance and flavor. Sometimes a sauce is used to improve the food's appearance by adding color. A simple white sauce, for example, adds creaminess to overly firm or dry foods. Gravy on potatoes moistens them and enriches flavor. A hollandaise sauce on a vegetable adds attractive color, richer flavor, and appealing tartness. Many very plain foods, simply prepared, can be transformed into deluxe fare through the wise choice of a tasty sauce.

Choice of the right sauce for a particular food deserves thoughtful analysis. A sauce should never be taken for granted, never served or omitted without due consideration to its influence on the appealing quality of the food. Skill in the use of sauces has brought fame to many chefs and their establishments. Sauces may add substantially to food cost and increase preparation and service labor. It is desirable, therefore, to use them only when they justify their cost by the degree to which they enhance the quality of the foods with which they are served. Too many sauces in a meal detracts from its quality and adds extra motions in service.

Sauces used with foods are customarily indicated on menus. This is done to let customers know the mode of preparation and serves to make menus more interesting. Familiar examples of menu names that indicate the sauce used include Roast Beef Au Jus, Lobster Newburg, Asparagus Hollandaise, Cauliflower a la Mornay, Roast Duck with Orange Sauce, Peach Melba, and Apple Cobbler with Spicy Cream.

Because of the great variety and fame of sauces, many believe their preparation to be mysterious and difficult. Some of the most delectable sauces are very simple to prepare. A sensitive taste, a gentle hand, and mastery of the techniques in the preparation of a half-dozen basic sauces are all that is necessary to produce many fine products. The basic sauces include (a) simple

Figure 7.1   A tasty sauce adds interest and appetite appeal to a simple meal. (Courtesy of the American Daily Association.)

sauces, such as pan-gravies and heat-and-serve sauces; (b) butter sauces; (c) bread sauces; (d) those thickened with eggs; (e) tart or savory sauces, such as those used for barbecues, marinades, and cocktails; and (f) starch-thickened sauces, which include white and brown sauces. Sweet sauces may be considered as an additional group or considered under the classification of the six listed, according to contents and methods of preparation which resemble that used in any of the six. Sweet sauces include butter sauces, egg- or starch-thickened sauces, purees, creams, and simple syrups.

SIMPLE SAUCES

Pan-gravies, purees of fruit or vegetables, and canned soups that are merely heated and served are the easiest to prepare. Pan-gravies (au jus) are prepared from the natural, unthickened juices of cooked meat. The liquid used to dissolve the browned particles in the pan, may be stock, wine, or water. The excess fat is drained off, then the liquid is added, and the browned material is dissolved by stirring over heat.

Purees are made by pressing cooked food through a sieve or China-cap strainer. Foods for a puree sauce are chosen for distinct flavor quality and appealing color. Favorite foods for pureeing include green peas, tomatoes, asparagus, raspberries, strawberries, cranberries, and apricots. The purees are seasoned to taste and may or may not be lightly thickened.

Concentrated canned soups may be used without diluting. They may be used alone or two or more flavors blended for the special flavor quality desired. Additional seasoning may or may not be added. Some of the most popular selections include mushroom, celery, cheese, and tomato. They are served hot. A small amount of milk or well-flavored stock may be added if needed to thin the consistency.

BUTTER SAUCES

Butter and margarine add richness and flavor as a sauce and are good carriers for additional seasonings. They may be used in melted form or the flavoring materials may be worked into softened butter or margarine. When the firm sauce is placed on hot foods, it melts quickly and disperses the seasonings into the food. It is well to follow proper procedures in making these simple sauces. The butter should not be melted, but softened until it can be beaten with a whip or in a mixer. Add the flavoring material and stir or beat until it is light, fluffy, and well blended. The sauce may be used in this softened form or it may be shaped into sticks, refrigerated until firm, then sliced for adding to individual portions of food. If the butter sauce is smooth enough to pass through a pastry tip, individual portions may be formed, chilled until firm, and used as a garnish. Table 7.1 gives examples of butter sauces with the ingredients suggested for use with one pound of butter.

BREAD SAUCES

Bread sauce varies in dryness from browned and buttered dry bread crumbs to a moist sauce in which bread crumbs are used as a thickening agent. Browned crumbs that have been prepared by being stirred and browned in a hot skillet with melted butter or margarine are used to add flavor, rich brown color, and crisp texture to casserole dishes. Minced mushrooms and a little lemon juice added to browned crumbs of meal-like fineness make a delicious sauce for fresh asparagus, broccoli, and other vegetables. A moist sauce can be prepared by using proportions of 2 ounces of dry bread crumbs to thicken 1 quart of stock. Stock, wine, or cream may be used to moisten a dry bread sauce. Flavoring of the sauce can be varied through the addition of minced onion, celery, horseradish, or dry mustard.

TABLE 7.1 MODIFICATIONS OF BUTTER SAUCE

Name of Sauce	Ingredients for Use with 1 lb Butter	Use to Accompany
Anchovy	¼ lb anchovy paste, 2 tbsp lemon juice	Baked or broiled fish
Caper	¼ c capers, 2 tbsp vinegar, ¾ c minced parsley	Lamb, steak, fish
Garlic	8 to 10 cloves garlic (parboil 30 sec, peel, rinse, and put through press), 2 tbsp minced parsley	Broiled meats, canapes
Mustard	¼ c prepared mustard	Meats, sandwiches
Parsley (Maitre d'Hotel)	½ c minced parsley, 2 tbsp lemon juice	Meats, fish, soups, vegetables
Green onion	Boil 1 c Vermouth or white wine and 1 c brown stock with ¼ c green onions until reduced to 1 c. Add ¼ c minced parsley.	Steaks and chops

SAUCES THICKENED WITH EGGS

The richest of all sauces are those thickened with egg yolk. They include those that have a mayonnaise base, such as tartar sauce, and cooked sauces such as hollandaise and bearnaise. Each contains a high percentage of fat and egg yolk. Hollandaise is frequently referred to as the queen of sauces. An important aspect in its preparation is the cooking of the egg yolks in a way that promotes their taking up and holding the butter. In order for the egg yolks to do this, they must be cooked slowly and never allowed to reach simmering temperature. Higher temperature causes the egg yolks to become hard and granular and to separate from the butter. One egg yolk will absorb a maximum of 3 ounces of butter, if the butter is beaten gradually into the *warm*, creamy, thick yolk.

The following recipes illustrate that bearnaise sauce is similar to hollandaise except in flavoring. The recipe given for each sauce requires approximately 1 pound of butter. Begin by melting 12 to 14 ounces of the butter or margarine over moderate heat, then set it back in a warm place until needed. Prepare the flavoring as follows:

For hollandaise sauce, blend 2 tbsp lemon juice
$\qquad$ 2 tbsp cold water
$\qquad$ $\frac{1}{4}$ tsp salt

For bearnaise sauce, boil until reduced to 4 tbsp, cool and strain
$\qquad$ $\frac{1}{2}$ c vermouth or white wine
$\qquad$ $\frac{1}{2}$ c wine vinegar
$\qquad$ 2 tsp dry tarragon (or 1 tbsp fresh)
$\qquad$ $\frac{1}{2}$ c minced young onions
$\qquad$ $\frac{1}{4}$ tsp salt
$\qquad$ pepper to taste

Proceed with the recipe as follows:

1. Place 6 egg yolks in the top of a double boiler and whip until thick. Beat in the flavoring for hollandaise *or* bearnaise according to the sauce desired.

2. Slice and add 1 ounce of cold butter. Heat the mixture gradually in the double boiler over very slowly simmering water. Beat with a wire whip until the mixture becomes as thick as heavy cream. Be watchful that the eggs do not thicken too rapidly or become too firm. When the mixture begins to coat the wires of the whip, remove it from the heat.

3. Slice and beat in 1 ounce of cold butter. This helps lower the temperature of the mixture and helps prevent overcooking of the egg yolks.

4. Beat in the melted butter or margarine in small droplets. Start with less than half-teaspoonful, beating continuously. The mixture will thicken as the butter is added, until it is as thick as heavy cream. The butter may be added more rapidly toward the end. Do not add the milky residue from the butter in the bottom of the pan.

5. The sauce is best if used immediately. It may be held during service over lukewarm water. If it breaks or curdles, beat in 1 tbsp of cold water. This sometimes helps it to blend and thicken it again.

Egg yolks promote thickening in mayonnaise as an emulsifying agent. (See Salad Dressings.) In addition to the many salad dressings that use mayonnaise as a base, it is used in fish, egg, and vegetable sauces for which extra richness is desirable. Tartar sauce, containing chopped pickle and flavorful vegetables, is popular with fish dishes. Remoulade sauce is another favorite with egg and fish dishes. It contains chopped pickle, anchovy fillets or paste, capers, and herbs.

Mayonnaise thickened with gelatin may be used as a shiny, flavorful coating or shaped with a pastry tube into forms to decorate buffet foods. The flavoring items should be selected to harmonize with the specific foods with which the sauce is to be used. The following recipe serves as an example of the proportions of ingredients to use in preparing a decorative coating.

DECORATIVE MEAT, FISH, OR POULTRY COATING   3½ c

Ingredients	Weight	Volume
Well-flavored stock (meat, fish, or poultry)	2⅔ oz	⅓ c
Vermouth or other white wine	1½ oz	3 tbsp
Vinegar or lemon juice	1 oz	2 tbsp
Granulated gelatin—Sprinkle over the liquid and allow to hydrate for several minutes, then heat, stirring until completely dissolved. Cool until it begins to thicken. Beat gradually into	½ oz	2 tbsp
Mayonnaise	1 lb, 8 oz	3 c

The mixture must be used before it becomes stiff. Pimento, green pepper, pickle, or other brightly-colored foods may be cut into attractive shapes and applied for decoration before the coating has set. The decorative forms shaped with a pastry tube serve as an attractive sauce when served with foods.

SAVORY OR TART SAUCES AND MARINADES

Tomato-flavored barbecue sauces are among the most popular of this group. They may be used with baked, broiled, and grilled meat, poultry, and fish. For some recipes, the ingredients may be blended quickly and used immediately. Other recipes call for slow simmering of ingredients until the sauce is thick and flavors are rich and well blended.

HAMBURGER OR FRANKFURTER SAUCE   1 qt (32 1-oz portions)

Ingredients	Weight	Volume
Catsup	10 oz	1¼ c
Cooked or combination salad dressing	8 oz	1 c
Pickle relish	12 oz	1½ c
Prepared mustard	2½ oz	¼ c
Salt	¼ tsp	¼ tsp

(Add vinegar to taste if the pickle relish and catsup are lacking in acid.) Blend well and serve.

The barbecue sauce for spareribs or lamb riblets should be simmered until thick enough to coat and cling to the ribs. Because of the fat content of pork, spareribs should be roasted covered for approximately 1 hour and the fat should be poured off before the barbecue sauce is added. A tasty sauce for basting 10 pounds of ribs, roasted uncovered until tender, can be made by boiling the following ingredients for approximately 5 minutes.

BARBECUE SAUCE		2½ pt
Ingredients	Weight	Volume
Catsup	1 lb	1 pt
Light molasses	1 lb, 5 oz	1 pt
Vinegar	2 oz	¼ c
Salad oil	2 oz	¼ c
Chopped onion	12 oz	1 pt
Cloves of garlic, minced	1 oz	4 cloves
Orange rind, chopped	1½ oz	½ c
Whole cloves	½ tsp	½ tsp
Prepared mustard	2 tsp	2 tsp
Salt	1 tsp	1 tsp
Cayenne pepper	1 tsp	1 tsp
Soy sauce	½ oz	½ oz
Worcestershire sauce	2 tsp	2 tsp
Orange juice	4 oz	½ c

Figure 7.2 An exotic meal in which halibut is served with a sweet and sour sauce and accompanied with sesame buttered sweet peas and crisp noodles. (Courtesy of Pacific Kitchen.)

Marinades are used with meats to impart seasoning and for the tenderizing effect of the acid. It is well to blend the ingredients and allow the marinade to stand for a few hours for the flavors to blend before adding the meat. The meat may be soaked for a period of 4 to 12 hours or longer before cooking, depending on the seasoning and tenderizing desired and the size of the pieces. When preparing a wine marinade, it is suggested that a white wine, such as sauterne or vermouth, be used for chicken or veal, and a red wine employed with beef, ham, and lamb.

WINE MARINADE   1 qt

Ingredients	Weight	Volume
Sugar	¾ oz	1½ tbsp
Tabasco sauce	⅛ tsp	⅛ tsp
Salt	½ oz	1 tbsp
Fresh marjoram	1 tsp	1 tsp
Fresh thyme, chopped	2 tsp	2 tsp
Onion, minced	6 oz	1 c
Cloves garlic, crushed	¼ oz	3 cloves
Lemon juice	6 oz	¾ c
Salad oil	12 oz	1½ c
Wine	12 oz	1½ c

Tart, spicy sauces are relished with seafood and vegetable cocktails. Fruit juices, wine, and carbonated beverages are used as sauces for many of the fruit cocktails. Additional flavor and sparkle may be developed in fruit cocktails through the use of bright colored, rich-flavored gelatin cubes. Most of the cocktail sauces are carefully blended but not cooked. The following table gives ingredients for 12 sauces and the type of cocktail with which each may be used.

TABLE 7.2 COCKTAIL SAUCES AND TYPES OF COCKTAIL ON WHICH TO USE THEM

Name of Sauce	Ingredients	Type of Cocktail
Celery and Onion	1 c minced celery, ¼ c grated onion, ¼ tsp salt, 1 tbsp horseradish, 1 tbsp Worcestershire sauce, ½ c catsup and ½ c lemon juice.	Meat, fish or vegetable.
Chili cheese	½ c chili sauce, 1 c mayonnaise, ½ tsp salt, ¼ c lemon juice, 3 oz cream cheese.	Avocado, celery rings, and grapefruit sections; celery rings and crabmeat or shrimp.
Chili-catsup	1 c chili sauce, ½ c catsup, ¼ tsp Tabasco, 1 tbsp horseradish, ½ c minced celery, 2 tbsp minced green pepper, ½ tsp salt.	Meat or fish and celery rings.
Cucumber-tarragon	2 c grated cucumbers, 3 oz minced green pepper, ½ c honey, ½ tbsp tarragon vinegar, and ½ tbsp malt vinegar.	Grapefruit, pineapple or tomato and celery.
Grenadine	1 c grenadine syrup, ¼ c lemon juice.	Pear, pineapple, and maraschino cherry; watermelon and green grapes.
Gingerale	1½ c gingerale.	Pear, pineapple, and maraschino cherry; melon balls; orange segments and green grapes.

167

TABLE 7.2 (*Continued*)

Name of Sauce	Ingredients	Type of Cocktail
Mayonnaise	2 c mayonnaise, ¼ c catsup, ¼ c chili sauce, 2 tbsp lemon juice, 1 tbsp tarragon vinegar, 2 drops Tabasco sauce, ½ tsp salt.	Seafood, vegetables, or grapefruit.
Piquant	1½ c catsup, 1½ c tomato puree, 1 tbsp onion juice, ¼ c horseradish, ½ tsp salt, 2 tbsp lemon juice, ½ tsp Tabasco sauce, 1 tsp Worcestershire sauce.	Fish, cucumber and celery, or mixed vegetables.
Pineapple juice	1½ c pineapple juice, ½ tbsp lemon juice.	Melon balls and raspberries.
Pineapple mint	1½ c pineapple juice, ½ tbsp lemon juice, ⅛ tsp mint flavoring and drop of green coloring.	Pineapple and canteloupe or grapefruit.
Sherry	¾ c sherry, 1½ c apricot juice.	Fruit either mixed or alone.
Tomato cream	1 c tomato puree blended with ½ c mayonnaise, 2 tbsp lemon juice, folded into ½ c whipped cream with salt to taste.	Orange, avocado, grapefruit, pineapple, and cucumber.

SAUCES THICKENED WITH STARCH

Starch thickened sauces are the sauces used in largest quantity. They are generally popular, readily adaptable and easily varied. Success in their preparation calls for an understanding of the characteristics of starches and the influence that certain ingredients and conditions have on their thickening power.

There are two types of starch commonly used. One is cereal starch, such as that from wheat, corn, and rice, and the other is root starch, such as potato, tapioca, and arrowroot. When added to liquid, the root starches begin swelling when heated at 150 to 160°F and the gelatinization or swelling is complete before boiling temperature (212°F) is reached. If heating or boiling is continued, the starch granules break up in such a manner as to make the mixture thinner and sticky. The cereal starches require a boiling temperature to complete gelatinization or thickening that results from the absorption of water and the swelling of the starch granules. It is necessary to continue the cooking of cereal starches until they become translucent and have lost the raw-starch flavor.

The thickening quality of starches vary. Only half as much (by weight) waxy-maize starch is required to produce a consistency comparable in thickness to one produced by flour. The waxy-maize starch mixture thins slightly, however, when it is heated above 195°F. It retains a smooth consistency when frozen and later reheated, without syneresis (weeping). This is a valuable quality in products that are to be frozen and held. Comparable thickness of 1 gallon of liquid can be obtained with 8 ounces of pastry flour, $5\frac{1}{2}$ ounces of cornstarch, 4 ounces of waxy-maize starch, or 7 ounces of tapioca. The root starches produce a more tender gel than the cereal starches.

The desired standard for starch mixtures is a glossy product of smooth consistency. Undercooking produces a dull product. Excess fat rising to the top, yielding a greasy sauce, and lumpy sauces indicate the use of the wrong techniques in the sauce preparation. The lumping of starch granules can be avoided by observing one of the following techniques and by stirring continuously while the mixture is cooking:

1. Separate the starch granules with fat before adding liquid. A common practice is to make a roux by blending equal volumes of melted fat and flour. The fat is melted in the saucepan, the flour is added and thoroughly blended before adding the liquid. This method is followed when making white sauce and gravies. When a cooked sauce is found to be thinner than desired, a blended mixture of starch and butter or margarine or other soft fat may be added in small amounts and stirred into the hot mixture until the desired consistency is obtained. The name used for this fat and flour mixture is *buerre manie.*

2. Starch granules may be separated by mixing the starch with other dry ingredients. Cornstarch mixed with sugar, for example, goes into solution smoothly as the sugar dissolves.

3. A fluid mixture can be made by gradually beating a cold liquid into flour or other dry starch. Thorough stirring is required to remove lumps and to evenly moisten the starch. The fluid mixture can then be stirred into hot liquid. This mixture, as well as the buerre manie, is useful for adding extra thickening to hot mixtures.

Blond and White Sauces

These are starch thickened sauces in which the flour used is not browned. Some of the cooking of the starch is done in the roux and additional cooking is done after the liquid has been added. Flavor goodness requires that sufficient cooking be done to remove any raw or harsh taste from the flour.

The liquid for white sauces may be milk, milk and cream, light cream, and/or white stock. The term "white sauce" refers to a sauce made with milk, and "cream sauce," correctly speaking, is one containing cream. Bechamel sauce contains part milk or cream and part white stock. (See Chapter 8 for the preparation of stock.) Velouté is a blond sauce made with white stock and it contains no milk or cream.

The purpose for which the sauce is to be used influences the thickness desirable. Recommended proportions of flour and fat to be used in sauces of different thickness, with 1 gallon of liquid, 1 ounce of salt, and 2 teaspoons of pepper, are as follows:

WHITE SAUCE PROPORTIONS

Thickness	Flour	Fat	Use
Thin	4 oz (1 c)	8 oz (1 c)	Cream soups
Medium	8 oz (2 c)	1 lb (2 c)	Casseroles, vegetables
Thick	12 oz (3 c)	1½ lb (3 c)	Souffles
Very thick	1 lb (4 c)	2 lb (4 c)	Deep-fry mixtures, croquettes

Cold liquid may be added gradually to hot roux or hot liquid to cold roux while stirring vigorously to avoid lumping and develop a smooth mixture. Fat may come to the top of the sauce if the starch is not fully gelatinized. In order to incorporate the fat, heat the mixture to boiling and stir well.

Figure 7.3   Preparation of soft custard. (*a*) Scald milk in saucepan over low heat. (*b*) Stir milk gradually into blended eggs and sugar. (*c*) Cook, stirring constantly, over low heat until the mixture coats spoon. (*d*) Cover custard with foil, plastic, or waxed paper to prevent skin forming over the top. (Courtesy of the Poultry and Egg National Board.)

When sauces are very thick it is sometimes necessary to add a little additional liquid, in order to blend the fat into the mixture so that it does not rise to the top of the sauce.

White, bechamel, and velouté sauces provide bases for the many delicious and well known sauces shown in Table 7.3. The quantity of ingredients suggested are in the amounts that should be used with 1 quart of sauce.

TABLE 7.3 MODIFICATIONS FOR WHITE, BECHAMEL, AND VELOUTE SAUCES

Name of Sauce	Ingredients	Foods with Which Used
	White Sauce, 1 qt	
Cheese	½ lb grated sharp cheese (cheddar), 1 tsp dry mustard, 1 tsp Worcestershire sauce.	Vegetables, eggs, fish, pastes, rice.
Cucumber	1 c grated cucumber, dash of Tabasco sauce.	Fish.
Curry	2 tbsp curry powder	Chicken, eggs, rice.
Dill	1 tbsp dried dill seed, ⅛ tsp nutmeg	Green beans, bland meat, or fish.
Egg	4 sliced hard-cooked eggs, 1 tsp prepared mustard.	Ham croquettes, fish.
Mustard	2 tbsp prepared mustard.	Cauliflower, cabbage, fish.
Parsley	1 c finely minced parsley.	Meat or fish loaves.
Green pea	¼ c chopped pimento, 1 c cooked peas.	Salmon loaf, omelet, fish.

TABLE 7.3 (*Continued*)

Name of Sauce	Ingredients	Foods with Which Used
	Bechamel Sauce, 1 qt	
A la King	2 c sliced, sauted mushrooms, ½ c minced green pepper, ⅓ c pimento cut into strips. Add 4 slightly beaten egg yolks mixed with ½ c cream. Cook until thickened and remove from heat.	Chicken, eggs, ham, seafood.
Almond	1 c blanched, shredded almonds, 2 tbsp lemon juice, dash of cayenne.	Chicken, fish, vegetables.
Creme	1 c whipping cream—gradually beat in 1 tbsp lemon juice.	Croquettes, chicken, casseroles, fish.
Mornay	½ c shredded Swiss cheese, ½ c grated Parmesan, dash of nutmeg.	Eggs, poultry, fish.
Newburg	3 c cooked crab, lobster or shrimp meat, ½ c sherry. Heat well, then add 4 beaten egg yolks mixed with ½ c cream. Stir and cook slowly until thickened. Remove from heat.	Toast cups, rice omelet.
Ravigote	1½ tbsp chopped chives, 1 tbsp chopped parsley, 1 tbsp chopped green onion, ¼ c tarragon vinegar.	Chicken, crabmeat, fish.
Tomato	3 tbsp tomato paste (2 tbsp minced fresh basil or tarragon may be added if desired).	Eggs, veal, fish, chicken, vegetables.

173

TABLE 6.2 (Continued)

Name of Sauce	Ingredients	Foods with, Which Used
	Velouté Sauce, 1 qt	
Allemande	Add 4 slightly beaten egg yolks mixed with ½ c cream, cook until thickened and add 1 tbsp lemon juice. Remove from heat.	Fish, patties, vegetables.
Caper	2 tbsp capers.	Fish, veal, lamb.
Horseradish	¼ c well drained prepared horseradish, 1 tbsp prepared mustard.	Boiled or cold beef, pork or veal.
Supreme	1 c whipping cream beaten in until sauce is of desired consistency, 1 tbsp lemon juice.	Eggs, fish, poultry, vegetables.
Soubise	Cook 2 qt sliced white onions until soft, drain and put through a sieve. Add pulp to sauce.	Pork, lamb, and veal dishes.

Brown Sauces

The chief ingredients of a brown sauce (espagnole) are a well browned roux, richly flavored stock of beef that has been cooked with chopped mixed vegetables (mirepoix) and seasonings (bouquet garni or sachet). The mixed vegetables may include carrots, celery, leeks, onions, turnips, and possibly cabbage. The seasonings include herbs such as bay leaf, parsley, thyme, and marjoram. These are tied in a cheesecloth bag for easy removal from the broth after cooking. The fat used for the roux should be a mild, sweet-flavored fat that blends well in flavor with the foods with which the sauce is to be used. Cooking oils and hydrogenated cooking fat with a fairly high smoking point are best. The flour should be blended into the fat, stirred, and allowed to cook until it has become a uniform nut-brown color. Wheat flour, because of richness of flavor, is the thickening agent used for the majority of meat dishes. One of the other starches (cornstarch, arrowroot, potato starch, or rice flour) is used for sauces in which greater translucency is desired, such as fruit or wine sauces.

The sauces thickened with flour should be allowed to simmer slowly until all of the raw taste has disappeared. Flavors mellow and blend during the longer cooking. This long-simmered brown sauce made with meat stock is called espagnole, and may be used as a base for other sauces. If excess fat or scum collects on the sauce as it cooks, it should be skimmed off. Strain the sauce through a wire strainer or a china cap before serving. Sauces thickened with arrowroot or cornstarch need not be simmered more than 5 minutes. These sauces depend for flavor on a richly flavored stock or other liquid such as wine. If the sauce is to be cooled and held for later use, it is well to treat the top to prevent a skin from forming. This may be done by covering with melted butter, a liquid such as wine, cream, or water, or by floating plastic or waxed paper on the top.

TABLE 7.4 MODIFICATIONS FOR BROWN SAUCE

Name of Sauce	Ingredients	Foods with Which Used
	Brown Sauce (Espagnole), 1 qt	
Bordelaise	¼ c minced green onion, ¼ c chopped beef marrow, 2 tbsp minced parsley, ¼ c red wine.	Steak.
Curry	2 c chopped onions cooked slowly in 2 tbsp oil or butter, 4 tbsp curry powder, ¼ c minced parsley, 2 tbsp lemon juice.	Chicken, eggs, rice, lamb dishes.
Madeira	1 c Madeira boiled until reduced to ½ c.	Veal, eggs, ham, chicken livers.
Mexican	Saute ½ c minced onion and ¼ c minced green pepper in ¼ c butter until tender. Add 2 c tomato catsup and cook until thickened. Add salt, pepper, and celery salt to taste.	Omelets, fish, meats.
Mushroom	Saute 1 lb (1 qt) minced mushrooms and ½ c minced green onions in 3 oz butter. Add ¼ tsp Worcestershire sauce.	Hot meats, chicken, rice, pastes, eggs.
Piquant	½ c chopped sweet pickle, ¼ c capers, 1 tbsp vinegar, 2 tbsp minced onion.	Pork, tongue, veal, boiled beef, fish.
Provencale	1½ c chopped tomato and 3 cloves minced or crushed garlic.	Meat, vegetables, spaghetti, noodles.
Robert	½ c minced onion, ¼ c prepared mustard, ⅓ c pickle relish, 1 tbsp vinegar.	Hamburger, pork, boiled beef, ham.
Tomato	Saute ½ c chopped onion and ½ c chopped green pepper in 2 oz butter. Add 3 c tomato sauce and cook until thick, simmering slowly.	Veal, egg dishes, cheese souffle.

SWEET SAUCES

The consistency of sweet sauces varies considerably. Some are as fluid as juice, some have body as a natural quality of the products used, as with purees, and others are thickened with starch or eggs. Butters, purees, and creams are included among sweet sauces. Although the sweet sauces are separately listed here, the techniques required in their preparation are described earlier in this chapter under other headings.

Simple purees may be made by pressing fresh or frozen fruit through a sieve or China-cup strainer, then sweetened to taste. Many fruits benefit from the addition of lemon juice. Sieved jam, especially apricot, makes an excellent sauce or glaze. Fruit purees are popular for use on angel and chiffon cakes, custards, ice creams, and puddings. Fruits that have a stimulating balance of sugar and acid, such as apple, cranberry, and cherry, add appealing flavor to meat and poultry dishes as well as to various desserts.

The hard sauce commonly served with steam pudding and mince pie is made by blending butter, sugar, and flavoring. The butter is creamed until soft, and sifted confectioner's sugar is beaten into it until the desired consistency is attained. The sauce may be made stiff enough to hold a sharp form when pressed through a pastry tip, or softened with cream, rum, or wine until it can be spooned easily. A fluffy hard sauce can be made with the addition of eggs. The following is a recipe for 25 portions of 2 scant tablespoons of sauce:

FLUFFY HARD SAUCE		25 portions
Ingredients	Weight	Volume
Butter	5 oz	1 cube or ½ c plus 1 tbsp
Powdered sugar	1 lb, 4 oz	4⅓ c
Eggs, separated	4 oz	2 large or ½ c
Boiling water	1¼ oz	2½ tbsp
Vanilla	1 tsp	1 tsp
Lemon extract	½ tsp	½ tsp

PROCEDURE:

Cream the butter and sugar until smooth.
Beat the egg yolks and slowly add the boiling water while continuing beating.
Add egg yolks to the butter and sugar mixture.
Whip the egg whites until stiff, but not dry, and fold into the sauce with the flavorings.

Foamy sauce is a fluid sauce of comparable richness to the hard sauce. It contains whipped cream instead of butter or margarine.

FOAMY SAUCE		25 portions
Ingredients	Weight	Volume
Eggs, separated	5 oz	3
Powdered sugar	4 oz	⅞ c
Whipping cream	12 oz	1½ c
Vanilla	1½ tsp	1½ tsp

PROCEDURE:

Whip the egg whites until stiff but not dry, and gradually add the sugar. Fold in the beaten egg yolks and the cream whipped until stiff. Add the vanilla and chill.

This sauce, which is very easy to make, is a delicious one to use with steamed puddings and simple cakes that can be improved by the added flavor and richness.

Soft custard sauce (Crème Anglaise) is an especially good one to serve with stewed pears, simple puddings, and ice cream. It should be made in a double boiler or kettle in which the temperature can be controlled (185 to 189°F). Custards need to be cooked below simmering temperature to produce best quality. The cooking process can be shortened by scalding the milk and adding it gradually (in a thin stream) to the beaten egg yolks. Continue cooking, stirring, until the custard is thick enough to coat the spoon. Cornstarch is used in some recipes, as a safeguard in obtaining a smooth custard with a minimum of separation (syneresis). Cornstarch custards, which depend largely upon the starch for thickening, may be used as sauces (Figure 7.3).

Crème brûlée is a soft custard sauce made with whipping cream instead of milk, and has half as much sugar as the regular custard. Zabaglione or sabayon sauce contains wine as the liquid in the custard. The proportions call for 6 egg yolks, beaten until thick and light, 2 to 4 tablespoons of sugar beaten into the yolks, and ½ cup of sherry or Madeira warmed and beaten into the mixture. The sauce is cooked over hot water, below simmering, until thick. This is a deliciously rich sauce for souffle desserts and either stewed or fresh fruit.

Flavored syrups of sugar and water serve as a foundation for numerous sauces. Acid, such as lemon juice or cream of tartar, or corn syrup may be used in them to inhibit the formation of sugar crystals. They are cooked to the degree that produces the thickness or body desired (such as the soft ball stage). Milk or cream may be used in making the syrup and it may be thickened lightly with starch to give it body and creaminess.

Flavored whipped cream is a popular sauce for puddings, fruits, and cakes. It may be varied by the addition of different toppings. Syrups may be poured over the whipped cream, or foods that add interesting flavor or texture may be sprinkled over it. Popular toppings include crushed peanut brittle or peppermint stick candy; fresh raspberries, strawberries or blueberries; and sprinkles of chocolate, tiny candies, or toasted coconut. Sweetened sour cream may be used on certain puddings and cheesecakes. It is often sprinkled lightly with nutmeg.

SUGGESTED LABORATORY EXPERIENCE

1. Prepare three kinds of butter sauce. Shape each into a stick by rolling it in wax paper. Refrigerate it for later use.
2. Prepare a hollandaise or bearnaise sauce. Evaluate the sauce in relation to foods with which it may be served.
3. Prepare and compare sauces made with flour, waxy-maize starch and corn-starch, according to proportions given in the text for thickening 1 gallon of liquid. Note proper temperature and preparation method to be used with each.
4. Prepare a white sauce using a roux and another thickened with flour and milk mixture. Compare the quality and ease of preparation of the sauces by the two methods.
5. Brown the same amount of flour as that used for preparation of the white sauce, and prepare sauce with stock according to directions. Note the consistency of the sauce as compared with the white sauce, using the same amount of liquid.
6. If the sauce is thinner than that of a medium sauce, prepare a buerre manie using 4 ounces of softened butter and 3 ounces of flour. Add small amounts to the sauce until it is of the same consistency as a medium thick sauce. Note amount of additional thickening required.
7. Prepare a velouté sauce using chicken soup base. Make a Soubise sauce using a china-cap strainer for pureeing the onions.

REVIEW QUESTIONS AND ANSWERS

1. When is it desirable to use a sauce?

When it improves food quality sufficiently to justify cost.

2. Name three simple sauces and indi-

Au jus with roast beef, concentrated

cate foods with which each may be served.

3. What are butter sauces?

Butter or margarine used alone or with flavoring materials blended into them.

4. Give examples of bread sauces.

Bread crumbs browned in butter. Flavoring material such as mushrooms, onion, cinnamon, or wine may be added.

5. What special precaution should be taken when cooking egg sauces?

To cook slowly at temperature below simmering.

6. Name the two best known warm sauces that are thickened with eggs.

Hollandaise and bearnaise sauces.

7. On what principle is the preparation based in blending the egg yolk and butter?

Egg yolk cooked slowly at low temperature holds a larger amount of fat than yolk cooked at a temperature that makes it firm or hard.

8. What is a marinade?

A seasoned liquid in which a food is soaked for the purpose of adding flavor or developing tenderness.

9. Is a sauce and a marinade the same?

A sauce may be used as a marinade in which a food is soaked. A marinade may be brushed on the food while it is cooking. If it is served over the food it is a sauce.

10. What are the two types of starches used for thickening sauces?

Cereal starch and root starch.

11. Give examples of each.

Cereal—wheat, corn, and rice starch; Root—potato, tapioca, and arrowroot.

12. Which type should be cooked at lower temperature?

Root starches should be cooked below 190°F and cereal starches should be allowed to boil (212°F)

13. What is the result when root starches are cooked at higher temperatures?

They become thinner and sticky.

14. What effect does acid have on the starch during the cooking process?

The acid tends to hydrolize the starch so that it will not thicken.

15. How does sugar influence starch mixtures?

It lessens the thickening power and makes the sauce more translucent.

16. What methods can be used to prevent the lumping of starch granules?

By separating the granules with fat, dry ingredients, or water, and by continuous stirring while they are cooking.

17. How much general purpose flour is required to thicken 1 gallon of liquid for white sauce for each of following consistencies: thin, medium, thick, and very thick?

Thin—4 ounces; medium—8 ounces; thick—12 ounces; and very thick—1 pound.

canned soup with casseroles, and whipped cream with desserts.

18. Differentiate between a blond, white, and cream sauce.

A blond sauce is made with light colored stock, white sauce with milk, and cream sauce is made with cream.

19. What liquids are used in making white, bechamel and velouté sauces?

White sauce is made with milk, bechamel contains part milk and part light colored stock, and velouté contains stock only.

20. What is a roux?

It is a blend of fat and flour, usually in equal volume.

21. How can a fluid mixture be made for adding thickening to hot soups or sauces?

By adding cold liquid gradually and stirring vigorously to prevent lumps forming.

22. How do brown sauces differ from light sauces?

The flour is browned for the roux and the liquid is a brown stock.

23. What important effect does browning have on the flour?

It lessens its thickening power.

24. How do cake flour, waxy maize, and cornstarch compare in thickening power?

To thicken 1 gallon of liquid for a thin sauce of comparable thickness—4 ounces of waxy maize, $5\frac{1}{2}$ ounces of cornstarch or 8 oz of cake flour are required.

25. How can the formation of skin on top of a sauce be prevented?

By covering top with melted butter, liquid, or by floating waxed paper or plastic on it.

26. What is hard sauce?

A blend of powdered sugar and butter.

27. What is Crème Anglaise?

A soft custard sauce.

28. What precaution is needed in its preparation?

Use of a slow temperature (below simmering) for cooking.

29. How do crème anglaise, crème brûlée and zabaglione or sabayon sauces differ from each other?

Crème anglaise is made with milk, crème brûlée with whipping cream, and zabaglione or sabayon is made with wine.

30. What qualities are desirable in foods for purees to be used for sauces?

The food should be soft enough to puree well, and should possess distinctive flavor and an appealing color.

8.

Soup Preparation

The steaming fragrance of flavorful soups have universal appeal. When they are well made and appropriately served they do much to stimulate the appetite. The nutritive value of soups have a considerable range. Some are hearty enough to serve as the main nourishment of a meal, while others are light in calories but sufficiently rich in flavor to serve as appetizers. Good soups have two qualities that are essential for gustatory enjoyment: (a) rich, appealing flavor and (b) a positive temperature, either piping hot or refreshingly cold. Appetizing soup has magnetism in attracting patronage to a food establishment, while watery, insipid mixtures served at tepid temperature can dissipate pleasure in an otherwise delicious meal.

Soup making is not a difficult part of food preparation, but it calls for sensitive judgment in the handling of materials and in the blending of flavors. It requires the unhurried extracting of flavorful substances from foods into the broth or liquid that is to be used for soup making. Many of the edible, but less tender, cuts and trimmings of meats and vegetables can be utilized by large kitchens at a quality and cost advantage. These and other by-products in large-quantity food service, such as small amounts of leftovers, can be utilized at low cost for preparation of soups that give interest and distinction to meals.

A slowly simmering stock pot on the back of the range was a familiar sight in the important kitchens of the past. The cooking procedure in making stock continues, but the steam kettle has supplanted the range-top stock pot. Modern meat marketing methods have affected soup preparation, also. Prepared-for-use meat has eliminated the excess of bones and trimmings available for stock in the average kitchen. Now, users buy only the materials desired for specific needs. Many usable by-products for stock are still available in large-quantity food production, however, and can be utilized at an economic advantage through wise planning. Usually, additional meat and bones need to be purchased to be combined with them.

There has been an increase in the use of commercially prepared soup bases. Some of the soup bases are satisfactory for enriching the flavor of soups and sauces; others detract from the quality of any product in which they are used. For this reason, if a commercial soup base is to be used, the selection should be made very carefully. Any soup base chosen should justify its cost in proportion to the extent to which it improves food quality and adds to the convenience of preparation. Even the best of commercial soup bases is second in quality to freshly and properly made soup stock. Caterers who emphasize high quality do not depend on the use of commercial soup bases. They use them only when it is necessary to provide flexibility and convenience in the satisfactory seasoning of food.

Selection of a satisfactory soup base calls for a keen, alert judgment of flavor. It is easy for a novice to be misled in judging flavor value by the flavored salts, such as celery and onion, or vegetable concentrates in the base. The rich, pleasing essence of meat is the flavor that is the most costly to produce and the one that has the greatest value in use. The principle ingredients in soup bases are listed in order of the quantity of an item contained in the base, from the largest amount of the smallest. Those that contain a large percentage of salt can be expected to sell for a lower price per pound. The lower price, however, may be a high one for salt.

When selecting a soup base, all of the brands under consideration should be tested at the same time and compared for appealing flavor, strength of flavor, and cost. In order to test them, brew a given amount of each in a given amount of boiling water. A soup base of satisfactory strength should yield a gallon of stock with 4 ounces of base, or 2 tablespoonsful per quart of water. In evaluating the soup bases for appetizing aroma and full, rich, appealing flavor of meat, the meat flavor must be carefully discerned from the vegetable flavors. Comparative strength and cost should be noted.

KINDS OF SOUP

Soups may be classified in various ways. They may be grouped into milk or stock base soups, thick or thin soups, soups that contain specific ingredients such as meat, fish, poultry, and vegetables, or soups that are hearty or light. Many soups contain both milk and stock, and others such as fruit soups, may contain neither milk or stock. A soup is selected for a specific place in a meal and should harmonize with the other foods in the meal. The share of nourishment that it provides, its flavor, and its general character should fit agreeably with the foods with which it is served.

The classification that appears most useful is in terms of the place of soup in a menu, with added information relating to its chief ingredients. As menu components, soups may be identified as appetizers or main-dish soups. The appetizer soups are those that are used as the first course preceding a full meal. They should be stimulating and light or served in small quantity so as to provide limited calories in the meal. The main-dish soups should be more nutritious in substance and generous in size of portion. Knowledge of ingredients in the various soups is helpful in guiding the menu maker in choosing suitable accompaniments and in fitting them into meals.

Hearty, main-dish soups are served for luncheons or suppers. They take the place of an entree and should be as satisfying as a casserole or stew. A salad or sandwich and dessert may complete the meal. The portion size needs to be at least 8 or 10 ounces in order to be adequately satisfying for a normal appetite. Bisques, chowders, cream soups, and gumbos are typical examples of main-dish soups.

The chief function of the appetizer soup is to refresh and alert the appetite and stimulate interest in food. These soups should be light and have a definite and appealing flavor. Appetizer soups include such thin clear soups as consommés, bouillons, and broths, and the light, delicate creams and purees. They are served in bouillon cups at luncheons and informal dinners and in rimmed soup plates at more formal meals. The portion should be approximately 6 ounces. Jellied clear soups may be served in glass bowls. It is attractive to serve them in a small bowl on an ice bed in a larger bowl set on an underliner.

Broth, bouillon, consommé, and stock have specific qualities that distinguish them. The liquid in which the meat and/or vegetables have been slowly simmered before it has been clarified and seasoned, is known as broth. Bouillon is the clarified liquid from simmered, browned beef. The flesh and bones of beef only are used. Consommé is a clear stock of lighter color. It is made, not alone of beef, but also may include flesh and bones from chicken, veal, and possibly a small amount of pork. Bouillon and consomme are made from stock. Stock differs from broth in that it has been clarified and the fat removed. It may be cooked down as much as the concentration desired. Stock that has been concentrated by boiling down provides rich flavor for seasoning soup, sauces, casseroles, and vegetable dishes.

Although bisques, purees, and cream soups are thick soups with certain points of similarity, they also have many differences. A puree is made with sieved meat, fish, poultry, or vegetables. Stock may be added for flavor, for example, ham stock in split-pea or bean soups. Water, or the liquid in which the pureed product was cooked, is usually used as the liquid in the soup. Purees may be very heavy and nutritious or light enough to use as appetizers. Cream or bechamel sauce is added to the pureed food when making a bisque. With the exception of tomato bisque, the puree in bisques is usually lobster, shrimp, salmon, or another seafood. Bisques and purees are smooth in consistency. In cream soups the flavoring foods may be either pureed or in pieces, and the liquid may be light cream or milk and thickened with bechamel, cream, or velouté sauce.

Other hearty soups that qualify for service as a main dish are chowders, gumbos, stews, and bouillabaise. These soups are like stews and contain larger particles of the chief flavoring ingredients than the cream soups. Most of the chowders are made with light cream or milk and contain onion, diced potatoes, and bacon or salt pork. Stews have one chief flavoring ingredient, such as oysters, plus a milk or light cream base and seasonings. Gumbos and bouillabaise contain the liquid in which a mixture of flavoring foods were cooked, plus the possible addition of a wine.

Chilled soups include those that are jellied by the natural gelatin in the meat stock or added gelatin, and those that are thickened with a starch or puree. Sparkling, jellied consommé served with a slice of tart lemon is a refreshing beginner for a dinner on a hot day. Cold vichyssoise, gazpacho, and borsch are flavorful, delicious, and hearty. Fruit soups may be served hot, but are more often served chilled. They are made with cooked dried or canned fruits and are slightly thickened with starch or tapioca. Their flavors combine well with cheese sandwiches or chicken salads for summer luncheons.

PREPARATION OF STOCK

The majority of soups and many sauces benefit from the addition of a richly flavored stock. The dominant flavor of the stock or base, such as beef, chicken, or ham, should be one that blends well with, and enhances the quality of, the dish in which it is used. Chicken stock is more appealing than beef stock in delicately flavored cream soups. Beef stock adds a hearty flavor to many of the vegetable soups, and the ham flavor is a favorite with split peas and beans.

The preparation of stock calls for understanding care and discerning taste. The skill used in its preparation and use marks the difference between persons who merely cook and connoisseurs who are sensitive to flavors and use good judgment in seasoning foods. Long, slow simmering of foods used for stock is required to draw out the flavor-giving substances from the foods into the liquid. The best stock is not made in an hour or a day. After cooking, it needs to ripen for a day because it has a fuller flavor on the day after the initial cooking.

Stocks are classified as brown and light or white. The brown stocks are made from browned meat and cracked bones of beef and vegetables. The browning may be done in a hot oven or in hot fat, before the products are placed in the stock kettle. If a deep color is desired in the stock, all of the meat and bones should be well browned. If a lighter, amber color is preferred for the stock, only half of the total to be used should be browned. White or light stocks are made from flesh and bones of veal and chicken, and are not browned before cooking. White fish stock can be made from the flesh and trimmings of fish and shellfish. Seasonings that do not deepen or change their color should be chosen for the light stocks.

Kitchens that do not have sufficient bones and trimmings from the preparation of their meats to use for stock are advised to purchase shank and neck of beef, knuckle of veal, and fowl from which to prepare well-flavored stock. Meats of the lower grades are wholesome and satisfactory for stock and are likely to be the most economical. The fatter cuts can be utilized also. The fat of meats contain aromatic substances that give flavor richness. The choice of meat for stock has considerable influence on flavor goodness. Fowl or mature chickens have more flavor than young chickens. The flavor of chicken broth is generally preferred over turkey broth; it is milder and blends well with more foods. Stock of lamb bones and trimmings has limited popularity because of the distinctive and dominant lamb flavor. Pork imparts a sweetish flavor that is not generally liked if used alone, but small amounts can be added to other meats for stock. Experience in cooking and sampling is needed to determine proportions of the different meats, vegetables, and seasonings that are most agreeable to the specific group being served.

The meat should be cut into small enough pieces to expose cut surfaces to the water for drawing out nutritive and flavor-giving substances. The bones should be sawed into 3- or 4-inch pieces for the same reason. The meat should not be cut so fine that it is difficult to remove from the stock (hamburger, for example). Simmer the meat slowly in the stock until the meat is very tender. The meat may be divided into particles and added to the soup or it may be utilized in making salads and sandwich fillings that are seasoned and enriched with dressings.

The preparation of stock requires from 5 to 6 pounds of meat and bones for each gallon of stock. Use 1 pound of mixed vegetables, such as celery, onion, carrots and turnips, and 5 quarts of lightly salted water for this amount. A bouquet of a bay leaf, a sprig of marjoram, thyme, and parsley, and a few peppercorns may be tied in a cheesecloth and added to season the stock. Warm water is more effective in dissolving the flavorful substances from meat and vegetables than either cold or hot water. In order to prolong the soaking or extracting time it is recommended that the meat and bones be started in cold or warm water and slowly brought to a slow simmer, 180 to 185°F. Beef bones and meat should be allowed to simmer slowly for 6 to 8 hours; veal and chicken for approximately 4 hours; and fish for only $1\frac{1}{2}$ hours. Longer cooking of fish tends to make the stock cloudy. Rapid boiling of stock and meat coagulates some of the nutrients in the flesh so that they are not drawn into the broth.

After cooking, the bones and foods in the stock may be removed by pouring through a colander or by fishing them out with a skimmer (a utensil with a perforated disc fastened to a long handle). Cool the stock as rapidly as possible. Large containers of stock may be placed in a sink in a bath of cold water and stirred to speed cooling. Some steam kettles are designed to permit cold water to circulate inside the jacket around the kettle, and have a paddle for stirring that is electrically powered. Refrigerate the stock overnight or until needed at 35 to 40°F. Chilling causes the fat to congeal on the top; this allows it to be removed with a skimmer.

Clarify the stock after all of the fat has been removed. This can be done by decanting (pouring the liquid off of the sediment in the bottom, being careful not to roil the sediment), unless a very clear stock is required. Meat stocks usually contain sufficient gelatin to gel. It is most effective to decant the liquid when the gelatin is of a syrupy consistency. The food particles or residue are left in the bottom of the kettle.

A more complete clarification can be obtained with the use of egg white and ground raw meat. The slightly beaten egg white and meat should be stirred into cool broth and the broth slowly brought to boiling. When it is stirred into the broth, the egg white rises to the top as it coagulates and carries the solid food particles with it. The mass that is formed is called a raft. It may be carefully removed with a skimmer, or the stock may be drawn off through the draw-off faucet at the bottom of the kettle. The hot stock should be poured through several layers of cheesecloth to remove any particles that may remain.

The stock may be concentrated through continued cooking. When the moisture has evaporated until the stock is reduced to about one half of its original volume, it is called demi-glace. If further reduced to a fourth in volume it is called glace. The flavor is pronounced and, when cold, the consistency will be thickened until it is heavy and rubbery. This concentrate may be frozen for delayed use in flavoring soups and various other dishes.

DEVELOPMENT OF BODY IN SOUP

Body is an important score point for evaluating either a soup or a beverage because of its influence on palatability. When a suitable body is lacking, even in clear soups, the consistency is regarded as watery. Bouillons, consommées, and other stock soups derive their consistency from the body developed in the stock from the substances extracted from the foods with which it was made. Additional thickness may be developed through the use of a thickening agent or foods such as poultry, meats, fish, and vegetables, that are added to the stock.

It is desirable that thickened appetizer soups be light, delicate, and of creamlike consistency. The hearty soups may be thicker with puree, a thickening agent, or an abundance of the protein foods and vegetables. The starchy foods like rice, the pastes, and dumplings, are commonly used to give body to soups. The thickening agents most generally favored are flour, starch, and eggs.

The majority of cream soups contain a thickening agent. In the cream soups made with a stock, it usually is best to add the thickening in a velouté sauce. High temperature and any acid present in the food may cause the milk to curdle. The starch in a velouté sauce can be thoroughly cooked and blended with the flavoring foods without danger of curdling because it does not contain milk. If milk is desired in the soup, it can be added a few minutes before the time of service.

For soups in which added richness of flavor and nutrients are desired, a liaison mixture of one part beaten egg yolk to three parts cream may be stirred into the soup shortly before service. Gradually add some of the hot soup to the egg and cream mixture, and then stir the egg and cream mixture vigorously into the hot soup. It is important that the temperature of the soup be held below simmering and that it be served within a short period of time after the egg mixture has been added.

Heavy bechamel and cream sauce can be used for thickening soup in fashion similar to the velouté sauce. Both contain milk and greater care must be used to prevent curdling during cooking or prolonged holding. The amount of flavoring material, such as puree or minced foods, should be in the proportion of two cups per gallon of soup. It should be blended with the sauce, and then the blend is stirred vigorously into the hot milk or cream.

Purees that are smooth and thick can be made with such mealy vegetables as peas, lentils, beans, and potatoes. Those that are more watery when cooked require the use of some starch to obtain the desired consistency. Tomato, asparagus, celery, and carrots are flavorful in soups, but have a tendency to separate in the soup unless a little starch is used to hold the pulp in a smooth mixture. These soups may have cream or milk added or may contain only stock for a base.

Egg yolk adds interest, nutrients, and good flavor when used in bouillon or consommé. It may be added in different forms. One of the easiest is to allow the beaten yolk to drizzle slowly through a sieve into the hot soup. Another is to form balls of cooked, seasoned, sieved egg yolk that are bound together with raw beaten yolk. These cook quickly when added to the hot soup, and the temperature should be held around 190°F. Results are best if the soup is served at once.

SERVICE OF SOUP

The manner in which soup is served may strongly influence the pleasure which it gives. Few people enjoy either lukewarm soup or a tepid beverage. It is important for either of these to have a "positive" temperature when served. A "positive" temperature calls for soup containers for service that are heated so that they do not chill the soup served in them, or prechilled if used for cold soup. The temperature of hot soup at time of service should be 150 to 160°F; chilled soup should not be higher than 40 to 45°F.

Appropriate garnish and accompaniment add greatly to the enjoyment of soup. (See Table 3.4 in Chapter 3 for suggestions.) They will add appealing flavor and decoration if skillfully used. A dash of paprika, a little minced parsley, or a sprinkle of golden cheese helps to transform a too-white soup and adds to the flavor. Fine shreds of ham or chicken, thinly sliced frankfurter or sausage, or bits of meat add important nourishment and make soups more enticing. An accompaniment in the form of some kind of bread item is welcomed by most diners except for the strictest calorie counters. Although soda crackers are readily accepted, wide variety is possible through the numerous wafer items on the commercial market.

SUGGESTED LABORATORY EXPERIENCE

1. Evaluate different brands of soup base. Compare at least three commercial brands of chicken base and three commercial brands of beef base. Prepare by steeping 1 ounce of base in 1 quart of boiling water. Stir well and serve in cups or bowls. Score each according to the following:

Score Points	Score Values					Rating
	20	15	10	5	0	
General flavor	Very appealing	Appeal-ing	Accept-able	Objection-able	Very objection-able	
Strength of meat flavor	Very strong	Strong	Accept-able	Weak	Very weak	

Score Points	Score Values					Rating
	20	15	10	5	0	
Color	Very attractive	Attractive	Acceptable	Poor	Very poor	
General appearance	Very appealing	Appealing	Acceptable	Poor	Very poor	
Cost	Very good value	Good value	Acceptable value	Poor value	Very poor value	
Total						

2. Prepare a light stock and a brown stock. Degrease and clarify the stocks. Compare the stocks with the best one of the commercial bases. How do the scores and the costs compare?
3. Prepare tomato soup with a velouté sauce and with a cream sauce. Compare flavors, appearance, and ease of preparation.
4. Prepare a puree of salmon using a china cap. Use the salmon in a bisque. Serve the salmon bisque with the garnish that makes it most attractive.
5. Prepare a jellied consommé. Serve in appropriate manner with attractive garnish and accompaniment.

REVIEW QUESTIONS AND ANSWERS

1. Should bones and meat be boiled when preparing stock?

No. They should be simmered slowly in order to draw the nutrients into the liquid.

2. Should the bones and meat be started in hot or warm water?

In warm water.

3. What kind of bones and meat are used in preparing brown stock?

Largely beef. Veal and some lamb and pork may be included.

4. What determines the color of the stock to the largest degree?

The browning of the bones and meat. All are well browned for dark stock and part are browned for lighter stock.

5. Are vegetables used in brown stock?

Yes.

6. How does the preparation of light stock differ from that for brown stock?

Light stock is made with the bones and flesh of veal and/or chicken, and is not browned.

7. Are lamb bones and flesh used alone for stock?

Only for special soups such as Scotch broth.

8. Are pork bones used for stock?

A small percentage may be used for brown stock.

9. Why should the bones be cracked and the flesh cut into small pieces?

To expose more cut surface for extraction of nutrients into the stock.

10. What are the characteristics of an appetizer soup?

Stimulating flavor and small amount of nourishment.

11. What is an appropriate portion of an appetizer soup?

6 to 8 ounces.

12. What is the customary size for a portion of a hearty soup?

At least 8 to 10 ounces.

13. What is the difference between a broth and a stock?

Broth is the liquid from cooked meat or vegetables before the fat is removed and the liquid clarified, and stock is the liquid after it is degreased and clarified.

14. What is the difference between bouillon and consommé?

Bouillon is the clarified liquid from browned beef and bones. Consommé is lighter in color and may be made from a mixture of other kinds of meat and bones in addition to those of beef.

15. Of what are bisques made?

They are usually made of seafood purees plus a bechamel or cream sauce or light cream.

16. Of what are purees made?

They may be purees of meat, fish, poultry, or vegetables with stock added.

17. When is it appropriate to serve a chowder, gumbo, or bouillabaise?

When it serves as the main dish in the meal.

18. How may a stock be clarified?

By decanting. Further clarification may be done by stirring a mixture of egg white and raw beef into cool broth and slowly heating it to boiling. The egg carries the solid particles to the top as it coagulates.

19. What is a raft?

The egg mixture that rises to the top as the stock is being clarified.

20. Should stock be allowed to cool at kitchen temperature overnight?

No, this is hazardous from the standpoint of sanitation. It should be cooled as quickly as possible in circulating water (as water bath in a sink) and then refrigerated.

21. Is it safe to freeze stock for delayed use?

Yes. It is well to concentrate it first.

22. What is a demi-glace? A glace?

A demi-glace is stock that has been reduced through cooking until it is half its original volume, and glace is one fourth of the original volume.

23. How can body be developed in soups?

By drawing out the gelatin and other nutrients in the stock, by adding gelatin, by use of starch or flour to thicken, by adding pureed food, and by use of eggs, starchy foods, and vegetables.

24. What is a liaison mixture?

Mixture of egg yolk and cream.

25. Why are sauces used in soups?

To add flavoring and to develop body.

26. Which sauce should be used for blending flavoring material into soups that contain acid ingredients?

Velouté, because it does not contain milk that might curdle.

27. How should a liaison mixture be added to a hot soup?

It should have a little of the hot mixture added to the egg mixture and then the egg mixture should be stirred gradually into the hot mixture. It should be stirred vigorously and removed at once from the heat.

28. What are two qualities important to palatability of soup?

Rich, appealing flavor and a "positive" temperature.

29. What precautions need to be taken when serving soup to insure good quality?

Use proper holding temperature, rotate the preparation of soups that are likely to curdle so that they are served within a short time, heat or chill bowls to insure right temperature.

30. Why is the preparation of stock or selection of a soup base of special importance?

Because the stock or base strongly influences the quality of soups in which it is used, and a stock or base is used in the majority of soups.

BIBLIOGRAPHY

Beck, Simone, Louisette Bertholle, and Julia Child, "Mastering the Art of French Cooking," New York: Alfred A. Knopf, 1961.

Cleveland Range Company, "Operators Directions, Form No. 2F2," The Cleveland Range Co., 971 East 63rd Street, Cleveland, Ohio.

Cooperative Extension in Agriculture and Home Economics, "Rules for Cooking Vegetables" and "Time Table for Cooking Vegetables in Quantity," Michigan State University, East Lansing, Michigan.

Culinary Institute of America, Inc. and Editors of Institution Magazine, "The Professional Chef," Chicago: Institutions Magazine, 1964.

De Gouy, Louis P., "The Gold Cook Book," New York: Greenberg, 1947.

General Electric Company, Owner's Information Manuals for Automatic-High-Compression Steamer and for Electronic-Control Trunnion Kettle, General Electric, Chicago Heights, Illinois.

Gordon, J., and I. Noble, "Effect of Cooking Method on Vegetables," *The Journal of the American Dietetic Association*, Chicago, 35, 578–581 (1959).

Griswold, Ruth M., "The Experimental Study of Foods," Boston: Houghton Mifflin, 1962.

Hubbert, B. H. & Son, Inc., "Specifications of Tilting and Stationary Kettles," Baltimore: B. H. Hubbert & Son.

Kotschevar, Lendal H., "Quantity Food Production," Berkeley, Calif.: McCutchan, 1964.

Kotschevar, Lendal H. and Margaret E. Terrell, "Food Service Planning: Layout and Equipment," New York: Wiley, 1961.

Lowe, Belle, "Experimental Cookery," New York: Wiley, 1955.

Lundberg, Donald and Lendal H. Kotschevar, "Understanding Cooking," Amherst: University of Massachusetts, 1965.

Market Forge Co., "Operating Instructions Market Forge Steam Cooking Equipment," Everett, Mass.: Market Forge Co.

McWilliams, Margaret, "Food Fundamentals," New York: Wiley, 1966.

Montagne, Prosper, "Larousse Gastronomique," New York: Crown, 1965.

Shank, Dorothy E., Natalie K. Fitch, and Pauline A. Chapman, "Guide to Modern Meals," New York: Mc-Graw-Hill.

Terrell, Margaret E., "Large Quantity Recipes," Philadelphia: J. B. Lippincott, 1951.

SECTION III

The Pantry

CHAPTER 9   Pantry Equipment (Refrigeration Equipment, Work Tables, Slicing Machine, and Beverage Equipment)

CHAPTER 10   Salads and Salad Dressings

CHAPTER 11   Sandwiches

Bibliography for Section III

9.

Pantry Equipment

REFRIGERATION EQUIPMENT

Satisfactory refrigeration equipment is highly important in large kitchens. It is essential in preserving the proper sanitation of food and in reducing food spoilage. Its placement or location in relation to work areas influences the steps required in the production of food. Large kitchens usually require some walk-in type refrigerators for the handling of bulk supplies, such as crates of eggs, cans of milk, cartons of butter, and foods that are handled in cart-load quantities. Smaller, reach-in refrigerators should be placed within reach of work centers for highly perishable foods that must be kept under refrigeration and that require frequent trips to a refrigerator for supplies. The three areas of the kitchen where this has special importance are the cooking section, the pantry, and the bake shop.

The walk-in refrigerators are usually constructed of concrete, and installed when the building is being constructed. Aspects that strongly influence their performance include the refrigeration system used, the placement of the floor drain and the pitch of the floor to the drain, a safety device to prevent a person's being locked in the compartment, an easy-opening and firmly closing door, and a level with the floor outside the refrigerator that permits carts to be rolled into the compartment. Selection of the refrigeration system should be done in conference with the building engineer and should include consideration of reliable maintenance of desired temperatures, circulation of air, defrosting of the unit, and the periodic care required in maintaining the unit.

Circulation of air within compartments is essential for effective cooling. Food should be stored in a manner that permits air to flow around it. Food should not be placed against the sides of compartments or heaped in corners in such a way as to block the free flow of air. Natural convection (movement of air) occurs as cold air drops and warmer air rises. Forced convection, in which a fan or blower is used to move the air, improves the speed of cooling.

Figure 9.1   Refrigerators may be equipped with shelves or slides for modular pans. (Courtesy of Koch Refrigerators, Inc.)

Reach-in refrigerators are available in a variety of designs, sizes, and materials. They may open on one side only or may be the pass-through type. They may have fixed shelves, removable shelves, slides for modular pans, or may be of a design and size to permit roll-in carts. The materials of which institution refrigerators are usually constructed include enamelled steel, stainless steel, and aluminum. Cleanability, durability, convenience for use, and appearance are important points for consideration when selecting refrigerators.

The pass-through type refrigerator helps to reduce handling when it is placed between the preparation and service areas for portioned foods, such as salads and sandwiches. It helps maximize the time that the food can remain under refrigeration. The number of portions required influences the desirability of having a refrigerator that can accommodate roll-in carts or modular containers, such as trays. Commercial refrigerators are currently designed to accommodate the following utensils as modules: baking sheets (18 × 26 inches), steam table pans (12 × 20 inches), and cafeteria trays (14 × 18 inches).

Figure 9.2   Pass-through refrigerators between the production and serving areas save steps.

The size of the door should be appropriate for the size of the material to be placed in the refrigerator, but not larger than is necessary for convenience. The nature of the work calls for frequent opening and closing of the door. Warm air rushes in each time it is opened. The rise in temperature results in moisture being drawn from the food because warm air absorbs more moisture than cold air. The warm air promotes the development of bacteria and causes a drying effect on the food. The frequent opening of the compartment also causes extra work for the refrigerator motor and shortens its service life. Therefore, the best refrigerator opening is one that is no larger than required for use, and it should not be opened and closed more often than is necessary.

Use and Care of Refrigerators

Foods must be protected from absorbing off-flavors. Odorous foods should be carefully wrapped or enclosed in containers that confine their odors and protect them from absorbing flavors from other foods. Odorous foods should not be stored with dairy products or other mild flavored foods that absorb other flavors readily. Plastic wraps or containers are helpful in confining odors and in protecting foods from drying. Meticulous cleanliness is important in maintaining a sweet smelling refrigerator.

Warm water and baking soda are satisfactory for daily cleaning of the refrigerator interiors if food has not been allowed to dry on the surfaces. The use of abrasives and soaps that have an odor should be avoided. Spillage should be wiped up immediately so that it does not have time to congeal or dry. All surfaces of the interior, including the door gaskets, should be cleaned weekly and thoroughly rinsed with clean water. Wipe the exterior with a damp cloth, using a mild soap for washing the exterior if needed. Wipe with a soft cloth. If it is necessary to use a scouring powder for cleaning stubborn spots from exterior metal surfaces, the rubbing should be done in the direction of the polish lines and not across the grain of the metal. Let the powder dry and polish off with a soft cloth. The large size of kitchen refrigerators make them important features in the appearance of a kitchen and when they are given proper care their appearance adds to the attractiveness of the workshop.

WORK TABLES

The work tables need to be planned or selected carefully in relation to the work that is to be done in the specific work unit. Work requirements affect choice of best height, amount of space or size of the table, facilities needed for storage of small equipment and food supplies, and the material of which the table is constructed. Production workers spend a large percentage of their working time at the work table and a well-planned table can save excess motions and reduce fatigue in the progress of work.

Height and Work Space

A worker should be able to stand erect in an easy posture while working. He should not have to stoop over or reach too high while working. Since tables are reasonably permanent items of equipment, this means that the tables need to be selected in relation to the height of persons usually employed. If men are normally employed to do certain types of production, the work surface of the tables used by them may need to be an inch or two higher than that required for women workers. Characteristic height of workers is likely to be affected by nationality. For example, the Latin people tend to be shorter in stature than Nordic people.

There is a simple test for arriving at a comfortable working height. Have a person who is the average height of the workers normally employed make the test. The best working height for the majority of tasks is the one on which this person can place his hands flat with wrists bent and elbows straight while standing erect. Certain jobs are exceptions to this rule. Rolling of biscuits or pie crust by hand, for example, calls for the person to lean forward, putting pressure on the rolling pin. This work progresses more easily if the working height is a little less than normal. If kitchen tables are normally 34 inches high, it would be well for the pastry table to be 32 inches in height if very much hand rolling is to be done. Another exception may be caused by additions to the table height, as happens with the extensive use of a thick cutting board.

There are two considerations to keep in mind when determining the length and width of the work table. One is the span of the worker's reach and the other is in terms of space required for equipment and supplies during the normal progress of work. Work convenience requires keeping the work center compact and materials located within the span of normal reach. Where a large volume of food is being processed it is often better to store supplies on a cart beside the worker rather than to allow extra table space for holding it. Normal reach of a 5-foot, 4-inch person is less than 4 feet and maximum reach is somewhat less than 6 feet.

When selecting the table size, it is well to visualize the way in which the work normally progresses. Plan the flow of work so that it moves smoothly with a minimum of motion. (See Chapter I, "Plan for Progress of Work.") The following sandwich unit designed for preparation of trayloads of sandwiches exemplifies the method for projecting plans for flow of work and space needs. The space allowed in the plan is 30 inches wide and may be 48 to 60 inches long, depending on the size of the containers used.

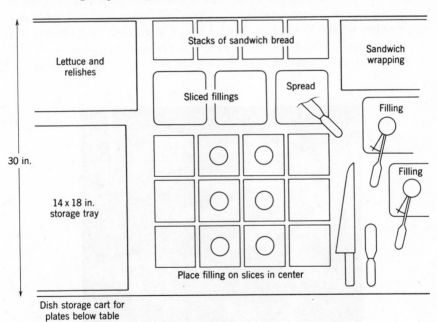

Figure 9.3 Suggested arrangement for sandwich making on a table 30-inches wide. For a 24-inch wide table, place the storage tray on a cart at the left of the worker, the sliced fillings and lettuce at the left of the sandwiches, and the wrapping paper in a drawer under the table top or on a shelf above the table.

(a) Arrange materials and equipment for two-handed activity, with all of the things to be used within easy reach of the worker's hands, and those items used most frequently located nearest the heart of the work area. (b) Split open the bread packages near the center of the loaf, exposing slices, and place both halves at the top of the board. This is to make it possible to reach the bread and take slices in both hands, dropping them in straight rows one at a time from the top of the board toward the worker. For six sandwiches, arrange slices in rows four across the board and three down. (c) The containers of spread and fillings should be placed at the right for a right-handed person. (d) Filling is placed and spread on the two center rows. (e) The outside rows are spread, and then turned over the center rows with both hands (see Figure 9.3).

Storage Needs

Labor saving calls for the storage of certain food supplies and equipment on, or immediately adjacent to, the work tables. Cooks' and bakers' needs for flour, milk solids, and spices is such that it is desirable to provide storage for these as a part of the work-table unit. Flour, salt, sugar, and milk solids may be in either rolling- or tilt-type bins. It is well to provide small tilt-type bins in a high shelf position for the numerous spices most frequently used. The highly perishable nature of sandwich fillings calls for the use of refrigerated

Figure 9.4 Baker's table with spice bins in a high-shelf position.

filling containers in situations where fillings must be exposed for an extended period of time. This is characteristic of restaurants in which a variety of sandwiches are made to order, as opposed to one in which a large volume of sandwiches is completed quickly and the sandwiches are immediately refrigerated.

Each work center has need for specific items of equipment to be stored in or on the work table. Drawers located immediately below the work surface are commonly needed for storage of spatulas, spoons, ladles, scoops and other utensils required in the manipulation of food. Knives may be in a rack in a drawer or on the side of the table. An ingredient and portioning scale may be on, or adjacent to, the production work table. Storage may be desirable for the most frequently used pans. Tables that are used for portioning the food (as in salads, sandwiches, and desserts) need a storage place for the dishes to be used. Mobile dispensing units that fit under the work surface or are located adjacent to it are better for this than shelving under the table top.

Material

Stainless steel is a preferred material for the majority of work surfaces in kitchens. It is durable, easy to clean, and retains a bright appearance. In work centers where a great deal of chopping, slicing, or cutting is done, a work surface that has less of a dulling effect on knives than metal should be made available. The surface may be supplied as either a table top or a cutting board. In salad and sandwich centers, hard rubber or one of the new durable plastics causes less damage to cutting edges than the stainless steel. Cleanability is important for surfaces on which food is prepared. The laminated maple tops have a tendency to pull apart and do not provide surfaces that are fully cleanable.

Cleaning and Care

During processing the food is often placed directly on the work surface. The cleanliness of the table is as important as the sanitation of any utensil or dish used for food. The sanitation is often impaired by the placing of soiled packages or other containers of unknown cleanliness on the work surface. It is better to place market packages on a cart, or on a tray if they must be placed on the table. The work surface should be washed with soap and rinsed with clear water after each use. The storage drawers should be regularly cleaned, and any spillage or droppings of food particles should be wiped out immediately.

SLICING MACHINE

A slicing machine may save the price paid for it through controlling portions of such expensive food items as meat, and by saving labor. The uniform thickness of slices adds to attractiveness. Both cooks and sandwich makers who require many sliced foods find slicing machines valuable aids. In securing portions of a specific weight, the thickness of slices can be controlled through a simple adjustment. This adjustment is made by means of a calibrated knob that raises and lowers the table or gauge plate in relation to the knife.

Some slicing machines have the knife set vertically, and others have the knife set at an approximate angle of 45 degrees. The "angle slicer" is generally preferred. The slices falling from a vertical blade tend to fold down in a manner that makes thin or tender slices difficult to handle without tearing or breaking, but food falling from an inclined blade tends to fall flat without folding. The slices from the "angle slicer" look more attractive and are easier to handle.

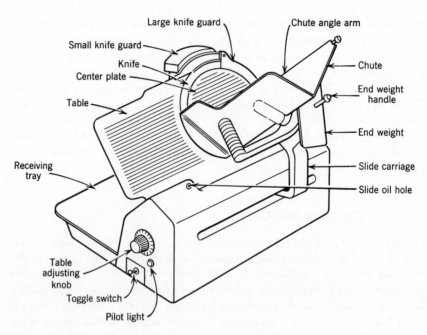

Figure 9.5 Diagram showing the parts of a slicing machine. (Courtesy of the Globe Slicing Machine Company, Inc.)

Machine Operation

The food to be sliced is placed on a carrier or chute, and is moved against a rapidly revolving disc-like knife. The end of the food in the chute rests against the gauge plate. One should consult the chart for the number of slices or portions per pound that are to be secured before starting to slice. Next, the adjusting knob on the face of the machine is set. The end weight or holding device is then moved into position against the upper end of the food. This device furnishes the right amount of pressure for uniform slicing to the end of the piece. *The hands should never be used to press food against the slicing blade* because this causes a lack of uniformity in the slices and places the operator in danger of seriously cutting his hand.

The product should be placed on the carrier in a position that causes it to be sliced to the best advantage. Meat slices are the most tender when sliced across the grain. The shape of the slices may be affected also.

When all preparations are completed, the motor is turned on. This causes the knife to revolve. The carrier, with its load of food, may be moved manually or electrically. In the manually operated, the operator grasps the chute handle and pulls the carriage toward him and then pushes it back to bring the food against the revolving knife blade. The electrically powered machines move the carriage automatically. The first or second slice should be examined for thickness to determine whether its weight meets the portion allowance and is large enough to be satisfying.

Figure 9.6   The end weight helps to hold food and provide proper pressure for uniform slicing. (Courtesy of the Globe Slicing Machine Company, Inc.)

Cleaning and Care of The Slicing Machine

When the operator changes from slicing one material to another, he should wipe the blade and the chute. Before wiping the blade, he should turn the adjusting knob to zero. This moves the table so the blade is least exposed for cutting. Then he should start the motor and hold a cloth that has been folded several times against the blade until it is clean. He then can turn off the motor and wipe the chute and receiving tray.

The slicing machine should be washed with soap and water daily. Caution: Do not use caustic or strong soaps on any anodized aluminum surface. The revolving knife tends to throw particles of food during the slicing process and these are likely to lodge in the knife guard and on other areas of the machine. Before dismantling the machine to clean it, the operator should be sure that the motor is off or disconnected from power. He then loosens the bolts and removes the knife guards and the chute. They, and all other surfaces of the machine, should be washed with soap and water, rinsed well, and dried thoroughly. It is very important to remove and wash the center plate over the knife after slicing soft or juicy foods. The slicer should be reassembled immediately so that it will be ready for use when needed.

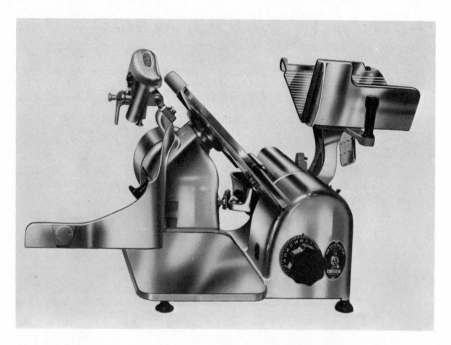

Figure 9.7 Slicer opened for cleaning. (Courtesy of the Globe Slicing Machine Company, Inc.)

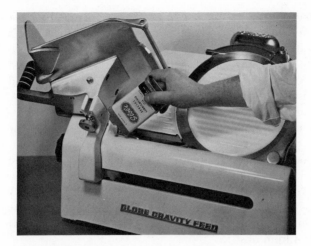

Figure 9.8   Lubricate with tasteless, odorless mineral oil of light viscosity. (Courtesy of the Globe Slicing Machine Company, Inc.)

If a slicer is given proper care, it will serve well for many years. It is important to follow the manufacturer's directions for oiling, using a good grade of tasteless and odorless mineral oil of light viscosity and not a salad or other kitchen oil that will become thick and gummy.

The condition of the knife is very important to the usefulness of the slicer. The slicing of cracked wheat breads, hard crusts, small meat bones or other

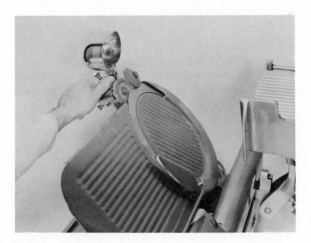

Figure 9.9   Stones in position for sharpening. (Courtesy of the Globe Slicing Machine Company, Inc.)

products that quickly dull or knick the sharp edges of the knife should be avoided. The knife is kept in condition by sharpening it lightly at frequent intervals so that it does not become dull enough to require heavy grinding. For this light sharpening, (a) place the stones in position for grinding so that both stones operate simultaneously. (b) Turn the motor on and bring the stones against both sides of the knife with a light pressure; hold for 15 to 30 seconds or until the knife is sharp. (c) Wipe both blade and machine to remove the carborundum that sifted off during the grinding process from the stone.

The sharpening stones also require proper care to do the best job. This includes having the knife clean before sharpening, so that the stones do not become greasy. Stones that have become soiled can be cleaned by brushing them with a stiff brush and ammonia water and rinsing thoroughly. The stones should be returned to their storage position where they are enclosed and protected from dust.

BEVERAGE EQUIPMENT

The equipment for preparation and service of beverages is more often located in the service area than in the pantry section of the kitchen. Since service equipment is not covered in this book, beverage equipment is included here because of the importance of beverages as a part of food preparation. When beverages are made in the kitchen, this activity is usually performed in the pantry area. Suitable equipment, properly maintained, is requisite for consistently good quality and influences labor saving.

The majority of public food establishments are equipped for making and/or dispensing three chief mealtime beverages, coffee, tea, and milk. The same piece of equipment is often used for making coffee and for heating water for brewing tea. Milk service requires equipment that provides reliable refrigeration and convenience in storing and dispensing milk. The milk equipment may consist of a refrigerated cabinet for half-pint cartons or a refrigerated dispenser for bulk milk (in 2 to 5 gallon cans).

Selection and Use of Coffee Equipment

Coffee equipment is chosen for size in terms of volume of prepared coffee needed, desired frequency of brewing, and anticipated speed of service. The two main types are urns and the vacuum type which utilize 6- to 12-cup decanters. Urns are generally preferred for cafeteria lines where fast service, a large volume, and a minimum of motion are desirable. In table service, frequent brewing and the use of decanters by waitresses for pouring coffee

Figure 9.10   Cut-away of an automatic twin urn. (Courtesy of S. Blickman, Inc.)

at the table may be preferred. Quantity needs of either type are met through choice of unit size and number of units required. Ranges for multiple unit decanters are terraced for ease in reaching individual units. The range unit may be equipped with a hot water tank to supply water for coffee making and for steeping tea.

Good coffee can be made in both manually operated and automatic equipment. The automatic equipment is recommended for labor saving and for greater uniformity in coffee making. In either type of operation good quality requires the following:

1. Clean equipment.
2. A weighed amount of coffee for the number of cups of coffee desired.
3. Good drinking water of medium hardness (neither too hard nor distilled).
4. A measured amount of water (proper quantity for the strength of brew desired.

Figure 9.11   Step-up two-burner range. (Courtesy of Bloomfield Industries, Inc.)

5. The water poured over the coffee of suitable grind at proper temperature (205°F).

The water as well as the coffee influences the flavor of the brew. In many metropolitan areas it is advisable to have a fine filtration system to help eliminate the conditions in the water that adversely affect the odors and flavors in the coffee.

The blend of coffee and the holding temperature determine how long a brew may be held satisfactorily. Some blends develop bitterness more quickly than others. This aspect should be considered when testing coffee before purchase. The flavor that is savored depends in large degree on escaping aromas. This lessens as coffee cools. Coffee temperature should be high enough when served (185 to 190°F) for the best enjoyment of flavor and to offset the rapid cooling of the small cup quantity. The water in the urn jacket should be maintained at 190 to 200°F. A uniform holding temperature helps to maintain best quality. For this, thermostatically controlled, adequate heating supply is required.

A sparkling brew, for which a filtering system is needed to remove the

Figure 9.12   Different types of coffee filters. (*a*) Stainless steel tri-saver filter. (*b*) Fine stainless steel mesh to be used with a coarse grind of coffee. (*c*) Cloth bag and frame. (*d*) Filter paper and holding frame. (*e*) Enlarged cut-a-way view of tri-saver filter. (Courtesy of S. Blickman, Inc.)

grounds, adds to coffee enjoyment. The leachers or filters may be made of two stainless steel perforated disks in which perforations of one disk fit against the solid area of the second. The liquid moves edgewise by capillary attraction leaving the grounds on the upper disk. Cloth bags with a flannel section and filter papers may be used in a holding frame.

An adequate supply of water heated to proper temperature must be available for making urn coffee. The weighed amount of coffee is placed in the leacher or coffee basket. If the urn is automatic, it can be set in action and left to complete the necessary action. If it is not automatic, a few additional steps are required.

1. Allow a measured amount of hot water (205 to 212°F) to spray over the coffee.

2. Remove the leacher with the coffee grounds as soon as the water has had time to run through (4 to 6 minutes).

3. Draw off and repour some of the coffee, (approximately one-third) to agitate and even out the strength of the brew.

4. Check to determine whether there will be sufficient hot water to make another urn of coffee when needed.

5. Allow coffee to ripen approximately 10 minutes before serving.

Figure 9.13 Automatic brewing equipment and holding range for use with decanters. (Courtesy of Bloomfield Industries, Inc.)

The decanters for vacuum type coffee makers may be made of glass or stainless steel. The following steps are required for making coffee with this equipment.

1. Fill the lower bowl or decanter with the right amount of fresh water, and place on the heat.

2. Fasten the filter in the upper bowl and add the proper measure of coffee for the volume of water in the decanter. Be sure that the rubber gasket is firmly and smoothly in place.

3. As soon as the water is heated to boiling, place the upper bowl on the decanter, pressing the upper bowl with the gasket, firmly into the neck of the lower bowl. The heat will cause sufficient expansion of the contents of the lower bowl to force the water to rise into the upper bowl over the coffee. Stir it with one circular motion as soon as it has risen.

4. After approximately 20 seconds, remove the decanter from the heat. The change of temperature in the lower bowl will create a vacuum to draw the brew from the upper bowl. As soon as the vacuum is exhausted and all of the liquid is in the lower bowl, remove the upper bowl and discard the coffee grounds.

5. The bowl and filter should be rinsed well with hot water.

6. The decanter of coffee should be placed on a thermostatically controlled heating element to maintain a temperature of approximately 185°F.

Cleaning and Care of Coffee Equipment

Clean equipment is essential for good coffee. Grounds should be emptied from the leacher as soon as the coffee is made. If a cloth filter is used, it should be washed thoroughly in hot water, covered with cold water, and stored conveniently for next use. Cloth filters absorb coffee oils and covering them with cold water during storage prevents rancidity from developing. A cloth filter should never be used after it has been washed with soap; it should be discarded for coffee making before rancidity can develop. Metal leachers should be thoroughly brushed to remove all particles of coffee that may adhere to them. The metal leachers, frames, and bowls for vacuumtype coffee makers should be thoroughly washed with hot water and soap and well rinsed with clean, hot water.

A long handled brush that reaches to the bottom of the urn and a gauge brush of suitable size to fit through the faucet opening and through the gauge glass are needed for urn cleaning. All surfaces of the urn and faucet should be thoroughly washed with hot water and a brush daily. The interior of the urn should be thoroughly rinsed with hot water, using a brush as needed before making a fresh batch of coffee. A fresh batch should never be made on top of an old one. After it is brushed and the water drawn off, the urn

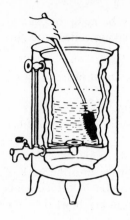

Drain off contents of the urn. Fill with two gallons of fresh, hot water. Scrub all surfaces with a long-handled brush. (Use urn cleaner twice weekly.) Drain and scrub all surfaces again. Drain.

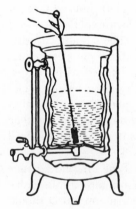

Remove cap at end of faucet and scrub faucet thoroughly with slender brush. Run brush through gauge glass.

Use slender brush to clean fitting in bottom of liner. Flush faucet, fitting, gauge glass, liner, and urn cover thoroughly with fresh hot water. Rinse two or three times after using urn cleaner. Leave gallon or more of fresh water in the urn until it is time to make fresh coffee.

Figure 9.14   Steps in cleaning a coffee urn. (Courtesy of S. Blickman, Inc.)

should be rinsed well with clean, hot water. If the urn is to stand for a time, a gallon or two of fresh water should be left in it. This water is drained out just before the next lot of coffee is prepared.

The urns should be cleaned with an urn cleaner every two or three days, depending on their use. To do this (a) fill the urn jackets approximately three-fourths full with water and heat to 200°F; fill the urn interiors or liners about two-thirds full. (b) Add urn cleaner in the quantity recommended by the manufacturer, and allow the solution to stand in the urn for about 30 minutes. (c) Use the long handled brush to scrub the entire interior, including the inside of the cover. (d) Drain off the solution, and open and thoroughly brush the inside of the faucet and the gauge glass. (e) Rinse with fresh water three or four times, being sure that the faucet, gauge glass, pipes and interior are thoroughly rinsed and free of the solution. Allow a gallon or more of fresh water to remain in the urn until time for use.

Hard water deposits can interfere with efficient heating of urns, may lead to burning out of heating elements, or cause other equipment difficulties. In hard water areas, therefore, it is well to regularly rinse out the water tank to lessen such mineral deposits or "scale" from forming, or to use a solution or device to prevent them forming. The sludge is flushed out by opening the water faucet completely and the inlet valve sufficiently to keep the water level in the gauge constant. This should be done for a few minutes daily. Inquiries of the local equipment or soap company should be made if a device is desired that will inhibit the mineral deposits from forming.

Source of Hot Water for Tea

The preparation of tea of enjoyable quality depends on three things: (a) the quality of the tea used, (b) good drinking water that is freshly heated, and (c) the boiling temperature of the water when the tea is steeped. If the water for tea steeping is to be drawn from the urn, the water in the urn must be fresh and the temperature held at or near boiling (212°F). The pots in which the tea is made should be heated and rinsed with boiling water just before making the tea. Normal delays in service often result in the tea becoming too strong before it reaches the patron. For this reason it is preferable to have a source of boiling water for use in making tea, such as a decanter on a hot plate, in the dining area close to point of service.

In the past only a very small percentage of patrons have chosen tea as a beverage but the number has greatly increased in recent years. When the number was small the service was regarded as an inconvenience and handled in a fashion that prohibited good quality. A common practice has been the placement of the tea packet beside the cup or pot to be plunged into the hot water (not boiling) by the patron. Better quality and convenient service results when the tea is steeped in freshly boiling water in a glass decanter and held at a uniform temperature (190°F) for service in cups or pots as needed for 4 to 6 patrons.

Selection and Care of Milk Service Equipment

Points of special interest in choosing milk-handling equipment are (a) sanitation, involving cleanliness and refrigeration, and (b) convenience for service. Available equipment includes the upright refrigerator, chest-type cabinets with or without a leveling device for raising cartons to convenient height, and dispensing units for service of bulk milk. Storage of milk in sealed cartons presents very limited sanitation problems except for maintenance of 35 to 40°F temperature and general cleaning of the storage compartment. The temperature of the carton-milk may not be as cold as that from a dispenser because of less care in keeping the cartons refrigerated.

Figure 9.15   Dairy products dispensing units. (Courtesy of the Sweden Freezer Manufacturing Company.)

Milk from refrigerated dispensing units have special points of advantage. When serving a large number of individual portions, the elimination of the separate cartons is of particular value. Several hundred cartons require a sizable refrigeration area and present considerable bulk for disposal. The dispensing units can be located on counter or table height for convenient operation. It is well to be sure that the surface on which they are placed has sufficient sturdiness to support a weight of approximately 250 pounds. The Norris Dispenser has a copper tube projecting under the base of the dispenser that is for the purpose of draining the cabinet interior. This should have a tubing connection to a suitable drain area. The refrigeration equipment requires an electrical outlet (110 volt, 60 cycle).

When filling the dispenser, the full milk containers are placed in the dispenser, the sanitary tube folded at the bottom of the container is freed, and

Figure 9.16 Milk dispenser showing position of tube in the Manhattan valve from either dispenser can or single service container. (Courtesy of Norris Dispensers, Inc.)

the container set so that the marking indicating location of valve is immediately above the valve. The valve is opened and the tube, when uncovered, is dropped through the valve allowing it to hang freely. The valve is then closed and the surplus tubing is cut off flush with the bottom of the valve.

When the container is empty there are three operations in removing it from a Norris Dispenser: (a) placing a container under the valve, opening the valve, and tipping the can forward in the dispenser to drain out the milk that remains in the can; (c) removing the tube from the open valve and removing the can from the dispenser; and (d) detaching the tube from the milk container and discarding it to insure against its re-use.

Milk does not come in contact with the cabinet or the valve. General cleaning of both is desirable for general sanitation. The cabinet may require defrosting periodically (if frost is more than $\frac{1}{8}$ inch thick on the cabinet interior). To defrost complete the following:

1. Disconnect the service cord.
2. Remove all milk cans, making sure they are empty.
3. Leave cabinet door wide open.
4. When frost has melted, wash interior with warm, soapy water, rinse and wipe dry.
5. Close door, reconnect service cord and allow about one hour for cabinet to cool before installing fresh milk cans.

The valve can be removed from the cabinet by loosening a thumb screw that holds it to the cabinet. Both the valve and the cabinet should be washed with soap and water and rinsed well, and the cabinet should be polished dry with a soft cloth.

SUGGESTED LABORATORY EXPERIENCE

1. Visit a production unit and observe amount of refrigeration and uses. Check temperatures of the refrigerated areas.
2. Calculate refrigerated space needed for serving 100 persons three meals daily.
   1. Carton milk or a comparable amount of bulk milk.
   2. List supplies and calculate space needs for (a) salad materials and (b) portioned salads.
3. Compare slicing sandwich meat or cheese by hand and by machine, making slices as closely as possible of comparable thickness. Note time required for slicing and the number of slices obtained per pound, and the ounces per slice.

4. Use a thermometer to register the temperature change in (a) a walk-in refrigerator that has the door open for 1 minute, and (b) a reach-in box that has the door open for 30 seconds.
5. Outline the motions to be made and arrange the work table for a good flow of work for (a) making and arranging salads, and (b) preparing sandwiches.
6. Prepare coffee in a coffee urn following the procedure described in the text.
7. Clean the urn and leave the equipment in the condition recommended.

REVIEW QUESTIONS AND ANSWERS

1. On what conditions does complete refrigeration depend?

Low temperature and good circulation of air.

2. How do changes in temperature affect food quality?

It takes moisture from the food.

3. What is meant by forced convection?

Air is forced to circulate by a blower or fan?

4. What is meant by modular equipment?

Equipment that has a common measurement with other items of equipment, such as refrigerators and carts that will accommodate standard size pans.

5. Why is the sanitation of table tops and other working surfaces of special importance?

Because food, during preparation, is likely to be placed directly on the surface and may become contaminated.

6. Of what advantage, other than labor saving is a mechanical slicer?

It makes slices of uniform thickness, thus yielding better appearance and portion control.

7. Where is the food placed for slicing?

On the carrier or chute.

8. Is it well to hold the food and press it firmly against the blade?

No, do not use the hand to press food against the blade. This causes the slices to be irregular and may result in the hand being badly cut.

9. How is the thickness of slices controlled?

By adjusting the Table Adjusting Knob that raises or lowers the table in relation to the location of the knife.

10. What is an "angle slicer"?

One in which the knife is tilted at an angle of approximately 45 degrees.

11. When should the blade be wiped?

After slicing each type of food and after using the sharpening stones.

12. How should the wiping be done?

Use a damp cloth, folded several times, turn the adjusting knob to zero, and hold

13. What other cleaning of the slicer should be done regularly?

the cloth against the side of the blade while the knife is revolving.
It should be taken apart after use, daily and washed with soap and water, rinsed thoroughly and wiped dry.

14. What type of oil should be used for oiling the slicer?

Light-weight, tasteless mineral oil.

15. Can salad oil be used?

No, because it tends to become gummy upon standing.

16. How can the knife be protected?

Avoid use in slicing dulling foods, such as breads with a heavy crust or cracked grains, and knicking on small bones. Keep the blade sharpened with frequent light sharpening so that heavy grinding is not required.

17. How should the sharpening stones be protected?

Do not use them to sharpen a dirty knife. Keep the stones clean and cover to protect from dust when not in use.

18. How may a convenient working height for a person be measured?

By measuring the level from the floor at which a person standing upright can place hands flat on the surface with elbows straight.

19. What aspects are to be considered in determining length and width of the work center?

A person's normal and maximum reach in relation to the food and equipment essential to the progress of the work.

20. What mealtime beverages are served in the majority of public food service establishments?

Coffee, tea and milk.

21. What are the two chief types of coffee making equipment?

Urns and vacuum units.

22. On what factors does a good cup of coffee depend?

(a) Clean equipment, (b) accurate amount of good coffee for the strength of brew desired, (c) good drinking water, (d) accurate amount of water for strength of brew desired, and (e) poured over the proper grind at 205°F.

23. What are the different types of filters used in urns?

(a) Perforated stainless steel, (b) cloth bags on a frame, and (c) filter papers.

24. How is the vacuum created in a vacuum-type coffee maker?

The gasket helps to form an airtight seal when the upper bowl is pressed into the neck of lower bowl, and when the contents of the lower bowl are heated, the air expands and forces the air and liquid into the upper bowl. When the heat is reduced and the air contracts it forms a vacuum that pulls the liquid back into the lower bowl.

25. Can coffee grounds be re-used for making coffee?

No, they should be discarded immediately. Most of the solubles that give flavor (85%) will have been taken from the coffee on the first brewing process.

26. Is it necessary to clean the urn between making different batches of

Yes. Coffee oils adhere to the sides of the urn that will affect the flavor of the next batch unless the sides of the urn are brushed down and rinsed well between batches.

27. What daily cleaning is necessary with the urns?

All surfaces of the urn and faucet should be washed thoroughly with hot water and a brush and rinsed well daily.

28. How often should an urn cleaner be used?

Every two or three days, depending upon the heavy use of the urn.

29. How can hard-water sludge be flushed from the water urn?

Open the water faucet completely and the inlet valve just enough to keep the water level in the gauge constant. Allow the water to flow for a few minutes each day, in hard water areas, where deposits tend to form readily.

30. What are the three essentials for preparing good quality tea?

(a) Proper quantity of a good blend for the strength of brew desired, (b) good drinking water, freshly heated, and (c) boiling temperature of water for steeping the tea.

31. What are two important points to consider in choosing milk service equipment?

(a) Sanitation, involving cleanliness and refrigeration and (b) convenience of portioning for service.

10.

Salads and
Salad Dressings

Freshness and stimulating flavor are characteristics desired in salads. Most foods that are not sweet may be used in salads. There are certain qualities, however, that set salads apart as something special. Except for a very few hot, savory mixtures, such as hot potato salad or wilted lettuce, salads are most appealing when well chilled. Cold, crisp, piquant, colorful, well-seasoned, and attractive are adjectives applicable to well-prepared salads. They supply valuable nutrients to the diet, especially when they are made of fresh fruits and vegetables. (See color insert for Figure 10.1.)

Salad preparation involves working with foods that possess highly perishable qualities in ways that may readily result in contamination. In order to insure safety and good quality, meticulous cleanliness and careful, continuous refrigeration are essential. A large share of preparation calls for cutting and arranging foods by hand. Clean hands, sanitary methods of work, and protection of foods and equipment from contamination are highly significant.

Materials selected for salads and the size of the portions need to be governed by the salad's role in the menu. Salads may be used as appetizers, as an accompaniment to the main course, as a separate salad course, as the meal's main dish, or as a party refreshment. When served as a part of a meal, they should harmonize with the other foods with which they are served. They may have as few calories as a lettuce leaf without dressing or they may be as hearty as meat and potatoes. Their arrangement should be simple rather than elaborate, with a natural rather than set appearance. Arrangements that are exact, uniform or perfect tend to connote over-handling of materials. Salads are adaptable and may be varied in materials, arrangement, and service.

Appetizer Salads

Salads are often served as the first course or appetizer for luncheons and dinners. This economizes by eliminating the appetizer course. It is especially favored for low-cost meals and by the short-order restaurants where patrons must wait for their food to be prepared. Preportioned salads or those requiring simple arrangement can be served as soon as orders are placed. Hungry patrons can enjoy their salads while other preparation is underway. This helps to speed service and to pacify impatient diners.

These first-course salads should be of a type that arouses the appetite. They should be light, crisp, and cold. The dressing should be tasty and piquant. Tossed green salads are popular and widely used. They may become very trite unless a special note of interest is introduced. It is well to use special care to prevent this delicious and important food from becoming tiresome

Figure 10.2   Appetizer salad with Alaska King Crab, salad greens, and a dairy sour cream dressing. (Courtesy of Pacific Kitchen.)

and lacking in appeal. Varying the kind of crisp, cold greens used in a combination can help. There are many kinds from which to choose and combining two or three varieties adds interesting variation in color, texture, and flavor.

The appetite is not given much of a lift from nibbling on bare salad greens. Stimulation needs to be added in the form of a piquant dressing and/or garnishes of richly flavored foods. Some of the foods that may be used to add appetizing goodness include crumbled crisp bacon; strips of salami, ham, or chicken; bits of crabmeat, lobster, shrimp, tuna, or salmon; grated cheese; or croutons flavored with cheese or garlic. Even a small amount of such foods adds interest.

As an appetizer that combines the cocktail and salad courses, the salad is an introduction to the meal. It creates the first impression and is likely to set the attitude toward the food. The colors, form, and arrangement should be attractive, and the food combinations interesting. It does not need to be large, but it should appear plentiful. The flavors should excite the appetite.

Accompaniment Salads

The accompaniment salads are served with the main course, and provide a relish with the main-course foods. The selection of foods used should harmonize in color, texture, and flavor and complement the foods in the meal with

Figure 10.3   Accompaniment salads should provide relish with the main course foods. (Courtesy of Pacific Kitchen.)

which they are served. Satisfaction of appetite and nutrient balance are to be considered. Salad greens, cabbage salads, tart fruits, savory vegetables, and many milder fruits and vegetables make up a generous list of appropriate salads from which to choose. Heavy foods, such as potato, macaroni, dry beans, and meat salads, are suitable only if other items in the main course are very light and lack similar foods. In making selections one should remember that to fulfill its purpose the salad must be tasty, adding zest of flavor to the meal. Avoid foods that are too smooth or too sweet, or that have an insignificant flavor. A good salad must add relish to the meal.

Separate-Course Salads

Salads are served as a separate course following the main course in the more formal types of service. This service is customary in clubs, hotels, and restaurants that feature fine dining and a leisurely atmosphere. A salad that follows a heavy course should be light and refreshing. It should provide a change from the main-course foods, and should refresh the appetite. Some kind of wafer or other bread item should be served with this course. Well-dressed salad greens, savory vegetables, and fruit salads are popular choices for the separate-course salads.

The plates on which this salad is served should be larger than those used for salads that accompany the main course. The accompaniment salad may be served in a bowl or on a plate approximately $6\frac{1}{2}$ to 7 inches in diameter. As an accompaniment, it is important that the dish not overcrowd the arrangement with the other dishes used in the main course. The separate-course salad should be served on a plate about $8\frac{1}{2}$ to 9 inches in diameter. The service of the separate-course salad on a larger plate need not mean that it is a larger salad. It should be arranged, however, in such an attractive manner so that it appears important in quantity and is not dwarfed by the plate.

The Main-Dish Salads

Hearty salads are used to furnish the chief nourishment for luncheons and dinners. The volume and richness of these salads should be adequate to satisfy the normal appetite. A main dish salad served with bread may constitute the complete luncheon. It may be arranged in a bowl or on a luncheon-size plate (9 to 10 inches). The plate may contain one large salad or an assortment of three to five small ones. Foods rich in protein (for example, chicken, fish, eggs, ham, veal, and cheese) are chosen for these salads. A popular example of a main dish salad is one made with large chunks of tender chicken and seasonings folded into a piquant whipped-cream dressing. It

Figure 10.4   An artichoke supplies a delicious salad base and may be filled with poultry, sea-food, or ham salad to serve as the main dish for a luncheon. (Courtesy of Pacific Kitchen.)

may be garnished with plump segments of grapefruit and salted almonds. This salad makes a hearty and delicious luncheon when served with assorted hot breads.

Party Salads

Sweet salads and many of the rich mixtures (such as frozen whipped-cream salads) are rarely appropriate for mealtime service, but may be enjoyed as party fare. Party refreshments should be selected with the specific group and the particular function in mind. The size of the salad needs to be

Figure 10.5 Sweet salads and rich mixtures are often enjoyed as party refreshments. (Courtesy of Pacific Kitchen.)

governed both by the way in which it is to be served and whether there is a generous assortment of other items. It may be served in bite-size cream-puff shells or small lettuce cups, or it may be the main feature of an afternoon tea. Finely cut crabmeat or chicken salads are favorite mixtures for serving in small cream puffs or tiny lettuce cups. When served as the main item after a club or bridge session the salad filling may weigh 4 to 6 ounces, depending on its richness. It is usually arranged on a plate with enough space for a small sandwich or wafer beside the salad. Favorite choices for these salads include fruit mixtures, molded salads, frozen-fruit salads, and salads of chicken, ham, lobster, crabmeat, or shrimp.

CHOICE AND PREPARATION OF SALAD GREENS

Lettuce holds top popularity as a salad green. Several varieties are available for choice. The crisp or iceberg type is used in largest volume. Its crispness and availability the entire year adds to popularity. The color is pale green and white and the head may be fairly loose or very firm. The butterheads, such as Big Boston and Bibb lettuce are darker green and cream yellow in color. The heads are looser, the leaves are thicker and richer in flavor with higher oil content; it is less crisp than iceberg lettuce. These varieties are available in the market all year.

Cos lettuce or romaine forms an elongated semi-head. The leaves separate readily and have a crisp stem. The flavor is rich and sweet. The color shades from dark green to pale cream. The elongated leaves do not cup well for forming a salad base, but add rich flavor and crisp texture to tossed salads. The heavier texture of the leaves retain crispness in a dressed salad longer than the more fragile lettuce. This type is available all year and is usually marketed in 20-pound crates.

The leaf lettuce varieties are fragile, and need to be handled with care. The Grand Rapids, Bronze, and Oak Leaf are among the more popular varieties. The market supply comes mainly from greenhouses in the winter. The color, form, and flavor add interest and variety to salads. The fragile leaves require protection from dehydration and they wilt quickly in salad dressing. It is necessary, therefore, to arrange these salads shortly before they are to be served. With proper care, their beauty and flavor are rewarding.

Two members of the chicory family are salad favorites. These are the French endive and the curly chicory. Escarole, which is also a member of the chicory family, has a harsher flavor and is used more often as a potherb. All

Figure 10.6 Spinach leaves and curly chicory make an attractive combination as a base for a salad-sandwich plate. (Courtesy of Pacific Kitchen.)

three have a mild bitterness that adds an interesting seasoning quality to mixed salads. The curly chicory is the most plentiful of the three in the year-around market. It is in largest supply from October through December. The finely cut or curly aspect of the leaves with their white stems adds eye appeal to salads. The color of the outer leaves and tips is dark green, and bleaches to yellow green and white toward the heart of the bunch. The French, Belgian, or Witloof endive that is grown from Chicory roots away from the light is bleached a creamy white. The best quality forms a small, firm, cone-shaped bundle about 4 or 5 inches long and approximately 2 inches in diameter at its widest part. The crisp, tender leaves are separated and used whole as a salad base, or broken and mixed in tossed salads. It is available in many markets from November through April.

Cress is a spicy delight for salads. The best known of this group is watercress which grows into attractive, dark-green sprigs with small, thick leaves. It is available all year in some markets and only in spring in others. Field cress is another type; it has oval, dark-green, deeply notched leaves with a spicy flavor. Pepper grass or pepper cress is sometimes in the market and worth watching for. Its spicy taste adds interest to tossed salads.

Two fresh herbs that add interest and flavor distinction are dill and anise. Both have feathery foliage. Anise has a mild, licorice flavor that blends in an interesting way with green or vegetable salads. Dill foliage and seed tops are delicious blended with vegetable salads and tossed greens. Anise (fennel

Figure 10.7   Herb leaves and seeds add delicious flavor to salads.

or finochio) is in the large markets from October through April. Dill is available in late summer and fall.

Many of the tender leaves of potherbs are also delicious in salads. The list includes spinach, beet greens, Swiss chard, mustard, turnip, and dandelion. These dark-green vegetables are rich in vitamins C and A. The deep color forms an appealing contrast to the pale lettuce and their tangy flavor adds special interest and character to salads. Chinese or celery cabbage is creamy white in color and crisp and rugged in texture. Its flavor is mild and it blends well with other vegetables. Both white and red cabbage, celery, parsley, and chives are dependable salad favorites that are available the entire year.

SALAD MAKING

Salads of best quality are clean, cool, crisp, and tasty. The greens must be cleaned long enough in advance of making the salad to allow them to drain well. Dressing to season the salad will not stick to wet leaves, and liquid draining off the leaves after the salad is arranged lessens its enjoyment. Coolness calls for keeping salads refrigerated and crispness requires freshness and protection from dehydration. The direct contact of a worker's hands in arranging salads makes clean hands and clean work habits essential for clean salads.

Certain pieces of equipment are useful in salad making. (See Chapter 2, for small equipment used in salad and sandwich making.) Before beginning salad preparation assemble the items that are required immediately. At least three knives are usually needed, (a) a French knife, (b) a stainless, slender-bladed salad knife, and (c) a paring knife. If paring is to be done a swivel-action parer may be needed. Mixing bowls of proper size, measuring equipment, and a cutting board is likely to be required.

A chilled board and serving dishes help in maintaining low temperature in the salads. A mobile, dish-storage unit that can be rolled into a refrigerated area facilitates chilling. When it is not in use, the board might be stored on top of the dish storage unit. "Keep it cold" is a good slogan for salad makers. Enough refrigerated space for salad supplies, serving dishes, and the salads as soon as they are arranged until they are required for service, is needed in the salad department.

The chief ingredient of a salad is usually indicated on the menu, but with little information concerning its garnish or method of preparation. Special treatment is often required to develop savory qualities desirable in a salad. Most cooked vegetables are improved by marinating in a tasty French dressing. Bland fruits may need flavor and crispness added. Colorless or drab foods may be made more appealing with bright garnishes or by molding in colorful gelatin.

Figure 10.8   Iceberg lettuce is crisp and firm and may be made into different shapes for salads. The top display shows the head with shredded lettuce and a wedge, and below a slice known as a club cut or raft and the slice cut into chunks. (Courtesy of Western Iceberg Lettuce, Inc.)

Tossed green salad may be counted as America's favorite salad in terms of the volume served. Numerous restaurants throughout the country offer it with or without a choice of dressing. The frequency of its service emphasizes the need for sufficient variation of ingredients to make it interesting. The term tossed green salad may mean either lettuce only or a mixture of salad greens. The use of at least three different salad greens in a combination helps to produce an appealing variation in color, texture, and flavor. There is an extensive list of combinations that may be used. The following are examples of such combinations:

1. romaine, French endive, and watercress;
2. iceberg lettuce, romaine, and curly chicory;
3. iceberg lettuce, spinach, and Bibb lettuce;
4. iceberg and Boston lettuce and fennel;
5. romaine, red cabbage, and spinach;
6. iceberg lettuce, watercress, and celery cabbage; and
7. romaine, spinach, and curly chicory

Salad greens should be dry when the salads are made so that water does not dilute the dressing, and so that the dressing can cling to the leaves and season them. Leaves may be dried by patting them with absorbent towels when there is insufficient time for them to fully drain. Salad greens are more attractive when torn into bite size pieces rather than cut. Dressing destroys the crispness and should not be added to the salads until time for service. These tossed green salads can be given added interest, richness, and flavor by garnishing them with certain flavorful foods at the time of service.

A food, or a combination of several foods, that makes a satisfactory garnish may be chosen from the following:

Artichoke bottom, canned, cut in wedges

Artichoke hearts, canned, quarters, halves

Avocado—diced or sliced

Bacon—crisp, crumbled

Celery—rings or dices

Cauliflower—small flowerlets

Cheddar cheese—grated or slivered

Blue cheese—crumbled

Carrots—curls or julienne strips

Almonds—whole or slivered

Onions—separated rings or thinly sliced

Green beans or peas—cooked, marinated

Fish—crabmeat, salmon or tuna flakes, shrimp, sardines, anchovies, lobster

Swiss cheese—cut in fine strips

Cucumber—diced or sliced

Dill or anise—snipped fresh herb

Chives—snipped

Citrus sections—orange, mandarins, grapefruit, tangerine

Meats—thin strips or dices of ham, chicken, luncheon meat, turkey, salami, frankfurters, pepperoni

Croutons—garlic or cheese flavored

Chips—corn or potato, crumbled

Radishes—strips, slices, or small whole

Tomatoes—quartered or sliced cherry, quarters of large tomatoes

Eggs—chopped, quartered, sliced hard cooked

Walnuts or pecans—coarsely chopped or broken

The Salad Base

Arranged salads usually have a base, such as a lettuce leaf, on which they are placed. Head lettuce (iceberg, Boston, and Bibb varieties) furnish the most attractive cups. The lettuce cups help to shape or confine salads that are composed of loose particles of food. They give height and provide a frame for the salads. Molded salads, filled salads like avocado and tomato, and those that arrange well without spreading are attractive when arranged on loose leaf lettuce, romaine, spinach, curly chicory, and endive. A level base may be made by slicing across a firm head of iceberg lettuce. The thickness of the slice may be varied according to ingredients to be used on it. It may be sliced fairly thick if it is to be served with dressing only. A nest of cole slaw is delicious and attractive when used as a base for orange or tomato salads.

The salad base should not be so large that it dominates the appearance of the salad, but should be in pleasant proportion to the main ingredients. It should set well in proportion to the plate. It should never be so large or so limp as to hang over the edge of the plate. The frilly edge of lettuce or the highest part of the lettuce cup should be displayed on a counter or in front of a guest at the back of the plate. This exposes the main part of the salad to the patron.

Iceberg lettuce is the salad base used in greatest quantity. There are seasons when the heads are very firm and the leaves are difficult to separate without breaking the cups. Tapping the core gently against the table to loosen it and then twisting the core from the leaves to remove it, helps to loosen the leaves. They may be further separated by allowing a strong flow of water to pour into the opening from which the core was removed, because the water tends to force the leaves apart.

All of the crisp, tender leaves of the lettuce should be used. Large outside leaves often do not cup well. They may be made to cup by breaking or splitting the leaf part of the way from the stem side toward the outer edge, and overlapping it. When setting up salads for a large number of servings, it is well to separate the entire head and combine some of the tenderest inner leaves with the coarser outer leaves in each salad. The firm, heart leaves should not be neglected. These crisp, tender parts may be broken and added to the center of the cup. They should not be shredded. Crispness is one of the desirable characteristics of a salad and shredding destroys crispness and makes stringy particles that are tedious to eat.

Salad Arrangement

The topography of a salad has psychological value. Appropriate height lends importance. A flat salad tends to appear limp, small, and unimportant. Height can be built into a salad in various ways. Even flat segments of fruit can be made to stand up through artful use of the tiny heart leaves of lettuce to support them. Chunks of firm lettuce or similar fillers are sometimes needed to give an impression of plentiful size.

A salad should have a main point of interest. This may be either the chief ingredient or a garnish with special appeal. A well-known fruit salad can be given extra interest by garnishing it with a first fruit in season, such as a fresh strawberry or raspberries. Salad ingredients should be chosen and treated in a manner that complements other foods in the meal; for example, tart fruits or crisp, savory vegetables are better with main course foods than such items as bananas, pears, cottage cheese, beans, peas, and macaroni.

Arrangements are most attractive when they are simple and natural in appearance. Seasoning foods, such as onions and celery, may be minced, but the chief materials in a salad should be large enough to be identifiable. The overly industrious saladmakers who dice and chop all of the materials destroy desirable crispness and good appearance. The chief salad materials should be bite size or of tender materials that are easy to cut with the salad fork. Firm apple, for example, requires cutting before use in a salad. Most stewed or canned fruits are tender enough to use whole or in large pieces. Salads containing foods that require cutting with a fork should be served on a salad plate, not in a bowl. It is a good idea to vary the form when cutting salad materials. Interesting variation in form may also be secured through selection of ingredients. A combination salad, for example, might include green beans, tomato wedges, and celery rings. A fruit salad might have julienne cuts of

Figure 10.9   The salad size should be in attractive proportion to the plate and have a dressing that harmonizes in flavor, richness, and piquancy. (Courtesy of Western Iceberg Lettuce, Inc.)

apple, tidbits of pineapple, segments of citrus fruit, and a garnish of chopped red and green pepper.

Setting a food on a lettuce leaf or other salad base does not make it a salad. To qualify as a salad, food must possess piquancy or relish value. Some foods have a stimulating flavor, while it must be developed in others. Marinades may be used to season such foods and give the flavor a lift. Citrus and pineapple juices for fruit, and seasoned marinades for vegetables, help to add piquancy. Spices, herbs, and flavorful vegetables may be used for seasoning. Seasoned croutons, watercress, capers, spiced foods and other savory garnishes may be used to add flavor and the desired relish qualities.

The dressing selected should be one that harmonizes and makes a pleasant addition to flavor and piquancy. Slightly sweet dressings are usually preferred for fruit salads and tart ones for vegetables. Many patrons prefer salads without dressing, and it is well to permit this option by offering the dressing in a manner that permits self-service. In informal service this may be done by serving the dressing in a souffle cup beside the salad. In formal service, it should be presented in a bowl from which the guest may serve himself.

Well chosen garnishes add interest and attractiveness to salads. Dressings that have enough body to hold their shape may be used for color. Garnishes should contrast in color, form and texture with ingredients in the salad. The flavor should harmonize, but it may be one stronger or more pronounced.

TABLE 10.1 SUGGESTED SALAD COMBINATIONS

Salad Ingredients	Dressing	Garnish
Fruit salads		
Diced apple, celery rings, chopped pecans	Mayonnaise or cooked dressing	Salad cherry or bright berry
Diced apple, half sections of orange	Fruit	Strips of date
Apple julienne, pineapple tidbits, orange and grapefruit sections	French	Chopped red and green pepper
Apple, orange, and grapefruit segments in alternating arrangement	Poppyseed and honey	Green-pepper ring
Apricot halves, pineapple tidbits	Fruit	Spiced prune
Avocado, pineapple, and orange segments	French	Sliced stuffed olive
Avocado and grapefruit sections	Celery seed	Sliced kumquat
Banana chunks rolled in chopped peanuts with pineapple slice	Fruit	Orange sections
Molded cranberry and orange	Fruit	Frosted green grapes
Bing cherries, mandarin oranges, and slivered almonds in black cherry gelatin	Fruit	Slivered almonds

TABLE 10.1 (*Continued*)

Salad Ingredients	Dressing	Garnish
Grapefruit and red-apple sections	Honey	Seeded Tokay halves
Grapefruit and pineapple sections with chopped green pepper and diced cucumber	Honey	Tarragon jelly cubes
Orange diced, shredded carrot, and raisins	Sour cream	Celery rings
Peach half filled with cranberry relish	Fruit	Green grapes
Diced pineapple, orange, and celery in lime gelatin	Fruit	Salad cherry
Pineapple ring, honeydew-melon balls, and orange sections	Fruit	Fresh berries
Pineapple fingers, sliced orange, green grapes	Fruit	Shredded coconut
Pineapple chunks and green grapes	Fruit	Fresh strawberry
Pineapple tidbits with grapefruit and apple segments	Poppyseed	Crumbled blue cheese
Pineapple chunks, celery rings, chopped nuts	Fruit	Stuffed prune
Spiced prune with pineapple ring	Honey	Mandarin orange
Crushed pineapple and diced cucumber	Fruit	Slivered almonds

237

TABLE 10.1 (*Continued*)

Salad Ingredients	Dressing	Garnish
Main dish salads (cheese, egg, fish, meat)		
Asparagus tips with chicken salad	Mayonnaise	Stuffed olive
Avocado filled with chicken or crab salad	Mayonnaise	Grapefruit sections
Cottage cheese, herb flavored with sliced tomato	Combination	Watercress
Cottage cheese with pineapple ring or peach half	Fruit	Salad cherry
Chicken salad, grapefruit segments	Mayonnaise	Whole salted almonds
Jellied chicken with pineapple and slivered almonds	Mayonnaise	Pepper ring
Egg salad and tomato wedges	Combination	Parsley sprig
Frozen cream cheese and fruit	Fruit	Walnut halves
Ham salad with asparagus tips	Combination	Tomato wedge
Crab Louis—crabmeat, hard-cooked egg, and tomato slices, wedges, or cherries	Thousand island	ripe olives
Kidney beans, chopped celery, onion, and pickle	Combination	Julienne ham and Swiss cheese
Club—macaroni, hard-cooked egg, chopped pickle, olives, celery, onion, and green pepper	Combination	Parsley and cherry tomato

TABLE 10.1 (*Continued*)

Salad Ingredients	Dressing	Garnish
Salmon flakes, diced celery and eggs, chopped pickle	Mayonnaise	Ripe olives
Shrimp salad with avocado slices	Mayonnaise	Ripe olives
Lobster salad with tomato slice	Mayonnaise	Pickle slice
Potato, frankfurter, hard-cooked egg, cucumber, and minced onion	Combination	Stuffed olive
Tuna salad with cucumber slices	Combination	Sliced hard-cooked egg
Chef's salad—iceberg and romaine lettuce; chopped green onion; celery rings; julienne beef, ham, tongue, or chicken; Swiss cheese, and anchovy fillets	2 parts mayonnaise and 1 part French mixed	Part of the julienne meat and cheese
Vegetable salads		
Asparagus tips, tomato and cucumber slices	French	Shredded cheddar
Marinated asparagus cuts, celery rings, and tomato chunks	Sour cream	Sliced green onion
Grated carrot, celery rings, and raisins or peanuts	Combination	Spanish peanuts
Cabbage, celery, and chopped green pepper	Combination	Orange slice
Shredded carrot, pineapple tidbits, diced celery	Mayonnaise	Nuts
Shredded cabbage, radish slices, celery rings	Sour cream	Green pepper ring
Perfection—molded chopped cabbage, celery, green pepper, and pimento	Combination	Pimento strip
Whole-kernel corn, cut green beans, chopped celery, onion, green pepper, and pimento	Combination	Stuffed olive

239

TABLE 10.1 (*Continued*)

Salad Ingredients	Dressing	Garnish
Cole slaw	Cream	Tomato wedge
Cucumber and sweet onion slices	Sour cream	Chopped parsley
Green limas, sliced green onions, celery rings	Combination	Carrot curl
Kidney beans, chopped pickle, onion and sliced celery	French	Cauliflowerlets
Three bean—kidney, and/or garbonza beans, green and waxed beans, chopped pickle, onion, celery and pepper	French	Sweet onion ring or carrot curl
Tossed romaine, iceberg, and curly chicory	French, Thousand islands, or blue cheese	Cheese or garlic croutons
Caesar—Romaine, parmesan and blue cheese, peas, chopped pickle, celery, and pimento	Garlic flavored oil, raw egg, and lemon juice	Croutons and anchovy fillets
Green Goddess—salad greens, grated cheddar, and shrimp or crabmeat	Green Goddess	Tomato wedges
Broken iceberg lettuce and fresh spinach, chopped onion and celery	French	Chopped hard-cooked egg
Long green beans, beet slices, marinated limas and snipped chives	Mayonnaise	Shredded cheddar cheese
Tomato and cucumber slices	French	Sliced young onion
Tomato aspic with vegetables	Mayonnaise	Ripe olive
Sliced zucchini, tomato wedges, celery rings	French	Chopped hard-cooked egg

SALAD DRESSINGS

Salad dressings are sauces that are blended to complement and season foods with which they are served. Their function is to add well seasoned flavor, richness, and piquancy. The dressing selected for a specific salad should harmonize well with the salad ingredients; for example, a mustard dressing would not be enjoyed if served on a fruit salad but would be welcome with egg, potato, or meat salad. Likewise, a sweet whipped-cream dressing is not the best selection for a vegetable salad.

Ingredients for salad dressings should be chosen carefully for good flavor. The oil should be mild and sweet, free from rancidity or off-flavor. The acid, such as fruit juices or vinegar, selected for tartness or piquancy should have a good natural flavor and not be too sharp. There are numerous herb flavors that may be chosen to give interest, subtlety, and variety. Tarragon, dill and poppyseed, and celery seed are among the favorites. Others that blend well with, and bring out desired flavors in, foods they accompany may also be used.

Salad dressings are classified into four general types. Each has numerous variations. (a) French dressing is a temporary emulsion of oil, vinegar, and seasonings. (b) Mayonnaise is a permanent emulsion containing oil, vinegar, seasonings, and an emulsifier, that is chiefly or entirely egg yolks. (c) Cooked dressings have a thickening agent, such as eggs or starch, to thicken the liquids, which may include an acid ingredient, water, and/or fruit juice. Seasonings are added. (d) Cream dressings may be made with either sweet or sour cream. Whipped sour cream contains natural acid and may have lemon juice added for additional tartness. The simple addition of salt and other seasonings make this type an easy-to-make and popular dressing. Whipped-cream dressings may merely have lemon juice and seasonings added, or they may be folded into a starch-thickened, fruit-juice mixture.

French Dressing

French dressing may not contain any emulsifying ingredients other than the small amount of seasonings. The emulsion consists of small drops of oil suspended in the water and vinegar. The surface tension of the oil causes the oil droplets to coalesce (blend together into one) and, being lighter than the water and vinegar, the oil rises to the top of the mixture as a separate layer. When beaten or shaken vigorously it again forms a temporary emulsion. Ingredients may be added that interfere with the coalescence of the oil droplets and cause the French dressing to become a semipermanent emulsion. Those commonly used include honey, condensed soup, gelatin, gum arabic, and gum tragacanth.

Mayonnaise

Mayonnaise contains oil, water, and vinegar plus an emulsifying ingredient that prevents the oil droplets from coalescing. Egg yolk is the most commonly used and effective emulsifier. Whole eggs may be used, but this makes the product thinner because the whites have less stabilizing power than the yolks. Gelatin or cooked starch may also be used as a part of the emulsifying ingredients, but egg yolk remains the most effective and satisfying for producing a superior dressing. The yolks may be either fresh or frozen, but mayonnaise made with frozen egg yolks tends to be somewhat thicker.

In mayonnaise the oil droplets are suspended in the water and vinegar. If the acid in the vinegar is too sharp it may cause the emulsion to break. It is important for the ingredients to be in proper proportions. There must be sufficient moisture to carry the oil droplets, but without an excess of either the vinegar or oil. Mayonnaise is prepared by whipping the yolks at medium mixer speed until well beaten, then adding the mixed dry ingredients and about half of the vinegar. Next, the oil is added in small amounts (a slow drizzle if a mechanical oil dropper is used). Beating continues until most of the oil has been added. Toward the last, the oil may be added more rapidly. The remaining vinegar may be added after all the oil; the beating is continued another 5 minutes. Mayonnaise that has separated may be re-emulsified by beating it gradually into a small amount of beaten egg yolk.

Cooked Salad Dressings

These dressings contain much less oil than either the French or mayonnaise dressings. A combination of starch and egg yolk may be used for thickening. The mixture may be thick enough for dilution with whipped cream or for blending with another type of dressing. The goal is to produce a smooth, well-blended, and well-seasoned product.

When preparing cooked dressing, the dry ingredients should be mixed and blended with cold liquid, then gradually added to the hot liquid, which should be stirred constantly. It should be heated in a double boiler until the starch is well cooked. The butter and vinegar or lemon juice should be added after the mixture has thickened. If eggs are used, they should be beaten and added at this time with continuous stirring. The mixture should be removed from the heat as soon as it has thickened and the eggs are cooked.

Combination dressings are usually a combination of cooked dressing and mayonnaise. The proportions may vary according to taste, from 2 parts cooked dressing and 1 part mayonnaise to half and half. A cooked base made with fruit juices and combined with whipped cream is a favorite for fruit salads. Various flavorful fruit juices may be used if they are not excessively sweet and have enough tartness to give character to the dressing. Extra lemon juice may be needed to point up those that are too mild. The following proportions may be used for 1 gallon of dressing:

FRUIT SALAD DRESSING	Approximately 100 1-oz portions	
Ingredients	Weight	Volume
Fruit juice (pineapple and orange)	3 lb	1½ qt
Lemon juice	4 oz	½ c
Cornstarch	1¼ oz	¼ c
Sugar, granulated	3 oz	5 tbsp
Salt	1 tsp	1 tsp
Eggs, beaten	1 lb 2 oz	10 large
Whipping cream	2 lb	1 qt

PROCEDURE:

1. Heat the juices to boiling. Blend the dry ingredients and add to the hot juices, stirring constantly. Cook until the moisture thickens and the starch has lost its raw taste.
2. Add a small amount of the hot mixture to the beaten eggs, and then add the egg mixture gradually to hot mixture, stirring constantly. Cook until thickened and eggs are done (about 5 minutes over slow heat). Cool thoroughly.
3. Whip the cream and fold into the fruit mixture.

Cream Dressings

The dressings that are made with sour cream, cream cheese, or whipped sweet cream need to be well seasoned if they are to harmonize with, and add the required seasoning to, the salads on which they are used. Salt is needed and often a little lemon juice. The use of spices depends upon the individual taste. Nutmeg or cinnamon may add a delicious flavor and may be folded in or sprinkled on top of the dressing. These dressings may be varied by the addition of such ingredients as chopped nuts, minced olives, snipped chives, grated cheese, chopped pickle or pickle relish, and chopped eggs.

All salad dressings should be well chilled before service. They should be added to salads immediately before service unless they are used as a marinade or a part of the salad mixture. Acid and oil wilt salad greens and reduce the firmness of texture of citrus and certain other fruits. The viscous dressings have a nicer sheen and are more attractive when they are freshly served.

SUGGESTED LABORATORY EXPERIENCE

1. Compare ease of removing leaves of iceberg lettuce for salad cups from a head (a) merely washed and drained, (b) cored by tapping core area on table and then twisting core out, and (c) core is cut out in cone shape and water is forced into head from a strong spray or from moving head up and down in a large amount of water.
2. Prepare and compare attractiveness of salads using different salad bases— various types of lettuce, chicory, watercress, and spinach.
3. Prepare and compare palatability of vegetable salads that are marinated in French dressing with those that are not.
4. Arrange different types of salad and evaluate appearance, appropriateness, size, and cost.
5. Make French dressing with and without a stabilizer. Compare length of time the emulsion holds.
6. Prepare mayonnaise. Recover one that has separated.

REVIEW QUESTIONS AND ANSWERS

1. Name the courses in which a salad may be served.

As an appetizer for the first course, as an accompaniment with the main course, as the main dish, as a separate course after the main course, and as a party refreshment.

2. List the desirable qualities for a salad.

Cold, crisp, clean, piquant, harmonious with the meal in color, flavor, and texture, and attractive.

3. What are the special characteristics needed in an appetizer salad?

It is in place of the cocktail and should have stimulating flavor and few calories.

4. What qualities are desirable in an accompaniment salad?

It should complement the main course foods in color, texture, nutrients, and flavor.

5. What are the requisites of a main dish salad?

Volume and nutrients sufficient for the main dish of the meal; well seasoned and attractive.

6. When is it appropriate to serve sweet salads?

As a party refreshment.

7. Why are they rarely suitable as mealtime salads?

Because their sweetness satisfies rather than stimulates the appetite.

8. What are the chief varieties of lettuce used for salads?

Iceberg, Boston, Bibb, romaine or Cos, oak leaf, Grand Rapids, and bronze.

9. List salad greens that may be used for a base.

Lettuce, chicory, spinach, cabbage, watercress, and possibly Swiss chard.

10. List five spicy or flavoring greens.

Watercress, dill, anise, chive, and parsley.

11. How can dehydration of greens be prevented?

By cleaning as soon as they arrive in the kitchen, and then storing in plastic bags or covered containers in a refrigerator.

12. What knives should be available for salad making?

A French knife, a stainless salad or fruit knife, a paring knife, and a swivel action parer.

13. When should salad materials be refrigerated?

Every minute they are not in preparation or service.

14. Why is refrigeration important?

To prevent spoilage and to insure the most palatable temperature and freshness.

15. In addition to refrigeration, how may coldness be protected?

By preparing on a cold board and serving on cold dishes.

16. What is a salad base?

The foundation, such as a lettuce cup, on which the main ingredients are served.

17. What are the chief functions of salad dressing?

To season, increase piquancy, add flavor, and increase interest and variety.

18. What is a semi-permanent emulsion?

One in which the separation of the ingredients is delayed for a time through the use of ingredients that interfere with the coalescence of the oil droplets.

19. What is the chief emulsifying agent in mayonnaise?

Egg yolks.

20. What ingredients can be used to produce a semi-permanent emulsion in French dressing?

Honey, catsup, condensed soup, gelatin, gum arabic and gum tragacanth.

21. Can mayonnaise be recovered after it has separated?

Yes, by beating it gradually into a small amount of beaten egg yolk.

22. What is a combination dressing?

A mixture of cooked dressing and mayonnaise.

23. Should sour cream and sweet cream be seasoned when used as dressings?

Yes, they should have salt and perhaps some lemon juice.

24. When should salad dressing be placed on salads?

Immediately before serving, so that the acid and oil have the least possible time to wilt the salad greens.

25. Why is it important for salad greens to be dry when salads are arranged?

Salad dressing does not adhere to wet greens; moisture on the greens dilutes the salad dressing and tends to run off onto the plate.

26. Why are clean hands and clean habits of the worker of special importance in salad making?

Because of the hand contact with the salad materials in cutting and arranging the salads.

27. What effect do temperature changes in a refrigerator have on salad greens?

It robs them of moisture and causes them to wilt and lack crispness.

11.

Sandwiches

Sandwiches hold a position of popularity and high volume in American food service. Their characteristics permit very fast service and the wide selection of fillings satisfy a variety of tastes. Many kinds can be prepared well in advance of service and wrapped, stored, or transported without serious deterioration. The use of precooked foods or short-order methods of preparation allows many popular kinds to be made to order. When considering sandwiches nutritionally, both the bread and the filling should be evaluated. Enriched bread should be selected and adequate protein should be used in the filling if the sandwich is to provide the chief protein in the meal.

Qualities essential to sandwich popularity include (a) rich, fresh flavor; (b) moist texture; and (c) sufficient piquancy to stimulate appetite. For best enjoyment, the bread should be neither dry or soggy. It should be tender and well flavored. The filling should be well seasoned and tasty. Because of the frequent dryness of bread, special care needs to be taken to insure having fillings that are palatably moist. If foods used for fillings, such as meats and cheese, are too dry, it is advisable to chop and blend them with dressing to relieve the dryness. Fillings, though moist, should not be so wet that they run or drop from the sandwich making it difficult to eat. They should not be so wet as to soak into the bread and make it soggy. The filling should be spread to the edges of the bread, but should not project beyond it.

Sandwiches should look "good enough to eat." The appearance should be neat and attractive. The manner in which they are cut can add to attractiveness. The pieces should be of a size that makes the sandwich easy to handle. There are many forms into which they may be cut. Large quantity handling calls for quick, simple strokes of the knife and limited motions in assembling the pieces on the plate for service. Figure 11.2 illustrates six popular cuts and their arrangement for service.

Figure 11.1 Toasted cheese sandwiches are luncheon favorites at the Air Force Academy, where 5000 are grilled in 45 minutes for 2180 cadets. (Courtesy of the American Institute of Baking.)

SANDWICH MATERIALS

Bread

Good bread is essential for top quality sandwiches. Major attention is likely to be focused on the fillings with only casual thought given to the bread. It is well to remember that the bread makes up the major part of the sandwich and its richness, flavor, and general condition strongly influences the quality of the sandwich.

There are many kinds of loaf breads, rolls, and buns from which to choose. White and whole wheat breads have top popularity. French bread, rye, raisin, herb, cinnamon, fruit, and nut breads offer appealing variety. Consider the flavor of the filling when selecting the bread, and choose one that harmonizes with and enhances the flavor goodness. Certain breads have become somewhat traditional as choices for particular fillings, such as ham or corned beef on rye bread, peanut butter and marmalade on raisin bread, and cream cheese on fruit or nut breads. Yeast breads are favored for the majority of hearty sandwiches and for most of the tea and fancy sandwiches. Specialty rolls and buns, such as hamburger and hot dog buns and crusty rolls, add to the list of breads that are appropriate for sandwiches.

The bread needs to be fine textured and reasonably tender. A coarse or porous bread tends to soak up moisture from the filling and becomes soggy. In storage it dries or stales more quickly than fine-textured bread. The texture should be firm enough to spread well, and it should not become pasty

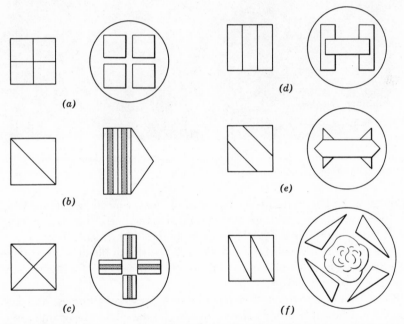

Figure 11.2 Six easy and popular sandwich cuts and arrangements. (*a*) Cut in half vertically and horizontally. Squares may be separated on plate with the garnish in the center, or overlapped in a semicircle with salad or garnish at the side. Arrangement shown on 7-inch plate. (*b*) Cut in half diagonally. Wrap or place on plate to display the filling. (*c*) Cut in quarters diagonally. Set triangles with cut side up to show filling. This is an attractive cut for salad-sandwich plates. Arrange on 9-inch plate. (*d*) Divide into three equal rectangles. For best display of filling, arrange crust edges toward center on bottom and center cut across top of other two pieces. (*e*) Cut diagonally into three pieces. Arrange cut sides toward edge of plate and center piece across top of the other two. (*f*) Divide into four triangles by first cutting in half vertically and then cutting each rectangle diagonally into two equal triangles. The pieces may be laid on their sides or set around salad or relish with the cut side up. Salad and sandwich arrangement shown on 9-inch plate.

Figure 11.3   Good bread is essential for top quality sandwiches and there are many varieties from which to choose. (Courtesy of the American Institute of Baking.)

in the mouth. The rich nut-like flavor of the wheat or other grain of which the bread was made, adds greatly to sandwich goodness. The flavors of the bread and the filling should harmonize for best enjoyment. The flavor of white and whole wheat breads is sufficiently neutral to blend well with most food flavors. The more pronounced flavor of rye bread calls for savory rather than sweet or fruit flavors.

Bread should be stored in a manner that preserves freshness and good flavor and where it is within convenient reach of the sandwich-making center. The waxed paper or plastic wrap helps to preserve freshness and should not be removed until time for the bread to be used. Bread absorbs other flavors readily and its goodness can be spoiled by storing in a musty or dirty cabinet. Bread may pick up off-flavors (onion or tobacco, for example) from work surfaces or the worker's hands. Bread stales less rapidly stored at room temperature (75 to 85°F) than when refrigerated. If bread is to be held for several days or longer, it should be frozen to preserve freshness.

Commercial breads vary in size and shape of loaves and in thickness of slice. The pullman shape provides a $4\frac{1}{2}$-inch square slice that is popular for sandwiches. It has a fine texture and a firm tough crust. The spring top loaf contains the same amount of dough but, because it is allowed to expand more, it yields a larger slice, a more open texture, and a thinner, more tender crust. (See Table 11.1 for the average number of slices from the standard commercial loaves.)

TABLE 11.1 NUMBER OF SLICES IN COMMERCIAL LOAVES OF BREAD

Variety	Ounces in Loaf	Slices in Loaf*	Thickness of Slice (in.)
Egg sesame	22½	22	⅜
Egg sesame	15	15	⅜
Honey wheat	22½	22	⅜
Raisin	15	16	½
Rye, regular	16	23	⅜
Rye, regular	32	33	⅜
White, pullman	32	28	½
White, pullman	32	36	⅜
White, pullman	48	44	½
White, pullman	48	56	⅜
White, pullman	20	19	⅝
White, pullman	24	24	⅝
Whole wheat, regular	16	16	⅝
Whole wheat, regular	32	28	½
Whole wheat, regular	48	44	½
Whole wheat, regular	48	56	⅜

*Number of sandwich slices not including the ends.

Loaves of quick breads are usually made in the 1½- or 2-pound loaf pans in the individual kitchens. They slice into 20 slices ⅜-inch thick per each 28-ounce loaf.

Butters and Fillings

A spread of butter or margarine not only adds to the palatability of sandwiches but also helps to prevent moist fillings from soaking into the bread. The spread should be softened and stirred enough to spread smoothly and evenly but not melted because this would cause it to soak into the bread. Mayonnaise may also be used as a spread for sandwiches that are to be used immediately. It does not protect from soaking as well as butter or margarine. Butter volume may be increased by mixing with evaporated milk, using

8 ounces of evaporated milk to 1 pound of butter. The milk should be added gradually to softened butter, while it is being beaten in a mixer or with a rotary beater. Three pounds of this or another spread is sufficient for 100 sandwiches, allowing approximately $1\frac{1}{2}$ teaspoonsful per slice of bread.

A savory butter may be used to season meat and cheese sandwiches. Various savory additions are suggested in Table 11.2; amounts are those to be used with 3 pounds of butter or enough for 100 sandwiches.

TABLE 11.2 SUGGESTED FLAVORINGS FOR SANDWICH SPREADS
(in amounts for use alone or in combinations with 3 pounds of spread)

Flavoring	Amount	Flavoring	Amount
Celery, minced	1 c	Horseradish, grated	1½ tbsp
Chili Sauce or Catsup	1 c	Lemon juice and	
Chives, minced	¼ c	grated rind	2 tbsp
Green pepper, minced	½ c	Mustard, prepared	1½ tbsp
Parsley, minced	1 c	Onion, grated	1½ tbsp
Pimiento, minced	½ c	Watercress	½ c

Meat dries and loses flavor more rapidly after it is sliced. It is best therefore, to slice it shortly before it is to be used in sandwiches. The thickness of the slice needs to be governed by the characteristics of the particular meat, and the cost allowance for the sandwich. The less-tender beef roasts, when thinly sliced and placed on the bread in layers or a looped arrangement, are more tender to eat and give the appearance of a more generous portion of meat. These sandwiches need to be protected from drying by careful wrapping as soon as they are made if they are not to be served immediately. Thinly sliced meat may be protected before being made into sandwiches by being tightly wrapped and refrigerated, or a little richly flavored stock may be sprinkled over them. Thicker slices of meat should be thick enough to provide a satisfying, moist, flavorful sandwich.

An appropriate cost should be determined for each type of filling and specified in ounces per sandwich. (See Table 2.4. Scoop size Number 30, which holds 1 ounce as a popular size for sandwich fillings.) The thickness of sliced meat to yield the specified weight can be controlled by the setting of the thickness regulator on the meat slicer. Adjustments can be made in relation to the diameter and the characteristics of the meat, in order to yield the weight and tenderness desired. Care should be taken when slicing to have full, well-formed slices and to avoid crumbling or scrappiness. The cost of the sandwich is largely determined by the number of sandwiches prepared from the total weight of the meat as purchased, including trim or scrappy parts that may not be used. The cost of the bread, the spread, and the relish or garnishes are included in the total cost.

Hot sandwiches are more often prepared at the grill or in the cook's unit than in the sandwich section. Hamburgers and frankfurters are among the most popular of these. Hot meat sandwiches, with hot gravy over the meat and bread, grilled cheese, and baked sandwiches are often made in the cook's unit for service in cafeterias. Baked-cheese sandwiches have a custard mixture poured over them and are baked slowly, as in the cooking of other custard mixtures.

Hamburgers rate very high in quantity served when compared with other types of sandwiches. Size and quality varies widely. The best quality is made of sweet flavored, freshly ground beef, without any bread crumb or cereal filler. The ground beef must be fresh for it deteriorates rapidly and absorbs off flavors readily, especially if it is handled carelessly or stored with strong-flavored foods. Palatability calls for the right amount of fat. If there is too much fat in the meat there is a high percentage of shrinkage and too much fat on the grill. When there is too little fat in the meat, the hamburger is dry and lacking in flavor richness. A fat percentage of 18 to 20% is generally satisfactory.

A beef quality graded "Good" or better is recommended for tenderness and good flavor. Purchases should be regularly checked by taste-testing and evaluated in terms of cost and yield. Commercially portioned ground beef may be procured to yield from 2 to 10 portions per pound. The jumbo size (8 to 10 oz) has a very limited demand except as a dinner entree. Many restaurants that feature high-quality hamburgers use 4 ounces of high-grade beef containing 18% fat. The economy hamburgers may be made of a lower grade of beef and portioned 8 or 10 servings per pound of a meat containing from 20 to 30% fat. These must be fairly rare to prevent frying out; they are served on a smaller bun. In choosing the best type to serve, the specific clientele, their taste, and willingness to pay costs must be considered. The food-cost allowance within the specific selling price must be determined, and the meat cost adjusted accordingly.

When making hamburgers, the split buns should be opened and placed inside down on the warm portion of the grill to heat while the hamburger is cooking. This helps to freshen the bun and heats them to a palatable temperature. Preportioning of lettuce and the other additions to the sandwich promotes speed in assembling.

There is an extensive list of food combinations for making delicious fillings; some of the more popular ones are listed in Table 11.3. Fillings are usually mixed with salad dressing, cream cheese, butter, peanut butter, or another

TABLE 11.3 SUGGESTED FOOD MIXTURES TO USE FOR SANDWICH FILLINGS
(in amounts for 24 hearty sandwiches, with 48 slices of bread, ¾ pound of spread, and 24 lettuce leaves)

Name	Ingredients
Beef and onion	Arrange 3 lb sliced roast beef, 1 lb sliced sweet onions.
Sliced meat	Arrange 3 lb sliced meat, 1 c drained pickle relish mixed with ½ c mayonnaise.
Meat and egg salad	Blend 2 lb ground cooked meat, 1 c chopped hard-cooked eggs, ½ c minced pickle, 1 c minced celery, and 1 c combination dressing.
Roast beef and avocado	Serve open with beef on one slice and tomato and avocado on other. Arrange 3 lb thinly sliced roast beef, 6 sliced avocados, 6 thinly sliced tomatoes, spread bread with 2 c chopped pimientos and 1 c mayonnaise.
Chicken and tongue	Arrange 1½ lb sliced tongue, 3 lbs sliced breasts of chicken or turkey, ½ c pickle relish, and ½ c mayonnaise.
Frankfurters and beans	Combine 1 lb thinly sliced frankfurters, 1 lb softened cheddar cheese, 1 lb crushed baked beans, ½ c chopped onion, and ¼ c chili sauce.
Reuben	Arrange on rye bread: 2 lb sliced corned beef, 1½ lb sliced Swiss cheese, 3½ c drained sauerkraut, 1 c Thousand Island dressing.
Corned beef and egg	1½ lb chopped corned beef blended with 6 chopped hard-cooked eggs, ½ c pickle relish, and ½ c combination dressing.
Corned beef salad	2 lb ground corned beef, 1 c chopped onion, 1 c garlic dill pickles blended with ½ c catsup and ½ c cooked dressing.
Chipped beef and cheese	Blend 6 oz chopped chipped beef, 1½ lb cheddar cheese, 3 oz chopped ripe olives, and 1½ c combination dressing.
Bacon and tomato	Arrange 2 lb (48 slices) crisp bacon, 24 slices (4 lge) tomatoes, and 1 c combination dressing.

254

TABLE 11.3 (*Continued*)

Name	Ingredients
Peanut butter and bacon	Blend 1½ lb crumbled crisp bacon, 3 c peanut butter, 1 c combination dressing.
Peanut butter and banana	Blend 3 c softened peanut butter with 1½ c mayonnaise and spread on bread; arrange lengthwise slices of 12 bananas on it.
Ham and cheese	Spread bread with 1 c cooked dressing mixed with 1 tsp prepared mustard and arrange slices of 3 lb sliced ham and 1½ lb sliced cheddar cheese.
Chef	Use 1 c mayonnaise for spread. Arrange 24 slices ham (2½ lb), 2 lb sliced breast of chicken, 24 tomato slices, 72 cooked asparagus spears. (May be served hot or cold. If hot substitute 1½ qt hot cheese sauce for mayonnaise.)
Denver	Blend 1½ lb ground cooked ham, 2⅔ lb (24) raw eggs, 1½ c minced onion, 1½ c minced green pepper, 1½ c milk, salt and pepper to taste. Stir well and saute to order.
Bologna and cheese	Soften 8 oz cream cheese with 1 c combination dressing and spread bread. Arrange 3 lb sliced bologna and 3 c well-drained cole slaw.
Chicken and bacon	Arrange 2 lb sliced chicken, 48 strips crisp bacon, and 1 c mayonnaise.
Chicken salad	Blend 2 lb chopped cooked chicken, 3 oz chopped celery, 3 oz chopped sweet pickle, 1 tsp prepared mustard, 2 tsp lemon juice, and 1½ c cooked salad dressing.
Tuna salad	Blend 1½ lb flaked tuna, 1½ c minced celery, ½ c minced onion, ½ lb shredded American cheese, 1 c chopped ripe olives, and 1 c cooked salad dressing.
Egg and bacon	Blend 1½ doz chopped hard-cooked eggs, 1 lb chopped crisp bacon, and 1 c combination dressing.
Egg and olive	Blend 1½ doz chopped hard-cooked eggs, 3 oz chopped stuffed olives, and 1 c combination dressing.

255

TABLE 11.3 (*Continued*)

Name	Ingredients
Cream cheese and egg	Blend 2 lb cream cheese, ¾ c chopped onion, ¾ c chopped green pepper, ½ c chili sauce, 2 c chopped walnuts, 12 chopped hard-cooked eggs, and 1 tsp salt.
Pimiento	Blend 1½ lb shredded American cheese, 1 c chopped pimiento, and 1 c cooked dressing.
Cheese and ripe olive	Blend 1½ lb shredded American cheese, 2 c chopped ripe olives, 1 c chopped green onions, 1 tsp curry powder, 1 tsp salt, and 1 c mayonnaise.
Date, carrot, and nut	Blend 1¼ lb chopped dates, 1¼ lb shredded carrots, 8 oz chopped walnuts, and 2 c combination dressing.
Date, nut, and orange	Blend 1½ lb ground dates softened with ½ c orange juice, 1 lb chopped nuts, 2 tbsp grated orange rind, and ½ c mayonnaise.
Apricot and cream cheese	Blend 2 lb cream cheese, 1 lb pureed apricots, 2 tbsp grated orange rind, and ½ c mayonnaise.
Carrot, raisin, and peanut	Blend 3 lb grated carrots with ½ lb chopped raisins, ½ lb chopped peanuts, and 2 c mayonnaise.
Apricot nut	Blend 1½ lb chopped cabbage, 1 lb chopped dried apricots, ½ lb chopped walnuts, and 2 c mayonnaise.

binding material. Desirable qualities for such food mixtures are ease of spreading and a consistency that makes them appetizing and easy to handle. The cut particles should be bound together strongly enough that they do not shatter and fall apart. Excessive moisture that dampens the bread and makes it soggy is to be avoided.

SANDWICH MAKING

The large amount of hand work in sandwich making emphasizes the need for proper sanitation practices and an equipment arrangement that promotes efficient work motions. Clean hands, clean equipment, continual refrigeration of perishable products, and careful methods of preparation are all necessary. The essential equipment should be assembled before sandwich preparation is begun. Items commonly needed include:

A large cutting board or table surface	Sharp French knife
Container for trimmings or refuse	Paring knife
Shallow bowls for ingredients	Swivel action parer
Scoops—appropriate size for fillings	Short, wide sandwich spreaders
Wrappings, if needed (waxed or plastic)	Spatula
Pans for storage	Plates and trays for service
Slicing knife or slicing machine	

Prepare spread, lettuce, and fillings. The butter or margarine for the spread should be kept at room temperature, neither melted nor too hard for smooth, easy spreading. Whip it to a consistency of heavy whipping cream. Arrange washed, dry, refrigerated lettuce in sandwich size pieces. Prepare mixtures for fillings and refrigerate them. Determine portion allowance for sliced foods and adjust slicer for proper number of slices per pound. Note whether the thickness of the slice is the best one for tenderness and satisfaction.

Arrange materials and equipment for two-handed activity; all the things to be used should be within easy reach of the hands during preparation, with the most frequently used items nearest the heart of the work area. Split open the bread packages near the center of the loaf, exposing slices, and place both halves at the top of the work area. This is to make possible, reaching the bread, taking a slice in each hand, and dropping them in straight rows, one at a time, from the top of the work area toward the worker. For six sandwiches to be arranged at one time, arrange slices four in a row across the board or work area and three down. The containers of spread and fillings should be placed at the right where they can be reached easily with the right hand. (See arrangement suggested in Figure 9.3.) Plan the flow of work so that it will move smoothly with a minimum of motion.

Figure 11.4 A refrigerated table to keep perishable fillings cold is desirable for preparation continued over an extended period of time. (Courtesy of the American Institute of Baking.)

Tastiness and satisfaction in a sandwich calls for adequate filling, but suitable economy requires portion control. Fillings made of spreadable mixtures should be measured into the sandwich by means of a standard size scoop. Sliced foods may be measured by the number of slices per pound. Chipped materials or those that have several thin slices per sandwich should be weighed and separated into portion quantities with waxed paper. This promotes speed in assembling the sandwich. The butter or margarine spread adds richness of flavor to sandwiches and helps to prevent moisture of the filling from soaking into the bread. If the sandwiches are to be stored, the spread should be used on both slices, but if they are to be used immediately, it is satisfactory to have spread on only one slice when the filling contains dressing and is suitably moist. When working with the three rows of four slices, spread the center slices on which the filling is to be placed.

Simplify motions in spreading and assembling sandwiches. There are two

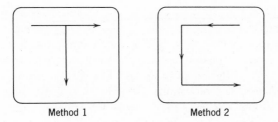

Method 1   Method 2

Figure 11.5 Simplified motions used when applying spread.

spreading movements recommended by experienced sandwich makers. (a) Pick up approximately 1 tablespoon of butter on the spreader and, starting at the top left-hand corner of the slice, deposit the butter by moving across the slice toward the right. Turn the spreader on the edge and spread the butter to the bottom of the slice, using care to cover the corners. (b) Start with the load of butter at the top, right-hand corner of the slice and move in a sweeping motion toward the left and down, counter-clockwise, and finish at the bottom right-hand corner. Try both methods and select the one that seems easiest. Avoid time-consuming, short, dabbing motions.

When making six sandwiches at a time, place the filling on the six center slices of bread. The filling should be placed at one time for as many sandwiches as are lined up on the board. Scoop filling mixtures onto the center of the bread slice. If it is soft enough to spread easily, two strokes, one toward the top of the slice and the other toward the bottom, are sufficient to spread the filling to the edges of the bread. Thicker fillings require four spreading motions, one from the center toward each of the four corners of the slice. Place the lettuce on the filling. Working with both hands, lift the outside slices and place them on top of the sandwiches. Cut the sandwiches and arrange them for service.

CANAPES, HORS D'OEUVRES, AND FANCY SANDWICHES

Canapés and hors d'oeuvres are savory morsels served as appetizers preceding a meal. Canapés are similar to fancy sandwiches and are prepared on some

Soft filling   Firm filling

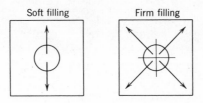

Figure 11.6 Motions used for spreading fillings.

kind of bread base. Fine textured breads, pastry, and crackers are commonly used. Hors d'oeuvres are tidbits of food, such as an assortment of fresh crisp vegetables, pickles, stuffed eggs, bits of fish, salami and other cold meats, attractively arranged without a bread base. Fancy sandwiches, although similar to canapés, differ in purpose and in ingredients; they are used as refreshments at teas and receptions. It is appropriate for fancy sandwiches to be more satisfying and less stimulating to the appetite. Many of the same foods may be used for either canapés or fancy sandwiches.

There are various terms used in different countries to denote the morsels of food used as appetizers preceding a meal. These include *zakouska* in Russia, *antipasto* in Italy, *t'i wei ping* in China, *smorgasbord* in Scandinavian countries, and *hors d'oeuvres* in France. In some of the countries these foods may constitute the major part of the meal. The French term is generally used in America. Food items for hors d'oeuvres may be used alone (bits of cheese, pickled herring or smoked oysters) or in various blends or combinations (foods combined on a pick, or stuffed foods like celery).

Dainty size and appearance makes a special appeal to appetites and is an important quality for canapés, hors d'oeuvres, and fancy sandwiches. The size should be small, the flavors delectable, and the appearance attractive. These foods are commonly eaten with the fingers and should be sufficiently firm to handle easily without crumbling or dripping. If the foods are damp or sticky, a fork or pick with which to eat them should be supplied. Assortments that present interesting contrasts in form, color, and flavor are

Figure 11.7 Toasted sandwiches rolled in cheese, minced chives, green pepper or onion, chopped nuts or sesame seeds may be used as a canape or an appealing accompaniment for soup or salad. (Courtesy of the American Institute of Baking.)

Figure 11.8   The bread is rolled around the filling and fastened with a pasty mixture, such as cream cheese, or skewered until the form is set.

desirable. This adds to attractiveness and provides sufficient variety to appeal to different tastes.

Foods used for canapés and hors d'oeuvres should be spicy, piquant, and/or savory. Well-seasoned butters are used as spreads for canapés. These may may be made with such stimulating foods as anchovy, caviar, devilled ham,

Figure 11.9   Sandwiches are filled with condensed bean soup, buttered on the outside and rolled, then dipped in a flavorful food and toasted. (Courtesy of the American Institute of Baking.)

liverwurst, and rich flavored cheeses. Herring, smoked oysters or clams, salami, marinated shrimp, cuts of cheese, savory bits of meat, olives and pickles are popular for hors d'oeuvres. Garnishes that add zest and interest include capers, tiny pickled onions, pimiento, cucumber pickles, tomato olives, young onion slices, and chutney bits. Canapés may be served either hot or cold.

Tiny pastry turnovers are popular when served hot. The pastry may be cut with a 2-inch biscuit cutter or into 2-inch squares and folded to form a triangle. Five suggestions for fillings are (a) caviar, minced onion, and lemon juice; (b) minced cooked chicken livers, crumbled crisp bacon, chopped hard-cooked egg, minced parsley, and mayonnaise; (c) smoked oysters, minced celery, and mayonnaise; (d) chopped ham and hard-cooked eggs, minced sweet pickle, mustard, and cooked salad dressing; (e) chopped lobster and mushrooms, shredded cheddar, horseradish, chopped stuffed olives, and mayonnaise.

Figure 11.10   There are numerous cutters and garnishes for fancy sandwiches. (Courtesy of the American Institute of Baking.)

Figure 11.11 Variety can be given through use of different fillings and garnishes. (Courtesy of the American Institute of Baking.)

Variety in color and shape adds appeal when arranging an assortment. To combine dark and light and bright and neutral colors helps enhance appearance. A few very dark items, such as black olives, prunes, or caviar, are needed to give strength and emphasis. Bright colors like those of tomatoes, bright fruit, and jelly, add gaiety and catch the attention. Cool colors and light, neutral shades are needed for contrast. Some of the sandwiches may be closed, and others open-faced. A wide variety of shapes is possible. The variety should be limited to produce an orderly rather than conglomerate appearance. The number to be served and the size of the trays on which the sandwiches are to be displayed influence the amount of variety that is desirable.

TABLE 11.4 COLORFUL FOODS APPROPRIATE FOR CANAPES AND FANCY SANDWICHES

Green

Asparagus tip	Arrange on top of cheese spread or sliced egg and garnish with pimiento strip.
Broccoli flowerlet	Cook until barely tender, marinate in French dressing, use with cheese spread or tomato slice.
Capers (tiny pickled buds)	Use to garnish fish, cheese and/or eggs.
Green celery rings	Arrange on meat, cheese, or egg spreads.
Chives	Snip and use as garnish on egg, cheese, or fish.
Cucumber, fresh and pickled	Slices may be used flat or cut half way through and twisted to form an attractive shape. If tender, the peel may be cut to simulate leaves in arrangements.
Green pepper	A bright, green color and pronounced flavor that may be used with fish, egg, and cheese mixtures.
Green olives	Stuffed with pimiento they supply attractive form and gay color for decorating many foods.
Watercress	The spicy, refreshing flavor harmonizes with many foods. The color is a rich green and the tiny leaves are dainty.

Red

Cherries	Fresh Bings, maraschino, salad cherries, and cooked, sweetened and thickened pie cherries are delicious and bright for decorating. These combine well with cream cheese.
Pimiento	The bright color and mild pepper flavor combines well with meat, cheese, vegetables, and eggs.

TABLE 11.4 (*Continued*)

Radish	Thin slices or small cuttings may be used for spicy flavor and bright color. Prepare shortly before serving.
Salami	This and other red cooked sausages may be used minced, sliced, or cut in forms. Slices may be stacked in alternate layers with cheddar or formed into tiny cornucopias filled with blue cheese mixture. Useful for decorating spreads.
Sweet red pepper	Use small cuts for rich color and pepper flavor.
Tomato	Slice cherry or 2-inch tomato, carefully remove seeds, place on 2-inch bread rounds spread with cream cheese and fill seed cavities with cream cheese with a pastry tip.

Pink

Apricots	Fresh, canned, or dried apricots combine well with cream cheese.
Ham	May be either sliced or minced.
Salmon	Freshly cooked or canned red salmon flakes or paste.
Shrimp	Tiny Alaska, sliced large, or shrimp paste.

White and Creamy White

Cauliflowerlets	Use raw or slightly cooked and marinated in French dressing.
Egg whites	Use in rings or minced.
Crabmeat	White shreds give variation in form as well as attractive whiteness.
Cream cheese	Softened and salted cream cheese is useful as a spread and as a garnish when put through a pastry tube.

TABLE 11.4 (*Continued*)

Swiss cheese	May be made into a spread, sliced, or slivered.
Onion	Tiny pickled slices of young onion, and small rings of sweet, mature white onions may be used.
Sesame seed	Flavor blends well with cheese, meats, and dried fruits. It may be sprinkled on top or rolled on the spread edges of sandwiches.
Yellow	
Egg yolk	Sieved yolk of hard-cooked egg is feathery and bright in appearance, and adds flavor richness.
Cheddar cheese	A mellow color and rich flavor that blends well with other foods.
Peaches	Spiced peaches combine well with cream cheese and chicken.
Pineapple	A light, creamy color and stimulating flavor to use with meats, cheeses, and other fruits.
Brown and Black	
Anchovy fillets or paste	Either flat or rolled fillets may be used. The flavor blends well with egg, asparagus, tomato, and cucumber.
Caviar	Costly, but attractive garnish for use with egg or onion, either fresh, minced or pickled whole.

TABLE 11.4 (Continued)

Chicken livers	Whole, minced, or made into paste; may be combined with pickle, egg, tomato or onion.
Black olives	May be cut into strips, sliced, or minced for garnish. Flavor blends with many foods.
Poppy seed	May be sprinkled on top or used to coat spread on sides of sandwiches. Flavor especially good with ham or cheddar.
Sardines	Use tiny whole or chunks with a savory spread; may be minced with celery and onion.
Spiced prunes	May be pitted and stuffed as an hors d'oeuvres or cut into forms for use as a garnish.
Truffle	An expensive mushroom form that is attractive as a garnish for meat, cheese, or egg sandwiches.
Sauted mushrooms	These may be minced, sliced, or cut into forms for garnishing meat, cheese, and egg sandwiches.
Smoked tongue	Use sliced or chopped.
Smoked oysters	Use whole or chopped with minced celery or cheddar spread.
Raisins	Plump with hot water and drain well for use whole, or grind for use as a paste or spread. Flavor blends well with cream cheese.

267

Flavor and richness of fancy sandwiches should be varied enough to please different tastes. Flavors may be piquant or sweet, delicate or pronounced, richly satisfying or light and stimulating. A social group may include calorie-watchers who wish light refreshments as well as those with hearty appetites. Light, refreshing, and colorful sandwiches may be made with tomato, cucumber, minced carrot, fresh berries, bright plums, and green grapes. Fresh fruits arranged on cream cheese spread and piped with cream cheese are especially colorful and appealing on a tray. A little powdered sugar blended into the cream cheese adds a welcome amount of sweetness with the fresh fruit. Dried fruit and nut mixtures, fish pastes, cheeses, and meats offer many choices for rich sandwiches. Some people favor sweet refresh-ments at teas and others prefer the more savory and stimulating meat, fish, and cheese mixtures.

Variation in texture and consistency adds to enjoyment. Pastes, spreads, and cream cheese so often used for fancy sandwiches are soft and smooth. Special care should be used to provide crispness. This may be supplied through crunchy fillings or a crisp bread base. Pastry cheese sticks or rolled fingers of bread that are filled and toasted may add welcome crispness. Nuts and crisp vegetables used as garnishes add texture in an assortment. Meat and fish salad mixtures in bite-size cream puffs are popular in texture and flavor.

Choose fine textured, day-old bread for fancy sandwiches. Slice it approxi-mately $\frac{1}{4}$-inch thick and the length of the loaf. The long slices permit more convenient and economical cutting into small shapes. The shapes may be made with biscuit cutters, cutters for fancy shapes, or cut into straight forms by using a sharp knife. A good appearance requires the shapes to be clean cut and well formed. Trim off the crusts to form straight edges. The crusts and trimmings may be saved for use as bread crumbs. Use a ruler for measuring to ensure accuracy and good form. Figure 11.12 shows measure-ments for cutting a 4 × 12-inch bread slice into small sandwiches. When making diamond shapes, a chubby shape is better than an elongated one, as slender tips of soft bread tend to break easily and are difficult to handle when covered with a soft, moist spread.

Last minute preparation is reduced if part of the sandwiches are of a type that can be made in advance. Pinwheel and ribbon sandwiches afford this advantage. They may be made the day before if refrigerated, and held for several days if frozen. Chilling makes the filling firm enough to slice well. Choose fillings and breads that are attractive in color. If artificial colors are used to intensity the natural colors in fillings (red with pimiento or green with parsley, for example) use special care to preserve a natural appearance. Sharp, unnatural colors should be avoided.

Ribbon sandwiches are pretty when made with alternate layers of dark

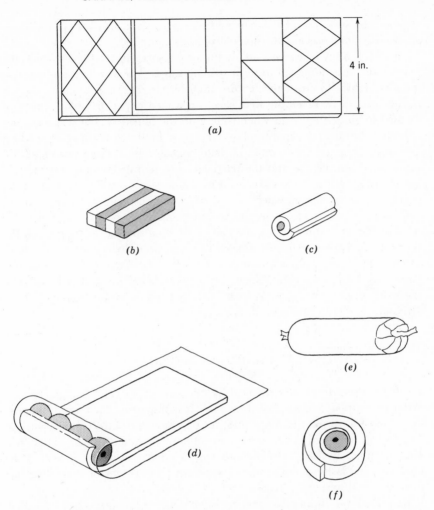

Figure 11.12   The shaping of fancy sandwiches. (*a*) Small diamonds $1\frac{1}{2} \times 2$ inches; rectangles $1\frac{1}{2} \times 2\frac{1}{4}$ inches; large diamonds $1\frac{3}{4} \times 2\frac{1}{2}$ inches; squares $1\frac{3}{4} \times 1\frac{3}{4}$ inches; diagonal cuts of $1\frac{3}{4}$ or 2-inch squares may be used for triangles. (*b*) Ribbon sandwich with alternate slices of dark and light bread. (*c*) Bread rolled around cheddar-cheese filling, to be toasted and served warm. (*d*) Pinwheel sandwich with olive center, to be chilled and sliced. (*e*) Finished pinwheel rolled in wax paper for chilling. (*f*) Sliced pinwheel.

and light bread, and put together with colorful fillings. Different fillings may be used for the separate layers. If different fillings are used, combine those that provide an appealing harmony in flavor. It is important for the spreads or fillings to be sufficiently pasty in consistency to hold the layers together when sliced. If chopped materials like meats, fish, eggs, olives, and pickles are used, be sure to add enough binding materials in the form of butter or cream cheese to prevent the layers from falling apart.

Pinwheel sandwiches are made with a long slice of bread from which the crusts have been removed to form straight edges. Use a rolling pin and roll the slice lightly to crush the texture slightly. Use care not to compress soft breads too much. Place the long slices on waxed paper or a cloth that can be used to guide the bread when rolling up the pinwheel. Use a spread that is both colorful and capable of serving as a binder to hold the pinwheel in shape; chopped foods must be held together by a large percentage of butter or cream cheese and the particles must be fine enough that they do not interfere with slicing. A colorful food that slices readily should be used for the center for the pinwheel; a row of stuffed olives tightly placed end to end, or long strips of sweet pickle and pimiento serve nicely. Place the material for the center across one end of the long slice of bread and roll the sandwich around it. The bread slice needs to be rolled smoothly and with enough pressure to form a roll similar to a jelly roll. Wrap it tightly in waxed paper or plastic and chill thoroughly before slicing into sandwiches. The slices should be from $\frac{1}{2}$- to $\frac{3}{4}$-inch thick, depending on the diameter of the roll and the size of sandwich desired.

SANDWICH MERCHANDISING

Sandwich appeal can be enhanced by the manner in which sandwiches are arranged on plates or displayed for sale. It is important for them to appear neat, colorful, fresh, and moist and not dry, soggy, or crushed. Patrons are especially interested in the kind and amount of filling. Recognizing this, modern merchandisers exhibit sandwiches so that the fillings appear in the most enticing fashion, either through the cut and arrangement on the plate or in the transparent wraps for display.

Readiness for immediate service is an aspect that appeals to patrons. Ensuring speed often requires preportioning of fillings. This may help to reduce material cost and standardize quality as well. Proper service materials and wrapping techniques help to promote speed and good appearance.

Figure 11.13 Sandwich buyers like to know what kind and how much filling is in a sandwich. This can be promoted by putting the bread together with filling on top in a transparent wrap. (Courtesy of the American Institute of Baking.)

Figure 11.14   A variety of sandwich wraps are available to fit specific needs in selling hot or cold sandwiches. (Courtesy of the American Institute of Baking.)

Figure 11.15 Sandwich bags, made of plastic films, glassine, wet-waxed paper, or foil are ideal for wrapping sandwiches. Purchase only those which seal easily and are moisture-vapor proof. Either cut or uncut sandwiches can be wrapped in bags. The first step is to place the sandwich bag so that the short edge of open end faces up from counter top toward worker. (Courtesy of the American Institute of Baking.)

Figure 11.16 Flat sheets of wrapping material can be neatly folded to provide attractive packages for either flat or triangular sandwiches. (Courtesy of the American Institute of Baking.)

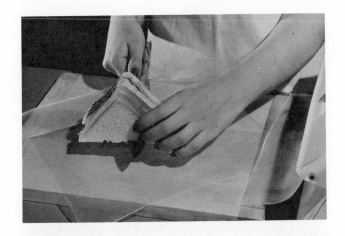

SUGGESTED LABORATORY EXPERIENCE

1. Examine different varieties of bread and rolls from the standpoint of their suitability for sandwich making. Consider fillings most appealing for each variety.
2. Test drying factors—use slices from the same loaf, prepare them in the following ways, and allow them to stand the same length of time (at least two hours, preferably over night).
   (a) In a waxed paper bag or wrap.
   (b) In a plastic bag or wrap.
   (c) On a serving plate in refrigerator covered with a waxed paper.
   (d) On a serving plate in refrigerator with waxed paper wrap covered with a damp cloth.
3. Count the number of sandwich slices in the loaves of bread judged suitable for sandwiches and determine the cost per slice according to the current price.
4. Prepare a sandwich spread. Measure the quantity required to spread one slice, starting with $\frac{1}{2}$ tablespoon and increasing or decreasing according to need. Calculate the cost of the spread.
5. Prepare a filling mixture. Measure the quantity needed for a tasty sandwich. Determine quantity in relation to volume of a standard scoop. Calculate cost.
6. Practice motions in spreading that covers corners and edges of bread as well as center. Which proves simplest and easiest?
7. Prepare pinwheel and ribbon sandwiches. Wrap, store and freeze for later use.
8. Cut, prepare, and decorate fancy sandwiches. Record time and evaluate cost.
9. Slice meat and slice cheddar into suitable sandwich portions. Calculate cost.

REVIEW QUESTIONS AND ANSWERS

1. Enumerate qualities desirable in sandwiches.

Fresh, rich satisfying flavor, moist texture, piquancy, and trim appearance.

2. What flavor is desirable in bread?

Rich cereal flavor.

3. How should bread be stored to protect quality?

In its original wrapper, either at room temperature or frozen.

4. What is a pullman loaf?

A square shaped loaf, baked in a covered pan.

5. What are the most popular breads for sandwiches?

White and whole wheat or graham.

6. What is a spring-top loaf?

A loaf baked in a pan without a cover, which has been allowed to expand and form a rounded top.

7. How much spread is required for 100 sandwiches?

About 3 pounds.

8. What is a savory butter?

One to which flavoring ingredients, such as lemon, parsley or chives, have been added.

9. How much filling is contained by a Number 30 scoop?

Approximately 1 ounce or $2\frac{1}{5}$ tablespoons.

10. Should the leanest meat only be used for hamburgers?

Some fat is needed for rich flavor and juiciness.

11. Approximately what percentage of fat is desirable?

About 18 to 20%.

12. What are the results when using hamburger with 25 to 30% fat?

High shrinkage and excess fat on the grill.

13. What is a canapé?

A small sandwich made with savory foods on a bread base.

14. How does it differ from a fancy sandwich?

It should be stimulating rather than satisfying to the appetite. It is used as an appetizer rather than a refreshment.

15. What are hors d'oeuvres?

Savory tidbits of food that stimulate the appetite.

16. Should hors d'oeuvres be large or small?

Dainty size adds to good appearance and appeal to the appetite.

17. Describe steps in preparing pinwheel sandwiches.

Slice day-old bread $\frac{1}{4}$-inch thick the length of the loaf. Roll it lightly with a rolling pin and spread with a flavorful, colorful food, place a food across one end to form center and roll sandwich firmly around it. Wrap and chill before slicing.

18. How are ribbon sandwiches made?

Use slices of dark and light breads. Spread them with colorful filling that is pasty enough to hold them together, and arrange them in layers to form an attractive ribbonlike appearance. Wrap in paper and chill before cutting.

19. Why is sanitation of special concern in sandwich making?

Because of the hand contact with foods in preparation, and because the foods are highly perishable and favorable to bacterial growth.

20. Describe motions used in applying spread.

(a) Deposit butter in motion from left to right across top of slice, then rake with edge of spreader from top to bottom.

(b) Spread top half in motion from top right moving toward top left and down to left bottom of slice and then to right bottom corner.

21. How should filling mixtures be added to sandwich?

Scoop with appropriate size scoop, to the center of slice which has been spread with butter, margarine or mayonnaise. If filling is soft, spread filling top half from center to top of slice and lower half with motion from center to bottom of slice. If filling is firm, spread in four motions toward each corner.

22. How can filling portions be controlled?

Moist fillings can be controlled through use of standard size scoops for applying filling, and sliced fillings by weight of slice, and if particles are small as with thin slices by separating weighed amounts with waxed paper.

23. What should be included in the portion cost for a sandwich?

Slices of bread, spread used, filling, lettuce, and garnishes.

24. What points are to be considered when choosing a plan of cutting?

Appearance of arrangement, ease in handling, and simplified motions in cutting and arranging.

BIBLIOGRAPHY

American Institute of Baking, Consumer Service Department, "Modern Sandwich Methods," Chicago, 1952.

American Institute of Baking, Consumer Service Department, "Turn to Sandwiches," Chicago, 1957.

Band, Asta and Edith Rode, "Open Sandwiches and Cold Lunches," Jul. Gjellerups Forlag, Copenhagen, 1955.

Beard, James, "Hors d'Oeuvres and Canapés," New York: Barrows, 1941.

Carson, Byrta and MaRue Carson Ramee, "How to Plan and Prepare Meals," New York: McGraw-Hill, 1962.

Cronan, Marion L. and June C. Atwood, "Foods in Homemaking," Peoria, Ill.: Chas. A. Bennett, 1965.

Cushman, Edith M., "Here's How to Select and Use Refrigerators," School Lunch Journal, June, 1957.

Finance, Charles, "Buffet Catering," New York: Ahrens, 1958.

Globe Slicing Machine Co., Inc., "Specifications and Service Manual," Stamford, Conn.

Good Housekeeping's Sandwich Manual, New York: Hearst, 1961.

The Hobart Manufacturing Company, "Slicing Machine Instruction Manual," Troy, Ohio.

Kotschevar, Lendal H., "Quantity Food Production," Berkeley, Calif.: McCutchan, 1964.

Kotschevar, Lendal H. and Margaret McWilliams, "Understanding Food," New York: Wiley, 1969.

Kotschevar, Lendal H. and Margaret E. Terrell, "Food Service Planning: Layout and Equipment," New York: Wiley, 1961.

Litman, C. K. and Louise A. K. Frolich, "Portion-planned Refrigeration," *Volume Feeding Magazine*, **8** (6) 26, June, 1957.

National Restaurant Association, "Sandwich Maker's Album," Chicago, 1956.

National Restaurant Association, "Sandwich Meals are Profitable," Technical Bulletin 122, Chicago, 1956.

Shank, Dorothy E., Natalie K. Fitch, and Pauline A. Chapman, "Guide to Modern Meals," St. Louis: McGraw-Hill, 1964.

Sunkist Growers, Inc., "Fresh Citrus Quantity Handbook," Los Angeles, 1959.

U.S. Department of Health, Education and Welfare, "Dressings for Foods," Washington, D.C.: Food and Drug Administration, June, 1957.

U.S. Department of Health, Education and Welfare, "Quantity Food Preparation, A Suggested Guide," Washington, D.C., 1967.

SECTION IV

Cooking Section

CHAPTER 12   Meat Preparation and Cooking Equipment

CHAPTER 13   Dairy Products and Eggs

CHAPTER 14   Poultry

CHAPTER 15   Fish and Shellfish

CHAPTER 16   Selection and Preparation of Beef

CHAPTER 17   Selection and Preparation of Veal

CHAPTER 18   Selection and Preparation of Lamb

CHAPTER 19   Pork and Variety Meats

Bibliography for Section IV

12.

Meat Preparation and Cooking Equipment

A golden brown color and crisp crusty surface adds delectable qualities to many foods. Dry heat cooking or deep fat frying are common means for producing these qualities. The caramelization of the surface of meat with dry heat adds to the richness of the meat flavor. Browning makes the appearance more appealing. Broiling and grilling are quick cooking methods that permit preparation to order and are especially favored by restaurants that cater to a fluctuating patronage.

These methods of cooking are not new. Cooking over an open fire or on hot stones predate ranges, grills, and broilers in culinary history, and are small-quantity methods currently used for pleasure or necessity. In camping or where need is acute, simple ranges are sometimes made out of empty cans or with a metal sheet or rack balanced between bricks, stones or wood blocks. The terms grill and griddle are used interchangeably for cooking on a flat hot surface.

Equipment to prepare protein foods has special importance. The protein products are generally the most costly and labor to handle them is paid the highest rate in the average kitchen. They are foods that are highly perishable. It is best economy, therefore, to have the proper equipment for meat cutting and storage, and to keep it in satisfactory condition. Carelessness can lead to serious cases of food poisoning. Flavor changes that lead to dissatisfaction with quality as well as decomposition can result in sizable expense. Meat should not be allowed to remain out of refrigeration and at temperatures favorable to the growth of bacteria. All utensils used in handling meat should be well washed, rinsed, and air dried.

283

MEAT PREPARATION EQUIPMENT

Sharp tools and a suitable surface on which to work are important in meat cutting. Where very much cutting is to be done, it is well to have a meat block. If the practice is to purchase pan-ready meats, a heavy cutting board may meet needs adequately. Meat blocks range in size from 18 × 18 × 10 inches to 35 × 35 × 18 inches, and are supported on legs of a length to furnish the desired height for working (30 to 34 inches). Heavy cutting boards of laminated maple or hard rubber are available in thickness varying from 1 to 3 inches and in several dimensions in length and width.

Where a block is used, a knife holder may be fastened to the side of the block so that the knife handles do not project above the surface of the block. This arrangement is useful in protecting the sharp cutting edge of knives and for holding them in convenient position for use. A table drawer adjacent to the cutting area may be preferred. The sharp edges can be protected by arranging a strip of wood in the bottom of the drawer that will hold the knives apart. Use a wood strip 1 × 2 inches wide and as long as the width of the drawer or area to be used. Saw notches approximately $1\frac{1}{4}$ inch deep on 2 to 3 inch centers and of sufficient width for the knife blades to fit into them easily. Locate the guide a distance from the front of the drawer, sufficient to readily accommodate the longest handle to be stored.

Few kitchens cut enough meat to have a power saw. Cutting tools must be kept sharp for the best trimming and slicing (see Chapter 2 for methods of sharpening). This includes the cleaver, which is more likely to shatter bones if it is not very sharp. The cleaver should be used as little as possible because of the possibility of causing bone splinters in the meat surrounding the bones. A hand saw is a better tool to use for brittle bones in the legs or ribs. A saw with a 20 to 25-inch blade is satisfactory for use in the average large kitchen. A power saw is not needed unless a great deal more meat cutting is done than is customary in most large kitchens today.

Cleaning and Care of Meat Equipment

Proper care of the cutting surface is essential for sanitation and good quality in the meat. Meat particles and blood left on the cutting surface in a warm kitchen will promote bacterial growth that may be a serious health hazard. The delicate flavor of fresh meat can be spoiled through picking up off-flavors from the meat block or other surface on which it is laid. The block or cutting board should be cleaned after each use and before a product of a different kind is placed on it; for example, if the block has been used for cutting beef, it should be cleaned before cutting lamb and veal. Off-flavors are often blamed on the product that should be credited to careless handling and improper cleaning of meat equipment.

The cleaning of the meat block requires a good metal scraper and a steel brush. Water should not be used, because it softens the wood, causes it to expand, and weakens the glue that holds the laminated wood together. The block is to be kept dry. The scraper and the brush removes the juices, soil, and a small amount of wood surface. Care is needed to use the entire surface of the top and to occasionally give the block a quarter turn to promote even wear.

The scraper and brush are *not* to be used on the cutting boards. These may be washed but should be wiped dry immediately. They should never be placed in very hot water or allowed to soak. This weakens the glue and allows the wood to pull apart, thus making lodging places for soil. When not in use, the cutting boards should be stood up in a fashion that allows air to circulate around them to evenly dry the entire surfaces.

Meat tools of wood or that have wood handles need to be cleaned with similar care. They should be thoroughly washed in detergent solutions, rinsed, and dried. Wood should not be subjected to extremely hot water or allowed to soak. Hot water soaks into the wood and causes it to expand, and when it dries it tends to crack and openings are enlarged so that it is less sanitary.

Observe safety precautions when handling cutting tools. Avoid greasy hands or tool handles that may cause slipping. Do not set meat or pans on top of cutting tools on which the fingers may be cut when the objects are picked up. Do not overcrowd work areas so that work must be done at a disadvantage. Keep the "holding hand" in a safe position when handling the cleaver. The free, or holding hand, should be as far as possible from the path of the cleaver. Use the proper tool for the job to be done; use a boning knife for boning, and a slicer for slicing. Clean up any bits of meat or fat that may fall to the floor before they are the cause of falls.

RANGES

Ranges are favored for kitchens where menus call for a variety of pan-cooking of foods, such as the pan-frying of fish, eggs, and poultry, and for sauce making. The type and volume of preparation required governs the size of range and type of cooking top needed. There are four types of cooking tops generally available which vary in sturdiness and intended purposes. (a) The fastest heating and lightest weight have open elements. The heating elements in the electric models are in circular open coils with a reflector plate underneath. Gas models have an open grate and the flame comes in direct contact with the cooking containers. These models are favored by those who wish fast heating for short periods of cooking.

(b) Sturdiness to support cooking containers is added by covering the heating elements with a light weight steel plate. This slows speed of heating to the extent that the steel plate must be heated before the cooking container becomes hot. (c) Heavy-duty ranges have cast steel, sectional plates that are much heavier, and require much longer to preheat. It is well to allow them to preheat for 10 to 15 minutes before cooking is begun. The plates are sturdy and when fully heated supply a steady, uniform heat over a larger surface. This is the best type for use with heavy pots and where continuous cooking with a variety of pan sizes are used. (d) The fourth type is the one with a griddle top used by placing the food directly on the cooking surface. Only food, never pans, is to be placed on a griddle surface. Later in this chapter the use and care of griddles are discussed.

A range may or may not include an oven. The advisability of having an oven depends on need and the amount of other oven space available. A high shelf for the range is optional. If considerable frying or other cooking from which there is a great deal of smoke, steam, and fumes is to be done on the range, a high shelf-type hood is recommended. The hood with filters located

Figure 12.1 A heavy-duty range with a sectional top. (Courtesy of the General Electric Company.)

below high shelf height are low enough to the cooking surface for ventilating efficiency. It is also low enough for ease in cleaning. Removable filters may be cleaned thoroughly with soap and water at the pot sink or washed in the dishwasher. Those with baffles need to be regularly scrubbed down inside and wiped dry.

Cleaning of the Range

There is likely to be considerable dripping and spattering of food in the normal use of a range. Some of the food particles become charred and may be brushed free with a heavy bristled brush, steel wool, or a scraper. Other particles cling, clog, or build up as soil that requires more vigorous cleaning. For best performance of the range and for satisfactory sanitation, it is important to keep it clean. The grease troughs and drip pans should be removed and cleaned daily. They can be washed at the pot sink in the same manner as a utensil. Spillage on any exterior area should be wiped up as quickly as possible to prevent hardening through cooking or drying. The open grates and the round plates should be cleaned weekly, or more often according to need, with a damp cloth or brush and scouring powder. Any carbonized material should be removed with steel wool. The heavy duty plates should be cleaned weekly or oftener, depending on use and soil build up, with a fine-grit griddle stone. Use a little grease and rub with the grain of the metal while the surface is still warm. *Do not use steel wool* as it may damage the surface and leave particles that could get into the food.

Spillage and the general accumulation of soil necessitates special cleaning under open types of heating elements. The reflectors should be washed and kept bright and the areas under the elements wiped with a damp cloth. Make sure that openings in burners of a gas range are unclogged and permit free flow of the fuel for a good flame. Many burners are designed for easy removal for thorough cleaning as necessary. Scrub them with a brush and soap and water. Be cautious of using scouring powder that may clog the small holes. Reassemble the burners after they have been thoroughly dried. Check the flame for a uniform blue flame. If the flame is yellow, the air mixer slide should be adjusted to admit less air until the flame is blue. A yellow flame supplies less heat and deposits black discoloration on the cooking utensils.

Use of the Range Top

Efficient use of fuel for range top cooking calls for the proper utensils. Select utensils with flat bottoms, straight sides, and tight fitting lids. Warped pans do not heat quickly and evenly. Iron heats more slowly but gives an even distribution of heat. Stainless steel is spotty in heat conduction; this results in "hot spots" that stick and burn. Pans with aluminum or copper core or clad surface distribute heat more evenly. High heat may be used to bring the heat of the cooking surface to desired temperature for cooking and then the heat reduced to moderate or low temperature for continued cooking.

GRIDDLES

Separate griddles are available in many sizes ranging from one with a cooking top approximately 16 inches square to one from 22 to 24 inches from front to back and as long as production capacity requires or labor is available to properly handle. Foods cooked on griddles are of a type that require individual portion handling. There is a limit to the number of items one grill cook can tend satisfactorily. Long griddles may be custom built or specific lengths may be secured through placing two or more griddles end to end, each of which may measure 30, 36, 48, or 72 inches long. Important selection points for griddles include uniform heating of the cooking surface, speed of temperature recovery, sectional control of heat that provides different temperatures simultaneously for cooking different products, reliable thermostatic control, suitable retention of heat, sturdiness of the griddle, adequate provision for the removal of grease, and ease of cleaning.

Use of the Griddle

Before placing food on a new griddle, clean it with a damp cloth and a mild detergent and rinse it with a damp cloth rung out of clean water. Wipe it dry and season it. Griddles should be seasoned before use and after each time that they have been thoroughly cleaned. This is of special importance before cooking any food that contains little fat. To season a griddle, preheat it to 400°F, brush with a thin film of cooking oil, and allow the oil to remain 2 minutes. Wipe off the surplus oil and brush with a fresh film of oil and allow to remain on the hot griddle for 2 minutes. Again wipe free of surplus oil. The griddle is now ready for use. Preheat to the temperature required for the specific preparation.

Cleaning and Care of the Griddle

Clean the griddle surface with a wire brush or flexible spatula after each use to remove excess fat and food. Thoroughly clean and wipe out the grease trough daily or as needed. Wash the drip tray and wipe dry. Empty and wash the grease pan daily. The cooking surface of griddles that are

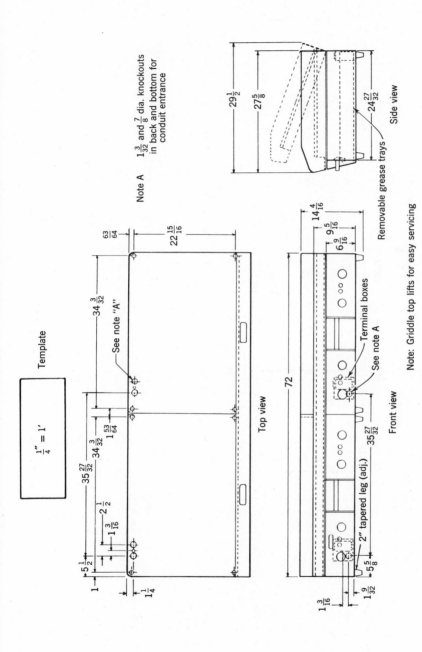

Figure 12.2   Top, front, and side views of a 72-inch griddle. (Courtesy of the General Electric Company.)

TABLE 12.1 SUGGESTED TEMPERATURES AND TIME FOR GRIDDLE COOKING

Food	Control Setting*	Time in Minutes**	Food	Control Setting*	Time in Minutes**
Ham salad sandwich	375	3 to 4	Canadian bacon	350	2 to 3
Hamburgers	350	3 to 4	Sausage links	350	3
Cheeseburgers	350	3 to 4	Sausage patties	350	3
Cheese sandwich	375	3 to 4	French toast	350	2 to 3
Frankfurters	325	2 to 3	Pancakes	375	2
Minute steaks—Med.	400	3 to 4	American fries	375	3 to 4
Club steak—1 in. thick	400	3 to 5	Potato patties	375	3 to 4
medium			Scrambled eggs	300	1 to 2
Ham steak	375	3 to 4	Hard-fried eggs	300	3
Boiled ham	375	2	Soft-fried eggs	300	2
Bacon	350	2 to 3	Sunny-side-up eggs	300	2

*Grill temperature Control Dial should be set approximately 50° higher than griddle temperature to obtain products of desired brownness and doneness.

**Time given is for griddling only. When using the grill section of a Griddle-Grill, allow foods to cook only half of this time.

(Courtesy of the General Electric Company.)

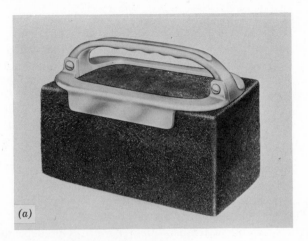

Figure 12.3 Griddle bricks (*a*) with and (*b*) without handle. (Courtesy of Bloomfield Industries, Inc.)

used a great deal should be thoroughly cleaned at least once each week. Rub the metal with pumice or griddle stone, rubbing with the grain of the metal, while the griddle is warm. *Do not use steel wool.* Clean with a damp cloth as described for a new griddle; wipe dry and reseason.

OVENS

Selection

An oven is one of the most important pieces of cooking equipment in the average kitchen. It should be selected to fit the special uses and capacity of the particular establishment. Variation for selection includes type of fuel for heating, type and size of decks, decks that move or are stationary, compartment heights, and conventional or convection heating. Regardless of the type chosen there are certain qualities essential for good performance. These include:

1. Adequate temperature delivered uniformly throughout the oven compartment. This is required for uniform baking of products without having to move them during baking.

2. A suitable range of temperature. The high temperature should be hot enough for baking pastry and low enough for cooking meat or holding food hot for service. Calibration from 100 to 500°F is recommended.

3. Reliable temperature control. This involves a reliable thermostat and effective insulation to prevent heat loss.

4. Speed of temperature recovery. This depends on the quantity and quality of the heating elements. Both loads of cold food and opening the door for inspection lower oven temperature. If recovery is slow, the baking temperature may not be the one that is best for the specific foods.

Figure 12.4   A reel oven with six shelves, each with capacity for five bun pans provides for a large number of meals.

5. Level, easy-to-reach shelves. Fluid mixtures, such as cake batters, custards, and pie fillings require a level shelf for even depth. Easy-to-reach shelves, that do not require the use of a peel, saves labor time when filling the oven. The single, bun-pan depth of the cabinet oven and the shelves of the reel oven are examples of easy-to-reach shelves.

6. Appropriate capacity. A frequent complaint in large kitchens is "too little oven space." Use care in estimating needed capacity.

7. Easy to operate and to maintain. Simple directions are easiest to under- and lessen chances of error. Cleanability is important in maintenance.

Certain special features improve convenience or usefulness of ovens and should be evaluated when selecting one. A glass in the door and inside lights facilitate inspection of products. A timer to guard baking time saves labor time and may prevent overcooking. A steam connection in the oven is desirable when baking crusty breads.

The kind of preparation to be done influences choice of conventional versus convection heating. The forced-air heating, by means of a fan in the oven, causes faster penetration of heat and reduces cooking time. The forced circulation of heat makes possible a more compact arrangement with more

Figure 12.5 A convection oven provides compact baking facility. Fan for moving the air is located in back of oven. (Courtesy of the General Electric Company.)

shelves in a given space. The oven compartment accommodates an 18 × 26 inch bun sheet and may have from 6 to 11 shelves. Meat research seems to indicate that slow penetration of heat yields a more tender product than fast penetration at the same oven temperature. Penetration of heat is speeded up when metal skewers, steam, or convection are used. Conventional ovens are preferable for roasting and a convection oven has special value in quick heating of casserole dishes, toasting sandwiches, and baking of cakes and quick breads. Each type of oven has strong points in its favor and selection calls for evaluation in terms of the use for which the oven is required.

Operation

Preheat the oven in ample time before it is needed. The heavy-duty ovens require from 45 minutes to an hour to heat to 425°F. Many kitchens never turn electric ovens off completely, but turn them to low for standby or overnight. This enables the cook or baker to raise the oven temperature more quickly for breakfast preparation, thus saving several minutes of labor time. When the oven is heated from cold or room temperature, allow the oven

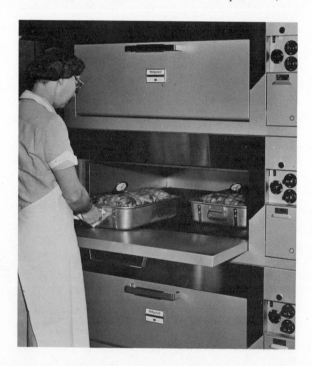

Figure 12.6   Cabinet oven showing 12-inch roasting decks and protective stainless steel trim.

Figure 10.1 Salads should be crisp, cold, colorful, and attractively arranged. (Courtesy of Western Iceberg Lettuce, Inc.)

Figure 15.1 Fish provides a delicious addition to meals as soup, salad, or entree. (Courtesy of the U.S. Fish and Wildlife Service, Bureau of Commercial Fisheries.)

Figure 16.1 Rib roast of beef is a favorite meat. (Courtesy of the National Livestock and Meat Board.)

Figure 21.1 Bread, a universally liked food, is a valuable medium for improving nutrition for both rich and poor. (Courtesy of the American Institute of Baking.)

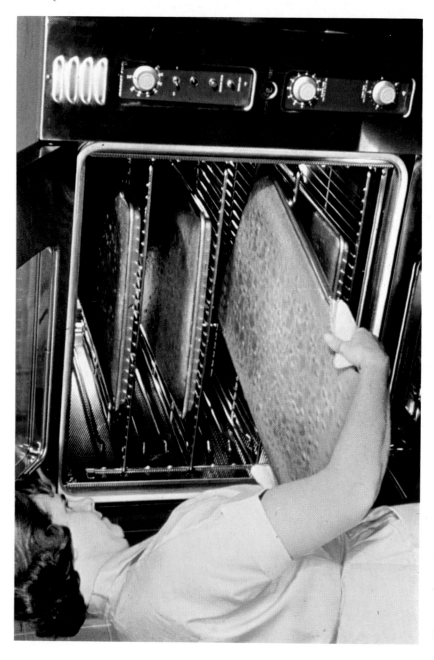

Figure 22.1 A golden sheet of cake with good contour calls for (*a*) proper blending of ingredients, (*b*) suitable weight of batter for size of pan, (*c*) correct baking time and temperature, (*d*) even distribution of heat in oven, and (*e*) a level oven shelf.

door to be open during the first 10 minutes of heating to avoid water condensation in the oven. Set the thermostat to the temperature required for baking.

Load the oven evenly, spacing pans away from each other and the sides of the oven, to ensure uniform circulation of heat. In a gas oven load the compartment that contains the thermostat element first. This is usually the lower compartment. As soon as the oven is loaded, set the timer to the required baking time. When setting a timer, turn it to the 10-minute setting, continue on for a higher setting and turn it back for a lower setting. It is not good practice to add cold food to the compartment after baking has started, and doors should be opened as little as possible to prevent lowering the baking temperature. When baking has been completed turn the oven off or set at the standby temperature.

Maintenance

Keep the oven interior and shelves wiped or brushed clean. When necessary use a long-handled scraper, wire brush, or spatula to remove soil from the shelves or decks. *Do not pour water or use a soaking wet cloth inside the oven.* Sprinkle salt on hardened food particles, close the door and heat the oven to 450°F and allow to stand until the particles have carbonized, then scrape clean with a spatula. Shelves in many models can be removed for special scrubbing at a pot sink. After they are scrubbed and dried, be sure that they are replaced with all of the clips correctly attached; this helps prevent warping. Heat the oven to 350°F with the door open to completely dry the shelves.

The interior finishes of ovens differ in material and require certain variations in cleaning methods. The finish on aluminized or painted steel liners will be removed if coarse abrasives and caustic solutions are used in cleaning. Use one of the cleaners that is recommended for this type of finish, such as Mr. Clean, Soilax "A," Tide, or Superglo. When finishes have disappeared through wear, then use a wire brush and grease solvent to clean them and remove the residue of finish. Refinish the interior with a heat-resistant aluminum paint. Use sudsy water and a damp sponge or soft cloth for cleaning a teflon interior, then sponge it off with clean water and wipe dry.

Use care to remove food, grease, or carbon deposits from valves, door handles, and edges of doors. A complete, even closure is necessary for proper heating and utilization of fuel. When doors do not close fully, escaping steam and vapors cause deterioration of the exterior finish around the door.

The exterior finish may be black iron, a "Permalucent" enamel, or stainless steel. The black-finish should be cleaned with a cloth saturated with a light oil when the oven is cold, then wiped dry with a clean cloth. Use a cloth and warm water with a mild detergent for cleaning enamel finishes, follow with a clear water rinse, then wipe dry. If grease stains occur that cannot be removed with regular cleaning, use a silicone-base polish and follow directions given for the particular polish. Do not use scouring pads or other abrasive material. Stainless steel can be cleaned with soap and water, rinsed, and wiped dry. A self-soaping scouring pad may be used for stubborn stains, but always be careful to rub with the grain or polish lines in the steel.

Adjustment

Oven temperatures should be checked for accuracy regularly. A competent service man from the manufacturing or utility company should check thermostat calibration and make the necessary adjustments of the heating elements. Follow manufacturer's directions closely for the initial lighting of pilots or starting and conditioning of the ovens.

BROILERS

Chief differences between broilers are related to the fuels used for cooking. The fuels commonly used are charcoal, electricity, and gas. Broilers may be designed for the meat to be laid on a grid above the heat source or below it.

Figure 12.7 A small electric char-broiler. (Courtesy of the General Electric Company.)

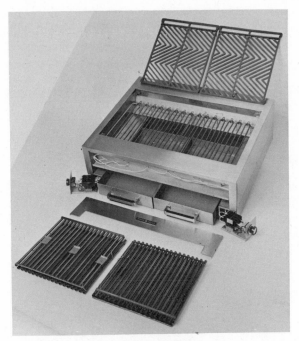

Figure 12.8   A char-broiler showing removal of parts for cleaning. (Courtesy of the General Electric Company.)

Charcoal is favored by many people for the flavor imparted to the meat from the charcoal smoke and from the smoke from the burning fat that drips from the meat during cooking. Hardwood charcoals that have a good flavored smoke are favored, but are somewhat difficult to use because of flaming. Briquets do not produce a good flavor but are easier to use because they flame less. Managing the heat as well as the broiling calls for skill.

Electric and gas char-broilers have grids above the source of heat in a similar fashion to the charcoal broilers. Fats, dripping from the meat during cooking, burn and produce some smoke flavor in the meat. The heat is easier to control than with charcoal, but with either method, if the heat is too intense and flames are allowed to lick up around the meat, the meat will be dry and firm.

There are many makes of broilers available that have adjustable grids and the heat source above the grid. They may be selected from sizes that range from the small back-shelf or salamander type, with capacity for 25 steaks per hour to the large, heavy-duty models that can process 140 or 150 12-ounce steaks per hour. When selecting a broiler, it is well to choose one that will handle the required load and that is convenient to use. Convenience includes having a grid at a height that is easy to reach for loading or viewing during cooking, and that can be readily exposed for turning or tending the meat. It should be easy to adjust for desired temperatures. Grease should not be allowed to collect in grease trays, which should be easy to remove often enough for safety and good sanitation. Broilers should be installed with proper ventilation facility to remove smoke and fumes from cooking. The baffles and/or filters should be within easy reach for frequent and thorough cleaning.

Operation

Broilers should be preheated at high temperature before use. This, with the electric model shown in Figure 12.9 calls for turning both switches to *high* for approximately 13 minutes. The time to preheat broilers of different makes

Figure 12.9   Electric broiler and cabinet. (Courtesy of the General Electric Company.)

varies from 5 to 30 minutes. After preheating, the temperature control should be adjusted to that desired for cooking. If the broiler is to be used for bar-becuing at low temperature and a long time, slow cooking is required.

Before broiling it is well to rub the grid with suet or oil to prevent sticking. This is especially important when broiling fish. The food may be marinated in oil. Excess oil should be shaken off before it is placed on the grid. If deep-brown grid marks or branding is desired on steaks, raise the empty grid to a position close to the source of heat and allow it to remain from 5 to 10 minutes to become very hot. Place the oil-dipped meat on the grid, and locate the grid at the proper position for broiling according to the degree of doneness desired. Approximate distances recommended for the placement of the grid from the source of heat (when broiling meat) are listed below.

Rare: Place from 1 to 2 inches from heat for fast browning of exterior before heat is conducted to interior.
Medium: Place 3 to 4 inches from heat to allow more cooking of interior before complete browning of outside.
Well done: Place 4 inches from the heat.

Broil meat on one side for approximately half of the total cooking time. When browned, season and turn meat, and brown the other side. Place on a

Figure 12.10   For large volume production at Annapolis, steaks are cooked on a traveling belt in infra-red broilers. (Courtesy of Food Management In Schools and Colleges.)

heated plate and serve as quickly as possible. If it is necessary to hold the food before service, as when serving a large group at a banquet, place the food in a warming cabinet or oven at a temperature of 140 to 160°F immediately after cooking. The lower temperature is the one to use for rare steaks and the higher one for well done ones.

Care and Cleaning

Keep broilers clean. Grids and baffles may be scrubbed with detergent and a brush. The inside of the broiler should be wiped with a damp cloth and a long-handled brush and a scraper should be used to remove food particles. *Do not use water or abrasives* in the broiler. The grid may be removed for scouring by pulling it forward and lifting it at a 45-degree angle to release the roller guides from the slot. Wash the outside of the broiler with a non-caustic cleaning compound and water, rinse, and wipe dry.

(a)

DEEP FAT FRYERS

A sizable percentage of the cooking done in many restaurants is done in deep fat fryers. The golden color and crispness of the food and the speed of cooking are points which have promoted its use. Those interested in reducing the amount of fat in the diet oppose its extensive use. Factors that determine satisfactory use are quality of the equipment, quality of the fat used, and the skill in food handling. Important selection points for a fry kettle are (a) appropriate capacity for required cooking load; (b) fast temperature recovery; (c) accurate temperature control; (d) economical method of heating; (e) economical use of fat in proportion to frying capacity; and (f) ease of emptying and cleaning.

It is better for kitchens that have peak periods or who serve a fluctuating patronage to have two smaller kettles than one large one. This allows one to be closed down when it is not needed. The service life of fat is shortened in proportion to the length of time it is held at a high temperature. The two kettles also provide flexibility in terms of the different items that may be prepared at the same time. The frying capacity of fryers is frequently expressed in terms of the quantity of French fried potatoes they fry per hour. This figure is influenced by both load capacity and recovery time.

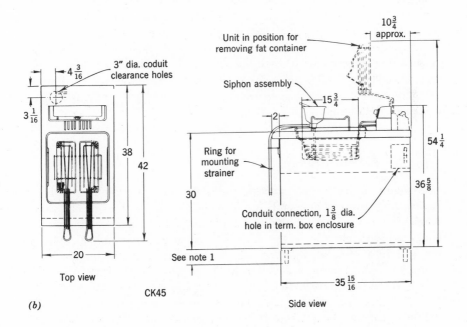

Figure 12.11 (Left and above)   Electrically heated deep-fry kettle. (*a*) Photo of front view, (*b*) diagrams showing top and sides views. (Courtesy of the General Electric Company.)

The size of the deep-fat fryer needed is calculated on the basis of the number of portions of fried foods needed during a peak hour of service times the average size of portions. If 120 4-ounce portions are needed per hour this means 30 pounds of food. Next, determine the frying and handling time in minutes and the number of loads that can be handled per hour. Divide the total weight by the number of loads that can be handled per hour for the weight to be fried at one time. If 4 minutes are required for frying and 1 minute for unloading and reloading the fryer or a load every 5 minutes, then divide the 30 pounds by 12 loads per hour for the amount required in a single load, which would be $2\frac{1}{2}$ pounds.

There is a best temperature for cooking the various foods. The temperature needs to be high enough to seal in the juices and develop a crisp surface, but low enough to permit adequate cooking without over-browning the exterior. The cooking time for deep-fat fried food is short, even for frozen items. Temperatures that are too low result in fat soaked products that are not properly browned. Repeated loads of cold foods and a short cooking period emphasizes the need for fast heating that ensures proper cooking temperature throughout most of the short cooking period. The quality of the product and of the fat requires a temperature control that prevents temperature going beyond that required for cooking.

Satisfactory models are available for either gas or electric power, and with considerable range in capacity and amount of fat required for frying. Economy in the use of a fryer involves power required for heating, amount of fat needed in frying, and labor required in handling and cleaning. The fat should be filtered after use and the kettle thoroughly cleaned. The fat may be removed from small kettles by pouring out and from large ones by draining or siphoning. When selecting, examine the kettle for ease in reaching all areas for thorough cleaning.

Fat for Frying

The quality of the fat influences the cooking results. The fat chosen should have a high smoke point and should have little or no flavor. The smoke point is lowered each time the fat is heated, and continued holding at high temperature shortens its service life. Shortenings and vegetable oils that do not contain an emulsifier (mono- and diglycerides) have the highest smoke point. The smoke point of these fats is 430 to 440°F on the first heating but it is lowered to approximately 365°F after one use. The temperatures at which the majority of foods are fried is from 350 to 375°F.

Proper care of the fat can prolong its service life. Some of the simple precautions to follow include the following:

1. Heat fat only to the temperature and for the time required for cooking.

2. Keep the fat clean (food particles and sediment should be filtered out after use and the kettles carefully washed and dried).

3. Replace about 15 percent of the used fat with fresh fat.

4. Keep salt out of the fat (do not salt food until after frying).

5. Have food defrosted, dry, and in small enough pieces for quick cooking. And

6. Use deep fat rather than shallow fat (the greater the exposed surface, the faster the decomposition of the fat).

The fat used can be a medium for introducing objectionable flavors in fried foods. Before re-using fat or after frying various foods in fat, it is well to cool and taste a small amount of the fat to determine whether the flavor is sweet and mild enough to produce good products. Fat that bubbles excessively before food is added or that has a gummy substance which collects on the frying basket and heating elements should be discarded along with any fat that has an off-flavor.

Use of the Fryer

Procedures in using a fryer are relatively simple. It is important that they be followed carefully to ensure good products, to preserve the quality of the cooking fat, and to prevent the operator from being seriously burned. A careless operator may be burned by the splashing or bubbling up of hot fat or by grasping hot basket handles without a holder.

1. Check the outlet to be sure that it is closed.

2. Fill the fryer with fat to a level at least 2 inches above the heating elements and turn on the heat. It is important to have the fat extend above the heating elements whenever the heat is on. Use enough fat to completely submerge the food to be fried.

3. Set the thermostat at 250°F until enough fat has melted to cover the heating elements, then set it at the temperature for cooking. If liquid fat is used the thermostat may be set directly at frying temperature. Preheating to 350°F requires approximately 5 minutes. Heat the fat, only at such time as it is necessary for cooking, and turn off the heat as soon as it is not needed in order to preserve the quality of the fat. At no time should the fat be heated over 400°F.

4. Fill the food basket (not more than two-thirds full) with the food to be fried. Be sure that wet foods are well drained or wiped dry and that pieces are uniform in size for even cooking.

5. Submerge the baskets into the hot fat cautiously, in the event that the quality of the fat or the moisture of the food causes the hot fat to bubble up.

6. During frying, keep pastry covered foods submerged and turn doughnuts and fritters once. When frying foods that tend to adhere to each other, such as French fries and onion rings, shake the basket occasionally to separate them.

7. At the end of the cooking period, hang the basket to drain for an instant and then remove the food to an absorbent paper towel or paper to take up excess fat. Be cautious of the heat of the basket handles.

8. Turn off the heat as soon as the frying is completed. During idle periods turn the thermostat to 200°F.

Care and Cleaning

Fat that is free of food particles and a clean fryer are both required for producing good quality fried foods. Proper care of the fat can prolong its service life. Depending on its use, the following procedures should be followed daily:

1. Remove the baskets to the pot sink for washing.

2. Attach a filter bag or several layers of cheesecloth at the end of the drain pipe.

3. Place a clean receptacle of sufficient capacity for the fat beneath the drain.

4. Open the drain valve slowly to avoid splashing of hot fat.

5. As the well empties, flush walls with drained hot fat.

6. Remove the basket support.

7. If the unit is electrically heated, swing the heating units up until they are locked in an upright position. (Fat and residue may be burned from these units by turning the thermostat to 400°F and turning on the power. After they are burned off and grease is free the power may be turned off.)

8. Remove particle accumulator or strainer, empty, and wash.

9. After fat has drained out, close the drain valve.

10. Wash the fryer with detergent and hot water. Rinse with a vinegar solution ($\frac{1}{4}$ cup vinegar to 1 gallon of water) and rinse again with water. Be sure that all traces of fat have been removed. Dry the fryer and heat elements with a soft cloth.

11. Reassemble the fryer by (a) placing strainer in fryer well (if specific model requires one); (b) lowering heating units (if an electric model); (c) placing basket support over heating elements (if required).

SUGGESTED LABORATORY EXPERIENCE

1. Visit a large kitchen or a hotel equipment supply house to examine
   (a) meat block, heavy cutting boards, and meat knives;

(b) ranges designed for different fuels and with tops for different purposes;

(c) griddles (note sizes, heating elements, and controls);

(d) ovens with different sizes in bun-pan capacity, type of heating, deck material and height, calibration, and finishes;

(e) Fryers (note heating, capacity, method for removing fat, cleaning possibilities);

(f) Broilers (note type, method of heating, controls, sizes, convenience).

2. Demonstrate operation of each type of equipment.

3. Disassemble for cleaning, clean and reassemble for use—range, broiler, and fryer. (Note use of equipment in preparation of protein foods in following chapters.)

REVIEW QUESTIONS AND ANSWERS

1.	Of what materials are meat blocks constructed?	Laminated maple.
2.	How are they cleaned?	By using a steel brush and/or scraper.
3.	Should they ever be washed with soap and water?	No.
4.	Why?	Water weakens the glue binding the blocks and softens the wood.
5.	Should a scraper and steel brush be used on a cutting board?	No.
6.	Should wood handled cutting tools or boards be soaked in hot water?	No. It is best to wash them, rinse well, and wipe dry immediately.
7.	What are the four types of tops for ranges?	(a) Open elements, (b) elements covered with light steel plate, (c) cast steel sectional plates, and (d) griddle top.
8.	Do all ranges have an oven?	No, an oven is optional and also the high shelf.
9.	How often should the grease troughs and drip pans of ranges be cleaned?	Daily.
10.	How should heavy duty tops be cleaned?	With a fine-grit griddle stone, using a little grease and rubbing with the grain of the metal while the surface is warm.
11.	What special precaution should be taken when cleaning gas burners?	That openings are unclogged for the free flow of gas.
12.	How may they be cleaned?	Scrub with a brush and soap and water. Avoid scouring powder that may clog burners.

13. How do griddle tops differ from sectional plates?

They are cast in one solid sheet and designed for suitable drainage of fat from cooking.

14. What are the important selection points that relate to heating?

Uniform heating of the surface, speed of temperature recovery, sectional temperature controls, reliable thermostat, and suitable retention of heat.

15. What are the three additional points for selection?

Sturdiness, suitable facility for grease removal and ease of cleaning.

16. How should a new griddle be conditioned?

Clean with mild detergent and water, rinse and wipe dry. Heat to 400°F, brush with cooking oil and let stand for 2 minutes. Wipe off surplus oil and brush with a fresh film of oil and let stand for 2 minutes. Wipe off excess oil.

17. How should the griddle be cleaned after each use?

Scraped with a spatula or wire brush to remove excess fat and particles of food.

18. What daily cleaning should be done?

Empty, wash, and dry grease troughs and pan.

19. How should the griddle surface be cleaned?

Rub metal with pumice or griddle stone, rubbing with grain of the metal, when the griddle is warm. Clean with damp cloth, wipe dry and reseason.

20. Should steel wool be used on a griddle?

No. Particles of the metal may remain and get into the food.

21. What are the important selection points for an oven?

Adequate, uniform temperature, suitable range of temperature, reliable temperature control, speed of temperature recovery, level, easy-to-reach shelves, appropriate capacity, and easy to operate and to maintain.

22. How much time is required to preheat many heavy duty ovens?

From 45 minutes to an hour to 425°F.

23. What precautions should be observed when loading an oven?

To load it evenly, allowing space between pans and between pans and oven sides for proper circulation of heat.

24. What is the major difference between conventional and convection ovens?

Convection ovens have forced circulation of heat and conventional ovens do not.

25. What are the chief fuels used for broiling?

Charcoal and briquets, gas and electricity.

26. Where are the grids placed in relation to the heat?

They may be either above or below the heat.

27. What should be done to prevent meat from sticking to the grid when broiling?

Keep grids clean and rub with suet or oil before broiling, if meat is not marinated in oil.

28. What are the important selection points for deep fat fryers?

Appropriate capacity, fast temperature recovery, accurate temperature control, economical use of fuel, economical use of fat, and easy to empty and clean.

29. What are two important qualities of fat used for frying?

Mild flavor and high smoke point.

30. How can service life of fat be prolonged?

Do not heat higher than necessary. Do not heat longer than necessary. Keep free of sediment and salt. Replace 15% of used fat with fresh fat. Defrost and dry foods and use deep fat with limited exposed surface.

31. At what temperature should the thermostat be set for standby time?

200°F.

32. How should the fat be cared for after use?

It should be drained from the fryer through several layers of cheesecloth, into a clean receptacle.

33. How should the fryer well be cleaned?

It should be washed with detergent and hot water, rinsed with vinegar solution and next with clean water.

34. What other parts of the fryer should be cleaned?

All parts of the fryer should be washed with soap and water, rinsed well and wiped dry, including the basket, particle accumulator, drain faucet and exterior.

13.

Dairy Products and Eggs

Dairy products and eggs are nutritionally valuable foods that are low in cost as compared with other foods rich in protein. Their value in the diet as well as their natural goodness makes proper preparation of these foods of special merit in order to promote their use. Milk and eggs contain vitamin A, thiamine (B_1), riboflavin (B_2), niacin and varying amounts of vitamin D. Commercial milk is enriched with vitamin D. The vitamin D content in eggs varies in relation to the amount of exposure of the hens to sunshine. Egg yolks are important sources of iron and phosphorus. Milk contains phosphorus and a trace of iron and is a rich source of calcium. Nutritionists recommend that adults have at least a pint of milk daily and that growing children have one and a half to two pints daily. Both adults and children should have four or five eggs weekly.

The uses and the principles of preparation tend to link dairy products and eggs. They are used in combination and the protein content of each tends to impose certain common rules for their preparation, for example, the use of low temperature for cooking. They are versatile foods that can be used in every meal and in every course from appetizers to desserts. Eggs and dairy foods lend themselves to the simplest forms of preparation or may be used as a part of the most elaborate cuisine.

Eggs and milk products are perishable and should be continuously refrigerated when they are not in use. The money spent in procuring top quality items can be wasted quickly by allowing them to remain out of refrigeration. A warm kitchen can soon make a Grade B egg with a weak white out of one purchased as Grade AA. Proper protection calls for refrigerators to be located adjacent to areas where these products are used; workers should be instructed to take out only those quantities needed for immediate use.

SELECTION AND CARE OF PRODUCTS

Dairy products and eggs are available for selection in different forms. Persons responsible for procurement need to know products available and those best suited for specific purposes. The fresh Grade AA eggs, for example, are best for breakfast eggs, not only for their fresh, sweet flavor, but also for attractive form or appearance. The thick white stands high for frying and holds firmly together for poaching, without washing out raggedly into the water. If kitchens use large quantities of eggs for baking, egg meats may be purchased at a saving in price and will reduce labor required for opening eggs. Dry egg and milk solids are also useful in the preparation of bakery formulas. Such items yield good products and offer greater convenience at a lower cost than fresh milk and eggs.

Eggs

Eggs in the shell are graded for quality and for size. Three quality grades for fresh eggs are defined by the U.S. Department of Agriculture as (a) U.S. Grade AA or Fresh Fancy Quality, (b) U.S. Grade A, and (c) U.S. Grade B. The grades are determined by the condition of the shell, the size of the air cell and the centering of the yolk. Top quality has a clean, fine-textured, unbroken shell, an air cell less than $\frac{1}{8}$ inch deep, a yolk that is close to the center of the egg, and the entire meat free from defects. A coarse or porous shell permits more rapid deterioration. The size of the air cell denotes age. As the moisture evaporates from the egg, the air cell becomes larger; it may be up to $\frac{3}{8}$ inch in a Grade B egg. When the white is firm, as in a very fresh egg, the yolk tends to be well centered. As the egg is held the white weakens and the yolk is more mobile and may move to the side or end.

The names for the size grades and the weights per dozen eggs are stated by the U.S. Department of Agriculture as follows: Jumbo—30 ounce, Extra Large—27 ounce, Large—24 ounce, Medium—21 ounce, Small—18 ounce, and Peewee—15 ounce. In order to determine whether egg meats of one size compare favorably in price with those of another, divide the price per per dozen by the number of ounces per dozen for eggs of the particular size. The price per ounce is the basis for comparison. In other words, Jumbos priced at 90 cents, Large eggs at 72 cents, and Peewees at 45 cents per dozen would all cost the same 3 cents per ounce. In large kitchens where several pounds are required for bakery or entree mixtures, the labor time in opening the eggs would be a cost worthy of consideration.

Egg meats may be purchased either fresh or frozen. One pound of whole egg meats is equal to eight large or nine medium-sized eggs. Frozen yolks and frozen whites are available, also. There are 12 to 15 whites per pound

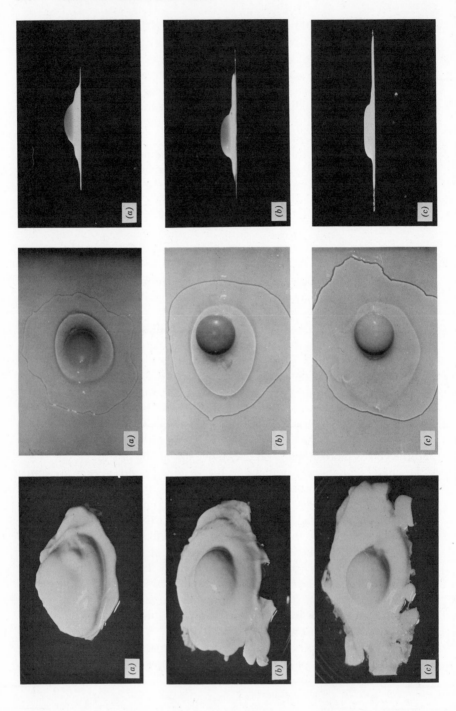

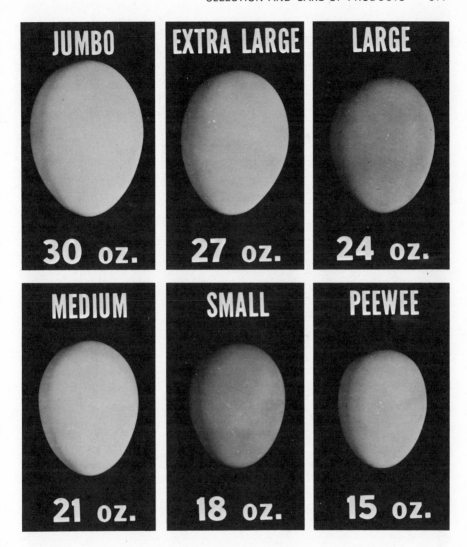

Figure 13.2 (Above)   Size grades recognized by the United States Department of Agriculture.

Figure 13.1 (Left)   The United States Department of Agriculture describes eggs for quality in this manner: (*a*) Grade AA—those which cover a small area, have whites that are thick and stand high, and yolks that are firm and yellow; (*b*) Grade A—those which cover a moderate area, have reasonably thick whites that stand fairly high, and yolks that are firm and high; (*c*) Grade B— those which cover a wide area, have a small amount of thick white, and yolks that are flattened and enlarged.

TABLE 13.1 MARKET PACKAGES AND FORMS OF MILK

Milk Item	Definition	Packages
Fresh Milk		
Certified	Milk produced by 100% healthy herd under very sanitary conditions as set forth by Amer. Assoc. of Medical Milk Commission. It may or may not be pasteurized.	½ pt, pt, qt, gal
Homogenized	Milk forced through fine openings that break up fat globules fine enough to stay distributed throughout the milk.	½ pt, pt, qt, gal
Pasteurized	Milk heated to a high enough temperature to kill disease-causing bacteria, then rapidly cooled.	½ pt, pt, qt, 1, 2, and 5 gal
Raw	Milk that has not been heated or otherwise treated.	½ pt, qt, gal
Skim (fat-free)	That with most all of the fat removed.	½ pt, pt, qt, gal
Skim (fortified)	Skimmed milk to which nonfat milk solids and perhaps vitamins have been added.	½ pt, qt
Chocolate	Whole milk plus cocoa or chocolate syrup.	½ pt, qt
Cream		
Commercial or coffee	18 to 20% butterfat (64 tbsp or servings per qt).	½ pt, pt, qt
Half and half	Fat content approximately 12%.	pt, qt
Whipping	Fat content varies from 30 to 40% (7 or 8 c per qt when whipped).	½ pt, pt, qt
Sour cream	Soured by lactic-acid bacteria, has been homogenized, and has about 18% fat.	½ pt, pt, qt

TABLE 13.1 (*Continued*)

Milk Item	Definition	Packages
Fermented Milk		
Sour	May be raw or pasteurized, soured by lactic-acid bacteria.	pt, qt
Buttermilk	Liquid after butter has been churned.	½ pt, qt
Cultured buttermilk	Pasteurized skim milk made into buttermilk by use of lactic-acid bacteria.	½ pt, qt
Yoghurt and acidophilus	Custardlike clabber formed by special acid-forming bacteria.	½ pt, qt
Milk with Water Removed		
Condensed	Whole milk with about 60% of water removed and sugar added. Sterilized and sealed in cans.	6 to 13 oz cans No. 10 cans
Evaporated	Whole homogenized milk with about 60% of water removed. Sterilized and sealed in cans. (To reconstitute use an equal amount of water.)	14½ oz and No. 10 cans
Nonfat Dry	Practically all water removed, powdered. (To reconstitute use 1 lb plus water to equal 5 qt.)	1, 50, and 200 lb
Dried Whole	Practically all water removed, powdered. (To reconstitute use ¾ to 1 c plus 4 c water for 1 qt liquid milk.)	5, 50, and 200 lb

313

and 18 to 22 yolks. Eggs are frozen in 30-pound cans and require two days to thaw at 40°F. They can be used in recipes in the same manner as fresh eggs. The yolks have a tendency to thicken unless sugar, glycerin, or salt is added prior to freezing. This reduces gummy or lumpy particles from forming as they thaw.

Dried eggs are available as whole egg solids, egg white solids and egg yolk solids. Low storage temperatures are recommended for holding these products. Changes occur in flavor, color, odor, and solubility when yolks or whole egg solids are held at temperatures above 40°F. The freshly dried egg solids held at 0°F are best. The U.S. Department of Agriculture recommends their use only in foods that are thoroughly cooked, because Salmonella organisms are likely to be present. They can be used successfully in popovers, batter cakes, custards and similar dishes. The quantities equivalent to one pound of fresh egg products are as follows:

$4\frac{1}{2}$ ounces of whole egg solids plus $11\frac{1}{4}$ ounces of water,

$2\frac{1}{4}$ ounces of egg white solids plus $13\frac{3}{4}$ ounces of water, and

$7\frac{1}{4}$ ounces of egg yolk solids plus $8\frac{3}{4}$ ounces of water.

Dried eggs settle and should be stirred before measuring. When reconstituting them, spread the solids slowly into lukewarm water, stirring constantly with a wire whip or mixer. Allow to stand a few minutes before using and then stir again. This allows the solids to take up the water.

Store fresh eggs in covered containers away from strong or odorous foods. Keep them refrigerated, bringing out only those to be used immediately. Do not wash eggs before storage as they naturally possess a film that helps to protect them from spoilage. To keep leftover egg yolks, cover with water to shut out air and prevent drying. Checks, or cracked eggs, should be used as soon as possible and not held more than a couple of days.

Dairy Products

Market milk is available in the many forms shown in Table 13.1. The American public spends approximately 15% of their food dollar for milk and milk products.

Butter and cheese are valuable for enriching and flavoring other foods as well as enjoyed as separate foods. Because of their flavor-giving values it is well to give special consideration to this aspect when selecting them. These foods absorb other flavors readily, and can be the cause of introducing an objectionable flavor in foods in which they are used as a seasoning. To insure good quality, select products with a good, sweet flavor and store in a manner that preserves their goodness.

The U.S. Department of Agriculture has established standards for grades of butter. Grade AA is of highest quality and is made of pasteurized sweet cream. Grade A is high in quality, but may have a slightly less palatable flavor or body. Grades B and C are of wholesome quality but have less desirable flavor. The Cooking Grade is recommended for use only where delicate flavor is not important. Good butter has a delectable flavor that is special unto itself. It can be frankly acknowledged that other mild-flavored fats are preferable for cooking to the lower grade butters that may introduce off flavors. Margarine that has been fortified with vitamin A and D may be as nutritious as butter.

The kinds of cheese available are sufficiently numerous and varied in character to permit connoisseurs to choose one that is well fitted for specific uses. There are over 400 varieties from which to choose. Cheese is a high quality protein food. Flavor, texture or body, and color are important points in selection for use. Each kind of cheese is enjoyed for its characteristic flavor, which may be mild, strong, or cultural. Soft cheeses, such as cream and cottage cheese, are highly perishable. They should be held for short periods only, carefully refrigerated, and protected from strong-flavored foods or refrigerator odors because they absorb off-flavors readily.

Cheese should be selected with the intended use in mind. This is particularly true of cheddar. Cheddar, which is called American cheese, cracker-barrel cheese, and rat cheese, has a wide variety of uses in food preparation and is available in many forms and qualities. It may be in its original or natural form or a processed form. Processed cheddar is ground, blended,

Figure 13.3 There are numerous varieties of cheese to satisfy individual tastes. A clear cellophane cover on cheese when displayed preserves sanitation and prevents drying or "oiling." (Courtesy of the American Dairy Association.)

TABLE 13.2 COMMON CHEESE VARIETIES AND THEIR USES

Use of Varieties	Description	Package Size
Canapes and Hors d'Oeuvres		
Cream	White, spreadable cheese, may be softened for use in pastry tube.	3 oz, 8 oz, 3 lb
Cheddar	Yellow, firm enough for dicing, may be softened for spreading.	1 to 22 lb
Swiss	Creamy color, nutlike flavor, may be diced or shredded.	1 to 22 lb
Blue	Cream white with blue veining, may be crumbled or softened for spreading.	3 oz to 12 lb
Cooking Ingredient (Sauces and Casseroles)		
Cheddar	Well cured cheddar with rich flavor and waxy texture, that will melt smoothly.	1 to 22 lb
Grating (for Topping)		
Cheddar	Sharp, well cured cheese, yellow color, hard texture.	1 to 22 lb
Parmesan	Yellow, hard cheese, grates well.	1 to 12 lb
Sap Sago	Greenish color, flavored with clover-like herbs, extremely hard, grates well, used for soups.	4 to 6 oz
Salad		
Blue	Popular for crumbling over salads or for blending in dressings.	3 oz to 6 lb
Cheddar	Firm enough to shred or dice, rich flavor and yellow color.	1 to 22 lb

TABLE 13.2 (*Continued*)

Use of Varieties	Description	Package Size
Cottage	White, soft cheese with or without cream added.	1 to 5 lb
Swiss	Mild, nutlike flavor, may be shredded or diced.	1 to 32 lb
Sandwiches		
Brick	Medium firm slicing cheese, creamy color and slightly acid flavor.	4½ to 5 lb
Cheddar	Medium firm, well cured, rich flavor, waxy.	1 to 22 lb
Cream	Soft, white, spreadable cheese with mild flavor.	1 to 6 lb
Edam	Creamy yellow, firm, mild flavor, slices well.	1 to 32 lb
Swiss	Creamy white, nutlike flavor, slices well.	5 lb
Processed	Blended cheese, may be flavored with Swiss, cheddar, brick or limburger cheese formed in Pullman shape.	
Dessert		
Blue	Moist, foil wrapped, well veined or rich flavored.	3 oz
Brick	Serve in slices or dices of creamy white, medium firm cheese.	4½ to 5 lb
Camembert	Soft to semifluid cheese of creamy white color.	8 oz box
Cheddar	Yellow color, medium firm, waxy texture, serve softened for spreading or in dices or slices.	1 to 22 lb
Edam	Small red balls used to center cheese tray, or yellow cheese diced or sliced in semi-circles.	1 to 6 lb
Gruyere	Creamy colored triangles of Swiss cheese that have been cured in wine.	6 1-oz pkgs

317

pasteurized, and remolded into loaves after it has been cured. This loaf cheddar is usually a blend of young and well-cured cheddar. It is shaped in convenient Pullman form for sandwich making. It tends to have a more gummy texture and a milder flavor than a well cured cheddar which has not been reworked. It is less desirable for cheese sauces or for flavoring dishes than a well-cured cheddar which has a more pronounced flavor. Cheese for grating needs to be dry and firm enough to grate into fine particles, similar to parmesan. It is well to test products for the specific purpose for which they are intended before purchase. Determine how well the flavor carries into products in which they are to be used and how satisfactory the cheese is for melting, blending, grating, or slicing.

PREPARATION OF MILK AND CHEESE DISHES

When cooking milk and cheese products use low temperatures. The scum which forms from the coagulation of certain of the proteins when milk is heated, is increased in amount and toughened by high temperatures and long cooking. It can be minimized by whipping the milk to form a foam on top or by tightly covering the pan and heating it below boiling temperature. The low temperature also prevents scorching of proteins that adhere to the sides and bottom of the container in which milk is heated.

When making sauces, puddings, and beverages that contain starch which requires thorough cooking for complete gelatinization, methods are used in which the starch is cooked separately and added to the hot milk. Cocoa and chocolate contain starch. It is best to combine them with the sugar, salt, and a little water and cook them well before adding them to the milk. The thorough cooking lessens the amount of sediment that settles to the bottom of the beverage. The starch for sauces is cooked in the roux before the milk is added.

Foods that contain acids and tannins tend to cause curdling when combined with milk. The tannins in potatoes, for example, often cause the curdling of the milk used in scalloped potatoes. Salt promotes curdling and calls for special care when preparing cured pork or fish dishes. Ways in which to lessen the tendency of curdling in milk dishes are by limiting the salt used, adding the milk in a medium white sauce, keeping the temperature below boiling, and shortening the cooking time. The form of milk used also makes a difference. Milk that has not been homogenized curdles less than homogenized milk. Evaporated milk is generally more stable against curdling than fresh milk, but curdles more readily when used in scalloped potatoes.

Because of its convenience and low cost, nonfat dry milk is used in considerable quantities in large kitchens. Custards, puddings, sauces, and baked products made with it have good flavor and consistency. Where desirable it permits enriching products with extra milk solids. Excessive amounts that lower the palatability of the product should not be used. When using dry milk it should be measured by weight as the volume varies between the regular and the instant dry milk. Regular dry milk measures 4 cups per pound and the instant $5\frac{3}{4}$ cups.

Rennin may be used to form a smooth, custardlike coagulation of the casein in fresh milk. It is obtainable in powdered or tablet form. The milk should be lukewarm when the rennin is stirred into it. It should be allowed to set without further stirring. The rennin is an enzyme that is killed at temperatures higher than body temperature, so that it does not form the coagulation. This product is most often used for infant feeding and for persons who are ill because it is easy to digest.

Whipped cream adds flavor richness and delectable lightness to many foods. It provides a means of incorporating air into molded salads and desserts, of fluffing dressings and sauces, and of adding an appealing garnish. Cream containing at least 30% butterfat forms the most stable foam, with stability increasing as the percentage of butterfat is increased. It whips best when it is not homogenized, and when it is aged two or three days before whipping. Bowl, beater and cream should be chilled at a temperature below 40°F for best results. Stability, particularly of the creams having lower butterfat content, can be increased by adding one and one half ounces of instant dry milk per quart of cream, before aging. Sugar and flavoring should be added after the cream has reached the desired volume or consistency.

Nonfat milk solids can be whipped for uses where a product lower in calories is desired. This product is not as stable as whipped cream and therefore does not hold up as long. Use 1 quart of instant dry milk and 1 quart of ice water and whip rapidly until it is stiff enough to form soft peaks. Add 1 cup of lemon juice and continue beating until stiff. Fold in 2 cups of sugar and the desired flavoring.

Low temperature and a short cooking period are recommended for the preparation of cheese dishes. High temperature and prolonged cooking toughens the proteins and causes the fat to separate and drain from the cheese. When possible, foods should be prepared so that the cheese can be added near the end of the cooking period in a manner that does not expose the cheese to the direct heat. Shredding or finely dicing cheese helps in blending it with other foods. In many delicious combinations it can be incorporated with fully cooked foods and baked only long enough for thorough heating. Use a double boiler when melting cheese or making cheese sauce, and use shredded cheese. When used as a topping it should be protected with a generous sprinkling of buttered bread crumbs.

Butter used for sauteing imparts good flavor. It will brown or burn less

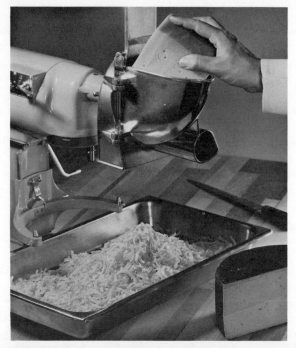

Figure 13.4   When preparing cheese sauce, (*a*) shred the cheese, (*b*) prepare the cream sauce, (*c*) lower temperature or remove sauce from heat, and (*d*) stir cheese into hot sauce until smoothly blended. (Courtesy of the American Dairy Association.)

Figure 13.5 Clarify butter by melting and decanting the clear fat from the milk solids. (Courtesy of the American Dairy Association.)

quickly if clarified. Butter contains milk solids or proteins that discolor and give off an objectionable odor when heated to a high temperature. To clarify butter, melt it, allow the milk solids to settle to the bottom of the pan, and then pour off the clear fat from the top for use in sauteing. If desired, vegetable oils may be blended with the clarified butter for use in frying.

EGG PREPARATION

Eggs possess properties that make them useful in many ways in the preparation of food. They are used as a thickening agent in many puddings and sauces. They serve as an emulsifying agent (mayonnaise). Many entrees contain eggs as a binder (meat loaf, croquettes, and timbales). Eggs and milk are used to coat foods that are breaded. Whipped whites afford leavening for batters and souffles and they are used for whips, garnishes, and meringues. Eggs are used alone as an important protein dish in meals.

Time and temperature are important factors in cooking eggs successfully. Time has an important influence on quality from the time that an egg is laid. Membranes weaken and flavor changes as time passes. Egg grades reflect degree of freshness of the eggs at the time of candling. The size of the air cell indicates amount of evaporation and the position of the yolk shows extent of weakening of the membrane which occurs with aging. Holding temperature affects speed of deterioration. Day-old eggs held at room temperature may not have better quality than week-old eggs that have been properly refrigerated.

Freshness is essential for good flavor and a strong membrane is requisite for good appearance in eggs prepared as whole eggs. In poached eggs a weak membrane allows the white to spread into the water, and in a fried egg the entire egg flattens out and the yolk is not well centered. The large air cell and an off-center yolk spoil the shape and appearance of eggs that are hard cooked. The dark ring around the yolk (ferrous sulfide) is more pronounced in the older eggs if they are cooked at high temperatures and for prolonged periods.

At 158°F the egg white and yolk coagulate into a firm, tender jell-like mass. The egg becomes more firm and less tender as the temperature is increased. Temperature affects other qualities than tenderness and influences decisions relating to the best temperature to use for specific types of preparation. Eggs that are fried or poached spread excessively if cooked at too low a temperature. The time factor in supplying short-orders tends to make higher temperature and shorter cooking time desirable, as long as the temperature is sufficiently moderate to produce a good product that is not brown or tough.

Poached Eggs

Quick coagulation helps to prevent the egg whites from spreading into the water. The water temperature should be simmering (212°F) when the eggs are dropped into the water. The addition of salt (1 tbsp) or vinegar (2 tbsp) to 1 gallon of water increases the speed of coagulation and protects the shape. However, it also dulls the sheen so that the egg white is less shiny than when cooked without salt and vinegar. The eggs should be slid into the hot water with the least possible disturbance of the white. It is well to break them onto a saucer or platter and then allow them to slide into the water toward the side of the pan.

When poaching in large quantity, a steam table pan deep enough to permit a water bath that amply covers the eggs may be used. Pans approximately 4-inches deep are recommended for ease of handling without spilling the water. The poaching may be done on the range top or in a steam cooker.

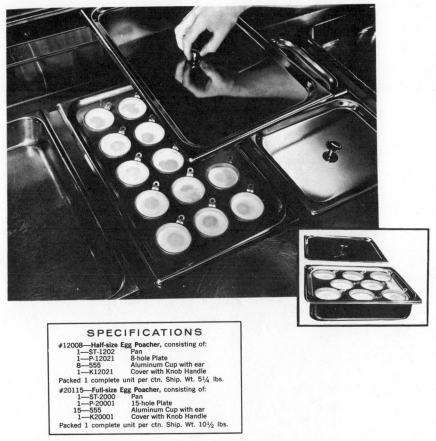

SPECIFICATIONS

#12008—Half-size **Egg Poacher,** consisting of:
    1—ST-1202   Pan
    1—P-12021   8-hole Plate
    8—555   Aluminum Cup with ear
    1—K12021   Cover with Knob Handle
Packed 1 complete unit per ctn. Ship. Wt. 5¼ lbs.

#20115—Full-size **Egg Poacher,** consisting of:
    1—ST-2000   Pan
    1—P-20001   15-hole Plate
    15—555   Aluminum Cup with ear
    1—K20001   Cover with Knob Handle
Packed 1 complete unit per ctn. Ship. Wt. 10½ lbs.

Figure 13.6 Eggs can be steamed or poached on the steam table during service. (Courtesy of Bloomfield Industries, Inc.)

It is desirable to use a timer to ensure a satisfactory degree of doneness. From 3 to 5 minutes are required for soft cooked eggs. A perforated spoon may be used to remove them from the water. Allowance may need to be made for the hot temperature during the time that elapses between cooking and presentation to the customer.

Fried Eggs

The largest percentage of orders is for fried eggs. The temperatures satisfactory for frying eggs range from 260 to 278°F. The white spreads more at lower temperatures. This may be prevented by cooking in small fry pans

Figure 13.7   Fry pans with slanting sides permit eggs to slide out readily. (Courtesy of Serv-O-Lift Corporation.)

that are just large enough for one or two eggs (4- and 7-inches in diameter at the bottom of the pan). The pans should have slanted sides that permit the egg to slide out readily when cooked. The pans when conditioned should be kept for egg frying only.

Fry pans may be conditioned by scouring them with scouring powder and steel wool. Wash, rinse thoroughly, and dry. Heat pans until too hot to barely touch with the bare hand. Rub with cooking oil and put aside for several hours or a day. Before using, sprinkle with about a teaspoon of salt and rub vigorously for a minute with a paper towel. Wipe out the salt with a fresh paper towel. The pans are then ready for use. After use, wipe clean with a paper towel; do not wash them. If they are washed, again rub them well with salt to prevent sticking.

The fry pans may be heated either on the range top or on the griddle. The eggs may be fried directly on the griddle, which is heated to 300 to 325°F. Since the whites are not confined there is a greater tendency to spread and the higher temperature is advisable. The eggs are less compact and trim in appearance when cooked on the griddle than when cooked in pans.

Use ample fat to prevent sticking, without an excess to make the eggs greasy. Clarified butter added to the fat, or as the fat used, adds a good flavor. Eggs, country style, are prepared in a manner that coagulates the white over the yolk. This may be done by covering the pan so that the steam cooks the top of the eggs, or by dipping hot fat over the eggs. Pans may have a tight fitting cover. When cooked on the griddle, the eggs may be covered by turning a shallow pan, such as a pie pan, over the eggs. Use an egg turner when lifting the pan.

Eggs Cooked in the Shell

Eggs placed in 212°F water are soft-cooked in 3 minutes, medium in 4 minutes, and hard-cooked in 12 minutes. Eggs are less likely to crack when placed in the hot water if they are at room temperature. Those taken from refrigeration that are to be cooked immediately, should be placed in luke-warm water for a few minutes before placing them in the hot water. At the end of the cooking period, plunge eggs into cold running water for an instant to halt the cooking process. This helps eliminate the development of a ferrous-sulfide (greenish) ring around the yolk.

Hard-cooked eggs shell most easily immediately after cooking and as soon as they have cooled in the cold running water. The air cell is likely to be at the large end of the egg, and this is a good point at which to start the peeling. When shells are difficult to remove, holding them under running water often helps. Those that are particularly tenacious can be eased away from the shell by slipping a teaspoon between the shell and the white.

The extra large and the extra small eggs have certain display value when used as garnishes or stuffed hors d'oeuvres. The Peewees, cut across rather than split lengthwise, appear especially dainty as a salad garnish or appetizer. The very small eggs tend to be seasonal because they are laid by pullets at the beginning of their laying season, which is chiefly in the fall. During the fall there are likely to be more small eggs and some price advantage.

Scrambled Eggs

Scrambled eggs are popular as a form when serving eggs to a large group because of ease of preparation and less argument about the degree of cooking.

Eggs of a lower grade than AA may be used if the flavor is sweet and whole-some. The eggs should be beaten only enough to blend the yolks and white with the added liquid. Liquid, such as milk or cream, should be added in proportions of 1 cup (8 oz) to 1 dozen (1½ lbs) large eggs. Scrambled eggs for cafeteria service are held for longer periods of service. It helps quality if a medium white sauce is used as the liquid; this lessens firming and bleeding out. The proportions to use are 1 cup of white sauce to 1 quart of whole eggs.

Cook the scrambled eggs over low heat, stirring them occasionally. Fre-quent stirring breaks up the smooth mass into small particles that appear less attractive. For best appearance, the particles should approximate ¼ to ½ inch in size. The eggs *should not* be permitted to brown, and should be tender and moist when cooking is completed. Overcooking results in rubbery curds from which the water separates. Control the holding temperature of the serving table.

Figure 13.8 The plain or French omelet (lower) compared with a fluffy omelet (upper). (Courtesy of the Poultry and Egg National Board.)

Omelets

Plain or French omelets have the same ingredients as the scrambled eggs. The chief difference is due to manipulation during cooking. The egg mixture for these is not stirred after it is in the pan. Allow the mixture to coagulate underneath; then slip a spatula carefully under the coagulated area and lift it gently to allow liquid egg to flow under it. Tip the pan as necessary for all of the liquid mixture to flow through to the pan. Allow it to brown slightly. If a filling is desired, such as chopped ham or crumbled bacon, it should be spread over half of the omelet at this time, and the other half of the omelet folded over it. The pan in which the omelet is cooked should be well greased so that the omelet can be moved easily and turned onto the plate without breaking.

Fluffy omelets have water instead of milk as the liquid and the eggs are separated. The use of an acid such as lemon juice or tomato juice as a part of the liquid helps to stabilize the egg white foam. It is important to work quickly to complete the omelet as soon as preparation is started to ensure a minimum of drainage and layering when cooked. Have the oven temperature at 325°F. For a two- or three-egg omelet, use a conditioned steel or aluminum fry pan 7 inches in diameter with 2-inch slanting sides. Heat the pan with 2 tablespoons of oil or clarified butter just hot enough to make a drop of water sizzle immediately before the omelet is poured into it.

A three-egg omelet may be made in the following manner. Whip the yolks until very thick and lemon colored. Add $\frac{1}{2}$ teaspoon of salt, pepper to taste, and 2 tablespoons of water. Whip the whites with 2 teaspoons of lemon juice until stiff and shiny, but moist enough for peaks to bend over when the beater is lifted. Gently and quickly fold the yolk mixture into the whites. Liquid will drain out if this mixture is held. For best quality it should be cooked at once. Pour into the fry pan and cook over low heat until puffy and the underside is golden brown. (About 5 minutes.) Set the omelet in the the fry pan in the oven and allow it to bake for 12 to 15 minutes (until the center springs back when lightly pressed with the finger tip). Cut omelet across the center, part way through. Loosen with spatula around the edges and turn one half over the other. Grip the plate in the right hand and the handle of the fry pan in the left, and rock them together in such a way as to roll the omelet onto the plate or platter.

Souffles

The procedure for the preparation of souffles resembles that for fluffy omelets. A thick white sauce is used as the fluid instead of either water or milk. The egg yolks are whipped with a fork until well blended. A small amount of the

Figure 13.9 (*a, above*) The plain or thinner French omelet is most attractive and easily handled when folded in thirds. (*b, right*) The fluffy omelet when taken from the oven should be creased across the center with a spatula and folded in half.

hot white sauce is added to them and then they are added to the white sauce. This mixture is then folded into the egg whites which have been beaten until moist-stiff. A souffle ($6\frac{1}{2}$ pound quantity) baking in a pan 12 × 20 × $2\frac{1}{2}$ inches at 300°F requires 65 to 75 minutes. It is done when a silver knife thrust into the center comes out clean.

When souffles are baked in casseroles to be taken to the table or in serving pans to be displayed on a cafeteria counter, extra height has certain psychological advantage. The souffle may not be lighter but it appears lighter if it extends well above the container in which it was baked. Do not grease the sides of the pan. Provide a paper collar extending above the height of the container, against which the souffle can rise, that can be removed before service. Shrinkage or collapse is likely to be less if the change in temperature is gradual. Allow the souffle to set on the oven door for a minute before moving it to service.

Custards

Stirred custard is used in sauces, desserts, and in numerous side dishes in which it is desirable to use eggs as a thickening agent. Best success is obtained by cooking at a low temperature and just enough to coagulate the egg protein. The water in a double boiler should be started well below boiling

(b)

and the temperature gradually increased until the water is at simmering temperature, and never boiling. The custard is done when it is like a smooth heavy cream and will coat a metal spoon. The custard should be stirred constantly but gently while cooking, and should be poured into a chilled container or cooled rapidly over a pan of cold water. This is to prevent overcooking that may occur with a large volume of hot custard.

Eggs for custard are beaten only enough to blend the yolk and white. They should not be beaten enough to foam. The cooking time of stirred and baked custards can be shortened by scalding the milk before combining with the eggs. At first the hot milk should be added to the eggs in order to blend the mixture smoothly and avoid overcooking particles of the egg with the scalding liquid. The baked custard should be baked at 325°F for 30 or 40 minutes, or until a knife inserted in the center will come out clean.

Timbales and Fondues

Timbales are custards that are used as carriers of other foods. They may be used with protein foods, such as fish or chicken, to serve as the main entree,

Figure 13.10 Souffles that have height are the most appealing. (Courtesy of Pacific Kitchen.)

or with vegetables, such as corn or spinach timbales. Custards used in this way have similar proportions of egg and milk to dessert custards, but the sugar is omitted.

A fondue may be mistaken for a souffle because of its lightness and similar flavor. The lightness of the fondue is imparted by bread or bread crumbs used in a custard mixture. It is less likely to collapse upon standing then a souffle, and for this reason is favored over the souffle for cafeteria service. Ham, cheese, chicken or other protein foods and seasonings may be added for flavor and added nourishment.

Egg White Foams

The low surface tension of egg white allows it to stretch around air bubbles when the whites are whipped, and the low vapor pressure holds down the evaporation from the exposed surface. Egg white is moist when whipped into a light foam, and it is elastic. The nature of the egg white changes as

TABLE 13.3 CHARACTERISTICS AND USES OF THE DIFFERENT EGG WHITE FOAMS

Stages	Characteristics	Uses
Blended	Beaten enough to blend thick and thin white. It will flow smoothly, is slightly foamy and transparent.	Thicken custards or sauces, clarify soups, brush bakery products, and for coating.
Beaten	Moist consistency, peaks bend over and will not stand, shiny surface, white color, slips easily in bowl, liquid will separate upon standing.	Angel food cakes, meringue for pies and garnishes.
Stiff Foam	Smooth and moist with small air cells, forms peaks, is shiny and white, will slip slightly in bowl.	Meringue shells, tortes, sponge cakes, divinity candy, souffles, cake frostings, omelets.
Dry Foam	Very stiff and dry, has lost its sheen and elasticity, flakes separate readily, air cells are very small, too dry to blend well with batters.	Little use in preparing dishes, might possibly be used for shirred eggs.

beating continues, and it becomes less moist and less elastic. Characteristics of the foam at the various stages of stiffness need to be considered in relation to proposed use. A foam that is moist blends more readily with other ingredients than a dry one. If the foam is depended on to supply leavening, the bubbles need to be fine, moist enough to blend well, and elastic enough to stretch when swelled with heat. Meringue shells are made with whites that are beaten until they form stiff peaks. There is little use of foam in food preparation that has been beaten drier than this stage.

There are certain conditions and ingredients that affect the stability of egg white foams. The temperature of the white, whether room temperature or refrigerated, seems to have little influence. Egg whites foam more quickly when they are at room temperature, and appear to have as much stability as the refrigerated whites. Very fresh whites are slower to whip than older ones but furnish a more stable foam. Dilution with yolk interferes with foaming and lessens stability. The addition of acid (cream of tartar) adds stability and increases time required for beating. The addition of salt decreases stability and volume and adds to the beating time. The addition of sugar adds to beating time, increases stability and results in a fine textured foam.

Meringues may be soft, as those used for pies or baked Alaskas, or hard, as those use for cookies or meringue shells. The stage of beating and the amount of sugar used differ. Soft meringues have equal weights of egg whites and sugar and the hard meringues have twice as much sugar as egg white by weight. Three ounces of egg white or three egg whites are adequate for one 9-inch pie, plus $\frac{1}{8}$ teaspoon of salt added with the final addition of sugar, and $\frac{1}{4}$ teaspoon of cream of tartar added to egg whites at the beginning. Beat the egg whites and cream of tartar until frothy, then gradually add sugar (fine granulated) a little at a time. Stop beating before they reach Stage 3, Stiff Foam. The peaks should bend slightly. Swirl on to the hot pie, sealing meringue against the crust and brown in oven at 350°F. For baked Alaska use oven preheated to 450°F to speed browning and shorten the baking time. For hard meringue, use 6 or 8 ounces of sugar for the 3 ounces of egg white. Add the $\frac{1}{4}$ teaspoon of cream of tartar to the whites and beat until frothy. Gradually add half of the sugar to form a soft meringue, then slowly add the other half and beat until the foam forms a stiff peak. Shape into shells and bake (on brown paper) at 250°F for approximately an hour, or until dry but not brown.

SUGGESTED LABORATORY EXPERIENCE

1. Prepare 1 quart of medium white sauce, and divide when completed into three parts. To one part add 4 ounces of shredded processed cheddar,

to the second add 4 ounces of shredded mild, green cheddar and to the third add 4 ounces of shredded sharp, well cured cheddar. Note how well each blends into the hot sauce. Evaluate the flavor quality of each. Compare price.

2. Prepare baked custard using (a) fresh whole milk, (b) evaporated milk and (c) dry milk solids. Reconstitute the milk, from which water has been removed, to yield 2 cups of milk. (1 cup of evaporated milk plus 1 cup of water or $1\frac{3}{4}$ ounces of nonfat milk solids plus $1\frac{7}{8}$ cups of water.) Recipe: Scald the 2 cups of milk with $\frac{1}{4}$ cup sugar and $\frac{1}{8}$ tsp salt. Blend 2 whole eggs with $\frac{1}{2}$ tsp vanilla and $\frac{1}{8}$ tsp nutmeg. Pour scalded milk in a very small stream into the egg mixture while beating constantly, until well blended. Pour into a baking dish or custard cups, and set dish or cups in a pan of hot water in a 325°F oven. Bake until custard is set. Compare flavor and consistency of the three custards.

3. Clarify butter. Fry an egg using clarified butter and another using butter that has not been clarified. Compare browning and flavor of the two.

4. Compare results with eggs hard cooked in the shell, using Grade AA and Grade B (or eggs held at room temperature for 2 days), prepared in the following ways:
    (a) Cook below simmering (175 to 180°F) for 30 minutes, then place in cold water.
    (b) Start in warm water and bring to boiling and boil for 13 minutes, chill in cold water.
    (c) Place in warm water in a steam cooker and cook for 7 minutes, place part of eggs in cold water immediately and allow others to cool at room temperature. When cool, shell eggs and note difference in ease of shelling. Evaluate eggs for appearance and tenderness.

5. Compare ease of handling and tenderness of eggs prepared as follows:
    (a) Place in boiling water directly from the shell.
    (b) Break into a saucer and slip gently into boiling water.
    (c) Slip from a saucer into boiling water to which salt has been added (1 tablespoon to 1 gallon of water).
    (d) Slip from a saucer into boiling water to which vinegar has been added (2 tablespoons to 1 gallon of water).
    (e) Slip from a saucer into water that is not boiling, and cook below boiling.

6. Condition a fry pan for frying eggs. If possible, compare use of a conditioned pan with one that has not been conditioned.

7. Prepare a fluffy omelet. Beat whites to stage 2 until peaks will bend over and are not stiff. Work quickly to prevent drainage, and note when the omelet is cooked how much layering is shown. Note length of time before omelet collapses.

8. Make 25 portions of cheese souffle with the following ingredients:

Butter or margarine	6 ounces	Make white sauce of first 4 ingre-
Flour, all-purpose	5 ounces	dients. Melt cheese in hot sauce.
Hot milk	$3\frac{1}{2}$ cups	Add a small amount of hot mixture
Salt	$\frac{1}{2}$ ounce	to egg yolks and then stir yolks into
Shredded cheddar	$1\frac{1}{2}$ pounds	remainder of hot mixture, stirring
Egg yolks,		constantly. Cool mixture while beat-
slightly beaten	19 ounces	ing whites. Beat whites to a foam,
Egg whites		add cream of tartar and beat until
Cream of tartar		stiff *but not dry*. Fold cooled mixture

into whites. Pour into 12 × 20 inch serving pan that has been greased on bottom *only*. Bake at 300°F for about $1\frac{1}{4}$ hours (until knife inserted in center comes out clean).

9. Prepare soft meringues and hard meringues. Note the difference in the stages of beating and the effect of the sugar in the meringues.

REVIEW QUESTIONS AND ANSWERS

1. Why is it necessary to keep eggs and milk refrigerated?

They are highly perishable and depreciate in quality at warm temperature.

2. What are the quality grades for eggs?

U.S. Grade AA, U.S. Grade A, and U.S. Grade B.

3. What are the size grades and weights set by the U.S.D.A.?

Jumbo, 30 ounces; Extra Large, 27 ounces; Large, 24 ounces; Medium, 21 ounces; Small, 18 ounces; and Peewee, 15 ounces.

4. How may comparative values be determined for different sizes according to prices charged?

By dividing price per dozen by the ounces, and comparing cost per ounce for each.

5. What is the difference between homogenized and pasteurized milk?

Homogenization is a treatment to break up the size of fat globules and pasteurization is a heat treatment to kill harmful bacteria.

6. What is the difference between coffee cream and half-and-half?

Coffee or commercial cream has 18 to 20% butterfat and half-and-half has 12%.

7. What qualities are desirable in a cheese for cooking?

Rich flavor, good color; it should melt well and blend smoothly.

8. What qualities are needed in a grating cheese?

Firm enough to grate into fine particles, and rich flavored.

9. What causes curdling of milk in scalloped potatoes?

The action of the tannins in the potatoes.

10. How can curdling be reduced or avoided?

Reduce salt, use cream sauce and shorten cooking time.

11. How can whipping cream with low butterfat be stabilized?

Through addition of nonfat dry milk in proportion of $1\frac{1}{2}$ ounces per quart of cream.

12. Name two factors important to good quality in cheese cookery.

Low temperature and short cooking time.

13. What happens when cheese is cooked at a high temperature and for a prolonged period?

The protein in the cheese is toughened and the fat tends to separate from the protein.

14. How may butter be clarified?

Melt at a low temperature and allow milk solids to settle to bottom of the pan. Carefully pour off clear fat from the top, leaving solids in the pan.

15. Which browns more quickly, regular butter or clarified butter?

Regular butter which contains the milk solids. The solids burn readily and produce an objectionable flavor and odor.

16. Name the two important factors to remember in egg cookery.

Short time and low temperature.

17. In what ways does time affect egg quality?

Membranes in eggs gradually weaken from the time they are laid. Whites weaken until they are watery and spread out when poached or fried. Long cooking hardens the protein and promotes the development of ferrous sulfide (greenish ring) around the yolk.

18. What conditions help in preventing white from spreading when poaching eggs?

Have water boiling, add salt, use very fresh eggs and slip them into the water gently.

19. How do eggs Country Style differ from regular fried eggs?

Country Style eggs have the white over the yolk coagulated.

20. How may the white over the yolk of a soft cooked egg be coagulated?

By tightly covering pan while it is cooking or by laving hot fat over the egg.

21. How may one prevent development of greenish ring around yolks of eggs hard cooked in the shell?

Use very fresh eggs, limit cooking time and temperature, cool in cold water as soon as desired degree of doneness is reached.

22. In what ways are scrambled eggs and French omelets alike?

Ingredients are the same in items and amounts.

23. How do they differ?

Scrambled eggs are stirred occasionally while cooking, but the omelet as it cooks

24. How do French and fluffy omelets differ?

is lifted gently while cooking to prevent breaking and to allow liquid egg to flow next to the pan.

In French omelets, whole eggs are beaten together and milk is used as the liquid. In fluffy omelets, eggs are separated and whites are beaten separately, and water is used as the liquid.

25. How does the fluffy omelet differ from a souffle?

White sauce is used as the liquid in a souffle. It is more stable than the omelet.

26. How may a custard or a souffle be tested for doneness?

When pierced with a knife, the knife will come out clean.

27. In what way are custards, timbales and fondues alike?

All three have a custard base.

28. How do souffles and fondues differ?

The lightness of souffles is due to the beaten egg whites and in fondues it is due to bread or bread crumbs. The eggs for fondue are not separated.

29. To what stage should eggs be beaten for custards?

Only enough to blend the yolks and whites.

30. What is the test for egg whites when they have been beaten enough for angel food cake or pie meringue?

They appear white and shiny and the peaks bend over.

31. How much should the whites be beaten for souffle and hard meringues?

Until they form peaks and the texture is fine and shiny.

32. How do egg whites look when they have been beaten too much?

They are dry and stiff and have lost their sheen.

33. In what ways are eggs spoiled for food preparation when they have been whipped to this stage?

They do not blend well with other foods, and the white loses its elasticity.

34. What is the effect of acid and of sugar on egg whites for meringues?

Acid or sugar makes egg whites more stable when beaten.

35. Should more sugar be used in soft meringues or in hard meringues?

More sugar is used in hard meringues.

36. What quantity of sugar is used in each?

The weight of sugar in soft meringues should equal the weight of the whites and twice the weight of the whites in hard meringues.

14.

Poultry

The five kinds of poultry commonly available in markets throughout the United States are chicken, turkey, duck, goose, and guineas. Specialty items such as squab and pheasants are periodically available in large markets. Poultry supplies high quality, easily digested, well-liked protein food that is acceptable to the majority of people. Chicken and duck have long been regarded as year-around meats, but only in recent years has turkey been made readily available and accepted on an all-year basis. Prices vary with the seasons as affected by the supply ready for the market.

When buying poultry there are six points that need to be specified. The buyer should state kind, such as chicken or turkey, type, such as fresh or frozen, class, such as broiler, roaster or stewing, size of the individual poultry or item, style, such as New York dressed or pan-ready, and grade, which pertains to quality. The type and style of poultry purchased influences the time and method of handling in the kitchen. Poultry frozen in large units requires considerable thawing time before preparation and fresh poultry requires immediate attention or preparation.

There are various classes for each kind of poultry, based chiefly on age and sex. Various sizes are packed with limited variation in weight within a wholesale package. Small birds such as broiler chickens and guineas may have a range in weight of $\frac{1}{4}$ pound and larger chickens may have a range of $\frac{1}{2}$ pound. The weight range of turkeys in a package may be 2 pounds. The same type, class, style, and grade of poultry are in a package. Prices are quoted per pound and vary for each kind and style in terms of weight and grade.

Three grades of dressed and ready-to-cook poultry are recognized by the U.S. Department of Agriculture, Grade A, Grade B and Grade C. They are based on (a) conformation or shape of the bird or part and its freedom from deformity; (b) fleshing or depth of flesh as affecting percentage of flesh to bone; (c) fat covering in terms of adequate, uniform distribution without ex-

337

TABLE 14.1 CLASSES AND WEIGHTS OF POULTRY

Class	Age	Average Wt of bird	Wt Variation of birds in pkg	Purchase Wt per Portion	Preparation Method
Chicken					
Rock Cornish Hen	5 to 7 wk	¾ to 2 lb	¼ lb	¾ to 2 lb	Bake or barbecue
Broiler or fryer	9 to 12 wk	¾ to 2½ lb	¼ lb	¾ to 1¼ lb	Broil, fry, or barbecue
Roaster	3 to 5 mos	2½ to 5 lb	½ lb	¾ to 1¼ lb	Roast or fricassee
Capon	Under 8 mos	3½ to 9 lb	½ lb	¾ to 1¼ lb	Roast
Stag	Under 10 mos	3½ to 6 lb	½ lb	½ to 1 lb	Stew or braise
Stewing hen or fowl	Over 10 mos	3½ to 6 lb	½ lb	½ to 1 lb	Stew or fricassee
Cock or rooster	Over 10 mos	4 to 6 lb	½ lb	¼ to ½ lb	Soup, stew, or minced chicken
Turkey					
Fryer-roaster	16 wk	4 to 9 lb	½ lb	¾ to 1 lb	Barbecue, roast, or braise
Young hen	5 to 7 mos	8 to 12 lb	2 lb	¾ to 1 lb	Roast
		12 to 18 lb	2 lb	½ to ¾ lb	Roast
Young Tom	5 to 7 mos	8 to 12 lb	2 lb	¾ to 1 lb	Roast
		12 to 16 lb	2 lb	¾ lb	Roast
		16 to 20 lb	2 lb	½ to ¾ lb	Roast
Old hens	8 to 15 mos	10 to 20 lb	2 lb	½ to ¾ lb	Roast or stew
Old Toms	8 to 15 mos	12 to 30 lb	2 lb	½ lb	Roast or stew

TABLE 14.1 (*Continued*)

Class	Age	Average Wt of bird	Wt Variation of birds in pkg	Purchase Wt per Portion	Preparation Method
Ducks					
Broiler or fryer	Under 8 wk	2 to 4 lb	¼ lb	¾ to 1¼ lb	Broil or bake
Roaster duckling	Under 16 wk	4 to 6 lb		¾ to 1 lb	Roast
Mature	Over 6 mos	6 to 10 lb		¾ to 1 lb	Roast
Geese					
Young or mature	6 to 12 mos	6 to 12 lb	2 lb	1 to 1½ lb	Roast
Guineas					
Young or mature	6 to 12 mos	1¼ to 2½ lb	¼ lb	1 to 1½ lb	Roast or poach
Squab	3½ to 4½ wk	½ to 1 lb		½ to 1 lb	Roast or poach

339

Figure 14.1   United States Department of Agriculture grade and inspection stamps.

cess abdominal fat; (d) and (e) freedom from pinfeathers and defects, such as bruises and skin breaks; and (f) freedom from freezer burns. The poultry that has been Government graded and inspected bears a grade mark and an inspection stamp.

Poultry is highly perishable. An unbroken skin helps to protect the flesh from the invasion of bacteria. Before markets had improved refrigeration facilities, most of the poultry on the fresh market was New York dressed (killed, bled and the feathers removed. The head, entrails and feet were not removed). The largest percentage of the present market supply is in ready-to-cook form. It may be purchased whole or cut up and packaged in assorted or segregated pieces of the carcass. Although much of the poultry is marketed frozen, it is usually also available fresh.

Allow adequate time for defrosting frozen poultry. The best method of defrosting it is in the refrigerator at 35 to 40°F in its original wrapper. There is less loss of natural juices when defrosted in this way. When it is necessary to shorten the defrosting time, leave the birds in the original wrapper and place in cold running water. In the running water the birds require 2 to 6 hours to thaw, depending on size. Defrosting in the refrigerator requires 2 or 3 days for large turkeys, 1 or 2 days for chickens and other small birds, and 3 to 9 hours for cut up parts, depending on the size of the package. The birds should be thawed enough to be pliable before cooking, except for frozen stuffed birds which should be roasted from the frozen state. For large quantity use, it is considered better not to stuff birds before freezing. Many managers believe it is much better not to stuff them at all, but to bake the poultry and dressing separately.

Holding temperature is important to quality of the preservation of the poultry. Chicken should be neither frozen nor cooked for 4 to 6 hours and

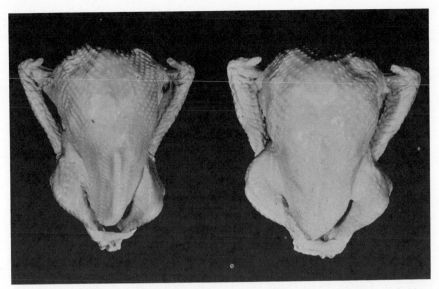

Figure 14.2   Grade B and Grade A poultry illustrating differences in conformation, fleshing, and color.

turkeys for at least 12 hours after slaughter and during rigor mortis, or the flesh will be tough. Fresh birds should be refrigerated at 34 to 36°F until frozen or cooked. Frozen birds should be held at 0 to 5°F until time for use. Do not allow cooked poultry to remain at room temperature for prolonged periods of time. Special care needs to be used with sandwich and salad materials, and left-over poultry on serving counters.

The best cooking method to use for poultry depends upon the size of the bird and the nature of the flesh. Some birds are young and tender and lacking in fat and others are tough and require moist heat for tenderizing. Older fowl have richer flavor to impart to soup and creamed dishes than young chickens. Characteristics of the meat has led to special methods of preparation for the specific classes of poultry; chicken pie or chicken and dumplings made with fat fowl, roast young tom turkey with dressing, and golden brown fried chicken are among the popular examples. Tenderizing mature birds through moist cooking, seasoning with added flavor where flavor is lacking, and enriching with fat in the frying of tender, lean, young birds add to palatability.

ROASTING

Roasting is one of the favorite methods of cooking the different kinds of poultry. Chicken and turkey have two kinds of flesh. The light breast meat is lower in fat than the dark leg and thigh meat. The breast tends to be drier and is improved by having some protection during roasting. A double fold of cheese cloth laid or tied over the breast and basted with fat two or three times during the roasting helps to moisten the flesh and enriches the flavor. The use of plastic film or aluminum foil is not recommended because they keep the juices in and the bird stews rather than roasts. This produces a pot-roast flavor which is less satisfactory than that produced by the use of a cloth covering. The covering should be removed 20 to 30 minutes before the bird is done in order to permit attractive browning.

A satisfactory roasting temperature for either chicken or turkey is 325°F. Low-temperature roasting (250°F) results in lower shrinkage and may be used for birds that are not stuffed. Roasting large turkeys at 250°F requires enough time for heat penetration to allow multiplication of bacteria in the warm dressing to a degree that may be hazardous to health. It is better, therefore, not to stuff birds that are to be cooked at low temperature. Roasting at high temperature (450°F) dries and toughens the meat. The flavor, also, is less desirable than that developed when the poultry is roasted at a moderate temperature.

A meat thermometer is the surest test for doneness. It should be inserted into the thickest part of the breast or the inner part of the thigh muscle, and to a point where the bulb will not be resting against a bone. Temperature should register 185 to 195°F according to the preferred degree of doneness. If the thermometer is inserted into the stuffing, the temperature should register 165°F. Note in Table 14.2 the extra cooking time required for roasting stuffed birds over those that are not stuffed. In large quantity cooking it is preferable to roast birds without stuffing. Dressing browned separately presents a better appearance and is easier to serve.

When planning for the roasting of large turkeys, give thought to the height of the roasting deck. Large cabinet ovens, used in institutions, may have roasting decks that are approximately 12 inches high or baking decks that are only 8 inches in height. Large turkeys will need to be split into halves or quarters for roasting in bake ovens with shallow decks. It is important to the quality of the meat, particularly that of the breast, that it not be too close to the heating elements or hot oven surface.

Allow sufficient time for poultry roasts to be removed from the oven and to stand from 15 to 30 minutes, depending on size, before slicing. This permits the hot juices to be absorbed into the meat and become set, so that they flow less freely when the slicing is done. The flesh firms upon standing so that it can be sliced with less tearing or crumbling. If bones from the breast thigh and leg are removed, the meat can be sliced on a meat slicer. Portions may be weighed and the 2 or 3-ounce portions arranged on predipped mounds of dressing in a serving pan, ready for quick service. If the sliced poultry is to be held several minutes for service, it should be carefully covered

TABLE 14.2 APPROXIMATE TIME FOR THAWING AND ROASTING

Kind of Poultry	Ready-to-Cook Weight Lb	Thawing (40°F) Frozen Birds Hr	Roasting Time (325°F)	
			Stuffed Hr	Unstuffed Hr
Chicken				
Cornish hen	1 to 1½	8 to 11	1½ to 2	1 to 1½
Broiler or fryer	1½ to 2½	8 to 11	1¼ to 2	¾ to 1½
Roaster	2½ to 4½	10 to 12	2 to 3½	1½ to 2¾
Capon	4 to 8	10 to 12	3 to 5	2 to 3
Duck	3 to 5	13 to 18	2½ to 3	
Goose	4 to 8	13 to 18	3 to 3½	
	8 to 12	20 to 30	3½ to 5	
Turkey				
Fryer-roaster	4 to 8	10 to 12	3 to 4½	2 to 2¼
Roasters	6 to 13	12 to 15	3½ to 5	2½ to 3
	12 to 16	15 to 24	5 to 6	3½ to 3¾
	16 to 20	20 to 26	6 to 7½	3¾ to 4½
	20 to 24	22 to 30	7½ to 9	4½ to 5½
Halves,	3½ to 5	10 to 12	3 to 3½	
quarters, and	5 to 8	12 to 15	3½ to 4	
half breasts	8 to 12	12 to 15	4 to 5	
Guineas	1½ to 2½	8 to 11	1½ to 2	1 to 1½

to keep it moist and placed in a slow oven or warming cabinet to keep it warm.

Kitchens that are required, on occasion, to serve an unusually large number of meals with limited staff and equipment will find the cooked and frozen turkey logs of special advantage. The logs may be entirely of white meat or have a combination of 60% white meat and 40% dark meat. These may be sawed, by means of a power saw, into 2 to 3-ounce portions while still frozen. The portions arranged on mounds of dressing in a serving pan should be moistened with stock, tightly covered with a lid or foil and thoroughly

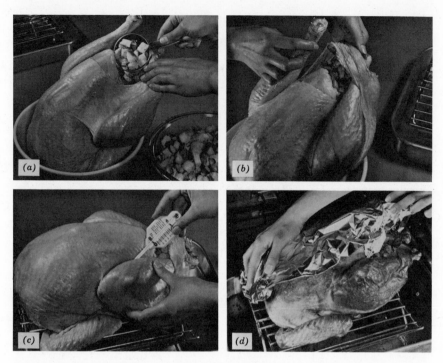

Figure 14.3   (*a*) After turkey is stuffed, (*b*) legs can be tucked under band of skin, (*c*) a thermometer placed in the fleshy part of thigh (avoiding contact with bone), and (*d*) roasted until half to two-thirds done before covering with tent of foil to prevent over-browning. (Courtesy of the Poultry and Egg National Board.)

Figure 14.4   A turkey log with an interesting sauce is an attractive, easy-to-serve buffet food. (Courtesy of Swift and Company.)

heated in an oven or steam cooker. For palatability, it is important for the dressings to possess extra richness and the gravy to have rich color and flavor. The lack of drippings for gravy make necessary the use of a tasty chicken base and browned roux in preparing the gravy.

The dressing served with poultry can add or detract from interest and palatability. The dressing should be light in texture and just moist enough to hold together when spooned onto the plate. Use care to avoid a hard or soggy dressing. A suitable portion of dressing is 2 to 3 ounces or $\frac{1}{3}$ to $\frac{1}{2}$ cup (rounded 12 or 16 scoop). The following recipe is for a simple bread dressing:

Ingredients	Weight	Volume	
Butter or margarine	1½ lb	3 c	Melt butter
Chopped onions	1 lb	3 c	Saute vegetables
Chopped celery	1 lb	1 qt	until tender
Chopped parsley	1 oz	¼ c	
Salt	½ oz	1 tbsp	Blend in
Pepper	2 tsp	2 tsp	seasonings
Poultry seasoning	2 tsp	2 tsp	
Bread, day-old, cubed	5 lb	1½ gal	Toss together with bread cubes
Stock (fresh or with chicken base)	4 lb	2 qt	Moisten with stock and mix well

This dressing recipe may be varied by adding ingredients as follows:

1. **Almond-bacon.**   3 c of sliced almonds, and 2 c of crisp, crumbled bacon.
2. **Chestnut.**   3 c of chopped, roasted shelled chestnuts.
3. **Giblet.**   1 qt of cooked, chopped giblets.
4. **Cornbread.**   Substitute 2 lb of cornbread crumbs for 2 lb of other bread, and 1 c of beaten raw eggs.
5. **Mushroom.**   Saute 1 qt of sliced mushrooms with the vegetables.
6. **Sausage.**   Omit butter or other fat and use only 1 tsp of poultry seasoning. Brown 2 lb of sausage and saute vegetables in the fat.

When roasting goose and duck, which are rich in fat, it is well to start them in a hot oven for the first 15 or 20 minutes and then reduce the heat. This reduces the fat and helps to develop a golden brown color. The brown color can be developed further by brushing the skin with a mixture of 3 parts honey and 1 part soy sauce about 10 minutes before roasting is completed.

Small birds may be roast-broiled or oven broiled. Little young birds are lean and require frequent basting with fat. They should be rubbed with seasoned butter before placing in the oven, and turned and basted every 5 minutes while roasting. Tender young birds such as squab, broilers and Cornish hens require approximately 30 minutes at 400°F to cook or 1 hour at 325°F. For best enjoyment of this method of preparation, use care to have them very tender, well seasoned, and moist.

BROILING AND BARBECUING

Only the tenderest young birds should be prepared by broiling. The pieces should be small or thin enough for complete penetration of heat in the time allowed for browning. Brush with melted butter or margarine and season with salt and pepper. For barbecued chicken, brush with barbecue sauce at the beginning and each time the chicken is turned. The broiler rack should be placed from 7 to 9 inches from the direct heat and the poultry should be allowed to cook slowly. Turn frequently to permit even cooking and browning, and baste with fat. Allow 50 to 60 minutes for cooking.

PAN FRYING OR SAUTEING

Large cast iron or heavy aluminum skillets containing $\frac{1}{2}$ inch of cooking fat and at moderate heat are needed for pan frying. Fryers or small roasters weighing from 2 to $3\frac{1}{2}$ pounds are meaty sizes that yield satisfactory pieces when disjointed. The larger breeds of chickens, such as Plymouth Rock, New Hampshire Red, and Wyandottes, are more satisfactory for frying than small breeds such as Leghorns. The Leghorns are a naturally small, very active breed with firm muscles and mature early. The larger breeds are tenderer and juicier.

Dip the pieces of chicken in milk and dredge with seasoned flour (containing 2 tablespoons of salt and 1 tablespoon of paprika to 1 pound of flour). Brown and turn until the pieces are well browned on all sides. Cover the pan and allow to cook slowly for an hour, or place in a serving pan and finish in a moderate oven. The chicken should be turned while cooking or covered with a lid or foil to prevent the top pieces from becoming dry.

OVEN FRYING

Chicken, cut in halves, quarters or pieces, can be browned nicely in the oven without turning. Allow $1\frac{1}{4}$ to $1\frac{1}{2}$ hours for cooking at 325°F. Serving pans 12 × 18 in. or baking sheets 18 × 26 in. may be used. Melt a thin layer of fat to cover the bottom of each pan. Proceed according to one or the other of the following methods:

1. Place the chicken seasoned with salt and pepper in the pans and brush each piece with undiluted evaporated milk or undiluted canned mushroom soup and sprinkle generously with slightly crushed cornflakes.

2. Dredge each piece in mixture (proportions 2 cups dry milk, 2 tablespoons of salt, 2 teaspoons of paprika, and 1 pound of flour). Place close together in the baking pan and brush the top with melted butter or margarine.

DEEP FAT FRYING

Deep-fat fried chicken is favored over pan fried in many large kitchens for two special reasons. Deep-fat frying produces an attractive golden brown color uniformly around the pieces of chicken and requires less handling during the frying operation than pan-frying. Halves, quarters, and pieces of young birds may be prepared in this manner. Tenderness and palatability are improved by oven baking at 325°F for 20 to 30 minutes after the poultry pieces have attained a rich golden color in the deep fat (325°F for 10 to 12 minutes).

Poultry for deep frying may be prepared by breading or dipping in a batter. Breading consists of four steps. (a) Dredge the pieces with the seasoned flour, (b) dip them in milk or beaten egg to which a little water has been added, and (c) in fine bread crumbs. (d) Place the pieces apart on a rack to drain and set. This last step is important for good results and about 15 minutes should be allowed for it. Chicken a la Kiev is boneless breast that has been stuffed with butter or cheese and fried in this manner.

Poultry for batter frying may be poached before dipping and then fried until golden and the batter fully cooked, or it may be dipped and fried from the raw state and finished in the oven for 20 to 30 minutes at 325°F. A batter for dipping approximately 50 portions may be made with $1\frac{1}{2}$ cups (6 large) well-beaten eggs blended with 2 cups of milk and $\frac{1}{4}$ cup melted fat, stirred into a mixture of dry ingredients containing 12 oz (3 cups) flour, $1\frac{1}{2}$ tsp salt, and 2 tsp baking powder. After dipping pieces allow them to drain for 10 to 15 minutes on a rack, before frying. Fry at 325°F for 5 minutes if precooked and 12 to 15 minutes if raw, and finish in the oven. Boneless breasts of chicken are especially good prepared in this manner and served with a fruit sauce.

FRICASSEEING OR BRAISING

A fricassee is prepared by dredging the pieces in a flour mixture and pan frying them, then a small amount of water is added and they are allowed to simmer covered until tender. This method of preparation is frequently used for birds that are more mature and less tender than fryers. Disjointed roasters or young fowl are very good prepared in this manner. The poultry may or may not be well browned before adding liquid, according to the individual taste. The liquid from cooking is used for preparing a cream gravy to serve over it.

POACHING, SIMMERING, AND STEAMING

Poaching and simmering or stewing may be done in a steam jacketed kettle, in a stockpot on the range, or in a deep pan in the oven. Steaming is done in the steam cooker. Poaching or stewing produces a better product than cooking in the steam cooker, particularly if the pressure used is greater than 4 or 5 pounds. Shrinkage is at least 20% less in poultry that is poached over that which is roasted, and the tenderness and juiciness is greater. The difference between poaching and stewing is chiefly in terms of the amount of water used. Use only a small amount for poaching, just enough to cover the bottom of the container from approximately $\frac{1}{4}$ to $\frac{1}{2}$ inch. When stewing, the poultry is covered with water.

Disjoint and bone poultry for poaching. Set aside the bones and boney parts such as the back, neck and wings for stewing and for stock. Place the boned pieces in the pan with the legs and thighs on the bottom and the breasts on the top. Slicing of the pieces after they are cooked is most satisfactory if the pieces are placed so that they lay fairly straight while cooking. Season the liquid in the proportions of 1 tablespoon of salt to 1 gallon of water. Turn the pieces during cooking and add liquid as needed. Turkey requires approximately 3 hours for cooking.

The poultry for stewing or simmering may be either left whole or disjointed. If the chief purpose of stewing poultry is to produce soup stock, then add cold water and slowly bring the temperature to simmering. If more flavor in the poultry is desired, cover the poultry with boiling water and quickly bring it to simmering temperature (185 to 195°F). Season the water as indicated under poaching or in proportions of 2 teaspoons of salt for every 5 or 6 pounds of poultry. Additional flavor may be imparted by adding 1 onion, 1 carrot, and 1 stem of celery, 2 peppercorns, and $\frac{1}{2}$ inch of bay leaf per gallon of liquid. Fowl requires approximately $2\frac{1}{2}$ hours and turkey approximately 3 hours of simmering to attain tenderness.

When steaming fowl or turkey, the same proportions of seasoning are used. The birds may be cut up or whole, placed in a pan, and covered with water. If steamed at 5 pounds pressure the cooking requires about one half hour less than for simmering in a steam kettle. The higher temperature in cooking results in firmer or tougher meat.

The poached, simmered or steamed poultry should be chilled before slicing, in order to obtain the most satisfactory slices for cold cuts or sandwich meat. It may be sliced after chilling, either by hand or on a mechanical slicer. The broth should be cooled quickly and refrigerated as soon as possible. For safety, the meat and the broth should not be held beyond three days unless they have been frozen.

SUGGESTED LABORATORY EXPERIENCE

1. Write specifications for 50 portions of the following poultry: (a) chicken for fricassee, (b) Cornish hens, (c) creamed chicken, (d) roast turkey, (e) chicken stock, (f) barbecued chicken, (g) roast goose, and (h) fried chicken.
2. Poach turkey, cool and slice for sandwiches. Calculate cost of portion. Compare quality with that of a commercial turkey roll.
3. Pan-fry and oven-fry 2 to $2\frac{1}{2}$ pound chickens. Compare palatability and appearance. Note time required in preparation of each.
4. Deep fry poultry, part with batter and part breaded. Compare palatability of the two treatments.
5. Prepare stuffing, stuff and roast Cornish hens. Note roasting time for tenderness at 325°F and 400°F.
6. Prepare stock using (a) fowl and (b) young chickens. Compare flavor.
7. Carve one half of a roast turkey using a sharp knife and the other half using the meat slicer for the breasts and thighs. Compare portion weights and appearance.

REVIEW QUESTIONS AND ANSWERS

1. What five kinds of poultry are usually available in most large markets?

Chicken, turkey, ducks, geese, and guinea hens.

2. What are the three U.S.D.A. grades for ready-to-cook poultry?

Grade A, Grade B and Grade C.

3. On what points are the grades based?

Conformation, fleshing, and fat, plus freedom from defects, pinfeathers, and freezer burns.

4. What is the desired conformation?

Blocky, rather than angular shape, and freedom from deformity.

5. What are common defects?

Bruises and skin breaks.

6. When ordering, specifications should include what 6 points?

(a) Kind, (b) type, (c) class, (d) size, (e) style, and (f) grade.

7. Which point indicates quality?

Grade.

8. To what does type and class refer?

Type refers to whether fresh, frozen, cooked or canned. Class is based on sex and age.

9. Why is class important?

It will influence preparation method.

10. How do New York dressed and pan-ready poultry differ?

New York dressed are not cleaned or eviscerated, but merely bled and de-feathered. Pan-ready are cleaned and may be whole or cut into pieces.

11. Which is the more economical in portions per pound, a 12-pound or a 20-pound turkey?

The 20-pound turkeys have a greater per cent of flesh to bone. A 12-pound bird requires $3/4$ to 1 pound A.P. per portion and a 20-pound bird $1/2$ to $3/4$ pound as purchased.

12. What is the best way to defrost frozen poultry?

In a refrigerator at 35 to 40°F.

13. How much time is needed to defrost whole turkeys by this method?

Two or three days.

14. What faster method may be used?

Defrost in original container under cold running water, or water changed frequently to keep it cold.

15. How completely should it be thawed before cooking?

Completely or until pliable, except when frozen-stuffed.

16. What are the best methods for the less tender poultry?

Poaching, braising, stewing, and fricasseeing.

17. What points are to be considered when choosing a cooking method?

Age of the bird, size, flavor, and amount of fat it contains.

18. What is a satisfactory roasting temperature?

325°F.

19. Why is it hazardous to sanitation to roast large, stuffed birds at 250°F or lower?

Because it permits time for bacteria to develop in the warm dressing before a safe internal temperature has been attained.

20. Should poultry be carved as soon as cooking is completed?

No. It should be allowed to stand 15 to 30 minutes depending on size, until juices have become set.

21. Why is it good practice to have large turkeys split before roasting?

It shortens cooking time, makes them easier to handle and keeps the breast from being so close to the hot oven surface.

22. How may a rich brown surface be developed on duck or goose?

By roasting for a few minutes at a high temperature and by rubbing skin with a mixture of 3 parts honey and 1 part soy sauce 10 minutes before the end of roasting.

23. What is the difference between pan-frying and fricasseeing?

Pan-frying is sauteing in fat until done and in fricasseeing water is added after browning and simmered until tender. Sauce is made after fricasseeing and served over the poultry.

24. What is the difference between poaching and stewing?

Poaching is done in a small amount of water ($\frac{1}{4}$ to $\frac{1}{2}$ inch in bottom of pan), and in stewing the poultry is covered with water.

25. What is Chicken a la Kiev?

Boneless breast of chicken stuffed with butter or cheese, breaded and fried in deep fat.

26. Should stewed poultry be boiled rapidly or simmered? Why?

Simmered. High temperature toughens the meat.

15.

Fish and Shellfish

The public taste for fish has increased as methods of preparation have improved. Satisfactory preparation calls for an understanding of the qualities of the flesh and the fat content of the specific fish. Fish, like eggs, are a protein food that requires gentle heat. High temperature causes it to be dry, hard, and unpalatable. Fish does not contain tough connective tissues that call for tenderizing methods of preparation. Lean fish are delicious deep-fat fried and fish that have enough fat to keep them moist while cooking are better baked, sauted in a little fat, or poached. All of the shellfish are low in fat. Clams and shrimp contain 1.4% fat and crabs 2.8%. Herring and salmon are among the fat fish, with salmon being 16.5% fat. (See color insert for Figure 15.1.)

Numerous varieties of fish and shellfish can be purchased fresh, frozen, and canned. When selecting fresh fish, be sure that it is firm and elastic to the touch and has a bright and shiny appearance. It should have little odor. When fish is held too long in the market, the flesh becomes soft and somewhat slimy, the color fades, the eyes sink in the head and become cloudy and a strong odor develops. Frozen fish should be bright in appearance, sweet smelling, and solidly frozen. A brownish tinge and fishy odor indicates poor quality. The meat of shellfish as that of other fish should be bright in color, firm, and with a very mild, sweet odor. Shucked oysters and scallops should not have an excess of liquid in the package.

Federal grades have not been established for fresh fish, but four grades or standards are designated for certain frozen items. The items include fish sticks, raw-breaded fish portions, raw-breaded shrimp, fish blocks, haddock fillets, cod fillets, ocean perch fillets, flounder fillets, sole fillets, halibut steaks, fried scallops, and salmon steaks. The grades are U.S. Grade A—denoting high quality in flavor, odor, color, depth of flesh, uniformity of size, shape and weight, and with limited defects; Grade B—reasonably good in quality, uniformity and processing; Grade C—applies only to raw headless shrimp of reasonably good quality, but rating lower in uniformity and defects than Grade B; and Substandard Grade denotes that which does not measure up to requirements for Grades B and C. Grade A is usually the wisest choice for economy and satisfaction.

Forms or Cuts of Fish

Large kitchens rarely procure fish in the *whole* (or round) and *drawn* forms. The first is just as it came from the water and the second has been eviscerated only. The head, fins, tail and scales are still on the fish and need to be removed before cooking. The edible portion of the whole fish is about 45% and of the eviscerated or drawn fish between 48% and 50%. Cleaning labor and waste should be considered when comparing market prices for these and other forms of fish.

Food departments in hospitals, clubs and charitable institutions may be recipients of fish as gifts, and it is well to know how to dress them. To scale a fish, lay it on the table, grasping the head firmly with the left hand. Hold the knife almost vertical, and starting at the tail and working toward the head scrape off the scales. Soaking the fish in cold water for a few minutes before descaling helps in removing scales more easily. The entrails may then be removed by cutting the length of the fish from the vent to the head. Cut off the pelvic fins. Remove the head and pectoral fins by cutting above the collarbone. A large backbone may be severed by cutting down to it on both sides of the fish and then by breaking the bone at the cut over the edge of the table. Cut it free and cut off the tail.

Figure 15.2   Removing scales from a fresh fish. (Courtesy of the U.S. Fish and Wildlife Service, Bureau of Commercial Fisheries.)

Dressed fish have had the scales and entrails removed, and usually the fins, head, and tail are removed also. The fish is ready for baking or cutting into portions or fillets. It may have the backbone removed so that it will lay open and flat. This is known as *book style* and is popular for barbecuing. The skin and flesh on the outside of the backbone are not cut, but serve to hold the fish together. This style subjects more of the flesh to the heat and smoke in broiling or open-fire barbecuing. The yield of edible meat in dressed fish is about 67%.

Steaks are a popular market form. The edible yield is approximately 86%. They consist of slices made across the fish. When sizing portions make them thick enough for satisfactory cooking, even though they must be cut in half for allotted portion weight. Thin steaks tend to be too dry for palatability. Have them at least $\frac{5}{8}$ to $\frac{3}{4}$-inch thick.

Fillets are the sides of the fish cut away from the backbone. This removes the main bones in the fish, so that it is practically boneless, and yields 100% edible fish. In order to fillet a fish, use a sharp knife and cut along the back from the tail to just behind the head. Cut down to the backbone above and along the collarbone. With the knife flat and in line with the bones cut away the flesh from the bones, cutting from the head to the tail. Avoid cutting into the flesh and, also, leaving flesh on the bones. Lift off the entire side. To skin the fillet, turn it skin side down on the cutting board. Cut away the flesh for about an inch from the tail end. Hold the exposed skin firmly

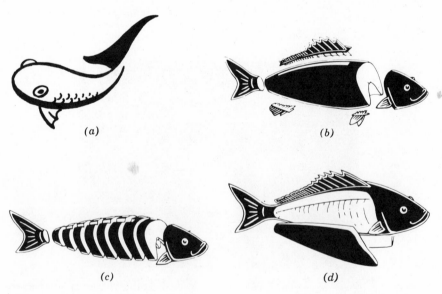

(a)   (b)

(c)   (d)

Figure 15.3 Forms or cuts of market fish: (*a*) whole or round, and drawn; (*b*) dressed; (*c*) steaks; (*d*) fillets.

Figure 15.4   Method of filleting a fish. (Courtesy of the U.S. Fish and Wildlife Service, Bureau of Commercial Fisheries.)

against the board, and with the knife held almost flat with the edge turned only slightly toward the skin, cut the flesh free by firmly pushing the knife along the skin.

The fillets may be cut into *fish sticks* or *fish portions*. The sticks are usually about an inch wide by three inches long. They may be procured raw, raw and breaded, breaded and precooked, and frozen. Fish portions are larger cuts appropriate for a given size serving. They are available in similar treatment to that of the sticks.

Common allowance of portions per pound of fish is as follows:

1. Steaks, fillets, sticks or portions—3 portions ($5\frac{1}{3}$ ounces) or 4 (4 ounces)
2. Dressed fish—2 portions ($5\frac{1}{3}$ ounces) or 3 ($3\frac{2}{3}$ ounces)
3. Whole and Drawn—1 portion ($7\frac{1}{4}$ ounces) or 2 ($3\frac{5}{8}$ ounces)

Forms and Edible Portion of Shellfish

Clams, crabs, lobster, and oysters may be purchased alive in the shell. If shells of hard-shelled clams and oysters are open and the gaping shells will not close, it is a sign that they are dead and not usable. Crab and lobster may be cooked by plunging them into boiling salted water ($\frac{1}{4}$ cup salt to 1 gallon of water). Clams and oysters may be opened and served on the half shell with a cocktail sauce, or steamed until the shells open (5 to 10 minutes). Clams and oysters are sold by the dozen and crab and lobster by the pound.

THE EDIBLE PORTION OF SHELLFISH

Clams	14 to 20%	Serve 6 per portion or approximately 2 to 3 oz of meat
Crabs	10 to 18%	A portion is 1 to 2 lb as purchased
Lobster	35 to 37%	Serve 1 to 2 lb as purchased
Oysters	8 to 11%	Serve 6 medium or 4 large oysters per portion

Shucked clams, oysters, and scallops may be purchased ready for cooking. These entirely edible products may be fresh or frozen. The frozen products should not be thawed until time for use and should never be refrozen. They should be plump, natural color, with clear liquid and free from shell particles. They are sold by pint, quart, or gallon and according to type or size. Types refer to soft or hard clams, sea or bay scallops and Easter, Pacific Coast or Olympia oysters. Oysters are graded for size as follows:

1. *Counts* or *Extra Large* having not more than 160 per gallon.
2. *Extra Selects* or *Large* with not more than 161 to 210 per gallon.
3. *Selects* or *Medium* containing not more than 211 to 300 per gallon.
4. *Standards* or *Small* having not more than 301 to 500 per gallon.
5. *Standards* or *Very Small* with over 500 per gallon.

Usually only the tail section of shrimp is marketed, and is sold according to size or grade. About 50 or 60 per cent of the weight is edible. The shrimp may be fresh, cooked, or frozen. The size designations are jumbo, large, medium, and small. The jumbo size has 12 or 15 shrimp per pound and the small size may have 60 or more per pound. Specific use and labor time for cleaning and deveining are important considerations when buying. Peeled, cleaned, and breaded shrimp are also available.

Cooked meat of lobster, crab, and shrimp is available. These shellfish have been cleaned; the meat is ready for use and 100% edible. It is perishable and should be purchased very fresh, kept under refrigeration, and used as soon as possible.

Canned fish and shellfish are available in cans ranging in size from $3\frac{1}{2}$ ounces to 4 or 5 pounds. The products are of high quality and have usable meat.

Cleaning of Shellfish

Clams are dug from sand and an important part of cleaning is to free them of sand on and in the shell. Wash the shells well with clean sea water and then place the clams in enough clean sea water to cover them, or in a brine of $2\frac{1}{2}$ to 3 ounces of salt to a gallon of water. Change the water or brine several times, allowing 15 or 20 minutes between changes. This is to get the clams to cleanse themselves of sand. Wash them with fresh water and proceed to open them. The shells may be forced open by inserting a sharp, strong, slender-bladed knife between the halves of shell, while holding the hinged area against the palm of the hand. Cut around the edge using a twisting motion to force the shell open. Cut the muscles free from the two halves of shell. A second method of opening clams is to drop them into a small amount of boiling water, then covering it and allowing them to steam 5 or 10 minutes. As soon as the shells begin to open, remove the clams from the water, open them, and remove the meat.

Live crabs are cooked by plunging them into boiling, salted water and allowing them to cook about 15 minutes. The water may contain spices or other seasonings if desired. They are then cracked for picking. Lay the crab on its shell. Lift the shell-like flap with a knife, being careful to avoid being pricked by the prongs under the flap. Discard the flap and the prongs and pull off the top shell. Scrape off the spongy gills, remove the organs in the center of the body, and rinse cavity by allowing water to flow through it. Break into segments containing legs and body portions. Cut through the center to separate the two body halves. Crack the shells with a mallet or the handle of a heavy knife. For orders of cracked crab arrange the body portions with the legs attractively arranged around it.

Lobsters usually range in size from 1 to 3 pounds. They are boiled by

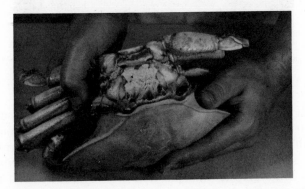

Figure 15.5   Removing the back from a crab. (Courtesy of the U.S. Fish and Wildlife Service, Bureau of Commercial Fisheries.)

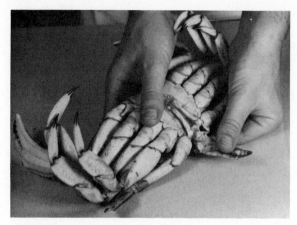

Figure 15.6   Removing the tail flap from the underside of the crab. (Courtesy of the U.S. Fish and Wildlife Service, Bureau of Commercial Fisheries.)

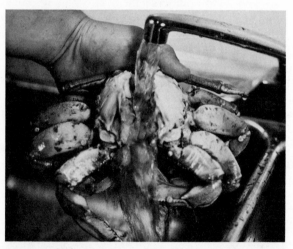

Figure 15.7   Removing the viscera with cold, running water. (Courtesy of the U.S. Fish and Wildlife Service, Bureau of Commercial Fisheries.)

plunging them head first into boiling salted water. The small lobsters require approximately 7 minutes to cook and the large ones 12 to 20 minutes. Cut them in half to clean them. Place the lobster on its back and with a strong sharp knife split it in half lengthwise. Remove the stomach, which is just back of the head, and the intestinal vein which runs from the stomach to the tip of the tail. The liver is green and the roe is coral in color. These are delectable parts and should not be removed. The claws may be cracked with

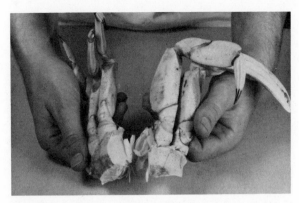

Figure 15.8 Separating the legs and the body. (Courtesy of the U.S. Fish and Wildlife Service, Bureau of Commercial Fisheries.)

Figure 15.9 Place a lobster on its back and split lengthwise with a sturdy French knife. (Courtesy of the U.S. Fish and Wildlife Service, Bureau of Commercial Fisheries.)

a mallet or a nutcracker. Arrange the lobster on a plate or platter and serve with melted butter.

Shrimp heads and thorax contain practically no meat and are usually cut off and discarded on the fishing boats or in the packing plant. They may be cooked before or after shelling. To shell the shrimp, grasp the shell on the inside leg area and lift the shell back. If the tails are to be kept intact, lace the thumb and forefinger near the tail and break the shell loose at this point. Devein the shrimp before they are cooked by inserting a skewer or pick under the vein in the middle of the back and carefully lifting the vein out. If the vein breaks, insert the skewer at the center of the remaining section and pull it out. They may be deveined after cooking by cutting lengthwise

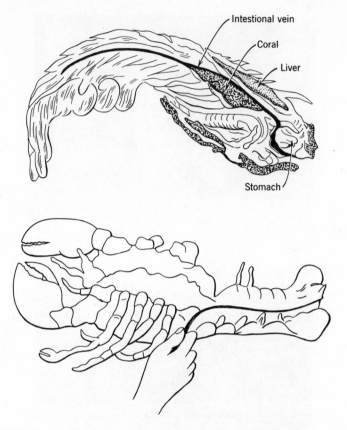

Figure 15.10   Remove intestinal vein which runs from stomach to tail without breaking the shell and remove stomach from high in the body shell.

along the back with a small knife with a sharp point, and removing the exposed sand vein.

The oyster shells should be washed thoroughly and rinsed before opening. To open, lay the oyster on its flat side, hold it firmly with the left hand and insert a knife near the thin end. Cut the large muscle close to the flat, upper shell and remove the shell. Cut the lower end of the same muscle from the lower shell, so that the oyster rests loose in the shell. Examine oysters during shucking to be sure that no shell particles are adhering to the oysters.

STORAGE AND HANDLING OF FISH AND SHELLFISH

Fish is a fragile food in terms of spoilage. The practice of fish vendors of wrapping fish in moisture-proof containers or wrappings or packing it in

Figure 15.11   Shell shrimp by grasping shell on inside of leg area and lifting it back. (Courtesy of the U.S. Fish and Wildlife Service, Bureau of Commercial Fisheries.)

Figure 15.12   Shrimp may be deveined by cutting along the back and removing the exposed vein. (Courtesy of the U.S. Fish and Wildlife Service, Bureau of Commercial Fisheries.)

ice is highly desirable. It protects the fish from dehydration, oxidation, and the absorption of off-flavors. When fish are exposed to the air, oxidation that causes rancidity occurs. This increases odor and spoils flavor. Loss of moisture injures both the texture and appearance of the fish. Such changes lessen palatability.

Fresh fish should be refrigerated at temperatures below 40°F, preferably

TABLE 15.1 SUGGESTED PREPARATION METHODS OF FISH AND SHELLFISH

Kind	Size	Amount of Fat	Flavor	Texture when Cooked	Method of Cooking
Albacore tuna	10 to 25 lb	Moderate	Rich	Meaty, firm	Bake, poach, steam or barbecue
Bass, giant sea	5 to 500 lb	Very low	Mild	Tender	Saute, fry, broil, and lave with butter
Chicken halibut	6 to 10 lb	Very low	Very mild	Very tender	Saute, poach, broil, fry
Halibut	10 to 75 lb	Very low	Mild	Tender	Broil, bake, fry, poach, saute
Cod	3 to 20 lb	Very low	Mild	Soft, breaks easily	Poach or broil
Lingcod	5 to 29 lb	Very low	Delicate	Very tender	Saute, fry, bake, poach or steam
Mackerel	1 to 2 lb	Moderate	Pronounced	Firm	Barbecue, bake
Rockfish (sea bass, red snapper)	2 to 5 lb	Very low	Mild	Flakes readily	Saute, broil, fry
Salmon (King or silver)	6 to 40 lb	High	Rich	Firm	Barbecue, bake, poach, oven fry
Shad	1½ to 7 lb	Moderate	Meatlike	Boney and firm	Bake or poach
Smelt	¾ to 2 oz	Low	Rich	Fine firm	Saute, broil, fry, oven fry
Sole (petrale, rex, flounder)	¾ to 7 lb	Very low	Delicate	Fine and firm	Saute, broil, fry, oven fry

TABLE 15.1 (*Continued*)

Kind	Size	Amount of Fat	Flavor	Texture when Cooked	Method of Cooking
Sea perch	½ to 3 lb	Very low	Mild	Firm	Saute, fry, broil
Sturgeon	15 to 300 lb	Low	Rich	Compact, firm	Barbecue, broil, bake
Swordfish	200 to 600 lb	Low	Rich	Meatlike, firm	Barbecue, broil, bake
Shellfish					
Clams		Very low	Definite	Slightly chewy	Soups, stews, fry
Crabs		Very low	Mild	Tender flakes	Boiled for meat plain or in cocktails and casseroles
Lobster		Very low	Mild	Firm	Boiled to eat plain or in made dishes
Oysters		Very low	Definite	Soft	Stews, saute, fry, cocktails and casseroles
Scallops		Very low	Mild	Firm	Saute, fry, and in made dishes
Shrimp		Very low	Mild	Firm	Fry, cocktails and made dished

363

at 30 to 32°F. Well-wrapped in moisture proof paper it is not likely to impart flavor to other foods in a refrigerator. If fresh fish cannot be refrigerated, it should be cooked at once and reheated for service. Frozen fish should be kept wrapped and held at 0°F or lower and not allowed to thaw until time for use. When thawing frozen fish, thaw it just to a condition that permits ease of preparation and cooking. Cooking may be done from the frozen state if adequate allowance is made in the cooking time.

When thawing frozen fish, use either of two methods. The first and the preferred method is to thaw it in the refrigerator at 37 to 40°F. The other is to leave it in its moisture proof wrappings and thaw it in cold running water. Thawing at room temperature is not recommended, because it allows time for bacterial action and an excess loss of moisture that results in drier fish. Thawing in the refrigerator requires 18 to 36 hours depending upon the size of the fish. A 1-pound fillet thaws in 18 hours in the refrigerator and in a half hour in cold running water.

FISH COOKERY

The best method of preparation for fish depends upon the characteristics of the specific fish or fish product. A considerable range in size, texture, form, percentage of fat, and strength of flavor are represented. As much sensitive care in protecting the palatability of this protein product is required as in egg cookery. Protect freshness and avoid high temperatures and overcooking. Serve it as quickly as possible after the cooking has been completed. Rotate preparation to prevent overcooking on the hot serving table.

The stimulating flavor of fish makes it suitable as an appetizer. Pickled and smoked fish, as well as the six kinds of shellfish shown in Table 15.1 are suitable to use for cocktails and hors d'oeuvres. Both fish and shellfish are popular for stews, chowders, and bisques. They blend well with other foods in the preparation of casseroles, and are a delicious entree when prepared in the simplest manner. The chief methods of preparing fish and shellfish are baking, broiling, barbecuing, deep-fat frying, pan-frying or sauteing, oven-frying and poaching, boiling or steaming.

Baking

Fat fish, such as mackerel, salmon, and tuna are best for baking. The whole fish or thick fillets or steaks are the most satisfactory. The whole fish should be sprinkled with salt, pepper and lemon juice. It may or may not be stuffed as desired. When preparing steaks or fillets for baking, dip them in a mixture of melted butter or margarine and lemon juice, sprinkle them with salt and

Figure 15.13 Pan-frying can be done on baking sheets in the oven. (Courtesy of the U.S. Fish and Wildlife Service, Bureau of Commercial Fisheries.)

Figure 15.14 Serve the golden portions while they are crisp and hot. (Courtesy of the U.S. Fish and Wildlife Service, Bureau of Commercial Fisheries.)

pepper and place them in a greased pan. When preparing fish that is not high in fat, it is well to score the skin and lay a strip of bacon over it to add fat during baking. Bake in a moderate oven (350°F) until the fish flakes easily when pierced with a sharp-tined fork. For a whole fish this requires from 40 to 60 minutes. Beware of overcooking. Serve with maitre d'hotel butter.

Broiling and Barbecuing

The fish, unless quite small, should be prepared book style so that they lay flat and open on the broiler rack. Grease the rack well before placing the fish on it, and lay the fish on the rack skin side down. Brush the surface well with a mixture of clarified butter and lemon juice, and sprinkle with salt and pepper. Place the rack six or eight inches from the source of heat, and broil for 7 to 10 minutes, depending on the thickness of the fish and the distance from the heat. In broiling large whole fish, turning the fish over is easier if a second rack is greased and placed on top of the fish and the two racks, with the fish between, are turned over together. If the fish is very large, it may be necessary to have two persons hold and turn the two racks.

Outdoor barbecuing of fish is done in a similar manner. A pit is needed for the fire. It may be dug into the ground or built up approximately 30 inches high out of concrete blocks or a frame. The racks may be made of heavy $\frac{3}{4}$-inch chicken wire with pipe around the four sides to give rigidity. The fire should be made of hardwood that has a sweet flavored smoke such as alder or apple wood. The fish is first placed on the rack flesh side down to cook slowly and absorb the flavor of the smoke. The time required for cooking depends on the distance from the heat, the thickness of the fish, and the amount of heat. Before turning the fish, cover it with a sheet of foil large enough to fully cover the fish and allow the edges to be crumpled into a rim to retain the juices. Place a second rack over the top and turn the two so that the fish is resting skin side down on the foil. Continue cooking until the underside is done. The top rack should be removed and the fish brushed with a mixture of melted butter and lemon juice and seasoned with salt and pepper during the second period of cooking. Onion juice and a small amount of oregano may be added, if desired.

Poaching

Cooked fish is very tender; when poaching fish protect its form by wrapping it in cheesecloth. Poaching may be done in a flat pan on top of the range or in the oven. The liquid to cover it may be court bouillon or water seasoned with a bouquet garni. A well-seasoned liquid may be prepared by simmering

Figure 15.15 A poached salmon, skinned and garnished for the buffet service at The Wind-jammer Restaurant, Seattle. (Courtesy of the U.S. Fish and Wildlife Service, Bureau of Commercial Fisheries.)

1 gallon of water or fish stock, $1\frac{1}{2}$ tablespoons of salt, 2 cups of sliced onion, 1 teaspoon of whole black peppercorns, $\frac{1}{2}$ teaspoon whole allspice, 1 bay leaf and 1 cup of lemon juice or vinegar for 15 or 20 minutes. Two cups of white cooking wine may be added for extra flavor. Place the cheesecloth-wrapped fish in the pan and pour the boiling liquid over it. Allow it to simmer until the fish is fork tender. The fish may be served hot or cold. This is a good way to prepare fish for salads and sandwiches.

Pan-frying or Sautéing

The use of clarified butter or mild flavored cooking fat and slow cooking temperature are recommended for pan-frying. The fish may be coated by dipping in seasoned flour (2 tablespoons salt, 2 teaspoons paprika to 1 pound flour) then into a liquid mixture (2 beaten eggs and 1 cup milk) and then into fine cracker meal (12 to 14 ounces for 50 portions), or in seasoned corn-meal or bread crumbs. Pan-frying is a good method for preparing small, whole fish, steaks or fillets. Cook just until fork tender. Serve on a hot plate, sprinkle with lemon juice and chopped parsley, and spoon butter

Figure 15.16   Trout can be sautéd or stuffed and baked. (Courtesy of the U.S. Fish and Wildlife Service, Bureau of Commercial Fisheries.)

Figure 15.17   Pan-frying is a good method of preparing small whole fish. (Courtesy of the U.S. Fish and Wildlife Service, Bureau of Commercial Fisheries.)

from the pan over the fish. To prepare fish a la Amandine, add slivered almonds to the butter in the pan after the fish is removed. Brown them slightly and serve the butter and almonds over the fish.

When preparing for large numbers, the pan-frying can be done on baking sheets in the oven. The pan should be covered with a generous coating of clarified butter, and the portion-size pieces of fish prepared with the desired coating. Dip the top of the pieces in the butter and place in the pan without crowding. Bake for 10 to 15 minutes in a hot oven (400°F), turning once if necessary for even browning. Serve at once while hot and crisp.

Deep-fat Frying

Deep-fat frying is one of the favorite methods of cooking sticks and portions of lean fish and shellfish. Prepare the products by dipping in seasoned flour, liquid-egg mixture, and fine cracker meal as is described under pan-frying. Let stand on a rack for 15 minutes to dry and set. Fry at 350°F until nicely browned. The approximate times required are as follows:

frozen breaded shrimp	4 min	fresh breaded scallops	4 min
fresh breaded shrimp	3 min	breaded fried clams	1 min
frozen fish fillets	4 min	breaded fried oysters	5 min
fresh fish fillets	3 min	frozen fish sticks	4 min

Figure 15.18 Deep-frying is a favorite method of preparation for lean fish and shellfish. (Courtesy of the U.S. Fish and Wildlife Service, Bureau of Commercial Fisheries.)

SUGGESTED LABORATORY EXPERIENCE

1. Dress a fish. Remove scales, eviscerate, remove head, fins, and tail.
2. Fillet a fish, and cut fillets into portion size pieces according to a given weight and cost per portion.
3. Weigh a crab. Clean the crab and pick the meat. Weigh the meat and calculate the percentage of meat in the total weight.
4. Cook, husk, and devein shrimp.
5. Clean and open clams and oysters.
6. Cook bones and trimmings of the fish, add seasonings as described for Court Bouillon. Poach part of the fillets. Prepare a Mornay sauce to serve with them.
7. Pan-fry or oven-fry part of the fillets and the oysters.
8. Deep-fry shrimp and part of the fish fillets (cut into fish sticks).
9. Prepare bouillabaise with the clams, clam nectar, and remaining seafood.

REVIEW QUESTIONS AND ANSWERS

1. In what ways does the handling of fish resemble that required for eggs?

Both are highly perishable protein foods that deteriorate rapidly out of refrigeration and both are toughened by high temperature in cooking.

2. In what stages of preservation are seafoods available?

Fresh, frozen, canned, smoked, and pickled.

3. Which of these are graded for quality?

Frozen and canned.

4. What are the forms or cuts of fish?

Whole or round, drawn, dressed, book style, steaks, and fillets.

5. What is a fillet?

It is the fleshy side of fish cut away from the bones. It may or may not have the skin removed.

6. What is a fish stick?

It is a slender piece of fish cut from a fillet, and may measure approximately 1 × 3 inches.

7. How are clams and oysters sold?

By the dozen in the shell and by the pint, quart, or gallon if shucked.

8. Are clams and oysters in the shell alive or dead?

They should be alive in the shell. If dead, they are not usable and should be discarded.

9. How can one tell whether they are alive or dead?

Live oysters and clams tightly close their shells. If shells are loose or open and won't close they should be thrown away.

10. What are the size grades for oysters?

Counts or Extra Large, Extra Selects or Large, Selects or Medium, Standards or Small and Standards or Very Small.

11. How are lobster, crab, and shrimp sold?

By the pound and count. They may be alive or cooked and in the shells or meat only. The picked meat is sold by the pound.

12. What are the sizes for shrimp?

Jumbo, Large, Medium, and Small ranging from 12 or 15 to 60 per pound.

13. What is the method to get clams to cleanse themselves of sand?

By placing them in clean seawater or brine.

14. How are live crabs and lobsters cooked?

By plunging them into boiling salted water.

15. Which shellfish may be served raw?

Clams and oysters.

16. At what temperature should fish be stored?

Fresh fish at 32°F and frozen fish at 0°F or lower.

17. How should frozen fish be thawed?

In the refrigerator or in the original wrapping in cold running water.

18. How much time is required for the thawing?

In the refrigerator—18 to 36 hours depending on the size of the fish.

19. Should the majority of fish be cooked at high or low temperature?

At low temperature, because high temperature toughens and dries it.

20. What are the best methods for cooking fat fish?

Baking, broiling, and poaching.

21. Which fish are high in fat?

Salmon, mackerel, and tuna.

22. What is meant by book style fish?

Fish with backbone removed so that it lays open and flat for broiling.

23. What quality is desirable in fish for deep-fat frying?

It should be low in fat content.

24. Are shellfish high or low in fat?

Very low.

25. Why should fish be wrapped in cheesecloth for poaching?

To protect the shape of the tender fish and make it easier to handle.

26. Describe method of oven-frying fish for a large group.

Use a baking sheet with a generous amount of clarified butter, coat fish with dipping mixtures, dip top of pieces in butter in baking sheet and arrange on the pan without crowding. Bake at 400°F for 10 to 15 minutes.

16.

Selection and Preparation of Beef

Meat is the heart of the meal for the majority of people, and in the United States the favorite meat is beef. It claims a major share of the average food budget, with an average per capita consumption of about 90 pounds of beef per year. Both the cost of the product and the enjoyment potential emphasizes the importance of selecting beef wisely and preparing it well. More research has been done to discover best cookery methods of beef than with any other food product. (See color insert for Figure 16.1.)

Tenderness and amount of fat in the tissues influences cooking method and eating quality. These qualities depend in large degree upon grade and cut of beef. The best beef is from young, fully grown steers of the beef breeds. Beef cattle, such as Angus, Hereford, and Shorthorn, are blocky in build. The chucks, ribs, loins, and rounds are well filled out with a fine depth of flesh, and the neck and shanks are short. Milk breeds, such as the Holstein and Guernsey, tend to be more angular and paunchy in build with less depth of flesh in the back and leg muscles. Beef animals are prepared for the market by lot or stall feeding for a minimum of six to eight weeks. The longer the period in which animals are well fed and held from ranging for food or exercising their muscles, the better the quality of the meat. Prime cattle are reasonably confined and well fed from birth. Extended feeding is required for fat to be distributed throughout the muscle tissues.

GRADES OF BEEF

Federal inspection and grading provides valuable protection for consumers. Regulations governing this have been established by the United States Department of Agriculture. The Federal Wholesome Meat Act requires that states enforce a meat inspection program equal to the government program for wholesome meat prepared under sanitary conditions. Meat that has been Federally inspected carries a round stamp (of vegetable dye) with the legend "U.S. Insp'd & P'S'D" (U.S. Inspected and Passed), indicating that the meat is wholesome for human consumption. The grade stamp is shield-shaped and has the letters USDA and the name of the grade. (Figure 16.2.)

There are six grades of market beef: Prime, Choice, Good, Standard, Commercial, and Utility. (a) Prime beef is young, well-marbled, velvet-grained meat that has good depth of flesh in lean areas. (b) Choice grade is produced in larger quantities and is sold at a slightly lower price than Prime. It is preferred by many consumers because the meat is tender and well marbled but has less fat and has less trim or shrinkage than Prime. (c) Good grade is considered to be a thrifty one. The cuts are well fleshed and relatively tender with a fairly good amount of fat distributed through the tissues. It has less fat trim and less loss from shrinkage because of fat in cooking. The Good Grade animals often have been specially fed for a shorter period and sell for a lower price. (d) Standard grade has a high proportion of lean meat and is less juicy than the higher grades. It has a mild, good flavor and if it is larded during roasting it has a fine degree of palatability. (e) Commercial grade beef may be from lean, older cattle that have had little or no lot feeding and from animals which have not responded well to special feeding. It provides economical meat that can be made delicious with long-period, low-temperature cooking and proper seasoning. (f) Utility grade beef has little or no fat. It tends to be dry unless well larded and/or cooked by slow, moist-heat methods. It is a source of wholesome, economical meat that can be made into tasty soups, stews, pot roasts, and ground meat dishes. Added richness, suitable flavoring materials, and tenderizing methods of preparation are required for greatest palatability.

The grade stamp serves as a clue to quality and guide to best preparation method. When the grade is not indicated, quality can be judged from the appearance of the meat. Flesh of top-grade beef is firm and fine-grained and has a velvety tenderness. It is bright cherry-red in color and has marbling of light-colored fat. There is a layer of firm, flaky fat on the outside edge. The bones are porous and reddish rather than white and flintlike. Young

Figure 16.2 Stamps indicating United States Department of Agriculture grades for meat quality.

animals have blood in their bones but older animals have bones that are whiter and more solid in texture. Top-grade beef is butchered when the animal is one and a half to two years old, or as soon as it has attained full growth. The lower grades are largely made up of dairy cows and breeder stock that are older. Beef from the older animals requires tenderizing methods of preparation.

An animal's muscles strengthen or toughen as they are used. Normal activities in living cause some of the muscles to be used more than others. The muscles along the back, for example, are used less than those in the legs that are required for walking. The length of the fibers and the amount and kind of connective tissue also influence tenderness. The distribution of fat as marbling is greatest in the least used and tenderest muscles. This can be observed readily in the rib and loin areas of top quality beef.

The shape of the bone serves as a clue to tender cuts of beef. The long rib bone connected to the chine bone is easy to discern in the rib area. The bones in the loin area are somewhat T-shaped as seen in the T-bone and porterhouse steaks. The pelvic bone in the sirloin area is wedge shaped. The less tender cuts have the round bones of the arm (front leg) and leg, the three-pronged bone of the shoulder blade and the smaller neck bones.

CUTS OF BEEF

The cost and shortage of skilled labor for meat cutting has brought about pronounced changes in the meat buying practices for large kitchens. Formerly beef was bought as sides or quarters of the carcass, and in primal or wholesale cuts. A person employed as a butcher or the chef cut and prepared the meat for cooking. The general practice today is to buy pan or oven-ready meat that requires a minimum of cutting by the chef or cook. Both the buyer and the person who prepares the meat can perform their functions more successfully if they know something of the anatomy of beef and have judgment

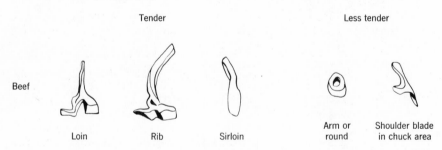

Figure 16.3   The shape of the bones furnishes a clue to the cut of meat.

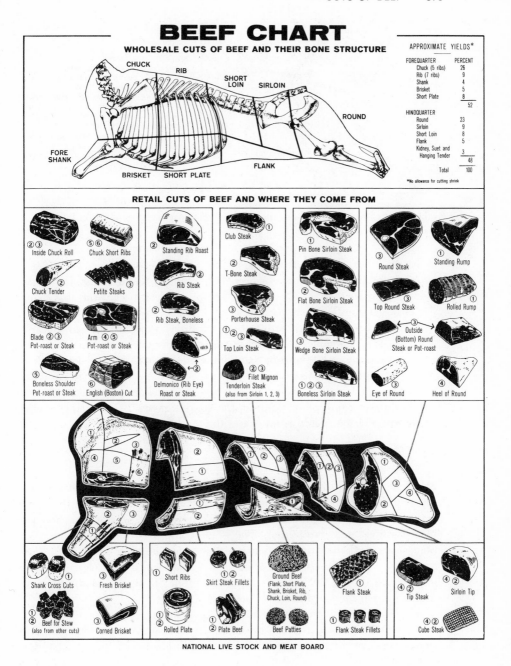

Figure 16.4   Cuts of beef. (Courtesy of the National Livestock and Meat Board.)

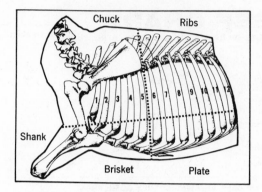

The accepted way to count ribs in all meats is to start at the front (anterior) and count to the rear (posterior). In a side of beef there are 13 ribs. Twelve of them are shown in the bone chart at the left. The 13th rib is in the hindquarter. The chuck contains five ribs (1 to 5). The rib has seven ribs (6 to 12).

Much confusion and misunderstanding will be eliminated when meat men, educators and consumers recognize and use this method of counting ribs.

Figure 16.5 Bone structure in the fore quarter of beef. (Courtesy of the National Livestock and Meat Board.)

of values, plus an understanding of the characteristics and preparation methods for the various cuts of beef. It is useful to know something of the shape and tenderness of muscles, the layers of fat and lean, the shape and size of bones, depth of lean areas and direction in which fibers lay.

A side of beef is divided into the fore and hind quarter between the 12th and 13th ribs. The one rib remaining on the hind quarter serves as a framework to keep the soft flesh from wrinkling while it is still warm from butchering. This improves the appearance of the cut and makes it easier to cut when cool. The wholesale or primal cuts in the fore quarter are the chuck, rib, shank, brisket, and plate, and in the hind quarter are the loin, round (including the shank and rump), and the flank.

Chuck

There is considerable difference in the way wholesale cuts are divided for the retail trade and for large quantity food establishments. For the retail trade, the chuck is made into arm and blade roasts, shortribs, and boneless meat for stew and hamburger. The blade roast is cut across the shoulder blade bone and the arm roasts across the round bone of the fore leg. The roasts may range in thickness from 2 to 4 inches. The muscle bundles in either roast do not lay in a common direction. Slicing across the fibers to improve tenderness is difficult to accomplish.

For large quantity use, the chuck is divided into six or seven boneless roasts or pot roasts that have muscle fibers in a more consistent direction (lengthwise) for greater ease in slicing. Institution buyers need to be alert to the skill used in removal of excess fat, bone, and hard connective tissue and cartilage. The fibers should be in a reasonably lengthwise position and

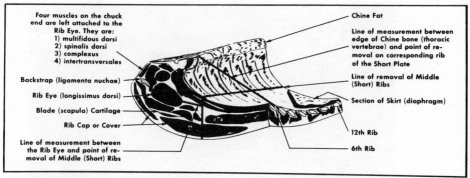

View of beef rib from chuck (anterior) end

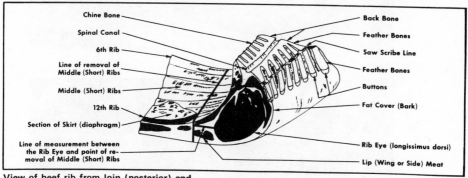

View of beef rib from loin (posterior) end

Figure 16.6   Nomenclature for the rib section of beef. (Courtesy of the National Livestock and Meat Board.)

firmly tied for ease in slicing. The roasts from the different areas of the chuck differ slightly in texture or grain, amount of fat in the tissues, and flavor. The buyer needs to become sufficiently familiar with the qualities to be able to specify preference when buying.

A square-cut chuck (chuck minus brisket and shank) may be cut into six or seven easy-to-carve roasts.

Cuts 1 and 2. Remove the arm bone by cutting along the top of it, around it, and cutting it loose from the shoulder joint. Next, cut from the socket of the joint, along the outside ridge of the shoulder blade. Let the knife follow along the flat area of the blade and cut along the edge of the blade back to the socket. Pull the flesh (clod) away from the blade. Cut into two or three roasts according to the size desired. Trim as needed, then roll each roast tightly and tie it.

Cut 3. Remove the meat from the other side of the ridge of the shoulder blade to the top of the chuck. Roll and tie this.

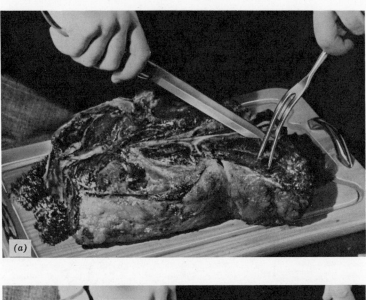

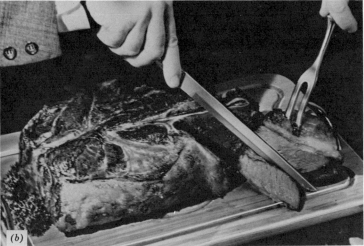

Figure 16.7 Carving across the muscle in a blade roast. (Courtesy of Swift and Company.)

Cut 4. Remove the triangular muscle that lies along the inside of the ridge of the shoulder blade (the Scotch tender). Shape up the remainder by removing the blade bone, cutting off the lower part for shortribs and the neck area about 1 inch above the first rib.

Cuts 5 and 6. Remove the top muscle by cutting flush against the rib bones

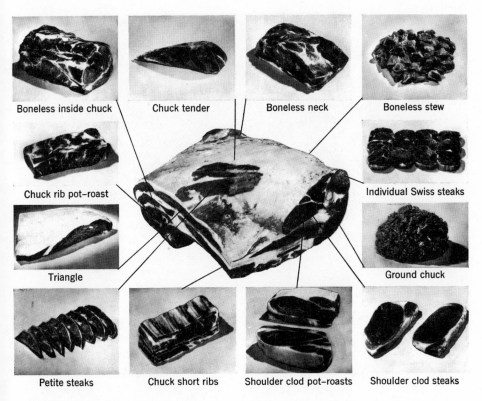

Boneless inside chuck   Chuck tender   Boneless neck   Boneless stew

Chuck rib pot-roast   Individual Swiss steaks

Triangle   Ground chuck

Petite steaks   Chuck short ribs   Shoulder clod pot-roasts   Shoulder clod steaks

Figure 16.8 Cuts from the muscle-boned chuck. (Courtesy of the National Livestock and Meat Board.)

until the natural separation is reached, then peel it from the heart of the chuck. Divide and tie it into two roasts.

Cut 7. Trim the heart of the chuck from the backbone. Roll and tie it.

Brisket and Plate

The brisket and plate are composed of alternate layers of fat and lean muscle. The fat layers and cartilage in the brisket are known as a deckle. The brisket may be purchased with or without the deckle. This meat has a very good flavor and is usually prepared by boiling or braising. A high-grade brisket makes a delicious roast if roasted until tender at a low temperature (250°F) to an internal temperature of 180°F. It is well to continue cooking for at least another 20 or 30 minutes at 180°F for further tenderizing.

The upper part of the plate and the lower part of the rib section are used

Figure 16.9   A high grade brisket makes a delicious roast when properly cooked. (Courtesy of Swift and Company.)

for shortribs. These are cut across the rib bones. They are prepared by braising. When purchasing brisket or plate cuts it is necessary to allow 47 to 50% for trim and shrinkage on the bone-in cuts and 23 to 25% on boneless, well-trimmed cuts. It should be noted that these percentages are reflected in the price quotations.

Shanks and Boneless Meat for Stew and Ground Beef

Shanks contain much connective tissue. If sliced perpendicular to the bone and cooked slowly in water, they are useful in making rich flavored stock. The meat may be cut up and used in soups or chopped for use in sandwiches after cooking. The bone marrow as well as the meat enriches flavor.

Boneless meat from the chuck, plate, brisket, flank, shanks, and that resulting from trimming other beef cuts may be used for ground beef and stew meat. Stew meat should be cut into reasonably uniform pieces and should not contain more than 20% fat. Fat on the individual pieces should be trimmed so as not to exceed $\frac{1}{4}$ inch in thickness. It is well to designate the maximum fat content acceptable when purchasing ground beef. It may vary from 12 to 30%. Many markets designate difference in fat content as (a) ground beef or hamburger, 25 to 30% fat; (b) ground chuck, 18 to 20% fat; and (c) ground round, 12 to 18% fat.

Rib

The rib of beef is tender enough for dry roasting and the top grades are well-enough marbled with fat and tender for broiling. Rib steaks have the shortrib area removed and may be cut with or without the remaining bone. For roasts or steaks, the rib bone should be cut so that it will not extend more than 3 inches from the extreme tip of the rib eye (longissimus dorsi). When made into steaks it is desirable, at the chuck end of the rib section, for the shoulder blade bone and connected cartilage and the outer muscles (a, b, c, d, e, and f, Figure 16.10) to be removed. These steaks with the bone in will weigh 8 to 16 ounces or 4 to 12 ounces without bone, depending upon thickness and portion size desired. Market or Spencer steaks are made from the eye of the rib (longissimus dorsi).

It is common practice to separate the rib from the chuck between the 5th and 6th ribs, and from the loin between the 12th and 13th ribs. This leaves five ribs in the chuck and seven in the standing rib. Severed at this point

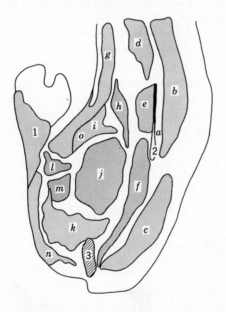

Figure 16.10 A cross-section at the rib end of the chuck (between the fifth and sixth ribs) showing location of bones and muscles. (*a*) infraspinatus, (*b*) latissimus dorsi (rose of Sharon), (*c*) trapezius, (*d*) and (*e*) seratus ventralis, (*f*) rhomboideus, (*g*) intercostal muscles, (*h*) serratus dorsalis, (*i*) longissimus costarum, (*j*) longissimus dorsi, (*k*) spinalis dorsi, (*l*) intertransversalis, (*m*) complexus, (*n*) multifidus dorsi, (*o*) lavatores costarum, (1) thoracic vertetra, (2) scapula (shoulder blade cartilage), and (3) ligamentum nuchae (back strap).

between the chuck and the rib, cartilage from the tip of the shoulder blade is in the chuck end of the rib section. The wholesale rib, as it is broken out of the fore quarter, contains both very tender meat and some that requires tenderizing methods of preparation. A tender back muscle (longissimus dorsi) extends in a carcass from the chuck to the sirloin. This muscle can be readily observed at the loin end of the rib section. At the chuck end of the rib there are less tender muscles that lie outside or above the eye of the rib (Note a, b, c, d, e, and f in Figure 16.10). The lower part or the shortrib section of the standing rib is composed of layers of fat and lean and rib bones. The meat has excellent flavor but is less tender and is best prepared by braising. When dividing a standing rib for cooking one needs to (a) allow for the best method of cooking according to tenderness of each part, (b) plan for the most attractive appearance, and (c) prepare it for ease of portioning and serving.

There are several methods commonly used in preparing the wholesale rib for roasting. (a) Two strips, each 2 to $2\frac{1}{2}$ inches wide, may be removed from the plate end of the rib section, for use as shortribs. The remainder may be roasted with very little additional trimming except for excess fat. (b) All of the bones, cartilage, back strap, and excess fat may be removed, and the meat rolled around the rib eye and firmly tied. (c) The shortribs may be removed approximately 1 inch from the extreme end of the rib eye and the backbones removed. The backbones or a layer of fat may be tied over the area from which the backbones were removed, to protect the meat from drying while roasting. This covering is removed before placing the roast on the counter or buffet table for slicing. (d) The quality of the roast may be improved in tenderness by lifting the natural fat covering and removing the muscles that lie above the rib eye at the chuck end of the rib. The covering is then tied back over the cut area. This method of cutting yields more uniform tenderness and slices that are more uniform in diameter. The uniform diameter of slices promotes more accurate portion control. (e) A more deluxe treatment of the rib for roasting is done by removing all of the bones and

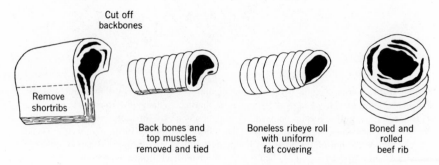

Cut off backbones

Remove shortribs

Back bones and top muscles removed and tied

Boneless ribeye roll with uniform fat covering

Boned and rolled beef rib

Figure 16.11   Methods of preparing beef ribs for roasting.

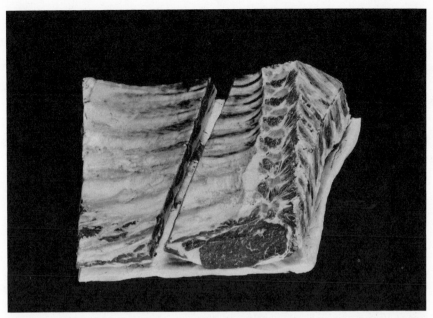

Figure 16.12   Rib of beef, loin end view, with chine and feather bones and backstrap removed. Cover and cap meat separated and natural seam and shortribs severed from rib 2 inches from rib eye. (Courtesy of the National Livestock and Meat Board.)

Figure 16.13   Boned and rolled rib of beef. (Courtesy of the National Livestock and Meat Board.)

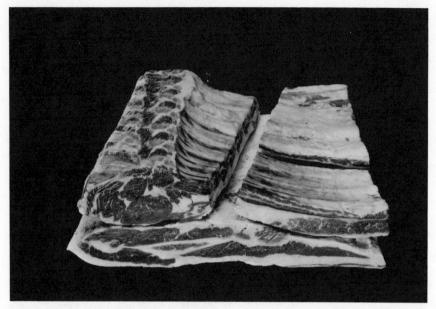

Figure 16.14 Chuck end view of beef rib showing cap meat and cover separated from rib eye at natural seam. (Courtesy of the National Livestock and Meat Board.)

the less tender muscles, leaving chiefly the eye of the rib. An even covering of tender fat, approximately $\frac{1}{4}$-inch thick, is wrapped around the lean rib eye. This is an especially good treatment for lean, lower grades that are not well marbled. In addition to the fat tied around the roast, strips of fat may be put through the eye muscle with a larding needle.

Loin

The full loin, as cut in many markets, includes the short loin, the loin end or sirloin, and the sirloin tip. The short loin yields club, T-bone, and porterhouse steaks. There are two very tender muscles, the tenderloin and the loin eye or strip, which are the chief ones in the short loin. The loin strip has a fairly uniform size and shape from one end of the short loin to the other. The tenderloin, on the other hand, is largest at the sirloin end but diminishes in size until little or none appears at the rib end of the shortloin. Therefore club steaks, which are cut from the rib end of the shortloin, contain little or no tenderloin. The T-bone steaks taken from the center of the shortloin have a small diameter of tenderloin and the porterhouse steaks cut from the sirloin end of the shortloin have the largest tenderloin area of the three steaks. The loin end or sirloin area is the source of sirloin steaks. The steaks may be

Figure 16.15   A deluxe rib roast, with beef for grinding, shortribs, and defatted cap meat. (Courtesy of the National Livestock and Meat Board.)

Figure 16.16   Boneless rib eye roll, with grinding meat, lean cap meat, and shortribs. (Courtesy of the National Livestock and Meat Board.)

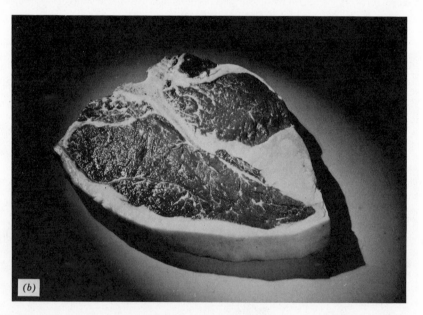

Figure 16.17   Loin steaks, in order from the rib end of the loin, include (*a*) club, (*b*) T-bone, (*c*) porterhouse, and (*d*) sirloin steaks. (Courtesy of the National Livestock and Meat Board.)

(c)

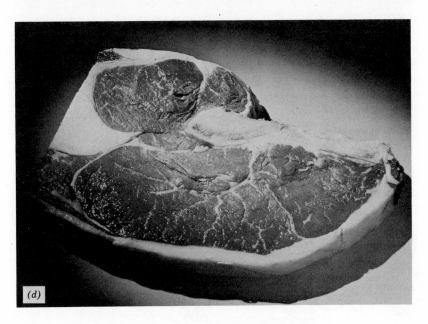

(d)

cut with a specified amount of the flank edge. An intermediate steak is cut with 3 inches from the outer tip of the loin eye muscle; a short cut, 2 inches; an extra short cut, 1 inch; and a special cut follows the contour of the eye muscle.

The top muscle of the short loin may be stripped out so that it is boneless. This cut may then be sliced for strip steaks or used whole as a roast. The tenderness and good flavor of this cut has given it a very high popularity rating. It can be cut into individual portions that are thick enough to broil well and has a size and shape that appears attractive on a plate. The uniform size and shape of the loin strip permits fairly uniform portioning and more exact timing when broiling.

The tenderloin is a smaller muscle and the tenderest in a beef. It has a milder flavor than the loin strip. Special names have been given to the steaks cut from the different areas of the tenderloin. The tenderloin butt is located in the loin end or sirloin area. The chateaubriand is from the porterhouse area of the shortloin. The filets are next, then tournedos, followed by filet mignon and the tenderloin tips. All are of equal flavor and tenderness; the names used designate diameter of the tenderloin. They may be cut with different thickness. The chateaubriand is usually cut 2-inches thick.

The short loin, with tenderloin only removed, is called a shell loin. Establishments that sell a large number of strip steaks may buy shell loins and have them held at a suitable temperature and humidity for aging (33 to 35°F and 85 to 87% relative humidity). There is a certain amount of tenderizing and development of rich meat flavor during the aging process, and some loss from evaporation. The bones and covering protect the flesh during the aging period (1 to 3 weeks).

A steak needs to be thick enough for broiling to develop a crisp, well browned exterior while retaining a juicy interior. When steaks are thin, it is

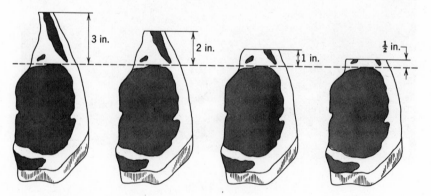

Figure 16.18   Specify length of tail from loin eye muscle to flank end.

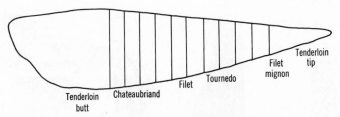

Figure 16.19 Steaks from the tenderloin of beef.

impossible to brown them without their becoming too dry inside. A steak for broiling needs to be at least ¾ inch or more in thickness. Club, strip and tenderloin steaks can be cut to satisfactory thickness and still be suitable for one portion. T-bone, porterhouse, and sirloin steaks cut thick enough for proper broiling (1 or 2 inches thick) are large enough for two or more generous portions. When it is necessary to economize on portion size, it is better to have one steak of suitable thickness for broiling and cut it into portions than to have two steaks that are too thin to process well. An allowance of 6 to 8 ounces per portion should be considered minimum for steak. If this means a portion cost that is too high, then a less expensive cut that affords appetite satisfaction should be used.

TABLE 16.1 SUGGESTED PORTION WEIGHTS FOR BEEF STEAKS

Cut	Ounces per Steak	
	With Bone	Boneless
Cubed		3 to 8
Round steaks		3 to 10
(inside or outside and knuckle)		
Rib steak	8 to 16	8 to 12
Ground patties		3 to 8
Club	8 to 16	8 to 12
T-bone	8 to 28	
Porterhouse	12 to 32	
Loin strip—Intermediate	8 to 28	8 to 24
Short cut	8 to 24	6 to 20
Extra short cut	8 to 24	6 to 20
Top sirloin butt		4 to 28
Center cut		4 to 16
Tenderloin		4 to 14

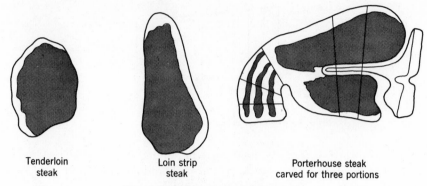

| Tenderloin steak | Loin strip steak | Porterhouse steak carved for three portions |

Figure 16.20 Portion cuts of loin steak.

When serving one large T-bone, porterhouse, or sirloin steak to more than one person, it should be remembered that there are different degrees of tenderness in the steak. It should be carved so that each person has some of the choicest part as well as some of the less tender portion. Carving is made easiest by cutting around the bone first, so that the meat is free from the bone. Divide the back muscle, the tenderloin, and the tail of the steak into as many pieces as there are persons to be served. Give a cutting from each area to each person.

Round

The sirloin tip (knuckle) that extends into the front of the leg from the sirloin is tender enough for roasting in young, top grades of beef. Sirloin tip roasts of good grade and lower should be cooked at low temperature and for a long enough period to tenderize them. This cut is boneless and 1 pound as purchased yields from 10 to 12 ounces of cooked meat. The boned and rolled rump of beef may be prepared in similar fashion and the portion yield of a boneless cut as purchased is about the same as that for the sirloin tip.

The muscle bundles in the round of beef form certain natural divisions. The top round or the inside of the leg, separates from the bottom round or outside of the leg through the center from the round bone to the back of the leg. Top round in the top grades of beef is tender and juicy enough for dry roasting. Grades good and lower should be cooked slowly at low temperature (250°F to an internal temperature of 160 to 180°F), or may have liquid added and slowly pot roasted. This cut is excellent for Swiss or braised steaks. The bottom round or outside of the leg has two natural divisions. The smaller one which is at the back of the leg is known as the eye of the round. The bottom round is less tender than the top round and requires long-period, low-temperature cooking or moist-heat preparation for palatable tenderness.

Figure 16.21 Method of carving a thick, tender, sirloin steak. (Courtesy of Swift and Company.)

The heel of the round is the lower back part of the leg. It contains a high percentage of firm connective tissue (collagen) that requires tenderizing methods of preparation. This cut contains very little fat, even in the top grades. It is usually ground or cut up for stew and mixed with beef from cuts that have more fat and less connective tissue.

COOKING OF BEEF

Cooking by moist heat and by dry heat are the two basic methods of preparation. It has been generally believed that dry heat methods are best for tender cuts and that moist heat should be used to tenderize the less tender cuts.

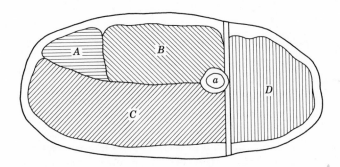

Figure 16.22 Divisions of the round of beef: (*a*) bone, (*A*) eye of the round, (*B*) outside of bottom round, (*C*) inside or top round, and (*D*) sirloin tip (knuckle).

Research has shown that the less tender cuts can be as tender when cooked by dry heat methods if the temperature is low (175 to 250°F) and sufficient time is allowed for the roast to tenderize at the temperature desired as the internal temperature (160 to 180°F). Tenderizing appears to occur most satisfactorily with a slow penetration of heat. Low temperature has less of a tenderizing effect if penetration of heat is speeded up by mechanical means such as the use of metal skewers.

It is desirable when cooking the various cuts and grades of beef to use methods that (a) preserve nutrients, (b) develop rich flavor, (c) give a good appearance, (d) develop tenderness, and (e) preserve juiciness, thus resulting in the least shrinkage. A specific method may be effective for one quality but interfere with another. It is necessary in such instances to choose the method that yields values that give the most satisfaction. Browning of meat in braising, for example, may increase shrinkage but adds to flavor and appearance. The browning of a roast to be displayed on a buffet is important for appearance, even though the browning increases shrinkage. If the roast is to be sliced in the kitchen and not displayed before patrons, the slices appear just as attractive and the shrinkage is less if the roast is not browned.

The use of meat thermometers for determining the internal temperature of roasts adds valuable precision in the cooking of meat. A desired degree of doneness can be determined by the temperature indicated, for example at 140°F the meat is rare, at 160°F it is medium, and at 170 to 185°F it is well done. The center of a roast is cooking when the internal temperature has reached 135 to 140°F. The proteins will have coagulated and denaturation has taken place when the internal temperature has reached 170 to 175°F. The internal temperature of roasts continues to rise after the meat has been removed from the oven because of the transfer of heat from the surface area. The rise is greatest in the largest roasts and in those roasted at high temperatures. When placing a thermometer in meat, be sure that the point of the thermometer reaches to the heart of the thickest part of the flesh without touching bone at any point.

Moist-Heat Cooking

Braising and boiling or stewing are methods of cooking in which liquid is used. To braise meat, brown it first in a skillet or on a griddle at a high temperature (475°F) and then place it in a pan on a range or in an oven and add a small amount of liquid. An oven temperature between 250 and 300°F is satisfactory for continuing the cooking. An internal temperature of 185°F and cooking continued at 185°F for 30 minutes yields good flavor and tenderness in braised roasts or pot roasts. If the internal temperature is increased to 200 or 212°F, the meat will be more tender but less juicy.

Boiling or stewing differs from braising largely in the amount of water used. A small amount of water is used when braising meat and enough water to cover the meat is used when stewing or boiling. Boiling is a familiar term denoting a method of preparation, but is a misnomer in terms of the temperature to be used. The temperature for cooking the meat should be 185°F, or below boiling. Meat for stews may be dredged with seasoned flour and browned before stewing. The caramelization in browning gives a deeper color and a richer flavor.

Steaming is a third way to cook beef with moist heat. Steam penetrates rapidly and a large piece of meat cooks more quickly by this method than by braising in the oven or simmering on the range. Beef cooked in the steamer, however, is less tender and juicy. Steaming may also be done by wrapping the meat in heavy foil and cooking it in the oven. The beef cooked by either steaming method loses more weight, is less tender, and has a less satisfactory flavor than that cooked by braising uncovered in the oven.

Braising and stewing or simmering are variations in preparation that are welcomed for specific recipes, to add interest to menus. Tenderizers, (an acid, for example), may be added as a part of the liquid. Many believe that moist-heat cooking is necessary to change the collagen or connective tissue into gelatin, thus tenderizing the less tender cuts and grades of meat, but research has shown that there is enough moisture in the tissues of these cuts to do this. Meat cooked slowly by dry heat for a longer period of time is more tender and juicy and has a better flavor.

Dry-Heat Cooking

Roasting means cooking without liquid and without a cover. When roasting, it is not necessary to sear the meat unless a well-browned appearance is desired. Roasts cooked at a constant temperature (250°F) until the desired internal temperature is reached are as palatable in flavor and have lower shrinkage. An increase in tenderness can be developed by continuing cooking at the temperature of the desired degree of doneness (140°F for rare, 160°F medium, and 170°F for well done). Ovens that supply temperatures calibrated from 100°F make these low temperatures possible. Research has shown that a standing rib, browned for an hour and a half at 350°F and then with the heat reduced to 140°F, reaches an internal temperature of 140°F in about three and one half hours. Tenderness of the roast continues to develop and is most palatable at the end of 24 hours, but it retains a juicy red interior for service as rare meat up to 48 hours. Tenderness at the end of 48 hours is too great for best palatability.

The pan for roasting should be appropriate for the size of the roast. It should be deep enough and extend sufficiently beyond the meat to catch the drippings, but not so large that the drippings are shallow enough to dry and char during roasting. A rack that holds the roast out of the drippings should be provided unless the roast has bones (as in a rib) that provide its own rack. The roast is placed on the rack with the fat side uppermost, then pierced with the oven thermometer in the center of the deepest muscle; the thermometer should not rest in a layer of fat or touch the bone.

Preheat the oven to the temperature desired. Sear the roast at 450°F only if a browned appearance is important for display. After browning, reduce the oven temperature to 250°F and continue roasting until the desired internal temperature is reached. When roasting less tender cuts or lower grades of beef, continue the roasting at the desired internal temperature for at least 30 minutes after the desired internal temperature has been reached. It is well to remember that there is a transfer of heat from the outside of the meat after the oven temperature has been reduced. Therefore, if an internal temperature of 160°F is desired, the oven heat should be reduced when the meat thermometer registers 145 to 150°F (depending on the size of the roast). Schedule time for roasting to permit the roast to stand 15 or 20 minutes after removal from the oven before slicing for service.

A roasting test was made on a boneless, commercial grade of beef brisket weighing 6 pounds. It was roasted without searing at an oven temperature of 250°F until an internal temperature of 175°F was reached. Roasting was continued at an oven temperature of 185°F for another 30 minutes. The entire roasting time was 6 hours. When sliced, the meat was tender enough to cut with a fork. The flavor and juiciness were good. The roast was lightly browned in appearance.

Grilling or Griddling

Large grills or griddles are used extensively for cooking steaks and hamburgers. It is desirable that the ground beef for hamburger have about 18 to 20% fat. This amount of fat seasons and enriches the flavor without causing excess shrinkage and too much fat on the griddle. A broad, offset spatula is needed for turning the hamburgers and for raking excess fat from the griddle as it accumulates. The cooking should be done at a moderate temperature, from 325 to 350°F, depending on the thickness of the hamburger. The lower temperature is used for the thicker hamburgers. Hamburgers should never be pressed against the griddle with the spatula, as this presses out the juices and results in a dry product.

Experience is needed in discerning the degrees of doneness when griddling. A hamburger should be allowed to brown on one side until juices rise to the top, and then it should be turned and cooked until done on the other side. For a well-done hamburger it is necessary to turn it once more, if juices rise to the top after the first turning. Many people like the hamburger medium rare and relish its juiciness when it is turned only once.

Grilled or pan broiled steaks appear to be juicier than those that are broiled. In kitchens where economy limits the steak thickness to ³/₄ inch or less, cooking steaks on a griddle may be preferred over broiling for juiciness. For steaks, as for hamburgers, a lower temperature (325°F) should be used for cooking the thicker steaks. The fat edge of steaks should be slashed to prevent curling as they are cooking. Salt may be used on the griddle, if needed, to keep the steak from sticking. Seasoning is done after the steaks are removed from the griddle.

Broiling

The tenderest and most expensive cuts of beef are most often prepared by broiling. Tastes for specific degrees of doneness are frequently very definite. There are numerous points in coping with different thickness of meat and differences in broilers where special skill is required. Practice is needed in controlling temperature and time in cooking steaks of different thickness to different degrees of doneness. Good looking grid markings on steak add to attractiveness. Skill is needed in turning them so that the markings make the desired pattern. Lines should angle across steak that is turned once only. When turned twice for each side, they should be placed on the grid in such a manner that a regular pattern of squares or diamonds is formed.

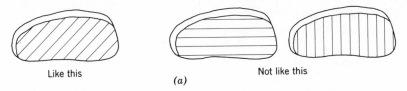

Like this   Not like this
(a)

Figure 16.23a   Grill markings on steaks that have been turned once.

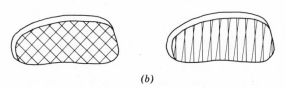

(b)

Figure 16.23b   Grill markings on steaks that have been turned twice. Notice that the one pictured on the left is much more attractive than that on the right.

The temperature can be controlled in the cooking of the steaks by the distance the steaks are placed in relation to the heat source. With a movable grid, this can be managed through the control of the grid. With a charcoal broiler with a fixed grid, it requires placing steaks in relation to the hottest area of the heat. The temperature at the heat source may range from 550 to 1800°F. The best temperature for the cooking of the meat is 300 to 350°F. The thickness of the steak determines the best distance to use from the source of heat. With a movable grid, a thick steak should be placed so that the top of it is 4 to 6 inches from the heat source. This allows for conduction of heat to cook the inside of the steak before the exterior is too brown and crisp. Place a 1-inch thick steak about 2 inches from the heat source so that the exterior browns before the interior becomes too done for juiciness.

Air must circulate in a broiler to prevent accumulation of steam from the meat as it cooks. Commercial broilers are designed to provide for this. When broiling in an electric oven, the door should be left open to allow for the ventilation needed. Gas ovens are regularly designed for more air circulation. It is important for fat drippings from broiling meat to drain away, so that the meat does not fry in the fat. This is also necessary to lessen the danger of its catching fire. It is not wise, therefore, to broil meat on a flat pan or cover the broiler grid with a sheet of foil.

Broil the steaks until brown on the one side, season, turn, and complete broiling on the second side. Lower the grid so that the top of the steak is 3 or 4 inches from the heat when cooking less tender meat or steaks that are to be well done, and allow extra time for broiling. Preheat the broiler before cooking begins. The schedule in Table 16.2 is suggested for steaks of different thickness and degrees of doneness.

Seasoning

Salt delays browning of meat. It is best, except when stewing meat, to season it after it is cooked. The penetration of salt on roasts or other large pieces of meat is too slight to season it. A mirapoix or garni of herbs may be used in stews or simmered meat to add extra flavor. Steak and shish-kebabs for broiling may be given added flavor by marinating them in garlic-flavored salad oil, French dressing, or some other marinade. Allow the excess to drip off before placing on the grid or griddle. Oil on the surface of the meat aids in browning, keeps the meat from sticking to the grid, and gives the meat a bright appearance. Vinegar marinades (used in sauerbraten) tenderize and flavor the meat. Because of the very slow penetration, it is necessary to pierce the meat and to allow several hours for marinating.

There are numerous seasonings that may be used on steak immediately before service. Flavored butter is a quick easy way to add certain flavoring

TABLE 16.2 TIME TABLE FOR BROILING STEAK

Steak Thickness	Distance from Heat	Minutes Rare	Minutes Medium Rare	Minutes Well Done	Kind of Steak
			For Each Side		
1 in.	2 in.	5	6	7 to 8	Prime, choice, good from short loin, individual cuts from loin end, and eye of the rib
1½ in.	3 in.	9	10	12 to 13	
2 in.	4 in.	16	18	20 to 22	
1 in.	3 in.	10	12	14	Full sirloin cut, and steaks from good, standard, and commercial grades
1½ in.	4 in.	12 to 14	14 to 16	18 to 20	
1 in.	3 in.		9	10 to 11	Ground-beef patties or hamburger
1½ in.	4 in.		12	15 to 18	

materials. Minced chive or parsley and lemon juice, blue cheese, anchovy paste, or chopped mushrooms may be worked into softened butter, molded into sticks, chilled and then sliced for serving on top of hot steak. A tablespoon of vermouth or sauterne wine poured over the broiled steak adds delicious flavor. Herb-flavored salt and pepper are popular with many diners. Very thin slices of roasts stacked for desirable thickness is a way to serve less tender cuts of beef. These served on crusty French bread with rich, hot broth or au jus have won popularity. (See Figure 16.24.)

The natural flavor of beef has a savory quality that is generally enjoyed. When selecting flavors for seasoning, care should be taken to choose those that harmonize with, and enhance natural goodness, and not those that mask it. Stews and simmered beef often need the enrichment of a sauce. A caramel coloring improves the eye appeal if the sauce or gravy color is too pale to appear rich flavored.

Terms in Common Use

There are numerous terms in common use for cuts or methods of preparation of beef. An understanding of those used most frequently helps in preventing confusion.

1. Beef brochettes, "kabobs" and shish-kabobs are terms used for cubes of beef (approximately 1-inch) threaded on skewers, alternately with mushrooms and vegetables and broiled or baked. They may be marinated in garlic

Figure 16.24 Slicing thinly helps to tenderize less tender meat. (Courtesy of Swift and Company).

French dressing or another marinade from 30 minutes to several hours before broiling.

2. Delmonico steak is cut from the rib end of the loin and corresponds with the club steak. It is boneless.

3. Beef a la Mode is a less tender cut of meat, marinated in wine and seasonings, drained, browned, and pot roasted with the marinade used for liquid. Vegetables are added near the end of the cooking period, and served with the sliced pot roast.

4. Planked steak is broiled until almost done, then placed on a heated plank garnished with a frill of mashed potato and assorted vegetables such as peas, tiny carrots, and small onions. The planked steak is then placed under the broiler to brown the potato and complete cooking the steak.

5. New England boiled dinner is simmered brisket of beef to which carrots, turnips, cabbage and onions are added when it is near the end of the cooking period. The cabbage is cut in wedges and the other vegetables are cooked and served whole.

6. A minute steak is made from a thin slice of a less tender cut of beef that is cubed by machine or scored with a knife to cut the fibers and improve tenderness. It is usually pan-broiled or sauted.

7. Swiss steak is made from $3/4$-inch thick slices of round, rump or chuck. It is dredged with seasoned flour and sauted until well browned. Liquid is added and it is baked until tender. Tomato juice and other seasoning may be added as a part of the liquid.

8. Roulades are made with $3/8$-inch slices of beef round or chuck. They are spread with a mixture of seasoned chopped beef or sausage and bacon, rolled and tied. They are dredged with seasoned flour and sauted until well browned. Liquid is added and they are baked until tender.

9. Sauerbraten is a pot roast from the round or chuck, that has been marinated for two or three days in a vinegar and spice solution. It is braised, with the marinade serving as the liquid during roasting.

10. Hungarian goulash, French ragout, and Irish mulligan are all varieties of beef stew. Cubes of beef from the less tender cuts are used, dredged with seasoned flour and browned in a small amount of fat. The vegetable combinations and seasonings differ. Wine, tomato juice, or water may be used as the liquid.

SUGGESTED LABORATORY EXPERIENCE

1. Identify the various cuts of beef. State how each should be prepared.
2. Compare grades of beef, point out qualities on which each grade is based.
3. Write specifications for a beef roast for 50 people, and explain reason for each of the specifications.

4. Dry-heat roast a less tender cut of meat.
5. Broil or grill chopped beef that has 15, 20, and 25% fat. Shape each to the same weight before cooking, and weigh after cooking. Compare quality and amount of shrinkage.
6. Prepare a beef stew, being sure that the meat is properly browned and cooked until tender, and the gravy is well flavored and of good color.
7. Prepare shish-kabobs. Marinate the meat and broil until thoroughly cooked and tender.
8. Identify the different steaks. Broil steak to different degrees of doneness.
9. Prepare Swiss steak using flank, bottom round, top round, and chuck. Compare the steaks and quality of the steaks. Calculate the portion cost of each.
10. Use eye-of-the-round steaks of comparable size for testing the various methods of tenderizing; (a) without special treatment, (b) marinate in French dressing, (c) marinate in pineapple juice, (d) use a commercial tenderizer, (e) pound with mallet or edge of a heavy saucer. Broil the steaks the same length of time and evaluate for flavor and tenderness.

REVIEW QUESTIONS AND ANSWERS

1. What are the Federal grades for beef?

Prime, choice, good, standard, commercial, and utility.

2. On what are the grades based?

Texture and tenderness of the meat, amount and distribution of fat, color, depth of flesh in the lean areas, and texture and quality of the bones.

3. Are the lower grades less wholesome than the top grades?

No. The lower grades result from difference in breed, feeding and age of the beef. The meat must be wholesome to pass Government inspection.

4. How can a buyer be sure that the meat has been government inspected?

By the appearance of a round stamp in purple, vegetable dye on the meat with the words "U.S. Insp'd & P'S'D."

5. How are the grades indicated?

They appear on the meat in a shield-shaped stamp with the letters USDA and the name of the grade.

6. How many ribs are usually in a standing rib cut?

Seven.

7. In what wholesale cuts do the other ribs occur?

Five are in the chuck and one is in the short loin.

8. Why is it desirable to remove the shortribs from the standing rib before cooking?

The shortrib area contains less tender meat that requires different treatment in cooking to tenderize.

9. Why is it good practice to remove the top muscle from the chuck end of a rib before roasting?

In order to make the quality of the meat and the diameter of the slices more uniform. Portion size is easier to control.

10. What is a Market or Spencer steak?

It is one cut from the eye of the rib.

11. What is the name of this muscle?

Longissimus dorsi.

12. Name the steaks in the short loin.

Club, T-bone, and porterhouse are full cuts across the loin including the bones. When boned, the top muscle yields strip steaks and the tenderloin muscle is divided into chateaubriand, tenderloin filets, tournedos, filet mignon, and tenderloin tips.

13. What steaks are cut from the loin end?

Sirloin.

14. What is a shell loin?

One from which the tenderloin has been removed.

15. What is the eye of the round?

A muscle bundle that is located at the back of the leg.

16. Are steaks from the sirloin tip and the top sirloin equally tender?

No. Top sirloin is the more tender cut.

17. What is the best method to use in cooking the tip and the top sirloin steaks?

Top sirloin is tender enough to broil, but the tip needs to be braised or cooked at a low temperature for a longer period.

18. What is the top round and why is it called top round?

It consists of the muscles on the inside of the leg, and was named from the way it is usually laid on the butcher's block.

19. Can a round of beef be roasted successfully?

Yes. Remember that there is little fat in or on the round. It is well to lard the roast (wrap beef fat around it) and cook it at a low temperature (250°F or lower) until tender.

20. Is it necessary for tenderness to boil, braise or pot roast such less tender cuts as brisket?

No, they may be dry roasted if cooked at a low temperature (250°F or lower) until tender.

21. What is the difference between braising and simmering?

In braising the meat is first browned and a small amount of water is added. The meat is not browned and is covered with water when simmered or boiled.

22. Why is it well to use a roast thermometer for meat?

In order to more accurately gauge degree of doneness for control of cooking.

23. Should beef roasts always be seared?

Only if a browned appearance is desired.

24. What is meant by grilling or griddling?

Cooking on a hot griddle.

25. Why is griddle cooking used more often for hamburgers than broiling?

It is easier to control the preparation of a large quantity at one time, and it has less of a drying effect on the meat.

26. Should thin steaks be cooked slowly or rapidly?

Rapidly, so as to sear the exterior and lessen time for cooking the inside.

27. How can a broiled steak be branded with the grid?

By heating the grid close to the heat source until it is very hot, before placing the steak on it.

28. Should steaks be salted before broiling?

No. Salt interferes with browning. Broil, season, turn, and broil the other side.

29. Should roasts be salted well before roasting?

No. The salt does not penetrate sufficiently to season the roast.

30. Should steaks be dipped in oil before broiling?

Yes. Flavoring may be added in this way, and the oil helps to keep the steak from sticking to the grid.

17.

Selection and
Preparation of Veal

Veal is a delicately flavored meat from immature bovine animals. Its availability in food markets is strongly affected by certain economic factors. It is more plentiful than beef in markets where the cost of food for animals is high and the supply is scarce, and where a major emphasis is on production of dairy products. This may be noted in many European markets as compared with the supply in either North or South America. The market supply in the United States includes some specially fed, high-grade veal of beef breeds and a large number of bull calves of dairy breeds, also calves that do not give promise of finishing well as beef in terms of growth or grade.

Veal grades are based on conformation, finish, quality, and weight. The best conformation is compact, having a good depth of flesh in the legs, loin, and ribs. The shank and neck are short. Top-grade veal is commonly described as blocky. Young growing animals that have been well fed have good depth of flesh and are firm to the touch rather than flabby. They are not fat, even though they may be well fed and plump. The flesh of the best veal is light pink in color, firm, smooth, and fine grained. The quality grades established by the United States Department of Agriculture are Prime, Choice, Good, Standard, Utility, and Cull.

The weight of a veal carcass may be 40 to 350 pounds. The best weigh 80 to 100 pounds. A carcass weighing more than 150 pounds, from a young animal more than 12 weeks old, is classified as calf. The very light veal tends to be watery and lacking in flavor. Heavy veal or calf gives a better yield per pound but the flavor may be too old for good veal and too young for beef. Weight may provide a clue to finish and age. The most desirable weights of veal carcasses (with the skin on) for the different grades, are as follows: Prime and Choice, 90 to 100 pounds; Good, 75 to 95 pounds; Standard, 65 to 80 pounds; and Utility, 50 to 75 pounds. A young animal of a beef breed that is six or eight weeks old and weighing 150 pounds dresses out at about 100 pounds.

Top grades are usually four to eight weeks old. Buyers who wish the delicate flavor of young veal need to develop sensitive awareness of color as a clue to age. The flesh of very young veal is pale pink. As the animal ages the flesh deepens to a rosy pink and then to red. The points which a buyer should specify when ordering veal are (a) grade and class; (b) total quantity and cut; (c) unit weight, such as that of portion or roast; and (d) whether fresh or frozen veal is desired.

Veal has a short storage life. It is well to hold it at temperatures between 31 and 36°F, and not more than 5 or 6 days. The high water content results in loss of weight as it is held and the flesh darkens as it is exposed to the air. The hide is frequently left on the veal carcass until final cutting in order to protect it from dehydration and darkening. Unlike beef, it does not have a fat covering to protect it. Retail cuts should be covered loosely with waxed paper or plastic while in storage and used as soon as possible.

VEAL CUTS AND THEIR PREPARATION FOR COOKING

A side of veal yields six wholesale cuts, namely: leg, loin, rib, shoulder, shank, and breast. Figure 17.1 indicates the retail or pan-ready cuts that may be made from each of these. Selection is usually made on the basis of the specific type of preparation intended and the particular food cost allowed per portion. The cut selected for roasting might be the leg, loin, rib, or shoulder. The portion yield per pound as purchased, the cost per pound and the desirability of these cuts differs. Palatable tenderness and attractiveness of the cuts on the plate are also likely to differ. Portions per pound as purchased are greater and more easily controlled in boned-rolled-and-tied leg or shoulder than in bone-in rib or loin. The price per pound is likely to be highest for loin and rib and lowest for shoulder. Acceptance of price and portion by clientele are to be considered.

The leg of veal is an excellent cut for roasting. The roast can be cut into attractive slices of firm meat. A boneless leg roast should yield approximately three 3-ounce portions of cooked meat per pound as purchased. A boned-rolled-and-tied shoulder is likely to be lower in price per pound than the leg and yields a similar number of portions per pound as purchased. The rolled shoulder provides a good roast of tender meat that can be sliced easily, but it requires careful handling to prevent slices from separating. The well-cooked meat has a tendency to fall apart because of the natural muscle divisions in the shoulder and the cuts made for removal of the bones. The

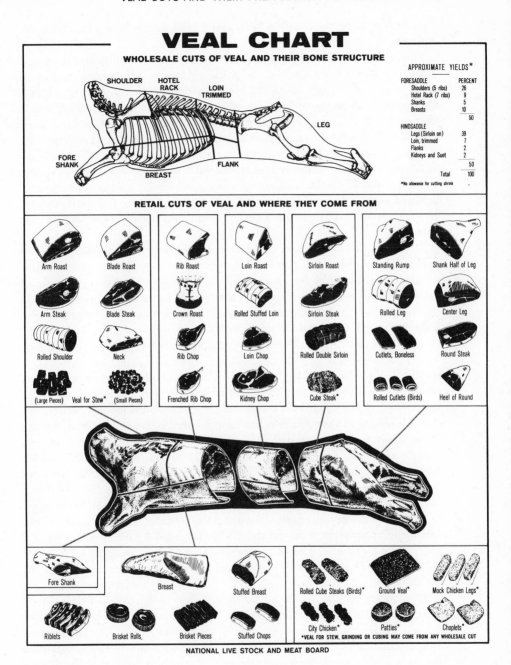

VEAL CHART

WHOLESALE CUTS OF VEAL AND THEIR BONE STRUCTURE

SHOULDER   HOTEL RACK   LOIN TRIMMED

LEG

FORE SHANK

BREAST   FLANK

APPROXIMATE YIELDS*

FORESADDLE	PERCENT
Shoulders (5 ribs)	26
Hotel Rack (7 ribs)	9
Shanks	5
Breasts	10
	50
HINDSADDLE	
Legs (Sirloin on)	39
Loin, trimmed	7
Flanks	2
Kidneys and Suet	2
	50
Total	100

*No allowance for cutting shrink

RETAIL CUTS OF VEAL AND WHERE THEY COME FROM

Arm Roast	Blade Roast	Rib Roast	Loin Roast	Sirloin Roast	Standing Rump	Shank Half of Leg
Arm Steak	Blade Steak	Crown Roast	Rolled Stuffed Loin	Sirloin Steak	Rolled Leg	Center Leg
Rolled Shoulder	Neck	Rib Chop	Loin Chop	Rolled Double Sirloin	Cutlets, Boneless	Round Steak
(Large Pieces) Veal for Stew* (Small Pieces)		Frenched Rib Chop	Kidney Chop	Cube Steak*	Rolled Cutlets (Birds)	Heel of Round

Fore Shank

Breast

Stuffed Breast

Rolled Cube Steaks (Birds)*   Ground Veal*   Mock Chicken Legs*

Riblets   Brisket Rolls   Brisket Pieces   Stuffed Chops

City Chicken*   Patties*   Choplets*

*VEAL FOR STEW, GRINDING OR CUBING MAY COME FROM ANY WHOLESALE CUT

NATIONAL LIVE STOCK AND MEAT BOARD

Figure 17.1 Cuts of veal. (Courtesy of the National Livestock and Meat Board.)

slicing needs to be done with a very sharp knife, taking care to prevent any separation as it is sliced.

The skill used in preparing pan-ready cuts influences quality and economy. Meat purchased from careless or untrained meat cutters may be low in price per pound as purchased but high in per portion cost. It is important, for example, when purchasing boned-and-rolled cuts that cartilage, coarse connective fibers and other undesirable parts be removed and a firmly tied roll made that is fairly uniform in diameter from one end to the other. The goal is to secure roasts that provide (a) attractive portions of satisfactory dimensions (proper diameter and thickness); (b) meat that is free of bones, cartilage, major arteries, discolored meat, and glands; (c) portions that can be sliced across the grain of the meat; (d) slices that do not fall apart readily; and (e) servings that can be afforded within an appropriate portion cost allowance.

The diameter of the rolled shoulder and the firmness with which it is tied influence ease of handling and satisfactory portioning. The eye muscle in a shoulder roll should be lengthwise and the roast should be tied girthwise at 2-inch intervals. After roasting, the roast should be allowed to stand outside the oven for at least 15 minutes before slicing. The slices hold together best if the full slice is used and not cut in half for portioning. It is well, therefore, to specify the maximum diameter acceptable for the shoulder roast, such as 4 or 5 inches. There are various ways in which a butcher may meet such specifications. The shoulder roast may be made from the entire square-cut chuck of small veal, boned and rolled; from the rolled shoulder clod only of larger veal; or the square-cut chuck with the bones and clod removed.

Portioning of the loin and rib roasts is influenced by the bones which remain in the roast and interfere with slicing. The portions of meat per pound as purchased range, depending on the size of the veal, from 6 to 16 ounces. These cuts, if boned and rolled for roasting, permit better regulation of portions but many people prefer the appearance with the bone. To facilitate portioning of the bone-in, tender meat after roasting, the back bones need to be removed when preparing the roast for cooking. The cut surface from which the bones were removed should be protected from drying by tying a covering of fat over it. The rib bones should be short enough to appear well on the plate. They should be cut not more than 3 inches from the ribeye to the flank end.

The rib sections of veal may be shaped into crown roasts to provide a more spectacular style for buffet meals. The crown is made with two sets of six ribs (hotel rack) taken from the small or loin end of the rib section. Remove the back bones. French the ends of the rib bones (remove flesh from the ends of the bones) for approximately $1\frac{1}{2}$ inches. Bend the ribs so that the fleshy side is inside the crown. Tie the half circles of ribs together with a

TABLE 17.1 SUGGESTED SIZES FOR PAN-READY VEAL CUTS

Item	Ounces per Portion									Pounds per Roast			
	3	4	5	6	8	10	12	16	Under				
Cubed steak, regular	•	•	•	•	•								
special	•	•	•	•	•								
Rib chop		•	•	•	•	•							
Shoulder chop		•	•	•	•	•							
Clod steak		•	•	•	•	•							
Loin chop		•	•	•	•	•	•	•					
Cutlet, regular		•	•	•	•								
special	•	•	•	•	•	•							
Chuck, square-cut, bnls, tied									10	10 to 15	16 to 22	23 and up	
Shoulder clod, roast-ready									6	6 to 8	9 to 10	11 and up	
Chuck, square-cut, clod out, bnls, tied									6	6 to 8	9 to 10	11 and up	
Legs, bnls, tied, roast-ready									10	10 to 15	16 to 22	23 and up	
Veal for stewing					Amount and cut as specified								

Figure 17.2   Crown roasts of lamb or veal are spectacular meats for buffet service. (Courtesy of the American Lamb Council.)

cord put through the flesh and around the two ribs that come together. A lining on which to place dressing or other filling may be skewered in the bottom of the crown. The material selected for the lining may be the flexible skin of fresh pork or a piece of sturdy plastic. A filling helps keep the roast moist while it cooks. A paper frill or olive placed on the end of each rib bone after it is removed from the oven adds to the festive appearance.

Ribs may be cut into chops, by means of a power saw. The rib chops may range in weight from 3 to 10 ounces each and the loin chops from 3 to 16 ounces. The protruding chine bone, the blade bone, and the extending cartilage plus the flesh and fat above the blade bone should be removed and not included in the chop weight. Bone-in shoulder chops may be cut across the arm bone up to the knuckle bone, and across the blade bone to the juncture of the blade and the knuckle bone. These chops may be purchased in weights as specified from 3 to 10 ounces each. The rib, loin, and shoulder chops should not have a covering of surface fat deeper than $\frac{1}{4}$ inch.

Regular cubed steaks may be prepared from any part of the veal carcass

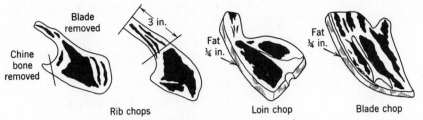

Figure 17.3   Cutting specifications for veal chops.

that is fairly free of cartilage, tendons, periosteum (connective tissue around the bones) and membranous tissue. Pieces may be knitted together but must not break when suspended from any point $1/2$ inch from the outer edge, and must be formed in a uniform shape. *Special* cubed steaks differ from the regular cubed steaks in that they must be made from the veal cut designated and the knitting of two or more pieces together is not permissible.

Cutlets are made from the leg muscles that have been separated at the natural divisions between the muscles. The membranous tissue and fat are removed. *Regular* cutlets may be cut at any angle. They must be cubed, but not more than twice, through a mechanical cubing machine, and may be folded during the cubing. *Special* cutlets are cut across the leg muscle slicing approximately perpendicular to the outside surface of the leg. They may or may not be cubed depending upon request by the buyer. If cubed, they are to be passed twice through the mechanical cubing machine. The knitting of two or more pieces together is not permissible for special cutlets.

The size of stew pieces may be designated by the buyer. The stew meat may be prepared from any part of the veal carcass and must be free of bones, cartilage, tendons, shank meat, periosteum, and major ligaments. The cutting of the meat may be done by hand or by machine. Ground veal may also be made from any part of the veal carcass.

THE COOKING OF VEAL

Characteristics to remember when preparing veal are (a) its delicate flavor, (b) the high moisture content of the meat, (c) the lack of fat in the tissues, and (d) that it is flesh that is toughened by high temperatures. The delicate flavor responds readily to added flavor and combines well with other foods. The light quality of its flavor compares with that of chicken. The moisture content and the lack of fat in veal calls for cooking methods that add richness and prevent drying. Recipes that involve roasting, braising, and stewing have been the most popular. Broiling is not a desirable method of cooking veal.

TABLE 17.2 COOKING SCHEDULE FOR VEAL (AT APPROXIMATELY 325°F TO 180°F INTERNAL TEMPERATURE)

Cut	Size	Cooking Method	Approximate Time
Leg, bone-in	5 lb	Roasting	3½ hr
	8 lb	Roasting	4½ hr
boned	20 lb	Roasting	8 hr
Loin, bone-in	5 lb	Roasting	2¾ hr
	8 lb	Roasting	3½ hr
Shoulder, bone-in	5 lb	Roasting	3½ hr
	8 lb	Roasting	4 hr
boned-and-rolled	5 lb	Roasting	3¾ hr
	8 lb	Roasting	4½ hr
boned-and-rolled	5 lb	Braising	3 hr
Chops (loin or rib), steaks and cutlets	½ to ¾ 1-in. thick	Braising	¾ to 1 hr
Breast	¾ to 1 lb	Braising	1¾ to 2 hr
Knuckle	1½ to 1 lb	Boiling	2 hr
Heart	¾ to 1 lb	Boiling	2¼ hr
Tongue	1¼ to 1½ lb	Boiling	2½ hr

Veal recipes utilizing specific flavoring materials have become popular. It is expected that persons who prepare food for the public will be familiar with those that are repeated most often; for example, Veal Scallopini, Weiner Schnitzel, Veal Parmigiana, Mock Chicken Legs, City Chicken, Hungarian Goulash, Veal Birds, and Veal Cordon Bleu. Eggs, ham, cheeses, herbs, wine, mushrooms and vegetables blend well with veal flavor and are commonly used for enrichment. Weiner Schnitzel is made with veal cutlets that are breaded with an egg wash, sauted until well browned, then braised until tender. They are served with a slice of lemon. In Veal Parmigiana, both mozerella and parmesan cheeses are added. City Chicken calls for slices of veal and pork arranged in alternate layers rolled to form drumsticks and skewered, breaded, and braised. Mock drumsticks are made with ground veal and bacon molded into the form of chicken legs on a skewer. They are rolled in fine crumbs, browned in hot fat, and baked until tender.

The following recipes provide examples of the use of different flavoring materials. Note that moderate temperatures are specified and that veal is cooked until well done. These recipes are in quantities of sufficient amount for 50 portions for adults, and call for approximately one pound of veal as purchased for every three portions.

VEAL CUTLETS CORDON BLUE   50 portions (5 oz)

Ingredients	Weight	Volume
Veal cutlets, sliced ¼ in. thick	17 lb	100 slices
Swiss cheese, 1-oz slices	3 lb, 2 oz	50 slices
Ham, sliced	5 lb	50 slices
Flour, all-purpose	1 lb, 8 oz	1½ qt
Nutmeg, ground	2 tsp	2 tsp
Cloves, ground	1 tsp	1 tsp
Eggs, slightly beaten	1 lb	9
Milk	1 lb	1 pt
Dry bread crumbs	3 lb	3½ qt
Cooking oil	8 oz	1 c
Clarified butter	8 oz	1 c
Dry white wine (or white stock)	8 oz	1 c
White stock	4 oz	½ c

PROCEDURE:

1. Pound cutlets with meat hammer until very thin. Sprinkle with salt and pepper.
2. Place 1 slice of ham and 1 slice of cheese on a cutlet and arrange another cutlet on top of it. Pound the edges of the veal cutlets together to encase the ham and cheese.
3. Blend the flour and spices.
4. Mix the eggs and milk together.
5. Blend the oil and butter together in a heavy skillet and heat.
6. Dip both sides of the cutlets in the flour mixture, then in egg mixture and next roll in crumbs until well covered.
7. Saute in hot oil and butter until well browned on both sides. Place in a baking sheet. Moisten well with mixture of wine and stock.
8. Bake in 300°F oven for 1 hour or until well done.

HUNGARIAN VEAL GOULASH   50 portions (4½ oz)

Ingredients	Weight	Volume
Veal, boneless, cut into 2 oz pieces	17 lb	8½ qt
Flour	1 lb	1 qt
Onions, diced	4 lb	5 qt
Shortening	1¼ lb	2½ c
Salt	2 oz	¼ c
Pepper	2 tsp	2 tsp
Tomato puree	8 oz	1 c
Paprika	6 oz	1½ c
Cloves of garlic	3 cloves	3 cloves
Bay leaves	2 small leaves	2 small leaves
Caraway seeds	1 tsp	1 tsp
Parsley	1 oz	¾ c
Brown stock	10 lb	5 qt
Sour cream	1 lb, 8 oz	3 c

PROCEDURE:

1. Brown onions in shortening.
2. Flour veal pieces in mixture of flour, salt and pepper. Add to onions and brown lightly. Cover and allow to simmer for 20 minutes.
3. Tie garlic, bay leaves, caraway seeds and parsley in cheesecloth bag. Add with tomato puree and stock to veal and onions. Simmer for $1\frac{1}{2}$ hours. Remove bag of spices and herbs.
4. Add sour cream and serve.

VEAL SCALLOPINI   50 portions (4 oz)

Ingredients	Weight	Volume
Veal cutlets, about ½-in. thick	17 lb	150 pieces
Flour	2 lb	2 qt
Salt	2 oz	¼ c
Pepper	¼ oz	1 tbsp
Cooking oil	12 oz	1½ c

Clarified butter	8 oz	1 c
Mushrooms, fresh, sliced	1 lb	1¾ qt
Sherry, cooking (or white stock)	1 lb	2 c
Water	1 lb	2 c
Chives, minced	2½ oz	1 c
Parsley, minced	1 oz	¾ c
Lemon juice	6 oz	¾ c
Marjoram, powdered	1 tsp	1 tsp
Rosemary, powdered	1 tsp	1 tsp
Tarragon, powdered	1 tsp	1 tsp

PROCEDURE:

1. Pound steaks with meat hammer until $\frac{1}{4}$-inch thick.
2. Blend flour, salt, and pepper; coat pieces of veal.
3. Saute in mixture of oil and butter until well browned on both sides.
4. Arrange in serving pan, overlapping pieces.
5. Saute mushrooms, and add remaining ingredients. Heat and pour over steaks.
6. Bake at 325°F for 30 minutes, or until tender.
7. Serve three pieces as a portion, with mushroom sauce spooned over them.

Note: Whole mushroom caps may be used in place of sliced mushrooms if desired.

SUGGESTED LABORATORY EXPERIENCE

1. Identify the various cuts of veal and state the best method of preparation to be used for each.
2. Write specifications for veal to be used in preparing 50 portions of stew, mock chicken legs, and veal cordon bleu.
3. Prepare each of the recipes given in the text (Veal Cordon Bleu, Hungarian Goulash, and Veal Scallopini). Calculate cost per portion.
4. Roast and slice rolled shoulder of veal. Calculate cost per portion.

REVIEW QUESTIONS AND ANSWERS

1. What is the weight of the best quality veal carcass.	A weight between 80 and 100 pounds dressed.
2. What are the grades of veal?	Prime, choice, good, standard, utility, and cull.

3. On what qualities are the grades based?

Conformation, finish, quality and weight. The best veal is blocky, well filled out, with fine textured flesh and heavy for its age.

4. Why is the hide often left on veal after slaughter?

To protect the veal from drying and darkening in color.

5. What are the wholesale cuts of veal?

Leg, loin, rib, shoulder, shank, and breast.

6. What cuts are used for roasting?

Leg, loin, rib and shoulder.

7. How many 3-ounce portions of cooked veal may be obtained from 1 pound as purchased (approximately)?

Three.

8. Why should shoulder roasts of veal be sliced with special care?

To avoid slices separating and presenting a scrappy appearance.

9. What in a butcher's preparation of a roast will influence quality and economy?

(a) Size or diameter of the roll; (b) satisfactory trim (removal of cartilage, major arteries, glands, etc.); (c) shaped so slices can be made across the grain; and (d) firmly tied so that cooked slices do not fall apart readily.

10. How long should roasts be allowed to stand after roasting, before slicing?

At least 15 minutes.

11. How should ribs and loins be prepared for roasting?

Backbones should be removed, and cut area larded to prevent drying.

12. What is the maximum measurement for length of rib bone in chop or roast?

Three inches from the edge of the ribeye to the flank end of the rib bone.

13. What is meant by Frenching of the rib bones?

Removal of flesh from the end of the bones (approximately $1\frac{1}{2}$ inches).

14. What part of the veal is used for a crown roast?

The hotel rack (rib section).

15. How is it formed?

Use two sets of six ribs, taken from the loin end of the rib section. Remove the backbones and French flank ends of ribs. Bend each set of six ribs into a half circle with fleshy side inside the circle. Tie two pieces together to form full circle. Skewer base inside for dressing.

16. What are the two kinds of shoulder chops?

Arm and blade. The arm chop is cut across the round bone of the fore leg and the blade chops across the blade bone.

17. What is the difference between Special and Regular cubed steaks?

Regular cubed steaks may be made from any cut of veal flesh and two or more pieces may be knitted together or folded and knitted. Special cubed steaks must be from the cut designated and knitting of two pieces together is not permissible.

18. What is a cutlet?

A slice made from a leg muscle, that has been separated at the natural division between the muscles.

19. How do Regular and Special cutlets differ?

Regular cutlets may be cut at any angle and cubed through a cubing machine. Special cutlets are sliced across the grain of the meat, approximately perpendicular to the outside of the leg. They may be cubed on request. Two pieces may not be cubed together.

20. Is broiling a preferred method for cooking veal? Why?

No. Veal is lacking in fat and the high temperature dries and toughens it.

21. State important points to observe when cooking veal.

Cook slowly and thoroughly, and add moisture and enrich flavor with fat and seasonings.

22. What flavoring materials are commonly used?

Cheeses, eggs, ham, mushrooms, herbs, wine, fruit, and vegetables.

23. What oven temperatures are recommended for veal?

300 to 325°F.

24. How do mock drumsticks and city chicken differ?

Drumsticks are made with ground veal and city chicken with slices of veal and pork.

25. What is the classification of heavy veal, over 12 weeks old and weighing more than 150 pounds?

Calf.

26. What are the clues to the age of veal?

Weight and color. The flesh of very young veal is pale pink. As the animal gets older the flesh deepens in color from pink to red.

18.

Selection and Preparation of Lamb

Market lambs are young ovine animals that range in age from three to twelve months old. These constitute approximately 85% of the sheep slaughtered for food. There is about 5% that classify as yearlings and 10% that are older and are classified as mutton. There is a small supply of very young ones, known as "Hothouse lambs" that are from six to eight weeks old. The immature flesh is watery, but it is very tender and delicate flavored; these are produced for a special trade. The carcasses range in weight from 15 to 30 pounds. "Spring lambs" are three to five months old, with pink colored, firmer flesh, and delicate flavor. An average weight is 30 to 35 pounds.

"Lambs" are 6 to 12 months old. The flesh of young lamb is light pink, and darkens to red in older animals. The fat and flesh become firmer as the animal ages. Young bones are red with blood and change to white as the lamb grows older. The "break" joint in young lambs shows four definite, smooth, moist ridges. In older animals the break is hard and white in appearance. Weight of lambs may range from 28 to 55 pounds with the majority weighing 35 to 45 pounds. Yearling mutton, 12 to 14 months old, weighs from 40 to 60 pounds, and older mutton from 50 to 70 pounds.

Lambs are produced in considerable quantity in 30 states and are available in meat markets all year. The largest number are sold by growers in September and October as they come from the pastures. Those sold from April through October have been milk and grass fed. During the cold months from November through March, the lambs have been feed-finished. The care and feeding of the lambs strongly influences grade. Grades are based on conformation, in terms of a compact, well-filled-out shape with good depth of flesh in proportion to bones; finish, as shown by color of the flesh and the amount and distribution of fat; and quality, as it pertains to fineness of texture and juiciness of the flesh. The government grades are: Prime, Choice, Good, Utility, and Cull.

416

When purchasing lamb and mutton, a buyer should specify what is desired in terms of (a) class and grade, (b) total weight needed and cut, (c) weight or dimension of pieces, such as roast size or portion weight, (d) type of preparation, whether wholesale or pan-ready, and (e) the state of refrigeration, whether fresh or frozen. Specifications for lamb shoulder roasts, for example, might be written as follows: 50 pounds of fresh, choice grade, boned and rolled lamb shoulders (with excess fat, cartilage, major arteries, any discolored meat and glands removed) and each shoulder roll reasonably uniform in diameter, firmly tied and not more than $5\frac{1}{2}$ pounds in weight and $4\frac{1}{2}$ inches in diameter. The size of roasts influences preparation and portioning for service. The diameter of slices affects their appearance on the plate. If slices are so large that they must be cut in half to be portioned, the tender meat is more likely to fall apart when served. This tends to lower portion yield per pound as purchased and make portions appear scrappy.

Purchase lamb for immediate use. It is a perishable meat, and although the carcass may retain its bloom for a week the cuts deteriorate more rapidly. The smaller the cut the faster the deterioration. Ground lamb should not be held more than a day. Larger cuts may be held two or three days under favorable conditions. A consistent temperature from 30 to 32°F is desirable. Lower temperatures have a drying effect on the meat, and higher temperatures allow more rapid deterioration.

It is especially important when handling lamb to work on a meat block that is fresh and clean and to store cuts under refrigeration in clean containers away from strong flavored foods. Lamb absorbs other odors readily, and has often been blamed for flavors that were the result of poor handling. The scraper should be used on the meat block before and after cutting lamb. Lamb that is properly handled has a flavor that is sweet and delicate. The entire carcass of a young, tender lamb has sufficient tenderness, fat, and flavor to adapt well to most modes of meat cookery, whether broiling, roasting or braising.

CUTS OF LAMB

The lamb carcass may be purchased whole, if personnel with sufficient time and/or skill is available to do the cutting. The lamb carcass may be broken in various ways to meet specific needs. It can be divided approximately in half by cutting across the lamb between the 12th and 13th ribs, leaving only one rib on each side of the hindsaddle, or it may be divided into three approximately equal weights, yielding the legs, middle and the yoke or front.

The lamb yoke is often cut so as to include the breast and flank (shown in Fig. 18.1 by dotted line). This yoke is called a triangle, wing, or stew.

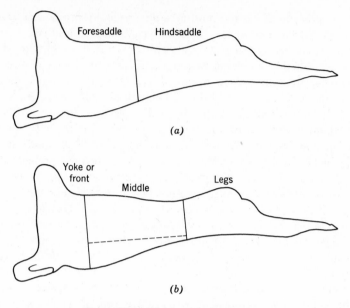

Figure 18.1   Divisions of a lamb carcass.

The middle section is called a back. It may be cut across at the loin end of the ribs to separate the rib section or rack from the loin. The full rack that has not been split is called a hotel rack, and if split along the back bones so it consists of only one side, it is known as a single-rib rack.

The majority of large kitchens lack skilled personnel and facilities for utilizing wholesale cuts of lamb. It is also difficult to meet specific needs for cuts of uniform size and character for a large number from the varied cuts available from a lamb carcass. The major demand in large kitchens, therefore, is for commercial cuts that are pan-ready. These cuts are popular as they provide an easily calculated portion cost within an established food-cost allowance, they yield attractive, uniform portions that can be handled quickly and easily and possess good appearance and quality appealing to patrons.

Legs of Lamb

The wholesale leg of lamb usually includes the sirloin area, shank and foot, as well as the meaty part of the leg. Neither the sirloin area nor the shank below the stifle joint yield satisfactory slices when roasted. The sirloin can be used more profitably as chops and the shank as a shank cut, stew, or

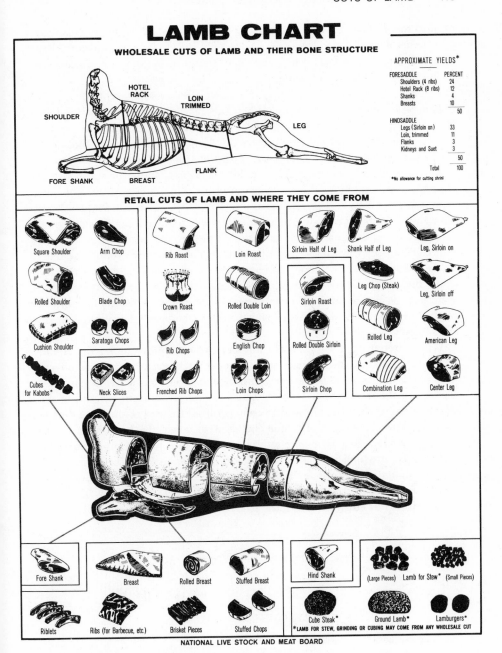

Figure 18.2   Cuts of lamb. (Courtesy of the National Livestock and Meat Board.)

ground meat. The remainder of the leg may have all of the bones removed and then rolled and tied, or it may have only the backbones and the pelvic (aitch) bone removed. The leg, also, may be sliced for steaks or cutlets for broiling, pan frying, or braising.

The round bone of the leg is easy to remove after cooking and many prefer that it be left in during roasting. When the carving is done in the kitchen, the round bone may be removed easily in the following manner: Grasp the roast by the shank end and stand it on the loin end. Beginning at the shank end, cut lengthwise next to the bone with the knife following the bone and removing the fleshy part (back of the leg). This cut, made the full width of the leg, exposes the bone down the center of the remaining portion. The part removed is boneless and can be sliced into attractive, horseshoe-shaped slices. To remove the bone from the remainder of the leg, make a shallow cut equal to the diameter of the bone on each side of it. Lay the knife down, take the shank end in the right hand and place the left hand firmly around the back of the meat. Twist the bone to release the tender, cooked meat from the bone. Be sure to cut away the knuckle bone. *Caution*: This small bone at the stifle joint is heavy enough to damage a slicer blade. This second portion of the leg is boneless and can be sliced into attractive slices by hand or on the slicer.

When preparing a leg of lamb for service on a buffet table, the round bone may be left in, but the backbones and the aitch bone should be removed. The shank bone should be sawed off an inch or so above the break joint and the end of the leg Frenched (by cutting the flesh away from the end of the shank bone) or the flesh allowed to contract from the end of the bone during cooking, after cooking a frill may be used to cover the bare bone. After roasting, make a slice or two lengthwise on the front part of the leg to form a flat base on which to rest the roast. The meatier part of the back of the leg should be uppermost for slicing. Slices are made by cutting down the width of the leg to the bone. The knife is then turned to follow the bone lengthwise, thus cutting slices loose from the bone (see Figure 18.3).

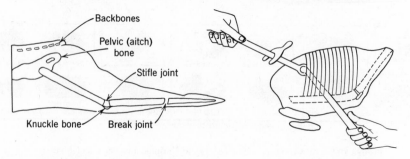

Figure 18.3   Positions of the leg bones and the carving of a lamb leg.

Cutlets made from the boneless leg of tender, young lamb are satisfactory for broiling, pan frying, or braising. When preparing cutlets from older lamb tenderness is increased if the cutlets are put through a steak machine. These cutlets should be cut thick enough to yield steaks about $\frac{1}{2}$ inch thick after cubing. Two or three pieces of lamb may be knitted together to make a good appearing and acceptable steak. Total fat in or on the cutlet should not exceed 25%.

Lamb Backs

The lamb backs are prized for chops. The back includes the hotel rack that is separated from the loin at the end of the ribs, and the loin. The rack may be cut so as to contain eight or nine ribs on each side. When preparing rib chops, the rack is split evenly along the backbones, and a parchment-like membrane known as the fell is removed. The shoulder blade is removed and the chops are cut according to the desired thickness, with a power saw. When ordering chops, specify the length of the rib bone from the ribeye to the flank end (3 to 4 inches) and the number of chops desired per pound.

French roasts and crown roasts require removal of the chine and backbones. When the meat is portioned after cooking, these bones would interfere with cutting. In Frenching, the flesh is removed for $1\frac{1}{2}$ to 2 inches from the ends

Figure 18.4   A French roast of lamb showing chop portions. (Courtesy of the American Lamb Council.)

of the ribs. The difference between the French roast and the crown roast is in shaping. The French roast is roasted flat and the crown roast is shaped into a circle using two or three half racks of 6 or 7 ribs each. In forming the crown, the half racks are bent into an arc with the fleshy part on the inside. The half circles or arcs are tied together by cord put through the flesh with a meat needle. If a base or lining on which dressing or other filling may be placed is desired for the crown, it may be made of pliable skin of fresh pork or a piece of heavy plastic. Skewers may be used to hold it in place.

The term loin is used here to denote the ribless portion of the back, and contains the back muscle or eye of the loin and the tenderloin. In some markets the term full loin is used to signify a cut that includes the ribs. It may or may not include the flank. In the preparation of a kidney chop an extra length of flank may be used to encircle the slice of kidney. The fell may be stripped off the loin before slicing or cut away from the individual chops with the excess fat trimmed after slicing. The exterior fat on the chops should not excess $\frac{1}{4}$ inch in thickness and the total fat should not be greater than 25%.

Loin chops of tender, young lambs are prized for broiling and are regarded as a prestige cut. They may be cut into single or double chops. The double chops are cut across the entire width of the unsplit loin and contain the flesh on both sides of the backbones. These are also called English chops. Either single or double chops may be fashioned into kidney chops. The whole loin is very rarely used for roasting. Thick, single chops from yearling mutton are sometimes featured by specialty restaurants as baked chops, and are cooked at a low temperature until nicely browned and well done.

When purchasing pan-ready chops or roasts, the unit weight or dimension

Figure 18.5 Stuffed breast of lamb choplets. (Courtesy of the American Lamb Council.)

TABLE 18.1 WEIGHTS COMMONLY USED FOR LAMB CHOPS AND ROASTS

Item	Ounces per Portion									Pounds per Roast				
	3	4	5	6	7	8	9	10	12	Under 4	4 to 6	6 to 8	8 to 12	Over 12
Rib chop (1 only) plain or frenched	•	•	•											
Rib chops (2) plain or frenched			•	•	•	•								
Rib chops (2 or 3) plain or frenched				•	•	•	•	•						
Shoulder chop (1) arm or blade		•	•	•	•	•	•	•	•					
Loin chop		•	•	•	•									
Loin chop (2)					•	•	•	•	•					
Shoulder, boned, rolled and tied										•	•			
Leg with shank, pelvic, back and tail bones removed, and tied											•	•	•	•
Leg, boned, rolled and tied											•	•	•	•

may vary according to the wishes of the buyer. It is well to base selection on (a) the cost allowance in the specific food unit, (b) a portion that gives satisfaction, (c) a size that provides a good standard of quality, and (d) a size that is suitable for preparation by the desired method. Table 18.1 shows weight variations that are in common use by different food establishments.

Good quality in a broiled lamb chop calls for a well browned exterior and a juicy, tender interior. A chop that is too thin will be dried throughout before a satisfactory degree of browning has been developed on the outside. If economy demands that the chop thickness be less than $\frac{3}{8}$ inch, the cooking method should be one that causes less dehydration than broiling, for example pan-frying or baking. It may be well to adjust portion size to one rib chop of adequate thickness for broiling rather than two thinner chops. Economy may be served by using sliced stuffed breast or another less expensive cut for broiling. For these a pocket is made the full length of the breast; it is filled with ground lamb and sliced crosswise into chop-shaped portions.

Yoke, Shoulder, Triangle, or Wing

The front part of the lamb is called by several names. In some markets it is called a turkey of lamb. The various parts are favored for different types of preparation. A square cut shoulder, minus the shank and breast, is often used for roasting. All of the bones and the excess fat are removed and it is tightly rolled with the back muscle (longissimus dorsi) the length of the roll. If the roast is properly tied, the flesh sets during cooking so that slices of roast hold together reasonably well for service.

Cubes of lamb for shish-kabobs may be taken from the leg, but are more often cut from the shoulder. A large part of the shoulder can be cut into steaks and chops. The blade chops are cut across the shoulder blade bone from the rib end of the chuck up to the knuckle bone. The bone-in arm chops are cut across the arm bone from the shank end of the chuck to the knuckle bone. These chops are satisfactory for broiling. The neck and trim from the chuck are used for stew and for ground lamb. The stew and ground lamb may be made from any part of the lamb carcass. It should be free of bones, cartilage, tendons, periosteum, and excess fat. The fat on any one piece of stew should not be more than $\frac{1}{4}$ inch and the total fat content in stew and ground lamb should not exceed 25%.

Lamb shanks that weigh from 12 to 20 ounces each are in demand for braising. This is a cut that does not divide well in portioning. Whole shanks larger than $1\frac{1}{4}$ pounds appear awkward when served on a plate unless sawed in half crosswise. Shank meat that is not used in this manner may be stripped from the bones and used in ground lamb or for stew. Although the

Figure 18.6   Square cut shoulder of lamb, boned-and-rolled shoulder, and cushion shoulder prepared for stuffing. (Courtesy of the American Lamb Council.)

breast of lamb is a thin cut, there are various ways in which it can be used for preparing delicious dishes, in addition to that shown in Figure 18.4. Riblets cut short into 1 to $1\frac{1}{2}$ inch pieces or into longer 3 to $3\frac{1}{2}$ inch strips are popular barbecued with a flavorful sauce. The breasts may be used for stew, with or without the bones. All of the bones and excess fat may be removed and the meat ground for patties.

Figure 18.7   Braised lamb shanks. (Courtesy of the American Sheep Producers Council, Inc.)

LAMB COOKERY

Lamb cookery calls for moderate to low temperatures. Oven roasts are better when cooked at a constant temperature from the beginning than when seared. Temperatures from 300°F are recommended. Browning adds to the flavor and appearance of roasts and chops, and can be produced through cooking to a medium or well done stage. A leg roast weighing 6 to 7 pounds or a shoulder weighing 5 to 6 pounds, requires from 30 to 35 minutes per pound at 300°F to reach an internal temperature of 170°F (medium) or 180°F (well done). A boneless shoulder weighing 4 or 5 pounds requires approximately 40 to 45 minutes per pound at 300°F. Roasting legs of lamb at a lower temperature (250°F) does not appear to improve tenderness.

Broiling is a popular method for cooking lamb. The tender cuts from most of the carcass can be prepared by broiling, even marinated riblets. The caramelization that takes place in the browning of the meat adds an agreeable flavor to the meat. When broiling, the location of the meat in relation to the source of heat and the cooking time is determined by the thickness of the cut. The thinner cuts are placed close to the heat and cooked for a shorter time so that the outside will be browned before the inside becomes overcooked.

Griddling appears to dry the meat less than direct heat cooking, as in broiling. It is a preferred method, therefore, for cooking patties and the thinner steaks and chops. The griddle should be moderately hot and rubbed with fat or sprinkled with salt before placing the meat on it, to prevent sticking. This is not necessary for meat that has been marinated in oil. A light garlic flavor may be added to the oil if desired. The chops should be

TABLE 18.2 TIME TABLE FOR BROILING LAMB

Cut	Thickness	Distance from Heat	Cooking Time (Min)*	
			Medium	Well Done
Rib or loin chops	1 in.	2 in.	12 to 14	14 to 18
	1½ in.	3 in.	18 to 22	22 to 25
	2 in.	3 in.	25 to 30	30 to 35
Leg steaks	1 in.	2 in.	12 to 15	14 to 18
Shoulder chops	¾ in.	2 in.	14 to 16	16 to 18
Lamb patties	¾ in.	3 in.	15 to 28	20 to 25
Riblets	1 in.	3 in.		20 to 25

*Half of the total time is used for each side. The meat may be seasoned after turning or when broiling has been completed.

Figure 18.8 Lamb stew with vegetables is a flavorful entrée. (Courtesy of the American Sheep Producers Council, Inc.)

Figure 18.9 Barbecued lamb riblets cooked in rich tomato sauce with onion and lemon. (Courtesy of the American Sheep Producers Council, Inc.)

Figure 18.10   Lamb cubes can be skewered with vegetables such as green pepper, onion, and tomato or with fruit such as apricot and cherries. (Courtesy of the American Lamb Council.)

allowed to develop an attractive brown color before turning, and should be turned once only. Season when the cooking has been completed.

Enjoyment of lamb dishes can be enhanced through proper seasoning. The flavor developed through browning of the meat adds appealing richness that is absent in boiled meat. Crisp bacon adds to this flavor quality and often is served with lamb as in a mixed grill. Seasoning with garlic and accompanying with mint sauce or mint jelly have been enjoyed sufficiently to make them traditional in the preparation of lamb. Lamb takes kindly to herb flavors, and much interest and variety can be developed through substituting oregano, thyme, rosemary, marjoram, basil, or parsley for the mint. Lemon juice or wine (sherry, Madeira, vermouth) helps to cut through any "furry" quality of the fat. Cranberries, tart fruit jellies, or marmalade may be welcomed as a change from the often used mint accompaniment.

When serving lamb, be sure that it is very hot or thoroughly chilled. When lamb is served at a lukewarm temperature, the fat in the mouth develops a

cottony quality commonly described as tallowy. The service of hot lamb requires right timing of preparation and serving, plus satisfactory holding
equipment. Timing calls for coordinating completion of preparation with
prompt service. Efficient holding equipment should maintain the desired
temperature for both the meat and the dishes on which the meat is to be
served. A cold plate of heavy institution china will quickly affect the temperature of its contents.

Lamb recipes range from low cost dishes to the top priced features of elite
restaurants. Certain selections stand out as common favorites. Among them
may be listed not only roasts and chops but also barbecued lamb riblets,
shish-kabobs, lamb curry, mixed grill, and Irish stew. Proper browning,
cooking at a moderate to low temperature, and thorough cooking for tenderness are important for best quality. The recipe for barbecue sauce given in
the chapter on sauces is a good one for use in preparing riblets and shanks
of lamb.

When preparing shish-kabobs, use $1\frac{1}{2}$-inch cubes cut from the leg or
shoulder of lamb and marinate overnight (at least six hours). Drain well.
Arrange on metal skewers with three items of fruit or vegetables that add
interesting flavor and color harmony. Three combinations that might be
used are pineapple chunks, mushroom caps, and cherry tomato; small onion,
green pepper squares, and mushroom caps; and tomato wedge, bacon, and
mushroom caps.

Figure 18.11 Skillfully slipping a shish-kabob from its skewer in front of the guest adds
showmanship. (Courtesy of the American Lamb Council.)

Lamb curry can have sufficient customer appeal to serve as a restaurant specialty. In order for it to qualify in this way, it must be more than a lamb stew with curry. (See recipe that follows.) It may be served over fluffy rice or a pilaf of bulgar wheat. If the rice is served with a scoop, make an indentation in the mound of rice with the back of the scoop to form a hollow in which to serve the curry. Patrons are pleased when they can serve themselves to a variety of accompaniments that always should include a good chutney and shredded coconut plus four or five of the following: chopped peanuts, crisp bacon bits, raisins, chopped egg whites, sieved egg yolks, slivered candied ginger, finely sliced young onion rings, banana chunks, pineapple tidbits, sliced kumquats (either fresh or candied), crisp prepared cereal. Choose the items for harmony of flavor, texture and appearance.

LAMB CURRY	**50 portions (4 oz)**	
Ingredients	Weight	Volume
Lamb, 1 in. cubes (leg or shoulder)	12 lb	6 qt
Shortening	6 oz	¾ c
Onions, finely chopped	2 lb	2 qt
Celery, finely chopped	3 lb	3 qt
Apples, fresh, pared, chopped	4 lb	3½ qt
Flour, bread	8 oz	2 c
Salt	2 oz	¼ c
Pepper	1 tsp	1 tsp
Curry powder	2 oz	½ c
Ginger	1 oz	¼ c
Tabasco Sauce	2 tsp	2 tsp
Worcestershire Sauce	4 oz	½ c
Water or stock	4 lb	2 qt
Fresh coconut, shredded and milk	36 oz	2 medium size (flesh and milk)

PROCEDURE:

1. Brown lamb in hot fat in heavy skillet. When almost browned, add onions, celery and apples and continue cooking.
2. Add flour, salt and spices and brown slightly. Add water or stock and simmer until tender (about 1 hour).

3. Shred fresh coconut, using a swivel-action parer. Chop slices slightly to make pieces about an inch long. Add to curry and cook for another 15 or 20 minutes.
4. Remove from the heat and permit curry to stand for about 3 hours, or even over night. Reheat to serving temperature when time for service.

Note: The amount of curry, ginger and sauces may be increased or decreased according to personal taste.

A Mixed Grill is a popular entree to serve for breakfast, lunch, or dinner. The items in the Mixed Grill may be a lamb chop, link sausages, and a slice of bacon, or the link sausages may be exchanged for sauted chicken livers. These are usually accompanied by a large mushroom cap and/or broiled tomato. A stuffed breast patty may be used instead of a rib or loin chop for a low cost Mixed Grill. Cooked-to-order and oven-hot lamb dishes are the most popular. It is well to remember that a sharp temperature is important to enjoyment.

SUGGESTED LABORATORY EXPERIENCE

1. Identify the different cuts of lamb and suggest ways in which each may be prepared.
2. Prepare specifications for lamb for 50 portions of (a) broiled shoulder chops, (b) loin chops, (c) boned-and-rolled shoulder roast, (d) lamb stew, (e) crown roast of lamb, and (f) roast leg of lamb.
3. Prepare the following: Broil—(a) 5-ounce loin chop, (b) 5-ounce rib chop, (c) 8-ounce shoulder chop, (d) 5-ounce shoulder chop. Pan-fry or griddle— 5-ounce shoulder chop. Evaluate tenderness, juiciness, flavor, appearance on the plate, and cost per portion. Determine situation when each is best to use.
4. Prepare a leg of lamb for buffet service, removing the aitch bone and Frenching the shank.
5. Prepare a crown roast from two half racks.
6. Barbecue a whole lamb shank (about $1\frac{1}{4}$ pounds) and shanks that have been sawed into 2-inch thick slices made across the bone and flesh. Weigh quantity of cooked meat in each portion. Compare meat quantity, cost or portion and appearance on the plate.
7. Prepare lamb curry. Try different accompaniments. Calculate portion cost including accompaniments.

REVIEW QUESTIONS AND ANSWERS

1. What is the age of the young, ovine animals classified as "spring lambs"?

   "Spring lambs" are 3 to 5 months old.

2. How old are those classified as "lambs"?

   They are from 6 to 12 months old.

3. What is regarded as a reliable indicator of a lamb's age?

   Appearance of the "break" joint. In young lambs it has four definite, smooth, moist ridges.

4. What are the government grades for lamb?

   Prime, choice, good, utility, and cull.

5. On what factors are the grades based?

   Conformation, finish, and quality.

6. What should a buyer specify when purchasing lamb?

   (a) Class and grade, (b) total weight and cut, (c) weight or size of pieces, (d) type of preparation, and (e) whether fresh or frozen.

7. At what temperature should lamb be held in storage?

   From 30 to 32°F.

8. What should be the time limit for holding (a) lamb carcass, (b) legs, (c) ground lamb?

   (a) 1 week, (b) 2 or 3 days, (c) 1 day.

9. What is a foresaddle of lamb?

   The front half of the carcass, containing the shoulder, ribs, shank, and breast.

10. How does it differ from a yoke?

    The yoke is the front $\frac{1}{3}$ and does not include the ribs.

11. What cuts are included in the hindsaddle?

    Loin, flank, leg, and shank.

12. What is a back of lamb?

    The middle third of lamb that contains the rib rack and loin.

13. What is a Hotel Rack? A half rack?

    The rib section cut across the width of the carcass, containing 8 or 9 ribs on each side. A half-rack is this rib section split along the backbones, containing ribs from one side of the lamb only.

14. What has added to the popularity of pan-ready cuts with purchasers?

    (a) Uniformity of portions, (b) saving on skilled labor, (c) expert cutting that yields good quality, and (d) easily calculated portion costs.

15. Which is the stifle joint and which is the break joint?

    The break joint is the first joint above the foot and the stifle joint is the next one above it (knee joint).

16. What is the aitch bone?

It is the pelvic bone, containing the socket into which the round bone (femur) of the leg is attached.

17. What wholesale cut of lamb is used for making a crown roast?

A 6 or 7-rib rack that lies next to the loin end.

18. What bones must be removed when preparing a crown roast?

The chine and backbones.

19. When preparing cutlets, chops or stew, how much fat may be on the individual pieces?

Not more than $\frac{1}{4}$ inch.

20. What is the maximum total fat acceptable in stew or ground lamb?

25%.

21. What are the minimum weights for rib chops, loin chops, shoulder chops?

Rib chops—3 ounce, loin chops—4 ounce, shoulder chops—4 ounce.

22. What precaution should be observed when cooking them?

Choose a method that permits browning and insures juiciness.

23. What method is generally preferred for cooking lamb chops and steaks?

Broiling.

24. When is griddling a better method?

When chops or steaks are sliced thinly.

25. Why is it preferred?

It tends to dry the meat less.

26. What seasonings are harmonious with the flavor of lamb?

Herbs—oregano, thyme, rosemary, marjoram, basil, mint, garlic, and parsley; Wines—Sherry and Madeira; and tart fruits and jam.

27. What temperature precautions should be observed in the preparation and service of lamb?

Cook at a moderate to low temperature, and serve either very hot or well chilled, never tepid.

28. How can proper service temperature be controlled?

By timing preparation and service to correspond, have efficient holding equipment for food and dishes.

19.

Pork and
Variety Meats

Pork is a mild flavored, tender meat that is liked by the majority of the American public. It ranks next to beef in the quantity consumed. The per capita use is approximately 70 pounds per year. Hogs are grown in all sections of the United States, with the largest number produced in the corn-growing states of the midwest. The animals mature quickly. A large percentage of the total production is slaughtered when they are six or eight months old, at which time they weigh around 200 to 240 pounds live weight. Dressed packer-style (split into sides, with head off, and kidney and leaf fat out), the yield is approximately 69%.

The quality of market pork is fairly uniform and less emphasis has been placed on grading than with beef, lamb, or veal. The U.S. Government grades for live animals became effective in 1952. The two major factors on which grades are based are (a) relative yield from a carcass of lean cuts, and (b) the quality of the meat. The lean cuts were identified as ham, loin, picnic, and Boston butt. Standards were established for three grades, U.S. Choice, U.S. Medium, and U.S. Cull. The Choice grade has three divisions that vary in percentage of lean cuts. Choice No. 1 yields 50%, Choice No. 2 45% to 48%, and Choice No. 3 less than 45% lean cuts. The Medium grade has a higher proportion of bone, less marbling of the flesh, and a softer texture than the Choice grades. The Cull grade from older or poorer animals is used chiefly for prepared pork products.

The appearance of the meat is a valuable aid in distinguishing quality. The flesh should be fine textured, firm, and greyish pink in color. Older animals have flesh that is a deeper rosy color and has a coarser texture. The fat should be abundant, well distributed throughout the flesh, firm, smooth, and snowy white. The bones of tender, young animals are red and spongy. Those of old animals are hard, white and flint-like. Good conformation in the carcass not only means a good yield of lean cuts but that individual cuts show a satisfactory proportion of flesh to bone.

The supply of pork is plentiful in the market all year, with the largest amount available between November and March. The price during these months is likely to be the lowest of the year. Pork, like other meats, is perishable and requires careful refrigeration. Both fresh and cured pork should be held at a temperature between 32 and 36°F. Fresh pork deteriorates rapidly and should not be held but purchased as needed. The mistaken idea that cured pork keeps without refrigeration has been the cause of many instances of food poisoning. The modern, quick-cured products are higher in water content and lower in salt than the earlier long-cured items, and they will support the growth of bacteria. Unlike the long-cured products, they do not require soaking to hydrate and remove excess salt. The "cure" is pumped into the arterial system before placing the meat in a pickling solution. The pickle may be injected into the muscles with needles. The pork is then smoked. The keeping quality is very little better than fresh pork. Smithfield-style hams are produced by the long-cure method.

When buying pork, the buyer should state (a) cut and total weight desired, (b) type of processing, such as fresh, cured, or canned, (c) portion weight or thickness of cuts or average weight or weight range for roasts, (d) market preparation, such as boning and/or tying, pocketing or other, and (e) state of refrigeration, such as fresh or frozen. Pork is sold in cuts rather than as a whole carcass. The cutting of the wholesale and many of the retail cuts are made at the packing house. The increased purchase of pan-ready meats and the fact that only about 35% of pork is sold as fresh meat has promoted this. The packing houses process the smoked hams, bacon, loins, picnics, pork products, and lard. Between 80 and 95% of the market supply of pork has been government inspected for wholesomeness and sanitation and all are included under the recent Wholesome Meat Act. All animals, processing methods, materials, and formulas for made-products are now checked for wholesomeness and sanitation.

CUTS OF PORK

Ham

The ham is the hind leg and includes the pelvic arch, rump, and leg to within an inch of the hock joint. The cut corresponds to the round and rump of beef. The weight of the majority of whole hams ranges from 8 to 24 pounds. Those weighing from 12 to 18 pounds are favored for baking and boiling. The larger hams tend to be coarser and less tender in texture, but they are

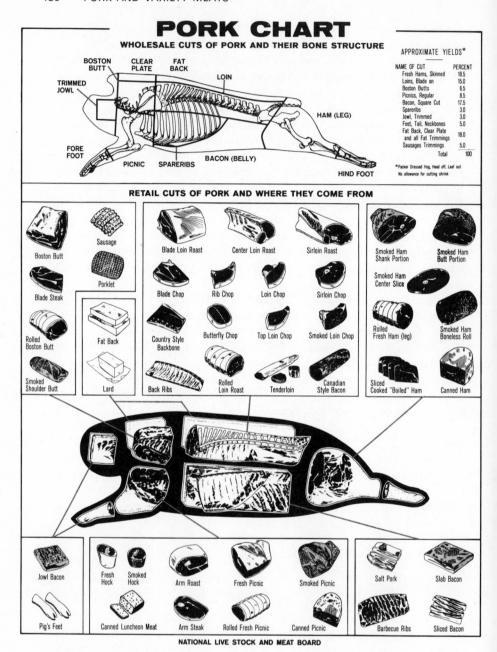

PORK CHART
WHOLESALE CUTS OF PORK AND THEIR BONE STRUCTURE

BOSTON BUTT · CLEAR PLATE · FAT BACK · LOIN

TRIMMED JOWL

HAM (LEG)

FORE FOOT · PICNIC · SPARERIBS · BACON (BELLY)

HIND FOOT

APPROXIMATE YIELDS*

NAME OF CUT	PERCENT
Fresh Hams, Skinned	18.5
Loins, Blade on	15.0
Boston Butts	6.5
Picnics, Regular	8.5
Bacon, Square Cut	17.5
Spareribs	3.0
Jowl, Trimmed	3.0
Feet, Tail, Neckbones	5.0
Fat Back, Clear Plate and all Fat Trimmings	18.0
Sausages Trimmings	5.0
Total	100

*Packer Dressed Hog, Head off, Leaf out
No allowance for cutting shrink

RETAIL CUTS OF PORK AND WHERE THEY COME FROM

Boston Butt

Sausage

Porklet

Blade Steak

Rolled Boston Butt

Fat Back

Smoked Shoulder Butt

Lard

Blade Loin Roast · Center Loin Roast · Sirloin Roast

Blade Chop · Rib Chop · Loin Chop · Sirloin Chop

Country Style Backbone · Butterfly Chop · Top Loin Chop · Smoked Loin Chop

Back Ribs · Rolled Loin Roast · Tenderloin · Canadian Style Bacon

Smoked Ham Shank Portion · Smoked Ham Butt Portion

Smoked Ham Center Slice

Rolled Fresh Ham (leg) · Smoked Ham Boneless Roll

Sliced Cooked "Boiled" Ham · Canned Ham

Jowl Bacon

Pig's Feet

Fresh Hock · Smoked Hock

Canned Luncheon Meat

Arm Roast · Fresh Picnic · Smoked Picnic

Arm Steak · Rolled Fresh Picnic · Canned Picnic

Salt Pork · Slab Bacon

Barbecue Ribs · Sliced Bacon

NATIONAL LIVE STOCK AND MEAT BOARD

Figure 19.1 Cuts of pork. (Courtesy of the National Livestock and Meat Board.)

usually lower in price and are an excellent choice for low-cost casseroles or other chopped ham dishes.

Ham may be procured in various market forms or types. It is necessary to be familiar with these in order to get the specific item desired. Fresh hams have not been treated in any way and are the fresh, raw product. Cured hams may have had a quick or a long cure, and may be regular, skinned, or skinless. The regular hams have the skin on. Skinned hams have 50 or 60% of the skin over the large part of the ham above the shank removed. Skinless hams have all of the skin and part of the fat removed.

The quick-cured hams cook more quickly than the long cured and have a mild flavor. The quick cured include those marketed as "tenderized," "ready-to-eat" and "fully cooked." The tenderized hams have been partially cooked, and the ready-to-eat have been cooked longer. Tenderized hams require further cooking. The ready-to-eat and fully cooked hams are safe to use without further cooking if they have been prepared under Federal inspection. These hams may have the bones in, may be partially boned, or fully boned, trimmed, rolled and tied.

Long-cured hams are more heavily salted and are smoked for a longer period. Although the various packers have their special process for these hams, there are two types that have become especially well known, the Smithfield and the Proscuitto. Those branded Smithfield must have been processed in Smithfield, Virginia. If produced elsewhere by a similar process, they must be labeled Smithfield-type. The Proscuitto hams are lean, flattened, and partially boned. The curing, drying, smoking processes used, when done under Federal inspection, make them safe for use without further cooking. The major supply of these hams for the American trade is produced in the United States by a formula originated in Italy.

Cooked hams, including those that are canned, are used in very large numbers. Although the price per pound may appear high, the cost per 3-ounce portion is likely to be comparatively modest. They are entirely usable without further preparation loss or shrinkage. The institution size canned hams are available in pullman and pear shapes. The pullman or square shape is particularly suitable for sandwiches. The pear shape, which follows the natural contour of the ham, is usually preferred when it is served as an entree. In addition to the large quantity of hams canned in the United States, a great many are imported from Denmark, Holland, Germany, and Poland.

The freshly cooked hams prepared commercially may be either boiled or baked. The boiled hams are the ones used in greatest quantity. Baking with sugar or molasses glaze is an added procedure and expense but most users prefer to add this process when the ham is heated immediately prior to service. The cooked hams may be purchased whole or sliced. Raw, cured hams are sold whole, halved, sliced, or in sections. The three sections are (a) shank end (low-priced, useful for flavoring soups and casseroles), (b) butt end (contains the aitch bone, next lowest in price, more meaty than the shank end, especially good for chopped ham dishes), and (c) center, which may be in one piece for baking or sliced for frying or baking.

When preparing either fresh or cured hams for slicing after they are cooked, they may be fully boned, rolled and tied, partially boned, or have the bones left in. The aitch bone should be removed before cooking because it is the most troublesome bone to remove when the meat is hot. The round bones may be removed, or the meat hand sliced against the bone in the same manner as that described for lamb legs in Chapter 18.

Middle

The middle of pork extends from the shoulder to the ham, and includes the loin, the fat back that lies on top of the loin (1 to 3 inches thick), and the belly. The belly, which corresponds to the plate and flank of beef, yields the bacon strip and spareribs. The spareribs and a large percentage of the loins are sold fresh. The top muscle of the loin that lies above the backbone is called Canadian-style or back bacon when cured. The boneless cuts of this tender meat sells for prices considerably higher than that for ham. It may be purchased whole or sliced.

Fresh loins for roasting may be purchased whole or as center cut, rib end, and loin end cuts. Crown roasts may be prepared with the center cut pork loins in the manner described in Chapters 17 and 18 for veal and lamb. The loin bones are likely to be too short to French and dress with a frill after roasting. An attractive garnish to place at the end of each rib bone can be made with round toothpicks or skewers. Place bright colored fruit or vegetables on the skewers, such as pineapple tidbits, whole cherries, stuffed olives, cherry tomatoes, or cranberries.

As they are cut from the entire loin, chops of a given thickness vary a great deal in circumference, weight, ratio of fat and lean, and tenderness. Center cut chops are prized for their uniformity and good quality. Pan-ready chops of uniform portion size and quality can be specified. These may either have the bone in or be boneless. The tenderloin may be removed from the loin and used whole for roasting, or cut into slices for sauteing or braising.

The fat backs and the clear plate (fat layer of 1 to 3 inches that lies on top of the Boston butt) are mostly rendered for lard. Some may be cured for use in seasoning beans and other vegetables. The bellies are trimmed, cured, and smoked for bacon. The average weight of bacon slabs varies from 4 to 18 pounds. That which is from 6 to 10 pounds is generally preferred because of the width of the slice (8 to 10 inches) and the proportion of fat to lean. Bacon with a high percentage of fat shows greater shrinkage in cooking. The lean should be a bright, pinkish-red in color, and reasonably fine textured and tender. The fat should be white and firm. The slab bacon with skin on has the best keeping quality, but for uniformity and convenience the majority of institution buyers prefer to purchase it sliced. When buying bacon specify quality or brand and number of slices desired per pound (average). Hotel sliced has 28 to 30 slices per pound; Regular has 20 to 22; and Western ranges from 12 to 18. It is packaged in layers in a 6 or 12-pound carton.

Spareribs are trimmed from the inside of the pork belly and consist of the ribs and breastbone. There are $4\frac{1}{2}$ pounds of spareribs in an average-size hog. Although a small per cent may be cured and smoked, the majority are sold fresh. The sweet, tender meat is popular for barbecuing. Because of the large percentage of bone, 6 or 8 ounces of meat as purchased should be regarded as a minimum portion.

Head and Shoulder

The meat on the head of pork consists of the cheeks or jowls and the meat that is trimmed from the bones for use in head cheese or scrapple. The jowls are trimmed and cured. These are sometimes referred to as jowl bacon or "Dixie Squares." The shoulder consists of the clear plate, Boston butt, and picnic shoulder. The clear plate and the shoulder butt or Boston butt constitute the top part of the shoulder. The picnic is the lower end of the shoulder.

The Boston butt is separated from the picnic near the shoulder joint and contains most of the shoulder blade. It may be used whole for roasting or it may be sliced into blade steaks or chops. The roasts may be boned, rolled, and tied. The thick, lean area that lies inside the shoulder blade is sometimes cured and smoked. This cut is called cottage butt, daisy or Westphalia. Capicola butt is a boneless shoulder that has been cured, spiced, smoked, and dried.

Picnic shoulders are available fresh or cured and smoked. Muscles extend in different directions in this cut, and the cut contains more skin, bone, and connective tissue than ham. It has often been misnamed "picnic ham," "cala ham," and California ham. Those who are not familiar with differences between shoulders and hams are disappointed when they find that picnic shoulders cannot be sliced into horseshoe-shaped slices similar to those in a ham. The shoulders are sold with or without the shank or may be boned, rolled, and tied. Shoulder hocks or shanks are available fresh or cured and smoked.

TABLE 19.1 SUGGESTED SIZES FOR PORK CHOPS, STEAKS AND ROASTS (RAW WEIGHTS)

Item	Ounces Per Portion						Pounds Per Roast					
	3	4	5	6	8	10	4 to 6	6 to 8	8 to 10	10 to 12	12 to 14	Over 14
Regular chop	•	•	•	•								
Pocketed chop		•	•	•	•	•						
Center-cut chop	•	•	•	•	•	•						
Boneless chop	•	•	•	•								
Blade steak, bone-in		•	•	•	•	•						
Blade steak, bnls		•	•	•	•	•						
Smoked-ham slice, bnls		•	•	•	•	•						
Smoked ham, bone-in									•	•	•	
Smoked ham, bnls, tied								•	•	•		
Fresh ham, bnls, tied							•		•	•	•	•
Boston butt, bnls, tied							•					
Pork loin, bone-in									•	•	•	
Pork loin, bnls, tied								•	•	•	•	

Sausage

There are many varieties of sausage. Their differences pertain to the kind of meat and other ingredients used, the coarseness of the grind, whether raw, cooked, dried, or smoked, and the casings used. The meat may be pork only, beef only, or a combination of pork with beef, veal, lamb, or mutton. There are three or four classifications that are generally recognized:

1. Fresh sausage is ground raw meat that is sold in bulk, in packages, and in casings, or as skinless links. Pure pork sausage is finely ground and may be purchased in links, packaged patties, or in bulk. The country-style is

Figure 19.2 Numerous sausages varied in kind of meat, seasoning, shape, and cure add interest to meals. (1) Large bologna, (2) ring bologna, (3) Polish sausage, (4) beerwurst, (5) football minced ham, (6) blood ring, (7) liver sausage, (8) salami, (9) Polish sausage, (10) knackwurst, (11) peppered loaf, (12) cotto salami, (13) ring bologna, (14) souse, (15) sausage roll, (16) pickle and pimiento loaf, and (17) skinless wieners (frankfurters or hot dogs). (Courtesy of the National Livestock and Meat Board.)

coarsely ground and may or may not contain beef. This raw, ground meat is highly perishable and should not be held. It should be thoroughly cooked before eating.

2. Smoked and/or cooked sausage may be made of pure pork or pork and beef. It is made from seasoned cured meat stuffed into casings and lightly smoked and/or cooked. Typical examples are frankfurters and bologna. These sausages contain nonfat dry milk or other binder. The liver sausages belong to this group. Braunshweiger has a smoke flavor developed through the smoking of the sausage or use of bacon as an ingredient. They are ready-to-eat and should not be stored longer than 4 or 5 days from date of purchase.

3. Dry and semidry sausages are made from highly seasoned, cured meat that is stuffed into casings. They are made of pork or beef or a combination of the two. Some are smoked and dried, others are dried and not smoked, and some are cooked. They are commonly called summer sausages and have excellent keeping qualities. Salami, cervelat, and Thuringer are popular examples.

4. Cooked specialties include such examples as the ham loaves and pickle loaves. They are made of cured meat, cooked, and often set in gelatin. They vary widely in flavor, shape, and texture. These are used for sandwiches and salad plates or for cold cuts. They will keep under refrigeration for about a week from time of purchase.

VARIETY MEATS

The variety meats include sweetbreads, heart, kidneys, liver, tongue of beef, veal, lamb, and pork; and pigs' feet, pigs' ears, tail, and chitterlings. The

Figure 19.3 Hearts. In order of size: beef, veal, pork, and lamb. (Courtesy of the National Livestock and Meat Board.)

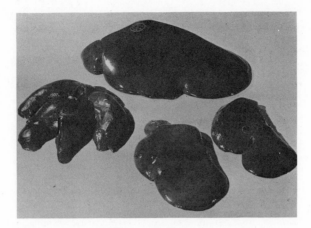

Figure 19.4 Livers. In order of size: beef, pork, veal, and lamb. (Courtesy of the National Livestock and Meat Board.)

chitterlings are thoroughly washed and rinsed large intestines. These are sold fresh, canned, frozen, pickled, and dry cured. Pigs' feet may be sold fresh, but the largest quantity are cured, cooked, and pickled. They may be purchased in bulk or packaged in jars. The sweetbreads are the thymus or pancreas of the animal, and have a spongy texture encased in a membrane. The sweetbreads, heart, liver, kidneys, and tongue are sold fresh by the pound and/or by count.

Figure 19.5 Tongues. In order of size: beef, veal, pork, and lamb. (Courtesy of the National Livestock and Meat Board.)

Figure 19.6 Kidneys, from left to right, (top) beef and veal; (bottom) pork and lamb. (Courtesy of the National Livestock and Meat Board.)

Figure 19.7 Beef brains (top left) and beef sweetbreads (lower right). (Courtesy of the National Livestock and Meat Board.)

CANNED AND COOKED PORK PRODUCTS

In addition to the canned hams and picnics, the list of canned items include deviled and minced ham, ham loaf and ham spread, liver paste and liver spread, pork with vegetables, and barbecued pork. Among the cooked pork products there is a variety of loaves, head cheese, scrapple, and souse. Scrapple is a popular breakfast and luncheon item on the east coast, but is practically unknown in the west. It is made of head meat, heart, and tongue thickened with cornmeal and other cereal flour. It may be purchased in bulk, packages or cans.

PORK COOKERY

Pork contributes important nutrients to the diet. It, like other meats, is a valuable source of protein, minerals, and vitamins. It is a richer source of thiamine than other meats. A 3-ounce portion of cooked pork supplies approximately one-third of the daily requirement of thiamine. Pork liver con-

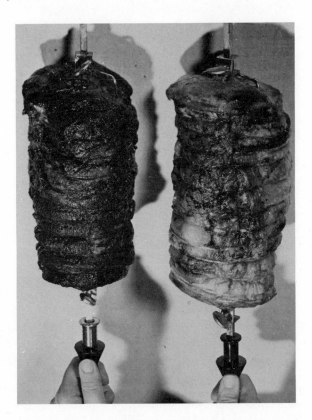

Figure 19.8   Too high a temperature and too long a cooking period causes excessive shrinkage. (Roast on left cooked to internal temperature of 200°F with 10% greater shrinkage was dry, and the one on right baked to 170°F internal temperature was juicy, flavorful, and attractive.) (Courtesy of Swift and Company.)

tains a greater supply of organic iron than does lamb, veal, or beef liver. Pork is completely digestible, although more slowly digested than the other three meats.

Significant points in the cooking of pork are (a) development of flavor, (b) preservation of tenderness, (c) destruction of the Trichinella spiralis organism, and (d) preservation of nutrients. The temperature at which pork is cooked and the end temperature to which it is cooked are important factors. The Food and Drug Administration accepts 137°F as a safe degree for the end temperature for cooking raw pork. It is well to allow a safety margin of from 10 to 15 degrees higher. As the end temperature is increased above the temperature of 150°F to the commonly recommended internal temperature of 185°F, cooking losses increase and the meat is less juicy and tender. However, taste panels rated the richness of flavor higher. Tenderness versus increased flavor calls for a decision based on personal preference.

Tenderness and the high percentage of fat are qualities that make many meats suitable for broiling. This is not true for pork, even though the pork is from young, tender animals and contains considerable fat in the tissues. Chops braised with or without added water are more tender, have a better flavor, and show lower cooking losses than those that are broiled. The chops that are braised without added water are generally preferred.

When roasting pork, oven temperature appears to have less influence on the tenderness than it does with beef. Cooking losses are less, however, if moderate to low temperatures are used. A constant temperature of 325°F is recommended for pork as well as for veal and lamb. The roast should be placed in an open pan with the fat side up, so that it is self-basting. Place a meat thermometer in the roast so that the bulb reaches the center of the meaty portion of the roast, and is away from the bone. (See Table 19.2 for a roasting or braising schedule for different cuts of pork or varying weights.)

When baking or boiling frozen meat increase the time allowance from 1 to 2 hours, depending on the thickness of the meat. Prepare in the same manner as unfrozen and rely on the meat thermometer for the desired internal temperature. When pan frying or braising frozen chops and steaks, start with a warm (not hot) skillet and a small amount of fat. Heat slowly, allowing the meat to thaw, then continue as for unfrozen meat. The cooking time should be increased according to the thickness of the pieces of meat and to the time required for reaching the proper degree of doneness or desired internal temperature.

When braising chops, spareribs, or other cuts of pork, allow them to brown slowly. The browning may be done in a skillet, on a griddle, or in the oven. When browning in the oven, use a temperature of 350°F. Use a small amount of liquid after browning. Do not drown the chops with the liquid because

TABLE 19.2 BAKING OR BRAISING SCHEDULE FOR PORK IN 325°F OVEN TEMPERATURE

Item	Approximate Weight (lb)	Approximate Time (hr)	Internal Temperature (F)
Fresh loin	3	2½	170°
	5	2¾	170°
	7	3	170°
Crown roast	7	3½	185°
Shoulder, bone-in, picnic, or Boston butt	4 to 5	4	185°
	8	5	185°
Shoulder, boneless	4	3 to 3½	185°
Ham	8	4¾	185°
	10	5½	185°
	14	5½	185°
Spareribs	1½ to 2	1 to 1½	185°
Chops	(6 to 8 oz)	¾ to 1	185°
Smoked Canadian bacon	1	¾	170°
	2	1½	170°
	4	2½	170°
	6	3	170°
Ham slice, 2-in.	2	1½ to 1¾	160°
¾-in.	1 to 1½	1 to 1¼	160°
Ham, whole, bone-in	6 to 8	3¼	160°
	10	3½	160°
	12	4	160°
	15	4½	160°
	18	5	160°
	22	6	160°
	24	6½	160°
Picnic	4	2½	170°
	6	3	170°
	8	4	170°
	10	4½	170°
Daisy	2	2	170°
	3	3	170°

TABLE 19.2 (*Continued*)

Item	Approximate Weight (lb)	Approximate Time (hr)	Internal Temperature (F)
Fully cooked ham	6 to 8	2¼	130°
	10	2½	130°
	12	3	130°
	14	3¼	130°
	16	3¾	130°
	4	1¾	130°
	8	2¾	130°
	10	3½	130°
Canned ham or picnic		(20 min/lb)	

this will rob them of color and richness of flavor. If the container is tightly covered and the temperature reduced to 325°F sufficient moisture may be retained and little or no additional moisture will be needed.

A glaze may be used to add flavor and attractiveness to hams used for counter or buffet service. The glazes may be fruit flavored, spicy, or sweet. They are added after the ham has been scored in a carefully made diamond pattern. Bits of fruit and long-stemmed whole cloves may be dotted over the ham in the center of the diamond patterns. After the glaze is applied, the

Figure 19.9   Loin of pork with featherbones removed. (Courtesy of Swift and Company.)

Figure 19.10   Carving of pork loin is easy with the backbones removed. (Courtesy of Swift and Company.)

meat is returned to the oven and the temperature is increased to 400°F for melting and browning the glaze. This takes from 20 to 30 minutes, or until a good color is produced.

Scoring the Ham

The scoring appears best when the size of the markings is uniform. Toothpicks arranged $1\frac{1}{4}$ inches apart along the two sides of the ham will serve as useful guides. Use a long, thin knife (such as a slicing knife) and make cuts about $\frac{1}{4}$-inch deep into the layer of fat. Start with the toothpick at the butt end on one side and make a diagonal cut to the third or fourth toothpick from the butt end on the other side of the ham. If the heel of the long knife is placed at the first toothpick it can be rocked across the ham to the other toothpick in a reasonably straight line. Continue to the next set of toothpicks, keeping an equal distance from the previous marking, until the entire ham has been scored. Turn the ham and continue the marking to form the diamond pattern.

Ham Glazes

Sugar in the glaze produces a rich brown color. Pineapple tidbits, cherries or other bright-colored fruit is more attractive when applied after the glaze has been put on the meat, so that they will remain bright and will not brown. Popular glazes, in amounts sufficient for one medium-size ham, may be made with the following:

1. For a plain, sweet glaze use either (a) 1 cup of honey drizzled over the

ham, or (b) 1 cup of honey drizzled over the ham and then sprinkled with
$\frac{1}{2}$ cup of brown sugar.

2. For a fruit flavor use (a) preserves—apricot, cherry, peach, pineapple,
or orange marmalade; (b) $\frac{3}{4}$ cup crushed pineapple and 1 cup brown sugar;
or (c) 1 cup of crabapple, cranberry, currant, or quince jelly.

3. For a spicy flavor use (a) 1 cup brown sugar and 1 tablespoon dry
mustard; (b) 1 cup sieved applesauce, 2 tablespoons prepared mustard, and
$\frac{1}{2}$ cup corn syrup; or (c) 2 dozen long-stemmed cloves stuck into the ham
plus one of the sweet glazes.

When cooking the short-cure hams or picnics in water, cover with hot
water and bring to boiling temperature, then turn the heat low and simmer
until done. Allow 25 to 30 minutes per pound for half hams and 18 to
20 minutes per pound for whole hams. Permit the hams to remain in the
broth until cool in order to insure the best flavor and juiciness. Save the
broth for use in soup or for seasoning. The long-cure hams like the Smithfield
should be soaked in cold water for 24 to 30 hours before boiling. Pork hocks,
neck bones, and spareribs should be simmered for $1\frac{1}{2}$ to 2 hours or until
fork tender.

The important pleasure qualities of bacon are its flavor and texture. Both
of these are affected by the method and degree of cooking. It should be crisp
but not brittle and evenly cooked from end to end. The fat should never be
heated to smoking temperature when pan frying. It should be placed far
enough from the source of heat in broiling so that it does not char readily
and the fat does not spatter badly. Broiling is believed to produce the best
flavor, and oven cooking requires the least handling. A shallow pan fitted
in the bottom with a wire rack is needed for broiling or baking in the oven.
Place the bacon on the rack with slices touching. Turn once, allowing 2 to
$2\frac{1}{2}$ minutes for broiling each side. The rack should be located at least
3 to $3\frac{1}{2}$ inches from the heat source. When baking in an oven at 400°F
arrange the bacon on the rack with the fat overlapping the lean. Cook without turning for 12 to 15 minutes or until satisfactorily browned. When pan
frying, the fat should be poured off as the bacon cooks, and the bacon should
be turned frequently. Allow 6 or 8 minutes for pan frying.

Juiciness in sausages is a desirable quality. It is best to use tongs for turning
them to avoid pricking them with a fork. When pan frying sausages, add a
small amount of water and allow them to steam for about 5 minutes before
browning. Drain the moisture and fat out of the pan and allow the sausages
to brown, turning them for even browning. Sausage links may be cooked in
a 400°F oven for 20 minutes and turned once during cooking. Sausage patties
should be allowed to cook for 30 minutes and turned after the first 15 minutes.

Brown 'n Serve sausage can be cooked enough in 3 or 4 minutes by pan frying or in 10 to 12 minutes in a 400°F oven.

COOKING OF VARIETY MEATS

Variety meats are enjoyed by the majority of the American public on an occasional basis and where they are used to add variety to menus. Liver and kidneys are sufficiently rich in iron, copper, and vitamins A, riboflavin, niacin, and thiamine to possess special value nutritionally. The mild flavor and tender texture of calves liver makes it favored over liver from beef, lamb, or pork. Pork liver, however, contains three times as much iron and lamb's liver has about four times as much vitamin A as the other three. Heart, sweetbreads, tongue, and tripe are also valuable sources of iron and vitamins but in smaller quantities than found in liver.

Enjoyment of these valuable foods depends in large degree on the manner in which they are prepared. Each has specific characteristics to be considered when choosing a method of preparation and foods with which they are to be combined in the menu. It is well for the foods with which they are used to harmonize in texture and flavor. *Heart*, for example, is a lean muscle without sufficient fat to keep it moist when cooked without liquid. If cooked in the oven it should be covered to prevent drying. Braising and boiling are best methods of cooking. If served with dressing, the dressing should be moist and have extra fat for richness, and should be well seasoned. Heart combines well with pork in chop suey and similar casserole dishes. The approximate weights of hearts are: beef, $3\frac{1}{2}$ to 4 pounds; veal, $\frac{3}{4}$ pound; pork, 1 pound; and lamb $\frac{1}{4}$ pound. There are 3 to 4 portions per pound as purchased.

When preparing boiled heart, begin by trimming away the coarse fibers at top and inside the hearts. Wash in cold water, and place in a kettle with enough hot water to cover. Add salt in proportion of 1 teaspoon per quart of water. Cover and simmer until tender. Veal and lamb hearts require from 1 to $1\frac{1}{2}$ hours and beef and pork hearts approximately 2 hours. When braising hearts, dip the pieces in seasoned flour, and brown in hot fat. When well browned, add water, cover, and allow to cook over low heat for about two hours, or until tender.

The variety meats are perishable and should be held frozen or used within 24 hours of purchase. Frozen items should be thawed in the refrigerator before use. Frozen brains or sweetbreads may be dropped in boiling water to thaw, then simmered and prepared in the same manner as fresh items. The fresh items should be loosely wrapped and held at 32 to 35°F.

Liver

Liver is a delicate meat that calls for gentle treatment for best results. Avoid high temperature that will cause it to be hard and dry, and do not soak or scald it before cooking. It should be peeled, evenly sliced, and the coarse membranes removed. Veal, calf, or lamb liver that is to be broiled should be sliced about $\frac{1}{4}$-inch thick. It may then be marinated in oil, French dressing, or brushed with melted butter and arranged on the broiler rack and cooked about 3 inches from the heat source. Broil about 5 or 6 minutes on each side, or until nicely browned. When pan-frying liver, dip the slices in seasoned flour until uniformly covered. Brown in hot fat, then reduce heat and allow to cook for 10 to 15 minutes longer. Two of the most popular accompaniments for liver are bacon and onions. The crisp texture and smoky flavor of bacon is appealing. French-fried onion rings add appealing appearance as well as crisp texture.

Sweetbreads

Sweetbreads are commonly regarded as party fare. They have a tender texture, delicate flavor, and a pale color. They are enjoyed most when prepared in ways that add texture, enhance flavor, and add color. Start preparation by precooking in boiling, salted water (1 teaspoon salt to 1 quart of water), cover and simmer for 25 minutes if they are veal or lamb and 35 minutes if beef. Drain. Let cold water run over them. Next, pull off the thin membrane; cut out the dark veins and coarse connective tissue. They may then be carefully sliced or broken into pieces for further preparation. If split in half, they may be rolled in crumbs, in beaten egg, and again in crumbs, and fried in hot deep-fat. This produces an attractive golden color and some crispness. If broken into pieces or cubed, they may be served in a rich cream sauce to which almonds have been added for texture. Ham, peas, mushrooms, oysters, or chicken are sometimes used for interest, color, and flavor. Pimiento and/or chopped parsley add color.

Kidneys

Kidneys may be cooked alone or as a part of lamb or veal chops. Beef steak and kidney pie is a well known entree. As a part of a chop, the flank end of the chop is skewered around the kidney, and they are broiled along with the chop. Veal and lamb kidneys require very little cooking. The outer membrane of the kidney should be removed and the kidney split in half. The veins and fat should be clipped out with scissors or cut out with a small sharp knife. The veal or lamb kidneys may be broiled or sauted. It is well to marinate them in French dressing or brush them with butter before broiling. Place them at least 3 inches from the heat source and allow them to broil 5 to 7 minutes on each side, or until nicely browned. Broiled tomato or crisp bacon are suitable accompaniments.

Beef and pork kidneys should have the membrane removed, split open and the veins and fat removed, and rinsed well in cold water. Simmer in salted water for about 30 minutes or braise by browning in fat and then cooking slowly in a small amount of water. If they are to be used in Beef Steak and Kidney Pie, they should be cut into 1-inch cubes before cooking. The kidney, steak, and onions may be browned and cooked together.

Tongue

Tongue may be served either hot or cold. It can be purchased fresh, cured, smoked, or pickled. It combines well with sharp flavored foods, such as sandwiches made with Russian rye or caraway bread, horseradish, coleslaw, sauerkraut, pickled beets, and hot potato salad. It is a favorite for service as a meat in assorted cold cuts.

When cooking fresh tongue, cover it with cold water to which salt (1 tablespoon for beef tongue), whole peppercorns, a small onion, and a medium-sized bay leaf have been added. If the tongue has been cured, smoked, or pickled omit the seasonings and cover with cold water. Bring the tongue to simmering temperature and cook until fork tender, allowing about one hour per pound. A beef tongue weighing $2\frac{1}{2}$ pounds requires about $2\frac{1}{2}$ hours and a veal, pork, or lamb tongue from 1 to $1\frac{1}{2}$ hours.

When tender, remove the tongue from the water and allow to become cool enough to handle easily. Remove the bones and gristle from the base of the tongue. Loosen the skin of the tongue at the thick end, using a paring knife. Using knife and fingers to grasp the skin, peel it off from the thick end toward the tip. Use care not to hack or roughen the surface of the tongue. The slices are most attractive and uniform in size when they are made slightly on a diagonal of the tongue.

Oxtails

Oxtails are sold disjointed and often are packaged and frozen. If fresh oxtails have not been disjointed, ask the dealer to do it, in order to facilitate preparation. Although they are a bony cut, they do contain quite a bit of muscular meat, and may be used to produce a fine flavor in soups and stews. Frozen oxtails should be allowed to thaw in the refrigerator before using. Wash the oxtails thoroughly in cold water. They may then be covered with salted water and simmered until tender. If they are to be used for soup or stew, added flavor may be developed by braising. Roll them in seasoned flour, brown in hot fat with onion, add water, and simmer until the meat falls from the bones (about 3 hours). For stew, the meat may be left on the bones, vegetables added, and the stew allowed to simmer for the last 30 to 45 minutes of cooking time. For soup, remove the meat from the bones, combine the meat with the vegetables, and cook until the vegetables are tender.

SUGGESTED LABORATORY EXPERIENCE

1. Prepare specifications for the following: pork for a low-cost roast, chops for stuffing, ham for a banquet, spareribs for barbecuing, liver for broiling to serve 50 people.
2. Weigh before and after cooking: a fresh pork picnic, Boston butt, and ham. Bake, slice, and compare portions per pound as purchased, appearance of slices, per cent of fat, and eating quality.
3. Grill, broil and bake bacon slices. Evaluate appearance and eating quality.
4. Prepare jambalaya using spiced ham as the meat in the recipe. Evaluate quality as a low cost casserole.
5. Cook heart and pork shoulder. Cut the meat and use in a pork chop suey. Serve with crisp noodles.
6. Prepare sweetbreads. Sauté part of them and cream others with almonds or vegetables. Evaluate flavor, texture, and appearance.
7. Cook oxtails and prepare oxtail soup or stew. (This preparation may be started during the class session one day and completed in the next.)
8. Pan-fry and compare beef, lamb, and pork liver.
9. Prepare and compare the different kinds of sausage.

REVIEW QUESTIONS AND ANSWERS

1. On what factors are the grades of pork based?

(a) Relative lean and fat cuts in a carcass, and (b) quality of the meat.

2. What are the grades?

U.S. Choice 1, 2, 3, Medium, and Cull.

3. What points in appearance indicate quality?

Fine texture, firmness, greyish pink color of flesh, snowy-white fat and reddish bones.

4. At what temperature should pork be held in storage?

32 to 36°F.

5. What should be specified when buying pork?

(a) Cut, (b) processing, (c) individual piece weight, (d) total weight, (e) market preparation, and (f) whether fresh or frozen is desired.

6. Name the wholesale cuts of pork.

Jowl, Boston butt, picnic, shanks or hocks and feet, fat back, loin, belly, spareribs, and ham.

7. What is Canadian style bacon?

Boneless, smoked loin of pork.

8. Differentiate between a regular, skinned, and skinless ham.

A regular ham is a cured ham with the skin on. A skinned ham has had 50 or 60% of the skin removed, and a skinless ham has had all of the skin and part of the fat removed.

9. What is the difference between a quick- and a long-cured ham?

Quick-cured hams have a milder cure and shorter smoke. Pickling solution is pumped into hams before placing in the pickle. Long-cured has heavier salt and longer smoking and require soaking and/or parboiling before cooking.

10. How should "tenderized" and "fully cooked" hams be prepared?

Tenderized hams are partially cooked and require more cooking before use. Fully cooked may be used without cooking, or may be heated to an internal temperature of 130°F if desired for service hot.

11. Where on a carcass is the fat back located and for what is it used in cooking?

It is the layer of fat that lies on the outside of the loin area, from the ham to the shoulder. It is used for seasoning and for lard.

12. What is the most popular size of ham for baking?

12 to 14 pounds.

13. How many slices of bacon are in a pound Hotel sliced, and Regular sliced?

Hotel sliced has 28 to 30 slices and the Regular sliced, 20 to 22.

14. What are "Dixie Squares"?

Trimmed and cured pork jowls.

15. What is a clear plate?

The fat layer on top of the Boston butt.

16. What is a Boston butt?

The top part of the shoulder, that contains most of the shoulder blade.

17. Is it correct to call a pork picnic a picnic ham?

No. It is the shoulder, not the ham, and is sometimes misnamed California ham.

18. What is fresh sausage, and is it composed of pork only?

It is ground raw meat. It may be pork only, or a blend of pork and other meats.

19. What are the classifications of sausage?

(a) Fresh sausage, (b) smoked and/or cooked sausage, and (c) dry and semi-dry sausage. (d) Chopped meat loaves that are cooked specialties may be considered as a fourth.

20. What is included under the classification Variety Meats?

Liver, heart, kidney, tripe, sweetbreads, tongue, oxtails, pigs' ears, tail, feet, and chitterlings.

21. What is the nutritional importance of variety meats?

Liver and kidneys are valuable for protein and for iron, copper and the vitamins A, thiamine, riboflavin, niacin and ascorbic acid. The other variety meats, also, have an appreciable amount of iron, thiamine, riboflavin, and niacin.

22. What are four significant points to remember when cooking pork?

(a) Develop flavor, (b) preserve tenderness, (c) cook thoroughly to destroy trichina, and (d) in a manner that preserves nutrients.

23. What are sweetbreads?

They are the thymus or pancreas.

24. Which method is preferable when cooking pork, broiling or braising?

Braising yields a more tender product with a better flavor.

25. What oven temperature is recommended for roasting pork? What internal temperature when cooking raw pork?

325°F. An internal temperature from 160 to 185°F depending on cut and curing.

26. When braising chops, should they be covered with water or only a minimum amount used?

Use a very small amount in order to produce the best flavor.

27. Is it necessary to parboil ham before baking it?

Only if it has had a long cure.

28. Describe the oven method of cooking bacon.

Place on a rack in a shallow pan, with the fat overlapping the lean. Cook at 400°F for 12 to 15 minutes without turning.

29. Describe pan-frying of bacon.

Place in unheated skillet and cook slowly. Turn often to cook evenly. Pour off fat as it accumulates.

30. What is the best way to cook in large quantity?

By baking at 400°F in an oven for about 20 minutes, and turning once during baking for even browning.

31. What precaution should be observed when cooking heart?

Cook it until fully tender in a way that prevents dryness.

32. Is broiling a desirable method for cooking liver?

Very tender liver such as that of lamb or calves may be broiled. Pork and beef liver is better when braised.

33. How can the palatability of sweetbreads be enhanced through cooking methods?

Color, flavor, and crispness can be increased by breading and sauteing. These qualities can also be increased through combining with other foods, such as almonds and/or vegetables.

| 34. How is a tongue peeled? | By loosening the skin at the base of the tongue (or largest part) with a small knife, and pulling it off using the knife and fingers, toward the tip of the tongue. |
| 35. How should a tongue be cooked? | By simmering slowly, allowing 1 hour per pound, in fresh water if cured or pickled and in water to which spices and vegetables have been added if it is a fresh tongue. |

BIBLIOGRAPHY

Adams, Charlotte, "1001 Questions Answered About Cooking," New York: Dodd, Mead and Co., 1963.

Aldrich, P. J., and G. A. Miller, "A New Milky Way for Your Own Favorite Quantity Recipes," Circular Bulletin 225, Agr. Experimental Station, Michigan State University, East Lansing, 1958.

Aldrich, P. J., and G. A. Miller, "Whole and Nonfat Dry Milk in Quantity Food Preparation," Circular Bulletin 223, Agr. Experimental Station, Michigan State University, East Lansing, 1956.

American Dairy Association Test Kitchen, "A Recipe Collection," 20 N. Wacker Drive, Chicago.

American Dry Milk Institute, Quantity Recipes, Bulletin 503; and "Nonfat Dry Milk in Quantity Food Preparation," Handbook No. 706.

American Lamb Council, Consumer Education Department, "Teaching Lamb Cookery," Bulletin No. 4, Denver, Colorado.

American Meat Institute, "The Story of Beef," "Beef Chart," "Pocket Guide To Beef," and "Beef Kit," 59 East Van Buren, Chicago.

American Sheep Producers Council, Inc., "Lamb Cutting and Merchandising Manual;" Bulletin No. 2, "Greater Profits with Rolled Shoulder of Lamb," Denver: American Sheep Producers Council, Inc.

Beck, Simone, Louisette Bertholle, and Julia Child, "Mastering the Art of French Cooking," New York: Knopf, 1961.

Bureau of Supplies and Accounts, Navy Department, "Meat Handbook," Washington, D.C.: U.S. Government Printing Office.

Carson, Byrta and MaRue Carson Ramee, "How You Plan and Prepare Meals," New York: McGraw-Hill.

Culinary Institute of America, Inc. and Editors of Institution Magazine, *The Professional Chef*, Chicago: Institutions Magazine, 1964.

Editors of Sunset Books, "Seafood Cook Book," Menlo Park, Calif.: Lane Books.

Eshbach, Charles E., and Kirby M. Hayes, "Increasing the Satisfaction from Fish and Shellfish," University of Massachusetts Publication 387, Amherst, 1963.

Food Service Magazine Editorial, "The Meat Market," Madison: *Food Service Magazine*, 2132 Fordem Avenue, March, 1968.

Fowler, S. F., B. B. West, and G. S. Shugart, "Food for Fifty," New York: Wiley, 1961.

General Electric Company, "Owners Manual," Commercial Equipment Department, Chicago Heights, Illinois: General Electric Company.

Gifford, Marie, "Pork Study Guide," "Study Guide for Ham and Bacon," and "Armour Processed Meats Study Guide," Chicago: Armour and Company.

Gillis, J. N., and N. K. Fitch, "Leakage of Baked Soft-Meringue Topping," *Journal of The American Home Economics Assoc.*, **48**, 703–707, Washington, D.C., 1956.

Greff, Joseph G., "Cooking for Managers," Dubuque, Iowa: Brown, 1967.

Griswold, Ruth M., "Experimental Study of Foods," Boston: Houghton Mifflin, 1962.

Kotschevar, Lendal H., "Quantity Food Production," Berkeley, Calif.: McCutchan, 1964.

Kotschevar, Lendal H., and Margaret E. Terrell, "Food Service Planning: Layout and Equipment," New York: Wiley, 1961.

Logan, Martha, "Martha Logan's Meat Handi-book" and "Bacon, the Meat of All Meals," Chicago: Swift and Co.

Longree, K. M., M. Jooste, and J. C. White, "Time-Temperature Relationships of Custards Made With Whole Egg Solids. III Baked in Batches," Chicago: *The Journal of The American Dietetic Assoc.*, **38**, 147–151, 1961.

Lundberg, Donald E., and Lendal H. Kotschevar, "Understanding Cooking," Amherst: The University of Massachusetts, 1965.

Martha Logan's Department, "Meat Handi-Book," Chicago: Swift and Co.

McLean, Beth Bailey, and Tora H. Campbell, "The Complete Meat Cookbook," Peoria, Ill: Bennett, 1953.

McWilliams, Margaret, "Food Fundamentals," New York: Wiley, 1966.

National Association of Meat Purveyors, Meat Buyer's Guide to Standardized Meat Cuts," Chicago: Nat'l Assoc. of Meat Purveyors, 29 South LaSalle Street.

National Dairy Council, "Newer Knowledge of Milk" and "Newer Knowledge of Cheese."

National Live Stock and Meat Board, "101 Meat Cuts," "Cooking Meat in Quantity," "Variety Meats," and "Meat Charts," Chicago: National Live Stock and Meat Board.

National Turkey Federation, "Turkey Handbook" and "Turkey Recipes for The Institutional Kitchen," Mount Morris, Illinois.

Poultry and Egg National Board, "Eggs are Cheaper," "Answers to Often Asked Questions About Eggs," "13 Easy Ways to Cook Eggs," and "Broiler-Fryer."

Roberson, John and Marie, "The Meat Cookbook," New York: Holt, 1953.

Restaurant Management Magazine Special Feature, "Lamb for Prestige and Profit," Chicago: *Restaurant Management Magazine*, March, 1959.

Seco Company, Inc., "Seco Food Preparation and Service Equipment," St. Louis: Seco Company, Inc., P.O. Box 7116.

Shank, D. E., N. F. Fitch, and P. A. Chapman, "Guide to Modern Meals," St. Louis: McGraw-Hill, 1964.

Swift and Company Hotel Dept., "Cutting Meats—The Beef Chuck" and "Facts You Should Know About Beef," Chicago: Swift and Co.

Terrell, Margaret E., "Large Quantity Recipes," Philadelphia: J. B. Lippincott, 1951.

U.S. Dept of Agriculture, "Eggs and Egg Products," Circular No. 583; "How to Buy Eggs"; "Handbook No. 51—Federal and State Standards for Composition of Milk Products"; "Turkey on the Table the Year Round," Home and Garden Bulletin No. 45; "Poultry Grading and Inspection," Agricultural Information Bulletin No. 173, 1961; "How to Buy Poultry"; "Know the Poultry You Buy"; "Poultry Inspection a Consumer's Safeguard"; "U.S. Grades of Beef"; "Pork, Facts For Consumer Education"; and "Institutional Meat Purchase Specifications for Portion-Cut Meat Products, Series 1000."

U.S. Government Printing Office, Fishery Market Development Series No. 8, "Let's Cook Fish"; and Test Kitchen Series, No. 1, "Basic Cookery for One Hundred," 1960; No. 2, "Basic Fish Cookery," 1948; No. 3, "How to Cook Oysters," 1953; No. 4, "How to Cook Salmon," 1951; No. 5, "Fish Recipes for Type A School Lunches," 1959; No. 6, "How to Cook Ocean Perch," 1952; No. 7, "How to Cook Shrimp," 1952; No. 8, "How to Cook Clams," 1953; No. 9, "How to Cook Halibut," 1959; No. 10, "How to Cook Crabs," 1956; No. 11, "How to Cook Lobsters," 1957; No. 12, "How to Cook Tuna," 1957; No. 13, "How to Cook Scallops," 1959, and No. 14, "Fish and Shellfish Over the Coals."

Wells Commercial Sales Company, "How to Use and Care for Wells Electric Fry Kettles," South San Francisco: Wells Commercial Sales Co.

Wolf Range Company, "Owners Manual," Compton, Calif.: Wolf Range Co., 19600 South Alameda Street.

SECTION V

The Bake Shop

CHAPTER 20   Bakery Equipment (Mixer, Dough Dividers and Rounders, and Dough Rollers, Moulders and Shelter, and Proof Box)

CHAPTER 21   Bread Baking

CHAPTER 22   Cakes, Cookies, and Frostings

CHAPTER 23   Preparation of Pies and Puddings

Bibliography for Section V

20.

Bakery Equipment

The characteristic activities in bake shops, involving measuring, mixing, cutting, shaping, and proofing, are time consuming. Equipment to relieve manual work, speed production, improve quality, and increase uniformity of products is welcomed by large-quantity producers of bakery items. The bake shop that is a part of a large kitchen usually follows a consistent pattern of activity according to the specific menu offerings. When selecting equipment and locating it in the layout, it is valuable to study the characteristic equipment needs and the customary flow of work.

The work in bake shops normally begins with adjustment of oven temperatures for the first products to be baked, and the assembling of food and equipment for the products at the work center. The measurement of ingredients, which follows as a next step, calls for a scale that provides accurate weights (see Chapter 2) and that is conveniently located between supplies in the work center and the mixer. The scale is used for measuring ingredients into the mixer and for scaling mixtures into pans. Although the later processing of products may vary according to the items made, practically all of the bakery mixtures follow these first steps in production.

Many of the dry ingredients used by bakers may be stored in or near the work center. When limitation of space prohibits keeping all of the supplies at the work center, it is well to analyze volume and frequency of use in choosing those that are to be stored there. Spice compartments or drawers in a high shelf location above the baker's table places these often used items where they are convenient (see Figure 9.4, p. 202). Rolling bins below the table top are commonly used for flours, sugars, and milk solids.

A small pantry, cabinet, or other storage area adjacent to a baker's work center is frequently desirable for a miscellaneous lot of small items that differ widely in size and shape, such as a variety of pans, cutters, sieves, sifters, coloring materials, extracts, and pastry tips. These are likely to present a dust-catching clutter when stored on or around the baker's table. Having a suitable place for them may save labor time that would otherwise be spent in searching for needed items or walking a distance to procure them.

MIXERS

A mixer is one of the most useful machines in the average kitchen. A pantry section may use one for making salad dressings; the cook who whips potatoes, strains soup, and blends casserole mixtures considers it an essential piece of equipment. It is also a necessary item of equipment in a bake shop for the production of good-quality products in large quantity. The number of mixers required by a kitchen depends largely on volume of output, the menu items prepared, and the extent of the preparation. A kitchen with small to medium-size output may find one mixer sufficient if it is located so that the various workers can use it without getting in each other's way or upsetting schedules of work. The location of the only mixer in a kitchen should be in or near the work section that uses it most frequently. This is likely to be the bake shop. It needs to be placed in relation to the work table or other equipment, so that the side on which the brake, clutch, and hand wheel are located is free for operating the mixer.

Size

Heavy-duty mixers are available in a range of sizes from approximately 5 to 140 quarts capacity. It is often desirable, in adjusting to volume for different functions, to have more than one size or capacity. A baker, for example, may need a 60 or 80-quart mixer for making cake or bread and a 10 or 12-quart capacity for whipping cream or making frosting. Some variation in size is possible through the use of an adaptor ring. An 80-quart mixer may accommodate 60, 40, or 30-quart bowls through use of the appropriate adaptor ring. A wider range in size is possible through two mixers of different sizes, such as a 60-quart mixer with a 30-quart adaptor ring and attachments, and a 20-quart mixer with a 10 or 12-quart bowl and attachments.

Certain factors other than volume required should be considered when choosing mixer size. For best quality, rotation of preparation should be used and smaller amounts mixed. Consideration should be given to the nature of the product. Weight of a large volume tends to interfere with best handling. Handling the weight of a large volume not only may prove a handicap to quality but may slow production and result in excess strain in lifting. Although bowl dollies or trucks are available for moving a heavy bowl and

Figure 20.1   Heavy-duty mixers are available in a range of sizes. (Courtesy of The Hobart Manufacturing Company.)

contents from one place to another, it is often necessary for it to be lifted to a convenient work level for processing, as when panning cookies.

Agitators

The agitators that are usually furnished as standard equipment with a power mixer are the whip and beater. These two items are used for the majority of whipping and blending operations. Additional agitators are available for specific purposes. These include a dough hook for bread doughs, a pastry knife, and wing whips for use where greater sturdiness is needed than the wire whips provide. The agitators are designed so that they may be slipped onto a shaft and clamped securely in position.

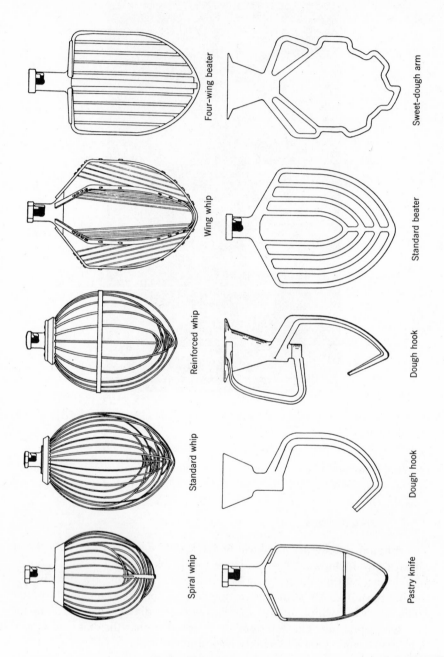

Figure 20.2 Mixer agitators.

Each of the agitators has special uses for which it was designed. The wire whips are for incorporating air and are used when whipping egg whites, cream, or frostings. Operate the mixer on second and third speed of a 3-speed mixer and on third and fourth speed of a 4-speed mixer. When working with materials that call for a mashing, creaming, and blending action use the beater. Start on first speed when adding ingredients, (for example, sugar or flour to cake mixtures or milk to mashed potatoes), then stop the mixer and scrape down the sides of the bowl if necessary. Change to second or medium speed to beat smooth and blend more thoroughly.

The Wing Whip and Beater have heavy frames that combine light creaming action with a whipping action. They are useful when mashing potatoes and making mayonnaise. The mixer is operated at medium and then high speed (second and third speeds of a 3-speed mixer, and third and fourth speeds of a 4-speed mixer). When making pie pastry, neither a rubbing nor a whipping action is desirable. The fat should be cut into the flour. The stirring action of the pastry knife cuts and combines the ingredients for pastry; it is used at first and medium speeds.

The preparation of yeast breads require a folding and stretching action. For this, the dough hook is used at low speed. The Sweet Dough Arm is used for the yeast mixtures that contain a higher proportion of fat and sugar. This agitator does a certain amount of creaming as well as folding and stretching. It should be operated at low speed.

Operation

Place the bowl of the desired size in position. There is a catch at the back (11) and a bowl pin (10) at each side on which the bowl must be set in order to be held securely in place. Many mixers are equipped with a bowl clamp to ensure holding the bowl in place more securely. When the bowl is in place, lower it to its lowest level on the slideway (17). Select the appropriate agitator, slip it on the shaft (18) and lock it in position. On some mixers it is locked in place by slipping the agitator up on the shaft over the driving pin, then turning it around until the driving pin reaches an L-shaped slot in the agitator shank, and allowing it to drop into the slot which holds the agitator in a locked position.

The bowl may be lifted into position as soon as the agitator has been placed. The lifting device may be a lever handle, a wheel, or a power lift. Small models are likely to be equipped with a lever handle and larger models with a wheel or power lift. The bowl should be lifted until the agitator is close to the bottom of the bowl but not touching it. The lever handle is likely to operate in a manner that is completely up or down, and controls the distance of the bowl from the agitator. In models where this is not true, lift the bowl until it touches the agitator and then reverse it slightly so that the bottom of the bowl is approximately $\frac{1}{16}$ inch from the agitator. The agitator should not scrape the bowl as it revolves.

Select the speed required for mixing, and move the Speed Selector Handle (1) until the indicator points to the desired number. The speed from low to high is indicated in numbers 1, 2, and 3. The power is to be off when shifting speeds. Models differ in the way the power release is handled. In some it requires turning the switch off and on, in some there is a brake which cuts off the motor, and in others, movement of the speed selector handle automatically turns off the motor. The operation necessary with the specific model should be ascertained before beginning the operation. It is important for the machine to slow or stop sufficiently for a smooth engagement of the clutches.

When the mixing has been completed, turn off the motor. Lower the

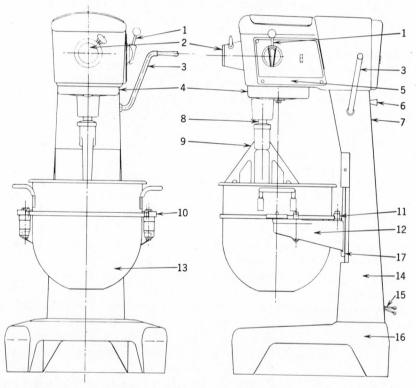

Figure 20.3 Power mixer parts: (1) speed selector handle, (2) hub for attachments, (3) bowl left handle, (4) oil-drip cup, (5) screw to hold drip cup, (6) cover knob, (7) access cover, (8) drive shaft, (9) beater, (10) bowl clamp, (11) back bowl catch, (12) bowl support, (13) bowl, (14) pedestal, (15) conduit connection, (16) base, and (17) slideway.

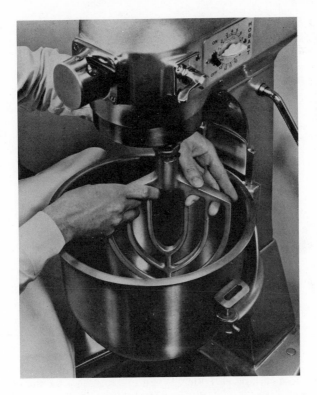

Figure 20.4 Placing beater in position. (Courtesy of The Hobart Manufacturing Company.)

bowl, remove the beater so that it will not be in the way of removing food from the bowl. The bowl may be lifted again to convenient working height on the machine or removed to a table. The height of rolling bins has been found to be convenient when dipping cookie dough from an 80-quart mixer.

Safety precautions when using a mixer require that the motor be stopped and the agitator still before attempting to scrape down the sides of the bowl or agitator. *Do not put hand or scraper in the bowl or near the agitator while the mixer is operating.* Use the correct speed to prevent splashing of food and poor volume in the product. Prevent damage to gears by allowing the agitators to stop before changing speeds.

Attachments and Accessory Equipment

A hub (2) is provided on the front of the mixer for the operation of various attachments by the mixer motor. The attachments include a dicer, coffee mill, colander and soup strainer, food chopper, juice extractor, tool sharpener,

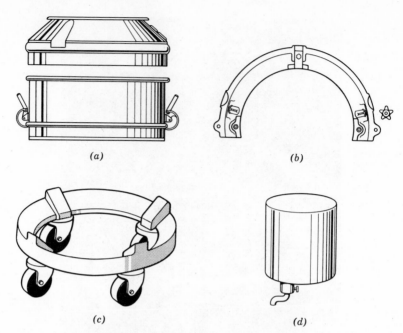

Figure 20.5   Items of mixer accessory equipment: (*a*) bowl extension ring and cover, (*b*) bowl adaptor ring, (*c*) bowl truck, and (*d*) oil dropper.

and vegetable slicer and shredder. When making the attachment selection, it is important to notice if the hub size of the mixer and attachments correspond. If the attachments are to be used on one of the other kitchen machines, it is well to make sure that the hub sizes are the same. (See Chapter 4 for use of attachments.)

Useful accessory equipment includes the bowl adaptor ring, bowl, and agitators to fit the specific size bowl. These are needed to adapt the mixer for the additional size, such as 30-quart capacity on a 60 or 80-quart mixer. A timer on the mixer is useful for guiding mixing time. A bowl extension ring and/or splash cover are convenient for use when whipping foods that have a tendency to splash over the sides of the bowl. The oil dropper is a worthwhile labor-saving device for kitchens that prepare mayonnaise. It controls the drizzle of oil into the egg mixture at the speed required, thus freeing the operator for other work. A bowl truck or dolly is highly desirable for handling any bowl larger than 60-quarts.

Cleaning and Maintenance

It is well to wash the bowls and beaters as soon as possible after use, before mixtures become dried and more difficult to remove. The bowls should be thoroughly washed with hot water and pot washing detergent, well rinsed, and scalded to remove oil film as well as to sanitize. After using them for oily mixtures such as mayonnaise or pastry, and before using them for whipping eggs, it is well to rinse them with a mild vinegar solution and then fresh water. Even a small amount of fat interferes with proper incorporation of air when whipping eggs.

Cast aluminum, tin or chrome-plated steel and stainless steel are the materials from which bowls and agitators are constructed. All of these metals can be washed with the usual pot-washing detergents. They should be rinsed well and allowed to air dry. Bowls of large mixers are usually made of tin-coated steel or iron. With heavy use the tin coating wears and the steel or iron rusts unless the bowl is replated with tin. This tinning is done by commercial companies which specialize in this service.

Many steps can be saved by having a place for the agitators and accessories to be stored near the mixer. It often is convenient to store large bowls in a space under the other pot storage so the bowl can remain on its truck. After removal of the beater, thoroughly wash and rinse the shaft and body of the mixer where it may have been splashed while operating. The oil-drip cup should be taken off occasionally and wiped clean. The main body of the mixer should be washed with warm water and mild soap, rinsed, and wiped dry. The finish of the body of the machine may be enamelled iron or anadized aluminum. Both retain a good appearance for many years if given proper care. The anadized aluminum is brighter in appearance and, with reasonable care retains the beauty of the finish for the life of the machine.

There are certain parts that require periodic lubrication. On installation of a new mixer, check that the transmission has the proper oil level (of special transmission oil) and that the oil in the planetary (oil for the planetary) is up to the filling opening. In order to do this, take off the drip cup and remove the plug. Inspection of the amount of oil here should be done routinely (weekly or as amount of use makes necessary). When using an attachment, add a drop of oil in the oil hole on top of the hub. Keep the bowl slideways, lift-screw, and gearing [(17), Fig. 20.3] lubricated. Graphite grease that is furnished with the mixer is used for this. It is necessary to take out the screw holding the apron and remove the apron that covers the slide-way in order to do this. In all of the lubrication, avoid using an excess amount of oil.

DOUGH DIVIDER AND ROUNDER

In bake shops that prepare a large quantity of rolls, the cutting, shaping and individual unit handling can be time consuming. One of the common aids to facilitate this work is a dough divider or cutter. The size of the roll is determined by the weight of dough placed in the divider. In the manually operated divider, the weighed amount of dough is placed in the divider pan, and spread to cover the bottom of the pan fairly well. An adjustment allows the plate that cuts the dough to be lowered. The knives are symetrically arranged within a circle and cut from 15 to 36 pieces of uniform size, in a slightly wedge-shaped form.

The cuts of dough may be used with very little additional shaping for cottage or pan rolls or may be shaped by hand into other forms. The electrically powered dividers and rounders are designed to shape individual cuts of dough into rounded forms. Before operating the divider and rounder, (a) adjust the setting for the number and size of rolls to be cut; (b) lightly knead back raised dough, allow it to recover but not prove; (c) scale amount for number and size of rolls to be cut; (d) place dough on moulding disc or plate and flatten by hand, working from the center toward the rim, so that the center is slightly higher and the dough extends to the middle of the outside circle of indentations; and (e) position disc in the machine, being sure that it is perfectly in place. Do not grease the plate or dust it with flour. Place moist side of dough on the disc. If the dough is soft, the top of the dough may be dusted with flour to prevent its sticking to the dividing disc.

The machine is operated by disengaging the locking plate and drawing the press lever downward. As the press lever is lowered a retaining ring moves into position to keep the dough confined on the plate or disc. This operation should be made quickly and lightly, without pressure that overly compresses the dough or causes it to stick to the disc. This operation spreads out the dough and removes air pockets. Next, complete the cutting by moving

Figure 20.6 A weighed amount of dough is flattened, placed on the plate, and slipped into the machine which cuts and rounds the rolls.

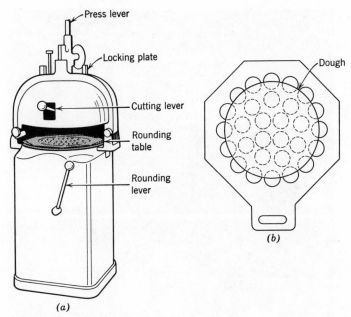

Figure 20.7   (*a*) Sample divider and rounder, and (*b*) moulding disk. (Courtesy of Eberhart-Nussex-Import Company.)

the cutting lever, and as soon as it is completed slowly depress the rounding lever. The movement of the rounding lever automatically switches on the motor to produce an oscillating motion to shape the dough. Only 5 or 6 revolutions are normally required. Return the press and rounding levers to their starting positions. Take out the moulding disc and remove the balls of dough to the table or baking sheet.

Cleaning

The pan, plates, retaining ring, and knives should be washed daily with warm, soapy water, rinsed thoroughly, and dried. In cleaning, a fiber brush, not steel wool, should be used. These parts are made of steel and should be oiled with a flavorless, surface oil (not a vegetable oil that becomes gummy) to prevent them from rusting, except for the moulding plate which should not be greased. It is necessary to handle the parts carefully according to the specific manufacturer's directions when they are disassembled for cleaning. It is important to the machine's operation that the retaining ring not be dented or bent. The dividing head may be broken if dropped.

DOUGH CUTTERS

There are various shapes available in rolling pin type cutters for use manually or on a machine. A few examples are shown in Figure 20.8.

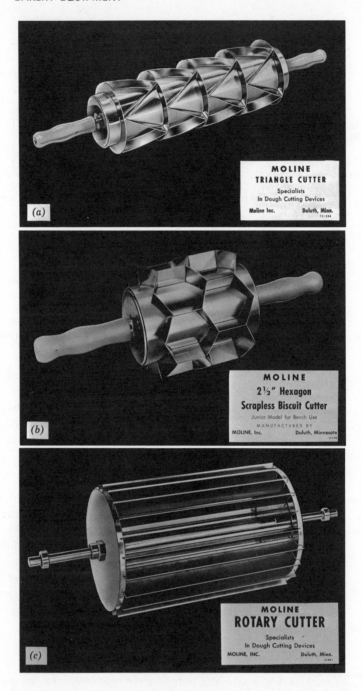

Figure 20.8 Examples of rolling-pin type cutters. (Courtesy of Moline Inc.)

Figure 20.9   Use of a rolling-pin type cutter. (Courtesy of Moline Inc.)

DOUGH ROLLER, MOULDER AND/OR SHEETER

Electrically powered machines are available for rolling and shaping doughs of different types. A bench-type pastry roller handles flat rolled doughs such as pie pastry, biscuits, and cookies. Thickness of the dough may be adjusted through movement of a lever. The rolling is done in two operations. A weighed amount of dough, sufficient for one pie crust and appropriate for the capacity of the machine, is flattened into a circular shape in the hands. First, it is passed through upper rollers that press it into an elongated shape. Both sides of the dough should be dusted lightly with flour and the piece should be turned so that the long side is fed into the lower set of rollers.

In the machines that have metal hoppers and platforms, the dough moves by gravity. In sheeters, canvas on rollers helps to carry or move the dough. The following procedure is recommended for sheeting Danish and puff pastry:

1. Start the operation with the machines at low speed.

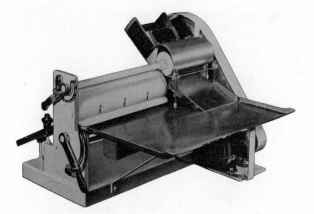

Figure 20.10   A bench-type dough roller. (Courtesy of Colborne Manufacturing Company.)

2. Set the rollers for the product to be rolled, such as No. 4 for Danish pastry and No. 3 for puff pastry.

3. Weigh out 12 pounds of dough and press out on a well floured 18 × 26-inch baking sheet until it covers the pan evenly.

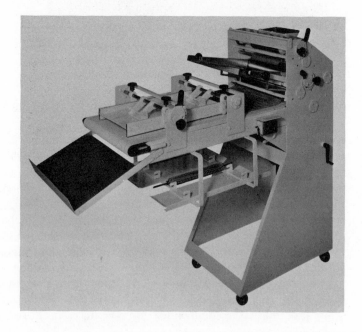

Figure 20.11   A roll sheeter. (Courtesy of D. R. McClain and Son.)

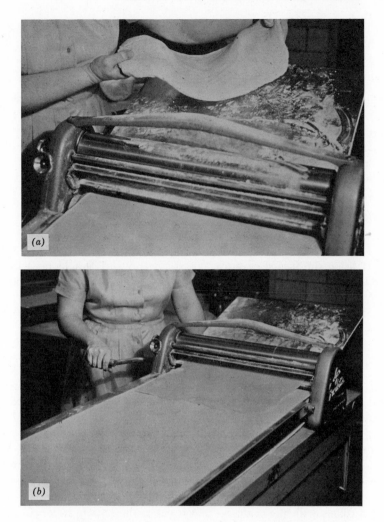

Figure 20.12   Rolling biscuit dough on a roll sheeter.

4. Spot roll-in two-thirds of the dough and fold in thirds.

5. Flatten slightly and turn pan so that the two open ends of the dough are on each side of you.

6. Lift the dough off of the pan with the hands and forearms, in a pincer fashion, and lay the dough on the floured hopper pan. Flatten slightly and keep it in shape but giving it a gentle shove without bunching at the rollers. A second shove helps to prevent the rollers from pulling the dough into an extremely long piece.

7. The piece may be folded while the machine is in motion, or the machine may be stopped before the dough is completely through.

8. When rolling Danish pastry three times it is well to let it rest for 10 minutes after the second rolling.

When working with soft doughs, pie pastry, and cookie doughs, refrigerate them thoroughly before machine rolling them. When shaping bread loaves it is important to have the bread pieces free of flour and crust so that they will seal properly. Bread doughs tend to tear if the feeding is too thick or too fast, or when the dough has not had sufficient rest.

When shaping loaves of bread, operate the machine at maximum speed. The approximate setting for 1-pound loaves is the following:

1. Set large rollers between $2\frac{1}{2}$ or $3\frac{1}{2}$.
2. Use heavy curling chain.
3. Use 8-inch plate, set pressure at $3\frac{1}{2}$.
4. If using the 9-inch pressure board, the pressure should be 3 to $3\frac{1}{4}$. (The longer the bread is to be pounded, the lower the setting would be.)

For $1\frac{1}{2}$-pound loaves, these settings are recommended:

1. Use 12-inch pressure board.
2. Set large rollers at $2\frac{1}{2}$ to 3.
3. The pressure on the board should be $3\frac{1}{2}$.

The pieces of dough should be narrow enough to enter under the pressure board without touching the side guards, in order to get a well shaped loaf. It should go under the pressure board at the exact center. For cross-grained bread, use the top rollers in a wide-open position, drop dough pieces in, catch them with the left hand, give a quarter turn, and send them through the bottom set of rollers. For bread made up on the 8-inch plate, feed it against the grain in the top rollers so that the piece of dough is not too wide to enter the pressure board freely. For the 12-inch bread, feed the dough into the top rollers with the grain, so that it enters the bottom rollers from 8 to 10 inches wide, thus eliminating the strain of pressing from very narrow to a 12-inch bread.

Cleaning and Maintenance

When doughs have been properly refrigerated before rolling and a dusting of flour is used to prevent sticking of soft doughs, cleaning of the crust roller and sheeter is very simple. Wiping with a damp cloth to remove all traces of flour is about all that is needed. Avoid an excess of water on the canvas or in the machine if more vigorous cleaning is required. In kitchens in which this equipment is used only once daily, it should be on casters so that it can be rolled away from the work center when it is not in use. It should be covered with a cloth or plastic to protect it from dust while stored.

The oil in the reducer should be checked every two months, and filled to low, as needed. Add a drop of oil to the motor once weekly. The fittings should have a little grease once a week. (There are two, one on the outside of the machine and one on the idler sprocket inside the machine.)

PROOFING EQUIPMENT

Proper proofing is an important aspect in the preparation of yeast breads. It has been said that one-fourth of all defective baked goods results from

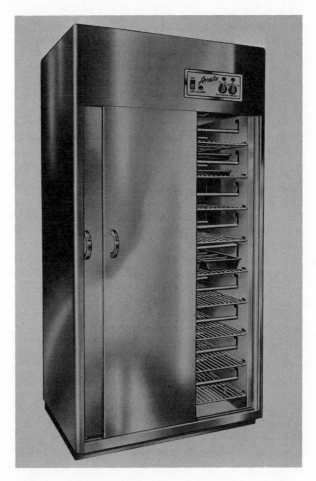

Figure 20.13   Proper proofing equipment helps to ensure good products. (Courtesy of Anetsberger Brothers, Inc.)

improper proof-box conditions. Temperature, humidity, and movement of air need to be controlled. The cabinet should be well insulated to prevent the condensation of moisture on the inside walls, from cold draughts of air, and to maintain a uniform temperature. The cabinet should have a tight, vermin-proof, easily cleanable construction.

The proofing equipment ranges widely in size from the single small compartment with a self-contained humidifier to a large capacity box, such as those used by large bakeries. The cabinet models, used in large kitchens that prepare a large quantity of yeast breads, may have air conditioners that are manually controlled steam operated, automatically controlled steam operated, or automatically controlled all-electric. It is important for the operator to understand the principles and have a schedule for the proving of the products that he makes.

Air absorbs more moisture at high temperatures than at low temperatures. A humidifier supplies moisture to sufficiently saturate the air so that moisture will not be drawn from the breads. The temperature and relative humidity most suitable for various products differ slightly. Table 20.1 lists those recommended for some of the commonly prepared products.

Evaporation has a cooling effect. A wet bulb registers a lower temperature than a dry one in air that is not saturated with moisture. Table 20.2 indicates the relative humidity when the temperatures registered by the dry and wet bulbs vary from 1 to 8 degrees. The relative humidity is the value found at the intersection of the dry bulb reading and the number of degrees difference between it and the wet-bulb reading; for example, if the top reading of 72°F for the dry bulb differed 8 degrees from the wet bulb registering 64°F, the relative humidity would be 65%.

TABLE 20.1 RECOMMENDED PROOF-BOX CONDITIONS

	Dry Bulb (°F)	Wet Bulb (°F)	Relative Humidity
White Bread (greased pans)	105	100	83
(glazed pans)	105	95	69
Whole Wheat Bread	105	100	83
Rye Bread	105	100	83
Water Rolls	90	80	65
Small White Rolls	100	95	83
Sweet Rolls	100	95	83
Coffee Cake (depending on richness)	80 to 90	70 to 79	61 to 71
Danish Goods (depending on richness)	80 to 90	70 to 79	61 to 71

TABLE 20.2 RELATIVE HUMIDITY PERCENTAGE

Dry Bulb Reading (°F)	Difference Between Dry and Wet Bulb Reading							
	1	2	3	4	5	6	7	8
72	95	91	86	82	77	73	69	65
73	95	91	86	82	78	73	69	65
74	95	91	86	82	78	74	69	65
75	96	91	86	82	78	74	70	66
76	96	91	87	82	78	74	70	66
77	96	91	87	83	79	74	71	67
78	96	91	87	83	79	75	71	67
79	96	91	87	83	79	75	71	68
80	96	91	87	83	79	75	72	68
82	96	92	88	84	80	76	72	69
84	96	92	88	84	80	76	72	69
86	96	92	88	84	81	77	73	70
88	96	92	88	85	81	77	74	70
90	96	92	89	85	81	78	74	71
92	96	92	89	85	82	78	75	72
94	96	93	89	85	82	79	75	72
95	96	93	89	86	82	79	76	73
96	96	93	89	86	82	79	76	73
98	96	93	89	86	82	79	76	73
100	96	93	89	86	83	80	77	73
102	96	93	90	86	83	80	77	74
104	97	93	90	87	83	80	77	74
106	97	93	90	87	84	81	78	75
108	97	93	90	87	84	81	78	75

The wet bulb is enclosed in a wet wick, which in turn is inserted in a water bath. The water may be supplied from a water line or a water bottle. Note which type of unit is in use. The water level should be ½ inch from the top of the trough, and the wick damp. In order to function properly the wicks must be clean so that they will absorb their full quota of water. They should be washed occasionally. Adjust the temperature and humidity controls, and allow the unit to operate 15 or 20 minutes. Check the readings on both the thermometers to determine whether the desired temperature and relative humidity have been attained. Adjust controls as necessary according to manufacturer's instructions for the specific model.

Cleaning and Maintenance

It is important for the proofing equipment to be clean and sweet smelling. The inside should be washed with a mild detergent solution and thoroughly rinsed. The outside, if finished with baked-on enamel may be wiped with a damp cloth, or washed when necessary with soap and water. Avoid the use of coarse abrasives. Be sure that the wicks are kept clean. The motor should be oiled every 60 days.

SUGGESTED LABORATORY EXPERIENCE

1. Visit a small bakery or a large kitchen to observe the items of bakery equipment in use.
2. Present a class demonstration, with appropriate materials, in the operation of the mixer with a beater and a whip.
3. Time the rolling of pie crusts by hand and by machine, demonstrating the use of the machine. Calculate the saving of time by the faster method. Calculate the amount of time required to pay for the machine according to the time saved if labor is paid four cents per minute.
4. Demonstrate and evaluate a dough cutter and rounder in a similar manner.
5. Demonstrate the operation of the specific proof box in use.

REVIEW QUESTIONS AND ANSWERS

1. What is meant by "flow of work"?

The order in which work activities are performed.

2. What are the first activities usually performed by bakers?

Check oven temperatures for first products, assemble equipment and supplies needed at the work center, measure and mix formulas for first products produced.

3. What factors influence the number of mixers needed in a kitchen?

Menu requirements, volume and frequency of use, extent of preparation done by the specific kitchen.

4. What factors should be considered when selecting mixer size?

Volume requirements, effect of volume handled on quality, weight of volume appropriate for employee handling.

5. Which agitators are usually supplied as standard equipment?

Beater and whip.

6. For what purpose should the whip be used?

For incorporating air into light material, such as egg whites or cream.

7. What is the purpose of the beater?

It supplies a mashing, creaming and blending action, such as those required for whipping potatoes or making cake.

8. How does this differ from a dough hook?

The dough hook supplies a folding, stretching action, such as that required for yeast doughs.

9. How does the pastry knife function?

It stirs and cuts fat into flour, without rubbing it into the flour or whipping air into the mixture.

10. Differentiate between an adaptor ring and an extension ring.

The adaptor ring is a heavy half circle used to adapt the capacity of a larger mixer to accommodate a smaller bowl, as in adapting a 60-quart mixer for a 30-quart bowl. An extension ring extends the depth of bowl in the form of a collar at the top of the bowl.

11. List the important safety precautions to be observed when using a mixer.

Be sure that (a) the bowl and agitator are firmly in place before operating the mixer; (b) that the bowl is lifted to the proper height; (c) that the power is off when shifting speeds; (d) that the proper speed is used for the specific agitator and material. (e) *Never* put hand or utensil in bowl while the machine is operating.

12. What metals are used for the construction of mixer bowls?

Tin-coated iron and stainless steel.

13. Describe the oil dropper attachment.

It is a graduated cylinder with a petcock that can be set to allow the flow of a small amount of liquid.

14. How should a mixer bowl be cleaned to insure freedom of oil in it?

Wash it with a detergent solution, rinse it with a vinegar solution, then clear water.

15. What is the difference between a dough divider and a dough divider and rounder?

The dough divider performs only the act of dividing the dough into the individual pieces. The divider and rounder cuts the dough and forms it into balls.

16. What determines the size of the rolls?

The weight of dough placed in the divider.

17. What function of the machine rounds the dough into balls?

The oscillation of the rounding table, which provides a motion similar to rotating a ball of dough in the hand on the work table.

18. Should the moulding plate be greased?

The moulding plate should *not* be greased or dusted with flour.

19. What parts should be oiled?

The pan, retaining ring, and knives.

20. May salad oil be used for this?

No, do *not* use a vegetable oil because it will become gummy. Use a flavorless, surface oil.

21. What should be the condition of the dough when it is cut?

It should be worked back lightly after proving, allowed to rest a few minutes, but not prove, then cut quickly and lightly and immediately removed from the cutter and plate before it has a chance to rise and stick together or to the plate.

22. What is the reason for refrigerating quick doughs before rolling them by machine?

To make them easier to handle and to keep them from sticking to the machine.

23. What causes bread doughs to tear when putting them through a moulder?

When they are fed in too thick or too fast, and when the dough has not had sufficient rest to be elastic.

24. What is the major function of proofing equipment?

To provide an atmosphere that promotes development of the yeast plants and protects the moist elastic surface of the bread.

25. What conditions are important for the desired atmosphere?

The right temperature and relative humidity.

26. How is relative humidity measured?

By the speed of evaporation, as shown by degrees of temperature difference between a dry thermometer bulb and a wet one. The drier the air, the faster the evaporation and the greater the temperature difference between the dry bulb and the wet bulb, for evaporation has a cooling effect.

27. Why is it important to keep the wick in proper condition?

The wick must be wet in order to accurately register the degrees of temperature difference.

28. What is the proper condition of the wick?

It must be clean to absorb its full quota of water, and water must be supplied in the trough to keep it wet.

21.

Bread Baking

The universal importance of bread as a food has led to its use as a symbol of nourishment. Its appetite-appealing aromas when baking have magnetic power in attracting patronage. The general acceptance of it as a food makes bread a valuable medium for improving the nutrition of both the rich and the poor. It holds an important place among the four basic food groups recommended for well-balanced daily nutrition: Milk and milk products, meats, vegetables and fruits, and breads and cereals. (See color insert for Figure 21.1.)

Science has made possible the enrichment of flour and bread with nutrients essential for health. In May 1941 the U.S. Food and Drug Administration set legal standards for the minimal and maximal standards for enrichment. Before 1954, 29 states and Puerto Rico required enrichment, and today "90% of all commercially baked standard white bread" is enriched. It is required that the wrapper on such bread carry a statement such as the following:

"One-half pound of this bread supplies you with at least the following amounts or percentages of your minimum daily requirements for these essential food substances—Thiamine (vitamin B_1) 55%; Riboflavin (vitamin B_2) 30%; Niacin (another B vitamin) 50%; Iron 40%."

One-half pound of bread yields about 8 or 9 standard slices. Optional additions that may be made per pound of flour are calcium (between 500 and 600 milligrams) and vitamin D (between 250 and 1000 U.S.P. units).

It is well to understand the terms "enrichment," "fortified" and "restored" as they refer to additions of nutrients to food items. Federal authorities limit the use of "enrichment" to the addition of nutrients to flour and bread. "Fortified" indicates addition of nutrients that are not normally found in appreciable quantities in a food item, such as iodine in salt. "Restored" means that nutrients removed by processing the food are replaced.

Enrichment of bread may be made through the use of enriched flour or through the addition of the vitamins and iron to the dough during mixing.

The vitamins and iron may be added in powdered form or may be dissolved in water (along with the yeast). The following recipe is a typical formula, presented by the American Institute of Baking, for enriched bread:

Ingredients	Parts
Flour	100
Water	68
Sugar	6
Nonfat dry milk	4
Shortening	3
Compressed yeast	2.5
Salt	2
Yeast food	0.5
Calcium propionate	0.2
Enrichment concentrate	1 measure

In the preparation of formulas for flour mixtures, it is common practice to use the weight of flour as 100% and calculate all other ingredients in percentages of that amount. This facilitates quick comparison of proportions of ingredients regardless of the size of the recipe. Table 21.1 illustrates percentage proportions for flour mixtures for different types of bread recipes.

TABLE 21.1 COMPARISON OF PROPORTIONS OF INGREDIENTS IN DIFFERENT TYPES OF BREADS

Ingredients	Yeast Bread	Muffins	Biscuits	Griddle Cakes
Flour, enriched	3 lb 100%	2¾ lb 100%	2½ lb 100%	2 lb 100%
Liquid, water or milk	2 lb 66.7%	2¼ lb 81.8%	1¾ lb 70%	2½ lb 125%
Eggs		8 oz 18.2%		12 oz 37.5%
Sugar	⅓ oz .7%	6 oz 13.6%		5 oz 15.62%
Salt	¾ oz 1.6%	2 oz 4.5%	¾ oz 1.8%	⅓ oz 1%
Shortening	4 oz 8.4%	6 oz 13.6%	10 oz	5 oz 15.62%
Leavening, B.P. or yeast (compressed)	1 oz 2%			

To obtain the percentages, convert the measure of all ingredients to ounces, multiply the number of ounces for each ingredient except flour by 100 and divide each of the resulting figures by the number of ounces of flour contained in the recipe.

TABLE 21.2 INGREDIENT PROPORTIONS IN SELECTED WHITE BREAD RECIPES

Ingredients	Recipe 1	Recipe 2	Recipe 3
Flour, enriched	100%	100%	100%
Liquid, water		14.9%	63.5%
Whole milk	66.7%	51.8%	
Nonfat dry milk			5.8%
Sugar	.7%	5.4%	4.2%
Shortening	8.4%	7%	5%
Yeast, compressed	2%	1.9%	2%
Salt	1.6%	1.9%	2%

Variation in recipes for a given product are clearly apparent upon comparison of proportion of ingredients that are shown in Table 21.2.

Products produced from flour mixtures may be classified in different ways. Many think of them in terms of their place in a meal, such as breads or desserts. Those who are responsible for production classify them according to the type of leavening used, as in quick breads or yeast breads, and in terms of the consistency of the mixture, such as batters and doughs. Batters are those mixtures that are sufficiently fluid to be poured or dropped from a spoon, and doughs are stiff enough to be kneaded or molded on a floured board. Griddlecakes and waffles are examples of pour-batters and muffins of drop-batters. Biscuits and yeast breads are doughs. The characteristics of flour mixtures are affected by specific ingredients contained and techniques of handling. To facilitate presentation of production requirements with flour mixtures, the discussion in this book has been divided into (a) breads, (b) cakes and cookies, and (c) puddings and pastries.

YEAST BREADS

Attention to details can have a considerable influence on quality in the production of yeast breads. Control of temperature is one of the more important details. It is best in promoting fermentation to maintain a dough temperature of 82°F. It is important to protect the dough from drafts. During processing, dough may be refrigerated to retard fermentation. Temperature can be used to adjust bread processing to fit worker time and the availability of equipment in a kitchen. Refrigeration and skillful scheduling can help in rotation baking to have a fresh supply of rolls as needed.

In order to control and utilize temperatures to the best advantage, it is necessary to know the specific temperatures involved. The baker should know the temperature of the materials and the room and the heat generated by friction from the action of the mixer. The degrees of heat developed in the mixing action are influenced by the length of mixing time and the type of mixer used. The liquid temperature is easy to control and is commonly used in controlling the temperature of the dough. The method used for determining the water temperature needed is to multiply the desired dough temperature by the total number of temperatures involved in the mixture. The temperatures are totaled and subtracted from this figure.

Dough temperature desired	82°F
Total number of temperatures involved	3
	246

Flour temperature	70°F
Room temperature	75°F
Degrees of heat created by friction	25°F
	170

Desired dough temperature times 3	246
Minus total temperatures involved	170
Water temperature needed	76°F

To test for the amount of heat created by friction in a specific operation start with the temperature of dough that has been produced by the machine. Multiply this temperature by the number of different temperatures involved in the mixture. Subtract from this total the total of all of the temperatures.

Temperature of the dough produced	80°F
Number of temperatures involved	3
	240

Flour temperature	70°F
Water temperature	75°F
Room temperature	70°F
	215

Dough temperature multiplied by 3	240
Minus the temperature total	215
Equals heat from machine friction	25°F

Ingredients

There are four essential ingredients in even the simplest of yeast breads— flour, yeast, water, and salt. Crusty French and Italian breads are examples in which little of any other ingredients are used. The character of their crust is important to their quality. The high protein flour used adds chewiness. Steam used in the oven during baking promotes the formation of a thick, crisp crust.

Wheat flour is a chief ingredient of most breads. It has special value in yeast breads for its content of the protein complex, gliadin and glutenin, that forms gluten when mixed with liquid. Gluten possesses elasticity that permits expansion of the dough by the leavening agent. It becomes "set" when baked, thus providing a cellular structure in the baked item. Both the liquid and the mixing are necessary for developing the gluten. Cohesiveness continues to develop with continued mixing or kneading until the optimum is reached.

Wheat flours differ in the quantity and quality of the gluten that may be developed. Flours high in gluten content are classed as "strong" and those with a small amount as "weak." The higher the content of gluten of good quality the higher the percentage of water it is capable of holding and the greater the bread yield for a given amount of flour. The gluten in high protein flour is more tenacious and harder to mix and requires longer to rise. Yeast breads require a strong flour made of hard wheat that contains a satisfactory amount and quality of gluten. A flour lower in protein is more satisfactory for making biscuits, cakes, and pastry because it yields a more tender product. This is flour made from varieties of soft wheat. The bakery sections of large kitchens frequently are supplied with three different blends of flour, a high protein flour for bread making, a general purpose or pastry flour that is lower in protein, and a cake flour that contains very little protein.

Flours blended by millers for specific purposes are carefully tested to determine flour quality in relation to use. Bread flour, for example, is test-baked to determine (a) processing time (strong flours may require more time to rise than a schedule permits); (b) tolerance of the dough (whether it will be hand kneaded or have to withstand beating by machine); (c) amount of liquid it will absorb; (d) potential loaf volume; and (e) quality of loaf in terms of flavor, texture, color, and crumb. Flours purchased for specific kitchens should be tested or carefully observed by the user to determine the blend that will work out most satisfactorily with specific formulas, methods of handling and equipment; for example, if yeast rolls are prepared by hand daily a fairly strong all-purpose flour may fit the strength and schedule of the baker better than a strong bread flour, if the products are of acceptable quality.

Physical, chemical, and biological leavens are used in the various breads, and the speed with which they leaven flour mixtures has led to the classifications of "Quick Bread" and "Yeast Bread." Yeast breads require a fermentation period during which the yeast plants multiply and produce carbon dioxide which leavens the dough. Food and moisture are needed for their growth. The plants grow best at temperatures between 80 to 90°F. Cooler temperatures retard their growth and a temperature as high as 110°F will kill the plants within an hour; 140°F will destroy them within 5 minutes.

The forms of yeast most commonly used are compressed and active dry yeast. The dry-yeast cake made of a compressed mass of dry, inactive yeast cells dried with cornmeal as a filler is rarely used today. The active dry yeast is a different product. It is formed of granules dried and sealed in packages. It is equal in action to the compressed yeast that is formed into cakes with cornstarch and contains 70% moisture. In determining amount to use, count on 1 pound of active dry yeast as equal to about $2\frac{1}{2}$ pounds of compressed yeast. When using either of these, prepare the yeast by sprinkling the crumbled yeast into lukewarm water and allowing it to stand for three or four minutes before stirring. A water temperature of 100°F is best for compressed yeast. The active dry yeast hydrates and responds more quickly in water at 110°F. Active dry yeast can be frozen and held or refrigerated at 40°F and retain its effectiveness for a year. Compressed yeast must be refrigerated and should be used within a week. It may be frozen and held for longer periods.

Sugar, shortening, and milk are additional ingredients commonly used in bread formulas. Each item influences specific qualities of the bread. Note in Table 21.2 the difference in amount of sugar used. Commercial bakers often use from 6 to 8% in white bread. Sugar in proper amount feeds the yeast plants and speeds fermentation so as to shorten processing time. If 10% or more is used it retards the growth of the yeast and slows fermentation. Additional yeast is used in sweet breads that contain higher percentages of sugar in order to offset this.

Shortening improves flavor, has a tenderizing effect on the crumb and crust, and in amounts up to 4 or 5% causes an increase in volume. The volume tends to diminish when more than 6% is used. Studies have shown firm fats to be more satisfactory than oils in their influence on volume.

The liquid used in making bread may be water, water in which potatoes have been cooked, or milk. The milk may be fresh whole or skimmed milk, or in the form of nonfat dry-milk solids. Milk improves both the nutritive value and the flavor of the bread. Commercial bakers and large kitchens use nonfat dry milk more often than fresh milk because of its lower cost and greater convenience. Although the percentage ranges from 0 to 8, the average used is about 4%. When bread is labeled as "Milk Bread," it must contain milk solids and butterfat equal to the amount that would be contained if whole milk was the only liquid used. Milk solids, as well as fresh milk, must be heated unless the dry milk solids have been specially treated. Evaporated milk has been heated in processing and does not require further heating. Milk contains a factor that is detrimental to bread quality unless it is inactivated by heat.

The amount of liquid required varies according to the amount of absorption by the specific flour. Too little liquid produces a heavy dough that is not as elastic as it should be and too much liquid causes the dough to be sticky. The mixture with the right amount of liquid is sticky at the outset before the gluten has been developed. Some experience with a specific flour is needed to discern how sticky the dough should be at the beginning of the mixing. At the start of mixing, before the gluten has developed, the dough sticks to the bowl or board. Be cautious about adding more flour at this point. When the flour is in the right amount, the dough changes in appearance from a bumpy, sticky mass to a smooth elastic dough. Dough that has been kneaded enough is not sticky and it has small air blisters under the surface.

Mixing, Kneading, and Fermenting

Yeast breads in large quantity production are most often mixed by either the sponge or straight dough method. In the sponge method, the yeast is softened in water and sufficient flour is added to produce a sponge of batter consistency, using about half of the flour in the recipe. The sponge is placed in a warm place (80 to 85°F) and allowed to rise until very light before the remainder of the flour is added and the dough is kneaded. In the straight dough method, all of the flour is added at one time and thoroughly mixed and allowed to rise until the dough doubles in bulk. The dough may be formed into loaves or rolls at this stage or kneaded lightly to remove excess gas and allowed to rise again until double in bulk, before shaping. The second rising is desirable for doughs made with strong flours. Doughs should be greased lightly before fermenting to prevent a crust forming.

The mixing and kneading are important to the development of the gluten. When mixing, use the dough hook attachment on the mixer. An elastic gluten is necessary for the bread to be light and to have satisfactory volume. A baker needs to be sensitive to the appearance and feel of the dough when it has had the right amount of mixing. Bread from either undermixing or overmixing is coarse and has poor volume. Overmixing is less of a hazard than undermixing, except where a heavy machine is used in the mixing.

After mixing, the dough should be placed in a warm, fairly humid place for fermentation to take place. A temperature of 80 to 85°F and humidity of 75% are desirable. The dough should be allowed to rise until double in bulk. A light pressure on top of the dough will indicate when it has risen enough. If a dent remains, this is a sign that the dough is ready for the next processing. If the dough has been made with a strong flour or mixed by the straight dough method, it may be desirable to punch it down and allow it to rise again before shaping. To punch it down, poke the fist down in the center of the dough and pull up the dough at the sides of the bowl and fold into the center. Next lift the dough and place the folded part on the bottom. Permit the dough to rise again until double in bulk.

Dividing and Shaping

The dough goes next to the work table or bench where it is divided. After being divided, it should stand without treatment for about 10 minutes to rest. It becomes more pliable and easy to handle after standing. When shaping the dough, there are certain precautions to remember. Be sparing in the use of flour so as to avoid flour streaks in the bread. In order to get a uniform texture, use enough pressure to remove the gas and at the same time avoid breaking or tearing the gluten strands that are important to the structure of the bread. Loaves may be shaped by rolling the weighed dough with a rolling pin or mechanical dough roller or sheeter. Rectangles are next formed into long rolls the length of the pans, the ends are sealed and placed in the pans with the seam side down.

If the dough is to be used for rolls it is divided into batch sizes. The batch depends on the method used for dividing into rolls. Where bun cutters are used the dough should be scaled into batches that yield rolls of the desired weight. The weight of dough for a cutter that makes 36 cuts, for example, should weigh 3 pounds for rolls $1\frac{1}{3}$ ounces each. This is an average size for a dinner roll. (Note description in Chapter 20 for handling dough for cutting in a mechanical cutter and rounder.)

The shaping of rolls is a pleasant art that adds variety and interest to breads. The balls of dough that have been shaped by hand or in a machine may be dropped into muffin pans without dividing or may be separated into two or three balls for twin or cloverleaf rolls. Balls of dough may be placed together on a baking sheet close enough to touch upon rising and have a small amount of crust when baked. Balls may be flattened for Parkerhouse rolls, creased in the center and folded over with one half on top of the other.

Many forms are shaped from dough that has been rolled flat, cut into strips, rectangles, or triangles. Fan tans or butter rolls are shaped from a thinly rolled rectangle that has been brushed with butter or margarine. The rectangle is cut into strips 1-inch wide and stacked with six or seven strips one on top of the other. It is then cut into $1\frac{1}{2}$-inch lengths from the stack and placed cut end down in muffin pans. Crescents are shaped by cutting 4-inch squares of dough, $\frac{1}{8}$-inch thick, from diagonal corners to form triangles or by cutting pie-shaped triangles from $\frac{1}{8}$-inch thick circles of dough that are about 10 or 11 inches in diameter. To form the crescent, begin at the width of one side of the triangle and roll the dough toward the point, keeping the point in the center of the roll. Place the roll on the pan with the point underneath and move the ends in a curve to form a crescent.

Dough that is to be cut into strips for shaping into rolls should be rolled to a thickness of about $\frac{1}{3}$ inch. The sharp edges of the cut may be eliminated and the diameter of the strip adjusted through twisting the dough. This is done by placing the two hands lightly on the dough and with a light pressure moving the hands in opposite directions, one forward and the other back, to twist the strip. A strip measuring approximately $\frac{1}{2}$ inch by 9 inches is needed to form knots or rosettes. When working with dough in shaping rolls or loaves of bread, it is important to work lightly and deftly, being careful not to overstretch or break the gluten strands.

Doughs for sweet rolls contain a higher percentage of shortening, sugar, and flavoring materials than plain bread and rolls. Some, like Danish pastry, contain eggs. Balls of dough are used for shaping Hot Cross Buns and Kolaches. The Hot Cross Buns contain spices and fruit, and a cross of sugar frosting is applied on the top after baking. Kolaches, flavored with lemon, have a depression made in the top of the ball of dough and filled with a spicy mixture of dried fruit. Butterhorns, made of rich dough, are formed with twisted strips of dough according to the size desired. The dough for cinnamon, butterfly, and pecan roll is rolled out to the desired thickness, brushed with butter or margarine, sprinkled with a filling such as cinnamon and sugar, rolled up jelly-roll fashion, and sliced. The diameter and thickness of the slices should be adjusted to yield rolls of the weight specified for an individual portion. The slices for shaping butterflies need to be approximately twice as wide as those for cinnamon rolls. A slice about $1\frac{1}{4}$ inches wide is used in forming butterfly rolls. Place a small rod or knife handle across the center of the slice parallel with the cut, and press down to force out the sides of the slice without cutting through the dough.

Proofing and Baking

Bread should double in bulk during the proofing period. Use care that it does not rise too long for if the gluten is stretched too much it results in an inferior product. It continues to rise during the first part of the baking period. The rapid rise or spring that takes place at this time results from the acceleration of fermentation and heat expansion of the gas. Oven temperature influences the quality of the bread. If it is too high the crust will form before it has reached its best volume. If it is too low the bread will continue to rise until it falls back or is coarse in texture. Preheat the oven, making the adjustments required for the specific oven to recover baking temperature upon receiving a cold load of food. If the oven is slow in regaining the desired baking temperature, it may be well to preheat it to a temperature 15 to 25° higher than that required for baking. Note the temperature indicated in the standardized recipe because there is a variation in the temperatures required for specific breads. The crust of the bread will be softer and more shining if rubbed with shortening when removed from the oven. Bread should be removed from the pan and allowed to cool on a rack away from a draft.

Storage

Bread may be stored for delayed use at different stages of preparation. The dough may be retarded by refrigeration or freezing after it has been divided for shaping or after it has been shaped before proofing. It may be baked just to the browning stage or fully baked and then frozen. For rotation baking of fresh rolls, doughs may be retarded at 40°F. High humidity (85%) is needed to prevent the surface from drying. Placing them in a moisture-vapor-proof bag helps prevent drying of the dough or the baked bread. When freezing dough or bread a temperature of − 10 to − 20°F is desirable, with the movement of air in the compartment about 500 feet per minute. Bread refrigerated at 40°F stales more quickly than bread held at room temperature. Freezing is the most effective method of delaying staling and preserving fresh flavor.

Quality

The quality of bread is judged by characteristics that make it appealing to the senses—appearance, aroma, flavor, and texture. Volume, good shape, and color influence attractive appearance. An approximate measure for desirable volume is 125 to 155 cubic inches per pound of bread. It should be made up of numerous, small, uniform cells with thin walls that yield a moist, tender crumb. The cells in bread of poor quality are not uniform, their walls are thick. The color of the bread is darker, and its texture is irregular and heavy. The flavor and aroma of good bread has a rich wheaty quality, somewhat nutty and slightly yeasty. It is free from any trace of a stale, sour, or musty quality.

QUICK BREADS

Quick breads offer wide variety in form, flavor, and general characteristics. Among them are included cornbread, popovers, pancakes, waffles, muffins, hot biscuits, and a wide variety of loaf breads and coffee cakes. The ease and speed of preparation with which they can be made tempts even novice cooks to try them. Pancakes, biscuits, and cornbread are the large volume items in terms of the amount used. Figures from the U.S. Department of Agriculture indicate that these breads are made in kitchens more often than either yeast breads or muffins. Many mixes are available for those who have limited time or who are uncertain of their skill. A little practice plus an understanding of essential techniques enables a cook to make products "from scratch" that are as good or better than those from mixes, and at lower cost.

Popovers

Popovers are leavened by steam and unlike other quick breads do not contain a chemical leaven. A good product is a fairly tender, crisp, golden brown, hollow shell. Good volume requires the use of flour with a fairly strong gluten, sufficient eggs, and the right amount of liquid. The gluten must be able to stretch without the strands breaking. If a small proportion of eggs is used the popover will lack volume and be muffin-like. The following recipe is suggested for trial, to be adjusted according to absorption of liquid by the specific flour used.

	POPOVERS	20–25 popovers	
Ingredient	Weight	Volume	
Bread flour	12 oz	3 c	(4 cs may be needed if all-purpose is used)
Whole eggs	8 oz	1 c	
Sugar	1 oz	2 tbsp	
Salt	⅓ oz	2 tsp	
Milk, fresh whole	1 lb	·1 pt	

PROCEDURE:

1. Beat the eggs, add sugar and salt and stir in milk until well mixed.
2. Beat liquid mixture into the flour gradually to form a smooth batter.
3. Deep muffin or custard cups made of iron, glass, china or aluminum may be used for baking. Grease lightly, avoiding an excess. Fill them two-thirds full.
4. Bake in oven preheated to 425°F for 15 minutes, then reduce heat to 350°F and continue cooking to brown exterior and dry interior of the popovers.

The high temperature is important to good results, and is for the purpose of developing the leavening steam before the popover structure is set. Lowering the temperature permits time for the popovers to dry out before becoming too brown. When they are done the inside should be moist but not soggy.

Griddlecakes

Griddlecakes, like popovers, are pour batters but the qualities desired in the finished products differ. A chemical leaven, a low protein flour, and some fat are used to produce a tender product that is light and has a fine, uniform texture. When mixing griddlecakes, sift dry ingredients together to mix well, blend beaten eggs, milk and melted fat together, and stir into the dry ingredients. The ingredients should be stirred only enough to yield a fairly smooth batter in which all of the dry ingredients are moistened. Bake them on a griddle that has been preheated to 375°F. The batter may be poured on the griddle or scooped with a number 16 or 20 scoop according to the size preferred.

Waffles

Waffles are leavened both with a chemical leaven and with air that is incorporated in beaten egg whites. The method of blending ingredients is similar to that for griddlecakes, except that the eggs are separated. The beaten yolks are blended with the milk and melted fat. These are stirred into the well mixed dry ingredients. The egg whites are whipped until stiff but not dry and folded into the batter. The waffle iron should be preheated. When preparing large quantities of this batter, results are likely to be best if not more than 3 or 4 pounds of flour (approximately 50 waffles) are mixed at one time. The batter should be handled lightly and with a minimum of stirring to prevent loss of the air incorporated with the egg whites. Refrigerate the batter when it is not in use. Waffles of top quality are light, crisp, tender, well-flavored, and golden brown.

Muffins

Thoroughly blend dry ingredients, separately mix the wet ingredients including melted fat, and then combine the wet ingredients with the dry ingredients with a minimum of stirring so that the dry ingredients are barely moistened. This is commonly known as the "muffin method" of mixing and may be used for certain coffee breads and cakes as well as muffins. Muffins of good quality are symmetrical in shape and have a rounded, pebbly top, a fairly even, somewhat coarse grain, and are tender. Careful proportioning of ingredients, avoidance of excess liquid, and stirring only enough to barely moisten the dry ingredients are important points in securing good results. Stirring develops the gluten strands in the flour, and in muffins this results in tunnels, toughness, and irregular texture. Low protein flour, such as pastry flour, should be used and sufficient fat and sugar for tenderness and good flavor. An excess of fat and sugar results in a cake like quality. Avoid extra stirring when filling the muffin pans. Scoop the batter into well greased pans using a number 16 or 20 scoop for a pan $2\frac{1}{4}$ inches in diameter, according to the size muffin desired. Bake at 400°F.

When using a mixer to combine large batches (10 pounds of flour yields 20 to 25 dozen muffins) thoroughly blend dry ingredients by sifting together *twice* into the mixer bowl. Stir the wet ingredients together until well blended. Pour the wet ingredients all at one time into the center of the dry ingredients. Allow the beater to revolve at low speed for about 15 seconds. It is best to bake muffins as soon as they are mixed and not hold the batter for delayed baking. The batter may be baked in muffin cups or in a sheet pan and cut into portions after baking. The product baked in sheets is equally light but lacks some of the crispness imparted by the extra crust on individually baked portions. It has special merit however, when speed is required and where there is a shortage of labor to fill or to clean muffin pans. Ten pounds of flour makes enough batter for 4 sheets measuring 18 × 26 inches, and when baked can be divided by six cuts lengthwise and ten cuts across into 60 pieces. Muffin batter may be varied through the addition of nuts, dried fruits, spices, and other flavoring materials.

Biscuits

Standards of excellence for biscuits vary according to personal preference. Technique of preparation also varies according to the qualities desired. The flour selected for their preparation may vary slightly. Those who prefer a soft, crusty biscuit, low in volume, use a low-protein flour, mix the dough only enough to blend the ingredients, and roll the dough fairly thin. Those who wish a more breadlike product with greater volume use a stronger flour, mix the ingredients well, knead the dough lightly, and roll the dough thicker. The liquid also makes a difference. Fresh whole milk yields a better thick biscuit than is obtainable with reconstituted dry whole milk, evaporated milk, or water. The amount of liquid required for a recipe depends on absorption by the flour used.

Care is to be taken to prevent overmixing when using a mixer to combine ingredients. Sift the dry ingredients together into the mixer bowl. Add the fat and operate the mixer (using the beater) at low speed until the mixture is slightly coarser than cornmeal. Add the liquid to different areas of the dry ingredients. Let the beater revolve slowly, noting consistency of the dough closely in order to control the amount of liquid required. The dough should be soft, but thick enough for kneading, with all of the dry ingredients moistened. Be cautious of overmixing as this overdevelops the gluten and results in a tough product. (The batter should not be mixed longer than 1 minute.)

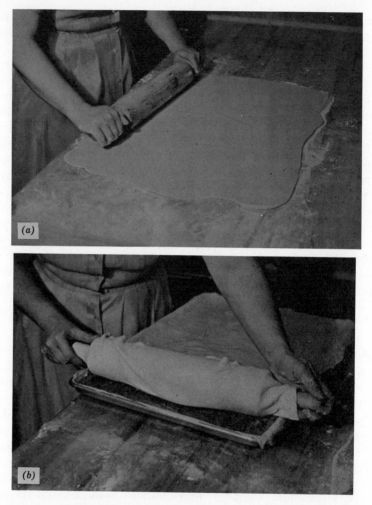

Figure 21.2   Biscuit topping for a baking sheet can be (*a*) rolled to suitable size and then (*b*) rolled around the rolling pin for transfer to the baking sheet. (Courtesy of Market Forge.)

Turn the dough onto a lightly floured board or bench for kneading. Use a light pressure in kneading. Do not compress the dough. Grasp the dough at the back edge and raise it and fold it toward the front, pressing down lightly. Turn the dough a quarter turn and repeat the folding motion 10 or 12 times. Use a very light sifting of flour on the bench as necessary to keep the dough from sticking. Roll out the dough to ½-inch thickness, using light, quick movements in one direction with each stroke. The shape of the biscuits is affected by uniform thickness of the dough and by the manner of cutting.

Use care in rolling the dough to uniform thickness and cut straight down with uniform pressure to obtain a straight sided biscuit. They may be cut with a knife or a rolling cutter into diamonds, squares or triangles. All of the dough can be used in this manner of cutting, thus eliminating the need to rework and roll the dough a second time. Extra handling and working tends to result in poorer quality. (See cutters, Figure 20.8, p. 474.)

Place the biscuits on a greased baking sheet about $\frac{1}{2}$ inch apart if a crusty biscuit is desired and barely touching if a soft biscuit is preferred. The biscuits may be baked immediately after placing on the baking sheet, or they may be allowed to stand for as much as 30 minutes or more before baking. For a deeper brown color, biscuits may be brushed with milk or an egg wash before baking. Bake in a hot oven (425°F) for about 15 minutes.

Biscuit dough may be cooked in broth or fruit juice in a kettle or a steamer for dumplings to use with stews or desserts. When used for shortcakes a little sugar and more fat should be used in the dough. A drop biscuit has added liquid to produce a dough that can be dropped from a spoon. These biscuits are not flaky and are rough in appearance. Scones are made of biscuit dough that is enriched with fat, sugar, and egg. They are mixed and kneaded in the same manner as plain biscuits. It is usual for them to contain currants, raisins or candied fruit. They are cut into triangular shape and brushed with an egg wash.

Coffee Cakes and Loaf Breads

The ingredients for coffee cakes and quick-loaf breads are mixed by the muffin method and are similar to a muffin batter. They contain a higher percentage of sugar, which interferes with the development of gluten strands, and there is less hazard to quality because of stirring. A wide variety of flavoring is possible. Fruit, nuts, and spice may be folded into the batter or used as a topping. Coffee cakes may be baked in the $1\frac{1}{2}$-inch deep baking sheets or in 12 × 20-inch pans that permit a cake about 2 inches deep, and loaves in loaf pans measuring approximately 4 × 9 inches.

Mixes

Labor time in large kitchens can be saved through the use of either commercial mixes or those prepared by the individual kitchen. Kitchens that serve quick breads daily can save time by blending dry ingredients at one time in sufficient quantity for a week. The mix should be stored in an airtight container. The amount required for one time can then be weighed out and quickly mixed with the liquid ingredients. Biscuit mixes may contain the fat as well as the dry ingredients, needing milk only to complete them. It is not recommended that amounts to last longer than a few days be mixed at one time.

SUGGESTED LABORATORY EXPERIENCE

1. Compare bread recipes by calculating ingredient percentages and evaluate in relation to the type of bread for which the recipe is intended.
2. Make a comparison of the absorption of liquid by bread flour, general purpose, and cake flours.
3. Divide class and prepare yeast bread in following six ways and compare time required, ease of handling, and quality of products.
   (a) Use compressed yeast, bread flour, and straight dough method. Punch down once after fermentation.
   (b) Repeat as above, except use the sponge method of mixing.
   (c) Use active dry yeast, bread flour, and straight dough method. Punch down once after fermentation.
   (d) Repeat as in (c), except use the sponge method.
   (e) Use compressed yeast, general purpose flour, straight dough method and do not punch down but make into loaves after first fermentation.
   (f) Repeat as in (e), except use the sponge method.
4. Make rolls and shape (a) with the cutter and rounder and (b) by hand. Compare time required.
5. Practice forming rolls in different shapes.
6. Prepare muffins, hotcakes, popovers, biscuits. Judge for quality and analyze results in relation to techniques used.

REVIEW QUESTIONS AND ANSWERS

1. What is meant by enrichment?

The addition of specified nutrients to bread or flour.

2. What nutrients are added?

Thiamine, Riboflavin, Niacin, and Iron.

3. How does "enrichment" differ from "restored"?

"Enrichment" is increasing quantity above that normally found and "restored" is the returning of nutrients removed in processing.

4. Why are the recipes for flour mixtures calculated with ingredients as a percentage of the total amount of flour used?

It facilitates enlarging or reducing a recipe accurately and the comparing of ingredient proportions regardless of the size of the recipe.

5. What is the difference between a pour batter and a drop batter?

The consistency of a drop batter is too thick to pour but is soft enough to drop with a spoon, and a pour batter is fluid enough to pour.

6. How do doughs differ from batters?

They are stiff enough to knead or mold on a floured board.

7. What does wheat flour contain that makes it useful in making yeast breads?

Gliadin and glutenin, which when mixed with water or other liquid forms gluten that is elastic in nature and permits dough to stretch or expand with leavening.

8. Are all flours equal in their gluten content?

No, some flours are strong in their content of this protein complex and others are weak in terms of their gluten content.

9. Is a strong flour preferable for every type of bread?

No, strong flours are best for yeast breads and popovers, but a low gluten flour is preferable for muffins and griddle cakes.

10. Are commercial flours made from one type of wheat only?

No, the flour is blended from strong and lower protein wheats to develop the desired baking qualities.

11. What are the qualities for which flours are test baked?

(a) Processing time, (b) bench tolerance, (c) absorption of liquid, (d) potential volume, and (e) loaf quality.

12. What are the forms of yeast used commonly in bread making?

Compressed yeast plants formed into cakes with cornstarch and active dry yeast which have been dried and are granular in form.

13. How should they be held for use?

Active dry yeast may be held at room temperature, but keeps better when refrigerated. Compressed yeast must be refrigerated and either may be frozen and held for longer periods.

14. How should the yeast be prepared for use?

Either type should be crumbled and sprinkled on the top of lukewarm water —100°F for compressed, and about 110°F for active dry.

15. At what temperatures do the yeast plants grow best? At what temperature are they destroyed?

At temperatures between 80 to 90°F. They are killed in 1 hour at 110°F and in 5 minutes at 140°F.

16. What temperatures are important in controlling the temperature of the dough?

Temperature of the materials used, room in which fermentation occurs, and heat created by friction in machine operation.

17. What ingredient temperature is utilized in regulating temperature of the dough?

Temperature of the liquid.

18. How is the desired water temperature determined?

Multiply the desired temperature by the number of temperatures involved and from this subtract the total of the actual temperatures of flour, room, and friction heat.

19. How can friction heat be determined?

Multiply the temperature of freshly mixed dough by the number of temperatures involved and subtract the total of the actual temperatures (flour, room, liquid).

20. What liquids are commonly used in making yeast bread?

Water, water in which potatoes have been cooked, and milk.

21. What treatment of the liquid is necessary when milk is used?

It must be scalded before use.

22. Why do recipes state amount of liquid in indefinite amounts?

Because the absorption of liquid by flours differ. High protein flours absorb more than weak flours.

23. How can a baker tell when dough has been kneaded enough?

When it ceases to be sticky and has small air blisters under the surface.

24. Which is likely to be the greater hazard, overmixing or undermixing?

Undermixing.

25. What is the best temperature for dough during fermentation?

82°F.

26. What are the tests that determine when it has risen enough?

It doubles in size and a light indentation made with the finger remains and does not return to original form.

27. Is shaping the only reason for rolling out the dough when shaping loaves?

No, pressure of the rolling pin or roller presses out bubbles of gas so as to form a more uniform texture.

28. What precaution is important when handling dough during shaping?

The dough should be handled gently, neither to compress it too much nor to break the gluten strands that give structure to the bread.

29. How can dough be retarded for delayed use?

By refrigerating at 40°F and by freezing.

30. What is the chief characteristic that distinguishes quick breads from yeast breads?

The use of a leavening agent that acts as soon as liquid is added to the mixture and the product is baked.

31. What is the chief leavening agent in popovers?

Steam.

32. Should they be baked at a high or a low temperature?

Bake at 425°F for the first 15 minutes to develop the leavening steam, reduce temperature to 350°F to avoid over browning and complete baking.

33. Is a strong or a weak flour used for griddlecakes and muffins? Why?

A flour is best that has a low gluten content, to produce a tender product and avoid the formation of gluten strands.

34. Describe the muffin method of mixing.

Dry ingredients are thoroughly mixed by sifting together, and the wet ingredients such as eggs, milk, and shortening are blended together and mixed into dry ingredients just enough to dampen them.

35. Is a similar method used for making baking powder biscuits?

No. The fat is cut into the combined dry ingredients and the liquid is stirred into mixture. Those who wish flat tender, crusty biscuits stir them only enough to blend, and roll and cut them without kneading. Those who like biscuits that are lighter and have greater volume and flakiness knead them lightly before rolling them.

36. What is the chief advantage of pre-mixing ingredients for quick breads?

To speed up production during a busy period of the day.

37. What is a chief hazard to quality in holding mixes for a long period or time.

Leavening agents may absorb enough moisture from the ingredients or atmosphere to activate them before time of use.

22.

Cakes, Cookies, and Frostings

Cakes are one of the most adaptable of desserts. They are appropriate to serve as a simple refreshment or may be elaborate enough to claim the center of attention on festive occasions. They may be classified according to two general types, shortened or butter cakes and foam or sponge cakes which contain little or no shortening. Each type affords numerous variations. In the butter type the shortening may be butter or other kind of fat and the leavening is chemical, plus air that may be incorporated in eggs and through the mixing process. Foam or unshortened cakes, such as angel food, contain no fat and gain their lightness from air incorporated in egg whites. Chiffon cakes contain oil, and are leavened with both chemical leaven and air beaten into egg whites.

Success in cake making is largely influenced by (a) the ingredients used, (b) accuracy in measuring the ingredients, (c) method of mixing, and (d) proper baking. Cakes of desired quality have satisfactory volume and contour, and a fine-grained appearance. They are light and have a soft, moist, velvety texture. The flavors most preferred are those resulting from an appealing blend of good materials and delicate flavoring. Precision is required in cake making, but the rules are not difficult to follow and the results are rewarding when rules are observed.

CHOICE OF INGREDIENTS AND AMOUNTS REQUIRED

Flour

Cake flour has characteristics that result in better volume and texture in cakes than obtainable with pastry or all-purpose flour. It is low in protein and is milled to a finer granulation than the other flours. Feathering or fineness of granulation increases its volume per given weight. Use special caution when measuring flour by volume if all-purpose flour is substituted for cake flour. Less all-purpose flour by volume is required. A given volume of cake flour is lighter than the same volume of all-purpose flour and the cake flour yields approximately $\frac{1}{2}$ cup more per pound. Cake flour measures approximately 5 cups per pound and all-purpose flour approximately $4\frac{1}{2}$ cups per pound. When the recipe specifies amounts in weights and weight is used for measuring the flour, the recipe can be followed as written. Flours vary within a classification and tests may show that slight adjustment of amounts need to be made for best results.

Shortening

The amount and type of shortening used, also affects the quality of cakes in terms of volume, tenderness, and flavor. Butter is a favorite for its rich flavor. As a shortening it yields a cake that is tender and flavorful, but one that has less volume than might be obtained through using a hydrogenated fat. Emulsifiers in the hydrogenated shortenings aid in the distribution of fat and fat soluble material throughout the batter. Fat is important in the formation of air cells in the batter, and the more completely it is distributed throughout the batter, the better the cake. Because of their mild flavor, lower cost, and better volume in cakes, hydrogenated vegetable fats are the most widely used for cake making in large quantity production. The new superglycerinated vegetable shortenings have brought about a change in cake formulas. Higher ratios of shortening, sugar, and eggs can be used successfully; this is illustrated by the following proportions which approximate those in general use:

Butter	Hydrogenated Shortening
Equal percentage shortening and whole eggs	Higher percentage of eggs and shortening
Equal percentage of sugar and flour	Higher percentage of sugar than flour
Combined weight of eggs and milk equal to combined weight of sugar and flour	Combined weight of eggs and milk may be equal to or slightly more than that of the weight of the sugar only.

Margarine and lard have been found less satisfactory than hydrogenated vegetable fats both in flavor and volume produced. Success with oil as shortening seems to depend on addition of stiffly beaten egg at the end of mixing, as in making chiffon cakes. Cakes in which oil is used for shortening are frequently mixed by the muffin method or the quick or one-bowl method, except for the egg whites and part of the sugar. The egg whites are whipped until stiff with part of the sugar and carefully folded into the batter as the final ingredients.

Sugar

The amount of sugar in the formula has an influence on the moistness, sweet flavor, and tenderness of the cake. The influence on tenderness is believed to be largely due to sugar's interference both with the gluten formation in the flour and with the coagulation of the egg protein. Most butter cakes contain a weight of sugar that is approximately equal to that of the flour (100%). This produces a cake that is palatably sweet. If the proportions of sugar are increased from 125 to 140% with proper balance of fat, eggs, and liquid, the cake will have a good volume and be more moist and tender. The finer the granulation of the sugar, the better the volume of the cake. Increasing sugar only does not produce a satisfactory cake. When sugar is increased more fat is needed for proper formation of air cells and to improve volume. Liquid is needed for dissolving the sugar, and egg for structure in the cake. It is necessary for satisfactory results that the liquid, egg, and fat be in balance with the amount of sugar used.

Eggs

Fresh, frozen, or dried eggs may be used for the preparation of cakes. Large kitchens commonly use fresh or frozen egg meats as this lessens labor time required for breaking the eggs. (See Appendix for Equivalent Measures of Food). Users are advised to make cost comparisons that include both cost per pound of ready-to-use egg meats and the labor time required to crack the eggs. Weight rather than number of eggs should be used for measuring because of the variation in egg size.

Eggs contribute to cake quality through enriching flavor and nutritive quality, and by giving structure to the cake. They have a toughening effect unless properly balanced in quantity with the sugar and shortening. Too large a percentage of sugar and shortening for the amount of eggs prevents sufficient formation of gluten in the flour and coagulation of the proteins to give satisfactory structure to the cake. The quantity of eggs must be increased for a proper balance when sugar and shortening are increased. The liquid must be in balance also, in order to produce desired volume. The liquid in the eggs should be considered as part of the total liquid in calculating the total liquid in a recipe. In other words, as the quantity of eggs in a recipe is increased the liquid should be reduced in proportion to the liquid content of the additional eggs used. The water content of egg whites is approximately 75%, whole eggs, 65%, and yolks, about 50%.

Liquid

Milk is the liquid most commonly used in cake making. It may be in the form of fresh whole milk, skimmed milk, sour milk, or nonfat dry milk. Because of its lower cost and greater convenience of storage, nonfat dry milk is widely favored in large quantity production. The solids may be reconstituted before use, or added as solids to creamed shortening and sugar or sifted with dry ingredients. Results appear to be better when the solids are reconstituted before use. Convenience is greater when they are weighed and sifted with dry ingredients.

The use of buttermilk, sour milk, or molasses as liquid calls for neutralizing the acid with the right amount of soda for proper leavening and palatable flavor. If the leavening is in excess of the amount required, the texture of the cake is coarse and irregular. Use $\frac{1}{2}$ teaspoon of soda to neutralize 1 cup of buttermilk, sourmilk, or molasses. In leavening power this is equal to 2 teaspoons of baking powder. Excess soda produces a bitter flavor and too little results in an acid flavor. When the right amount is used to neutralize the acid, the flavor resembles that of a sweet-milk cake.

Good volume and moist texture in cake requires the right proportion of liquid. It is important for the amount of liquid to be in balance with the ratio of sugar used. There needs to be sufficient liquid, not only to dissolve the sugar, but to supply liquid to develop the gluten in the flour and to gelatinize the starch. It is well for bakers to follow standardized recipes carefully; they also need to develop an appreciation of the appearance of the proper viscosity of a cake batter. This helps them in making the adjustments necessitated by differences in ingredients, such as difference in flours. Batters that are too thin or too stiff produce inferior cakes.

METHODS OF MIXING

Shortened or Butter Cakes

The shortened or butter cakes are general favorites and are prepared in greater quantities than foam cakes. Numerous studies have been made to find solutions to two problems that pertain to the methods of mixing. The first relates to production of good quality and the second, to ways of saving time and effort in the preparation of cakes. The way in which ingredients are combined can have a pronounced influence on quality. Simplifying the the method by which they are combined may call for some adjustment in the ingredients used.

The standard of quality desired is a cake that is golden brown in color and has a slightly rounded, even contour. The crust is thin and delicate, and not sugary. The crumb is tender, moist, and velvety. The texture should be made up of numerous, small, thin-walled air cells. The flavor and color should be those of natural ingredients. Materials may be used to support or enhance the natural ingredients. Both color and flavor should be delicate.

There are four methods of mixing that are commonly recognized. These are known as (a) the conventional cake method, (b) the muffin method, (c) quick, high-ratio, one-bowl, single step or simplified method, and (d) the pastry-blend method. An even dispersion of fat throughout the mixture has an influence in obtaining a tender, velvety crumb. The incorporation of beaten eggs with a minimum loss of air contributes to lightness. An increase of sugar in proportion to flour, with corresponding balance of fat, eggs, and liquid, may be used to offset conditions in simplified mixing methods. It is therefore recommended that when following a recipe one use the mixing method indicated as well as the quantity of ingredients prescribed.

In the *conventional cake method*, a first and important step is the creaming of the plastic fat and the addition and thorough blending with the sugar. Egg yolks or whole eggs may be incorporated with these. If the eggs are separated, only the yolks are blended in at this point, the whites are beaten and folded into the batter at the end, after the other ingredients have been added. The leavening agent, spices and other dry ingredients are sifted together and added to the fat and sugar mixture alternately with the liquid. This conventional method of mixing is more time and effort consuming than the following methods, but good results have made it one that is widely used.

The *muffin method* (described in Chapter 21, under "Quick Breads") is quick and easy to perform. The dry ingredients are sifted and mixed together. The wet ingredients, including the melted fat are blended separately and stirred into the dry ingredients. Cake batter may be more thoroughly stirred than a muffin batter. The higher ratio of sugar and fat to flour in the cake batter usually, is sufficient to prevent the formation of gluten strands and toughness as a result of stirring.

The texture of these cakes tends to be coarse and the cakes stale quickly. They are best when served warm. The ease and speed possible in combining these cakes may make the method a desirable one to use for morning coffee cakes or pudding type cakes (cottage or fruit pudding) that are to be served warm and often with a sauce. The muffin method, with some modification, is used for chiffon cakes. The egg whites and part of the sugar are not combined with the other ingredients but are beaten until stiff with the salt, cream of tartar and part of the sugar. This meringue is then carefully folded into the muffin-mixed batter.

The *quick, one-bowl, or simplified method* of cake mixing is often referred to as the high-ratio method because of the increased proportion of sugar and fat used. The dry ingredients, shortening (superglycerinated plastic fat, at room temperature), and part of the milk are combined and beaten (at medium speed) for two minutes. The remainder of the milk and the eggs are blended into this mixture for an additional two minutes. The quality of the cakes made by this method have been scored highest in preference tests when the proportion of sugar to flour was between 125 and 140% rather than 100%. The high ratio cakes have good volume, tenderness, appealing texture and flavor, and they are moist. The extra sugar promotes tenderness and retention of moisture but the extra sweetness slightly lessens the preference score for flavor.

The fourth mixing method is called *pastry-blend method*. In this, the fat and flour are blended before adding the other ingredients. The remaining ingredients are added in two steps. In the first, half of the milk, the sugar, and the baking powder are combined and blended into the fat and flour. The remaining milk and eggs are added next. Very good cakes can be made by this method, and it is a method of processing used by many commercial bakers.

Foam or Unshortened Cakes

The character of the egg whites and the way in which they are handled are significant to quality in preparing foam or unshortened cakes. Stability and a fine, uniform size of the foam, plus elasticity sufficient to swell without rupture during baking, are important for volume and tenderness. Procedures to promote desired qualities include (a) the use of thick whites (with a large proportion of thick albumen), characteristic in fresh, high quality eggs, (b) having whites at room temperature when beaten, (c) beating whites to the stage of soft or rounded peaks, (d) the addition of salt and cream of tartar to increase whiteness and stability, (e) addition of sugar when the whites are at the soft peaks stage of stiffness, and then continuing the beating until the whites are stiff but not dry, and (f) folding in the flour and/or other ingredients carefully to minimize loss of air from the foam.

The thinner whites of storage eggs whip more readily than fresh thick whites, but the foam is less stable and yields less volume when whipped in a power mixer. Fat of any kind interferes with foaming, such as that in a small amount of yolk, cream or even oil or grease on a mixer bowl that has not been properly cleaned. Acid (such as cream of tartar) and sugar have a stabilizing effect on the egg white foam.

It is well to divide the sugar required in a recipe, adding one part to the egg white foam after it has reached the soft-peak stage and the remainder to the flour. Sugar in the flour helps to blend the dry ingredients into the foam more easily and smoothly. It is usually preferable to fold the dry ingredients into the egg white foam by hand using a wire whip. If it is done in the mixer, operate at low speed and use special care to prevent overmixing.

The proportion of ingredients has an influence on cake quality. Too much flour causes the texture to be less tender. Sugar helps to make the cake tender, but an excess of sugar weakens the structure and the cake then falls. It is well to be cautious of recipes in which the weight of the sugar exceeds that of the egg whites. Sugar with fine granulation is best. Some recipes call for confectioner's sugar to be used for the part that is beaten into the egg whites.

BAKING OF CAKES

The leavening gas is not retained well in cake batters. The batter should be put into baking pans as soon as mixing has been completed and the cakes baked as soon as possible. Fast penetration of heat promotes better volume and texture. This is believed to be due to quick coagulation of the proteins in the batter. Attention is to be given to several details in the baking of cakes. Good results require that (a) baking containers of satisfactory material and finish be used, (b) pans be suitably conditioned before filling, (c) containers be filled to a proper level, (d) appropriate temperature and baking time be used, and (e) cakes be adequately cooled before removal from the pan (about 8 to 12 minutes for layers, 20 to 30 minutes for loaves and complete cooling for foam or sponge cakes).

Heat is absorbed and transmitted more rapidly in pans that are dark in color and have a dull finish than in bright, shiny pans. In the dark, dull pans the outer edges cook more quickly than the center, which continues to increase in volume. This results in a rounded rather than a flat center and in loaf cakes results in a crack along the top. The volume and crumb quality of these cakes has been judged superior to that of cakes baked in shiny pans that produce a more level contour. The bright, shiny pans reflect heat and the heat penetration is therefore slower. Glass transmits heat more slowly than metal, and it is difficult to get satisfactory browning on the bottom of the cake. This, plus the hazard of breakage, makes glass a less suitable material for cake baking. Metals from which selection may be made include aluminum, either bright or anodized, and steel or iron with tinned, japaned, or black-oxide finish. When selecting the material, one needs to decide which is of the greater importance, the level contour of the cake or its volume and good crumb quality. (See color plate insert for Figure 22.1.)

Depth of the pan and of the batter in the pan influences quality. Shallow cakes permit faster heat penetration and tend to result in better volume, more level contour, and tenderness. Round pans from 8 to 14 inches in diameter and 1½ to 2 inches deep, and baking sheets 18 × 26 inches and 1¼ to 1½ inches deep, are the popular sizes used in large kitchens for shortened cakes. The pans should be filled two-thirds full, but not exceed this amount. Fill to only half the pan depth for high ratio cakes. The loaf or pound cake pans should have a depth that yields a cake at least 2 to 2½ inches deep. Tube pans used for foam cakes may be 9, 10, or 12 inches in diameter according to size of slice desired for service. The pans may be filled three-fourths full. Some adjustment of temperature is needed for the different size cakes.

Choose pans with straight sides for shortened cakes. Use a pastry brush to grease the pans on the bottom and sides. Flour may be dusted on the bottom and the excess shook off, or the bottom of the pans may be covered with a waxed-paper liner. Do not grease foam cake pans, as these cakes need to cling to the sides of the pan for support when rising. Greasing interferes with volume and lightness of these cakes. Foil or brown paper lining is recommended for lining fruit-cake pans and aids in removing the cakes from the pans after baking and cooling.

TABLE 22.1 APPROXIMATE BAKING TIME AND TEMPERATURE FOR CAKES

Type of Cake	Size Pan	Weight	Temperature Degrees F.	Baking Time Minutes
Butter Cakes				
Cup cakes	2¼ × 1½ in.	1¾ oz	350	30
	2¼ × 1½ in.	1¾ oz	400	18 to 20
Round layer	9 × 1½ in.	22 oz	350	30 to 35
Sheet (plain, white, spice)	18 × 26 × 1 in.	7 to 8 lb	350	35
	18 × 26 × 1 in.	7 to 8 lb	375	25 to 30
Sweet (rich chocolate)	18 × 26 × 1 in.	7 to 8 lb	325 to 350	45 to 60
Jelly roll	18 × 26 × 1 in.	3 lb	375	12 to 14
Loaf	5½ × 10½ × 3 in.	2 lb	300 to 325	75
Fruit cakes	5½ × 10½ × 3 in.	3½ lb	300	120 to 180
Foam Cakes (in tube or loaf pans)				
Angel Food	10 in.	32 oz	300	60 to 75
Sponge	10 in.	30 oz	325	50 to 55
	10 in.	30 oz	400	35

Preheat the oven to the desired temperature for baking, making temperature adjustment for temperature recovery time if necessary (see "Ovens," Chapter 12). Place cakes in the oven so that heat can circulate around and between the pans. Follow the temperature recommended in the recipe for the type and size of cake to be baked. Table 22.1 is a guide to use in the event that a recipe has not stated the time and temperature for cakes of various kinds and sizes. Because of variations in oven temperatures and pan sizes, individual tests need to be made to determine the degree of doneness. The cake is done when the surface springs back when lightly touched with the finger, or when a toothpick inserted in the cake comes out clean.

Remove butter cakes from the oven to a rack and allow them to cool, for 10 or 12 minutes for sheet cakes and 8 or 10 minutes for round layers, before removing from the pan. Angel Food and sponge cakes should be inverted so that they hang upside down in the pan, and allowed to remain until they have fully cooled before removal from the pans. Butter cakes have a tendency to stick to the pans and are harder to remove if permitted to cool completely before taking them from the pans. They break easily if handled when they are hot.

COOKIES

Cookies may be classified as little cakes in terms of the type of ingredients required and methods of mixing. Numerous appealing varieties are possible through slight variation in ingredients and shaping. Limitation of their use in large quantity food service has been largely due to portion cost. A portion of cake for the same production effort may appear larger and more showy than cookies for similar cost. Part of the expense results from the dried fruits and nuts in the mixtures, and much of the cost is for labor time in individual portion handling.

Cookies may be classified according to ingredients, such as nut cookies, fruit cookies, and foam or butter cookies. They are more often classified in terms of the method of shaping. *Ball* or molded cookies are made with a dough that is fairly stiff, and can be handled easily for shaping. *Rolled* cookies are made with a stiff dough, also. The dough, when rolled by machine, should be well refrigerated, for firmness, before rolling. This is true for the *sliced* cookies, also. It is well for the rolls of dough to refrigerate several hours in order to be stiff enough to hold an attractive shape when sliced. The dough for these cookies may be frozen or refrigerated and held for several days, for use as desired. The dough for *pressed* cookies is a rich dough that should be soft enough to pass through the tips without excess pressure, but firm enough to hold distinct form after shaping. *Drop* cookies

Figure 22.2   Delicate ladyfingers arranged around a raspberry Charlotte Russe serve as a beautiful dessert for luncheon or tea. (Courtesy of Pacific Kitchen.)

are general favorites with the public and with those who are responsible for production. The dough for these must be soft enough for dropping from a spoon or scoop, but firm enough that they do not spread excessively. *Bars* and *squares* are made with a mixture that is soft enough to spread in the baking pan, and they are cut into portions after baking.

When choosing a mixing method for cookies, one may be guided by the ingredients, in a similar manner as with cakes. When a large proportion of egg white is to be used, as in ladyfingers, macaroons and kisses, it is best to proceed as in making foam cakes. Start with the egg white meringue and fold other ingredients into it. The largest number of cookies contain shortening and chemical leavening. It is best to mix these by either the conventional or simplified method for mixing cake batter.

Control the size of cookies when shaping them, in order to promote uniform baking and appearance, and to control cost. Standard size ice cream scoops are convenient tools for drop cookies. Size No. 30 makes a large hearty size that may be used for cafeteria portions. Size No. 40 is an intermediate size and No. 60 provides a small, dainty cookie suitable for teas. Sliced cookie size may be governed by the diameter of the roll ($1\frac{1}{2}$ to 2 inches) and the thickness of the slice ($\frac{1}{8}$ to $\frac{3}{16}$ inch). A measured number of cuts per standard baking sheet may be determined for bar or square cookies, and specified ounces of dough for use in those that are molded.

Bake cookies on bright, aluminum baking sheets or pans with low sides. Grease the pans with unsalted fat, unless the cookies are very rich in fat and the recipe specifies that the pans are not to be greased. Use the temperature stated in the recipe and preheat the oven before placing the cookies in it. Temperature requirements vary according to the shape and character of the cookies. It is well to be sure which one is specifically required, and the exact time for baking. Be careful to prevent overcooking because it dries out the cookies and spoils delicate flavors. Cookies should be lifted from the baking sheet as soon as they are baked, so that cooking cannot continue. Permit them to cool completely on a cooling rack. If they are to be held before use, store them in an airtight container.

FROSTINGS AND FILLINGS

Frostings and fillings are dressings for cakes, cookies, and coffee breads that are added to increase enjoyment of the product. Form, flavor, sweetness, texture, moisture, and general appearance of the products may be affected by the ones that are chosen. Give thought when selecting the dressing that it be in harmony with the character of the product and adds those qualities most desired. Those who like the delicacy and lightness of angel food for example, tend to enjoy a frosting that is equally delicate, such as a thin sugar glaze or whipped cream. The simple shortened cakes have flavor and texture that permit a wide variety of fillings and frostings. Interest and variety may be increased by adding fruit to fillings and/or frosting for those that do not contain fruit or nuts and smooth buttery or fluffy ones for those that do. Small cakes, such as petits fours, and cookies that are to be handled in the fingers need to have a nonsticky icing. When choosing both the cake and the dressing for it, is is well to consider whether it is to be complete as a dessert in itself or whether it is to be used as an accompaniment.

Frostings may be grouped generally into cooked and uncooked types. Each type may be used to create numerous interesting varieties. The uncooked frostings, prepared with confectioner's sugar, plus a moistening ingredient, are simple and easy to make. The fine grain of confectioner's sugar dissolves readily with a very little moisture and makes a smooth, velvety frosting. The moisture may be butter, cream, milk, fruit juice, egg white, chocolate, coffee, or cream cheese. Sufficient sugar is blended in to make it the desired consistency. Beating vigorously helps to make it fluffy and creamy. Fat in the mixture helps it to remain soft and creamy longer than if moisture is used that contains no fat. That which is mixed with water, fruit juice, and egg white becomes brittle when it dries. Those who wish a frosting that is not sweet may use melted semisweet chocolate to which a small amount of cream is added or whipped cream that is only lightly sweetened.

The versatile cooked frostings involve the use of a sugar sirup and may be grouped according to their resemblance to such candies as fudge, divinity, and fondant. The size of the sugar crystals in the finished product strongly influences quality. Fine crystals are essential for creaminess and for melting with palatable speed on the tongue. The sirup ingredients, cooking temperature and the handling of the sirup determine in large degree the size of the crystals in the finished product.

When cooking sirups either for frostings or candy include an ingredient that interferes with the formation of crystals. This ingredient may be a small amount of cream of tartar, which changes part of the sucrose to an invert sugar, or some corn sirup. Cook the sugar sirup to the temperature or test that yields the firmness desired. Sirup for fudge-type frosting, for example, is not cooked as long as that for candy in order to have a frosting that spreads easily. Confectioner's sugar may be used in this and in the divinity-type frostings to adjust consistency.

Prevent the hot sirup from being seeded with coarse crystals that promote the forming of similar coarse crystals. The seeds may be undissolved sugar crystals on the sides of the pan, spoon or thermometer. These may be washed down with hot sirup before the sirup has begun to boil, or the pan covered to steam them down. The spoon and thermometer should be removed from the sirup and the sirup permitted to boil without stirring. (See Table 22.2.) Vigorous beating of the frosting as it is cooling helps to separate the crystals and promotes smaller crystals and creaminess.

Fondant is boiled to 240°F and then cooled to 104°F before beating. The cooling should be done on a smooth surface such as polished marble, stainless steel or a china platter. Plain fondant is a richly sweet, snowy white, creamy mass of fine crystals, when it is properly made. It can be softened to pouring consistency by warming over hot water. Cream may be added to prevent its becoming brittle and to add to the flavor. It may be thinned with a liquid or made thicker with confectioner's sugar. It is the ideal frosting for petits fours, permitting them to be quickly frosted by pouring the fondant over them, and it is firm enough on cooling to avoid stickiness.

A divinity-type frosting is made by cooking the sirup to the firm ball stage and whipping it while hot, into stiffly beaten egg whites. One that is similar in fluffy consistency may be made by boiling the sirup just long enough to dissolve the sugar. The hot sirup is then added slowly to unbeaten egg whites, and beaten constantly at medium speed during addition of the sirup and then at high speed until the frosting will form stiff peaks.

Interesting fillings have special appeal when cakes are served as the dessert, and not as an accompaniment to a dessert. They have special appeal for persons who like the dessert to be less sweet than those filled with the candy-like frostings. Many of the gelatin or cornstarch thickened puddings serve as very good fillings. Dried fruits, such as dates, raisins, apricots or prunes may be ground, moistened with fruit juice, sweetened with a little of the

TABLE 22.2 TEMPERATURES AND TESTS FOR SIRUP AND CANDIES*

Product	Temperature At sea level (°F)	Test	Description of Test
Sirup	230 to 234	Thread	Sirup spins a 2-inch thread when dropped from fork or spoon.
Fondant Fudge Penuchi	234 to 240	Soft ball	Sirup, when dropped into very cold water, forms a soft ball which flattens on removal from water.
Carmels	244 to 248	Firm ball	Sirup, when dropped into very cold water, forms a firm ball which does not flatten on removal from water.
Divinity Marshmallows Popcorn balls	250 to 266	Hard ball	Sirup, when dropped into very cold water, forms a ball which is hard enough to hold its shape, yet plastic.
Butterscotch Taffies	270 to 290	Soft crack	Sirup, when dropped into very cold water, separates into threads which are hard but not brittle.
Brittle Glace	300 to 310	Hard crack	Sirup, when dropped into very cold water, separates into threads which are hard and brittle.
Barley sugar	320	Clear liquid	The sugar liquifies.
Carmel	338	Brown liquid	The liquid becomes brown.

*From Handbook of Food Preparation, American Home Economics Association, Washington, D.C. 1959, p. 31.

Figure 22.3 Boston cream cake with pastry cream filling and cherry topping. (Courtesy of Pacific Kitchen.)

frosting and used as fillings. Cream cheese softened with orange juice and flavored with grated rind make a flavorful less-sweet filling. The cream cheese may be used, also, with chopped pecans, butter and confectioner's sugar for frosting as well as filling. Semisweet chocolate and butter may be melted together over hot water and blended with sour cream and confectioner's sugar as a delicious frosting and filling for rich chocolate cake.

A glaze adds an appealing finish to coffee breads and simple cakes. These may be made with a sirup containing fruit pulp or juice, and may be thickened with gelatin or a starch. When thickened with the gelatin or starch, rather than the concentration of the sirup, they have a more palatable degree of sweetness and an attractive shine. A thin icing made with milk or cream and confectioner's sugar is often brushed on the warm coffee breads. The flavoring, vanilla or another favorite flavor, should be delicate.

Frosting the Cake

If the cake is to be frosted on the tray on which it is to be displayed, protect the tray with waxed paper under the edges of the cake that can be removed when the frosting is finished. Turn the layer that is to be on the bottom, with the top down on the tray. Be sure that all loose crumbs are brushed away. Spread the filling for the desired depth on the bottom layer. If the filling differs from the frosting, be cautious that it does not extend beyond the edge of the layer. Carefully brush away the crumbs from the layer to be placed on top, and place it top side up on the bottom layer. If the sides of the cake are to be frosted, frost the sides before frosting the top. Frost the top, spreading from the sides toward the center of the top. Swirled contours made with the frosting spatula are often more appealing in appearance than a surface that is carefully smoothed and level.

Conservation of labor time is important when frosting small cakes. There are various quick ways to handle cup cakes. One is to dip the top of the cup cake into soft frosting of the fluffy type. Use a slight twisting motion to cover the top of the cake and lift quickly to form a peak in the center. Some prefer to use the smallest size ice cream scoop, to scoop frosting of the butter type onto the cap and then spread it with a spatula. Others who are skillful in working with both hands use a spoon and spatula, and with quick motions are able to dip and spread soft frosting on cakes set on a tray. Tea cakes or petits fours are cut from sheet cakes. A fine textured cake should be used for these. Care is needed to cut them evenly, avoiding points or sharp edges that tend to break off. Peel the top, sugary surface from the cakes and brush off all loose crumbs. Place them on a rack over a tray, and frost them by pouring a fondant-type frosting over them.

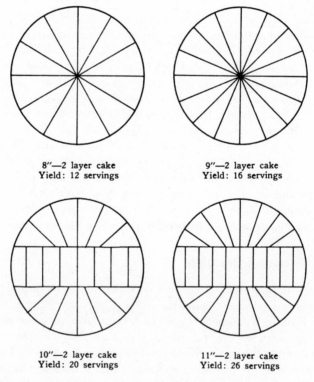

8"—2 layer cake
Yield: 12 servings

9"—2 layer cake
Yield: 16 servings

10"—2 layer cake
Yield: 20 servings

11"—2 layer cake
Yield: 26 servings

Figure 22.4 Suggestions for cutting cakes of different shapes and sizes. (Courtesy of the American Baking Institute.)

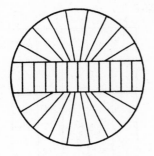

12"—2 layer cake
Yield: 30 servings

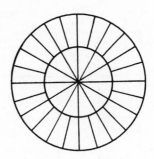

12"—2 layer cake
Yield: 36 servings

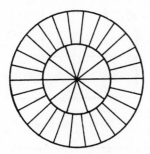

13"—2 layer cake
Yield: 36 servings

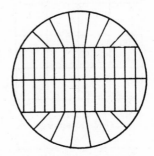

14"—2 layer cake
Yield: 40 servings

LOAF CAKES

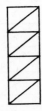

1 pound loaf cake
Yield: 8 servings

1 pound loaf cake
Yield: 8 servings

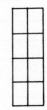

1 pound loaf cake
Yield: 8 servings

SQUARE CAKES

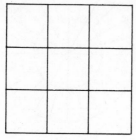

8″ x 8″
Yield: 9 servings

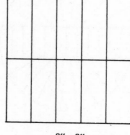

8″ x 8″
Yield: 10 servings

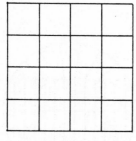

9″ x 9″
Yield: 16 servings

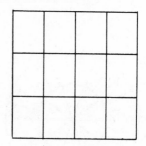

9″ x 9″
Yield: 12 servings

SHEET CAKES

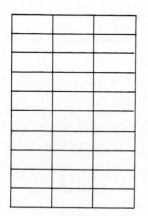

9″ x 13″
Yield: 30 servings

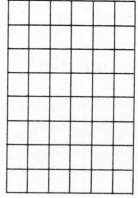

18″ x 25″
Yield: 48 servings

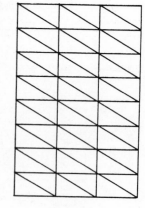

18″ x 25″
Yield: 48 servings

TIER CAKES**

A—Cut vertically through the bottom layer at the edge of the second layer as indicated by the dotted line marked 1; then cut out wedge-shaped pieces as shown by 2.

B—When these pieces have been served, follow the same procedure with the middle layer: cut vertically through the second layer at the edge of the top layer as indicated by dotted line 3; then cut out wedge-shaped pieces as shown by 4.

C—When pieces from the second layer have been served, return to the bottom layer and cut along dotted line 5; cut another row of wedge-shaped pieces as shown by 6.

D—The remaining tiers may be cut into the desired size pieces.

The average number of portions that various sized layers will yield are as follows:

14 inch layer will yield approximately 40 servings.
12 inch layer will yield approximately 30 servings.
10 inch layer will yield approximately 20 servings.
 9 inch layer will yield approximately 16 servings.
 8 inch layer will yield approximately 12 servings.

*Friel, Charles: Adapted from "Friel's Diagrammatic Cake Charts."
**Thelen, Ray: Cutting Wedding Cakes. Bakers' Helper, Vol. 89, May 15, 1948, Cakes and Pastry Section, p. 8.

Distributed by:
   Consumer Service Department
   American Institute of Baking
   400 East Ontario
   Chicago 11, Illinois

Figure 22.4 *Continued*

Decoration of cakes is a fascinating subject calling for fairly lengthy description concerning manipulation and artistry. It finds limited use in most large kitchens and is omitted here because of the limitation of space. The consumer sees the cake, in the majority of food service establishments, when it is in a portioned piece. It is important therefore, that portions be neatly cut and attractive in appearance. Portions should be standardized in terms of reasonable satisfaction and in keeping with cost allowance. Foam type cakes look best when cut with a tined cake breaker or serrated knife. Frosted butter or shortened cakes should be cut with a sharp thin-bladed knife that has been dipped in hot water. Shake off the excess moisture. A small amount of moisture keeps the frosting from dragging, but an excess spoils the frosting and dampens the cake. The cut of cake and size of serving plate should be in attractive proportions.

A fresh, moist texture is important to enjoyment of cake. It stales more rapidly when cut and especially after portioning. It is well, therefore, to delay arranging portions for service until immediately before service. Frosting aids in retaining moisture in cakes. Most cakes freeze well before they are frosted, and can be placed in airtight containers and held for delayed use. Cookies, also, in the dough or baked state may be frozen. The quality of most cookies appears fresher when baked after thawing of the frozen dough than when frozen after baking.

SUGGESTED LABORATORY EXPERIENCE

1. Prepare plain cake by the following methods and compare speed and ease of preparation and quality of the cakes:
   (a) conventional method (See Large Quantity Recipes, Terrell, p. 268).
   (b) pastry-blend method (See Food for Fifty, Fowler, West & Shugart, p. 90).
   (c) high ratio method (suggest use of recipe from manufacturer of high-ratio shortening).
2. Prepare a chiffon cake. Note the muffin type method of mixing.
3. Prepare and compare quality, mixing time and cost of angel food made with the fresh egg whites and with a well recognized commercial mix.
4. Prepare and frost cakes with each type of frosting (fudge, divinity, and fondant).
5. Calculate cost of cakes, including ingredients and labor time, and determine portion size in relation to portion allowance. Evaluate whether the portion is of attractive and satisfying size. Are portions competitive with those commonly served?

6. Prepare each of the four types of cookies. Take note of preparation time and ingredient cost. Portion according to appropriate use. Evaluate size in terms of appeal, cost and sale price.

REVIEW QUESTIONS AND ANSWERS

1. How do cake flours differ from all-purpose flours?

They have a lower protein content and are milled to a finer granulation.

2. What effect does this have on the volume of the flour?

The finer granulation increases the volume approximately $\frac{1}{2}$ cup per pound.

3. Why are they favored for cakes?

They produce better volume and texture in cakes than do the all-purpose flours.

4. Why is an emulsified fat preferred in cake making?

The emulsifiers aid in distribution of fat and fat soluble material in the batter.

5. Which produces better volume in cakes, hydrogenated fat, butter or lard?

Hydrogenated fat.

6. How does sugar affect cake quality?

It influences moistness, sweet flavor and tenderness.

7. What proportion of sugar is most often used?

Approximately 100%.

8. Under what conditions may the amount of sugar be increased?

By increasing fat, eggs and liquid so that they are in proper balance with the amount of sugar used.

9. What type of eggs are required for cake making?

The eggs may be fresh, frozen, or dried.

10. What form of milk may be used in cakes?

Fresh whole, skimmed, sour or buttermilk, or dry milk solids.

11. How may nonfat milk solids be added to cake batter?

Reconstituted and added in same manner as fresh milk, added as solids to creamed shortening and sugar, or sifted with the dry ingredients.

12. What is the best method?

As reconstituted milk.

13. How much soda is required to neutralize 1 cup of sour milk or buttermilk?

$\frac{1}{2}$ teaspoon.

14. This quantity is equal to how much baking powder in leavening power?

Two teaspoonsful.

15. In the event that more leavening is required than is needed to neutralize sour milk or buttermilk, should the amount of soda be increased?

No. The added soda would result in a bitter flavor in the cake. The added leavening should be added in the form of baking powder.

16. Why is it important to have the right amount of liquid in the cake batter?

The right amount of liquid is necessary to dissolve the sugar, supply liquid to develop gluten in the flour and gelatinize the starch and make a moist cake.

17. What are the two general types of cakes?

Shortened cakes that are chemically leavened and foam cakes that depend largely upon air incorporated in egg whites for the leavening.

18. What are the four methods of mixing shortened cakes?

(a) Conventional, (b) high-ratio or simplified, (c) muffin, and (d) pastry-blended methods.

19. What are the important points in mixing that affect quality of the product?

Thorough, even distribution of fat throughout the batter and incorporation of beaten eggs with minimum loss of air.

20. Why is superglycerinated, hydrogenated shortening used for the simplified method of mixing?

The emulsifier which they contain aids in the dispersion of fat in the batter.

21. What is the chief value that may be contributed by butter in cakes or cookies?

Rich flavor.

22. What are the common characteristics of a muffin-mixed cake?

Coarse texture and cakes that stale quickly. They are best when served hot.

23. What mixing method is used for chiffon cakes?

Ingredients, except for the egg whites and part of the sugar, are mixed by the muffin method. The whites are beaten and sugar is used to make a meringue that is folded into the batter last.

24. How does this differ from the method used for angel food?

Angel food is prepared by making a meringue with the egg whites and part of the sugar and the remaining ingredients are gently folded into the meringue.

25. What are the important points to follow in baking cakes?

(a) Preheat oven to proper temperature, (b) Use bright pans of satisfactory material, (c) Prepare pans with or without grease as required for the specific cake, (d) Fill pans with proper allowance for rising according to the type of cake, (e) Bake at the proper temperature just until done, and (f) Allow suitable cooling time after baking before removal from the pan.

26. What is a common method for classifying cookies?

Methods of shaping.

27. Name four types.

Ball or molded, rolled, sliced or refrigerator, pressed, drop and bar, or square cookies.

28. What methods are used for mixing cookies?

Methods for mixing cookies are similar to those used for cakes and are guided in a similar way by the ingredients.

29. Why is cream of tartar or corn sirup used in sirups for frostings or candy?

To interfere with the formation of large sugar crystals.

30. List points for consideration when frosting cakes.

Choose a frosting appropriate for the type of cake to be frosted, apply it neatly and in suitable proportion, and so that it appears well in the way it is to be displayed (whole or in a piece).

23.

Pastry,
Pie Fillings,
and Puddings

Pastries contain a high percentage of fat in proportion to flour. They are commonly classified into four groups as (a) pie or plain pastry, (b) puff paste, (c) chou paste (for cream puffs), and (d) Danish pastry. The dough for the Danish pastry is rich in eggs as well as fat, and has fat folded and rolled into the dough. It is a yeast dough used for sweet rolls. Puff paste is similar to pie pastry but has a high proportion of fat that is folded and rolled into the dough, to produce flaky layers. Chou paste is a rich egg mixture that is leavened by steam.

Figure 23.1 Apple pie, whether french apple (shown) or two-crust apple pie, is a favorite dessert. (Courtesy of Pacific Kitchen.)

Pie ranks as a most popular dessert, and the pastry with which it is made strongly influences its quality and popularity. Pie filling, served as a pudding and identical with that served in a pie shell, rates much lower in acceptance by the public. Many of the fruit and starch thickened puddings are similar in materials and manipulation to pie fillings. This is also true of those made with gelatin and eggs. Because of the points of similarity both puddings and pie fillings are included for discussion in this chapter.

PASTRY

Quality ratings for pastry allow the highest percentage (60%) for texture. The desired texture is one that is crisp, tender, and flaky. The preferred flavor, which receives a 15% score, is one that is bland. The best flavor is gained from the fresh wheaty flavor of the flour and the sweet, almost flavorless fat. The remaining scores are for appearance. These allow 10% for shaping and 15% for baking. The shaping calls for crusts to be evenly rolled, medium thin ($\frac{1}{8}$ inch), well fitted into the pan, free from excess shrinkage or buckling, and to have an attractively finished edge. A high score for baking requires thorough cooking and uniform browning to an attractive golden brown color.

Ingredients

The ingredients used, their proportions and manipulation influences tenderness and flakiness of pie pastry. Of the two qualities, tenderness is preferred over flakiness. The kind of flour, the type of fat and the proportions of fat and water affect tenderness. A pastry flour, commonly milled from winter wheat and possessing a low protein content, is considered the most satisfactory. Good pastry can be made from all-purpose and bread flour (10 to 14%), however, through the use of ingredients that offset the extra strength of the flour. When stronger flours are used, cornstarch may be added to lower the protein percentage or the amount of fat in the formula may be increased in order to produce the desired tenderness.

The four ingredients essential in the preparation of plain pastry are flour, fat, liquid, and salt. In blending these, the flour combines readily with the fat or the liquid. The gluten is developed in a mixture of flour and liquid and is weakened by the introduction of fat. When fat is mixed into the flour so thoroughly as to completely coat the particles of flour, the mixture will take up very little liquid. Such pastry tends to be mealy rather than flaky. Flakiness requires that the flour take up enough water for gluten strands to be formed. Upon baking, steam formed from the liquid forms layers between the gluten strands.

Fats that contain emulsifiers are not the best for pastry as they blend too readily with the liquid. This is a useful quality in cake making, but it is not desirable in pastry making. Steam-rendered lard produces a more tender pastry than the hydrogenated fats and butter or margarine. A firm grained lard that mixes less readily with the flour particles is a good shortening to use in producing flaky pastry.

The amount of fat in the formula needs to be adjusted to (a) the flour used, (b) the pastry qualities desired, and (c) the method used for handling the dough. An amount as low as 40% has been used with good results with all-purpose flour. Recipes in which stronger flours are used may call for from 60 to 75%. A dough that is overly rich for the amount of gluten in the flour breaks or crumbles easily and is hard to handle. The weight for a given volume of lard, butter and margarine differs from that of hydrogenated fats. The weight of the hydrogenated fats is about 7 ounces per cup and the other fats weigh 8 ounces per cup. The percentages in formulas are calculated on the basis of weight.

Cook book recipes frequently state quantities without indicating the type of materials used. It is important for the individual kitchen to try out different proportions with the specific materials to be used, until a formula is developed that is satisfactory for their service and methods of handling. The following formulas for pie pastry illustrate recipe differences for products that have been well accepted. Pastry flour was used in D and all-purpose flour in C. The others used unknown flour.

	A	B	C	D	E
Flour	100%	100%	100%	100%	100%
Fat	67	75	59	50	40 to 44
Water	33	38	22	33	25 to 40
Salt	2	2.3	1.8	1.8	2.17

The amount of water used in the dough influences the ease or difficulty in handling and the tenderness of the finished product. When too little liquid is used the mixture is crumbly and difficult to form into a dough that can be rolled and moved into the pan. The smaller the per cent of water used, however, the more tender the finished product. An excess of water results in a tough crust. The goal, therefore, is to determine the correct amount of water to use with a specific fat and flour mixture to form a dough that can be handled with reasonable ease. Milk may be used as the liquid in pastry, or for richer pastry a combination of eggs and milk. Salt in the formulas is to season and bring out the flavor, and is to be used in an amount satisfying to general taste.

Methods of Handling

The temperature of the ingredients at the time of mixing has some influence on the tenderness of the crust. Fats at room temperature coat the flour particles more quickly than do those that are firmer because of low temperature. The warm fats yield a tender pastry but one that is less flaky. When using room temperature materials (70°F), if flakiness is desired, it is best to have materials measured before starting the mixing, so that the entire mixing procedure can be completed without requiring the fat and flour mixture to stand for a time before the water is added. This has extra importance for doughs that have a high per cent fat. When warm fat permeates (or soaks into) flour particles excessively, flakiness is lessened, and the pastry tends to be mealy.

The action in combining the fat with the flour should be one of cutting or breaking the fat into the flour. When working with soft fats it is well to use the pastry knife attachment on the mixer. The beater is satisfactory when blending in a firm grained lard. Use low speed and allow to blend until the fat particles are the size of large rice grains, with a small amount that are the size of peas. Dissolve the salt in the water and pour entire amount in a manner to distribute it over the exposed area of the dry ingredients. (When mixing by hand, add liquid in small amounts to different dry areas, while mixing and tossing to moisten). Mix at low speed until the water is mixed in (approximately 40 seconds). Use care to avoid overmixing, for excess mixing develops gluten strands that make the pastry less tender. The mixer should be stopped when the water and dry ingredients are just barely combined enough to leave the bowl.

Dough is the most tender that is shaped and baked immediately after mixing, using a minimum of flour for rolling. Excess flour for rolling increases toughness. The dough is easier to handle if it is allowed to stand for 30 minutes. It continues to hydrate more uniformly, become more elastic and firm if held for 24 hours. Those who utilize a machine for shaping, rather than hand rolling, tend to feel that the slightly tougher quality of dough that has been held is justified by the greater ease in handling.

The two most popular sizes for pies are 8 inches and 9 inches in diameter. For service, the 8-inch pie is commonly cut into six portions and the 9-inch into six or seven portions per pie. When preparing crust for 8-inch pies, allow 5 ounces for the bottom crust and 4 ounces for the top. For the 9-inch pies, scale 8 ounces of dough for the bottom and 6 ounces for the top crusts.

Convenient utensils for cutting crusts can be fashioned from metal bands formed into hoops that resemble giant cookie cutters, of the specific diameter for the crusts to be used. Crusts rolled, cut, and stacked with parchment or plastic between them can be refrigerated until the time when they are needed. When assembling two-crust pies, it is desirable to use a marker for the top crust that will guide the cutting of uniform portions.

A uniform thickness of $\frac{1}{8}$ inch is desirable for crusts. Good appearance and proper fills calls for the bottom crust to be well seated in the pan. Allow the weight of the dough to fall into position by lifting the edges and dropping the dough against the sides and bottom of the pan, pressing it into position with a minimum of pulling. Pulling may result in the dough being thinner in certain areas and if very tender will result in breaking. Dough that is stretched when fitting it into the pan tends to shrink more during baking.

After cutting and filling the bottom crust, moisten the pastry around the rim with water to help in sealing it to the top crust. Fill the pie and place the top crust, in which perforations have been made for venting steam during cooking. Cut the edges, allowing a projection over the edge of the pie of approximately $\frac{1}{2}$ inch. Fold the projecting edge evenly under the bottom edge and flute the two edges together in an attractive pattern. This will seal the edges to prevent the filling from boiling out during baking.

The dough for single crust pies should be fitted into the pans loosely with a minimum of stretching. It is well to cut the edge at least $\frac{1}{2}$ inch beyond the rim. This provides dough that can be folded back under the edge and fluted to add depth to the pie. Prick sides and bottom with a fork to prevent steam blisters and buckling from steam formed during baking. A light weight foil pan pressed into the single shell helps in shaping, and may be left in place during baking until the crust is set. It may then be removed to permit browning.

Baking

Two different temperatures are frequently required for best results in the baking of pies. The pastry is best when baked in a hot oven, and the filling often requires longer cooking at a moderate temperature. For filled pies, it is best to place them in an oven preheated to 400 or 425°F for the first 10 minutes of baking time, and then to reduce the heat to 350°F for the remainder of the baking time. Single crusts should be baked at 425°F for 10 minutes or until nicely browned.

The custard-type fillings that are baked in the crust, present the problem of soaking the crust. Both the custard quality and the crispness of the crust are best when the two are baked separately and then put together. When baked together, a crust prebaked to the point of browning before the crust is filled, lessens soaking and results in a crust with a better color. This permits the crust to be well set at a high temperature and the custard cooked at a suitably low temperature. When baked and cooled the custard should have a jelly-like consistency that shows a tender, glistening surface free from weeping when cut and holds its shape.

CHOU PASTE

Cream puffs and eclairs are generally classified as French pastries. Because of the large proportion of eggs contained in the paste and the fact that they are usually filled with a whipped cream, Bavarian cream or pastry cream (cream pie filling), they may also be listed as egg and milk desserts. The pastry of which the puffs are made is known by the French as *pate a chou*, or cabbage pastry, because of its rounded shape. Chou (pronounced "shoe") paste is simple to prepare when the right proportion of ingredients and techniques are followed.

CHOU PASTE FOR CREAM PUFFS AND ECLAIRS		50 puffs (2 oz)!
Ingredients	Weight	Volume
Flour, all-purpose	1 lb, 2 oz	1 qt
Water	2 lb	1 qt
Salt	1 tsp	1 tsp
Sugar	½ oz	1 tbsp
Butter or margarine	1 lb	2 c
Eggs, fresh	1 lb, 12 oz	12 large or 14 medium

PROCEDURE:

1. Heat water, salt, sugar and butter or margarine until it is boiling rapidly and the butter is melted. Add all of the flour at one time, remove from the heat and stir the mixture rapidly until the mixture is smooth and leaves the sides of the pan.
2. Add the eggs, one or two at a time, to the hot mixture, stirring vigorously after each addition until well mixed.
3. Stir the entire mixture until it is smooth and shiny. Permit the paste to cool for 20 or 30 minutes. (The paste may be refrigerated for shaping later.)

*4. Portioning may be done with a No. 20 scoop or a pastry bag, using 2 ounces of paste per portion. Place on a greased baking sheet.

5. Bake in preheated oven at 400°F for 40 to 45 minutes until golden in color and adequately dried. (Crispness requires sufficient time for drying.)

*The 2-ounce puffs are an average size for dessert service. Tiny puffs, for use with appetizers or afternoon teas, may be made with a level teaspoonful of paste.

If the puffs are to be cut open for filling, the cutting should be done while they are warm, as they are more likely to break when they are cool and crisp. They should be filled shortly before service. The dessert puffs will require approximately $\frac{1}{2}$ cup of filling each or a total of $1\frac{1}{2}$ gallons.

PIE FILLINGS

Pies represent a partnership which depends in similar degree on the quality of the pastry and the filling for popular acceptance. They are grouped as to type into one crust and two crust pies. Preference ratings tend to be influenced by the calorie conscientiousness of the particular diners, and the skill of individual bakers in producing specific kinds of pie. Two-crust apple pie is commonly regarded as a general favorite.

Single Crust Pies

The fillings for these pies may be thickened with a starch, eggs or gelatin (review use of these materials in Chapter 7). The pastry shells may be filled with fruit and topped with a glaze or whipped cream. Foods may be folded into whipped cream and the filling firmed by freezing. The single crust pies may have a topping of whipped cream, streusel, or meringue (see *egg foams* in Chapter 13). Many combinations are possible to give interest and variety to these pies.

When preparing starch mixtures, flour, cornstarch, tapioca, or one of the waxy starches may be used. The starch granules in sufficient water, when heated, swell and thicken the mixture. Certain materials and conditions interfere with this gelatinization. The starch requires a certain amount of water for maximum swelling. Sugar introduced in the mixture may rob the starch of some of the liquid which it needs for complete gelatinization, and as a result the mixture may not become as thick as desired. When preparing mixtures that call for a large amount of sugar, it is well to reserve part of the sugar for addition after the starch is fully cooked.

Rapid heating of the starch mixture produces better thickening than slow heating. It is best to moisten the starch in a small amount of cold liquid and stir it into the hot liquid. Stirring, though continuous, should not agitate the material in such a manner as to break up the starch granules. Cook only until the raw taste has disappeared and the mixture has become translucent.

The addition of acid during the preparation of starch thickened fillings, as for lemon pies, is likely to result in hydrolysis that breaks up the starch molecules. As a result, the mixture will not thicken. When preparing such pies or puddings do not add the lemon juice or acid and butter until the starch mixture has thickened and has been removed from the heat.

The starches differ in the amount of viscosity upon cooling. It is desirable for cream pies to be tender and at the same time firm enough to hold an attractive shape. The waxy starches thicken at relatively low temperatures, thin when heated above 195°F and increase only slightly in viscosity upon cooling. The wheat flour and cornstarch pastes thicken sufficiently upon cooling to present a firmer appearance, and are more satisfactory for cream pie fillings.

There are strong reasons for not holding or storing these starch-thickened pastries, some of which pertain to palatability and appearance and some to good sanitation practice. There is a point upon cooling when the pastry filling is at its best in flavor, consistency, and appearance. Retrogradation of wheat or corn starch that causes excess firmness and some syneresis takes place on standing. The mixtures containing milk and eggs are mediums that favor the growth of bacteria. If it is necessary to hold these foods for any appreciable period it should be done under refrigeration.

When cooking fillings containing eggs, the chief hazards to quality are too-high temperatures and cooking for too long a time. When adding eggs to starch thickened mixtures, it is best procedure to cook the starch and then add the eggs just before removing the mixture from the fire. A small amount of the hot mixture should be added to the beaten eggs, and then the eggs added gradually to the hot mixture, while stirring constantly. They should remain on the heat just long enough to cook the eggs (about 5 minutes). The eggs continue to cook in a large volume of hot mixture, even after it is removed from the heat. Overcooking of soft or stirred custards is likely to cause curdling.

Scalding the milk helps to shorten the cooking time when making custards (see *custards* in Chapter 13). Either fresh milk or the nonfat dry milk may be used. Little difference has been observed in custards made with A, B, or C grade eggs. The oven temperature for baked custards should be 350°F, and when baked in cups, the cups should be set in a pan of boiling water. The baked custard should be considered done when a knife inserted into the custard at a point half of the distance from the rim to the center of the pie comes out clean. The center of the pie may still be soft, but will continue to cook with the heat in the pie, after it has been removed from the oven. A soft or stirred custard is cooked sufficiently when it begins to coat the spoon, and should be removed from the heat immediately.

Figure 23.2   Pearadise eggnog pie in a graham cracker crust. (Courtesy of Pacific Kitchen.)

Gelatin, either plain or flavored, is used for body or thickening of chiffon pies. Flavored gelatin may be dissolved in boiling water, but the plain gelatin requires hydration in cold liquid before adding it to hot liquids. It should be allowed to cool until it thickens slightly and then the other ingredients folded into it. The gelatin should be fluid enough that ingredients can be blended in smoothly without having rubbery bits of gelatin. Beaten egg whites or whipped cream may be folded into the mixture to give extra lightness, or the whipped cream may be used as a garnish. The chiffon pie should be firm enough to hold its shape when set and at the same time be light and tender.

Two Crust Pies

The fruit selected for two crust pies should have sufficient flavor and acid to give character to the pie, and to make a pleasant harmony with the bland, rich crust. Many fruits lack desired acidity, and palatability is improved by the addition of lemon juice, pineapple juice, orange juice, or vinegar. Summer fruits, like rhubarb, cherries, berries and tart apples, have sufficient acid to provide sparkle to the flavor. Raisins, without added acid, are overly sweet. Late storage apples tend to have lost their snap and require lemon or orange juice to improve the flavor. Sour cream may be used to add acid and to enrich flavor. Fruits that are too sharply acid may be mellowed by using eggs for thickening as well as increasing the amount of sugar.

Various thickening agents are used for the juicy fruits. The one most commonly used in institutions and in homes is cornstarch. Many use tapioca for berry and some apple pies. Many bakers and commercial restaurants favor waxy maize starch or a gum such as carboxy-methyl-cellulose or gum tragacanth, because of their greater translucency and shine. The waxy maize thickens at a relatively low temperature and on cooling retains a viscosity similar to that which it has when hot. Since it does not break down with freezing and thawing it is especially desirable for pies that are to be frozen and held for delayed service.

PUDDINGS

There is no classification of foods that offers a wider variety, range of richness, and interesting psychological reactions on the part of patrons than puddings. Puddings may be low in calories or extremely rich. They may be as simple as a scoop of ice cream or as fancy as the most elaborate sundae or baked Alaska. They may be easy or complicated to prepare. Puddings may be served in bowls, sauce dishes, sherbet glasses, fruit shells, maryanns, pastry crusts, meringue shells, casseroles, or flat plates. They may be as light as a whip and snow or as rich and solid as a plum pudding. When well chosen a pudding can supply nutritional balance and a satisfying finish to an otherwise inadequate meal.

The techniques to be observed in the preparation of puddings of different types have been described under other headings in this text. Classification of puddings according to the type of preparation includes those that (a) contain milk and eggs, (b) are thickened with starch, (c) or gelatin, (d) are made chiefly of fruit, and that (e) are prepared like biscuits, (f) or cake. Examples from the different types have been selected for discussion here to serve as a review of some of the principles which have been presented.

Egg and Milk Desserts

Custards, souffles, and cereal thickened puddings are popular examples of the egg and milk desserts. The quality and food safety is best at the time when preparation has been completed. It is advisable, therefore, to prepare them only in quantities required for immediate use. The cereal thickened puddings may be varied greatly by the addition of different ingredients and ways in which portions are prepared.

BAKED CUSTARD		50 servings (4 oz)
Ingredients	Weight	Volume
Milk, fresh whole	10 lb	5 qt
Eggs, whole	2 lb, 4 oz	1¼ qt
Sugar, granulated white	1 lb	2⅛ c
Salt	1 tsp	1 tsp
Vanilla	½ oz	1 tbsp
Nutmeg	2 tsp	2 tsp

PROCEDURE:

1. Heat milk to scalding temperature.
2. Beat eggs just enough to blend yolk and white (avoid foaming).
3. Stir sugar, salt and flavorings into eggs.
4. Add hot milk slowly to egg mixture, stirring constantly.
5. Fill 50 custard cups that have been set in serving pans (12 × 18 × 2¼ inches).
6. Place pans with cups of custard in the opening of oven preheated to 325°F.
7. Pour boiling water in the pans surrounding the cups of custard, and move them carefully into the oven.
8. Bake in oven at 325°F for 30 minutes, or until knife inserted into a custard comes out clean. Avoid overcooking. Remember that there will be enough heat in the custard and cups to continue cooking after removal from the oven.

VARIATIONS:

1. *Raisin Bread Pudding*: Reduce milk to 9 pounds and eggs to 2 pounds and add 1 pound seedless raisins and 1 pound dry bread cubes to hot mixture.
2. *Coconut*: 1 pound coconut to hot mixture.
3. *Coffee*: Omit vanilla and nutmeg and add ½ cup instant coffee to hot milk.
4. *Rice and Raisin*: Use half of the recipe. Blend hot mixture with 1 pound rice steamed with 3 ounces of butter and 1 pound of raisins.

A *soft custard* may be prepared by the above recipe, by reducing the quantity of milk to 8 pounds (4 quarts). Omit the nutmeg and add the vanilla when the custard is removed from the heat. The procedure of preparation should be as follows: Scald the milk in the top of a double boiler or kettle that provides controlled heat. Beat eggs just enough to blend yolks and whites and add sugar and salt. Slowly pour a small amount of hot liquid into egg mixture, stirring constantly. Gradually add egg mixture to hot milk in double boiler or kettle. (Water in double boiler bottom should be at a slow simmer.) Stir constantly while cooking, and immediately remove from the heat when the custard begins to coat the spoon. Blend in flavoring and pour into molds or set aside to cool.

Floating Island Pudding calls for separating the eggs and using some cornstarch for part of the thickening. The cornstarch gives increased stability to the custard.

FLOATING ISLAND PUDDING   50 servings (4 oz)

Ingredients	Weight	Volume
Milk, fresh whole	8 lb	4 qt
Sugar, granulated white	1 lb	2⅛ c
Salt	⅓ oz	2 tsp
Cornstarch	2½ oz	½ c
Egg yolks	1 lb, 2 oz	2 c (24 yolks)
Vanilla	½ oz	1 tbsp
Egg whites	1 lb, 8 oz	3 c (24 whites)
Sugar	12 oz	1½ c

PROCEDURE:

1. Scald the milk. Blend 1 pound of sugar, salt and cornstarch.
2. Stir a small amount of hot milk into cornstarch mixture and add gradually to scalded milk in top of double boiler or heat-controlled kettle.
3. Cook until partially thickened. Add a small amount of the hot mixture to well-beaten yolks, and add yolks gradually to hot mixture stirring constantly. Continue cooking until thickened.
4. Remove from the heat. Stir in vanilla. Pour portions into sherbet glasses or other serving dishes, or dip using a No. 12 scoop.
5. Beat whites and sugar until whites form soft peaks (Foam stage 2). Drop, in amounts appropriate for single portion garnish, on top of pans containing hot water. Bake in a moderate oven until set.
6. Lift meringues from the water with a fork and place on top of the portioned custard.

Figure 23.3   A fluffy jellied custard in a coconut crust with a pear half and garnish of toasted coconut. (Courtesy of Pacific Kitchen.)

CHOCOLATE SOUFFLE	50 portions (2 oz)	
Ingredients	Weight	Volume
Butter or margarine	8 oz	1 c
Flour, pastry	5½ oz	1⅓ c
Salt	1 tsp	1 tsp
Milk	3 lb	1½ qt
Chocolate, unsweetened, melted	8 oz	1 c
Sugar	10½ oz	1⅓ c
Egg yolks	10 oz	1¼ c
Egg whites	1 lb, 2 oz	2¼ c
Cream of tartar	2 tsp	2 tsp
Sugar	10½ oz	1⅓ c
Vanilla	¾ oz	1½ tbsp

PROCEDURE:

1. Make a sauce of the first four ingredients. Melt the butter or margarine in double boiler. Stir in flour and salt until well blended. Add milk and cook until the flour has lost its raw flavor and the sauce is thickened.
2. Add melted chocolate.
3. Beat egg yolks until thick and lemon colored; add $10\frac{1}{2}$ ounces of sugar gradually and then a small amount of the hot sauce to the egg yolks. Add the egg yolk mixture to the hot sauce and cook until the yolks are well heated.
4. Beat the egg whites and cream of tartar to a foam, and gradually add $10\frac{1}{2}$ ounces of sugar. Continue beating until the meringue is quite stiff but not dry.
5. Fold the chocolate sauce gently into the meringue until well mixed.
6. Portion into souffle dishes or custard cups, or scale $2\frac{1}{3}$ pounds into each of 3 ungreased pans (approximately 10 in. × 12 in. × $2\frac{1}{2}$ in.).
7. Bake at 325°F for 1 hour or until a knife when inserted will come out clean. The souffle is delicious when served with whipped cream garnished with slivered almonds or chocolate shot.

Variation in flavor, texture and cost can be obtained by reducing the quantity of eggs used for thickening the milk mixtures and substituting a cereal. Flour[1] and cornstarch,[1,2] are commonly used for cream puddings with some eggs for richer flavor. Delicious eggless cream puddings[2] are possible, also. Tapioca,[1,2] farina,[2] rice, cornmeal,[2] grape-nuts[2] and shredded-wheat biscuits[2] used as thickening agents offer interesting variety.

Principles of egg cookery apply to desserts that call for egg foams, such as meringues, souffles and whips. The whips, made with egg whites beaten until stiff and flavored with pureed fruit (dried cooked apricots, prunes or fresh berries) may be served chilled or portioned into custard cups and baked in a similar manner to custards. The souffles are similar to the whips, except that they usually have a starch-thickened mixture that adds to their richness and stability folded into the whipped egg whites.

Soft meringues for puddings or pies may be made with equal weights of egg whites and sugar. The meringues are more tender when 1 pound, 4 ounces of sugar is used per 1 pound of egg whites, but greater leakage is likely to result. The whites should be beaten at high speed from beginning to end of beating.

[1] Sina Faye Fowler, Bessie Brooks West and Grace Severance Shugart, Food For Fifty (Dessert Section), New York: John Wiley & Sons, Inc., 1961.
[2] Margaret E. Terrell, Large Quantity Recipes (Dessert Section), Philadelphia: J. B. Lippincott Company, 1951.

Add the cream of tartar at the outset and begin adding the sugar as soon as the egg whites have reached the foam stage. Stop beating *before* the whites have stiffened to "stage 3" stiff foam. Arrange on the hot pies or puddings, so that the heat of the hot mixture will help to firm the meringue. Select an oven temperature for finishing according to preferred results. A high temperature (425°F) yields a more tender and less sticky product, and a moderate temperature (325 to 350°F) results in lower leakage of fluid from the meringue.

The hard meringues, such as those used for shells, contain twice as much sugar as egg whites by weight. The cream of tartar should be added before beating. The beating should be done at high speed and the sugar added gradually after the whites have reached the early foam stage. The beating should be continued to "stage 3" stiff foam. They may be shaped with a spoon, scoop or preferably with a pastry tube in the desired size and form, on brown paper. Baking temperature affects results. When baked at a moderate temperature (315°F for 50 minutes) the meringues are moist and chewy, and at a low temperature for a longer period (275°F for 90 minutes) they dry out and become more dry and crisp.

Fruit Desserts

The dessert course is often a desirable place to use fruit in menus. The fruit may be in its whole, fresh, original form or made into a delectable pudding. The cooked fruits may be served simply as a sauce or have a topping of some type added. A topping of bread or cake crumbs, fat and seasonings make it into a betty. If a crumbly mixture of flour, fat and seasonings are used it is called a crisp. When the flour, fat, and seasonings are blended into a crust that is placed on top of the thickened sauce it becomes a cobbler. Rich biscuit dough or muffin and cake batters with fruit arranged on top and baked are called cakes, such as apple cake, prune or cherry cake.

Interest and variety may be developed by blending fruit with gelatin. If the mixture is not whipped it is known as jellied fruit or molded fruit. If it is whipped and egg whites are used for added lightness it becomes a whip or chiffon pudding. Whipped cream may be folded into the whipped fruit, milk and gelatin mixture for a Bavarian cream. If milk and eggs are combined with gelatin in a custard type pudding it is a Spanish cream. Gelatin desserts meet with special favor at the beginning of a fruit season when the specific fruit is very high in cost. It is a means of giving customers a satisfying taste of the "first fruit of the season" at a comfortable price. Strawberry Bavarian Cream, jellied rhubarb, orange Spanish Cream and pineapple whip can add interest and sparkle to menus lacking in the appetizing qualities of fruit.

DATE OATMEAL TORTE   48 portions (3 in. sq)

Ingredients	Weight	Volume
Rolled oats, quick cooking	14 oz	1 qt
Hot water	2 lb	1 qt
Butter or margarine	1 lb	2 c
Brown sugar	1 lb, 12 oz	1 qt, firmly packed
Granulated sugar	14 oz	2 c
Eggs	12 oz	1½ c
Cinnamon	4 tsp	4 tsp
Soda	4 tsp	4 tsp
Baking powder	2 tsp	2 tsp
Salt	2 tsp	2 tsp
Ground cloves	2 tsp	2 tsp
Ripe bananas, mashed	1 lb, 8 oz	2 c
Walnuts or pecans, chopped	10 oz	2 c
Dates, chopped	15 oz	2 c

PROCEDURE:

1. Pour hot water over the oatmeal, stir and set aside to cool.
2. Cream the butter or margarine with sugar, blend in eggs and beat until smooth.
3. Sift dry ingredients together and add gradually to creamed mixture, beating at medium speed until blended.
4. Blend in mashed bananas, oatmeal, nuts and dates.
5. Pour into greased baking sheet (18 × 26 inches) and bake in a moderate oven (350°F) for 40 minutes. Allow to cool in the pan. Cut into squares and serve with whipped cream garnish.

Cake-Type Puddings

Tortes, steamed puddings, simple cakes with rich sauces, fruit and nut filled mixtured, and rich, highly flavored cakes come under this classification. Boston Cream Pie, a plain cake with a thick layer of pastry cream filling and Cottage Pudding, a square of plain cake served with a sauce, are common examples of cake puddings. Brownie Pudding and Raisin Pudding[1] are baked

[1] Margaret E. Terrell, *Large Quantity Recipes*, p. 358.

Figure 23.4   A pretty shape adds interest to steamed puddings. (Courtesy of Pacific Kitchen.)

Figure 23.5   Pear-topped oatmeal cake. (Courtesy of Pacific Kitchen.)

with a sauce. Recipe directions are most often according to the conventional method for mixing cakes. Many of the steam puddings can be baked or steamed by covering in the oven. Certain of the cakes can be steamed in a steam cooker or cooked in a microwave oven successfully, if a brown color or the flavor of a caramellized surface are not desired.

Tortes are usually described as rich cakes containing fruit and nuts. They may be made with a simple, plain cake batter baked in thin layers and stacked with flavorful fillings of fruit, nuts and/or cream. Hard meringues may be formed in cake size layers, and after baking put together with various fillings. Rich nut and fruit filled batters, such as date torte may be broken and folded into whipped cream and served in sherbet glasses. A rich torte, such as the following recipe may be made like a cake and cut into squares for service.

Refrigerated Desserts

Most of the refrigerated desserts include wafers, cookies, graham crackers or cake crumbs as a part of the recipe, and are put together with whipping cream and flavoring materials. Whipped gelatin, marshmallows and beaten egg whites may be used to increase volume and give lightness to such mixtures. Cream pie filling (pastry cream) can be made into a simple refrigerator pudding by pouring it into a mold on top of a layer of graham cracker crumbs and sprinkling some of the crumbs on top. If molded in a pan it can be cut into squares after chilling and served with a whipped cream and a fruit, nut or chocolate garnish.

Refrigerator puddings provide an attractive way to utilize leftovers, save labor time, provide variety and dress up simple foods. The average large kitchen, on occasion, has choice leftover desserts that are insufficient in quantity for service to a group or need freshening or change of form. Ingenuity in combining a few simple materials can result in popular desserts with a minimum of labor. Danish Apple Pudding,[1] which combines cake crumbs, spices, applesauce and coconut, serves as an example of such a pudding.

SUGGESTED LABORATORY EXPERIENCE

1. Prepare plain pastry as follows, and compare quality of crusts: (a) use formula containing pastry flour with 44% lard, 33% water, and 2% salt; (b) use formula containing pastry flour with 50% lard, 33% water, and 2% salt; (c) use formula containing all-purpose flour with 59% lard, 22% water and 2% salt; (d) use formula containing bread flour with 75% hydrogenated fat, 22% water and 2% salt.
   Mix each formula in the mixer at low speed, using 1 minute to blend flour and fat and 40 seconds for adding water and salt. Divide the dough from each formula and roll and bake part immediately and refrigerate the remainder, and roll and bake it the following day.
2. Prepare formula (b) as stated above, except in mixing allow the mixer to operate for $1\frac{1}{2}$ minutes after adding the water. Compare with results from 40 second mixing time.
3. Repeat formula (b) doing all of the mixing by hand.
4. Compare time required and quality of crusts rolled by hand and with a dough roller. Fit crusts into pans, trim and shape edges and prick for single crust pies.
5. Prepare a cream pie and a double-crust fruit pie.
6. Prepare chou paste, scale and bake cream puffs and eclair shells.
7. Prepare soft custard using (a) fresh milk and fresh eggs and (b) egg solids and nonfat milk solids.
8. Prepare chocolate souffle.
9. Plan for and prepare a refrigerator pudding.

REVIEW QUESTIONS AND ANSWERS

1. What are the score points used in judging pastry quality?

Texture 60%, flavor 15%, appearance, shaping 10%, and baking 15%.

2. What characterizes a satisfactory texture?

Crispness, tenderness, and flakiness.

[1] Margaret E. Terrell, *Large Quantity Recipes*, p. 370.

3. What factors influence these qualities?

The proportion and type of ingredients and the method of manipulation.

4. What is the best flour to use?

One that is fairly low in protein, such as pastry flour.

5. Is it better to use lard or a fat that contains an emulsifier? Why?

Lard, which yields a flakier pastry because it does not permeate the mixture so quickly and completely.

6. Why is a low protein flour used?

Fewer and less tough gluten strands.

7. Is the weight of a given measure of lard and hydrogenated fat the same?

Lard weighs 8 ounces per cup and hydrogenated fat weighs 7 ounces per cup.

8. In calculating percentages should weight or volume be used?

Calculate percentages in formulas by weight.

9. Should cake flour be used for pastry to lessen formation of gluten strands?

Some gluten strands are required for flakiness.

10. How do gluten strands promote flakiness?

Steam formed in baking separate the gluten strands into layers.

11. What factors cause toughness?

High protein in the flour, low fat in the formula, excess water in the formula, overmixing after the water is added, excess flour when rolling and holding time before baking.

12. Approximately how thick should a crust be rolled?

$\frac{1}{8}$ inch.

13. What is likely to cause unevenness of crust thickness?

Lack of uniform pressure when rolling, and pulling when placing in the pan.

14. How can the edges of two-crust fruit pies be sealed to prevent leakage during baking?

Moisten edges of the bottom crust before placing the top crust and crimping them together with the edge of the top crust folded under the edge of the bottom crust.

15. What is the purpose of pricking edges and bottom of a single crust?

To prevent blistering or buckling due to the formation of steam in the crust.

16. What is a chou paste and how is the word pronounced?

It is pronounced as "shoe," and is a rich dough leavened by steam that is used for cream puff and eclairs.

17. What materials commonly used in starch thickened mixtures may affect thickening?

Sugar may rob the starch of sufficient water for complete gelatinization and acid may hydrolize the starch and prevent it from thickening.

18. How can this be prevented?

When the recipe calls for a high percentage of sugar, reserve a part for addition after the mixture has thickened. Add acid, such as lemon juice, after the mixture has thickened.

19. What are the hazards in holding pastry creams?

They change to a less desirable consistency, and are a medium favorable to the growth of bacteria.

20. Why is the milk heated when mixing custards for baking?

In order to shorten baking time.

21. What is the test for doneness of (a) a baked custard, (b) soft custard?

(a) A baked custard is done when a knife inserted in the custard comes out clean. (b) A soft custard is done when it coats a spoon or knife.

22. How does the preparation of a plain and a flavored gelatin differ?

Plain gelatin should be hydrated in cold water before being dissolved in hot water, and hot water may be added immediately to flavored gelatin.

23. What characteristics should pie fruit possess?

Enough strength of flavor and acidity to give character to the pie, balancing the qualities of the rich, bland pastry.

24. What qualities of waxy maize starch make it desirable for fruit pies?

Clarity and shine of the mixture, viscosity that is not too stiff when cool, stability when frozen and reheated.

25. Is it equally desirable for cream pies?

The viscosity is not sufficiently rigid to cut well as a pastry cream.

26. What thickening agents are used in the preparation of milk desserts?

Eggs, starches, cereals, cake and cookie crumbs and gelatin.

27. How do the proportions of egg white and sugar differ for soft meringues and hard meringues?

Equal parts of sugar and egg white are used for soft meringues and twice the amount of sugar to egg whites is used for hard meringues.

28. For what is each type of meringue used?

Soft meringues are used as pie topping and pudding garnish and the hard meringues for meringue shells and tortes.

29. What is a torte?

A rich cake or a cake or meringue put together with a rich filling.

30. What is a refrigerator pudding?

Mixtures that are arranged together and permitted to chill thoroughly in the refrigerator.

BIBLIOGRAPHY

American Home Economics Association, "Handbook of Food Preparation," Publication by the American Home Economics Assoc., 1600 Twentieth St., N.W., Washington, D.C., 1964.

Amendola, Joseph, The Bakers' Manual for Quantity Baking and Pastry Making, New York: Ahrens, 1966.

Anetsberger Brothers, Inc., "Proofing Manual," and model descriptions, Northbrook, Illinois.

American Institute of Baking, "Enriched Bread," "Cutting Guide for Batter Cakes," "Frozen Bread Dough," "Freezing Unbaked Fruit Pies," 400 East Ontario St., Chicago, Illinois.

Charley, Helen, "Food Study Manual," New York: The Ronald Press, 1961.

Colborne Manufacturing Co., Bench Dough Roller, 157 West Division Street, Chicago, Illinois.

Detecto Scales Inc., Catalog Number 556 and Series 1100, Brooklyn, New York.

Eberhardt-Nussex-Import Co., Bun and Roll Divider and Moulder, West Chester, Pa.

Fowler, Sina Faye, Bessie B. West, and Grace S. Shugart, "Food for Fifty," New York: Wiley, 1961.

General Mills Inc., "Betty Crocker's Cook Book," New York: McGraw Hill.

General Mills, Inc., Cooking As An Art Series.

Griswold, Ruth M., "The Experimental Study of Foods," Boston: Houghton Mifflin, 1962.

Halliday, Evlyn G., and Isabel T. Noble, "Hows and Whys of Cooking," Chicago: The University of Chicago Press.

The Hobart Manufacturing Co., Instruction Manuals for Mixers and "The Use of Hobart Mixers Attachments and Accessories," Troy, Ohio.

Kotschevar, Lendal H., "Quantity Food Production," Berkeley, California: McCutchan Publishing Corporation, 1964.

Lever Brothers Co., Consumer Service Dept., "Create a Finer Cake The New One Bowl Way," New York.

McClain, D. R. & Son, "Instruction and Suggestions for the Care and Use of the Rol-Sheeter," 4730 Durfee Avenue, Pico Rivera, California.

Merck & Co., "Enrichment," Merck and Co., Rahway, New Jersey.

Moline Inc., Pastry Production Cutters, P.O. Box 308, Duluth, Minnesota 55801.

The Pillsbury Company, "The Pillsbury Family Cook Book," "Cake and Frosting Mixes," and "Dinner Roll Make-up Methods," Minneapolis: The Pillsbury Company, 1963.

Standard Brands Incorporated, Educational Service, "Our Daily Bread," "When You Bake," "The Basic Cake Formula," Room 1212, 420 Lexington Avenue, New York.

Terrell, Margaret E., "Large Quantity Recipes," Philadelphia: J. B. Lippincott, 1951.

Wheat Flour Institute, "From Wheat to Flour," "Bread Basics," 309 West Jackson Blvd., Chicago.

Appendix

EQUIVALENT MEASURES OF FOODS

Food	Weight	Volume
Beverages		
Cocoa	1 lb	4 c
Coffee, regular	1 lb	5 c
Coffee, instant	2 oz	1 c
Postum	4 oz	1¼ c
Sanka, instant	2 oz	1 c
Tea	1 lb	6 c
Cereals and Cereal Products		
Barley	1 lb	2 c
Bran, All	2 oz	1 c
Bread crumbs, dry	1 lb	1 qt
Bread slices	1 lb	16 slices
Cake crumbs, soft	1 lb	1¼ qt
Cracker, crumbs	1 lb	6 c
Crackers, graham	1 lb	40
Crackers, small, square, sodas	1 lb	108
Cracked wheat	1 lb	3½
Cornflakes	1 lb	4 qt
Cornmeal	5½ oz	1 c
Cornstarch	5 oz	1 c
Farina	6 oz	1 c

Food	Weight	Volume
Flour, bread, sifted	1 lb	4 to 4½ c
buckwheat	5 oz	1 c
Cake, sifted	1 lb	4 to 5 c
Graham, sifted	1 lb	3½ to 4 c
Pastry, sifted	1 lb	4 to 5 c
Rye, sifted	1 lb	4 to 5 c
Whole wheat	1 lb	3 to 4 c
Hominy grits	1 lb	2½ to 3 c
Macaroni, cut, uncooked	18 oz	1 qt
Macaroni, cooked	1 lb	2½ c
Noodles, cooked	1 lb	2¾ c
Noodles, uncooked	12 oz	1 qt
Oatmeal, raw	1 lb	5 c
Rice, cooked	1 lb	2½ c
raw	7 oz	1 c
Spaghetti, raw, broken	1 lb	1 qt
Soya flour	1 lb	5 to 6 c
Tapioca, quick cooking	1 lb	2⅔ c

Dairy Products

Food	Weight	Volume
Butter or margarine	1 lb	2 c
Cheese, cheddar, grated	1 lb	1 qt
cottage	1 lb	2 c
cream, Philadelphia	8 oz	1 c
slices, Pullman or loaf	1 lb	16 to 20 slices
Cream	8 oz	1 c
Milk, evaporated	1 lb	2 c
fresh	1 lb	2 c
dry, instant	1 lb	5½ c
nonfat, regular	1 lb	4 c
sweetened, condensed	11 oz	1 c
Ice cream	4½ to 6 lb	1 gal
Sherbet	6 oz	1 c

Eggs

Food	Weight	Volume
Large eggs in shell	1½ lb	1 doz

Food	Weight	Volume
Eggs (*continued*)		
Medium eggs, whole, uncooked	1¾ oz	1 egg
whole	1 lb	2 c (9 eggs)
whites, uncooked	1 oz	1 white
whites	1 lb	2 c (16 whites)
yolks, uncooked	¾ oz	1 yolk
yolks	1 lb, 2 oz	2 c (22 to 23 yolks)
whole, cooked, chopped	1 lb	3 c
Dry eggs, whole, packed	6 oz	1½ c + 1⅞ c water equals 1 doz eggs
whites	1½ oz	¾ c + 1½ c water equals 1 doz whites
yolks	4 oz	1 1/16 c + ⅝ c water equals 1 doz yolks
Meringue, 8 9-in. pies	1 lb	2 c (16 to 18 whites)
Fats and Oils		
Butter, melted	8 oz	1 c
Oil	1 lb	2⅛ c
Shortening, hydrogenated	7 oz	1 c
melted	7 oz	1 c
Suet, chopped	1 lb	3¾ c
Fish		
Clams, meat	1 lb	2 c
Crabmeat, flaked	1 lb	3 c
Oysters, shucked	1 lb	2 c
Salmon, canned	1 lb	2 c
fresh, flaked	1 lb	3 c
Shrimp, cooked, peeled, and cleaned	1 lb	3¼ c
Tuna, canned	1 lb	2¼ c
Fruit		
Apples, fresh	1 lb	3 No. 113
peeled and sliced	1 lb	1 qt

Food	Weight	Volume
Fruit (*continued*)		
peeled and diced	1 lb	3½ c
canned, sliced for pies	¾ to 7 lb	1 No. 10 can (13 to 14 c)
canned slices	1 lb	2 c
Applesauce	1 lb	2 c
Apple, dry nuggets	1 lb	6½ c
dry, slices, regular	1 lb	4⅓ c
low moisture, slices	1 lb	8 c
Apricots, fresh	1 lb	8 medium
canned, halves	1 lb	2 c
dried	1 lb	3¼ c
Avocados, medium size	1 lb	2 to 2½
Bananas, whole AP, medium size	1 lb	about 2½ to 3
diced	1 lb	3 c
mashed	1 lb	2 c
Blackberries, fresh	1 lb	1 qt
canned	6½ lb	1 No. 10 can (7½ c drained)
Blueberries, fresh	1 lb	3½ c
canned	1 lb	2¼ c
Canteloupe	1½ lb	1 small
Cherries, fresh, stemmed	1 lb	2⅓ c
canned	4 lb, 6 oz	1 No. 10 can, drained, 10 c
canned, drained	1 lb	2¼ c
candied	1 lb	3 c, 120 cherries
maraschino, drained	1 lb	50 to 60 cherries
Citron, chopped	1 lb	2½ c
Cranberries, fresh	1 lb	1 qt
cooked, pulp	1 lb	2 c
canned sauce	6½ to 7 lb	1 No. 10 can (12 to 14 c)
dehydrated	1 lb	8½ c
Currants	4½ oz	1 c
Dates, regular, whole	1 lb	2½ c
pitted, chopped	1 lb	3 c
low moisture	1 lb	3½ c

Food	Weight	Volume
Figs, canned	6½ to 6¾ lb	1 No. 10 can, 8 c drained
dry	1 lb	1 qt
Fruit cocktail	about 6½ lb	1 No. 10 can, 8½ c drained
Grapefruit, fresh	1 lb	1 fruit, 12 sections
canned	7 oz	1 c
Grapes, whole, stemmed	1 lb	3 c
cut	1 lb	2⅔ c
Lemons, size 300	1 lb	4 lemons
juice	8 oz	1 c
rind grated	1 oz	3 tbsp
thinly sliced	5 oz	1 c
Oranges, size 150	1 lb	2 oranges
diced	1 lb	2½ c
grated rind	3 oz	1 c
ground rind	4 oz	1 c
Peaches, fresh, medium	1 lb	4 peaches
fresh, sliced	1 lb	3 c
canned, halves, 40 count	1 lb	6½ halves
canned, halves	about 6½ lb	1 No. 10 can (8 c drained)
canned, sliced and juice	8 oz	1 c
canned, spiced whole	1 lb	7 small
frozen, sliced	30 lb	50 c
dried, halves	1 lb	3 c
low moisture	1 lb	4 c
Pears, fresh	1 lb	3 medium
cooked, diced	7 oz	1 c
canned	about 6½ lb	1 No. 10 can (8 c drained)
Pineapple, canned slices	1 lb	8 to 12 slices
crushed	9 oz	1 c
tidbits, drained	8 oz	1 c
frozen chunks	30 lb	50 c
Plums, fresh	1 lb	8 plums
canned purple	about 6½ lb	1 No. 10 can (8 c drained)

Food	Weight	Volume
Prunes, 30/40	5 oz	1 c
cooked	1 lb	2⅓ c
pitted, chopped	8 oz	1 c
canned	about 6½ lb	1 No. 10 can (9½ c drained)
Pumpkin, cooked	1 lb	2½ c
Raspberries, fresh	1 lb	3¼ c
canned	about 6½ lb	1 No. 10 can (6 c drained)
frozen	30 lb	50 c
Raisins	1 lb	3 c
Rhubarb, raw, cut	1 lb	1 qt
frozen	26 lb	50 c
Strawberries, fresh	1 lb	3 c
frozen, sliced and syrup	1 lb	2¼ c

Meat

Food	Weight	Volume
Beef, raw, ground	1 lb	2 c
cooked, diced	1 lb	3 c
dried, packed	1 lb	3¾ c
Lamb, raw, ground	8 oz	1 c
cooked, diced	1 lb	3 c
Pork, fresh, ground	8 oz	1 c
sausage	1 lb	2 c
bacon, diced	1 lb	2¼ c
bacon slices, raw	1 lb	18 to 22 slices
ham, cooked, diced	1 lb	3 c
ham, raw, ground	1 lb	2 c
ham, sliced Pullman	1 lb	8 slices
Bologna	1 lb	10 slices
Frankfurters	1 lb	8 to 10
Liverwurst	1 lb	30 slices
Salami	1 lb	20 slices

Miscellaneous

Food	Weight	Volume
Baking powder	1 oz	2⅔ tbsp
Cream of tartar	1 oz	3 tbsp

Food	Weight	Volume
Chocolate, grated	4 oz	1 c
melted	8 oz	1 c
Gelatin, flavored	1 lb	2 c
Gelatin, granulated	4 oz	1 c
granulated	1 oz	4 tbsp
Marshmallows	8 oz	1 qt (40 large)
Sherry	8 oz	1 c
Soda	1 oz	2⅓ tbsp
Water	8 oz	1 c
White sauce	9 oz	1 c
Yeast, compressed	½ oz	1 cake
compressed	8 oz	16 cakes

Nuts

Food	Weight	Volume
Almonds, slivered	5⅓ oz	1 c
whole	1 lb	3 c
Coconut, medium shred	1 lb	6 c
Coconut, ground or fine shred	2½ oz	1 c
Filberts or hazel nuts, shelled	1 lb	3 c
Peanut butter	9 oz	1 c
Peanuts, chopped	1 lb	4 c
Pecans, chopped	5 oz	1 c
whole	4 oz	1 c
English walnuts, chopped	15 oz	4 c
whole	1 lb	4¾ c

Poultry

Food	Weight	Volume
Chicken, fryers, whole	2½ lb (average)	1 fryer
breast, raw	4.8 oz	½ breast
drumstick	3 oz	1 drumstick
thigh	3.2 oz	1 thigh
wings	2.5 oz	1 wing
stewed, diced	2.5 oz	1 c
livers, raw	1 lb	5 portions
Duck for roasting, AP	1 lb	1 portion
Turkey, cooked, diced	2.7 oz	1 c

Food	Weight	Volume
Relishes and Dressings		
Catsup and chili sauce	9 to 10 oz	1 c
Cooked salad dressing	8 oz	1 c
French dressing	1 lb	2⅛ c
Horseradish, grated	4 oz	1 c
prepared	8 oz	1 c
Mayonnaise	1 lb	2 c
Mustard, prepared	10 oz	1 c
Olives, small	1 lb	3½ c (135 count)
chopped	6 oz	1 c
Pickles, chopped	1 lb	3 c
relish	8 oz	1 c
slices, drained	6 oz	1 c
Vinegar	8 oz	1 c
Worcestershire sauce	9½ oz	1 c
Spices and Extracts		
Allspice, ground	1 oz	5 tbsp
Celery salt	1 oz	2 tbsp
seed	1 oz	4 tbsp
Chili powder	1 oz	6 tbsp
Citric acid	1 oz	2⅔ tbsp
Cinnamon, broken stick	1 oz	⅓ c
ground	1 oz	4 tbsp
Cloves, ground	1 oz	5 tbsp
whole	3 oz	1 c
Curry powder	1 oz	4 tbsp
Ginger, candied, chopped	8 oz	1 c
ground	1 oz	4 tbsp
Mustard, ground	1 oz	4 tbsp
seed	1 oz	3 tbsp
Nutmeg, ground	1 oz	4 tbsp
Paprika	1 oz	4 tbsp
Pepper	1 oz	4 tbsp
Peppercorn	1 oz	6 tbsp
Poppy seed	5 oz	1 c
Sage, ground	1 oz	8 tbsp
Salt	1 oz	2 tbsp
Tumeric, ground	1 oz	3⅓ tbsp

Food	Weight	Volume
Vanilla and other extracts	1 oz	2 tbsp

Sugar, Syrups, and Sweets

Food	Weight	Volume
Corn syrup	10 oz	1 c
Honey	12 oz	1 c
Jam and jelly	12 oz	1 c
Molasses	11 oz	1 c
Maple syrup	10 oz	1 c
Sugar, brown, packed	1 lb	2⅔ c
cubelets	5.5 oz	1 c (41 cubes)
granulated	1 lb	2⅛ c
powdered	1 lb	3½ c

Vegetables

Food	Weight	Volume
Asparagus, fresh, cut	1 lb	1 qt
fresh, stalks	1 lb	20 stalks
canned cuts, drained	1 lb	2½ c
Beans, baked	1 lb	2 c
small white or limas, dry	1 lb	2½ c
limas, fresh	1 lb	2¼ c
string, cooked	1 lb	3½ c
Bean sprouts	1 lb	1 qt
Beets, cooked, diced	1 lb	2⅓ c
Cabbage, raw, shredded	12 oz	1 qt
cooked, drained	1 lb	3½ c
Carrots, cooked, diced	1 lb	3 c
raw, ground	1 lb	3¼ c
Cauliflower	12 oz	1 medium size head
Celery, diced, raw	1 lb	1 qt
Corn, cream style	1 lb	2 c
whole kernel, drained	1 lb	2⅓ c
Chives	2½ oz	1 c
Cucumbers, diced	1 lb	3½ c
50 to 60 slices, ⅛ in.	1 lb	2 to 3 large
Eggplant, diced	1 lb	1 qt
sliced, 4 in. diameter	1 lb	8 slices
Garlic	1 oz	8 cloves
Lettuce, shredded	8 oz	1 qt
head, medium size	12 oz	1 head, 8 c

Food	Weight	Volume
Mushrooms, fresh, chopped	1 lb	6 c
canned	1 lb	2 c
Onions, chopped	1 lb	3 c
grated	1 oz	1⅓ tbsp
sliced	1 lb	1 qt
dehydrated	1 lb	9½ c
Parsley, chopped	1 oz	¾ c
Parsnips, cooked, diced	1 lb	2½ c
mashed	1 lb	2 c
Peas, cooked, drained	1 lb	2 c
frozen	1 lb	3 c
split, dry	1 lb	2⅓ c
Peppers, green	1 lb	6 medium
green, chopped	1 lb	1 qt
Pimiento	6 oz	1 c
chopped	8 oz	1 c
Potatoes, chips	3 oz	1 qt
sweet, cooked	8 oz	1 c
sweet, raw	1 lb	3 medium
white, cooked, diced	1 lb	2¼ c
mashed	7 oz	1 c
whole	1 lb	4 medium
dehydrated granules	7 oz	1 c
flakes	3½ oz	1 c
Pumpkin, cooked	1 lb	2½ c
Radishes, whole, cleaned	1 lb	1 qt
Rutabagas, cooked, diced	1 lb	3½ c
Sauerkraut, raw	1 lb	3 c
Spinach, canned	1 lb	2 c
freshly cooked	1 lb	2½ c
raw	1 lb	5 c
Squash, summer, cooked	1 lb	2 c
winter, cooked, mashed	1 lb	2 c
Tomatoes, canned	1 lb	2 c
fresh, peeled, quartered	1 lb	3 c
fresh, diced	1 lb	2½ c
Turnips, raw, diced	1 lb	3½ c
Watercress	1 oz	1 c

FOOD QUANTITIES FOR 100 PORTIONS

Item	Description	Portion Size	Amount for 100 Portions
Bakery Products			
Biscuits, baking powder	2 in., dough ready for baking		10 lb
Bread, white	1½-lb loaf, 24 slices	1 slice	5 loaves
whole wheat	1-lb loaf, 16 slices	1 slice	7 loaves
Pullman	2-lb loaf, 36 slices	1 slice	3 loaves
rolls	doz	1 roll	8½ doz
Bread sticks	32 count/lb	2 sticks	6¼ lb
Brown bread	canned, 11 oz/can	1 slice ½ in.	16 cans
Cakes, layer	2 layer, 10-in., butter	1/16	6¼ cakes
angel	10-in.	1/12	8½ cakes
sheet	18 x 26 in. pan, cut 6 x 10	1/60	1⅔ sheets
batter	butter cake, ready for baking		15 lb
Cookies, choc. chip	8-lb box, 160/box	2 cookies	1¼ boxes
fig bars	7-lb box, 108/box	2 cookies	4 boxes
gingersnaps	8-lb box, 260/box	2 cookies	1 box
choc. graham	5-lb box, 100/box	2 cookies	2 boxes
home made	¾ to 1½-oz each	2 cookies	17 doz
Crackers, Graham	5-lb box, 140/box	2 crackers	2 boxes
oyster	7-lb box, 751/box	6 crackers	1 lb
saltines	7-lb box, 475/box	2 crackers	½ box
soda	7-lb box, 238/box	2 crackers	1 box
Griddle cakes	batter ready for baking, using No. 20 dipper		13 to 15 lb
Muffins, bran	batter ready for baking, using No. 20 dipper		18 lb
corn	batter ready for baking, using No. 20 dipper		13 lb
plain	batter ready for baking, using No. 20 dipper		13 lb
Pies, 8-in.	fruit or cream	1/6	18
9-in.	fruit or cream	1/7	15

Item	Description	Portion Size	Amount for 100 Portions
Bakery Products (*continued*)			
crust	dough for 15 double crusts, 9 in.		13¼ lb
filling	fruit, 3½ c/9 in.		14 qt
	pie custard, 1 qt/9 in. pie		15 qt
	cream, 2½ c/9 in. pie		10 qt
	meringue, 2 lb egg whites		4 lb
Pudding	approx. 4 oz or ½ c each		25 lb
Beverages			
Coffee, instant	20 teacups c/oz	6¼ oz	5 oz
regular	2 gal water/lb	6¼ oz	2½ lb
Fruit juice	concentrates (3 water to 1 juice)	6 oz	8½ lb
	canned, 46 oz	6 oz	13 cans
	fresh punch	6¼ oz	5 gal
Tea	1 tsp/c	6 oz	½ lb
Cereals			
Barley	pearl, for use in soup		3 lb
Cornmeal		4 oz	4 lb
Farina		4 oz	4 lb
Flour	for bread or rolls		5 to 6 lb
	for roux for soup or sauce		1 to 1½ lb
	cake and cookies		2 to 4 lb
Macaroni or spaghetti	for casseroles	⅔ c	6 lb
Noodles	for casseroles	⅔ c	5 lb
Oatmeal	breakfast cereal	½ c	5 lb
Prepared	all-bran, flakes, krispies	1 oz	6¼ lb
Rice	for casseroles	⅔ c	6 lb
	steamed	½ c	7 lb
Tapioca	cream pudding	4¼ oz	1¾ lb
	soup		12 oz
Wheatena	breakfast cereal	½ c	4 lb

Item	Description	Portion Size	Amount for 100 Portions
Dairy Products and Eggs			
Butter	pats/lb 48, 60, 72 or 90	1 pat	1½ to 2 lb
Cheese	entree mixtures		4 to 6 lb
	sandwich slices	1 oz	6¼ lb
	cottage, salad, No. 16 scoop		12 lb
	blue for dressing		1 lb
	cream, garnish	½ oz	3 lb
	dessert, blue, gruyere, cream	¾ to 1 oz	4 to 6 lb
Cream	coffee, (19 to 22%) or ½ and ½ (12%)	1 tbsp	1½ qt
	whipping, for desserts	1 tbsp	1½ qt
Eggs	fresh, whole	1 large	8½ doz
	frozen, whole, 10/lb whites, 16/lb yolks, 24 to 28/lb	1	10 lb
	dried, whole, 1 lb sifted is 5⅓ c (plus 5⅓ c water equals 2⅔ doz eggs)	½ oz	3¼ lb
Ice cream	12% fat, bulk, 4½ lb/gal	½ c No. 16 rounded	3¼ gal
	sherbet, 4% fat	½ c	3¼ gal
Milk	Grade A, pasteurized, homogenized	½ pt	100
	fluid, for soup	1 c	4 to 6 gal
	for sauces and puddings		1 to 2 gal
	dry, nonfat, 1 lb/fluid gal		
	evaporated, dilute with equal part water		
Fats and Oils			
Lard	for pie pastry	⅐ of 9 in.	4 lb
Margarine	for table use, 72 pats/lb	1 pat	1½ lb

Item	Description	Portion Size	Amount for 100 Portions
Fats and Oils (*continued*)			
	for sauces, cakes, cookies		1 to 2 lb
Salad oil	vegetable		3 to 5 qt
Salad dressing	French	1⅓ tbsp	2 qt
	mayonnaise	1 tbsp	1½ qt
Shortening	hydrogenated, 426°F smoking point		1 to 2 lb
	for frying, amount required by kettle size		
Fish			
Fillets and steaks	4 portions/lb	4 oz	25 lb
Whole	cod, halibut, salmon, sword, bluefish, king-fish, sea trout	4 oz ½ or 1 fish	50 lb 75 lb
Frozen	cod, flounder, perch, salmon	4 oz	25 lb
Shellfish, clams	for chowder	1 c	1½ gal
	steamed, medium size	4	34 doz
crab	cracked	8 to 10 oz	50 to 60 lb
	meat for cocktail	1¼ oz	8 lb
	meat for salad	2 oz	12½ lb
oysters	fried, 125 to 150/gal	3	2½ gal
	fried, 175 to 200/gal	5	3 gal
	for stew	1 c	2 gal
scallops	fried, 175 count	5	3 gal
shrimp	fried, large 25 to 30/lb	5	20 lb
	salad	½ c	17 lb
	cocktail	1¼ oz	8 lb
Canned, salmon	1-lb cans	½ c	16 cans
tuna	13-oz can, salad	½ c	16 cans
	13-oz can, casserole	⅔ c	9 cans
Fruits			
Apples, dessert	medium size, 113/box	1	1 box
pie	9-in., peeled, sliced	½ pie	28 lb
salad	Waldorf	½ c	22 lb

Item	Description	Portion Size	Amount for 100 Portions

Fruits (*continued*)

Item	Description	Portion Size	Amount for 100 Portions
sauce	fresh, A.P.	½ c	33 lb
	canned, No. 10	½ c	4 cans
Apricots, fresh	12 medium/lb	2	17 lb
canned	pie, No. 10, 9-in. pie	⅐ pie	4 cans
	sauce, halves, No. 10 can	½ c	4¼ cans
	sauce, halves, No. 2½ can	½ c	15 cans
dried	sauce	½ c	8 lb
	pie, 9-in. pies	⅐ pie	12 lb
Avocado	medium size	½	50
	salad, 3 slices		10
Bananas	3 medium/lb	1	34 lb
	pie or pudding	5 slices	8 lb
Blackberries,	fresh	3 oz	10 qt
blueberries and	canned, No. 10, 9-in. pies	⅐ pie	4 cans
boysenberries	frozen, 25 lb can		1½ cans
Cherries, sweet	15 lb box	3 oz	20 lb
sour	pie, 9 in., canned, No. 10	⅐ pie	4 cans
	pie, 9 in., frozen, 30 lb can	⅐ pie	1¼ cans
Cranberries	fresh, sauce	¼ c	6 lb
	canned sauce, No. 10 (12 c)	¼ c	2¼ cans
Currants	cakes, puddings		1 to 3 lb
Dates	pudding		8 to 10 lb
	cookies		5 to 6 lb
Figs	pudding		6 to 8 lb
Grapes	Emperor, Ribier, Thompson seedless 28 lb box	4 oz	1 box
	salad		14 lb
Grapefruit	breakfast, 64 or 80 size	½	50
	salad, 12 sections/fruit	5 sections	41
	mixed salads	4 oz	25
Lemons	No. 360s, 8 wedges per fruit	1 wedge	13
	lemonade, 2 oz juice per glass	1 glass	9 doz

Item	Description	Portion Size	Amount for 100 Portions

Fruits (*continued*)

Item	Description	Portion Size	Amount for 100 Portions
	juice, ¾ c/lb AP		
Limes	4 wedges/lime	1 wedge	25
	limeade, 1/lime	1 glass	9 doz
Mangoes	fresh, cubed or diced	½ c	25 lb
Melons,	45 size	½	50
cantaloupes	salad slices		12
	fruit cup		10
	balls		30
casabas,			
honeydew and	6/crate	⅛ melon	13
persian	fruit cups and salad		3½
watermelon	approximately 35 to 40 lb	16 oz	3
Nectarines	fresh	1	25 lb
Oranges	150, 176 or 200 size	1	100
	salad, 9 sections/orange	5 sections	56
	salad, 6 slices/orange	3 slices	50
	mixed salad or fruit cup		3 to 4 doz
Peaches	fresh, 4 to 5 oz ea.	1 peach	25 to 30 lb
	canned halves, No. 10, 40 count	2 halves	25 cans
	canned halves, No. 2½, 6 count	1 half	17 cans
	pie, No. 10, 9-in. pie	½ pie	4 cans
	frozen sliced, 30 lb can	½ c	1 can
Pears	5 to 6 oz ea.	1 pear	34 to 38 lb
	salad, 8 to 10 slices/pear	3 slices	30 to 35 lb
	sauce, canned No. 10, 40 count	½ pear	3 cans
	canned No. 2½, 6 count	½ pear	17 cans
Pineapple, fresh	dessert, cubed	½ c	35 lb AP
canned	chunks and tidbits, No. 10	½ c	4 cans
	No. 2½	½ c	15 cans
	crushed, No. 10, 9 drained	½ c	4¼ cans
	sliced, No. 10	1 large	4 cans
	No. 2½ can, 8 slice	1 slice	15 cans
	No. 2 can, 12 slice	2 slices	17 cans

Item	Description	Portion Size	Amount for 100 Portions
Fruits (*continued*)			
frozen	chunks, 30 lb can	½ c	1 can
Plums, fresh	medium size, approximately 8/lb	2 plums	25 lb
canned	purple prune, No. 10, sauce	½ c	4½ cans
	No. 2½ cans	½ c	15 cans
Pomegranate	garnish	5 seeds	5 fruits
Prunes	dried, 30 to 40/lb	5 prunes	15 to 16 lb
Raisins	seedless, cake, cookies, or pudding		1 to 3 lb
	seedless, pie, 9-in.	⅓ pie	12 lb
	sauce	½ c	9 lb
Rhubarb	sauce	½ c	27 lb
	pie, 9-in. pie	⅓ pie	20 lb
Strawberries, fresh	dessert	4 oz	26 lb
	garnish, 30 berries/pt	1	4 pt
	pie, chiffon, 9-in. pies	⅓ pie	11 lb
frozen	sauce, 30-lb can	½ c	1 can
Tangerines	dessert fruit, approximately 144/crate	1	100
	salad, 10 sections/fruit	5 sections	50
Meats			
Beef, fresh	brisket, bone-in	3 oz	50 lb
	boneless	3 oz	34 lb
	chuck, boneless, pot roast	3 oz	35 lb
	ground (80% lean)	4 oz raw	25 lb
	hamburger (75% lean)	3 oz	25 lb
	heart	3 oz	48 lb
	kidneys	3 oz	48 lb
	liver	3 oz	28 lb
	oxtails for soup		6 lb
	ribs for roast, 7-rib standing	3 oz	50 lb
	round roast	3 oz	28 lb
	rump, bone in	3 oz	32 lb

Item	Description	Portion Size	Amount for 100 Portions
Meats (*continued*)			
	sirloin roast	3 oz	40 lb
	short ribs, 4 oz cooked meat/lb AP		50 lb
	steaks—flank	3 oz	25 lb
	loin strip	8 to 10 oz	50 to 60 lb
	top round	3 oz	27 lb
	swiss, boneless rounds	3 oz	27 lb
	sirloin		45 lb
	tenderloin	5 oz (raw)	45 lb
	stew, boneless chuck	⅔ c	20 lb
	tongue	3 oz	25 lb
Beef, canned	corned, 6-lb cans	3 oz	4 cans
	with barbecue sauce	2 oz	25 lb
	with gravy	2 oz	25 lb
Beef, dried	chipped	2 oz	10 lb
Lamb	breast, bone in, braised	8 oz (raw)	50 lb
	chops, cut 3 to 1 lb, loin	1 chop	34 lb
	cut 5 to 1 lb, rib	2 chops	40 lb
	ground lamb	2 oz	21 lb
	leg roast, bone in	3 oz	34 lb
	shoulder roast, bone out	3 oz	26 lb
	stew, boneless chuck	⅔ c	20 lb
	bone in	1 c	33 lb
	shanks for braising, 16 to 20 oz ea.	1 shank	100 to 125 lb
Pork, fresh	chops, loin, cut 3 to 1 lb	1 chop	33 lb
	rib, cut 4 to 1 lb	1 chop	25 lb
	ground	2 oz	22 lb
	ham with bone	2 oz	23 lb
	without bone	2 oz	18½ lb
	loin roast, bone in	2 oz	27 lb
	boneless	2 oz	18½ lb
	shoulder roast, bone in	2 oz	27 lb
	boneless	2 oz	18½ lb
	sausage	2 oz (cooked)	27 lb
	spareribs	2 oz (meat)	49 lb

Item	Description	Portion Size	Amount for 100 Portions
Meats (*continued*)			
cured (mild)	bacon, sliced (24 slices/lb)	2 slices	8½ lb
	(18 to 20 slices)	2 slices	12 lb
	Canadian bacon (20 slices/lb)	2 slices	10 lb
	ham, bone in	2 oz	23 lb
	boneless	2 oz	20 lb
	shoulder, picnic, boneless	2 oz	18 lb
	ground ham patty	2 oz	17 lb
Pork, canned	ham, sliced	2 oz	17½ lb
	luncheon meat, 6-lb cans	2 oz	13 lb
Variety meats, Bologna	10 slices/lb	2 slices	20 lb
frankfurters	10/lb	2 links	20 lb
	8/lb	1 link	13 lb
liverwurst	30 slices/lb	3 slices	10 lb
salami	20 slices/lb	2 slices	10 lb
Veal	chop, loin, with bone, 2-oz cooked meat	1 chop	21 lb
	rib, with bone, 2-oz cooked meat	1 chop	24 lb
	cutlet, with bone	4 oz	40 lb
	without bone	3 oz	33 lb
	ground	3 oz	30 lb
	chuck, boned, rolled	3 oz	35 lb
	leg, roast, boneless	3 oz	30 lb
	liver, calves	3 oz	22 lb
	stew, boneless, 2-oz cooked meat	⅔ c	20 lb
Meat products	canned beans with frankfurters	⅔ c	45 lb
	beef goulash	¾ c	38 lb
	beef stew	¾ c	38 lb
	chili con carne	¾ c	38 lb
	hash	¾ c	38 lb
	meat balls with gravy	4 balls	36 lb
	tamales with gravy	1 c	50 lb

Item	Description	Portion Size	Amount for 100 Portions
Nuts			
Almonds	slivered, for sauces, entrees, and vegetables	¼ oz	1½ lb
	whole, salads and desserts	½ oz	3 lb
Coconut, dried	shredded	¼ c	3½ lb
Pecans	whole or pieces, cookies and cakes	¼ to ½ oz	1 to 3 lb
Peanuts	whole or chopped, cookies	½ oz	3 lb
Peanut butter	sandwiches	1½ tbsp	2½ qt
		No. 30 scoop	8 lb
Walnuts, English	whole or broken, cookies, salad		1 to 4 lb
Poultry			
Cornish hens	weight 1¼ to 1½ lb ea.	1 hen	125 to 150 lb
Ducks	wt 4 lb ea.	¼	100 lb
Fryers, parts	breast halves 4.8 oz (average)	½	30½ lb
	drumstick and thigh, 6.1 oz ea.	1	38½ lb
	drumstick, 3 oz ea.	1	19 lb
	thigh, 3.2 oz ea.	1	20 lb
	wings, 2.5 oz ea.	2	32 lb
whole	1¾ to 2 lb average	½	75 to 100 lb
	2½ to 3 lb average	¼	75 lb
Stewing chicken	dressed, 2-oz cooked chicken/portion	⅔ c	37 lb
Turkey, whole	dressed, 3 portions/lb AP	2 oz	34 lb
breasts	whole, excluding skin	2 oz	26 lb
	halves, excluding skin	2 oz	28 lb
	halves, with skin	2 oz	23 lb
legs	drumstick and thigh, with skin	2 oz	26 lb

Item	Description	Portion Size	Amount for 100 Portions
Poultry (*continued*)			
roll	frozen, to be cooked	2 oz	21 lb
	frozen, cooked	2 oz	14 lb
Relishes			
Catsup	hamburgers, sauces, etc.	1 oz	No. 10 can
	14-oz glass bottle	2 tbsp	9 bottles
Chili sauce	hamburgers, sauces, etc.	1 oz	No. 10 can
	12-oz glass bottles	2 tbsp	10 bottles
French dressing	for salad	1½ to 2 tbsp	2 to 3 qt
Mayonnaise	for salad	1 tbsp	2 qt
Olives, green	whole	3	1 gal
ripe	whole or pitted	3	1 No. 10 can
Pickles		2 small	1 gal
Sugars, Syrups, and Jams, Jellies			
Sugar, brown	medium, 1 lb equals 2⅔ c		
cubed	box 250 cubes	2 cubes	2½ lb
granulated	1 lb equals 2⅛ c		
powdered	1 lb equals 3½ c		
Syrups, corn	10 oz equals 1 c or 12 tbsp		
grenadine	served with fruit	1 tbsp	2 qt
molasses	11 oz/c	1 tbsp	2 qt
pancake or	maple	2 tbsp	1 gal
Honey	12 oz/c, strained	2 tbsp	1 gal
Jam or jelly		1 tbsp	2 qt
Vegetables			
Artichokes	globe	1 medium	8½ doz
Asparagus	30# crate	3 to 5 stalks	38 lb
Beans, fresh	lima, shelled	½ c	20 lb
	green or wax	½ c	20 lb
canned	green or wax	½ c	4¼ #10 cans

Item	Description	Portion Size	Amount for 100 Portions
Vegetables (*continued*)			
	green limas or red kidney	½ c	4¼ #10 cans
frozen	lima, 2½ lb pkg	½ c	20 lb
	green or wax, 2½ lb pkg	½ c	20 lb
dried	small white, lima, red and blackeye	½ c	9¼ lb
Bean sprouts		½ c	4¼ #10 cans
Beets, fresh	topped	½ c	28 lb
canned	diced	½ c	4¼ #10 cans
	sliced	½ c	4½ #10 cans
	baby whole	3	4½ #10 cans
	shoestring	½ c	4¼ #10 cans
Beet greens		½ c	35 lb
Broccoli, fresh		2 med. spears	35 lb
frozen	spears, 2½ lb pkg	2 med. spears	10 lb
	cut or chopped, 2½ lb pkg	½ c	10 lb
Brussels sprouts, fresh		½ c	24 lb
frozen	2½ lb pkg	½ c	7½ lb
Cabbage	cooked wedges	1 wedge	24½ lb
	shredded	½ c	11 lb
	cut for slaw	½ c	16 lb
Carrots, fresh	topped, used for sliced or diced	½ c	24 lb
	for carrot strips	3 strips	17 lb
	for salad shreds	½ c	16 lb
canned	diced or sliced	½ c	4½ #10 cans
Cauliflower, fresh	for cooked flowerlets	½ c	35 lb
	salad pieces	¼ c	17½ lb
frozen	2½-lb box	½ c	20 lb

Item	Description	Portion Size	Amount for 100 Portions
Celery	for cooked cubed	½ c	24 lb
	for sticks, 4 × ½ in.	4 sticks	10 lb
	for salad, rings	½ c	20 lb
Celery cabbage	for salad, chopped	½ c	13 lb
Chard	untrimmed	½ c	36 lb
Chives	for seasoning		8 bunches
Corn, fresh	on cob, with husks	1 ear	50 lb
	on cob, without husks	1 ear	34 lb
canned	cream style	½ c	4½ #10 cans
	whole kernel	½ c	5 #10 cans
frozen	whole kernel, 2½ lb pkg	½ c	20 lb
Cucumbers	fresh, unpared, salad slices	3 oz	1½ doz
Eggplant	12 slices per 1½ lb fruit	3 oz	12½ lb
Endive, chicory,	French endive	3 to 4 spears	8 lb
escarole	curly	2 to 3 sprigs	12 lb
Kale, fresh	for cooking	½ c	19 lb
frozen	3-lb pkg	½ c	9 lb
Kohlrabi	cooked diced	½ c	40 lb
Lettuce, head	8 to 10 c/head	1 c	12 heads
	broken for tossed salad	½ c	12 lb
Bibb	6 to 8 c/head	1 c	18 heads
romaine	for tossed salads	½ c	9 lb
Mint	garnish	2 to 3 leaves	1 bunch
Mushrooms, fresh	sliced	½ c	24½ lb
	caps, (average) 20 caps/lb	1 cap	5 lb
canned	stems and pieces	½ c	4½ #10 cans
	buttons, 12½ oz cans	½	36 cans
Mustard greens		½ c	41 lb
Okra, fresh	sliced	½ c	22 lb
canned		½ c	5 #10 cans
frozen	3-lb pkg	½ c	9 lb
Onions, green	chopped for salad	¼ c	7½ lb
mature	chopped	½ c	20 lb
	sliced	½ c	14 lb

Item	Description	Portion Size	Amount for 100 Portions

Vegetables (*continued*)

Item	Description	Portion Size	Amount for 100 Portions
	whole or quartered, cooked		31 lb
Parsley	for garnish and seasoning		4 lb
Parsnips	cut in pieces	½ c	30 lb
Peas, fresh	in pod	½ c	51 lb
	shelled	½ c	25½ lb
canned		½ c	4½ #10 cans
frozen	2½-lb box	½ c	20 lb
Peppers, green	raw strips		12 lb
	chopped for salads		20 lb
	for stuffing	1 bell	25 lb
Pimientos, canned	chopped for seasoning		2 #10 cans
	chopped for seasoning		5 #2½ cans
Potatoes, sweet	candied	3 to 4 oz	25 lb
	baked	1 medium	36 lb
	mashed	½ c	35 lb
white	baked, size 2 to 3/lb	1	36 lb
	steamed	1	33 lb
	mashed	½ c	30 lb
canned	sweet or white	½ c	4½ #10 cans
Pumpkin, fresh	baked	2½-in. sq	50 lb
	mashed	½ c	43 lb
canned	whipped	½ c	4¼ #10 cans
	whipped	½ c	15 #2½ cans
Radishes, topped	relish	3	12 lb
Rutabagas	diced	½ c	25 lb
	mashed	½ c	35 lb
Sauerkraut		½ c	4¼ #10 cans
Spinach, fresh	untrimmed, for cooking	½ c	33 lb
	for salad	½ c	12 lb
canned		½ c	7 #10 cans
frozen	3-lb pkg	½ c	20 lb

Item	Description	Portion Size	Amount for 100 Portions
Squash, summer fresh	diced	½ c	29 lb
frozen	2½-lb pkg	½ c	10 lb
winter	acorn	½ squash	50 lb
fresh	hubbard, marblehead, butternut	2½-in. sq	45 lb
canned	mashed	½ c	4½ #10 cans
frozen	2½-lb pkg	½ c	20 lb
Tomatoes, fresh	small whole	1	25 lb
	salad slices	3 slices	25 lb
	diced	½ c	20 lb
canned	stewed	½ c	4½ #10 cans
Tomato paste	seasoning		3 #2½ cans
Tomato puree	seasoning		2 #10 cans
Turnips, fresh	diced	½ c	30 lb
Turnip greens	cooked	½ c	48 lb
Watercress	garnish	1 sprig	4 bunches

DEFINITION OF TERMS IN FOOD PREPARATION
with Pronunciation Guide for Foreign Terms

à la (ah-lah) French, meaning "in manner of."

à la carte (ah-lah-cart) French, menu item to order and priced separately.

à la mode (ah-lah-mohd) French, meaning "in the fashion," as pie with ice cream or beef marinated and braised.

allemande (ahl-mahnd) White sauce with stock, cream, egg yolk and lemon juice.

angelica Candied leafstalk of an herb that is used for dessert decoration.

antioxidant Substance capable of preventing oxidation in foods.

antipasto (ahn-tee-pahs-toe) Italian, "before the pasta." Refers to appetizers of fish, vegetables or cold cuts.

appetizer Small portion of food served before a meal or as a first course.

ascorbic acid (Vitamin C)—available in foods or in powder and tablet form.

aspic A jelly made with concentrated fish, meat or vegetable stock and gelatin.

au beurre (oh-burr) French, with or cooked in butter.

au gratin (oh-grah-tan) French, with topping of buttered crumbs and cheese, and browned.

au jus (oh-zhu) French, with natural juices of the meat.

baba French. Rich yeast cake, flavored with rum sauce or fruit juice.

bake Cook in the oven by dry heat.

barbecue Cook on a grill or spit over hot coals, basting with highly seasoned sauce. (May be done in the oven.)

baked Alaska Ice cream on sponge cake, entirely covered with meringue (to insulate) and browned quickly in a hot oven.

bar-le-duc Jam made from currants and honey. Originated in Bar-le-duc, France.

baron Double sirloin of beef.

baste Moisten meat while cooking with fat or liquid, to prevent drying out.

batter Flour and liquid mixture, possibly combined with other ingredients, thin enough to pour.

beat Mix ingredients rapidly with over and over motion with spoon, whip or beater, bringing under part to top and blending evenly. Purpose may be to make material smooth or to incorporate air.
Whole eggs, slightly beaten have yolks and whites mixed; well beaten, mixture is light and foamy.
Yolks, when slightly beaten merely breaks the shape; well beaten makes thick and lemon colored.
Whites, slightly beaten are foamy; well beaten are thick and will form peaks.

bearnaise (bay-ar-nayz') French. Sauce of egg yolks, vinegar, butter, onion, and spices.

bechamel (bay-sha-mel') French. White sauce made by stirring equal portions of chicken stock and light cream into a white roux.

beurre manie (burr-mahnee) Well blended mixture of butter and flour used to add thickening to hot sauces.

bisque (bisk) French. Puree of shellfish, meat or vegetables made into a thick soup, often with cream added. Ice cream dessert containing nuts, fruit or crushed macaroons.

blanch Immerse food in boiling water for varying length of time according to need, then into cold water. Done to loosen skins as with almonds or tomatoes, and to shrink bulky vegetables or to remove their pungency.

blanquette (blan-ket') French. White ragout of veal, lamb or chicken, with sauce of egg and cream and garnish of small onions and mushrooms cooked in court bouillon.

bland Smooth textured, mild flavored food; not stimulating to taste.

blini (blee-nee) Russian. Thin, light pancakes leavened with yeast and beaten egg whites.

boeuf (buff) French. Beef.

bonne femme (bon fem) French. Good home style soups and stews.

bombe (bahm) French. Melon-shaped mold of ice cream having center and outer layers of different color and flavors.

bordelaise (bawr-d'layz') French. Brown sauce with butter or marrow fat, meat stock and red or white wine, onion, carrot, bay leaf and other seasonings.

borsch (borsh) Russian. A mixed vegetable soup with a predominance of beets and served with thick sour cream.

bouchées (boo-cheez') French. Puff pastry patties, filled with various mixtures.

bouillabaisse (bou-yah-bes') French. A fish stew having five or six kinds of fish, white wine, garlic, parsley, tomatoes, saffron, pepper and bay leaf.

bouillon (boo-ee-yon) French. A clear, white meat stock.

bouquet (boo-kay') Volatile essential oils that give aroma.

bouquet-garni (boo-kay-garnee') French. Tied bunch of aromatic herbs, such as parsley, thyme, bay leaf, and rosemary, used for flavoring soups, stews and sauces, then removed.

braise (brays) French. Brown meat in small amount of fat, add a small amount of liquid and cook covered until tender.

brew (broo) Cook in liquid to extract flavor, as with beverages.

brioche (bree-ohsh') French. A rich, light, yeast bread used for rolls or babas.

broil Cook over or under direct heat as in a broiler or over live coals.

brochette, a la (bro-shet') French. Food arranged on a skewer and broiled.

brulé (bru-lay') French. Rich molded pudding with cream and egg yolks.

brunoise (broo-noyz) French. Finely shredded vegetables, such as carrots, turnips, leeks and celery for soups or sauces.

broth A thin soup or water in which meat or vegetables have been cooked.

buffet (boo-fay') French. A table, often tiered, displaying a variety of foods.

Café au lait (caw-fay'-oh-lay') French. Coffee served with hot milk.

canapé (can-ah-pay') French. An appetizer of meat, fish, egg or cheese arranged on some kind of a bread base.

candied Preserved or cooked with heavy syrup.

caper (kay'-per) Small pickled buds from wild caper bush, grown in France.

capon (kay'-pon) Castrated chicken, fed and grown to large size.

caramelize Melt and lightly brown granulated sugar.

cavier (cav-ee-ar') French. Salted roe of sturgeon or other large fish. May be black or red.

chantilly, a la French. Foods containing whipped cream, such as chicken a la chantilly or charlotte a la chantilly.

charlotte (shar'-lot) French. A dessert with gelatin, whipped cream and fruit or other flavoring, in a mold garnished with lady fingers.

chiffonade (shee'-fahn-ahd) French. With finely shredded vegetables, as in dressing.

chill Refrigerate until thoroughly cold.

choux paste (shoe paste) French. Cream puff batter.

chop Cut in pieces with knife or other chopping device.

chowder A thick soup of fish or vegetables and milk.

clarify Make clear by skimming or by adding egg white and straining.

cloche French. Glass bell used for covering food.

chutney (chut'-ni) A spicy relish made from several fruits and vegetables.

coat Cover entire surface with flour, fine crumbs, sauce, batter or other food as required.

coddle Simmer gently in liquid for a short time.

compote (kom'-poht) French. Stemmed serving dish or fruit stewed in syrup.

condiment (kon'-di-ment) Pungent seasoning, such as pepper, mustard, catsup or chutney.

consommé (kon-so-may') French. Clear broth made with chicken, veal or other meat.

cool Permit to stand at room temperature until heat is lost.

court bouillon (cort-boo-e-yon) French. Flavorful broth in which fish, meat and various vegetables are cooked.

cracklings Crisp pork bits after fat has been completely rendered.

cream Combine fat and sugar until completely blended and creamy.

creole Foods containing tomato, green pepper and onion.

crêpe (krayp) Thin, crisp pancakes.

crisp Make firm and brittle as in chilling vegetables or drying food in the oven.

croquette (crow-ket') Ground or chopped meat, fish or vegetables, bound together with thick cream sauce, formed into small cylindrical or cone shape, dipped in beaten egg and crumbs and fried in deep fat or baked.

croustade (krus-tad') A case or shell made of bread and toasted.

croutons (kroo-ton') Bread cubes, toasted or fried for use in garnishing soup or salad.

cube Cut into $\frac{1}{2}$-inch squares.

cuisinier (kwis-e-ner) French. Cook.

curry A spicy combination of tumeric and other spices and herbs, or a stew seasoned with this condiment.

cut in Cut fat into flour with knives or a blender until fat particles are of the desired size.

custard Egg, milk and other ingredients cooked slowly in a double boiler on top of the stove or baked at slow temperature in the oven, until thickened.

cutlet A slice from the leg, shoulder or rib of veal, lamb or fresh pork, or a croquette shaped like a cutlet.

dash Less than $\frac{1}{8}$ teaspoon of an ingredient.

deep-fat fry Fry in deep fat that completely covers the food.

demitasse (deh-mee-tahss') French. Small cup of black coffee served after dinner.

devil Prepare with hot seasonings or sauce.

dice Cut into $\frac{1}{4}$ inch cubes.

dot Scatter small bits of butter or margarine over surface of food.

dough A mixture of flour, liquid and other ingredients, thick enough to roll, knead or drop from a spoon.

drain Pour off liquid from the solids.

drawn butter Melted butter.

dredge Coat food by sprinkling liberally with flour or other mixture.

drippings Fat and liquid residue from frying or roasting meat or poultry.

dust Sprinkle lightly with flour.

duchess potatoes Mashed potatoes mixed with beaten eggs and forced through a pastry tube.

emulsify When small amounts of one liquid are finely dispersed in another, so as to be held in suspension, an emulsion is formed.

éclair (ay-klair') French. Finger shaped cream puff paste filled with whipped cream or custard.

eau (oh) French. Water.

enchilada (en-chee-lah'-dah) Mexican. Tortillas dipped in hot fat, then in hot sauce, filled with onion, lettuce and cheese, rolled up and topped with sauce, or made into a stack of three with filling between and topped with a fried egg.

en cocotte (ahn-ko-cot') French. In individual casserole.

entrée (ahn-tray') French. May be the main dish of an informal meal or a single dish served before the main course of an elaborate meal.

eviscerate To remove internal organs.

filet mignon (fee-lay'-mi-nyon') French. Slice from the tenderloin of beef.

fillet (fee-lay' or fil'et) French. Flat slice of lean meat or fish without bone.

flake Break into small pieces, usually with a fork.

flannel cake Thin, tender griddle cake.

flapjack A large pancake.

fold in Blend an ingredient into a batter by cutting into the batter with the spoon or spatula, turning and moving spoon or spatula toward edge of bowl and up, repeating the motion, turning the bowl until the ingredients are well blended.

fondant Sugar syrup cooked to the soft ball stage (234°F), cooled and kneaded until creamy.

fondue (fahn-du') Baked dish of eggs, milk, cheese and bread or a bread dip made by combining cheese and wine.

flan Custard; open tarts.

franconia potatoes Raw potatoes, pared and browned with the roast.

frappé (fra-pay') French. Mixture of fruit juices frozen to a mush.

French fry To cook in deep fat.

fricassee (frik-a-see') Meat or poultry, cut in pieces, browned and stewed in gravy.

frijoles (fre-hol'ayz) Mexican. Beans cooked with fat and seasonings.

fritter A batter containing meat, vegetables or fruit cooked by spoonsful in deep fat.

frizzle Pan-fry in small amount of fat until edges curl.

frost To cover with icing.

garnish Decorate food to make appearance more appealing, usually with another food that will add contrasting color or texture.

gherkin Small, cucumber pickle.

glacé (glah-say') 1. Coated with sugar syrup. 2. Frozen.

goulash (goo'lash) Hungarian. Thick beef or veal stew with vegetables and paprika.

grate Rub food against a grater to form small particles.

grease Rub lightly with butter or other fat.

grill Cook on a griddle over live coals or direct heat.

grind Put through a food chopper.

grits Coarsely ground corn or other grain.

gumbo A soup thickened with okra or file.

hasenpfeffer Rabbit stew cooked with wine and served with sour cream.

herbs Aromatic plants used for seasoning and garnishing foods.

hollandaise (hol'ahn-dayz) French, of Dutch origin. Sauce of eggs, butter, lemon juice and seasonings, served hot with vegetables or fish.

homogenize Process to break up fat globules, as in milk, so that they will remain evenly distributed throughout the liquid and not float to the top.

hors d'oeuvre (ohr-doe'vr) French. Small portions of meat, fish, poultry, nuts, cheese, olives or other foods served as appetizers before a meal or as the first course of a meal.

hush puppies Deep fried corn meal paste.

ice 1. Frozen dessert of fruit juice, water and sugar with gelatin or egg white. 2. Frost food.

ice cream Frozen dessert of cream, flavoring, sweetening and a stabilizer such as eggs or other solids.

icing A sugar mixture used for frosting cake or rolls.

Indian pudding Baked pudding with cornmeal, milk, brown sugar, eggs, raisins and flavoring.

jam A thick sugar and fruit mixture used as a spread.

Irish stew Lamb or mutton stew mixture.

jelly Fruit juice and sugar mixture congealed by pectin to form a clear spread.

julienne (shu-lee-en') French. Food cut into thin, long, match-like strips.

junket Milk dessert coagulated to custard like texture with rennet.

kebabs Marinated lamb and vegetables cooked on skewers.

kisses Small meringues.

knäckebröd (khnah-kah-broed) Scandinavian. Whole rye, flat, hard bread.

knead Work dough by stretching, folding and pressing and pushing with the knuckles or heel of the hand.

kosher Food handled according to Jewish religious customs.

kolachy (ko-lahch'-kee) Bohemian. Fruit-filled bun.

kuchen (koo-ken) German. A cake, such as coffee cake.

lait (lay) French. Milk.

lard 1. To insert strips of salt pork into lean meat to prevent dryness. 2. Fat from pork.

leavening Ingredient in batters and doughs that increases lightness and porosity by releasing or forming gas or steam during cooking.

leek Pungent onion-like bulb used for seasoning in soups and stews.

legumes Seed-pod vegetables such as beans, peas and lentils.

limpa (limp-a) Swedish. Bread.

lyonnaise (lee'oh-nayz) French. Sauteed with slices of onion.

macaroon Small cakes or cookies made from egg white, sugar and almond paste or powdered almonds.

macedoine (mah-say-dwan') French. Combination of fruits or vegetables cut in uniform pieces. Usually for salad or dessert.

maitre d'hotel (mai-tre-doh-tel') French. Head steward or cook.

marinade (mah-ree-nahd') Mixture of oil, acid and seasonings used to flavor and tenderize meats and vegetables.

marinate To let food stand in a marinade.

marjoram A flavoring herb.

marmalade Spread made from citrus peel and pulp.

marron (mah'rohn) A large sweet chestnut.

marzipan (mahr'zi-pan) Confection of confectioners sugar and almond paste, formed in fruit and vegetable shapes and colored.

Mask To cover completely with thick sauce, such as mayonnaise.

meringue (mah-rang') Stiffly beaten egg white and sugar mixture used as a dessert topping or for forming into cases or small cakes, and browned in the oven.

mèunière, à la (meh-nyair') French. Fish floured, sauteed in butter and served with butter sauce and lemon, sprinkled with chopped parsley.

mince To chop very fine.

minestrone (mee-ne-stroh'nay) A rich broth soup with beans, barley or pasta and vegetables, usually with cheese.

mirepoix (meerpwa) Vegetable mixture used in flavoring stock.

mix Combine ingredients by stirring.

mocha (moh'ka) Coffee flavor or combination of coffee and chocolate.

mornay (mohr-nay') French. Sauce of thick cream, eggs, cheese and seasonings.

monosodium glutamate (MSG) White crystalline material made from vegetable protein, used to enhance natural flavor in foods.

mousse (mooss) French. Frothy entrees or desserts made with whipped cream or beaten egg whites.

mulligatawny (mul-i-ga-taw'ni) East Indian chicken soup flavored with curry and other spices.

Neopolitan Dessert, such as ice cream, prepared in layers of different color and flavor.

Nesselrode (Russian) Desserts containing chopped candied fruits and nuts.

Newburg, a la With sauce of eggs, cream and sherry. Used with fish or shellfish.

pan-broil Cook in a hot skillet with very little fat, pouring off fat as it accumulates.

pan-fry Saute in a skillet with small amount of fat.

panocha, penuche (pah-noh'chah) Mexican. Candy made of brown sugar, cream and nuts.

parboil Boil until partly cooked.

parch Cook in dry heat until slightly browned.

pare Peel off outside with a knife.

parfait (pahr-fay') French. Frozen dessert of whipped cream, eggs, syrup and flavoring, frozen without stirring. May be ice cream layered into tall, steamed glasses with fruit or syrup.

paste Soft, smooth mixture of a dry ingredient and a liquid.

pasteurize To hold a liquid for a stated length of time at a temperature (140 to 180°F) that will destroy bacteria, as in pasteurizing milk.

pastrami (pahs-tram'-ee) Italian. Highly spiced corned beef brisket.

paté (pah-tay') French. 1. Pie or pastry. 2. Highly seasoned meat paste used as an appetizer.

paté de foie gras (pah-tay-d'fwah grah') Paste of fat goose livers.

patty shell Shell or case of pastry or puff paste used for individual portions of creamed mixtures, usually chicken or fish.

peel 1. Remove skin or outer surface. 2. Long handled, spade-like implement used for removing food from large ovens.

petite marmite (pe-teet-mahr-meet') French. A meat broth with meat and vegetables.

petits fours (pe-teet-foor') French. Fancy small cakes cut from sheet cakes, with melted fondant frosting and dainty decorations.

piece de résistance (pee-es de resee-stahns') French. The main course or special dish of the meal.

pilauf or pilau (pih-lahf') Turkish. Dish of rice boiled with meat, fish or poultry and seasoned with spices.

piquante (pee-kahnt') French. Sharply tart or highly seasoned.

pit The stone or pit in fruit or to remove stone in fruit.

pizza (peet'zah) Italian. Flat yeast bread covered with tomato and cheese sauce, dotted with bits of anchovy, mushrooms or spicy sausage and baked.

plank 1. Arrange meat or fish on a board, garnish with vegetables and mashed potato put through a pastry tube, and broil. 2. The board on which such food is prepared and served.

poach Cook food submerged in barely-boiling liquid, as in poaching eggs.

polenta (po-lent'ah) Italian. Thick cornmeal mush formed into cakes.

pot-au-feu (poh-toh-fu') French. Meat and vegetables boiled together in broth.

poultry Chickens, Cornish hens, turkeys, ducks, geese, guinea hens, pigeons and squab.

praline (prah'leen) French. Flat cake of sugar candy with nuts.

prawn Large shrimp.

preheat Heat oven or other cooking equipment to desired temperature before putting in the food.

proscuitto Italian ham, usually thinly sliced.

purée (pu-ray') French. Cooked, sieved fruits or vegetables or the process of putting them through the sieve or mill.

ragout (ra-goo') French. Thick stew of highly seasoned meat and vegetables.

ramekin Baking dish for individual portions.

rarebit Mixture of medium white sauce, eggs, seasonings and cheese.

ravioli (rav-vee-oh'lee) Italian. Bite-size cases of noodle dough filled with finely ground meat, cheese and spinach, poached in meat stock or water and served with a highly seasoned tomato sauce.

reconstitute Restore dried or concentrated foods to natural amount of liquid, as water in milk or fruit juice.

relish Flavorful foods served to stimulate the appetite.

render To liquefy fat in meat over low heat to free it from fibers.

rennet A substance which coagulates milk.

rice 1. A cereal. 2. To put through a perforated ricer or sieve.

rissole (ree-sall') French. Savory meat mixture encased in rich pastry and fried in deep fat.

roast Cook by dry heat, usually meat or poultry cooked in an oven; may include cooking with hot ashes, live coals, and hot stones or metal.

roe Eggs of fish.

rosette (roh-zet') French. Thin, rich batter baked in a fancy shape by means of a special iron. Cooked in deep fat and served with creamed foods.

roulade (roo-lahd') French. A thin slice of meat rolled around a filling of chopped meat or dressing and baked.

roux (roo) French. Equal parts of fat and flour mixed together for use in thickening sauces and soups.

sachet (sashay) Mixed seasonings (herbs and spices) tied in a bag.

saffron Pungent, orange-colored stigmas of saffron plant used to color and flavor food.

salt To cure or season with salt.

sauerbraten (sour-brah-ten) German. Beef marinated in spiced vinegar, pot-roasted and served with gingersnap gravy.

sauté (soh-tay') French. Cook in a skillet in a small amount of fat.

scald 1. Heat to temperature just below boiling. 2. Pour boiling water over or dip food briefly into boiling water.

scallion or shallot Young, bulbless onion.

scallop (a) A shellfish. (b) Food baked in a sauce or liquid, mixed together or in layers.

scone Scottish quick bread containing currants.

score Make shallow gashes in the surface of food, as in cutting outer edge to prevent curling or making design for surface decoration.

sear Brown surface quickly at high temperature.

season Add salt, spices, herbs or other ingredients for flavoring.

set Allowed to stand until congealed, as with gelatin, puddings or custards.

sherbet Frozen dessert made with fruit juice, sugar and milk or cream.

shirr Break eggs into dish with cream and crumbs and bake.

shortening Fat suitable for baking or frying.

shoyu or soy sauce Japanese or Chinese sauce made from fermented soy beans.

sift To pass through a sieve to remove lumps.

simmer Cook in liquid just below the boiling point, so that small bubbles form around sides of pan.

singe Hold over direct flame to burn off all hairs, as in singeing poultry.

skewer Pin of metal or wood used for fastening meat or poultry while cooking or long pins used for holding bits of food for roasting or broiling.

skim Remove surface from a liquid mixture, such as foam or fat.

sliver Cut into long, slender pieces, as in slivering almonds.

smorgasbord (smur-gahs-bohrd') Swedish. Flavorful tidbits or appetizers arranged on a table in an attractive assortment.

soubise (soo'bees) French. A thick onion sauce.

soufflé (soo-flay') French. A light, fluffy baked dish with beaten egg whites. It may be sweet or savory.

spaetzle (spet'zel) Austrian. Fine noodles made by running batter through colander into boiling water.

sponge (a) High, light cake leavened with air and steam. (b) A yeast batter.

specific gravity Weight of a given volume of material compared with an equal volume of water.

spoon bread Southern corn bread baked in a casserole and served with a spoon.

spumoni (spoo-moh'nee) Italian. Rich ice cream in differing layers, usually containing fruit and nuts.

steam To cook in steam, with or without water.

steep Cover with boiling water and stand to extract flavor and color.

sterilize Destroy microorganisms with boiling water, dry heat or steam.

stew Cook slowly in a small amount of liquid.

stock Liquid in which meat, fish, poultry or vegetables have been cooked.

stroganoff (strog'an-off) Russian. Sauted beef in sauce of sour cream, with mushrooms and onions.

strudel (stroo'dl) German. Pastry of flakey, paper-thin dough filled with fruit.

tabasco (tah-bas'koh) Mexican. Hot red pepper sauce.

table d'hôte (tabl-doht') French. Meal for a fixed price.

tacos (tah'cos) Mexican. Rolled sandwich of tortillas filled with meat, lettuce, onion and hot sauce.

tamale (ta-mah'lee) Mexican. Highly seasoned meat mixture rolled in cornmeal mush wrapped in corn husks and steamed.

tarragon Herb used for flavoring vinegar.

tartar sauce Mayonnaise to which chopped dill or sour pickles, green onions and chives have been added.

tart (a) Sharp or sour in taste. (b) Small pie or pastry.

thyme Pungent aromatic herb used in flavoring soups and vegetables.

timbale (a) A thin fried case for holding creamed entrees or creamy desserts. (b) Individual unsweetened custard or white sauce with minced fish, meat, poultry or vegetables that is baked.

torte A rich cake made with crumbs, eggs and nuts or meringue in the form of a cake.

tortilla (tohr-tee'yah) Mexican. Thin, unleavened cornmeal cake baked on a griddle or hot stone slab.

toss Mix ingredients lightly without crushing, as in salad making.

trifle (try'fl) English. Dessert made with sponge cake soaked in fruit juice and wine and covered with jam, custard, almonds and whipped cream.

truffle Mushroom-like fungus, dark in color, used as garnish and seasoning.

truss To tie or skewer poultry or meat so that it will hold its shape while cooking.

turnover Food encased in pie pastry and baked.

tutti-frutti Mixed fruit.

velouté (ve-loo-tay') French. White sauce made with veal or chicken stock.

venison Meat of deer, antelope, elk and moose.

viscosity The property of fluids that determines whether they flow readily or resist flow.

whip Beat rapidly to produce expansion through incorporation of air, as in cream or egg whites.

Wiener schnitzel (ve'ner-shnit-sel) German. Breaded veal cutlet served with lemon.

won ton Stuffed dumplings cooked in chicken broth.

Yorkshire pudding English Popover batter baked in roast beef drippings.

zwieback (tsvee'bahk) German. A kind of toasted bread or rusk.

LIST OF TABLES

1.1 Food Poisoning Causes and Prevention — 8, 9

1.2 Control of Disease-Carrying Pests — 10, 11

1.3 Temperatures Related to Food Safety — 12

1.4 Commonly Used Abbreviations With Weight and Volume Equivalents — 15

2.1 Scoop and Ladle Sizes — 43

3.1 Ingredient Substitutions — 58

3.2 Thickening and Jelling Agents — 62, 63

3.3 Suggested Uses of Herbs, Spices, and Other Seasoning Materials — 66–72

3.4 Topping, Garnish, and Accompaniment Suggestions — 73–76

3.5 Cooking Temperatures — 78–79

3.6 Approximate Storage Limits for Foods Held at 0° F — 81

3.7 Frozen Food Preparation — 83, 84

3.8 Boiling Point of Water at Different Altitudes — 85

3.9 Temperatures of Steam Pressures at Different Altitudes — 85

3.10 Ingredient Adjustment for Different Altitudes — 85

3.11 Cooking Temperatures for Candy at Different Altitudes — 86

6.1 Maintaining the Fresh Quality in Produce in Wholesale Warehouses — 135

6.2 Fruit and Vegetable Preprocessing With Typical Per Cent Loss — 137

6.3 Minutes Required for Cooking Vegetables — 152

7.1 Modification of Butter Sauce — 162

7.2 Cocktail Sauces and Types of Cocktail On Which to Use Them — 167

7.3 Modifications for White, Bechamel, and Veloute Sauces — 172–174

7.4 Modifications for Brown Sauce — 176

10.1 Suggested Salad Combinations — 236

11.1 Number of Slices in Commercial Loaves of Bread — 251

11.2 Suggested Flavorings for Sandwich Spreads — 252

11.3 Suggested Food Mixtures to Use for Sandwich Fillings — 254

11.4 Colorful Foods Appropriate for Canapes and Fancy Sandwiches 264

12.1 Suggested Temperatures and Time for Griddle Cooking   290

13.1 Market Packages and Forms of Milk   313–314

13.2 Common Cheese Varieties and Their Uses   317–318

13.3 Characteristics and Uses of the Different Egg White Foams   331

14.1 Classes and Weights of Poultry   338–339

14.2 Approximate Time for Thawing and Roasting Poultry   343

15.1 Suggested Preparation Methods for Fish and Shellfish   363–364

16.1 Suggested Portion Weights for Beef Steaks   389

16.2 Time Table for Broiling Beef Steaks   397

17.1 Suggested Sizes for Pan-Ready Veal Cuts   407

17.2 Cooking Schedule for Veal   410

18.1 Weights Commonly Used for Lamb Chops and Roasts   423

18.2 Time Table for Broiling Lamb   426

19.1 Suggested Sizes for Pork Chops, Steaks, and Roasts (Raw Weight)   440

19.2 Baking or Braising Schedule for Pork in 325°F Oven Temperature   447, 448

20.1 Recommended Proof Box Conditions   480

20.2 Relative Humidity Percentage   481

21.1 Comparison of Ingredient Proportions in Different Types of Bread   486

22.1 Approximate Baking Time and Temperature for Cakes   511

22.2 Temperatures and Tests for Sirup and Candies   516

APPENDIX

Equivalent Measures of Food   549

Food Quantities for 100 Portions   559

Definition of Terms in Food Preparation   574

Index

A

Abbreviations, 15
Accidents, 13, 14
Accompaniments, 61, 73–76
Accompaniment salads, 224
Acidity, 145, 146, 157
Adaptor ring, 464, 470
Agar, 62
Aitch bone, 420, 433
A la king, 173
Alaska, baked, 79
Alkalinity, 145, 157
Allemande, 174
Allspice, 64
Altitude, 82, 85
Aluminum, 23
Anchovy, 162, 266
Anise, 64, 229
Anthocyanins, 146, 157
Anti-oxidant, 144
Antipasto, 260
Ants, 10
Appetizer salads, 223
Apples, 236
Apricots, 81, 137
Artichokes, 226, 232
Ascorbic acid, 130, 133, 146
Asparagus, 81, 139, 152, 239, 264
Assembly, food cutter, 98, 101
    mixer, 467–469
    vegetable dicer, 102
Attachments, food cutter, 97, 100–104, 113
    mixer, 469–470
Au jus, 160, 179
Avocado, 236, 238, 254

B

Bacon, 436, 450

Bacon (*continued*)
    sandwich, 254, 255
    sliced, 439, 455
Bacteria, 7, 8, 9, 12, 60
Baker's table, 202
Bakery equipment, 29, 463–484
Bake shop, 4, 463
Baking powder, 57, 58, 85, 88
Baking, bread, 493
    cakes, 510–512
    temperatures, pork, 447
    vegetables, 148
Barbecued lamb, 427
Barbecue sauce, 70
Basil, 65, 66
Batters, 487, 501
Bay leaves, 64, 66
Beans, 139, 152
Beef, chart, 375
    chuck, 376
    cuts, 374–391
    dishes, 74
    grades, 372–374
    noodle casserole, 16, 17
    temperatures, cooking, 78
Beets, 152
Berries, 137
Beverage equipment, 208
Bins, 33
Biscuits, 55, 56, 497
Bisque, 184, 191
Block, meat, 284
Blueberries, 146
Boiling, 146
Bones, shape of, 374
Boston butt, 436, 439
Bouillabaise, 185
Bouillon, 184

Bowls, 27
  mixer, 464, 467, 471, 483
Brains, 444, 451
Braise, 348, 392-293, 401, 446-448, 456
Bread, baking, 493
  enrichment, 485-486
  kinds, 248-251
  kneading, 491
  making, 485-500
  milk, 490
  mixing, 491
  proofing, 483
  quick, 487, 494-500
  storage, 494
  yeast, 487-494
Break joint, lamb, 420, 432
Brisket, beef, 379
Broccoli, 152
Brochette, 398
Broilers, 296-300
Broiling, beef, 395-398
  lamb, 424, 426
Brownie pudding, 541
Browning, 120
Brucellosis, 8
Brussel sprouts, 152
Buerre manie, 169
Burns, 13
Butt, tenderloin, 388-389
Butter, 58, 312, 315, 319, 321
  sandwich, 251
  shortening, 505
Butterscotch, 86

C
Cabbage, 152
Cakes, angel, 83, 504
  butter, 504, 507
  cutting, 518-522
  flour, 504
  high-ratio, 508
  mixing methods, 508-510
  pans, 510-511
  shortening, 505
Cala ham, 439
California ham, 439
Calves, 403
Canape, 259-269, 277, 317
Cannisters, 30
Can opener, 27

Caper, 264
Caper sauce, 162
Capicola butt, 439
Capon, 338
Caramelization, meat, 393
Caramels, 86
Carborundum stone, 28, 40, 53
Cardamon, 64
Carotinoids, 146, 157
Carrots, 109, 111, 153
Carts, 30, 31, 52
Carving, beef, 391
  lamb, 420
  pork, 449
Casseroles, 28, 31, 73, 83
Cayenne, 70
Celery, 65, 153
Celery seed, 64
Centigrade, 78, 79, 88
Certified, 313
Chateaubriand, 388-389
Cheddar, 266
Cheese, 67, 312, 315-318
Chef, 5
Chemical leavening, 57
Chemical poisons, 9
Chervil, 65
Chicken, 67, 75, 337-349
  city, 410, 415
  salad, 238
  sandwich, 254, 255
Chicory, 229
Chili sauce, 70
China, 23
China cap strainer, 31, 32, 33, 177
Chlorophyll, 145, 156
Chocolate, 58
Chocolate souffle, 538
Chops, lamb, 422-424, 433
  pork, 440, 446
  veal, 406-408, 409, 414
Chuck, beef, 376-379
Cinnamon, 65
Citrus fruit, 138, 143
Clams, 352, 355-357
Claret wine, 71
Clarify, 187, 321
Cleaning agents, 6
Cleaning methods, coffee equipment, 213

Cleaning methods (*continued*)
  cooking equipment, 287, 288, 295, 300, 304
  dough divider, 473
  dough sheeter, 478
  food cutters, 99, 103–104, 107, 110
  fry pans, 35, 324
  meat equipment, 284–285
  mixer, 470–471
  proof box, 482
  refrigerator, 199
  slicer, 206–208
  steam equipment, 130
  vegetable peeler, 96
  work table, 203
Clear plate, 436, 439, 455
Cleaver, 38, 39, 284
Clostridium botulinum, 8
Cloves, 64
Cocoa, 58
Coffee cakes, 499
Coffee, equipment, 208–215
  making, 209–213-221
Collagen, 391–399
Collander, 27, 31, 32
Collect supplies, 17
Color, canapes, 264–267
  vegetables, 145, 146, 156
Combination salad dressing, 242
Commercially prepared foods, 4
Consomme, 184
Contamination, 9
Containers, food, 32
Cooked salad dressing, 242
Cooking section, 4, 28, 281
Cooking, beef, 391
  temperatures, 78
Cookies, 504, 512–514
Cook-manager, 5
Cooling, 7
Copper, 24
Convection oven, 293
Cordon blue, veal, 411
Coriander, 64
Cornish hen, 338
Cornstarch, 58, 63
Costs, 94, 134
Cottage butt, 439
Crab, 352, 355–359
  salad, 238

Cream, 58
  dressing, 243
  sauce, 173
  sour, 243, 245
Creme, anglaise, 178
  brulée, 178
Crown roasts, 406–408, 414, 421, 438
Cumin seed, 64
Curry of lamb, 430
Custard, baked, 536, 546
  soft, 537, 546
Cutters, 96–111, 113, 262
Cutter and slicer, 108–111
Cutter/mixer, 104–108
Cutting boards, 28, 36, 37, 52, 287

D

Dairy products, 308–321
Date oatmeal torte, 541
Decant, 187
Decanter, 210, 212
Decorative coating, 164
Deep fat, 302
Deep fat fryers, 301, 307
Deep fat frying, 149–150
Defrosting, fish, 362
  poultry, 340, 343, 351
Delmonico steak, 399
Demi-glace, 187
Desserts, 76
Dicer, 102–103
Dietitian, 5
Dill seed, 65, 66
Dispenser, milk, 216–218
Divinity, 86
Dixie squares, 439, 455
Dough, 487
  cutters, 473–475
  divider and rounder, 471–473
  hook, 466, 467
  roller, 475–476
  sheeter, 475–479
  shaping, 476–478, 492–493
  pastry, 529–530
Drains, 123, 126, 128
Dressing, combination, 242
  cooked, 242
  cream, 243
  French, 241, 245
  fruit, 243

Dressing (*continued*)
  mayonnaise, 242, 245
  poultry, 345
  salad, 241
Dried, eggs, 312
  fruit, 148
  vegetables, 148
Duck, 75, 339, 345

E
Education, 5
Eggs, 58, 62, 67, 309–312, 321–332,
      506, 539
  dishes, 73, 238
  sandwiches, 255
  sauces, 160–162, 172
  selection, 309
  whites, 309–322, 509
  white foams, 330–332, 336
  yolks, 312, 321
Eggplant, 153
Electrical power, 14, 118
Emulsifiers, 505, 528, 545
Emulsions, 241, 242, 245
Employment, 3
Equipment, 17
  bakery, 29, 463–484
  beverage, 208–218
  cooking, 28, 283–307
  measuring, 44–45
  pantry, 197–221
  receiving, 27
  salad, 27, 230
  sandwich, 27, 204, 257–259
  steam cooking, 115–130
  storage, 27
  vegetable preparation, 27, 93–114
equivalents, weight and volume, 15, 47
espagnole, 179
experience, 5
extension ring, 470

F
Fahrenheit, 78, 79, 88
Fat for frying, 302
Fat back, 436, 438, 455
Fennel, 64, 229
Filet mignon, 388–389
Fillings, 515–517
Filters, coffee, 211

Fish, 66, 67, 74, 81, 84, 352–371
  cookery, 362–371
  cuts or forms, 353–355
  fillets, 354
  frying, 367–370
  scaling, 353
  steaks, 354
  storage, 360–362
Fire, 13
Flies, 10
Floating island pudding, 537
Flour, 489, 527, 545
Flour sifter, 28
Foam cakes, 509
Fondue, 329–330
Food cutters, 96–111
Food director, 5
Food habits, 6–9
Food handling 6
Food preference, 87
Forequarter, beef, 376
Foresaddle, 418, 432
Forks, 30
Fortified, 485
Freezing, 7
French, dressing, 241
  fries, 74
  knife, 38, 40, 41
  roast, 421
Fricassee, 348
Fried eggs, 323
Frosting, 514–518, 525
Frozen foods, 77, 80, 81, 84
Fruit, fresh, 133–157
  frozen, 84
  pies, 534–535
  puddings, 540
  salads, 236, 237
  salad dressing, 243
Fryers, 301–304
Fry pans, 35, 37
Funnel, 28

G
Galvaneal, 25
Garbage, 10
Garnishes, 61, 73–76
Gauge, pressure, 117
Geese, 339, 345
Gelatin, 63, 534

Ginger, 64
Glace, 187
Glass, 23
Gluten, 489, 501, 545
Goulash, veal, 412
Grades, beef, 372–381, 400
  butter, 315
  eggs, 309
  fish, 352, 356
  lamb, 416
  pork, 434
  stamps, 373
  veal, 403, 413, 414
Grapefruit, 143
Grating cheese, 317
Griddle cakes, 496
Griddling, 394, 426
Grilling, 394
Guineas, 339
Gum tragacanth, 63

H

Habits, work, 7
Ham, 435
  fully cooked, 437
  glazes, 449
  long cure, 437, 450
  Proscuitto, 437
  quick cure, 437, 450
  regular, 437
  scoring, 449
  skinless, 437
  skinned, 437
  Smithfield, 437, 450
  tenderized, 437, 455
  weights, 435
Halibut, 363
Hamburgers, 394
  sandwiches, 253
Hard sauce, 177
Head cook, 5
Hearts, 445, 451
Herbs, 64–70, 88, 89
Homogenized, 313, 319
Honey, 59
Hors d'oeuvres, 259–262, 277, 317
Horseradish, 71
Hotel rack, lamb, 419, 432
Humidifier, 480
Humidity, storage, 135

Hungarian goulash, 412
Hydrogenated shortening, 505, 524

I

Ingredient measurement, 44
Ingredients, 16, 57
Insecticides, 6, 10, 11
Internship, 5
Irish moss, 63
Iron, enamelled, 24, 287
  retinned, 25, 471
  zinc coated, 25

J

Jelling agents, 60
Job titles, 4, 5
Job requirements, 14
Jowl, pork, 436, 439

K

Kale, 153
Kidneys, 444, 452
Knives, 13, 27, 38–43
Knife sharpening, 38–42
Knuckle, beef, 390, 391
Knuckle bone, 420
Kohl rabi, 153

L

Ladies, 42, 43
Lamb, 74, 416
  backs, 421
  break joint, 420, 432
  classes of, 417
  cookery, 426
  cuts, 417
  foresaddle, 418, 432
  grades, 416, 432
  hindsaddle, 417, 418
  hotel rack, 419, 432
  legs, 418–421, 426
  loins, 422, 438
  shanks, 424, 425
  shoulder, 424, 425
  specifications, 417, 432
  weights, 416, 417
  yoke, 417, 418, 432
Lard, 505, 545
Leavening, 57, 87
Left-overs, 7, 19

Lemon, 71
Lettuce, 144, 227–240
  Bibb, 227
  Cos or romaine, 227, 231
  iceberg, 231, 233, 234
  leaf, 228
  storage, 144
  washing, 144
Liaison mixture, 188, 192
Lice, 10
Lifting, 14
Liver, 443, 451, 453
Loaf, breads, 499
Lobster, 355–360
  salad, 239
Loin, beef, 384–390
Loin chops, lamb, 422
  pork, 440, 446
  veal, 406–409, 414
Longissimus dorsi, 377, 381, 382, 401, 424
Lubrication, 99, 107, 114, 118, 207, 471, 479

M
Mace, 64
Madeira, 428, 433
Marbling, 374
Margarine, 505
Marjoram, 64, 66
Marinades, 164–166, 235, 396
Material, use, 57
  substitution, 57
Mayonnaise, 163, 242, 251
Measuring, 44–48
  equipment, 44
Meat preparation, 283
  equipment, 284
Meat seasoning, 66, 67, 72
Meat section, 28
Melons, 137
Meringues, 332, 546
Meringue shells, 78, 332, 540
Metals, 23, 52
Milk, 59, 490, 507, 523, 533
  dispensing, 216
  equipment, 216–218, 221
Minerals, 133
Mint, 66
Mirepoix, 175
Mixed grill, 431

Mixer, 464–471
  agitators, 465–467
  attachments, 496–470
  cleaning and maintenance, 470, 471
  cutter/mixer, 104–108
  operation, 467–469
  parts, 468
  size, 464
  speed, 467
Mixing
  conventional method, 508
  muffin method, 508
  pastry blend method, 509
  quick, simplified, 509
Mixes, 499
Mobility, 34
Mornay sauce, 173
Mosquitoes, 10
Mustard, 64
Mutton, 416

N
Newberg sauce, 173
Nonfat milk, 319
Nontoxic metals, 52
Nutmeg, 64

O
Oil dropper, 470, 483
Okra, 153
Omelets, 326–327
Onions, 65, 153
Orange, 71
Oregano, 64, 66
Organization, large kitchen, 4
  work, 6
Osmosis, 147, 157
Oxtails, 453
Oysters, 356

P
Packaging, 80, 83
Paddles, 28
Pans, 29, 34, 35
Paprika, 64
Parasitic dysentery, 8
Parmigiana, veal, 410
Parsnips, 154
Parsley, 65, 67
Party salads, 226

Pasteurized, 313, 316
  milk, 8, 9
Pastry, 526–532
Peas, 154
Peelers, 94–97, 112
Pepper, 65
Pests, 7
Pesticides, 6
Pets, 6, 10
Pies, 83
  single crust, 532–534
  two crust, 534
Pineapple, 237
Pinwheel sandwich, 267–270
Plastics, 26
Poached eggs, 322
Poisoning, 8
Popovers, 495
Poppy seed, 64, 70
Pork, 75, 81, 434–456
  cuts, 435–440, 455
  fat back, 436
  grades, 434, 454
  long cure, 435
  quick cure, 435
  picnic, 439, 455
  sausage, 441, 442
  specifications, 435, 454
Portions, 16
Porterhouse, 384–390
Potatoes, 79, 112, 148
Pots, stock, 36
Pot washing, 26
Poultry, 67–72, 337–351
Power tools, 7
Practices, food handling, 6
  classes, 338–339
  frozen, 81, 84
Preliminary preparation, 4
Preparation for production, 6
Pressure, steam, 115, 118
Prevention, accidents, 7
Processing time, 20
Progress of work, 18
Puddings, 535
Puree, 160, 181, 184

Q
Quality acceptance, 56
  judgment, 55

R
Raisin pudding, 541
Raft, 187, 191
Ranges, 285–288, 305
Ravigote sauce, 173
Rib, beef, 377, 381, 385
Riblets, lamb, 425, 426
Receiving area, 27
Relative humidity, 185, 480–481, 484
Recipe, calculation, 15
  proportions, 15
  standardization, 15
Refrigeration, equipment, 197–200
  food, 7
Refrigerators, 197
  use and care, 199
Refrigerated puddings, 513
Restored, 485
Rennin, 319
Roaches, 7, 10
Roaster chicken, 338
Roasting beef, 393–394
Roasting poultry, 341–343
Rodents, 7, 10
Rolling bins, 463
Rolling pin, 29
Rosemary, 64, 67
Rotation preparation, 18, 22
Roulade, 399
Roux, 169, 170
Rutabagas, 154

S
Sabayon, 178
Safe food, 7, 8, 9
Saffron, 65, 70
Safety, 6, 14, 285, 469, 483
Safety valve, 121
Sage, 67
Salads, 222
  arrangement, 233
  base, 232
  combinations, 236–240
  dressing, 241
  equipment, 27, 230
  greens, 144, 156, 227–232
Salami, 265
Salmon, 265, 363–367, 371
Salmonella, 8

Sandwiches, 247
  arrangements, 249
  breads, 248–251
  butters and fillings, 251–257
  cheese, 248
  equipment, 27, 204, 257–259
  fancy, 259–270
  making, 257–259
  merchandising, 270–271
  pinwheel, 268–269
  ribbon, 268–269
  wraps, 270–275
Sanitation, 6–14, 222, 230, 257, 277, 283–285
Sauces, 159
  barbecue, 165
  bearnaise, 163
  bechamel, 170, 173
  blond, 170, 181
  bordelaise, 176
  bread, 161
  brown, 175–176
  butter, 161
  cocktail, 167–168
  creme anglaise, 178, 181
  creme brulee, 178, 181
  egg thickened, 162–164
  hollandaise, 162
  pan-gravy, 160
  puree, 160, 181
  Sabayon, 178
  simple, 160
  Soubise, 174
  starch thickened, 169–176
  supreme, 174
  sweet, 160
  tart, 164
  velouté, 170, 172
  white, 170, 172
Sauerbraten, 399
Sausages, 441–442, 450
Sauteing, 129, 150
Savory, 65, 67
Scales, 27, 44, 45, 53
Scaling, 44
Scallopini, veal, 412
Scoops, 27, 43, 53
Score, pastry, 544
Scoring ham, 449
Scrambled eggs, 325
Seasoning, 60

Seeds, 68, 70
Sesame seed, 65
Shank, beef, 380
Shanks, lamb, 424
Sharpening stone, 53
Sharpening steel, 28
Shellfish, 355–364
Sherry, 71, 428, 433
Shish-kabobs, 398, 424, 428, 429
Shortrib, 379, 382, 385, 401
Shortening, 490
Short loin, 384, 391
Shoulder, lamb, 424, 425, 429
  veal, 406, 410, 414
Shrimp, 265, 359–362, 369, 371
Sirloin, 384, 391
Sirup, 516
Skimmers, 48, 54
Slicer, 39
Slicing machine, 204–208
Souffles, 327–328, 334
Soup, 182
  base, 183
  body in, 187
  broth, 73, 184
  cream, 73, 184–185
  kinds of, 183–185
  preparation, 182
  service of, 189
Soy, 72
Spatulas, 28, 48
Spareribs, 436
Spices, 64–70, 88, 89
Spinach, 154
Spoons, 28, 29, 48, 49
Squash, 154
Soda, 59, 507
Standardization, recipes, 15, 507
Staphyloccus, 8
Starches, 169–170, 175, 180–181, 533
Stationary kettle, 123–126
Steak, beef loin, 384, 386–390
  pork blade, 440
Steam cleaning, 31
Steam, cookers, 115–121
  kettles, 121–131
  pressures, 85, 115, 118
Steamed pudding, 542
Steaming, 146
Steel, 25

Stew, beef, 392–393
    lamb, 427
Stifle joint, lamb, 420, 432
Stirring, 124
Stock, 72, 185–187
Storage, 81, 133, 134, 135, 148, 156
    bread, 494
    equipment, 27
Strainer basket, 122
Streptococcus, 9
Sugar, 59, 85, 506
    effect of, 147–148
Sweet potatoes, 154
Sweetbreads, 444, 452, 456
Swiss chard, 154
Switches, 14
Syneresis, 169
Systematic, 18

T
Tannins, 144, 156, 316
Tapioca, 59, 63
Tarragon, 65, 67
Tasting spoons, 7, 54
Tea, making, 215
Temperature, 7, 12, 88
    beef, 392, 394, 396
    cake baking, 511
    candy, 516
    cooking, 77
    dough, 487–488
    frying, 148, 157
    lamb, 426
    milk and eggs, 319, 322
    pork, 447, 448
    poultry, 343
    sirup, 516
    storage, 135
    veal, 410
    vegetable, cooking, 152–154
Tenderizer, 393
Tenderloin, 384–390
Testing laboratories, 13
Thawing, poultry, 343
Thermometers, 49, 54
Thiamine, 445
Thickening, 60, 88, 123, 169, 188
Thyme, 65, 67
Timbales, 329
Time requirements, 18, 20, 410

Timers, 49, 50, 54
Tomatoes, 59
Tomato sauce, 72
Tongue, 443, 453, 457
Toppings, 61, 73–76, 88
Tornedo, 387–388
Tortes, 541
Trichinella spiralis, 446
Trichinosis, 9
Truffle, 267
Trunnion or tilting kettle, 126–130
Tuberculosis, 9
Tumeric, 65
Turkey, 75, 337–351
Turnips, 154
Typhoid, 9
Thyphus, 9

U
Underwriters laboratories, 13
Uniforms, 6
Utensils, 23
Urn, cleaning, 213–214
    coffee, 208–215

V
Value, good food, 3
Variety meats, 442
    cooking of, 451–454, 456
    kinds, 442
Veal, chart, 405
    chops, 406–408
    cooking of, 409–411
    cuts, 404
    cutlets, 409, 411, 415
    grades, 403
    shoulder, 406
    steak, 408–409
    stew, 407
    storage, 404
Velouté, 170, 174
Vermouth, 72, 428
Vitamins, 133, 146, 156, 308
Volume measures, 44, 46, 47
Volume weights, 15

W
Waffles, 496
Watercress, 229, 264
Waxy maize, 62, 169

Weight and volume equivalents, 44
Weight, measurement, 44
Weiner Schnitzel, 410
Western sliced bacon, 439
Westphalia ham, 439
Wheat flour, 489
Whips, 50, 51, 54
    mixer, 466–467
Whipped cream, 319
White sauce, 170–172
Wine marinade, 166
Worcestershire sauce, 72

Wood, 26
Work, centers, 4, 18
    flow, 19
    tables, 200–203
    surfaces, 7

Y
Yeast, 59, 88, 490, 501
Yoke, lamb, 417, 424–425, 432

Z
Zabaglione, 178